Gertrude Stein:

The Language That Rises

1923–1934

Postcard of Gertrude Stein and George Hawkins, Louis Bromfield's secretary, in the garden of Bromfield's old *presbytère* in Senlis (Oise), probably photographed by Bromfield, sent to Stein in October 1938. Courtesy Hope B. Stevens and Ellen Bromfield Geld.

Gertrude Stein:

The Language That Rises

1923–1934

ULLA E. DYDO

WITH WILLIAM RICE

Northwestern

University Press

Evanston

Illinois

Northwestern University Press
Evanston, Illinois 60208-4210

Printed in the United States of America
10 9 8 7 6 5 4 3 2 1

ISBN 0-8101-1919-6

Library of Congress Cataloging-in-Publication Data

Dydo, Ulla E., 1925–
Gertrude Stein : the language that rises : 1923–1934 /
Ulla E. Dydo with William Rice.
p. cm. — (Avant-garde & modernism studies)
Includes bibliographical references (p.) and index.
ISBN 0-8101-1919-6 (alk. paper)
1. Stein, Gertrude, 1874–1946 — Criticism, Textual. 2. Women and literature — United States — History — 20th century. 3. Modernism (Literature) — United States. I. Rice, William, 1931– II. Title.
III. Avant-garde and modernism studies.
PS3537.T323 Z5885 2003
823′.912 — dc21
2002153016

The paper used in this publication meets the minimum requirements of the American National Standard for Information Sciences — Permanence of Paper for Printed Library Materials, ANSI Z39.48-1992.

Contents

Illustrations

Note to Readers

Readers will want to have access to the Stein texts I discuss. Much of Stein's writing is in print and available, but certain collections are not. The eight volumes of the Yale Edition of the *Unpublished Writings of Gertrude Stein* (1951–1958), *Portraits And Prayers* (1934), and others would be available only in libraries. In *A Stein Reader* (1993) and the two volumes of the Library of America *Writings of Gertrude Stein* (1998), readers will find many short works not included in other collections.

All quotations from Stein texts, with the exception of a few phrases, have been treated as follows: Stein passages, short or long, are offset so that they can be read and seen as Stein wrote them. Her paragraphs, indentations, capitalizations, and spellings are retained. With few exceptions, I have avoided excerpting quotations.

Stein's titles are listed with all words capitalized, as she wrote most of them, though they were inconsistently printed. As in *A Stein Reader,* I follow her practice of not discriminating between important and unimportant words.

Stein rarely dated letters. Where envelopes are preserved, postmarks add dates on which I rely without identifying them unless the context requires it. Where they are not preserved, I give approximate dates, sometimes with question marks.

Quotations from letters are from the Yale Collection of American Literature (YCAL) unless otherwise acknowledged, with sources.

To preserve the sense and sound of French texts, I quote them in the original, adding translations in footnotes rather than the reverse.

Acknowledgments

The Estate of Gertrude Stein, represented by Calman A. Levin, has generously made this book possible by granting permission to print published and unpublished work as well as letters of Gertrude Stein.

Donald Gallup, curator of the Collection of American Literature at the Beinecke Rare Book and Manuscript Library at Yale University, welcomed me when I began my study and offered me steady support and critical interest through his retirement and his last years.

Joan Chapman, who saw Stein regularly during World War II, still spends summers in Culoz, and knows many who knew Stein, gave me invaluable help, walked with me through the country, and became a friend during my trips to France.

Anne Lindbeck and her daughters, Ann and Kathy Lindbeck, offered me years of hospitality in Hamden that made possible the slow research on manuscripts at the Beinecke Library.

From 1980 on, I received generous support from Dr. Patricia Willis, curator of the Collection of American Literature at the Beinecke Rare Book and Manuscript Library, Yale University, and the staff, especially Anne Whelpley, Marjorie Grey Wynne, Stephen Jones, Lori Misura, Alfred Mueller, and Tim Young.

I acknowledge the cooperation of the following major archives and institutions in giving me access to collections and permission to quote:

Baltimore Museum of Art, Baltimore, Maryland
The Bancroft Library, University of California at Berkeley
Barnard College Archive, New York, New York
Bryn Mawr College Archive, Bryn Mawr, Pennsylvania
The Poetry/Rare Book Collection, University Libraries, State University of New York at Buffalo
Columbia University Rare Book and Manuscript Library and the Random House Papers at Columbia Rare Book and Manuscript Library, New York
Columbia University Seminar on American Civilization
Library of Congress, Manuscript Division, Washington, D.C.
National Portrait Gallery, Smithsonian Institution, Washington, D.C.
New York Public Library
Harry Ransom Humanities Research Center, University of Texas at Austin
Little Review Archives, Golda Meir Library, University of Wisconsin at Milwaukee
The Sophia Smith Collection, Smith College, Northampton, Massachusetts

Louis Bromfield Papers, Ohio State University, Columbus, Ohio
Rare Book Collection, University of California at Los Angeles
Elliot Paul Papers, Special Collections, The Library, University of Colorado at Boulder
Schlesinger Library, Radcliffe College, Cambridge, Massachusetts
Poetry Magazine Archive, University of Chicago Libraries
Pagany Magazine Papers, Special Collections, University of Delaware Library, Newark, Delaware
Bibliothêque Littéraire Jacques Doucet, Paris
Bibliothêque Nationale, Paris
Bibliothêque de l'Arsenal, Paris
Bodleian Library, Oxford, England
Fondation Le Corbusier, Paris

I acknowledge assistance from many friends and colleagues here and abroad. Of those whom I saw in earlier years who had known Stein and Toklas well and gave me invaluable help, many are no longer living; but all added immeasurably to the life of my work and are lively presences in this book. Thanks to Sir Valentine Abdy, David Antin, Paul P. Appel, Eleanor Apter, Denise Aimée Azam, Melinda Barlow, Joseph Barry, M. J. Beauvais, Nora Beeson, Charles Bernstein, Hélène Bokanowski, Bette Bourne, Stan Brakhage, Ellen Bromfield Geld, Edward Burns, John Cage, William A. Camfield, Linda Chapman, Lord David Cecil, Astrid Peters Coates, Lady Ann Cowdray, Judith Curr, Michael Davidson, Patricia Everett, Cheryl Faver, Vincent Faÿ, J. D. Fleeman, Charles Henri Ford, Allen Frame, Pie Friendly, Serge Gavronsky, Peter and Ruth Gay, Vincent Giroud, David Greetham, Robert B. Haas, Allanah Harper, Gilbert Harrison, Lyn Hejinian, Susan Howe, Lindley Hubbell, Germaine Hugnet, Myrtille Hugnet, Mrs. Schuyler Jackson (Laura Riding), Maria Jolas, Leon Katz, Bruce Kellner, Lawrence Kornfeld, James Laughlin, Angèle Levesque, Edward Lintz, Jackson MacLow, Marghretta McBean, James R. Mellow, Douglas Messerli, Steven Meyer, Larry Mitchell, Rosalind Moad, Richard Morrison, Shirley Neuman, Ochiishi Augustmoon, Lola Pashalinski, Marie-Claire Pasquier, Robert Paxton, Marjorie Perloff, Olga Picabia, Allan Price, Peter Quartermain, Arthur Raffel, Rosalie Raffel, Joan Retallack, Jean Rigg, Jacques Roubaud, Perdita Schaffner, Mildred Parker Seese, Louis Silverstein, Linda Simon, Sacheverell Sitwell, Carol Slade, Walter H. Slote, Julian Stein, Samuel M. Steward, Christopher Sykes, Allen Tanner, Anne Tardos, Virgil Thomson, Anthony Tommasini, Elinor Ulman, Steven Watson, Beatrice Wayne, Norman Weinstein, Monique and Philip Wiedel, Robert A. Wilson, and Brenda Wineapple.

Research for my study was supported in 1981–82 by a Fellowship for College Teachers from the National Endowment for the Humanities and in the summer of 1980 by a grant from the P.S.C.-C.U.N.Y. Research Award Program, both gratefully acknowledged.

I want to give special thanks to Susan Harris who signed the contract for this book and has been a friend since we worked on *A Stein Reader* in the early 1990s.

I am grateful to Susan Betz and her staff at Northwestern University Press for their considerate professional care in sending this book on its way.

Abbreviations

Gertrude Stein Texts

AABT	*The Autobiography Of Alice B. Toklas*
AFAM	*As Fine As Melanctha (1914–1930)*
A&B	*Alphabets And Birthdays*
AWD	*An Acquaintance With Description*
BTV	*Bee Time Vine And Other Pieces (1913–1927)*
EA	*Everybody's Autobiography*
FIA	*Four In America*
GHA	*The Geographical History Of America Or The Relation Of Human Nature To The Human Mind*
G&P	*Geography And Plays*
GMP	*Matisse Picasso And Gertrude Stein With Two Shorter Stories*
HTW	*How To Write*
HWW	*How Writing Is Written*
LA	*The Library of America Gertrude Stein*
LCA	*Lucy Church Amiably*
LIA	*Lectures In America*
LO&P	*Last Operas And Plays*
MOA	*The Making Of Americans*
NOTY	*A Novel Of Thank You*
MR	*Mrs Reynolds And Five Earlier Novelettes*
O&P	*Operas And Plays*
PL	*Painted Lace And Other Pieces (1914–1937)*
P&P	*Portraits And Prayers*
PGS	*A Primer For The Gradual Understanding Of Gertrude Stein*
R	*A Stein Reader*
RAB	*Reflections On The Atomic Bomb*
SIM	*Stanzas In Meditation And Other Poems (1929–1933)*
SOA	*Staying On Alone: Letters of Alice B. Toklas*
SW	*Selected Writings Of Gertrude Stein*
TB	*Tender Buttons*
TWO	*Two: Gertrude Stein And Her Brother And Other Early Portraits (1908–1912)*
UK	*Useful Knowledge*
WAM	*What Are Masterpieces*
WIR	*What Is Remembered,* by Alice B. Toklas

Other

HRC	Harry Ransom Humanities Research Center, University of Texas at Austin
LGS/CVV	*The Letters of Gertrude Stein and Carl Van Vechten*, ed. Edward Burns
LGS/TW	*The Letters of Gertrude Stein and Thornton Wilder*, ed. Edward Burns and Ulla E. Dydo with William Rice
SBW	*Gertrude Stein: A Biography of Her Work*, by Donald Sutherland
YCAL	Yale Collection of American Literature

Gertrude Stein:

The Language That Rises

1923–1934

Entrances

In 1976 Edward Burns, planning a Stein issue of *Twentieth Century Literature,* asked me to write an essay on "Stanzas In Meditation" of 1932, then an almost unknown text of compelling difficulty, which had long struck me as a peak of Stein's work and her last great accomplishment before she succumbed to writing to please readers, for fame and success. I did not write that essay. Instead, for some years, "Stanzas" became the text I studied. Yet the "Stanzas" are no longer the central focus of this book.

When in late 1979 I began to read the manuscript and the typescripts of "Stanzas" in the Stein Collection of the Beinecke Library at Yale, I started a journey magnificent in its confusion. I was groping in uncharted territory, in a landscape which would become wonderfully filled with discoveries that led me far beyond the poems. This book is the record of that journey.

Three discoveries changed my view of "Stanzas" and the scope of this book. The first, which began with the poems but went far beyond, was that Stein's manuscripts give us access to her creative process. They include not only the lines eventually printed but also other elements that I gradually learned to read: traces of the physical act of writing, movement of the hand in space, visual sequences of words, revisions, notes, paper, pen and pencil, lineation, erasures, doodles, names, addresses, phone numbers, and dog-eared corners of notebooks conveying messages—all contexts for her texts and her mind at work. These features, not found in typescripts or printed texts, had not been examined with care in chronological sequence and offered treasures of insight. They also taught me what it was, as Stein always insisted, to see and hear at once, to talk and listen at the same time. The sense of her language lifting off the page changed my approach to her work, my view of "Stanzas," and the scope of my inquiry. It also gave me a phrase from "A Long Gay Book" as a title: *The Language That Rises.*

The second discovery was finding in manuscript revisions that showed the only printed text, in *Stanzas In Meditation And Other Poems (1929–1933),* to be corrupt. I assumed that the revisions had to do with what the "Stanzas" were about, though I did not know how. I found the unrevised first and the revised second typescript of the poems, traced the textual changes in detail, wrote about them and eventually demonstrated how the printed text of "Stanzas" was adulterated. I looked for the events of 1932 that led to the alterations. Then, trying to disregard these, I began all over again to read the "Stanzas" in the unrevised, uncorrupted first typescript.

Continuing to search for an entry into the poems and hoping to discover steps that culminated in them, I extended my work backward in time, to her first attempt, in "An Elucidation" of 1923, to explain, by example, the evolution of her language. In spite of its title, this work is not a theoretical study but a single, unified text about *writing;* I think of it as a poem in several parts. Studying in manuscript all the works from 1923 to 1932, I realized that the texts, which had been assigned approximate dates in the Haas-Gallup numbering system based on Stein's own, inaccurate bibliography of 1929, could be dated exactly by internal textual and other evidence. I followed them in sequence from "An Elucidation" on and traced a coherent gradual evolution of her method through explanation, description, genre, vocabulary, grammar.

From "An Elucidation," I moved to the next elucidatory piece, the Cambridge and Oxford address of 1926, published later under the title *Composition As Explanation.* This text, like some of her later lectures, is an examination in retrospect of *her writing.* From the lecture on, I read and commented chronologically on all her texts up to 1932, preserving sequence and context unbroken. But this work also failed to open "Stanzas."

So I expanded the study forward to include *The Autobiography Of Alice B. Toklas,* written late in 1932, some six months after and perhaps, I thought, as a result of "Stanzas." Again I was wrong. The *Autobiography* was not connected and yielded no clearer understanding of "Stanzas." Yet how confusing to read, in "Stanzas," in successive poems,

> This is her autobiography one of two (IV, xiv)

and

> This is an autobiography in two instances (IV, xiii)

If the second instance is not *The Autobiography Of Alice B. Toklas,* what is it? What was she talking about?

The *Autobiography,* written in a voice entirely different from her own, was her first book of what she came to call audience writing, created to please readers, for success, rather than as writing for its own sake. It changed Stein's daily life, her writing, and her sense of herself. It became clear that I had to follow the whole group of texts following the *Autobiography* to its completion in the summer of 1934, including *Byron A Play, Blood On The Dining Room Floor* and related short pieces, "And Now," "The Superstitions Of Fred Anneday, Annday, Anday A Novel of Real Life," *Four In America,* and the writing, but not the delivery, of the lectures for the American tour.

The third discovery came very late. Having made the decision to move beyond the *Autobiography,* I gained a new perspective, not only on "Stanzas" but on Stein's work as a whole. I realized that by focusing on "Stanzas" and its many problems, I had spotlighted that text and isolated it from the body of her work. This only magnified the problems of "Stanzas" and took it out of its context, which is not the way to approach any Stein work. Her texts do not progress linearly from one concern, say, with grammar, or with the novel, to another, nor do they go as I had earlier thought, from "real writing" to public or audience writing. They never move away from real writing, and Stein's real voice was never lost. I now had to revise my approach radically. Consider works like "Brim Beauvais," of fall 1931, and "Bartholomew Arnold," written weeks before she began "Stanzas." And after "Stanzas" and the *Autobiography,* in the spring of 1933, she produced the play *Byron,* as fine a poetic achievement as we can imagine, not discussed or published in her lifetime and even now virtually unknown.

For some years I had thought of the lectures also as audience writing—the last of the many steps she felt driven to take toward self-realization, publicity stunts to charm an audience. Stein herself, when considering lectures, also feared them as temptations to indulge in audience writing, to abandon god for mammon and serious concern with writing for personality display.

Yet they are not audience writing. While the experience of audience writing provided her with important new ideas about writing that entered the lectures, the lectures themselves returned her to her work and her art. They became self-portraits in a new Stein voice, and they establish a new balance. They are not confession but elucidation, not about genius in America but about her own work—the written writing and the impulse to do it that is her genius. They are not in another voice or about another voice but in and about her own.

Between 1981 and 1985, I spoke and wrote about the scenario of 1932 and some of these textual problems in essays, listed in the bibliography, with interpretations that kept changing as I came upon new finds. I could have followed this road and written a largely biographical monograph. Yet the biographical context, whose importance I recognized, does not explain her work, which she insisted was not autobiographical and had to be read literally, as pure writing, without explanations or introductions. I wanted to understand the texts and what it is to read Stein.

What does it mean to read her literally? It does not mean to read her mimetically, representationally. She invented her own compositional methods but never used words only as signs. By the time her words are embedded in a text, they lose their referential thrust and are composed rhetorically. Sometimes they retain references that it is useful to understand, though they do not name subjects and do not explain the text.

Trying to come closer to what she wrote, I discovered how she wrote. Abandoning the printed texts, often full of errors, and reading in manuscript, I learned new ways of reading. I not only followed the moving hand and its shapings but also came upon unexpected contexts. Sometimes I overtook Stein playing games as she joined the words, or I found small writing events not visible in printed texts. Clues appeared that sometimes showed how she moved from word to word, line to line, piece to piece. I even came upon evidence, beyond what she wrote, of how she emptied words of meaning.

An example remains in the manuscript of "Business In Baltimore" of 1925. Business is about counting money, an absorbing, orderly, humorless activity, which she renders in monotonous, parallel, rhyming steps with the simplest vocabulary. The printed page looks flat, gray, and neutral. Here goes the nursery rhyme:

> This is the way they make the day they make the day they make the day this is the way they make the day, once a day and it is a reason for having heard of it.

It? Stein had first written "Pierpont Morgan," then crossed out the name, changed it to "him," and then replaced "him" with "it." The three words remain on the manuscript page. The disembodied "it" has more power here than any identification. Stein is rarely recognized as a master at neutralizing the language.

It had been thought that Stein abandoned the habit of note taking visible in her early studies for *The Making Of Americans.* However, at Yale there are some thirty pocket-size notebooks, most of the 1920s and 1930s—to distinguish them from the manuscript *cahiers,* I call them *carnets*—which in quality resemble the early notebooks, containing drafts, along with other notes. They show that while Stein mostly composed in the *cahiers,* she sometimes drafted in the *carnets,* copying from them. They also demonstrate that Toklas *copied* some of these drafts, not that she *composed* in the *cahiers.* My detective story, "Reading the Hand Writing," suggests how to read the clues. How Stein wrote is a central question of this book.

My study now encompasses far more than I had originally planned; not only its scope and its center of interest have changed. It has become an analysis that also traces many apparently obscure references to immediate daily life—people, places, events, observations, letters—leading us to the very origins of her writing. At one point she even uses the term "decontextuate," now a part of the vocabulary of critical theory, to describe how she neutralizes distracting details. Such changes, done in first writing or later, are not corruptions but true revisions of texts, which then become complete in themselves.

Questioning who she is and what her work is are inseparable aspects of her art in its active and reflexive condition, which Stein called meditation. But such writing is difficult for an audience whose expectations are conditioned by standards of representation alien to her intention and standards of reading counter to her own.

As Stein once wrote to Edmund Wilson, "all literature is to me me, that isn't as bad as it sounds." What she meant was consistent with her view of the creative process. She also said of Picasso that throughout his work he painted himself. The same was true of Stein: there was no other way to write. But this does not mean "through herself" as if she were an eye, a mirror, an ear, a recorder of reality. Nor does it mean "about herself" as subject or personality.

Reality for her was not separate from the perception and the perceiver of reality. Her portraits are perfect demonstrations of the identity of object and subject, perceiver, perceived, and perception. Likewise, when she did second portraits, it was at later moments, when both perceiver and perceived had changed. They were truly new.

I look at all of Stein's work not only as a series of separate texts but also, in a sense, as a single spiritual autobiography whose vocabulary is generated by the daily life but whose voice is uniquely hers. The relation of the disembodied texts to the bodied referential vocabulary is central to my reading.

What is new and different in my book? Earlier scholars—notably Donald Sutherland, Richard Bridgman, James Mellow, Marianne DeKoven—have in different ways surveyed Stein's work in its totality. Others—Leon Katz, Neil Schmitz, Wendy Steiner, Allegra Stewart, Jayne Walker, Brenda Wineapple—have followed one period, one theme, or one genre. Still others have unsystematically consulted some manuscripts, but no one has studied their revelations about the process of writing and, in sequence, sometimes down to the month, their exact time of beginning and ending composition.

All biographical studies suffer from excessive reliance on personality and the autobiographical books and insufficient attention to her texts. Yet inadequacies and unanswered questions in all these books can often be traced to the state of the Stein collection itself, for such a long time so difficult to tap in the Yale archive, so large, so various, and so wide in its scope—from literature to art, from America to France, from one place or person to another.

And behind it all was the still, small voice of Alice B. Toklas. For all the long late years she answered questions and gave guidance out of her own appropriation of Stein. She never breathed to anyone that the manuscript *cahiers* were of interest, wanted some early notebooks destroyed when they were found, and did not know that some *carnets* from the 1920s and 1930s had slipped into the collection. Even beyond her death, in an archive largely set up on her terms, her voice can still be confused with Stein's own.

I read the evolving sequence for a most productive period of Stein's maturity, revealing the roots of her later concern with audience. The difficulty of the texts makes it imperative to comment in detail as the only way to enter their world. I offer no survey and no "key" to the work but hope to open its voice in proportion to the depth of my reading and the reader's willingness to read with me.

I rely on manuscripts and other contexts, not on speculation, appreciation, or theory, tracing her creative process by showing how she composed, opening texts in sequence and following the intimate link between her life and her art. New discoveries in documents at Yale and other archives here and abroad should allow my book to stimulate new research on Stein and literary modernism.

My first interest is always in the texts. I offer readings of many that have received no critical attention and new readings of familiar works. For those who cannot spend years at Yale I give a full description of essential contexts and note errors in printed texts. In *A Stein Reader,* I assembled a selection in chronological order though without full continuity. My brief headnotes reached for a kind of textual essence from the work I had then done for the present book. Here, however, I include full detail and documentation for my readings in chronological order.

I trace the physical process of composing, commenting on auditory and visual punning, not only in English but in other languages when they enter. I discuss how Stein finished her texts, since total design and continuity were problematic for her. I follow chronology, correcting errors in dating and giving exact dates for their beginning and completion, tracing development to show how each work grows organically out of the preceding as a step in an evolution that can be understood rhetorically and biographically. Yet this book is not a biography. It documents how experience becomes material for composition and yields the vocabulary for her writing.

Everywhere in the Yale archives I consulted in search of Stein, I saw the pioneering work of retiring curator Donald C. Gallup, who had known Stein, had in late years transferred materials from Paris and received information from Toklas: the card catalog of works, with approximate dates; at the desk, a typed copy of the Haas-Gallup listing of texts, annotated and updated in pencil; a small wood box with cards listing books from the Stein library given to Yale by Alice Toklas and Allan Stein; related personal papers —of Alfred Stieglitz, Carl Van Vechten, Marsden Hartley, Mabel Dodge, Henry McBride—and Stein's letters to others—Mabel Weeks, Emma Lootz Erving, and many more—all gathered by Gallup while they were still living.

Just to find what was there, in an archive that those who work there now can hardly imagine, became a part of hewing out how to read—there was no way to be efficient. Here were manuscripts few had consulted, some complete and others whose pages had come loose from titled cover sheets; scraps one might find accidentally, with scribbles, most unidentified; boxes and boxes of letters dated by Gallup; and, if one knew how to call for them, two containers to wade in, marked "Uncatalogued." Scholars identified some papers and helped put them in order—or disorder.

The staff at the desk, relying heavily on memory, were always helpful, but until 1984, Beinecke curators, with part-time student assistants, did all the manuscript work for the library. The Beinecke had no catalogers. Two to four overworked archivists organized and recorded what they could of old papers and new materials pouring in through the 1970s and 1980s. No one was assigned the recataloging of the Stein Collection.

All that has changed since 1996, when the cataloging of all the Stein papers, a two-year project, was completed with exemplary care by Timothy Young under the guidance of Patricia Willis, the present curator of the Collection of American Literature, and Ralph Franklin, director of the library. Now readers can access information about papers whose very existence I had to discover. Details can be found, cross-referenced, on the computer, not only at Yale but on-line anywhere else. Now all the papers, including unidentified ones, are listed in delicate transparency for those who wish to penetrate Stein texts. It is possible to locate sources and find one's way in them. At the time Robert Haas and Donald Gallup made their list, the collection was not fully cataloged; now we can more accurately date the texts in sequence.

Groping in the archive paid off. Touching these texts in manuscript, I read hour by hour, week by week, word for word. Slowly words and phrases began to echo in my mind in shapes and sounds that sometimes made clear and simple sense. Learning to read among the papers in the archive took years. It also sent me in new ways to writing poems, to reading aloud and poetry readings, to art exhibits, art history, old and new experimental films, and music. I learned from many exchanges about Stein with poets writing now, and I followed new voices with growing interest. I read in libraries, an education in modernism and Stein criticism and scholarship as far as it went by the 1970s and 1980s.

What most astounds me after twenty years in the Stein opus with the growing, not diminishing, excitement that comes from familiarity are the steadily emerging intricate patterns and figurations which can be read in-numerable ways. Stein not only studied writing, painting, and human beings all her life but also studied the effects of her own writing.

Stein and Toklas carefully devised ways to maintain a social life designed to safeguard their privacy while also serving its public function. I shall in part enter the private life, a central context for Stein's capacity to meditate and write. It is far more important for her work than her better-known public life in the charmed circle that Mellow describes in detail.

The deceptive surface of the art collector, of the much photographed and painted subject, the charmed words of the famous—all the glitter recorded in the theatrical *Autobiography Of Alice B. Toklas*—conceal a human being who wrote with single-minded dedication. Her meditations, whose verbal genesis can be traced, arise from the vocabulary that daily life offered her, in the scraps of manuscript notes, in overheard talk, and in the hand we see forming the letters, playing with words and lines, and filling, as a painter fills a canvas, the manuscript notebooks that allowed her to be and know who she was. It is here, not in the biographies, that we gain access to her texts and her voice. It is the work that is the legacy of Gertrude Stein.

I could not have completed this book without the help of William Rice. Not only did he research endless puzzles of dating, sources, and inter-pretation, but he added to my reading his painter's eye and his work on Picasso's painting of 1905–07. In years of conversation, we talked and read our way into locked texts until we heard not only their words but their voice. Together we maintained the conviction that to accomplish the impossible is the only thing worth trying to do, as John Ashbery said in his 1957 review of "Stanzas."

The Voice of Gertrude Stein

The Context of Publication

What does Stein write? Novels? Plays? Poetry? Of course she wrote novels, from *Q. E. D.* to *The Making Of Americans,* to *Lucy Church Amiably, Ida,* and *Mrs. Reynolds.* But is she a novelist? Surely not as George Eliot or Henry James are called novelists. Nor are hers typical novels, although Stein plainly considered them so. She wrote plays from 1913 until the end of her life, starting with *What Happened,* which sounds like a takeoff on a play. Yet she is not a playwright like Ibsen or O'Neill. In what sense are her plays plays?

The title "Stanzas In Meditation" identifies poetry. "An Elucidation" sounds like the title of an essay, but it looks and sounds more like poetry than prose. Is *Tender Buttons,* which looks like prose, poetry, description? What *are* tender buttons? *An Acquaintance With Description* seems to announce a treatise on description but reads like an exercise in description. Preparing the first issue of *This Quarter,* Ernest Walsh, on March 10, 1925, wrote to Stein about her play *Capital Capitals* that, unless she objected, he was "running Capitals as poetry."

Apparently she did not object, for the piece appeared under "Poetry." On July 14, 1925, Walsh wrote that *Punch* "took a poke at him for putting Capitals in as poetry." The May 20 issue of *Punch* said "Capital Capitals" was poetry on a principle impossible to analyze. "It begins very well," *Punch* said, quoting the first seven lines. "And it ends very well," with the last nine. "And there are eight pages in between."

Our categories do not fit Stein's work. Yet she had no doubt that she was writing novels, plays, poems. She saw herself as a writer, not one kind of writer. She said she wrote literature, compositions, or simply writing. Creative ability was a matter of writing, not of what kind of work one wrote. Stein did not think in categories.

And her subjects? She wrote portraits of people whom her titles name, but they are not recognizable likenesses. Early titles name general subjects—*Three Lives,* begun as *Three Histories; The Making Of Americans,* subtitled *A History Of A Family's Progress;* the abstracted *Two,* identified in the subtitle as "Gertrude Stein and Her Brother," though it began as a study of her sister-in-law and her brother. On April 3, 1913, John Lane asked that for publication the title of *Three Lives* "be changed to something more generic"—something that sounded more like a novel and could be so promoted. *Objects Lie On A Table* suggests not the play it is but a still life. What can *A Novel Of Thank You* be?

"A Sonatina Followed By Another" is easy enough, but what of "Bee Time Vine"? Why does Stein call "Three Sitting Here" a narrative when it sounds like a portrait? Is "More Grammar For A Sentence" a treatise on grammar? How much more grammar? But these titles, like so many others, suggest her always playful mind. Titles aside, many say that Stein's work has no subject matter, but what then does it have? And why do others say that she is too much hard work?

Stein *is* hard work, for she challenges our capacity to read and our expectations of what written words and sentences are, what they do and how they do it. Her writing calls for a radical redefinition of genre, representation, language, reading, and writing. Yet such redefinitions were not undertaken systematically until long after she wrote, and then only gradually. Her work was pushed aside as offensive or silly, and all but a small group who understood and took it seriously ended up discussing her as a personality rather than as a serious writer.

No subjects. No genres. No sentences. She did not fit an editor's specialty, a magazine's layout, a publisher's categories, a bibliography, a library system—in short, she did not fit. On January 3, 1932, Lindley Williams Hubbell, a poet who worked at the New York Public Library, sent a fan letter for Stein to *transition* magazine in Paris. He told her that in 1922, at Frank Shay's bookstore on MacDougal Street, he had discovered "Vacation In Brittany" in the *Little Review,*

> I was really hearing *words* for the first time. . . . It made me understand the contours of a sentence and the texture of a word. . . . You have taught more writers how to write than any other writer in this century.

He spoke of the many who felt freed by Stein.

At the library, he discovered that her work was filed under "eccentric literature," a category that meant "books by people who are goofy." The result of his effort to reassign it was that *Tender Buttons* was put in the reserve collection as a rare book, no help to readers or to Stein. When Stein received his first letter, she immediately understood that as a staff member, he could help to promote her books. For years they exchanged letters and ideas about writing, and Hubbell placed orders, recommended outlets and publishers, and wrote about her.

But most publishers and editors refused her as illiterate or mad—a faker or simply a capricious lady. What little was published left many readers angry. They turned the tables on her, blaming her for writing incomprehensibly rather than themselves for failing to comprehend. They ridiculed her and her work. No one writes her off as a charlatan anymore. But anyone reading Stein must understand what it was like for an artist to live under incessant, condescending assaults upon herself as a writer, a person, and a woman.

Unlike Stein, Joyce can be analyzed and researched with the scholar's tools. In *Modern Music* for April 11, 1934, Gilbert Seldes wrote that Joyce "packs ten meanings into a word" whereas Stein "strips all meanings from words." Joyce's work allowed systematic searches for meanings in other languages, puns, etymology, Irish lore, Catholic doctrine, history, mythology. But Stein did not seem learned. Her primitive and childlike vocabulary provoked condescending smiles. Of course, Stein was aware of Joyce, although she made few public statements about him. In *The Autobiography Of Alice B. Toklas* she pointedly quotes Picasso likening Joyce to Braque, the two "incomprehensibles whom anybody could understand" (260). Implied was her own alliance with Picasso.

The Making Of Americans was completed by the end of 1911, but it remained unpublished until 1925. *Ulysses,* written between 1914 and 1921, was published on Joyce's fortieth birthday, February 2, 1922. In "A Birthday Book" (1924), the entry for Stein's birthday, February 3, reads,

> February second this second.
> February third Ulysses. Who Ulysses. Who Ulysses. Who Ulysses.
> February third. February third heard word purred shirred heard. Heard word. Who. (132)

Who had written the great modern novel? Among the Stein papers is a clipping of "Roots of Resentment," Oliver St. John Gogarty's review of *Finnegans Wake* in the *Observer* of May 7, 1939. Gogarty notes that Stein was the first to strive for the new style of suggestion by punning and contorted words. Marked in the review is the comment that Joyce's work had its "precedents in Lewis Carroll and Gertrude Stein."

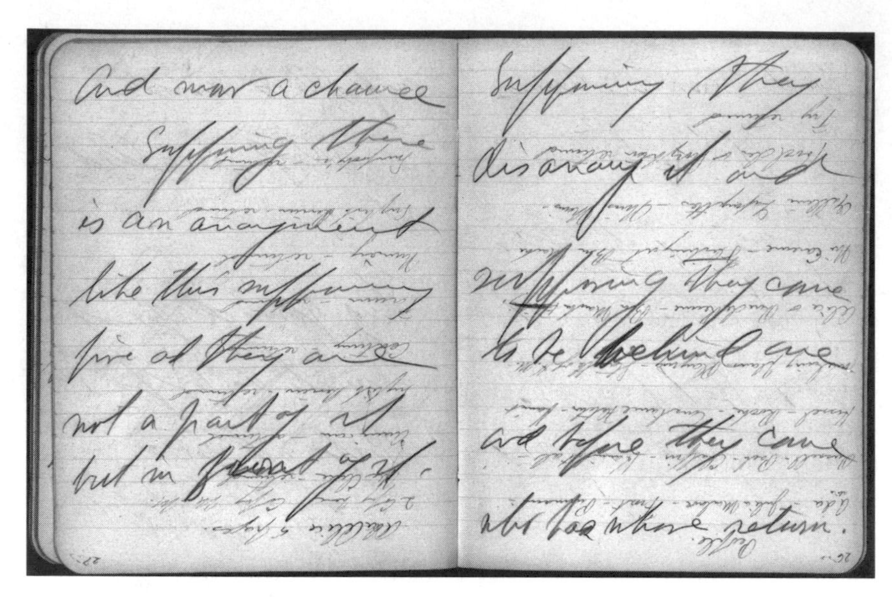

Figure 1. Double page from Stein's early "Book of Literature," 1910s, reversed and reused for writing "A Novel Of Thank You," 1926–27. Courtesy YCAL.

Stein submitted new works to magazine and book publishers as soon as she finished them. Among her papers is a fat black oilcloth notebook, a meticulous handwritten record, like a bookkeeper's ledger, of the number, location, and length of typescripts of her early texts, followed by lists of submissions to publishers. It also includes ideas for collections, with or without titles; twenty-two portraits under the title "People" were unsuccessfully submitted to Hodder and Stoughton and sent to Roger Fry. The title "One Volume" includes four longer portraits. She submitted virtually everything she wrote to major current magazines and publishers and almost immediately sent out again what was returned.

The absence of copies of letters of submission is not surprising. Few business letters are preserved except those that led to contracts, and few letters of rejection are among her papers. Yet from the record book we know that she submitted the 1911 portrait "Frost" to the *Atlantic Monthly* long before 1919, the year her published correspondence with editor Ellery Sedgwick begins. Inexperienced in publication, she submitted without success to the journals of the very literary establishment whose values her work challenged. Those were presumably also the magazines read by her family, whom Stein wished to impress as a serious and successful writer.

Her few early serial publications came about because friends placed her work: Mary Knoblauch contacted Stieglitz's *Camera Work;* Henry McBride gave her access to the *Sun* and *Vanity Fair,* Carl Van Vechten to *Rogue.*

time, it can also be described as "abstract," but that does not mean made-up or cut off from reality: it refers to the focus on essence rather than on detail. For example, she often eliminated nouns or names, always heavy with reference, and substituted pronouns. In a passage about blue paintings in "More Grammar Genia Berman" of 1929, the manuscript shows that she substituted "he" for "Picasso" to prevent an association with the painter.

Titles often sound abstract, although the texts do not. By not naming the person who is the subject of the portrait entitled "One," Stein prevents the intrusion of incidental personal detail and concentrates on the composition. The same is true of "Fourteen Anonymous Portraits." She is not interested in creating likenesses for parlor-game readers who enjoy solving puzzles, "Who is this?" Her manuscripts show how she decontextuates by destroying referential leads that we follow without thinking; for example, she substitutes the homophone "there" for "their" or even "three" for "there," or she bends "and so forth" into a new shape, "and so fourth." Abstraction sets in with punning as soon as the tie of word and reference is loosened.

The very words "composition" or "construction," which she used, suggest an abstracting process that concerns the perception of forms. Her commitment to that process is similar to that of Juan Gris, who never admitted decorative detail into a painting and believed "that the composition of a painting determines its subject and not vice versa," as Elliot Paul noted in the July 1927 issue of *transition* in an essay on Gris indebted to Stein.

It has been suggested that Stein decontextuated her work to conceal her lesbianism. Yet the need to conceal sexual references fails to explain her language. The many pieces that include sexual material are in fact extraordinarily explicit, as even a brief look at "Lifting Belly," "A Sonatina Followed By Another," or "Pink Melon Joy" makes abundantly clear. Sexual detail, such as the image of the cow, is clear, physical—and totally comical. The thrust toward abstraction goes deeper than sexual subject matter. It is compositional or constructive, not concealing.

Neutral words with minimal reference have more possibilities than colorful, referential words. Nouns and verbs have greater power as signs than connectives, pronouns, and auxiliary verbs. But they decline in power as signifiers in proportion to their gain in importance as word nuggets used as elements in patterns or designs.

Stein's disembodied words inhabit the enchanted forest of *As You Like It,* where figures join and part, marriages are made and unmade, names and identities change naturally. Free to change their referential ties, Stein's texts are written in the language of true comedy, where nothing is absolute, hierarchies are not respected, roles and identities can change, and the only authority is in the wide democratic freedom of the word that can move, make,

Here is the first notebook entry, the record of submission for *Three Lives:*

Duffield	returned
Bobbs Merrill	returned
McClure	returned
John Lane	returned
Kennerly	returned
Co[a]dy	taken away
John Lane	accepted published

The submission entry for "Ada," the five-page 1910 portrait of Alice Toklas, records two copies being "here," in Paris, and one with "M. M.," Mary Knoblauch in New York, who acted informally as Stein's agent in America.

McClure	returned
American	returned
English Review	returned
Century	returned
Forum	returned
[ ]	returned
English review	returned
Everybody's	returned

The notebook gives us information in a stark mood. The central word in the record book is "returned," relentlessly repeated. Painfully neat and orderly, the record speaks of Stein's unceasing, unsuccessful efforts at publication, nearly all ending with the same depressing refrain. The ledger looks not only like a matter of order but like a listing to keep herself going in the face of the steady "No" between the work and the readers she wanted. The last entry in this book—there may have been others—is "I Can Feel The Beauty" of 1917. By late 1925, she turned the half-filled notebook upside down, started from the end, and used it as the twenty-seventh manuscript book for *A Novel Of Thank You.*

To Strip Away the Context: The Primacy of Naked Words

Even in early years, Stein spoke of a writer's need to avoid what she called "associative habits." She meant unthinking, easy use of words, put down automatically and without consideration of exact meanings. By such habits, she said, words were cast into tired, worn forms that prevented perception. For her, questioning the forms of perception went with questioning the forms of language. As the modernist poet Mina Loy understood perfectly when she described her, Stein attacked language itself:

Curie
of the laboratory
of vocabulary
she crushed
the tonnage
of consciousness
congealed to phrases
to extract
a radium of the word
(*The Last Lunar Baedeker,* 26)

To free consciousness meant to free language or rather to free the word. The 1920 play *Photograph* puns on the need for renewing language:

A language tires.
A language tries to be.
A language tries to be free.
(*R* 345)

One way to free words was to remove them from habitual association and treat them as things rather than as signs. Repeating a word over and over gradually breaks the bond of word and reference. A form of punning, repetition gives body to the word and assaults meaning. What remains is, on the one hand, a physical compound of sound, tone, rhythm, length, weight, look, shape, thrust, or whatever one wishes to call these things, and, on the other, a meaning, which, abstracted from its carrier, tends to vanish. Free of convention and meaning, words can be used in new forms.

She did not use made-up or nonsense words, but she broke the vocabulary down into syllables until they became new words. *Selfish* became *sell fish,* two new words with new meanings—not no meanings—and new grammatical possibilities: an adjective turned into two verbs or nouns. And how quick we are to reconstruct *sell* and *fish* into a phrase about selling fish! *Disappointment* became *disappoint meant,* and we can imagine other ways of breaking it up. Such reductions create a double jolt, removing the meaning and destroying the anticipated grammatical behavior of a word.

The play *Photograph* raises the question of representation by exploring photographs as reproductions, copies, or twins. Act III was provoked no doubt by a snapshot:

A photograph. A photograph of a number of people if each one of them is reproduced if two have a baby if both the babies are boys what is the name of the street.
Madame. (*R* 346)

On rue Madame, a few steps from rue de Fleurus, lived Michael and Sarah Stein. Act IV continues,

We say we were warm. Guess McAdam.

Rue Madame was a paved, macadamized street.

Stein's young friend Bravig Imbs said that she "stopped at nothing in order to get at the essential naked language." That naked language is the result of a process of reduction accomplished by punning with elements of sound and sight, which shakes up stable syntax and meaning. Unhampered by meaning or grammar, treating English as a foreign language, Stein puns shamelessly from the visual to the auditory and back: "90 x 40" equals "nine tea time four tea," a series of new and unexpected phrases that refuse to stand still: tea time, time for tea, four o'clock tea. "Often away" is broken up as "often a way," "prism" as "pre-sun."

Punning recognizes no word boundaries, and Stein puns move from English to French and occasionally German. When "fountain" becomes *font tin,* it hovers between French and English. "A hole is a true" plays with French *trou* (hole). It is all made audible by rhymes which act in reverse in "St. Cloud and you. / St. Cloud out loud," where the first rhymes in French, the second in English. "Saint Therese seize" rhymes in English with the verb "seize," but "Saint[e] Thérèse seize" in French with the French word for "sixteen" (*seize*); and there are still other ways to hear it. Interestingly, "Finally George. A Vocabulary of Thinking" of 1928 was in part provoked by the problems encountered in translating sections of *The Making Of Americans* into French. For Stein, every word is a repository of ideas and unexpected possibilities.

Her stripped words cannot be joined by unthinking habit. Their exploration requires thought. Out of the physical properties uncovered by the process of reduction, she builds new, unstable and ambiguous forms and meanings. They sound strange precisely because they are new and unfamiliar. They are indeed anarchistic.

Her rejection of the rigid conventions of language led her gradually dissociate herself from all inflexible forms, including hierarchical thinki authoritarian organization, prescriptive grammar, and chronological na tive—aspects of the patriarchy. In a sense, all her work is a demonstr of possibilities of grammar for democracy. She was interested in spa living sentences.

To Decontextuate the Text

Over and over Stein said that she composed what she saw; s invent. All her work arises from the world in which she lived.

and remake itself. It is the world of here and now, which does away with all authority by asking, "What's in a name?"

The Context in the Text: The Autobiographical Presence

Stein's short works are meant, of course, to be read one at a time as discrete compositions. She wrote of ordinary daily life, and everything she wrote included the writer who shaped it. Experience yielded the vocabulary for writing. Composition shaped it in forms that evolved gradually one out of the other.

With the words, there enters into her work referential detail that speaks of the world and herself. Such details challenge us, as does all referential matter, to read representationally. Pointing out from the composed text to the world, they become centrifugal elements. But joined as words in a text, they become centripetal, creating patterns that point inward, to the composition. Reading Stein becomes both a centripetal, compositional task and a centrifugal, referential task, the two in constant, creative opposition.

The references ask us to attend to the world while the composition asks us to attend to the design. Her texts simultaneously pull us toward the compositional center and push us out into the world. But since her texts refuse to follow the conventions of representational language, they push us to hear, see, and connect words in new ways in a new verbal world of perceptions.

Stein's appear to be the perfect texts for deconstruction and doing away with the link between text and author. She did everything in her power to use her words in the service of composition, not information.

> To have rarely seen what is more and more an account of it. Everybody can change a name they can change the name Helen to Harry they can change the name Edith to Edward they can change the name Harriet to Howard and they can change the name Ivy to Adela. This makes it impossible for all of them to say what they mean. (*NOTY* 38)

These lines refuse paraphrasable meaning while teasing us, with substitutions of names in patterns that do not sound arbitrary, to read referentially. One thinks of the growing preoccupation with names and identities that finally leads her to reassign identities to Grant, Wilbur Wright, Henry James, and George Washington in *Four In America.* Anyone who knows of her interest in names wonders whether she is saying more than at first appears.

Although the biographical information in the work of the late 1910s and the 1920s never concerns major events or historical upheavals, the fragmented referential nuclei give body to Stein's life. They also help make audible the Stein voice. Biographers have relied for information on the late

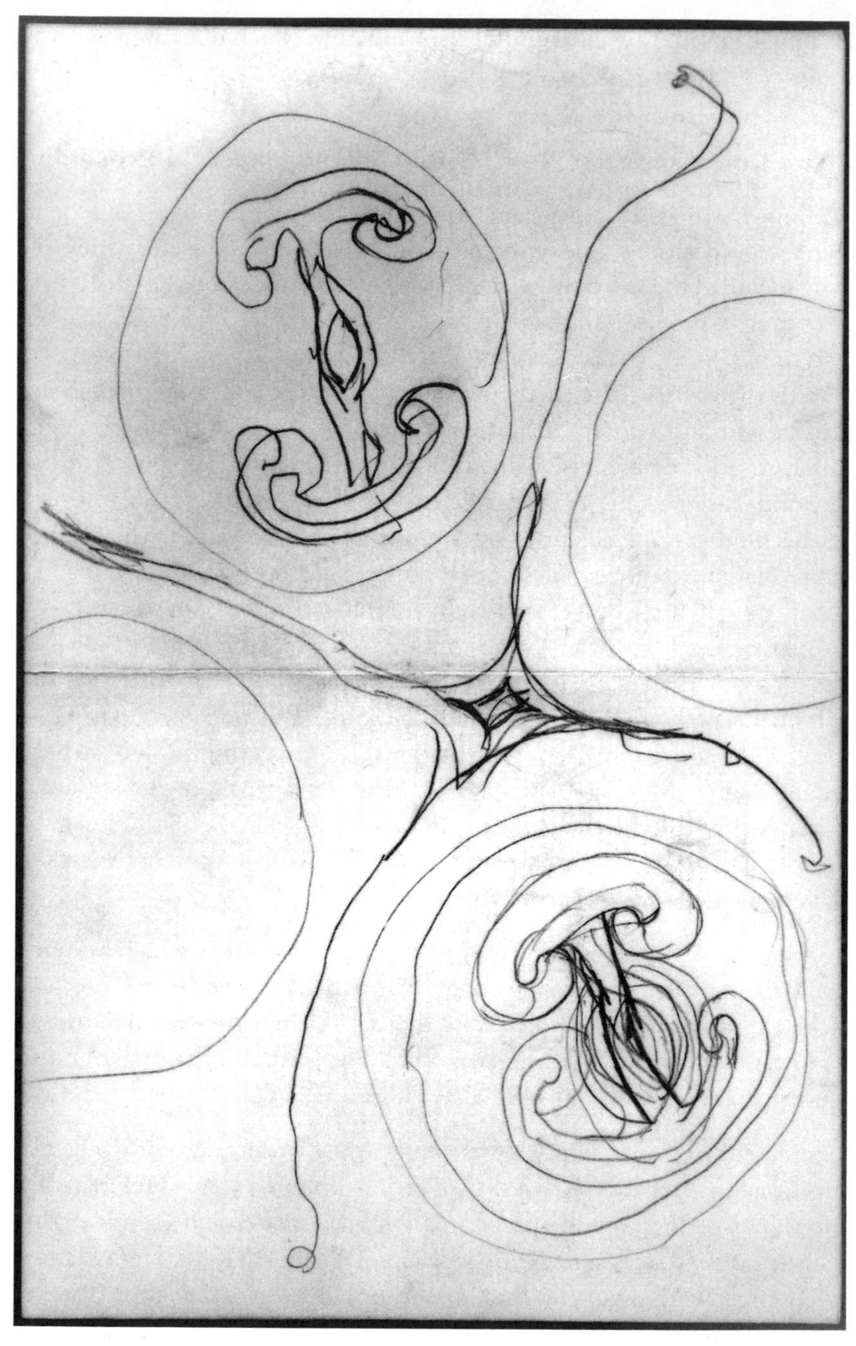

Figure 2. Len Lye, sketch for and final version of the logo for Seizin Press books, YCAL. Courtesy Len Lye and the Len Lye Foundation.

AN ACQUAINTANCE WITH DESCRIPTION

BY

GERTRUDE STEIN

Printed and published at The Seizin Press
35A St. Peter's Square Hammersmith
London 1929

autobiographical books from *The Autobiography Of Alice B. Toklas* to *Wars I Have Seen*. Forgetting that autobiography is not history, they often fail to check the "facts" trailed by the words, including the silent omissions. Most have shunned the early work because it is difficult to read, does not appear to be autobiographical, and refuses story, information, reference. Yet these manuscripts and texts are the untapped sources for her life. Barely audible, we can hear in them the voice of the "I" before it turns into the I that is "I not any longer" of the meditations.

"The Voice of Gertrude Stein" suggests both the voice of composed words and the voice of Stein's endlessly publicized personality. The two voices—of the work, of the person—not only are different but are often in conflict. Language itself has no voice but has the possibility of voice. Writing, the act of articulation, gives voice to words. When Stein read a piece aloud—she can still be heard on recordings—she read in an evenly paced, clear and neutral voice to allow the words to move freely in the auditory space of the text. For her, the voice of a work is not the personal, expressive voice of the author but the articulating voice of the composition.

Her work, though it is not religious, recalls the formulae of prayer. In her 1922 "Talks To Saints Or Stories Of Saint Remy," prayer is associated with saints; they speak not of and for themselves but, having overcome the temptation of the referential world, speak as an act of devotion in the tradition of the comic spirit, free of the regimentation of the world.

> Can you create the word and he created the word created. (*PL* 109)

When saints speak, objects and audience gradually drop away, and saints, like artists, offer devotions in words.

> Talks to saints.
> Have you heard of me.
> I am said to resemble them and they are said to resemble them and they are said to resemble me. Talks with me. Talk to me. Talk of me. Talk for me.
> Saints talk for me.
> Saints talk to me.
> Saints talk with me. Saints talk with saints.
> Talks with saints.
> Talks with saints mean more and more and more. Talks with saints mean more.
> Talks with saints.
> We feel it to be our gift. (*PL* 111)

Reading the Hand Writing

The Manuscripts Of Gertrude Stein

Outside the words of her works, Stein gave no clues to the reader who found her difficult. She kept no diary or journal. She added no prefaces or postscripts to her books. She rarely commented in letters. A composition was complete when it was self-contained, making explanation superfluous and paraphrase extrinsic. The logic of her position is clear and consistent, and though her work changed dramatically over the years, her commitment to language did not change. Her insistence upon composing each perception in its authentic immediacy in verbal forms that "emancipate thought rather than limiting it"[1] demands of the reader an attention that takes nothing for granted, an effort that always concentrates on the possibilities, not the habits of language. Yet precisely because her words are centripetal, pointing inward, to the piece, rather than centrifugal, pointing outward, to the world, readers find entry into her work difficult and look for help in a world that offers none.

Oddly enough, the most obvious source of information about how Stein wrote has hardly been explored: her manuscripts. Stein's printed books preserve what she wrote but are stripped of the process that gave them being. In the autograph manuscripts, however, that process is often preserved and can be "read" as detectives read stories in the smallest clues. What follows restores some of the process of writing—the context of the text.

This chapter is a revised reprint, with an expanded section on sexuality, from Bruce Kellner, ed., *A Gertrude Stein Companion* (New York: Greenwood Press, 1988), 84–95.

1. Georgiana King, "Gertrude Stein," *International* 7, no. 6 (June 1913): 157.

Among the Stein papers at Yale, most of her autograph manuscript notebooks for individual pieces are preserved. In these are the texts from which typescripts were prepared for submission and publication. In addition, as has been known since the 1950s, Stein from 1902 until 1911 kept voluminous notes—on pads, loose leaves, in school copybooks, large and small notebooks.[2] These early notes include observations, commentary, plans for books, quotations from reading, her typology of personality, identification of pseudonyms, advice to herself, responses to events, drafts of descriptions, and so on. All these form context for the various drafts of sections for her early books. Together, these notes and drafts represent the first stage of Stein's writing.

In the second stage, many but not all these drafts were transferred, with or without revision, into the individual manuscript books, where Stein also, however, composed directly, combining the drafted sections she or Toklas copied over with new writing composed on the spot to complete her texts. The complete text of each of her early works is preserved separately in one or more autograph manuscript books. There is also an almost complete collection of typescripts, which Alice Toklas prepared from all manuscripts after *Three Lives,* starting sometime between 1907 and 1909.

Unlike the texts, which were written for publication, the notebooks were private. They were never intended for publication and probably not even for inspection. Toklas, who had not read them although she knew of them, was distressed when she heard that they had turned up at Yale among the papers Stein had hastily assembled for shipment in the spring of 1946.[3] One reason was that they contained not only first drafts of Stein works, but raw personal comments, including detailed studies of friends and family members whom the notes identified although the books did not. Precisely because they are so informative, however, not only about persons but about the genesis of Stein's ideas, the sequence of her works and the steps in composition, the

2. In this summary, I refer mainly to her early notebooks for *MOA* and some of the early portraits, which Leon Katz and Jayne Walker date 1902–11. There are at Yale also notes long misidentified as being for *TB,* 1912–13, which Rosalind Moad in 1993 identified as being for work done in Paris, winter 1914–15, for "Pink Melon Joy," "Johnny Grey," "How Could They Marry Her," and "Possessive Case." I here give 1911 as terminal date since the early notebooks were first studied and documented by Katz. See Leon Katz, "The First Making of *The Making of Americans:* A Study Based on Gertrude Stein's Notebooks and Early Versions of Her Novel (1902–8)" (Ph.D. diss., Columbia University, 1963), i–iii; Jayne L. Walker, *Gertrude Stein: The Making of a Modernist* (Amherst: University of Massachusetts Press, 1984), xvii–xviii and n. 9.

3. Toklas to Carl Van Vechten, 4 June 1947.

notebooks make possible an understanding of Stein's early development that could not be achieved without them.

In the apparent absence of notebooks for works after 1913, it was thought that Stein ceased taking notes altogether and came to compose all her work directly in the manuscript books, as she had in part already done earlier.[4] Yet many of the manuscripts after 1913 show a hand so smooth, steady, and regular that I wondered whether it was possible to produce in first draft long and complex texts of such finished fluency. Some small emendations and changes began to look like minor copying slips rectified rather than revisions—wrong starts for single words, erroneous endings corrected, slips of the pen caught and adjusted. Other changes were visibly revisions—longer crossed out passages with new sections scribbled above them, deletions not replaced by new wording, changed titles, and so on.

Stein herself was interested in writing and in being read, not in explaining what she was doing. Among her papers, there are only two brief statements of principles of composition, both in drafts for letters; whether she actually sent the two letters is not known. Interestingly, one is to a professor and the other to a researcher; her consistent respect for professors and students is striking. The first comment appears simple enough:

> I do all my work in my head and only write down what it my head finally accepts.[5]

The statement is less clear than it seems: how much could Stein keep in her head at one time—a sentence one page long? How she built the sequence of phrases and sentences remains an unanswered question.

The other statement, answering Leonard B. Gandalac's inquiry of May 27, 1932, emphasizes the conscious and deliberate nature of her work. In awkward, self-conscious phrasing, she theorizes about

> exactitude of abstract thought and poetry as created by exactness and as far as possible disembodiedment if one may use such a word, creating sense by intensity of exactness. . . .[6]

Once, however, she described simply and concretely how she wrote. After the publication of *The Autobiography Of Alice B. Toklas,* in 1933, she tried in

4. Leon Katz, "First Making," 10.
5. Draft of an answer to Clarence E. Andrews of Ohio State University, probably 1926. The letter from Andrews, a teacher of Samuel Steward, is not preserved.
6. Draft of an answer to Leonard B. Gandalac, Montreal, after 27 May 1932.

"And Now" to return from "outside" or "audience" writing for success to serious writing from inside, and she concluded,

> I write the way I used to write in Making of Americans, I wander around and I come home and I write, I write in one copy-book and I copy what I write into another copy-book and I write and I write. . . . I have come back to write the way I used to write and this is because now everything that is happening is once more happening inside, there is no use in the outside. . . .[7]

No one has paid attention to these words. Yet they acknowledge notebooks prior to the final texts. The absence of notebooks, then, means not that there were no later notebooks but merely that they were not donated to the Yale Collection or that they were destroyed. The comment in "And Now" makes it impossible to consider her later manuscripts as the first and only versions of her texts.

Closer inspection of the Stein papers at Yale has uncovered over thirty of the first copybooks to which Stein refers. They date from the 1920s and early 1930s and contain sections of various Stein works, along with other notations. They differ in characteristics of notation from the early notebooks. Their texts focus more narrowly than those of the early notebooks on composition in progress and include almost no comments on her writing that are not drafts. Also, most are small pocket notebooks rather than a motley collection of scraps such as Stein often used in early years. Some scraps, however, are also preserved, and many others may have been lost or discarded. It is impossible to judge by the scraps now in the Stein collection.

Again unlike the early notes, these copybooks contain jottings about daily domestic life, including intimate details about her relationship with Toklas. The preserved notebooks do not constitute a complete series, and it is unclear why these and not other notebooks—there must have been hundreds more—ended up at Yale. However, the consistency of their matter and their manner, especially their nonverbal features, shows beyond doubt how Stein worked. Together, the preliminary notebooks, or *carnets,* and the manuscript books, or *cahiers,* open Stein's mature creative process.

Apparently Stein bought *carnets* in large numbers to make sure that they were always available. Varying in size from an average 3 1/4 inches by 4 3/4 inches, they are small enough to slip in a pocket or hold in the hand. That Stein carried them with her is suggested by small written exchanges with Toklas. For example, in a 1927 *carnet,* Toklas notes,

7. "And Now," 1933, early manuscript version.

If you can look *later* at the 3 people behind you. It's a Mrs. Belloc Lowndes.

The *carnets* are scribbled full, often starting from both ends, and the pages are covered with writing, sometimes in both directions, in an uneven hand, usually in pencil.

Jottings must have been made under all sorts of conditions, perhaps even in the dark, for they are often hard to read. They contain, in addition to text, letter drafts, shopping lists, guest lists, addresses and telephone numbers, doodles and small drawings, drafts of dedications for books, titles, calculations of income or expenditures, contents for proposed books, notes and jingles to Toklas, and so on. If the entries are more carefully followed than this random list suggests, however, they begin to speak of the process of writing.

Stein apparently worked often late into the night, even when she shared the studio with her brother. After 1910, when Toklas moved in, she continued working after Toklas went to sleep. The prospect of starting work sometimes left her anxious and unable to concentrate. In both the *carnets* and the *cahiers* she devised ways to help herself start. She began work in a *carnet* with little love notes, jingles, intimate addresses, and occasional drawings to Toklas.

A little new book always has to tell and to tell very well very well of my belle. . . . (1925)

or

[Stein] Dedicated to Baby . . . dedicated to she. . . .

[Toklas] . . . It is a nice thing to have a dedication from a husband with a decoration. It is a nice thing . . . to sit with a husband on the sand. (Nice, 1923)

To offset such notes from composition, they are often written in a tiny, thin, "secret" hand. None are literary; many are the kind of embarrassingly bad private verse full of sentimental diminutives that lovers keep to themselves or tear up. The notes become a kind of correspondence between "Mr. and Mrs. Reciprocal," as Stein calls them in one *carnet*. A new *carnet* was often inscribed for good luck with a few words to Toklas:

To dedicate and did eat cake to dedicate it all to wifie. (1925)

or

I have ordered fifty-two little books to write of my little Hebrew constantly. . . . (1923)

Seven of these fifty-two, which have distinctive, marbleized double covers, are preserved. The ritual of dedicating a *carnet* to Toklas allayed anxiety, enabled Stein to know who she was and to find her voice for writing. When something went wrong in her work, she might attribute the trouble to her failure to start with a word to Toklas.

> It all happened because the little book got started without . . . wifey. (1925)

Stein likens the creative act to the sexual act, associating it not only with lesbian sexuality but also with patriarchal gender. Again and again she writes notes to Toklas that describe making love to her in intimate detail and indeed *are* lovemaking. Always it is Stein, the husband, who makes love to Toklas, the wife, which culminates in her *having a cow,* or orgasm (the verb *to cow* also appears). Toklas' sexual fulfillment inspires Stein to write, which in turn represents sexual fulfillment for herself. It produces literature or what she at times calls *babies.* Toklas' *cows* are equivalent to Stein's *babies,* but both cows and babies are also their joint creations.

Toklas is both the beloved and the muse. As beloved, she induces Stein to create masterpieces of sexual fulfillment on the instrument of her body; as muse, she inspires Stein to create literary masterpieces with the instrument of language.

> She is . . . constantly going to have her cow now master pieces of yes, Oh yes master pieces oh yes master in pieces, oh yes. (1923)

Masterpieces and mastery also permit Stein to see her work as masculine, serious, and professional rather than as feminine, frivolous, and amateurish.

> Master pieces are quietly made at home ("The Pilgrims," 1930, *PL* 147)

refers to both literary and sexual activity.

In union, Stein wins fulfillment, freedom, and access to language.

> Husband is trying not a wife
> He is trying and succeeding
> trying his wife's cow
> and she and he are satisfied
> we call it three and free. (1925)

Stein's work with twos and threes throughout her career is in part sexual.[8] Two as one in union make a third, whose many possible forms Stein ex-

8. See also Leon Katz's introduction in Gertrude Stein, *Fernhurst, Q. E. D., And Other Early Writings* (New York: Liveright, 1971), viii.

plores, for example, in "A Third" (1925). Freed by this love from the vexing question of who she is—or, to put it differently, given definition by that love—Stein achieves her sense of being as "Baby." The creative act, linked with the sexual act, allows her voice. Identity literally dissolves in union.

Another third is an actual baby. A baby here is not a child raised by parents but a written work.

> She says she needs a word a third. (346)

In a note written at the end of a work session in a 1925 *carnet,* Stein warns Toklas,

> Do not read further they are mixed babies ! ! ! ! !

Mixed babies appear to be sections of writing for different pieces, which are not meant to be read consecutively.

Houses also can be thirds, being places created by two and for two to become one; English idiom sounds procreative:

> They had had a house. . . . (334)

Who makes houses or homes for lovers—or for married couples?

> He makes houses which are surrounded by trees. (*NOTY,* 34)

Stein makes houses in words, from outside, just as people build houses and plant trees. Toklas creates home living inside. Inside and outside, looking out and looking in, are partly sexual in origin. Finally, the third can be a new comer or intruder, the proverbial third that breaks up the union of two—and makes novels.

> Never leave out a third.
> Always put in a third. (345)

> A third is always first. That is for you to find out my fat wife. (340)

At the end of one *carnet* occurs a concluding epigraph to Toklas, similar to the opening dedications elsewhere,

> A noble cow, as a wife has a cow a love story and a wife has a cow which is truth no truth stranger than fiction is only diction not contradiction but a blessing. . . . (Nice, 1923)

The entire piece that concludes with "as a wife has a cow a love story"—not only its final section—*is* a love story. The conclusion of lovemaking is a cow; the conclusion of verbal union is a book. Cow and book are sexual and artistic creations, intimately related. *A Book Concluding With As A Wife Has A Cow A Love Story* (1923) is a portrait of Toklas.

Stein had written early portraits of the three friends most intimately associated with her art, "Picasso," in 1909 or 1910, "Ada," Alice Toklas, in 1910, and "One. Carl Van Vechten," in 1913. In Nice, in the late summer of 1923, she wrote in short succession second portraits of all three, "If I Told Him. A Completed Portrait Of Picasso"; *A Book Concluding . . .;* and two portraits of Van Vechten, "Van Or Twenty Years After" and "And Too. Van Vechten. A sequel to One." All, in a sense, are love stories, and all have to do with creation, mastery, identity, engenderment. The circular and punning *A Book Concluding . . .* begins and ends with love (wife, cow) but also begins and ends with writing (book, story). The subtitle, "As A Wife Has A Cow . . . ," is built into the "book" of the main title as an unfinished sentence. How is the sentence to end? As my wife has a cow, so I have—what? So I have a book. Or, "As my wife has a cow [so I have] a love story." *Res* and *verba* have become one.

Stein and Toklas made love in life and love in books.

> They Had.
>
> They had no children. They had no children but three sister-in-laws a brother which brother and no nephews and no nieces and *no other language.*[9]

The 1926 Juan Gris lithographs for the book extend Stein's verbal puns into elaborate, heterosexual visual puns. She must have explained her text to Gris, since he did not read English. Oddly, his illustrations have provoked almost no comment, perhaps because their connection with Stein's words has appeared unclear. Yet Stein's love story, like so many of her works, requires the simplest, most literal reading. Her opening doors, closets, windows, and books lead to his guitar and song, the guitar strings parallel to the lines of her text. They also lead to his final circular design that reflects the Stein composition whose end is tucked into its beginning.

With Toklas as beloved and as muse, her sexual fulfillment is described again and again in loving detail and lovers' verse—but her own sexual fulfillment lies in the perception of Toklas' sexuality. What this fact means for their sexual relationship and their marriage is a question that no biographer has so far even asked. What it means for Stein's writing is in part suggested in this book. The "unconventional" lesbian relationship, crisscrossed with conventional patriarchal marriage terminology, breaks usage open in indeterminate modernist texts.[10]

9. *A Book Concluding . . . , R* 457; emphases added.

10. The information in the *carnets* may surprise those who consider Stein and Toklas to have been squeamish Victorian ladies. They were formal and reticent about their private do-

Toklas understood what Stein was doing as a writer but also understood her need for validation and support. Occasionally—not very often—she wrote answers to Stein's notes. Some pick up Stein's style, her banter and her humor, but others play with her own.

A question mark is not admitted by us moderns,

Toklas in a 1924–25 *carnet* comments after Stein questions her ability to make Toklas happy.

Practice makes perfect
practice in appreciation makes perfect appreciation,

Stein writes in a 1925 *carnet,* next to a drawing of what appears to be a wild rose, and Toklas responds,

Lu et approvė. [*sic*][11]

Stein also asks Toklas to check facts—for example, in 1928 about Picasso:

When did he leave rue Ravignan?

Sometimes Toklas comments very personally upon Stein's work. On a torn, undated slip of paper, she writes,

> Sweet pinky, you made lots of literature last night didn't you. . . . You are doing most handsomely. Would you mind if I didn't think you a Post-Impressionist . . . you are not a Cubiste either. It's such a very orderly literature much more orderly than Pablo's. La Jolie is quite messy compared to this. . . .

When, in the course of writing, concentration again became difficult, Stein often regained her voice by writing a new note to Toklas or by diverting herself with verses composed on the small pages of the *carnets,* as in one of 1928:

Mon petit blanc et
mon petit toujours, mon

---

main. They also insisted on good manners, whose function was in part to maintain privacy. But that the private life was intensely sexual is beyond doubt. See Carl Van Vechten to Donald Gallup, 27 February 1954, YCAL, in Bruce Kellner, ed., *Letters of Carl Van Vechten* (New Haven: Yale University Press, 1987), 253.

11. The sentence, "Practice makes perfect," appears in "Natural Phenomena" (*PL* 196), parts of which Stein drafts in this 1925 notebook. It also refers to the draft for a review of Alfred Kreymborg's autobiography, *Troubadour* (New York: Boni and Liveright, 1925), that Stein was writing in appreciation of his inclusion of the "history of us" in his "history of himself."

petit blanc et mon
J'espere et je l'aime . . .

Taking off from Mont Blanc and from "petits bleus," the notes mailed by pneumatic tube in Paris, this verse speaks, with a slight echo of Toklas, always associated with blue, of the white dog Basket. Slim and unfinished as it is, it affords a glance into the transition from private life to writing. Stein often begins literally with descriptions of things seen, including Toklas. Very quickly these become elements of description, no longer elements of Toklas. By the time they are seen formally, as elements of composition, writing has begun.

One notation, begun as a description of Toklas or another woman, ends up in "Arthur A Grammar":

> She was photographed with trees. (1928, *HTW* 79)

This sentence is placed directly after a parallel phrase, perhaps about the same snapshot and perhaps reflected also in a drawing of earrings in a *carnet* of the same period,

> She was photographed with earrings.

In slightly different form, describing Alyse Gregory, the novelist and managing editor of the *Dial,* this sentence also appears in the play *Paisieu* of that year,

> Gregory Alice is photographed in earrings. (*LO&P* 157)

Joined in "Arthur," the two sentences have become a small grammatical paradigm—"she was photographed with": with what *was* she photographed? Stein has written, from life, a portrait and a grammatical miniature about the word "with."

What look like dog-eared corners at the outside top and bottom of many *carnets* appear to contain elaborate private signals from Stein to Toklas, showing her where to begin, what to do, how far to read or copy. Toklas apparently folded corners with return signals when she left the *carnets* for Stein to pick up again. Doodles and simple drawings also appear in this private correspondence in the *carnets* and sometimes in the manuscript *cahiers.* The doodles frequently play with repeated calligraphic shapes of letters or initials, sometimes in puns and rhymes, and are often carefully distributed in the space of a page. Some of the drawings are representational though they lack detail—earrings, flowers, animals, human figures, and especially birds, which appear to have a private significance that remains unclear to me.

Other drawings are abstract and sometimes suggest anatomical forms.

Never in the *cahiers* but only in the *carnets* appear simple, linked figures, alike except for a bun or long hair for the female, who is always larger. Suggestively erotic, they are drawn as if by children, with small circles for heads and larger circles for bodies, usually in groups of three, six, and sometimes four, alternating male and female. Irregularly scrawled circles under them suggest sexual activity—"wife having a cow now now now"—or excrement.

Not only the words *cow* and *Caesar* but also the name *Lindo* and a verb, *to lindo* (dildo?) describe sexual activity. The last echoes the Spanish adjective *lindo* (nice, elegant, sweet) and originated during their stay in Majorca in 1915, when in Palma they met James Lindo Webb.[12]

Finally, the love notes are often signed by Stein and Toklas in coded initials and abbreviations, especially *Y. D.* and *D. D.*, the initials Swift used in the *Journal to Stella,* which is replete with his "little language."[13] From the little *carnets,* in which she drafted text and wrote love notes, emerges a private ritual astounding in its elaborate consistency.

In addition to the devices for starting work, many other notes show Stein playing. Here, for example, she experiments with balanced expression and typographical design, using the alliterating names of her friends, Bernard Faÿ and Christian Bérard:

Bernard or Berard
balance believe balance
with

This exercise is followed by the draft of a 1928 letter to Laura Riding, praising the shapes in the logo designed by Len Lye for the Seizin Press, ready to publish *An Acquaintance With Description:*

> They have real weight and balance in them in some strange way.

The preoccupation with design, always important to Stein, leads from the names to the logo.

Many other personal scribbles—the kind anyone jots down on slips of paper or notepads—become sources of biographical information. Frequently jottings tell where Stein is—in Paris, in Belley, in Nice, where in one *carnet*

12. After teaching English in Palma, Lindo Webb became British vice consul for Majorca from October 9, 1915, to October 3, 1916. Stein became friendly with him and his wife, Lettie Lindo Webb. He appears in two Majorca plays, *He Said It. A Monologue.* (1915) and *For The Country Entirely. A Play In Letters.* (1916), and his name is in "A Sonatina . . ." and *NOTY* 31. There are letters at YCAL. See Rosalind Moad, "1914–1916: Years of Innovation in Gertrude Stein's Writing" (Ph.D. diss., University of York, England, 1993).
13. See *LGS/TW* 86n.

of 1923 she writes concurrently the beginning of the second Picasso portrait and the end of "Are There Arithmetics" while in another she works on a later section of the portrait and on "Geography." The notebooks also permit dating and identifying people.

One *carnet* contains English addresses and other English notes—as well as the beginnings of *An Acquaintance With Description* and of the portrait "Edith Sitwell And Her Brothers The Sitwells And Also To Osbert Sitwell And To S. Sitwell." The *carnet* and the manuscript *cahier* together make clear how the awkward title of this portrait came about. Both these pieces were begun during the visit to England in June 1926. But the *carnet* also shows later sections of both pieces, interspersed with notes about the Bugey, the region around Belley, and written after Stein's return to France. The last step in this sequence is in letters, which document when Stein sent the finished portrait to Edith Sitwell.

There are also various lists in both women's hands. Reading lists appear to be culled from reviews, from suggestions of friends, and perhaps from advice of librarians at the American Library. Of course, a title on a list does not necessarily mean that she read the book. The lists show Stein's special interest in biographies and personal as well as historical narratives, usually popular works.

Shopping lists show an interesting use of pronouns: Stein and Toklas, as husband and wife, using the personal pronouns *he* and *she*, not inflected and occasionally even capitalized, as their names. On such lists appear "Stockings for he" and "Material for she." Such data are as important for the biography as the drafts are for Stein's work. The *carnets* make clear how inseparable working and living were.

In order to establish the personal context of Stein's work that is visible in the *carnets*, I have left the drafts until last. They will also lead to the *cahiers*, for they were copied, sometimes with revisions, into the *cahiers*, where Stein often continued composing without preliminary drafts. One *carnet* of the summer of 1928 is an instructive example.

At one end of the *carnet* appear the original title and subtitle of Stein's play, *Paisieu*, in the form *Pasiue / A Play / A Work Of Pure Imagination In Which No Reminiscences Intrude.* Stein's original spelling of the title, *Pasiue*, corrected by Toklas to read *Paisiue*, probably conflates *Pugieu*, a hamlet near Belley, and perhaps *Peyrieu*, another hamlet, with *pays* (country) or *paix, paisible* (peace, peaceful). After the title, rhyming with *intrude*, appears the author's name, "Gertrude."

Stein liked writing her name. She signed even drafts of letters. Often she inscribed the student *cahiers* that had spaces for name, subject, class, or address, with her name and sometimes that of Toklas and all sorts of word and name play. The first twenty-five pages of the booklet show the beginning of the play. By page 26, perhaps at a different sitting, the writing changes in direction from the horizontal to the vertical and produces another section of the play, used later in the final text. This section, identified with the capital letter *P* as *Paisieu,* ends with the sentence "Definition made a hand." (*LO&P* 160).

The same sentence, copied over at the top of the following page, begins a section of "Arthur A Grammar" (*HTW* 80), identified with the letter *G* for "Grammar." A sentence used in one piece becomes an occasion for a meditation upon writing in another piece, a common situation for Stein in the late 1920s when side by side she wrote grammar pieces and portraits, plays, or other works. There follow in the *carnet* several letter drafts and further sections of both *Paisieu* and "Arthur A Grammar."

Stein's transfer of the texts into the manuscript notebooks led me to a startling discovery. The *Paisieu* manuscript book opens with the title and the beginning of the play—in Toklas' handwriting. After a few pages, the text continues in Stein's hand, only to change again later to Toklas' hand. What has happened? The manuscript sections of *Paisieu* written by Toklas are exactly those that Stein drafted in the *carnet.* Toklas copied them for Stein. Meanwhile Stein herself copied the grammar sections into the *cahier* of "Arthur A Grammar."

What happened next is a matter of conjecture. Either Stein composed directly into the *cahier* the next section of the play, the one written in her own hand in the *cahier,* or she wrote the next section first in another *carnet,* not preserved, and eventually herself copied it into the *cahier.* The presence in these passages of revisions, not merely corrections, suggests that Stein composed in the *cahier.*

Bridgman, after examining the notebooks for "Ada" and *A Novel Of Thank You,* which also show the hand of Toklas, as do some other manuscripts, concludes,

> given the manuscript in two hands; and given the conclusion that the two people are one, the evidence is persuasive that this was a collaboration of symbolic significance, sealing the relationship between the two women. (211)

What confusion of writing and love! Surely union in love is central for Stein and Toklas, but union in writing, especially in Stein's manner, including the beginning of a new piece? The very thought is preposterous. Where her hand is visible in the manuscripts, even with no first drafts preserved, it is because she copied, not because she composed.

The *carnets* that survive make clear how Stein worked, although many questions remain about particular pieces for which no drafts and no notes are preserved. Hundreds of *carnets* must have been filled. The scribbled notes tell what she did, what she saw, what she thought, where she went, and how she worked, all interlocked in the service of composition. The details are literally true and the process of writing is far more conscious and less spontaneous than has been thought.

By the time the drafts were transferred into the *cahiers,* the personal contexts visible in the *carnets* were left behind. What makes these so valuable is that they preserve these contexts. In a way, they constitute Stein's unwitting introduction to her work, the references from which she labored so hard to abstract her texts. For her, once the *carnets* had served their purpose—after text was copied into the *cahiers,* after the friends on the list had been invited for dinner, drafted letters copied over, groceries purchased, the car repaired, the addresses transferred—they became redundant. What remained, and what Stein intended to preserve, was her writing—self-contained and disembodied movement, lifted from the context between the covers of the *carnets.*[14]

The *cahiers* share some of the characteristics of the *carnets* but are also very different. Although they include some personal notes and verses to Toklas, they do not suggest the vast private context or the sexual details of the *carnets.* Yet they show far more than the typescripts or the printed texts and tell stories of their own.

A nearly complete collection of manuscripts is preserved. Although some are loose leaves or pads, most are standard copybooks, most commonly about 6 3/4 inches by 8 3/4 inches, available in any French stationery shop. Some are larger than others, some thicker than others. Some have graph paper, others lined or plain paper; some have stiff covers and others soft covers. Many are heavy black oilcloth notebooks. Some are composition books or *cahiers* for students with simple, stylized line drawings and titles on the front covers, a dragon with the title "Le Dauphin"; a sheaf of wheat entitled "Le Bon Grain"; a bird, "Avia"; "La Science Guidant le Travail" with a female figure reading instructions from a scroll to a laborer.

Other manuscripts are in thin student *cahiers* with colored front covers

14. It is unlikely that Stein should have considered giving the *carnets* to an archive. Either they must have been eliminated as she went along or, if they were kept, they must have been destroyed at a later time. The few that are among the papers at Yale must have been included by accident, as were the early notebooks. After Stein's death, Toklas burned papers at a friend's house, as is clear from a letter to Anne Low-Beer of 29 August 1955 (*SOA* 325). We do not know what she burned. But if further *carnets* had been kept, they might have been among those papers.

illustrating people in action and on the back covers explanatory text on educational subjects. These *cahiers* were published by Hachette and various other firms in titled series with numerous subtitles in each series. For example, the series *Mots Historiques* (*Famous Sayings*) includes pictures and stories from French history: *Souviens-toi du vase de Soissons* (*Remember Soissons*), the stern reminder of Clovis to a soldier who had challenged his authority, or *Madame, tout est perdu fors l'honneur,* François I's note to his mother on the evening of his defeat that all was lost but honor. The series *Les Phénomènes de la Nature,* which provided the title and starting point for Stein's "Natural Phenomena," included notebooks entitled *Volcan, Foudre,* and *La Marée,* on volcanoes, lightning, and tides. Unlike the stiff, stylized line drawings, these action pictures sometimes gave Stein ideas for writing.[15]

When Stein began writing in a *cahier* rather than in a *carnet,* she sometimes relied on the *cahier* to give her a start. Here she begins in a notebook on Lamartine from the series *Les Educateurs de la Jeunesse* (*Teachers of Youth*):

> I wondered how I would begin
> my Lamartine
> with a song about my queen.
> ("An Indian Boy," 1923, ms)

The jingle to Toklas is not included in the text; Lamartine helps Stein start but does not become a part of her work. Likewise, when she worries what to write about and decides that she will not write about a volcano, the cover of the notebook on volcanoes tells us where she got the idea, though we do not need the *cahier* to understand what she means.

As Stein gathered her resources by concentrating on the immediate, details might enter her work from anything she could see, including the notebooks. Some of these remain casual triggers of words. Others, however, determine composition, sometimes leaving the texts difficult to understand without the sources. Wendy Steiner has shown some of the ways in which such illustrations determine her portraiture, especially the portrait of Hemingway. Stein apparently was not aware of how impenetrable some of her pieces were that relied on details from the *cahiers.* How elements from the notebooks are absorbed into her work requires further study.

Many other matters beside the covers of the notebooks are visible in the manuscripts and must be "read" with care. For example, "A Little Love Of Life" (1932) literally enacts the purchase of a new pen by writing in pencil the word "pencil" and rewriting over the same word, in ink, the first three

15. See Wendy Steiner, *Exact Resemblance to Exact Resemblance: The Literary Portraiture of Gertrude Stein* (New Haven, Conn.: Yale University Press, 1978), 110–18.

letters, *pen,* so that a visual pun, which does not show up in print, exemplifies her literalism. We do not need this detail to understand the piece, but it is interesting to see it.

Stein drew ideas from the *cahiers,* as she did from everything that surrounded her, in innumerable surprising ways. A few examples will illustrate her range. "A Bouquet" (1927), incorporated in 1928 in the opera *A Bouquet. Their Wills.,* is composed in a notebook from the series *La Parole du maître: Connaissances utiles* (*The Master's Word: Useful Knowledge*) and subtitled *L'Art de faire un bouquet,* translated by Stein to begin the piece, "The Art Of Making A Bouquet." The picture shows a group of ladies busy arranging flowers on a terrace opening into a garden.

The text for this picture describes the art of assembling bouquets, reminding the reader that it requires taste, dexterity, talent, but mainly an artistic conception of the whole, like that of the painter or playwright—a statement of principles of composition. Stein treats it as a set of directions, which she follows by writing a single, totally composed, totally abstract sentence—a bouquet of words exemplifying the principles outlined in the *cahier.* What could be simpler?

"A Diary" (1927) uses a *cahier* from the series *Voyages autour du monde* (*Trips Around The World*), subtitled, *Un nuage de sauterelles en Algérie.* It shows three tourists on horseback riding into a "cloud of grasshoppers." Stein originally included in her own title a translation of the French title, "A diary and a storm of grasshoppers on a trip," but then crossed out all but "A Diary." In the spring of 1927, preoccupations with narrative and time may have led her to examine the diary form. Whether the suggestion of a travel diary on the *cahier* gave her the idea, or whether she chose the Algerian *cahier* to fit an idea she already had, cannot be known. But her steps are entirely clear.

Sometimes she composed with small details from the *cahiers.* The lion in the *Third Historic Drama* (1930) comes from a *cahier* about a famous lion hunter; she combines details about the lion with her own thoughts about being lionized. "Why is milk good" in Act III of *Say It With Flowers* (1931) comes from a notebook on nutrition; identifying the source is easy enough, but what does the sentence do in the play? The phrase "their origin and their history," which fits perfectly in the context of "Patriarchal Poetry" and also echoes the subtitle of *The Making Of Americans: Being A History Of A Family's Progress,* is a literal translation of *son origine et son histoire* from the title of a notebook in the series *Chants Patriotiques* (*Patriotic Songs*). The play with "patriarchal" and "patriotic" also derives from this title.

Stein's late 1925 word portrait, "Lipchitz," surely in part describes details from the illustrations of the *cahier* in which she composed it. It shows a young soldier in World War I standing behind a battlement at a lookout post, watching with patient concentration for the enemy. In 1920 Lipchitz had done a bronze head of her. In return, she now writes his portrait.

In her portrait, the phrases "he was so patiently then standing" and "[w]hen I knew him first he was looking looking through the glass" describe both the soldier and the sculptor who had looked at her with such concentration. Stein uses the intense "looking" of the soldier to lead into the "looking at the looking" of the artist and to echo "Through the looking glass." "I look at him for him" comes from the *cahier* and refers to both portraits.

The fact that a verbal element originates in a notebook does not mean that it cannot be interpreted beyond its origin, but clarifying its origin reveals context and can prevent misreading. The first question is *how* Stein uses the materials from the *cahiers*. The next and more difficult question is *how successfully* she composes them.

The *cahiers* also include textual revisions unrelated to the notebooks. While they are rarely extensive, they show Stein's attention to movement, rhythm, and phrasing. Revisions must be followed, where possible, from *carnet* to *cahier* and within the *cahier*. Often a passage crossed out and replaced by a revision can still be read and yields information. The use of certain words and phrases often dates pieces, for Stein discovered new words and constructive possibilities year after year. She also had an extraordinary verbal memory. A given phrase enters into her piece with its own history of occurrence in Stein's writing and with echoes and overtones that begin to compose meanings across pieces and years. There is pleasure in hearing the verbal echoes enrich reading as they enriched her writing.

Stein's technique of decontextuating in order to focus on essence can be documented by a study of her revisions. Often the manuscripts retain, crossed out, the original nouns or names for which Stein substituted more neutral pronouns in order to prevent attention from shifting to the references. "Business In Baltimore" (1925) is a relentless, bitter piece about the power of counting, which Stein associated with family, Baltimore, and money. Counting makes riches, and riches make weddings, which are not about people but about money.

> Anything that begins with r makes read riches and this is as twice and once and once. . . . This is the way they make the day . . . this is the way they make the day, once a day and it is a reason for having heard of it. (*UK* 70)

Do we hear echoes of "The king was in his counting-house / counting out his money"?

In "Regular Regularly In Narrative" (1927) Stein included a long portrait of Harold Acton. One sentence reads,

> Harold Acton can be finally withdrawn from Beatrice. . . . (*HTW* 234)

One might think that Harold Acton has somehow withdrawn from a girl he loves. In the manuscript, however, remains the original identification, crossed out:

> and so she might be Beatrice Beatrice [xd Cenci Cen] bent she she bent to bent to be bent to be he to be bent to be he to be bent to be Beatrice but to be he. (236)

Also in the manuscripts may be found revised titles and crossed-out subtitles that can help to place works in context. Why is *Lucy Church Amiably* subtitled "A Novel No. 2"? Why did Stein eliminate this subtitle from the final text? What is Novel No. 1?

The title of the play *Say It With Flowers* is revised. Crossed out in the manuscript notebook, entitled "L' Alouette" ("The Lark"), in the series *Le Monde des Oiseaux* (*The World of Birds*), is an earlier title, which refers to the title that describes the illustration—a lark hovering above a field with flowers. Barely legible, Stein's original title appears to read, *The ? World of Birds with Strange Flowers in It.* What does this title tell us about the play? When was it created, when revised? The answers to such questions help our reading. But it must first be discovered that there are questions to ask. Many questions are suggested, and some are answered by the manuscripts.

One more extraordinary aspect of Stein's manuscripts demands attention: writing as a physical act in space. What does the title "Five Words In A Line" mean? As usual, the phrase is literally true: in the *cahiers,* about five handwritten words fit on a line. She must suddenly have become aware of this fact and begun to play with it. There might even be an ironic echo of Tennyson's

> . . . and jewels five-words-long
> That on stretch'd forefinger of all Time
> Sparkle for ever. . . .
> ("The Princess," ii, 377–79)

By the time her pieces are typed or printed, the spatial quality of her handwritten work is gone. Yet to follow her hand shaping words, lines, and pages in the spaces of *carnets* and *cahiers* makes exhilarating contact with the act of composition.

She frequently wrote into given spaces. For example, she would sometimes draft answers on the back of the letters she had just received. Since such letters were usually folded in half, in thirds, or both, she tended to fill each half or each third, as if each were a separate page, rather than to open the sheet and write from top left to bottom right. It is important to know whether the format of a notebook or even a scrap of paper determined how she filled it. Some sections of "An Elucidation" and of "A Village" (1923) are drafted on a tiny pad, which results in very short lines and small units—including, in "An Elucidation," "Small examples are preferable."

Many manuscript notebooks are filled to the last line of the last page of the last cahier of any one work. Such completions cannot be accidents. In these *cahiers* Stein let space determine composition, as painters do when they fill a canvas. Drafts of these works cannot have been completed in a *carnet* and copied since it is impossible to plan the need for space from one notebook to another. Indeed, she often began or continued but hardly ever finished pieces in the *carnets.* Her artistic problem became to *complete* a composition within a given space, not simply to *stop* it.

Sections of what became the teasing, grammatical portrait "Bernard Fay" appear first in the long "Sentences" of 1928. Selected sentences are copied, with revisions, into a new illustrated *cahier* as the opening of this portrait, the last piece of 1928. It is continued in the notebook, revised and finished at the very end of the inside back cover. Completing works in the space of one or more manuscript books challenged her and forced her to confront the problem of endings.[16]

Finishing pieces was a source of difficulty. She was reluctant to plan endings that suggested the premeditated or the mechanical, and she refused to organize content chronologically or hierarchically. There is rarely a sharp end point, although her forms of rhetorical completion can be astounding. What I described earlier as the "instability" of her texts is visible in the verbal and mental "leaps" that her work so often requires. Stein's is a world—a space—of unending process, which does not unroll toward a climax or conclusion but *goes on,* steadily and simultaneously, in many forms.

The circles on which she so often relies complete pieces without the jolt of a stop. The discipline of a set space in the manuscript book offered a way to create endings with complete verbal flexibility. It is important to discover by what spatial or rhetorical means she completes her designs. The problem of endings returns to the questions asked earlier in different contexts, for only once we understand *how* Stein composed endings does it become useful to ask *how effective* they are. The answer must be rhetorical rather than representational.

What Stein meant to leave for posterity was her work—self-contained, disembodied words in movement, without clues or keys to the world. As she

16. See also *SBW* 113–14.

said over and over, she wrote literature, not references. It is the composition, not the references, that creates her art and her meaning. The little *carnets* and the larger manuscript *cahiers,* the links from life to literature, provide a partial dictionary for some of the references. Without the *carnets,* an understanding of some dimensions of her work would have remained permanently beyond reach.

And yet, in spite of what she believed about the autonomy of her work and her words, perhaps she also wanted to keep some slight tie to the referential world of identity in which her literature had been made. Perhaps the accident which preserved a few *carnets* along with the *cahiers* and the other papers sent for safekeeping was after all, as she had said in the fourth *Narration* lecture in 1935, "carrying out an idea which was already existing."

A sort of introduction to myself

—Stein to *Atlantic Monthly,* 15 February 1924

I am certain that so very many I am always knowing are not wanting to completely listen to me in my explaining and many are not understanding that they must be hearing me completely . . . I am full up now with knowing that mostly those to whom I am explaining are not completely hearing

—*MOA* 595

1. 1923

"An Elucidation"

In this chapter I am the reader of "An Elucidation," trying to enter the black and white. I start by facing the print from outside and follow myself slowly moving into the piece. I speak in the first person of my reading as I speak in detail of her writing. I comment not only on the text but also on what it is to read this text. For Stein's work, with its apparent gap between what it says and what it is, makes me ask both what I am reading and what reading Stein is, just as she, in writing, always ponders what writing and reading are. Her printed words remain mere black and white until my reading makes the language rise from the page. As Stein incorporated the act of writing into what she was writing, I read that act in the manuscripts as a part of the creative process of the becoming of her work. At this point text and context become enmeshed and are no longer easily separated. Reading Stein involves reading both.

Toward "An Elucidation": The Larger Context of 1923

In the nine years after 1912, when Stieglitz printed Stein's portraits of Picasso and Matisse in *Camera Work,* fewer than twenty short pieces by Stein appeared in print. Most were published with the help of friends who knew the editors of magazines. One book, *Tender Buttons,* printed by Donald Evans in 1914 at the suggestion of Carl Van Vechten, was widely ridiculed. Meanwhile, her major works remained unpublished and known only to friends: *The Making Of Americans, Two, A Long Gay Book, Many Many Women, G.M.P.,* most early portraits, and all early plays. Between 1916 and

1920, when *Three Lives,* first published by Stein herself in 1909, was printed in England by John Lane, Stein received no reviews at all. Publication, precarious from the beginning, was made more so by World War I.

Uneasy about the danger of life in Paris in wartime, Stein and Toklas from April 1915 until June 1916 went to live in Mallorca, where Stein did a good deal of writing, but without access to publication. Only after completing wartime relief work in Paris, Perpignan, Nîmes, and Mulhouse between August 1916 and May 1919 was Stein, back in Paris again, ready to return full time to her own work.

She reviewed what she had done and reconsidered her interest in art and literature ("Made A Mile Away," "Descriptions Of Literature"). She looked ahead and began to explore literary problems of language, genre, method, and organization, evident in many short studies whose titles often name her concerns, "Practice Of Oratory," "Studies In Conversation," *A List,* "Procession."

The end of the war also opened new contacts with American writers and editors who could again travel to Europe. In 1921, Stein met Sherwood Anderson and, through him at the end of the year, Hemingway. She knew Ford Madox Ford from before the war but now saw him again, with Stella Bowen and their daughter Julia, and as editor of the *Transatlantic Review.* Stein's "Vacation In Brittany" and "B. B. Or The Birthplace Of Bonnes" appeared in the *Little Review* in 1922. In 1923 Stein met the editors, Jane Heap and Margaret Anderson, whose serialization of *Ulysses,* March 1918 to December 1920, had led to a complaint of obscenity, heard in February 1921.

Kate Buss, from Medford, Massachusetts, sought Stein out in 1921 in the hope of writing about her and introduced her to Alfred Kreymborg, editor with Harold Loeb of *Broom,* and others. She met Ezra Pound as well as Robert McAlmon and William Carlos Williams, coeditors of *Contact* magazine and publishers of Contact Editions. Many others became friends in the course of the 1920s.

By 1920, to make a new start after the war and show the great variety and novelty of her work in retrospect and prospect, she was ready to print a new book at her own expense. By July 1921, Kate Buss made the contact between Stein and the Four Seas Company in Boston. On November 9, Four Seas received her collection, *Geography And Plays;* on January 24, 1922, she returned the signed contract to Boston. Sherwood Anderson, whose name the publishers felt would be helpful for reading and marketing, agreed to write a foreword. By August, Stein had supplied Buss with information for the jacket and read the galleys. A press release described the book as "examples of each of her experiences." It appeared on December 15, 1922.

Once Stein and Toklas had completed their work for the publication of

Geography And Plays, in late August 1922, they accompanied their friends, the sculptor Janet Scudder and her companion, Camille Lane Seygard, to Provence. Scudder wanted to look for property and enjoy a vacation. She ended up purchasing a house in Aix-en-Provence where she and her friend went to live after completing renovations while Stein and Toklas remained at their hotel in St.-Rémy. They returned to Paris by mid-March 1923 while Scudder and Lane stayed on at their "farm" through the summer. A country house was to become important to Stein as it did not to Scudder, who quickly sold the property as not suited to her way of living.

In St.-Rémy, Stein and Toklas were deeply in love and happy. They explored the land and their shared devotion in steady exchange. Upon the publication of a full, new collection of her work on December 15, 1922, and the discovery of Provence, Stein became enormously productive. She continued doing extraordinary new work after her return to Paris in the spring and on the trip to Nice in the late summer and fall of 1923. As will become clear in this chapter, the year before she turned fifty and her twentieth year of writing since *Q. E. D.,* her first, unpublished novel, it became one of the great years in her writing and her living. The phrase "twenty years after" in her work of this time reflects the mood of self-portraiture in review. In the world of Cézanne, Stein discovered new visions and new ways with words. Immersed in the landscape, she wrote a series of new plays conceived spatially rather than temporally, including *Saints And Singing* and *A List.*

The region where these ideas developed and where she had done wartime duty may also have returned her to her experience in Spain with Toklas in 1913. Restrictions fell away and opened the world—the geography—of detail, large and small, moving and still, rhythmic and melodious, each contributing equally to the landscape and so to composition. Upon the women's return from Provence to Paris, before March 15, 1923, reviews of *Geography And Plays* began to appear, the first by late March and early April 1923 but most in the course of the summer.

The landscape of St.-Rémy included rivers, canals, and ports with access to the Mediterranean. Water and movement entered her writing along with pastoral settings, religion, saints, music, singing, and thoughts about opera. Stein's saints, who are not necessarily canonized, wander in an extended landscape which allows them, in moving, to meditate or become objects of meditation.

One saint in "Talks To Saints Or Stories Of Saint Remy" of late 1922 or early 1923,

> had been a great wanderer. He had wandered all over France everywhere except in Paris. He did not like Paris because he had never been there. He

> had been a great wanderer. He had wandered all over Long Island. He had been a great wanderer he had wandered all over. I would like to talk to saints. As great a saint as that. I wish to pass from saint to saint. I wish to pass from saint to saint. (*PL* 113)

He appears, as saints surely do, conflated in several guises, as Whitman, and as a figure from World War I,

> a Negro wounded man whose name was Hannibal and he said that he had wandered all over Staten Island, well here in Europe they are just wanderers. . . . (*Wars I Have Seen* 134)

Perhaps he is also a wandering Jew. She played with figures and forms of language, explored order in series, conversation, procession, oratory, lists, and composed in twos, threes, and especially fours: capitals, villages, religions, people.

From Manuscript to Text

Stein said that if writing required explanation, it was not writing. Yet here is a piece, "An Elucidation," which I read in the face of her refusal to explain and my trouble in comprehending. Why, against her own principles, did she write it? What does it elucidate? What is difficult about reading it? How does elucidation explain—or become—composition, and what happens to the subject in the process?

Stein manuscripts open both text and context. In her *carnets* and *cahiers* are preserved some of the sources of her writing, the ways in which the text rose from these sources, the revisions, omissions, and deletions by which Stein concealed sources and decontextuated the piece, and the order in which she arranged it.

For "An Elucidation," an extraordinary wealth of manuscript material is preserved in three *cahiers* with final text and one tiny *carnet* with preliminary notes for what became five separate sections in the piece. Together, these exhibit most problems of manuscripts as contexts for texts. I read them here as a paradigm for the making of an astonishing text.

"An Elucidation" fills three *cahiers,* the last to the very end, which suggests that it served to frame and complete the text. The piece begins from the back in a notebook used from the front for a somewhat earlier piece, "Lily Life," whose title is on the front cover while the title and first line of "An Elucidation" appear on the back cover. Manuscript evidence suggests that "Lily Life" was written close to "An Elucidation." The second and third *cahiers,*

Baby necessary baby,
cow necessary cow.
They go together and the
cow comes out to-morrow
You sweet treasure of my love.
BaBy.

The intentionally erroneous *B* in the last word brings out the capitals *B B* (*bébé?*) and leads next to a little game demonstrating what a poor typist Stein would make, an implied tribute to Toklas as a good typist. Stein cannot even type, though of course she can write.

Baby's type writing
I! no not that
IT no not that
It yes thats it
ByBy no BaBY no
Ba!Y no Baby no
Baby yes

Toklas participates in Stein's creative gift with her sexual gift and her typing. Later in the *carnet* Stein asks,

> Now how can I express my love and delight

and answers,

> In this way by never being a nuisance with plans or excitements, by making nice babies for my wife and pleasing her in every way, giving her cows regularly and not making any preparations.

She concludes by initialing the section "Y. D.," with Swift's signature in the *Journal to Stella,* to label it private writing, not to be typed as composition.[4]

Babies and cows in these verses are two parts of one process. "Baby," capitalized, is Stein, but "babies" are compositions. Stein gives Toklas "cows," or orgasms. These enable Stein to produce "babies," or writing. Composition, not necessarily sexual in content, originates in sexuality. Love opens writing.

But the matter is more complicated. These verses provoke questions and speculations. Unless Stein writes the love verses after making love, what leads to babies may not be orgasm itself but writing about orgasm. Stein writes often and in detail about her lover's orgasms, which create sexual fulfillment and lead to babies. She never writes about her own orgasms, however, except

4. See *LGS/TW* 86n.

entitled "Victor Hugo" and "La Fontaine," are from a series on teachers, "Les Educateurs de la Jeunesse," including also Buffon and Lamartine.[1] References to these men occur in some pieces, for example, to Buffon in "Yes You Do." No such references appear in "An Elucidation."

The only *carnet* preserved is a tiny perforated notepad, 2 inches by 3 1/2 inches in size, in a cardboard holder into which replacement pads can be slipped. It contains preliminary notes and jottings used in "An Elucidation," the beginning of *A Village. Are You Ready Yet Not Yet* (1923), which follows "An Elucidation" and is textually related, and other notes. Further *carnets* that Stein may have used are not preserved.[2]

The texts and manuscripts show many sources for the bits and pieces of "An Elucidation," some from Stein's life with Toklas, some suggested by other writing of the period, as the many verbal cross-references show. She rearranged the samples. I do not know whether she had a purpose in wrenching sections from the order in the one preserved *carnet* and perhaps others that are not preserved. I have wondered whether she deliberately lifted the sections from private continuity, especially where Toklas plays a large part, and combined them with word ideas from recent work and daily life.

"An Elucidation" remains an immensely difficult work. A collection of small pieces of writing which seem to float unattached in midair, it does not appear grounded in a dominant principle such as the title suggests. With the title—or antititle—at the back of the mind, even if I know that it is a later addition, I keep searching for an illuminating idea and forgetting that under the light of such an idea, the words she wrote would pale. I make myself return to the school she had in mind when she wrote to Henry McBride about elucidating. In that school, children learn from examples to read, not to hear big ideas.

Slowly some words connect with others, but "An Elucidation" remains discontinuous reading, a loose assemblage of bits and pieces that explore words and their constructive possibilities. I want to know how she composed the piece. Any clues to its making must be in the words she wrote by hand in the manuscript.

1. Illustrations show the writers and major works on the front cover and brief biographical facts and lists of works on the back cover. The *cahier* on Victor Hugo is reproduced in Wendy Steiner's *Exact Resemblance to Exact Resemblance* (New Haven, Conn.: Yale University Press, 1978), 112.
2. The passages transferred from *carnet* to *cahier* are: "Disturb. / Seated here . . ." to ". . . a journey to and"; "Small examples . . ." to "He consolidated it. That you must not do."; "I know the difference between white marble and black marble" to "Can follow where they like"; "If in order to see incidentally . . ." to "Should you see me too."; and "To explain I will explain" to ". . . avail yourself of your opportunities."

I see in the incompleteness of my reading the life of my text. Only rereading will illuminate it, as rereading perhaps illuminated the empty pages and marble checkerboards. As Stein said in a phrase in the *carnet* not transferred to the final text,

> mysteries are marbled.

The tiny *carnet,* the only preliminary source preserved of this piece and indeed this time, was not meant to be kept. It is the repository of a private process that is yet so directly tied to composition that I must decipher what I can. In the final version, Stein covered the private tracks visible in these preliminary notes. My reading of these early notations led to speculations about that which she never states—not what she wrote, for that is in print, but where composition came from and how she made it.

The manuscripts show three important facts. First, "An Elucidation" originates in the love relationship of Stein and Toklas, which is revealed mainly in the *carnet.* Love frees the flow of words. The love verses, distinct from literary composition, are always personal and sexual. Love lines, sometimes followed by answers composed by Stein or answers written by Toklas, and further retorts from Stein, open writing. It is by no means clear that Toklas is present when such lines are being written, though she sometimes seems to respond later in her own hand to what she has read. For example,

> When there was a
> baby made.
> a little husband
> is ready she said,
> He said Oh yes
> She said Oh yes

After several pages of this sort of thing in the tiny *carnet* pad,

> she will
> go to sleep
> nicely and
> Washed de
> dishy.
> Oh you sweet.
> I will do what
> you entreat
> Oh yes

After more such lines, which include a cow coming out of a sweet belly like jelly, she signs "Y. D." and starts a new section,

> You are
> seated here.
>
> ———
>
> Disturb.
> Seated here.
> (433)[3]

Second, as is clear from this sample, mere traces of the sexual sources remain in the final text. Stein adjusts tiny details, omits a word or a line, changes a pronoun here or there in revisions so small that one hardly notices them. Yet they defamiliarize the writing, shifting the focus from private and sexual life to the words, which she removes from personal sources and composes in new forms. For example, here are two sentences, printed consecutively, on separate, indented lines.

> If in order to see incidentally I request to see.
> I see you I see you too. (438)

In the *carnet* appears between them "Baby Baby baby," omitted in the final text. Also omitted, in the "Tremble for small examples" section (434), is a phrase in the *carnet,* surely personal and sexual,

> their hand is a connection between them.

Third, the passages used as examples are radically rearranged so that the final order of "An Elucidation" is quite unlike the order in the *carnet.* Not all steps in the final order can be traced, because some passages may have been composed in the *cahier* or copied from *carnets* that are not preserved. But the details from the *carnet* we do have are entirely rearranged, removing any private continuity and further decontextuating the piece. "An Elucidation" becomes a defamiliarized, almost referentially neutralized text, continuous only in the irregular headings, "example," "instance," "another example." With no principle of order or selection to guide my progress, I read each section individually and intensively.

The love verses in the *carnet* surround the text of "An Elucidation." Embarrassingly bad and not at all what Stein called "literature," they are yet a context for the text. Here she begins with an invocation to herself as the lover of Toklas, "celebrated for . . . being the best cow giver in all the world." She goes on,

3. Quotations from "An Elucidation" are paginated throughout to *A Stein Reader,* 429–4

as babies, or writing. Her freedom in describing Toklas' sexuality and her cows is not equaled by freedom about her own sexuality. She offers Toklas a double gift in two joint creative acts. One is sexual fulfillment, or cows, the other artistic creation, or babies.

Her insistent preoccupation with sexuality, her repeated and repetitious love verses, and her inscription of notebooks to Toklas assume a magical power to ward off failure and propitiate creative capacity. An unsuccessful piece is blamed on her failure to inscribe a *carnet* to Toklas. Toklas represents Stein's love and her ability to give cows. She also becomes the guarantor not of Stein's capacity to achieve orgasm for herself but of her creativity.

Baby enjoys her partner's sexuality and her own sexual feelings and responses, visible in the texts and verses, which always have a babyish and cuddly tone. Baby does not experience orgasms but wants cuddling. For herself and Toklas, Stein coined the term "Mr. and Mrs. Cuddle-Wuddle," formulated in code as "Mr. and Mrs. C.-W."

As I read in the *carnet* the love verses that lead up to the first lines incorporated in "An Elucidation," I hear in new and poignant ways the overtones that rise from the double creative occasion in sexuality and writing, and Stein's double offering to Toklas of cows and babies:

> Disturb
> Seated here
> I know how to please her.
> (433)

The overtones also appear later, in "Small examples are preferable . . . ," and the charged "Tremble for small examples," which leads to the literary, "I hope you received the three volumes safely," in a line that joins writing and sexuality.

I return once more to the opening lines of "An Elucidation" in the first *cahier.*[5] On the front cover of this notebook appears at the top the title "Lily Life" and at the bottom two lines of love verses in the form of a playful dedi-

5. The *cahier* opens from the front with four pages of love verses, including the section quoted, about Stein as "cow giver," "necessary baby . . . cow," and "Baby's type writing." These pages are followed by evidence of three torn-out pages. On these pages, removed from the notebook and joined with other leaves, is the text of "Lily Life." The piece is heavily revised and visibly composed on, not copied onto, these manuscript leaves. Stein started this piece in the *cahier,* not in a *carnet,* which explains why love notes appear at the beginning of a *cahier.* From the front, this notebook is the only repository of text for "Lily Life," a slight and intimate love song, as is confirmed by its earlier title, "An Opera Tune," crossed out in revision.

cation to Toklas, written in pencil so light that it becomes secret and difficult to read:

> To the little river
> |for
> | me and for you
> |from
> Gertrude

If my reading of this faded, smudged notation is correct, the word "river" and the phrase "Halve [have] Rivers and Harbors" suddenly become simple, idiomatic, and literally true. The rivers and the harbors into which they flow join in giving and receiving, having and halving, creating the one and the other as one.

Creation in love becomes creation of words. The little river in the love verse on the cover of the *cahier* may go with "Lily Life" but may also be the beginning of "An Elucidation," which originally started, "Rivers and Harbors." Loving and writing collapse into one. To drive a wedge of conventional explanation between them is to destroy both. "An Elucidation" is autography, Stein writing herself, not about herself. It composes rivers and harbors and others for literal reading.

I spoke earlier of word games that are also love games. Unexpected traces and extensions of such games show up between the preliminary notes and the final text of "An Elucidation." The lines directly after "I know how to please her" are copied unchanged from *carnet* to *cahier,*

> If I know
>
> If you know how to throw how to throw or to go. I feel that you easily understand that preparation is not everything. I understand everything. And now to explain where preparation and preparing show this xpedition. An xpedition is a journey to and (433)

Here, without punctuation, the text in the *carnet* breaks off. It is followed by an empty page. On the page after that begins an entirely different section, used much later in "An Elucidation." But there is the unfinished sentence, and I wonder whether to add into my reading what I see: An expedition is a journey to an empty page. These words are not written, but the empty page is here, teasing me to read it as a referential actuality. Stein, always the literalist, uses everything, even an empty page—a blank passage, a thing not spoken of, a new piece of writing to come, and of course preparation for a cow.

In the *cahier,* however, there is no empty page, and Stein works only with words. To the unfinished "An expedition is a journey to and," she adds a single word. We may expect "fro" but Stein writes "for." It is not a slip of the pen but a three-letter jolt to make us think about what she is saying and what we do with words when we do not think. She refuses to fill in the next word from associative language habit.

In print, the passage of variations on "May we seat" (431) takes nine lines, ending "May I see." Only in the *carnet* is the last line carefully offset by itself on the page, which adds pauses, emphasis, and overtones to the reading. In the *cahier,* however, the first five lines are entered upside down, in a very small, fine hand, six pages beyond where they appear in the text. Neat and tiny, the writing resonates with private meaning. Stein tried out the lines and the spacing here, on this later, still blank page, before entering the lines in her text.

I read these lines as a tiny draft trying out how to write. Later, as she continued her piece, she wrote over them, in her regular hand and in the direction of her text, the passage she had come to that happened to fall on this page,

> If I know.
> If you know how to throw how to throw or to go. I feel that you easily understand that preparation is not everything I understand everything. (433)

In the *carnet* appears an earlier version of the offset sentence, "May I see," perhaps the one Stein originally heard and jotted down for later use. It is "May I see the baby," exactly the kind of sentence that would have appealed to her. It creates a tea party or reception with fitting bits of talk. The baby, of course, is a real baby, but since Baby is also Stein, I hear both "May I see the baby" and "May I see Baby." The two ask to see Stein, or her portrait, or the baby that is her work, the product of sexuality that also portrays her. The final text truly defamiliarizes the sentence by eliminating the baby.

One more visual game in the *carnet* does not appear in the final text. The end of the section on white and black marble and the next, on explanation that can "carry me across," are combined with the following,

> I think I won't
> I think I will

Here are the passages as they follow one another in print:

> I know the difference between white marble and black marble. White and black marble make a checker board and I never mention either.

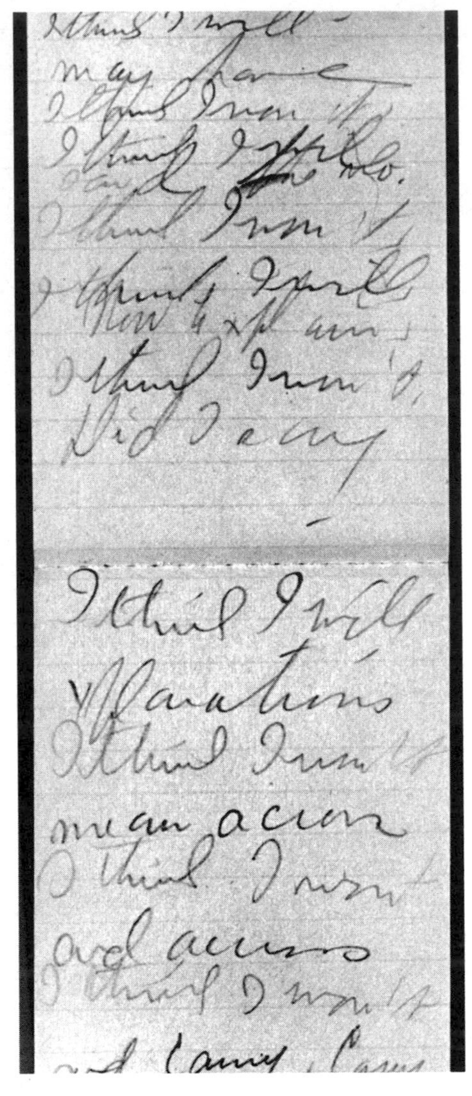

Figure 3. Manuscript pages for "An Elucidation" in a *carnet,* 1923. Courtesy YCAL.

Either of them you know very well that I may have said no.

Now to explain.

Did I say explanations mean across and across and carry. Carry me across.

Another explanation.

I think I won't
I think I will
I think I will
I think I won't . . . (436)

Between pairs of "I think I will / I think I won't," she enters sections of the preceding passage, reproducing the way the mind works when it thinks about one thing and another enters. Out of the two sections printed in sequence she makes a checkerboard of texts and voices alternating in double consciousness. She literally writes one passage across the other. Here is a sample as it looks in the little *carnet:*

. . . White
and black
marble make
a checker board
and I never
I think I won't
I think I will
mention either
I think I will
I think I won't
Either of them
I think I won't
I think I will
. . .
xplanations
I think I won't
mean across
I think I won't
and across
I think I won't
and carry. Carry
I think I will
I think I won't
me across
. . . .[6]

6. These examples of visual play appear related to boustrophedon writing, where alternate lines are written in opposite directions, as oxen pull a plow back and forth, reversing direction. I do not know whether Stein was aware of the origin of this form in the turning from one side of the orchestra to the other of the classical Greek chorus.

She explores writing visually and challenges single, inflexible conventions of vertical

Stein is always aware of the folds of paper, the spread of a line or page, the look of a meaning, for she is not only a verbal but also a visual literalist. An example is her portrait "Next." with the added subtitle, "Life And Letters Of Marcel Duchamp" (1920). The title word "Next" is written over a small "Next" since next is plainly not next unless it is next to another. In the manuscripts of "An Elucidation" she experiments with reversals, inversions, interlocked texts, and other visual and typographical possibilities in especially elaborate and inventive ways.

They are a natural extension of the elucidation of word problems in their visual dimensions. In her compositions, however, she disciplines herself sternly to work only with words and not with visual elements. She does not include the visual play in her final versions of texts, but it leads to the methods of concrete poetry.

The Text Itself

The title instantly creates expectations. To elucidate means to clarify or explain. The word "elucidation" raises hopes of a key, a credo, a guide. Perhaps what follows is a Jamesian preface, a "Philosophy of Composition," an *I Wanted to Write a Poem,* an *ABC of Reading,* a "How I Write." But the printed piece does not look like analysis or even personal recollection. It looks like poetry interspersed with prose.

Halve Rivers and Harbors

Elucidation.
First as Explanation.
Elucidate the problem of halve.
Halve and have.
Halve Rivers and Harbors,
Halve rivers and harbors.

You do see that halve rivers and harbors, halve rivers and harbors, you do see that halve rivers and harbors make halve rivers and harbors and you do see that you that you. . . . (430)

---

or horizontal direction. The *carnet* for "An Elucidation" begins with a magical inscription held in an S-shaped line with reversals, "Please remember me on my birthday / I do / conversation between / baby and its Jew." In various *carnets* she also plays visual games that reproduce exchanges with Toklas. Some have overtones of parlor games. For example, there is a ticktacktoe game with the Swift initials, "D. D." Stein's awareness of such forms must have begun early. Among her papers is also a letter written in college, in alternating lines, one by Stein and one by Mabel Earle, as young women friends writing truly "together." The circular "Rose is a rose . . ." is another such visual form.

Yet "Elucidation" sounds methodical, as do some details and other promising if odd headings—"Let me explain properly," "An instance," "More beginning," "First Example." But the pages look casual and unsystematic. They announce explanations but omit connectives and transitions. They are an odd mixture of concrete, often punning bits and abstract but illogical pieces, in sequences difficult to follow though visibly composed.

> Dealing in accelerated authority.
> Do not notice this.
> Dealing in their delight or daylight.
> Do not notice this properly.
>
> (433)

The phrase, "There is an excellent example," sounds as if Stein was elucidating by examples, an easy principle to understand, but examples of what?

The prospect of light diminishes line by line. Wordplay seems easy to understand, but where does the play go?

> There are four words in all.
> There.
> Why.
> There.
> Why.
> There.
> Able.
> Idle.
> There are seven in all.
>
> (432)

The use of four different words (the last two are four-letter words) among the seven, some of which appear more than once, is simple, but why these words and what do they mean? I try to read literally but am not sure how. Few are ready to read as Stein asks, word for word, without expectation about what comes next. In a first skimming, I grasp a few felicitous phrases and lines, but nothing about the whole. Thinking that I know how to read does not help me read a piece that supposedly explains what I do not grasp.

I return to the title. Why would anyone write an elucidation? Simple. Because someone asks for it. The elucidation answers a question. Its voice is personal and particular, an *I* speaking to a *you*.

> Elucidate the problem of halve. (430)

> I have an explanation of this in this way. (431)

> And now seriously to discuss. . . . (434)

> I completely introduce. Yes you do. (432)

And the question? Everyone knows the question, What do you mean? What does it say? Readers asked that question from her earliest work on, and she answered by continuing writing, not by explaining, though the second epigraph to this chapter shows how early she was aware of the question. But in the early spring of 1923 she began "An Elucidation." It looks as if it was provoked by reviews of *Geography And Plays.* But reviews did not even begin to appear until April 1923. By the time she wrote "An Elucidation," there had been virtually none.[7] The piece is not an answer to reviews. Of course, by 1923, Stein had not only readers curious about her method but young admirers eager for instruction, including Hemingway. In such personal situations she may have explained her procedure.

Hints about the speakers in the elucidation appear in both the text and the context. To Henry McBride Stein wrote in April 1923 from Paris,

> I have been working a lot a rather amusing thing called Elucidation, you know they used to elucidate in America and it is a nice word I hope some day to help myself so. It is a rather nice one with lots of examples.

Elucidation belongs in the school room, between a teacher who proposes paradigms and models, asks questions, anticipates difficulties, and pupils who demonstrate understanding. The teacherly voice makes the pupils "listen to an explanation" and tells them "now to seriously discuss." The voice that so often begs or commands, "Listen to me," pervades her work long before the phrase becomes the title of a late play. The teacher cajoles, prods, teases, threatens an examination, pokes fun at us. "Let me lead you to find this." "Do you all understand if you please." "If you know how to throw or to go. I feel that you easily understand . . ." "This is an example a very good example." "I begin you begin we begin they begin." "I know the difference between . . ." "Now do you see that this is a thing to erase and eradicate." The teacher even ridicules her own explanations, "I will now explain dishes [thises]. / I have explained that." She ends with the familiar, patronizing, "Yes you do."

"Yes you do" trails idiomatic expressions like "Do you," "How do you do," "No, you don't." But suddenly the phrase doubles in my mind. "Yes You Do" is also the title of a separate piece Stein wrote near the time of "An Elucidation." The phrase cannot be in "An Elucidation" by accident. One

7. In his letter of 30 March 1923, Carl Van Vechten wrote that Kenneth Burke's review, "Engineering with Words," had appeared in the [April] *Dial* (*LGS/CVV* 71–72). Stein probably received it later. But by late March, she had already written much of "An Elucidation."

text connects with another and spreads reading across more than one piece of this time.[8]

"Yes You Do" tells me something else.

> I completely introduce. Yes you do.
> Yes you do.
> Yes you do is the longest example and will come at the end. (432)

And later,

> Five examples and then the long example entitled Yes you do. (439)

The "Yes you do" section does come at the end. Stein, who claims she does not plan ahead, here knows in the middle what she is going to do at the end. Her procedure differs from what she says, for a text or at least a draft of the long example in her mind must be ready if she plans to insert it later.

Instruction in Stein's school includes fun and games, hide-and-seek, peekaboo, "Search for me," "Again search for me," "I see you I see you too." Almost like a counting-out game appears another familiar tag,

> I think I won't
> I think I will
> I think I will
> I think I won't.
> I think I won't
> I think I will
> (436)[9]

It is repeated with variations, including a few periods, twenty-seven times, in lines that spread over more than a page. This is the language that teaches. Any child knows what it means. "Yes you do."

8. "Yes You Do," though in the HG listing the last piece of 1922, in the order of typescripts directly follows "An Elucidation," presumably because it relates to its final section. In this chapter I identify numerous pieces related to "An Elucidation" but do not discuss them in detail. To send a reader of the difficult "Elucidation" also to other Stein pieces in different volumes, many out of print and available only in libraries, is discouraging. However, I point to links and echoes and to textual relationships among the pieces of which I know.
9. I read this set of lines about indecision as a version of the phrase, "I think I can," in *The Little Engine That Could,* by Watty Piper, first published as a book in 1930 but preceded by an early version in 1910. However, the story was apparently known as early as the 1880s and may have originated in oral folk tradition. See Priscilla A. Ord, "Watty Piper," *Dictionary of Literary Biography,* vol. 22 (Detroit: Gale Research Co., 1983), 276–81. Stein is not concerned with the rewards of perseverance but with repetition and variation of "I think I will," which she calls "a good example if you do not abuse it."

But nothing is stable in this piece. The school room becomes another room, the voice another, and talk goes on. Here is the language of polite society and formal exchange,

> May we seat.
> May we be having a seat
> May we be seated
> May I see
> May I see
>
> (431)

or

> An introduction and an explanation and I completely introduce as you please. (432)

It may also be the language of a lecture or a social function.

> Suppose or supposing that you had an invitation . . . supposing you had been inviting him to listen to an explanation . . . I can explain visiting. (434)

We are among guests assembling, apparently with "cause for congratulation," in a salon,

> and now I will explain away as if I have been sitting for my portrait every day. (432)

She invites those around her to listen to an explanation. Here we are, in Paris, in Stein's studio, facing the Picasso portrait of herself.

> If I say I stand and pray.
> If I say I stand and I stand and you understand and if I say I pray I pray to-day if you understand me to say I pray to-day you understand prayers and portraits. (432)[10]

10. Starting in 1923, Stein plays again and again with the phrase "portraits and prayers." "Portraits" goes back to earliest years; "prayers" appears in Provence, 1922–23. The two combined in a ringing title to make the words of Stein also the portrait of Stein, or the Stein who writes the Stein we read.

The book published in 1934 by Random House under this title, with the Van Vechten photograph of Stein on the cover, was the only one printed of a long series of collections with this title, planned with changing contents and unsuccessfully submitted over the years. The phrase appears in manuscripts and correspondence, for example, the manuscript notebook of "Harold Loeb" and "Fourteen Anonymous Portraits," of *A List,* and others. By 1926, after submitting the proposed volume to Duckworth, she included the title in a draft of a publicity sheet for *Composition As Explanation.* In the manuscript of

Stein stands there, before the Picasso portrait that represents her, before herself, speaking of herself and of the portrait, which is self-explanatory as is her work. The passage in the drawing room is Stein's introduction of herself as hostess, artist, subject, literature.

"An Elucidation" is a self-portrait with multiple visual and auditory refractions suggested by the phrase "portraits and prayers," first used here. It crosses over from painting to writing, from Stein as subject to Stein as artist, Stein seen from outside as hostess to Stein's writing seen from inside, with the Picasso portrait as focus for subject and construction.

Once more I go through the formal introductions.

> May I see
> May I see
> Martha
> May I see Martha.
> May I see.
> May I see.
>
> (431)

Martha? There is only one important Martha in Stein's work—Martha Hersland in *The Making Of Americans Being A History Of A Family's Progress.* The novel was in Stein's mind early in 1923. Writing from America on February 22, 1923, Carl Van Vechten thanked her for *Geography And Plays,* praised it, and asked,

> What has become of *The Family?* I want to show the mss to my publisher [i.e., Alfred Knopf]. It has occurred to me that the time is getting ripe for its publication now that you are a classic & have Imitators and DISCIPLES. Please do something about this!

On March 15, after her return to Paris, Stein responded to his proposal with warm pleasure. She suggested sending him one by one the early sections of the novel and added that she was writing an elucidation.[11]

"Or More (Or War)" she says that "all loose manuscripts make Portraits and Prayers." It is important to know this history when referring to *Portraits And Prayers* and to hear its echoes in Thomson's 1963 song cycle for voice and piano, *Praises And Prayers,* for Betty Allen.

11. It sounds as if she began "An Elucidation" after her return to Paris, but the context suggests that she began it in St.-Rémy. Her comments in letters on her work must not be read as exact dates. For example, she says she is writing "more plays and some religions," works done in St.-Rémy in the winter and spring 1922–23: *Saints And Singing, A Saint In Seven, Capital Capitals, A Village,* "Talks To Saints Or Stories Of Saint Remy," "Lend A Hand Or Four Religions," and others. She did not continue this kind of work in Paris.

On March 29, she wrote that she was sending him the first volume of the typescript and would shortly send the second and third of the eight that made up the complete novel. On March 30, Van Vechten, familiar with the problems of publishing the long novel, warned her, "Hope . . . nothing for the present." His letter of April 16 began, "Three volumes have arrived." Later in "An Elucidation" Stein writes,

> I hope you have received the three volumes safely. (434)[12]

This, unlike the spoken "May I see Martha," sounds like a sentence in a letter. It must have been in Stein's mind between the time she sent the volumes and the time Van Vechten acknowledged their arrival.[13]

Together, the letters and the text identify one occasion for the piece. When Stein wrote to McBride that she hoped to help herself with it, her unstated object was "to get published." Knowing McBride's wariness of success and fame, she did not name Knopf as the publisher she hoped for. McBride had warned her in a letter of November 13, 1920, underlining his words,

> There is a public for you but no publisher.

The ruminations of "An Elucidation" were provoked by the prospect of submission to Knopf, by the question of her language, perhaps underscored by the new book, *Geography And Plays,* and by the return to Paris and the portrait of herself on the wall of the studio. Not written for Knopf, the piece became a meditation upon writing, reading, explaining, understanding.

A few doors to text and context have opened. There is no one right way to read Stein, but eye and ear gradually discover how she moved from word to word and line to line. The world of her words opens when I listen more to how it speaks than to what it says. Often I play with her words to figure her out by following her figures in writing. Play on words, which changes the words as I read them, resists systematic analysis, gloss, and paraphrase. It respects no boundaries, not even the autonomy of a language. I cannot be both inside and outside a punning composition, for in "An Elucidation,"

> This is not originally said to frame words this is originally said to underestimate words. (435)

12. In the text, this sentence follows "Tremble for small examples," quite different in tone. If the three volumes are, as I suggest, the first three of the eight-volume typescript of *MOA,* the big book next to the "small example" becomes funny, as Stein no doubt knew.
13. See *LGS/CVV* 67–74.

The lines deconstruct themselves before my eyes. As she noted just before this comment,

> We understand that you undertake to overthrow our undertaking. (435)

Is Stein worth the effort to figure her out? Like those who read her when she first appeared, readers today still demand a key to her bewildering work or, in the absence of a key, they wonder whether there is anything to figure out. Recently, theoreticians have offered keys to Stein in feminist, lesbian, and other readings. Yet none of these accommodates more than selections of her texts. Stein remains more confusing and irritating than other modernists. We have learned to read Joyce, Pound, Olson, and others with the help of scholarly tools. But Stein, older than they, remains difficult because she is primitive and naïf. Her simple vocabulary requires little learning. Her refusal of the conventions of English defamiliarizes her writing and angers readers. She demands total concentration on the naked text before eye and ear. The rewards are as great as the effort is difficult.

And so I start again, this time with the opening,

Halve Rivers and Harbours

Centered in print, it looks like a subtitle and leads to

> Elucidate the problem of halve. (430)[14]

No, she does not use British spelling, though Toklas typed "harbours" with "ou" as was still accepted practice in publishing in America at the time. Nor are "halve" and "have" typing or printing errors. Stein plays with homophones, which always worry spelling. More puns and word problems come in the next section, "Madrigal and Mardigras."

To Americans, though not to the English, who sound the vowel of "halve" differently ("haf," not "hÆv"), "have" and "halve" are homophones. The two verbs become problematic when they take on objects, which create statements with meanings. Can I have rivers or harbors? Probably not; they—the

14. The manuscript gives help with the title. Stein apparently began the piece not with "An Elucidation" but with "Halve Rivers and Harbors," capitalized and twice underlined as title. She added "Elucidation" as a next step or subtitle. Later, on the cover, she changed "Elucidation," first to "An Elucidation of Style," then to "An Elucidation of My Style" and finally to the simple "An Elucidation," which became the title. At the bottom of the cover is also written, "The sad procession of the unkilled bull. And they stand around," probably copied into "An Elucidation" from "Talks To Saints Or Stories Of Saint Remy" (*PL* 110), where it first occurs.

water in them if not the river bed or the harbor bottom—would run away. Can I halve rivers and harbors? If I can, I no longer have them, and the region which has them cannot halve them though they might divide. I cannot even quite define rivers and harbors—the river bed and port as containers, or the water in them.

The words play. References aside, it may be impossible to have or to halve rivers and harbors, but it is possible to compose with these words—a "preparation," as Stein calls it, which sounds almost like a cooked dish. Finally, "harbor" in French is not only *port* but also *havre,* which joins with "halve," "have," and "harbor." Puns wonderfully multiply in crossing from language to language.

Rivers and harbors sound like St.-Rémy rather than Paris words. In St.-Rémy, rivers and harbors are a part of daily life and fit Stein's fascination with water. She may have written this section there, and the later sentence about the safe arrival of the three volumes after her return to Paris. I wondered about the phrase "rivers and harbors" and looked up "river" in the dictionary, which referred me to the Rivers and Harbors Bill, also known as the pork barrel, an American appropriations bill that now goes under a different name. No, Stein is not writing about this bill or about pork barrels. She is tapping her own vocabulary, which leads from the word "rivers" to the phrase "rivers and harbors" by a path I must discover in the dictionary whereas for her it moves from one word to the next in her own store.

"Have" and "halve" move from identical sound to different meaning. The two punning M names, "Madrigal" and "Mardigras," are visually nearly identical, but ambiguous sound makes different meanings. Moving from the auditory to the visual, Stein says that their initial letter M reminds her of

> Em which is a nickname for Emma. (431)

"Emma" may evoke Emma Lootz (Erving), a friend from medical school, or the mother of Alice Toklas. "Em" is also the letter *M* spelled phonetically, and *M* brings to mind the many possible *M* names, including Mary, Martha, Mabel, and so on, with which she played often over the years.[15] Finally, "em" is the square of a pica "m" used as a unit of measure in printing.[16] Behind

15. Martha also appears in *A List* (1923), whose characters all have *M+a* names. Some, like Martha and Mabel, come from personal associations but do not appear to function personally in *A List.* As always, she uses what is at hand, for example, (Caius) Marius, who defeated the Teutons at Aix and who is given a playful feminine counterpart, Maryas, making a pair that echoes Mary and Martha. In the play the names are largely but not completely freed of association.
16. M may also stand for "Hem," the Old English dative and accusative case of the personal

"have/halve" ring common idiomatic phrases like have "half," "haves and have-nots," "do things by halves," "break into half." I also hear echoes from other Stein pieces of this time.[17] "Halve/have," "rivers/harbors," "Mardigras/Madrigal" have a ripple effect generating play that animates piece after piece.

As I asked earlier about the source of rivers and harbors, so I ask now about Mardigras and Madrigal. Mardigras is Shrove Tuesday or Fat Tuesday, the beginning of Lent in February, when Stein was still in St.-Rémy. Madrigal is both a part-song and a pastoral poem, as Stein knew from her reading of Lodge, Greene, and Lyly. The double reference to poetry and music fits the work of St.-Rémy. However, Madrigal de los Altas Torres is also a town in Spain, between Valladolid and Avila.[18]

Finally, a woman named Margarita Madrigal in New York gave Spanish lessons to Sherwood Anderson. Though such references may not need pinning down, they make "Madrigal" ring and suggest that these lines were written in the south in February.

Between the two punning passages built on half harbors and Mardigras appears, perhaps for relief, "a new preparation." It sounds almost like a medical substance, made of four declarative sentences.

---

pronoun in the declension in h- rather than the colloquial abbreviation for (th)em evident in the spelling " 'em." Though the notion may seem far-fetched, this form may echo Hemingway, who had come to her that year for instruction such as fills this piece, and the portrait "He and They, Hemingway" of summer 1923.

17. See, for example, *A Saint In Seven, A Village, A Book Concluding* . . . and many later uses. Here is one illuminating passage:

> He searches for more than one word. He manages to eat finally and as he does so and as he does so and as he does so he manages to cut the water in two. If water is flowing down a canal and it is understood that the canal is full if the canal has many outlets for irrigation purposes and the whole country is irrigated if even the mountains are irrigated by the canal and in this way neither oil nor seeds nor wood is needed and it is needed by them why then do the examples remain here examples of industry of cowardice of pleasure of reasonable sight seeing of objections and of lands and oceans. ("A Saint In Seven," *PGS* 80)

18. On July 17, 1952, Toklas wrote on a postcard from Burgos to Virgil Thomson, "There is buried in the Cathedral one of its Bishops Alfonso Tostado de Madrigal, 1400–1455. What do you think?" This note not only refers to Madrigal but may also echo "Toasted Susie is my ice-cream," the last line of the early "Preciosilla," which Thomson had set to music. Toklas' late statements often include echoes and hints of details recalled, whose dimensions few readers would identify.

Do not share.
He will not bestow.
They can meditate.
I am going to do so.
(430)

She defines the four together by putting them into a sentence such as teachers use, adding an odd comment.

> I have an explanation of this in this way. If we say, Do not share he will not bestow they can meditate I am going to do so, we have organized an irregular commonplace and made excess return to rambling. I have always liked the use of these, but not particularly. (431)

Are "these" the joined words? These kinds (what kinds?) of statements? Ordinary sentences in succession, or talk, which of its nature is irregular, becomes an irregular commonplace. Joining words—what Sutherland calls "rambling about the ordinary"—is meditating or writing. She meditates about composition but immediately qualifies her liking—"not particularly."[19]

This is a vexing passage. The sentences, if they are sentences, name or describe nothing I can see. They are so simple and clipped that they seem unfinished or disconnected. No easy rhythm or sound softens and opens them. The first three use formal verbs—share, bestow, meditate—in auxiliary constructions of uncertain actions. The fourth refers back and ties up the group, creating a stark verbal space with possibilities I cannot name.

So I return to the words that give away nothing, as Stein must have intended. I could tell where rivers, harbors, and Mardigras came from, but I cannot tell where she got these. Forbidding text, rising from anywhere, it yields not even context and asks me only to read, read, and reread.

The difficulties of "An Elucidation" remain formidable. Often I am not even sure where one example ends and the next begins, or how to follow the sudden shifts in language. Yet Stein, methodical as a school teacher, is always preoccupied with order, though she never imposes a stiff grid or mechanical system.

19. Sutherland effectively shapes the last chapter of his 1951 study, *SBW,* in the form of a dialogue on ideas about writing that circles around "An Elucidation" as a central text. His dialogue uses what I think of as voices throughout Stein's work.

She is in and out
It is placed in there
(431)

leads to ideas of placement and order.[20]

Place. In a place,

A place for everything and everything in its place.
In place in place of everything, in a place. (431)[21]

It is not the mind that puts the words in order but the words that open the mind to possibilities of order. "Place," "in a place," "in its place," move her from line to line. She follows the sound, not the sense, of a sober school definition to a hilarious surprise:

To explain means to give reasons for in order. He adores her. (433)

As if doodling, arranging flowers or decorating a cake, she composes patterns with words.

A checkerboard is all orderly pattern. She separates the white and the black squares, then joins them.

I know the difference between white marble and black marble. White and black marble make a checkerboard and I never mention either. (436)[22]

20. Order and placement refer not only to writing but also to painting. Likewise, the phrase "portraits and prayers" physically locates the action in Stein's studio in front of Picasso's portrait of her, where she stands and explains as she composes her admiration of the work. "I explain wording and painting and sealing and closing . . . opening . . . reasoning . . . rolling . . ." See also the play with "place," "in the first place" and mixing up places in *A Village,* which of course is a place.

21. This passage appears also, without line breaks, in "Jonas Julian Caesar And Samuel," a piece occasioned by a 1923 summer reception of Yvonne Davidson, the sculptor Jo Davidson's wife, who designed clothes. From the reception it seems to collect social chitchat, which also appears, in different forms, in "An Elucidation." Here she explores the wish to be seen by the right people, which extends to modeling clothes and artists' models.

He sees me, and you see, when I see you whom do I see, I see you and you see me and he sees me and I see him. . . (*PL* 287)

22. White and black, perhaps with overtones of a checkerboard, chessboard, or crossword puzzle, or of writing, letters, prints, photographs, appear in the very punning "Next. Life And Letters Of Marcel Duchamp" (1920), in *G&P.* This portrait, which may have been in her mind when she wrote of the checkerboard, also speaks of "dark people" while "An Elucidation" uses

Brown and white. The nigger and the night . . . (435)

Word by word and line by line she composes order. Earlier I followed two forms of order by counting four words in one way and seven in another, to "There are seven [words] in all" (432). "In all" leads the ear to the next example,

A stall for each.
As tall as each one.

"Stall" opens words of spatial order—boxes, loose boxes (cubes?), boxes arranged with cement (houses? window boxes? painted boxes? papiers collés?). A vocabulary of space comes to mind—cattle stanchions, stalls in churches, boxes in theaters, bull pens.[23] And look at the order of time in that strange sentence that surely originates in St.-Rémy and lodges itself in the mind,

> The sad procession of the unkilled bull. And they stand around. (435)

In July 1927, a few weeks after the death of Juan Gris on May 11, *transition* no. 4 published Stein's portrait of him. Following it, in the same issue, was a piece by Elliot Paul on Gris, "A Master of Plastic Relations." He writes,

> [C]omposition of a painting determines its subject and not vice versa. . . . Stand before one of his still lifes as long as you like. Your vision will improve and the improvement will appear to take place in the painting. (163–65)

These words could almost be Stein on Stein writing. That is what reading "An Elucidation" is about.

My reading of "An Elucidation" goes beyond Stein's text, for I spell out what cannot be read in her work without the private notations. It is not that

---

However, checkerboard patterns were also prominent for years in the work of Juan Gris, which Stein followed closely. It is futile to look for a source for her checkerboard but important to recognize that such figures and themes appear both in painting and in her writing. Regular geometric patterns, placement, volume (stalls and boxes?), as well as muted color patterns (black and white, brown and white) are prominent in "An Elucidation."

23. Meanwhile, echoes appear from "I Feel A Really Anxious Moment Coming" (1922), about "stalls and boxes," and buildings, windows, walls, doors. Bridgman, following Sprigge (128), suggests that the changed room here is a hospital room and Stein is ill (164). I read her purchase of a painting, perhaps by Gris.

> I suddenly felt strongly impressed with the sentiment of a door of a window of a balcony of a curtain. And then I said. I will buy it. (*PL* 236)

The painting changes the room in which it hangs. Throughout 1921, Gris used the motif of the open window. By June 1921, Stein owned *The Table in Front of the Window*. But whether this is what changes the view cannot be known.

the words of the *carnets* are not real but that they speak of the sources of writing, not of her text. Never introspective or confessional, she intended us to read her text, not where it came from. My study, however, is about both her texts and their sources.

After a review of the *carnets,* the words of "An Elucidation" become more brilliant and resonant as elements of composition, not as descriptions of private life. Read for their apparent subjects, the sections pull apart, but read as assemblages of words, they come together as a construction requiring no explanation. Perhaps the moving waterways of the Rhône delta and the light on the land of Van Gogh and Cézanne illuminated composition in new ways for Stein.

Publication

Stein's first known attempt to publish "An Elucidation," in the *Atlantic Monthly,* was unsuccessful. What in her correspondence with editor Ellery Sedgwick between 1919 and 1933[24] is spoken of as her first submission to the *Atlantic Monthly* was in fact not her first. She unsuccessfully submitted "Frost," her portrait of A. B. Frost, the American illustrator, before World War I, as is evident in her early listing of submissions, described in "The Voice of Gertrude Stein." The exchange with Sedgwick on "An Elucidation" raises in stark form the difficulty of reading and explaining Stein texts.

However, "An Elucidation" was not printed until the first issue of *transition* in April 1927, where it introduced Stein as it also introduced Joyce to readers of the new journal, which then published numerous further Stein pieces between June 1927 and March 1932. She said in the *Autobiography* (295) that Elliot Paul chose the piece for inclusion; Stein probably had something to do with this choice.

In the process of setting up pages, the first two lines of several pages were erroneously combined with the following lines of different pages, with the result that continuity and unity of the examples were destroyed. Proofreaders missed the error. Stein demanded rectification, and a correct text was issued to subscribers as a separate sixteen-page supplement with an apology by Elliot Paul.

Stein included the piece as the last in *Portraits And Prayers* (1934) to end the volume with a summing up of principles that also shows the source of the collection's title. Only Donald Sutherland, in *Gertrude Stein: A Biogra-*

24. Presented to the Stein Collection by *Atlantic Monthly* and published by Donald Gallup in the *Yale University Library Gazette* 28, no. 3 (January 1954): 109–28.

phy of Her Work, his seminal study of 1951, confronted "An Elucidation" and Stein's disarmingly simple comment.

Geography: Everything in Its Place

Geography as the arrangement of words in compositional space appears in the work of St.-Rémy but is not confined to that work. It is in the title *Geography And Plays,* devised before Stein went to St.-Rémy, and in her conception of plays as landscapes which make everything visible at once rather than one by one in time. It is in "Geography," another piece of 1923, and it returns in later works, such as *The Geographical History Of America Or The Relation Of Human Nature To The Human Mind* (1935), which makes time spatial.

There are hints, in several St.-Rémy pieces, of a country house in a pastoral setting, more mountainous than Provence. A country house is always a part of the landscape. When Stein says,

> in a summer house the landscape has a different appearance ("Practice Of Oratory," *PL* 126),

she is looking from inside out upon the landscape, which in turn becomes a part of the house. She asks,

> How do you reside. ("Yes You Do," *PL* 119)

The wish for a country house of her own has been thought to begin after 1924, the first Belley summer, and to have led to active house hunting by 1926.

The idea of a country house, however, may have come to her by 1923, in part because in St.-Rémy she began to consider habitations and landscapes as inseparable and in part because of the purchase of a house in Aix by Janet Scudder. In "Talks To Saints," she records "Camille [Lane] and a wheel, farm, water" (*PL* 115); details of Scudder's "farm," described at length in letters from Camille Lane, may have furnished some of the elements in Stein's writing.

Stein was interested in landscapes of pronounced height, greater than most heights in Provence. Even in the writing of St.-Rémy there are references to mountains, snow, and Mont Blanc ("Praises," "Practice Of Oratory"). Perhaps as early as this time, Stein in her mind followed the Rhône River upstream in the direction where they eventually settled. The discovery of Belley may have been less accidental than has been assumed. However, only details in her writing suggest this interest in a landscape with verticals in the direction of Mont Blanc.

For Stein, *geography* is not about places visited during travels, though she writes about these. It is not setting or scenery. It is not the science of the earth. Geography is about words in relation in the space of the composition. A piece is never simply about what the words signify, but it is the realization of a word arrangement. The play *Capital Capitals* (1923) is an example. It uses geographical subject matter but also composes this matter into a carefully modulated arrangement of words which exist not merely as details of Aix, Arles, Avignon, and Les Baux, the four capital cities of Provence, but as elements of sound, sight, and sense realized in the geography of a compositional space.

Stein composes words somewhat as painters, with the tools of their art, model three-dimensional perceptions on canvas or paper to create pictorial space. Yet words, whatever their arrangement, always carry referential meanings, unlike brushstrokes, lines, and colors in a painting or rhythms, sound, and phrases in music. As a result, reference and representation bedevil the reading of Stein texts as constructions. The preliminary notebooks and manuscripts help us when they show the geographical process of Stein composing words.

A few months after "An Elucidation," Stein wrote "Geography," another piece about writing, first published in *PL* (239) and reprinted in *A Stein Reader* (467). It is illuminated by "An Elucidation" and in turn extends the context of composition for 1923. I conclude this chapter, which makes no attempt to discuss all her work of 1923, with a brief reading of this piece and the ones related to it, the second portraits of Picasso, Carl Van Vechten, and Alice Toklas, all composed in Nice in the early autumn of 1923.

After their return from St.-Rémy in March, Stein and Toklas spent about five months in Paris. Stein must have been busy with activities in the city and with the reactions to *Geography And Plays.* After a change of place, it always took her time to settle down to work. In Paris, she probably wrote the very abstract "Subject-Cases: The Background Of A Detective Story," perhaps about the reviews of *Geography And Plays,* and the play *Am I To Go Or I'll Say So,* about travel, probably in preparation for the August trip to the south.

She also wrote the portrait, "He And They, Hemingway," which she later, in a letter of February 1924, described to Sherwood Anderson as "a little skit I presented to him on going away." It is a send-off piece, a farewell-and-return salute upon his departure from Paris for America on August 16. Its tone is light and affectionate but also guarded, for Stein had reservations not about Hemingway's gift but about how he used it.

In the same notebook with this portrait, also written in Paris, is a second portrait of Carl Van Vechten that was not sent to Van Vechten and was neither typed by Toklas nor published by Stein. "And Too. / Van Vechten [now] / A sequel to One" was presumably written in response to Van Vechten's novel, *The Blind Bow-Boy.* The portrait, like Stein's letter about the novel, is filled with details of temporal and spatial relationships between the early "One" (1913) and the new "And Too"—now against then, does against was, "to follow one before the other," "[t]he man next to himself half rose to his feet."[25]

Late in August, Stein and Toklas went to the Riviera. They saw Picasso, who was in Antibes, and met his mother, who was visiting. Stein also saw Gris in Monte Carlo. Earlier, he had designed the decor for the "Fête Merveilleuse" organized by Diaghilev for June 30, 1923, in the Hall of Mirrors in Versailles.[26]

And in Nice, "[g]eography as nice. Comes next geography."[27] Again the school teacher speaks, "As geography return to geography, return geography. Geography. Comes next." Even the opening lines work with rhythms, repetitions, and phrasing that also appear, in different forms, in "If I Told Him / A Completed Portrait Of Picasso," her second portrait of the painter. "Geography" even includes a reference to Napoleon. Drafts of some sections of the Picasso portrait and "Geography," which are conceptually and textually related, are in the same *carnet.*

"Geographically to place" is not about stable location on a map but about movement in compositional space by shifts in rhythm, resonance, and point of view. Geography explores volume in auditory construction or in a swelling sheaf of writing. Look at where we are in this passage:

25. See *LGS/CVV* 82–86 and Appendix B, 855–66, where the portrait is printed.
26. From October 11, 1923, until the end of January 1924, Gris worked in Monte Carlo on the decor for Gounod's *La Colombe* and for Chabrier's opéra-bouffe, *Une Education Manquée.* Stein might have seen or discussed any of these works with Picasso or Gris. Nothing is known about the reason Stein and Toklas prolonged their stay until late November unless it was that Stein was writing with extraordinary intensity or that the crisis Gris underwent late in 1923 kept her in the Midi. The women left Nice for Paris on November 27, as Gris reported to Kahnweiler on November 26.
27. The geographical details of this time also lead to comparisons of north and south and of different places, probably first suggested by the two trips to the south of France in 1923, but in early 1924 extended to north and south in the United States, "Wherein The South Differs From The North," "Wherein Iowa Differs From Kansas And Indiana," and perhaps "The Difference Between The Inhabitants Of France And The Inhabitants Of The United States Of America," all eventually included in *UK,* a collection of texts about America. "Geography" refers to Iowa and Monte Carlo, the latter perhaps also connecting with Carl[o] Van Vechten.

Looking up under fairly see fairly looking up under as to movement. The movement described. Sucked in met in, met in set in, sent in sent out sucked in sucked out.

An interval.

If it needs if it needs if it needs to do not move do not move, do not touch, do not touch, do not if it needs to if it needs. That is what he is looking for. Less. Less threads fairly nearly and geography and water. Descriptive emotion. As it can be.

. . .

More geography, more than, more geography . . . (*R* 467)

She is writing from inside and under the surging, sucking waves, which are also in the Picasso portrait, as Stein said in the *Autobiography* (273).[28] The piece embodies the waves and the act of creation in steadily shifting forms. There is the rhythmic ritual of daily coming and going and sitting in intimacy by the sea. A note in the *carnet* reads, "It is a nice thing to have a husband to sit with his wife on the sand." In the draft, the lines about the waves are interspersed with love notes and take on sexual overtones as the waves join water to water in the cyclical seasonal space of water, snow, rain.

The creative act also rises in waves. Water turns rhythmically into watercolor on paper,

> Naturally and water color the color of water and naturally. Very naturally the color and very naturally. It is the best yet. (468)

Water takes on the color of what is behind it or the color the painter gives it. A surging incantation of adverbs builds the quality of creation.

> Immeasurably. Immeasurably and frequently. Frequently and invariably. Invariably and contentedly. Contentedly and indefatigably. Indefatigably and circumstances. Circumstances and circumstantially. (469)[29]

"Can you tell can you really tell it from here" opens into shifts of seeing and saying, closeness and distance, moving and hearing, writing and loving.

28. "Geography" employs a point of view from inside the moving, sucking, and ejecting wave. The second Picasso portrait renders the waves hitting the shore or a swimmer hitting the waves and being pushed up, in short, irregular, and sharp rhythms with half rhymes pivoting on short and long syllables, cannot/note, cannot/float.

29. Echoes of this passage return in the words of St. Ignatius in *Four Saints In Three Acts:*

> Foundationally marvellously aboundingly illimitably with it as a circumstance. Fundamentally and saints fundamentally and saints fundamentally and saints. (*O&P* 40)

> Can you tell can you really tell it from here, can you really tell it can you tell it from here. From here to there and from there to there. Put it there. Is he still there.
>
> If to say it if to see it if to say it. If to say it. (469)

At another moment the water is "spread as glass is, glass is spread and so are colours, colours and pretty ways." The water is smooth as glass, as a painting under glass. The calm sea has become a watercolor lying flat on the surface, not hanging on a wall.

"Geography" moves in changing dimensions and directions, rhythms and sounds, distance and closeness, outside and inside. Its verbal shape is far from the dry school subject of the title, as the final line shows. With one tiny, disciplined revision, Stein tightened the line she originally wrote in the *carnet,* "Geographically only not at all," to the line in the *cahier,* which puts a full stop to the surging activity, "Geographically not at all."

In the Midi, Stein continued the review of her career that had begun with *Geography And Plays* and led to the work of St.-Rémy. In a burst of inspired writing, she paid homage in second portraits to the three who had sustained her as an artist, a person, and a writer—Picasso, Toklas, and Van Vechten. Picasso is Napoleon, the builder of new empires and the conqueror of women. The waves in his portrait and in "Geography" become Stein's indecision about saying it to him, "If I told him would he like it." They become Picasso's changing relationships with women, the shifting "[s]hutters shut and open" of snapshots or portraiture that is "completed" in exact resemblance but that can never be complete. Picasso's protean genius becomes a rhythmic base for the portrait.

Toklas is the beginning and the end of every work. Her portrait is a book, just as each book Stein writes is also a love story that enfolds babies and becomes a portrait of Toklas and for Toklas. The very title, *A Book Concluding With As A Wife Has A Cow A Love Story,* folds the beginning into the end, writing into story, cow into love, sexuality into creation. The book that is her portrait will in turn become a new book.[30]

"Van Or Twenty Years After A Second Portrait Of Carl Van Vechten," in the same manuscript notebook as the second portrait of Toklas, looks back to Stein's first portrait of him done ten years earlier, in 1913. "Van Or Twenty" phonetically transcribes French *vingt* (twenty) to Van. "Twenty years after" may be the twenty years since Stein herself in 1903 began to

30. It is possible that even in Nice in the autumn of 1923 she discussed this book with Gris, who in 1926 did the illustrations for its publication by Kahnweiler's Galerie Simon.

write. She assembles ways of phrasing time—then and now, twenty years after, is and was, now to fairly see it have—into a punning series of auditory word modulations. Their realization is spatial since hearing takes place in space, where words can be taken in free of reference as physical things that relate, resemble, rhyme, attract, and repel and do their sibling punching and punning by sound and volume. When Stein sent Van Vechten the portrait, she described it in spatial terms, "It piles up."

These portraits include references to their subjects, but they are no longer representations or imitations. As Stein wrote to Edmund Wilson on October 3, 1923, from Nice,

> You are right there do exist portraits and stories but although imitation may be the highest form of flattery it isn't continuation . . . when you realize that to take the commonest example the bible lives not by its stories but by its texts you see how inevitably one wants neither harmony, pictures stories nor portraits. You have to do something else to continue. . . . References you see are association, one refers to one's associates but not to oneself, and all literature is me to me, that isn't as bad as it sounds.[31]

She refused representation. She wanted to write her perception from inside, not to make pictures of it, tell stories about it, or explain it from outside. Being inside a wave is radically different from seeing, naming, and recognizing the wave from here or from there. The vocabulary of reference and the grammar of the world's discourse may serve to picture the wave. It does not serve texts that have absorbed the wave. For Stein, whose texts were themselves worlds, the question was no longer what the world was like but what was geography, the world as writing.

From "An Elucidation" to "Composition As Explanation"

"An Elucidation" is a self-contained piece. Its references to the world from which it rises do not explain it, and it gives no information about the world

31. In the early summer of 1923, Wilson had reviewed *Geography And Plays* for the June issue of *Vanity Fair* 20 (4): 18. He also considered Stein's play *A List* for publication in *Vanity Fair.* On June 6, 1923, he asked for permission to print it in a cut version, which Stein refused. She explained in words that spoke not of plot but of spatial construction that the quality of the play was in "the way it fills itself out," which made cutting impossible.
    In "A Guide to Gertrude Stein," *Vanity Fair* 20, no. 7 (September 1923): 60, 80, Wilson paid tribute to her but also raised questions about her capacity to hold the reader once she abandoned story and verisimilitude. Further details about Wilson, along with the complete letter to him, are printed in *LGS/CVV* 66–88.

or about how Stein writes. It sometimes includes an I and a you, speaker and audience, but these are pronouns and voices in the composition, not people with whom we exchange gossip or news. The occasional tone of a lecture is a part of its compositional voice, but the piece is not a lecture.

A lecture to an actual audience, however, cannot be self-contained. The invisible writer of a text becomes on stage a personality who reads words to an audience and can be seen and heard, photographed and recorded. The voice of the words in the composition becomes the voice of the speaker. Stein had always wanted to be represented by her writing, not her personality. When her work did not sell itself, as she firmly believed it could, she was left in growing pain and dismay.

She finally agreed to promote her work—or was it herself?—through a lecture. What she later came to call "audience writing," work done to appeal to readers, begins with the 1926 lecture, "Composition As Explanation." In that lecture, she spoke about the principle of composition explaining itself. The principle was embodied in "An Elucidation," a text with a dramatic power of voice that could not be a lecture.

Do you all understand if you please.
Do you all understand why I explain.
Do you all understand elucidation and extra addresses.

I describe all the time.
—"An Elucidation"

2. 1926

"Composition As Explanation"

With these words, a teacher appears to address students in a classroom. Yet "An Elucidation" is not a lecture but a meditation upon writing. Everything in this difficult piece faces in upon itself. The audience addressed and the act of speech are inside the piece. The voice is internal to the composition, where the process of writing is inseparable from the matter written, portraits inseparable from prayers, speaker from substance, artist from work. Stein as creator, Stein as subject of a portrait on the wall, and Stein the writer as subject of an elucidation are the same. The urgency of "Do you all understand . . ." is a part of the composition, not an aside or a rhetorical question outside it.

Stein's next elucidation, the address at Cambridge and Oxford of June 4 and 7, 1926, not only is entirely different from "An Elucidation" but is also different from anything Stein had ever written. It is the first piece she wrote as a mature writer in something like conventional discursive prose for delivery to an audience.[1] Here a speaker addresses an audience outside the

1. Stein's only earlier lecture was "The Value of a College Education for Women," delivered to an unidentified women's group in Baltimore, probably 1898, long before she was a writer. The manuscript is in the Cone Collection, Baltimore Museum of Art. (See also Richard Bridgman, *Gertrude Stein in Pieces* [New York: Oxford University Press, 1970], 36n.) A related essay, "Degeneration in American Women" (probably written October 1901), was located by Brenda Wineapple among the papers of Mary Mackall Gwinn Hodder, Princeton University Library. Printed in the appendix to *Sister Brother: Gertrude and Leo Stein* (New York: G. P. Putnam's Sons, 1996), it is discussed in chapter 8.

An "address" and various puns on addressing are not only in "An Elucidation" but in

composition rather than inside it. Between the text of the address and its audience lies a context that is not fully absorbed into the text and requires comment. Unlike Stein's meditations, her public statements rest on such contexts. The lecture is often discussed as one of Stein's statements of principles—a key to her work. While it can be read apart from its own history, it becomes clearer and richer if read in context.

The title, "Composition As Explanation," speaks of an idea central to all Stein's work—that compositions are complete only if they are self-explanatory, requiring no interpretations beyond what they are. Unlike the pieces that she considered self-contained compositions, however, the lecture that announces this principle is in fact an explanation wrenched from the body of her early work, on which it rests. In the lecture, Stein offered her views of what she had tried to do in her early work.

Several contexts must be looked at. First is its history. Far from casual, the invitation to speak was a part of a campaign to promote her work among English readers. Her trip to England, the delivery of the lecture, the results all require commentary. Second, before Stein wrote the lecture, her anticipation of it entered not a diary or journal, which she did not keep, but work she was composing when the invitation arrived. The lecture is not only a text in its own right, but it is subject matter in other pieces that become contexts for it—*A Novel Of Thank You* and "Natural Phenomena."

Always one Stein piece engenders the next, so that each becomes a context for the next. Her life's work is not only a series of discrete pieces but also a single continuous work. Personal commentary is not separate from literary composition but is used, as she uses everything, for composing. Third is the text of the lecture itself, including its revisions, which is at the center of this chapter but can be read in depth only once its circumstances are established. These add to this chapter biographical and historical narrative, which forms with the text a single sequence of astonishing and dramatic consistency.

The History of the Address

In December 1925, the Cam(bridge) Literary Club invited Stein to lecture during the Easter term of 1926. The invitation did not come as a surprise.

---

other pieces of 1923 and later. See "Practice Of Oratory," 1923, incompletely printed in *PL* 124 but complete in *R* 443; "Jean Cocteau," December 1925 or January 1926, *P&P* 80.

Stein's lecture was announced at Cambridge and Oxford as "An Address." Only for publication in the Hogarth Press Essay Series did she, at the request of Leonard Woolf, devise the title *Composition As Explanation.* See Woolf to Stein, 11 June 1926. "Composition As Explanation," written January 1926, *R* 493.

It was a part of a campaign initiated by Edith Sitwell to promote Stein in England. Sitwell had become acquainted with Stein after writing a review of *Geography And Plays* in the summer of 1923; here she praised Stein for her bravery in giving "new significance to language" while also voicing reservations about the "silliness" of her expression. In "Subject-Cases: The Background Of A Detective Story" of that summer, Stein apparently reacted to the review with sharp puns on Sitwell's name:

> Sit and sit smell and smell. Go to hell go to hell. (*AFAM* 4)

By October 1924, Sitwell again wrote about Stein, paying her unstinting tribute. Soon afterward, the two met in Paris. With Sitwell a devoted admirer, they became friends. In the spring of 1925, Stein wrote the portrait "Sitwell Edith Sitwell." Sitwell's next piece echoes what must have been extensive discussion between them; it relies on "An Elucidation," which Stein had sent her for help with the review.[2] Soon Sitwell began a systematic effort to make Stein's work known. The invitation from Cambridge was the most important result.

Stein wanted to accept the invitation but was uneasy about speaking in public. Before the end of the year, she turned the invitation down.[3] On January 1, Sitwell wrote of her distress:

> I must tell you how bitterly disappointed I am . . . that you are not able to accept this invitation. I wish very deeply that you had been able to do so, because I do feel that your actual presence in England would help the cause. It is quite undoubted that a personality does help to convince half-intelligent people.

2. "Miss Stein's Stories," *Nation and Athenaeum* 33, no. 15 (14 July 1923): 492; "Three Women Writers" [Mansfield, Richardson, Stein], *Vogue* (London) 64, no. 7 (October 1924): 81, 114; "The Work of Gertrude Stein," *Vogue* (London) 66, no. 7 (early October 1925): 73, 98. For the first meeting, see Sitwell to Harold Acton in Edith Sitwell, *Letters 1919–1964*, ed. John Lehman & Derek Parker (New York: Vanguard Press, 1970), 31. Stein's portrait of Sitwell, written 1925, *R* 475, was first published in October 1926 by the Hogarth Press as one of the samples of Stein's writing following the address; it was later reprinted in *P&P.* Sitwell speaks of it in her letter to Stein of 24 April 1925.
3. The invitation from Cambridge, presumably by Geoffrey Gorer, the president of the Cam Literary Club, whom Sitwell knew, does not survive; presumably once Stein turned it down, she did not retain it. It can be dated and its contents inferred, however, from references in letters from Edith Sitwell and details in *NOTY,* discussed subsequently. Stein's answer, written before the end of 1925, is not preserved at Cambridge and is not among the papers of Sir Geoffrey Gorer, who wrote me in 1985 that in early years he did not keep letters.

Although Sitwell sounded as if she had accommodated Stein's refusal, she slyly made the prospect of lecturing more attractive by offering to "work up further invitations from Oxford and from University College, London."

Sitwell lectured and reviewed regularly, in part out of financial necessity.[4] Knowing how to hold the attention of an audience, she advocated precisely what Stein most distrusted—appeal by personality. She insisted that she shared Stein's conviction that literature was not an expression of personality[5] but justified reliance on personality as a necessity when confronting "half-intelligent" audiences.

Thirteen years younger than Stein, Sitwell apparently derived strength from Stein's convictions, whose consistency she understood, admired, and perhaps envied. At the same time, she enjoyed using her connections and her flair for drama to sponsor with English audiences and publishers an author of stature, senior to herself, who was reluctant to promote herself.

In background the two women were remarkably similar. Neither was conventionally pretty and neither was willing to live the life expected of women of her class. Both had had to free themselves from the expectations of their families. Both were liberated by female friends, Alice Toklas and Helen Rootham, and both had to struggle for recognition as serious professionals. Both had brothers important for their work, though Sitwell, unlike Stein, received support from her brothers. Finally, both were interested in painting, had important relationships with painters, and sat for many portraits. As Sitwell introduced Alvaro Guevara to Stein, so Stein introduced Pavel Tchelitchew to Sitwell. In addition, of course, they shared many acquaintances and interests.

To Stein, personal appearance before an audience, such as the lecture required, spelled self-display antagonistic to art. She wanted readers and wanted to lecture but shied away from appearing before an audience. As a woman, she was sure to be admired less for her work than for her personality. The letters of Stein and Allen Tanner hint at his understanding of her discomfort; his stage fright impaired his career as a pianist and reduced him

4. Stein did not lecture and wrote very few book reviews, only as personal favors. She found them difficult to write precisely because their subjects were given rather than created and because they involved personal relations with friends rather than purely artistic considerations. When she prepared the bibliography of her work for *transition* no. 15, for February 1929, she did not include reviews, for she did not consider them literature.

5. Sitwell was well aware of the problem of audience, which came to preoccupy Stein also. For example, for the performance of *Façade* at the Museum of Modern Art in New York in January 1948, Sitwell issued a statement explaining that masks were being used to prevent personality display, which interfered with the audience's concentration upon the words.

largely to recording. But Sitwell appealed to Stein precisely where she was susceptible:

> Do, if you can, reconsider this question of coming over here and *helping in the invaluable way that only you can, with the propaganda.*[6]

Stein reconsidered and sometime in January 1926 accepted the invitation. But the prospect worried and preoccupied her. On February 3—her birthday, as was surely no accident for such an announcement—Stein wrote to Van Vechten in New York,

> I think you will be pleased with my news. The literary society of Cambridge England, the Cam asked me some time ago to give them an address on myself, and I said no at first but now I have said yes, and now it looks as if I will also be going to give it at Oxford and London University, more than that I have written it and it is a pretty good address really it clarifies I believe.[7]

The calm, businesslike tone of this letter conceals both the elaborate Sitwell-Stein campaign and Stein's turmoil between receipt, refusal, and finally acceptance of the invitation. The ambivalence is in her texts for anyone to read who will look and listen.

As Sitwell had promised, an invitation from Oxford followed. On March 4, 1926, Harold Acton, the president of the Ordinary, the literary society, invited Stein to lecture. The University of London, however, did not issue an invitation; what exactly Sitwell had planned for London and to whom she may unsuccessfully have appealed remains unclear.[8]

6. Emphases added, 1 January 1926; printed in Donald Gallup, ed., *The Flowers of Friendship: Letters Written to Gertrude Stein* (New York: Alfred A. Knopf, 1953), 184–85.
7. *LGS/CVV* 126.
8. Oxford invitation in Gallup, *Flowers,* 186. Both at Cambridge and Oxford, the whole affair was carefully planned and no doubt monitored by Sitwell and her friends. Announcements of the address were published the week before in *Granta,* 4 June 1926, 420; *Oxford Magazine,* 27 May 1926, 507–8; *Oxford University Review* 1, no. 7 (27 May 1926): 264; *Isis,* 9 June 1926, 8. Oxford students were reminded that the speaker preceding Stein at the Oxford Ordinary, in the spring of 1925, had been Sitwell.

   The Cambridge *Granta* for 7 December 1925, 178, had carried a review of the Hogarth Press volume of Sitwell's *Poetry and Criticism;* that review in turn referred to Sitwell's lecture at the Cam Literary Club of the preceding spring.

   A similar series of events followed after Stein's lecture, when, upon her suggestion, René Crevel was invited by Geoffrey Gorer to speak to the Cam in November 1926. Crevel reported to Stein about his plans and was invited by her for Christmas 1926 with Gorer, who had come to Paris.

The Address in *A Novel Of Thank You* and "Natural Phenomena"

A Novel Of Thank You

Swings of mood from excitement to anxiety preoccupied Stein from January until June of 1926, when she finally spoke in England. From daily life, her worries moved onto the pages of *A Novel Of Thank You*[9] and "Natural Phenomena." In the first, the heroine envisages herself lecturing, wonders what she will say, wishes for success while shunning public exposure, anticipates fame but dreads a public name. The novel absorbed the worries as it absorbed other details of Stein's life. In the second, anxiety, distress, and conflict appear appropriately as natural phenomena.

Stein began *A Novel Of Thank You,* originally entitled *A Novel,* in the spring of 1925 and did not complete it until the fall of 1926. In 1925, she speaks of it as "my novel" or "my little novel." As a novel or a "little" novel—a ladies' novel?—it contrasts with the "long novel," *The Making Of Americans,* which, that spring and summer, was being reexamined, prepared for printing, and later proofread with the help of Toklas; it was published in October–November 1925.

The new work is a novel "of thank you" for publication of the long novel, and probably also for the help of Toklas in realizing this project. Unlike the history of Stein's family, it is "a long history of them" (140), Stein and Toklas, and it includes virtually "everything." It is filled with details of daily life, so that one easily reads it as a serial account of "everything" and forgets that this is exactly what Stein considered to be the novelties that make a novel. It is also a novel about the novel, or a novel about how, in the process of "tell[ing] it as it was" (151), actuality becomes fiction. Not a theoretical statement about the art of fiction, the book composes actualities into the constantly evolving shapes that make a novel.

In the portrait "Edith Sitwell And Her Brothers The Sitwells," Stein includes what must have been a part of a conversation about the work she was engaged in writing and the novel in general.

> Let me tell you about a novel a novel is an arrangement of their being there and never having been more glad than before and would they have liked to have it have had it and is it as if they could always like what they had, no and yes. (*PL* 298)

9. *NOTY,* reprinted by Dalkey Archive Press, 1994, with a helpful introduction by Steven Meyer, follows the same pagination as the first edition in volume 8 of the Yale Edition of the Unpublished Writings of Gertrude Stein. In this chapter I do not discuss the novel fully in its own right but concentrate on the evidence of the address in it.

The statement is followed by a definition of a poem and of description.

Alongside the novel and "Natural Phenomena," Stein in 1925 also wrote "A Third," which got its title from the fact that it was the third in progress that summer[10] but also that "a third" is what makes things happen in novels. A fourth 1925 piece, "Business In Baltimore" (*R* 479), is probably occasioned by the presence in France through that summer of Rose Ellen Stein, the wife of Stein's cousin, Julian, with their young son, Julian. It is a subtle but scathing satire on the power of business to effect marriages, promote real property, foster or prevent the accumulation of wealth and family power—in short, to determine lives, the material of novels. Two shorter pieces, "Early And Late" (*BTV* 241), one in a series of works on time, and "Or More (Or War)" (*UK* 115), which plays on the slogan "No more war," were also written that summer. These varied works turn out to be about closely related preoccupations.

Since Stein "used everything" in writing, it is not surprising that precipitates of actuality appear in these works. Though they are not "about" Stein's life and are not autobiographical in design, they absorb the vocabulary of her experience. Reading the referential details makes it possible to follow, in a raw state, what was happening to Stein, what she did and what she thought. Reading rhetorically follows the evolving construction of the words into completed texts. The two processes are not separate, though they can be considered separately.

The references to the anticipated lecture in *A Novel Of Thank You* and "Natural Phenomena" are startling not because of their inclusion but because of their number and quality. Theirs is frequently a shrill voice of personal distress. In seventy-five of the novel's 260 pages that Stein wrote between December 1925 and June 1926, when they were "back again from there" (173), the lecture returns constantly. In addition, once she is back in France, the success and her doubts about it remain preoccupations for much of the remainder of the novel. These alternately strident and flat references require an explanation, for they are not simply the stuff of a novel, absorbed into its fabric.[11]

When Stein received the invitation to speak, she had recently met and

10. See Stein to Anderson, n.d. [summer 1925], in Ray Lewis White, ed., *Sherwood Anderson/Gertrude Stein: Correspondence and Personal Essays* (Chapel Hill: University of North Carolina Press, 1972), 48–49.

11. Perhaps at the back of Stein's mind was also the sense that it was her brother Leo who, by endless lecturing and explaining, compensated for his "paucity of experiencing" (early notebook M-26). On page 179, in the context of resemblance, she comments, "Every little while they must resemble their brother . . ."

entertained Paul and Essie Robeson, Josephine Baker, and the cast of the Revue Nègre, all successful performers.[12] Singing, charm, fame, bows appear in the novel:

> Coming closer and the best way the best way by this time they have meant to be individually in unison and so Paul can be a name. (101)

> Now that they have allowed for it they need and do have more than all and alteration they can surround and be be doubtful are there fifty or seventy lions to their name. (103)

> They came to bow. (104)

These may be "about" Robeson but may carry over to Stein.

> Would they be afraid.
> One two three. Would they be afraid. (103)

Fame and performance are in the air. Sometime while composing pages 98 to 101 of the novel, Stein must have received the invitation. From then on, she keeps returning to fame and public appearances, describing performances by others or rehearsing her own.

A Novel Of Thank You absorbs the events of Stein's daily life, which in turn make her reconsider the nature of the novel. If its heroine goes to England, the novel will turn into a story of adventure, a story of departure (112), or a story of travel. She considers the journey to England. In phrasing that echoes Caesar's division of Gaul, Stein foresees her conquest of Britain, recalling at the same time *Boswell's Journal of a Tour of the Hebrides with Samuel Johnson,*

> often all Scotland has been known to be divided into Lowland and Highland. (235)

On page 116 appears "a visit to America." There is no evidence of a plan to go to America, although various friends at different times suggested lecturing there. Mabel Weeks, a professor at Barnard College, mentions lectures in a letter of May 15, 1923, and may have returned to the idea when she visited Stein in the summer of 1925. Emily Dawson, who also visited that summer, went to America in the autumn. Stein speaks of her immediately before the reference to the visit (115).

Her cousin Rose Ellen Stein, whom she saw often in 1925, repeatedly proposed lectures in America, but Stein did not wish to return home until she felt recognized as a major writer.

12. 6 November and 16[?] December 1925.

A visit to America. In visiting America they found themselves there and they said who is perhaps the most important and they answered you are perhaps the most important. . . . Just as well and pensive and answered and obliged and missing missing it who made flowers into bouquets who did. Who did make flowers into bouquets. And who did make flowers make flowers into bouquets of flowers who did make flowers into bouquets of flowers. And who did make flowers into bouquets. (116)

The bouquets, of course, applaud her as the most important author. The person who made flowers into bouquets is in part Stein herself, who makes bouquets of words, but bouquets are also associated with Stein's cousin Simon H., Julian Stein's brother, who died in 1913. He must have given her praise, support, and affection in early years. The bouquet certainly suggests that a visit to America connected with her family.

On 18 January 1926, Van Vechten commented on his efforts to finish his new novel,

I think, perhaps, when you read *Nigger Heaven* you will want to come to New York.[13]

This remark, written just before Stein composed the lecture, may also lie behind the "visit to America." After her triumph in England, Van Vechten on September 5 asked,

and when will you do this in America? I hope to hear you at Harvard, Howard and Lincoln.[14]

Lecturing in America may have been in her mind when she accepted the invitation, for she went to England with the hope that a successful lecture at the two great British universities might attract the public and publishers in America. Success in England led to success in America, she reminded Ellery Sedgwick of the *Atlantic Monthly* when she offered him the lecture.

In the novel, the vision of a visit to America leads to the phrase, "ferried ferried across" (119). The *cahier* in which Stein writes concerns the transatlantic luxury liner SS *France;* crossing may refer to the Atlantic or the English Channel. To compose, Stein uses whatever is at hand.

If she achieves fame, she will become historical and her novel will be a historical novel (116, 146). The historical novel is no doubt also the family history, published that fall, a belated but historic event for Stein. If she becomes historical, the new novel may become a history of flattery (159); if she

13. *LGS/CVV* 125.
14. *LGS/CVV* 132.

dresses well, it may become a novel of elegance (128). What fun she must have had exposing precarious genres by making up ridiculous subgenres of fiction! Does the addition of elegance or flattery make for a different kind of novel or does it remain simply a novel, thank you?

On page 113, she rehearses anxiously,

> He knew her address. He knew his address. And he knew his address. And he knew his address too.

She sees herself walking into the next room, eliminating the distance between the room she is in and the next—or between the room she is in and the auditorium where she is to lecture—or between Paris, where she is, and London, where she is afraid of going,

> It is an excellent idea to take away a distance to take away to a distance to make it a distance to make it in the distance. . . .

She admonishes herself,

> Go in there. Where. Having carefully arranged that they will never be frightened they have carefully arranged that they will never be frightened. . . .

She repeats the last sentence six times, as if to allay the anxiety that keeps her from exploring the unknown territory of a lecture.

The French manuscript *cahier* in which she here writes is one of a series entitled "Exploration." This particular one, entitled "Hommes d'action: engagement de porteurs," concerns the hiring of porters for expeditions into primitive colonial territories. In the text of the novel, Stein weaves together her own experience and the theme of the *cahier* to suggest advances into and retreats from dangerous terrain for explorer or writer.

> Everything that will be said in connection with porters will also have the same meaning in connection with carriers and subjects and animals and advancing and retiring and going and coming and will have a connection with paper and amethysts with writing and silver with buttons and books. (114)

Soon the fearful heroine, attempting to introduce herself, no longer knows whether she is coming or going. She was

> asked to go if it were not troubling her unduly was asked to come and if at that time there had been no use if at that time it had been of no use asking would it perhaps not be at all and more when there could be no

difficulty might she not present herself. And if she might what would she say and what would she say when she was attentive. . . . (123)

A few lines later begins Chapter CXXXI of the novel, which consists of three words reverberating with silent incapacity, "Invited to address" (124). The sentence—it is undoubtedly a sentence—is followed in the next chapter by a series of polite modulations masking her uneasiness:

> Invited to address them.
>
> They made them ask them ask him ask him would he be able to address them.
>
> He made them ask them would they be willing to have him address them.
>
> He made them ask them would they ask him would he be willing to address them.
>
> He made them ask him would he be willing if they asked him would he be willing to address them. (124)

Six pages later, Stein breaks through the anxiety with a single enabling word (131),

> She gave an address.
> Tenderness.[15]

The rhyme "address"/"tenderness" is not accidental. "Tenderness," a word that Stein uses with great care, has both personal and aesthetic meaning. It is one of two words naming feeling—rare with Stein—that recur throughout her work, *anxious* and *tender* or *tenderness*. Throughout the novel and "Natural Phenomena," Stein is beset by anxiety about the lecture. It is writing that finally frees her from the anxiety about going public and lecturing.

Tenderness, on the other hand—French *tendresse* is active in Stein's English word—validates the self and becomes a bulwark of ease against anxiety. In Stein's world, it is connected with Toklas, whose love confirmed Stein's right to be and allayed her existential anxiety. Knowing, through tenderness, that she was and who she was gave her access to words and enabled her to write her text. That text is not about tenderness, but tenderness is a condition for its creation that also allays anxiety.

Tenderness is also artistic receptivity. In "Lipchitz" (late 1925), Stein describes the sculptor as "so tenderly then standing." The cover of the *cahier*

15. Late in the portrait of "Jean Cocteau," written a little earlier, Stein says, "They must address with tenderness / Two him." The passage in the novel echoes the portrait, one of the examples of her work that Stein read at the end of the lecture. But the echo goes much further back, to "Ada," the early portrait of Toklas, where "tender" is already a key word.

in which this portrait is composed is entitled "Le Soldat au Créneau" and depicts a soldier patiently scanning the terrain from a battlement through the sight of his cocked rifle. She composes Lipchitz and the soldier into a unified sequence of sentences:

> When I knew him first he was standing looking looking through the glass and the chicken. When I knew him then he was looking looking at the looking. When I knew him then he was so tenderly then standing. When I knew him then he was then after then to then by then and when I knew him then he was then we then and then for then. When I knew him then he was for then by then as then so then to then in then and so. (*P&P* 63)

The sculptor is looking, tenderly and receptively, at the world from which he receives the impressions that allow him to create. Stein likewise must be tenderly receptive to the world whose words she composes.

Her need for tenderness explains why she raises and instantly rejects the idea of going to England and lecturing alone.

> Do you know why they both prefer it do you also know why they both want to come. They both want to come because later on later on they can and they cannot be left behind always to speak of it all alone. (120)

She needs Toklas with her. Tenderness is for two; anxiety is for one alone.

"Natural Phenomena" (*PL* 167–233)

A sixty-page work written alongside the novel between the spring of 1925 and 1926, "Natural Phenomena" takes its title from a series of the French *cahiers,* "Les Phénomènes de la Nature." Among the many phenomena that yield subtitles are thunder, volcanoes, tides, rainbows, and so on. She got the idea for the piece from the French series, which appealed to her as an acute observer of the world, especially while she was also exploring the French countryside.

What are natural phenomena? Stein tries out what we mean when we use the phrase,

> Used to natural phenomena. . . . Inclined to natural phenomena. . . . distrusted natural phenomena. (*PL* 213)

She composes concrete examples of natural phenomena that lead to

> A list of Phenomena of Nature and what they mean. (216)

The piece becomes a collection of exercises on natural phenomena. They provoke questions about recognition, representation, and description, including references to drawing and painting, especially of landscapes and still lifes:

> Natural phenomena means a chance to draw and to describe and to describe and to save to save and to idolise to idolise and to withdraw and to withdraw and to expect to expect and to return to return and to oblige to oblige and did he when he had he at best most. (232)

The anxious prospect of the lecture enters "Natural Phenomena" as it enters the novel. It may disrupt the flow of these pieces, but the disruption is a natural phenomenon, a part of the composing process. It must not be judged as disruption of a planned work. Stein tries to begin the address:

> Let us suppose that she spoke, she spoke to them, let us suppose that she spoke to them and she said what do you wish to have come here and there and why. . . . (219)

This start does not work well. She tries again, still uncertain, but becomes aggressive in self-display, her voice alternately strident and flat, as if she was not sure who she was.

> An address.
>
> I am taking it for granted that you are very much interested in what I have written and why and because and because I am very likely to be remembered. . . . (220)

Such loud rehearsals of herself are far from what she produced when she was in control of composition. As seductive as it is, the prospect of the lecture disrupts her capacity to compose and breaks her voice. Yet the tentative beginning also quickly leads to one of the central ideas in the lecture:

> Everybody always is the same the only thing that differs is what they look at not what they look like but what they are looking at. . . . (220)

For the final form in the address, Stein revises the phrasing,

> the only thing that is different is what is seen when it seems to be being seen, in other words, composition and time sense. (*R* 495; *SW* 514)

Time and change, central to "Natural Phenomena" and to the novel, become central also in the lecture she has now begun to draft.

> The sense of time is a phenomena of nature. It is what adds complexity to composition. (221)

In both *A Novel Of Thank You* and "Natural Phenomena," Stein at last succeeds in producing central sections of the address. Together, the two pieces offer a rare glimpse into a particularly troublesome composition. Richard Bridgman has pointed out that the second paragraph of the lecture appears also in the novel (131–32), but he says nothing about the other commentaries on the lecture in the novel and in "Phenomena."[16] No one has noticed the troubled attempts in these two works to write the lecture.

Stein herself, of course, did not comment on her difficulties in her first piece of audience writing. By the time she spoke about the lecture in 1932, in her next audience piece, *The Autobiography Of Alice B. Toklas,* she acknowledged only that "she was very upset at the prospect" of lecturing but continued,

> One cold dark afternoon she went out to sit with her ford car and while she sat on the steps of another battered ford watching her own being taken to pieces and put together again, she began to write. She stayed there several hours and when she came back chilled, with the ford repaired, she had written the whole of Composition As Explanation. (286)

How charming and easy it all sounds in this anecdote, composed for audience consumption to make light of the trouble, the temptation, and the struggle of the address. The truth of that struggle is recorded in *A Novel Of Thank You* and "Natural Phenomena," in two posthumously published volumes.

The Text

The manuscript of the address is not preserved. However, its composition can in part be pieced together from the novel and "Phenomena." Revisions in one of two typescripts will be discussed in this section.

The lecture falls into two parts, the first on modernism, the second on Stein's own work, which exemplifies the modern impulse. She begins with an apparent echo of postwar disillusionment ("nothing . . . makes a difference") but quickly moves to the problem of permanence and change in art and to modernism. In an astonishing performance, she addresses the English students as champions of modernism and readers most likely to appreciate her own work—in short, as those who are with the times.

> There is singularly nothing that makes a difference a difference in the beginning and in the middle and in ending except that each generation

16. Bridgman (167–68) says that the long section of *NOTY* after "She gave an address. / Tenderness," to which Stein in the manuscript added the marginal note, "Put in," was transferred from the lecture to the novel. But the second paragraph was transferred from the novel to the lecture. "Put in" directs Toklas for typing.

has something different at which they are all looking . . . composition is the difference. . . . (*R* 495; *SW* 513)

What changes is not life but the way we see life. The changes in perception from one generation to the next affect style in living as they also affect composition. By forcing us to respond to the times, war accelerates change everywhere.

"Or More (Or War)," written in the spring of 1925 (*UK* 115), plays on the slogan "No more war." Proceeding literally, it considers "war" and "more." Stein recapitulates elements of war by references to the Civil War, the Cuban, Mexican-American War, and then leads up to World War I. Wars, unlike ordinary life, have beginnings, middles, and ends. She then asks what makes for great or small wars, how quantity and quality relate, how wars are counted. She also, of course, implies a further question—what happens after the war? Is after a war before another war?[17]

Stein draws an analogy between war and art. In the second paragraph, transferred to the address from *A Novel Of Thank You* (131–32), she refers to Lord Grey.[18] As the British foreign secretary from 1905 to 1916, he

17. In the manuscript, the parenthetical phrase in the title appears to me to be not "(Or War)" but "(On War)." The question of after the war connects with many others about time, evident in such titles as "After At Once" (1924), *PL* 50, or "Early And Late" (1925), *BTV* 241.

18. Sir Edward Grey (1862–1933), Viscount of Fallodon, was foreign secretary when Stein and Toklas were in England at the outset of the war, a fact she no doubt recalled as she composed the lecture. Lord Grey had maintained good relations with the United States, had been friends with Theodore Roosevelt, president of the League of Nations Union from 1918 on, and ambassador to the United States, 1919–20. The American edition of his memoirs, *Twenty-Five Years: 1892–1916* (New York: Frederick A. Stokes Company) had appeared in September 1925 and was widely read.

> Lord Grey emphasizes again and again, as he had also done in speeches, that World War I marked the beginning of a new epoch and that on the Continent all the great Powers [were] thinking of war in terms of previous experience, and of the latter half of the nineteenth century. We were alone in foreboding that war in the twentieth century would be unlike anything that had preceded it. (2:32)

A literary man with an interest in words, Lord Grey frequently draws comparisons with Laurence Sterne's *Tristram Shandy* (New York, Modern Library, n.d. [1760–67]). He refers those who speak of a soldier's want of sympathy for his fellow man (67–69) to Uncle Toby's reply to Mr. Shandy (416–17), that man's propensity for war is not mere evil but is his gift for keeping ambition and turbulence within bounds. See also Lord Grey's *Fallodon Papers* (Boston: Houghton Mifflin), a collection of lectures published late in 1926, after Stein's address, but including lectures familiar to many before they appeared in a collection.

remarked that when the generals before the war talked about the war they talked about it as a nineteenth century war although to be fought with twentieth century weapons. That is because war is a thing that decides how it is to be when it is done. (*R* 495; *SW* 513)

War is planned on the basis of strategic experience of the past. Yet blueprints for strategy devised in the war academies do not enable us to win new wars with new, unprecedented conditions. To win a war, we must give up past practice and respond to present conditions. Stein appeals to her audience, some of whom may have been in the war while others are the children of the war, as those most in tune with the moment and therefore with modernism.

Like those who devised the winning strategies of World War I, those who created modernism in art are winners in the struggle to see the contemporary world as it is. She puts herself on the side of those who have won the war. Modern art, she implies, composes and speaks to the reality of their lives.

Artists are no more ahead of their time than the soldiers who fought in World War I. Artists and soldiers know, as those who are not in the front lines and who live by tradition do not, that total responsiveness to their world is needed if they are to survive. Genius, be it of a great artist or a great strategist, is the capacity to see truly, to close the gap between fact and perception—between what is and how we perceive what is.

Having shown war and art to be two forms of struggle, it remains to convince her audience that modern art—the work of the painters whom Stein considered authentically modern and her own writing—is not ugly, as it is often said to be. It appears ugly only to those who do not understand it. Modern art, she says, is rejected as ugly because it does not conform to accepted standards. Perceptions change, however, and suddenly what had appeared ugly is seen to be true and to show things as they are. At that moment, art that had been outlawed becomes accepted as classic.

In other words, Stein predicts that changing public taste, which lags behind artistic perception, will be open to the beauty of her art and that of the modernist painters. She is making a bid for acceptance as a classic author about to be recognized and understood by her audience.

When Stein first drafted the reference to rejection and acceptance of new artists, she attempted once more to use the analogy of art and war. The first typescript, which she sent to Carl Van Vechten in the summer of 1926, shows one paragraph with significant revisions of substance.[19]

19. Stein to Van Vechten, postmark 9 August 1926, *LGS/CVV* 345. All other revisions are stylistic.

In what follows, the sections excised in revision are italicized. The final version, which was printed, can be read by omitting the italicized sections. Which version she read at the universities or when she undertook the revisions is not known.

> For a very long time everybody refuses and then almost without a pause almost everybody accepts. In the history of the refused in the arts and literature the rapidity of the change is always startling. *It is like the United States re-electing Wilson because he kept us out of the war and two months after before the term for which he was elected for keeping us out of the war could begin they were all whole heartedly accepting war.* Now the only difficulty *not with their coming into the war but* with the *volte-face* concerning the arts *in times of peace* is this. When the acceptance comes, by that acceptance the thing created becomes a classic. It is *again* a natural phenomena a rather extraordinary natural phenomena that a thing accepted becomes a classic. (YCAL; *R* 496; *SW* 515)

By carefully excising the references to American entry into the war and to Wilson,[20] Stein eliminated not only a shoddy analogy but also a potential political indiscretion. Though she meant to speak of American entry into the war in a pro-British manner, the comment might have seemed to pit Britain against the United States and her audience against herself when she in fact wished to show Britain and the United States, her audience and herself, allied on the side of modernism. Stein's revisions are never casual but always deliberate and sophisticated.

One senses in the address the same discomfort on her part that pervades the sections on the address in *A Novel Of Thank You.* There she expresses hope for fame but fears publicity. Here she explains how outlaw artists become classics, but by the time a work is accepted as classic, she says,

> the composition of a time has become so pronounced that it is past. (*R* 498; *SW* 517)

Is becoming a classic to be passé or, worse, to be dead? Stein suffered from being an outlaw. Her commitment was uncompromisingly modern, but she

20. Stein's awareness of Wilson goes back to her 1904 fragment, "Fernhurst," incorporated into *MOA.* In Philip Redfern, the professor who clashed with Dean Thornton (Carey Thomas) at Fernhurst College (Bryn Mawr), she showed Wilson's personality traits. See Leon Katz, introduction to *Fernhurst, Q. E. D., And Other Early Writings* (New York: Liveright, 1971), xxiv–xxix. Stein's interest in political personalities and problems, including the League of Nations and Zionism, requires more detailed investigation than it has received. Nor has her acquaintance with members of the New York reform movement, including Alfred Hodder, Wilson's rival at Bryn Mawr, been studied in detail.

also wanted to be read, to be comprehended, to hear the "yes" of readers. Instead, she received rejection upon rejection when she submitted work and was ridiculed when published. She was left with despair about publication that sometimes turned bitter and aggressive. The fifth section of this chapter will suggest some of the responses to her efforts.

In the second part of the address, Stein reviews her own work. In 1926, she could not count on an audience's familiarity with her writing because little was in print. An audience was more likely to know about her as an eccentric writer who owned modern paintings than to have read her.[21] The announcement of Stein's lecture in the Cambridge *Granta* gave no information about her work. The notice in the various student magazines at Oxford, on the other hand, which was signed by Harold Acton, referred to *Three Lives, Tender Buttons, Geography And Plays, The Making Of Americans,* and the *Oxford Magazine* pieces.

Central to her summary of her efforts is the theme of the first part of the address—the modern effort to "be in the present." She acknowledges that when she produced her early work,

> nobody knew why it was done like that, I did not myself although naturally to me it was natural. (*R* 498; *SW* 518)

She groped for solutions rather than theorizing. Ex post facto, she creates in the lecture two critical terms to justify her procedure: the "prolonged present" and the "continuous present" (*R* 498; *SW* 517–18). She connects the first with "Melanctha," the second with *The Making Of Americans,* but the difference is not clear.[22]

21. Of her early work, by 1926 *Three Lives* (reprinted by John Lane, London, 1920) was in print as was *G&P* (1922). *MOA,* published in November 1925, was available but not widely distributed and not well known to students. *TB,* the portrait of Mabel Dodge, and the early portraits of Picasso and Matisse in *Camera Work* were no longer available. The portrait of the Cone sisters, "Two Women," had appeared in June 1925 in Robert McAlmon's Contact Collection, where Sitwell was also represented; the second portrait of Picasso, originally done for *Vanity Fair,* was published in *Tom Masson's Annual* in the United States in October 1925 but was not easy to find in England. Very few works had appeared in mostly small American periodicals until, starting in 1922, her writing appeared in *Broom* and the *Little Review.* Two pieces ("Two Cubist Poems. The Peace Conference," later retitled "More League," written 1920, and "A Portrait Of One. Harry Phelan Gibb," written 1913) had appeared in the *Oxford Magazine* of 1920.

    By 1926, nobody had even heard of other major works of the early years like "G.M.P.," "A Long Gay Book," "Many Many Women," "Two," and the many early portraits, all unpublished.

22. Sutherland attempts to define the difference by analogy with music, the prolonged present corresponding to development by recurrence and variation, the continuous present

She uses "prolonged present" once, as if groping for a term, but does not use it again. "Continuous present," on the other hand, remained in her vocabulary and in that of her students. Since Stein offers few theoretical terms to her often bewildered readers, they cling to the two words, hoping for distinctions that may not have been clear to Stein herself. The continuous present initially concerns narrative but later becomes an aspect of description.

In discussing her early work on time, Stein implies that the continuous present in her narration is realized by "using everything" and by "beginning again and again." "Beginning again and again" describes her repetitions, so-called, which create extended, unbroken continuity as well as gradual variety that opens into "insistence." "Using everything" refers to her reliance on minute details, including tiny inflections of language, to develop the evolving continuity of the present. Stein always insists on the importance of small things—an infinitude of tiny details rather than a collective totality.

Both "beginning again" and "using everything" involve similarity and difference. Repetition, never twice the same, creates difference and newness, not mere likeness. She associates her growing interest in difference with description, with the exercises in minute observation of *Tender Buttons* and with natural phenomena.[23] All these and the early portraits show her struggling to seize the differentia in all their exciting specificity.

Differentiation leads her to the work of 1923 with its new techniques for seizing difference by means of series or lists, with the list continuous but the details different; or of geography, with the earth unendingly one but particulars infinitely varied; and with second portraits, of the same subjects as the first and yet, years later, no longer the same as they were.

The end of the address returns her to the present of 1926—the postwar world of the peace that returned her to work. Peace brings an interest in equilibration and distribution of words as well as things. The peace, she says, will make time, the central problem of all composition, take new forms. To be contemporaneous is to realize the only certainty, the present. The future remains uncertain. She implies but never states that it lies with her audience.

The two concluding sentences are deceptively simple.

And afterwards.
Now that is all.

---

by making each successive passage entirely new, that is, "beginning again." The analogy with music is not helpful to the reader; Sutherland himself does not appear to be comfortable with it and finally says that both are "dimensions" of the present (*SBW* 51–52).

23. See "Natural Phenomena," *PL* 220–21, written at the time of the address.

Stein spoke them in one way. The careful reader hears in the mind all at once the innumerable ways in which they can be spoken and can have meaning.

Four Examples

With Sitwell's approval, Stein decided to conclude the address with four examples of her work: a poem, "Preciosilla" (1913); a play, *A Saint In Seven* (1922); and two portraits, "Sitwell Edith Sitwell" (1925) and "Jean Cocteau" (1925–26), all then unpublished. Perhaps referring to the pieces by genre, as she did not usually do, was meant to help her audience.

Stein read no example in her early abstract style with rhythmic repetitions and variations. She may have felt that *Three Lives* was well enough known as an example of the early work. "Preciosilla," like "Susie Asado," which opened *Geography And Plays,* had been written in 1913 in Spain, in the new style she had suddenly developed late in "A Long Gay Book" that had led to *Tender Buttons.* Its concrete words, its short phrases and multiple puns, which break up and recombine words in many ways, are particularly suited for reading aloud. It develops by sound and melody of words rather than by meaning. Hearing "Preciosilla" is listening to words that play, not to a story. The poem exemplifies perfectly the elements with which Stein began to compose in 1913. It also suggests the continuing importance of Spain.

A Saint In Seven, written in St.-Rémy in 1922, was originally entitled "Seven And A Saint." The title is full of echoes: the town of Soye-en-Septaine (Cher), the composer Saint-Saëns, who had died in 1921, the rhyme "seven / heaven," and the phrase "seventh heaven." The play develops by melodic phrasing, quite different from "Preciosilla," which builds by sharp verbal wit. *A Saint In Seven* opens with an epigraph that was surely appropriate for the English universities:

> I thought perhaps that we would win by human means. I knew we could win if we did win but I did not think that we could win by human means, and now we have won by human means. (*Primer* 75)

Like many of the pieces that Stein wrote in St.-Rémy in 1922 and 1923, the play makes words—names, saints, phrases—march formally and processionally. Time, which makes processions, here also becomes a visual element—"followed and not surrounded"—that does not escape toward a vanishing point but is contained in surrounding circles, repetitions, and rhymes. The piece introduces saints, always associated with Toklas but also with the lyrical meditation that Stein treasured, and with Spain.

The saint, "followed and not surrounded," is the figure which allows victory over time and suggests the meditating artist, tenderly receptive, active but not measurably productive. All the personages listed at the beginning of this play—a saint with a lily, a girl with a rooster, a woman leaning forward, and so on—are arrested in movement. The words are not spoken expressively by the characters themselves but are used descriptively to suggest pastoral scenes—one thinks of tableaux—with still figures.

The play also includes a small, humorous love scene, echoing Stein and Toklas, in a spoken, rhyming love duet:

> Saint.
> A Saint.
> Saint and very well I thank you.
> Two in bed.
> Two in bed.
> Yes two in bed.
> They had eaten.
> Two in bed. . . .

The saints are undoubtedly human saints in a human heaven full of humor, laughter, and activity, though not sequential action moving toward a prescribed end or resolution of a plot. In this play, time takes the form of verbal movement but does not go anywhere. Less than a year later, Stein returned to some of its themes and phrases. Its selection here suggests some of what was in her mind less than a bare year before she wrote *Four Saints In Three Acts.*

The two portraits of Edith Sitwell and Jean Cocteau that concluded the reading add to the lecture dramatic contexts reminiscent of the one explored in "An Elucidation." Stein had written "Sitwell Edith Sitwell" in the spring of 1925.[24] Reading the portrait during the lecture initiated by Sitwell was a tribute to Sitwell that both must have relished.[25] In addition, Sitwell as sub-

24. Sitwell acknowledged receipt of the portrait in a letter from Madrid of 24 April 1925. She expressed particular delight at the prospect of its inclusion in a proposed volume under the title *Portraits And Prayers* that Stein had submitted to Sitwell's publisher, Duckworth, who, however, eventually turned it down as "much too difficult to publish with success" (Thomas Balston, for Duckworth, to Stein, 1 May 1925). Sitwell praised the "inevitability" of the sound and rhythm of the portrait, which "exhilarated, stimulated but at the same time calmed our [her and her brothers'] nerves to the most extraordinary degree."
25. It is not clear whether Edith, Osbert, and Sacheverell Sitwell attended the lecture at Cambridge, though they all appear to have been at Oxford. It has been said that Sitwell (and her brothers?) sat on the stage while Stein spoke. However, since the Junior Censor's Dining Room at Christ Church, where the talk was given at Oxford, is not a large, formal lecture room, Sitwell presumably sat in front.

    Toklas (*WIR* 118–19) says that in London, presumably prior to the lecture, the Sitwells asked Stein to sit on the platform at a poetry reading they gave. I have not found

ject of the portrait could be seen and "read" directly by the audience while Stein read her own portrait of Sitwell, so that portraiture became performance. Stein read to those who were her own admiring audience about those who "sit when they sit around her," as she says of Sitwell's audience in the portrait. With their flair for drama, Stein and Sitwell must have enjoyed the performance.

Among the Stein papers is a small manuscript pad which shows in sections what must have been the nucleus of the portrait, written in short lines, small page by small page, dictated by the size of the pad. The first page reads,

> In a minute
> when they sit
> when they sit
> around her.

and the next,

> Mixed it with
> two who. One
> two two one
> two two. Mixed
> it with two two

and so on. The visual arrangement on the small pages makes rhythms prominent that are easily missed in the longer printed lines.

The portrait is begun on the tiny pages of this *carnet* and then substantially reworked. It connects Sitwell and Stein's old college friend Mabel Weeks: "Weeks and weeks able and weeks." Weeks, a professor of English at Barnard College in New York, had been in Europe in the spring and summer of 1925, presumably among those who sat admiringly around Sitwell. Stein connects Weeks and Sitwell by exploring their names literally. Sitwell is an immediate presence in space ("in a minute," "sit around," "look up . . . down and around") whereas Weeks comes out of past time and tense. There is a "change in time" between the early friendship with Weeks and the present friendship with Sitwell.

> Not to remember weeks to say and asking, not to remember weeks to-day.

The portrait, she says, is for Sitwell, not for Weeks; for the present, not the past; to Stein, Sitwell may have recalled Weeks as a type of personality. In

---

documentation for this reading. Of course, the idea of Stein on stage during a Sitwell reading and the Sitwells on stage during a Stein reading, which in addition includes the reading of Stein's portrait of Sitwell, has magnificent dramatic mirror possibilities.

the early notebooks there are extensive comments on Mabel Weeks. These observations may account for the movement from past to present and may make Weeks, who also was a faithful friend and correspondent of Leo Stein, a foil to offset Sitwell, "and now altogether different." In the portrait, Stein makes a concerted effort at seeing, beholding, realizing Sitwell, which creates one of those fine verbal miniatures that suddenly rise from the page:

> Fill my eyes no no.
> It was and held it.
> The size of my eyes.
> . . .
> To know it as well as there.

She brings together polite social introductions, which are presumably also introductions to writing. There is a knock at a door (a question?) and a key, whether to a door or to literary work. Door and key, opening and closing, question and answer, facing and agreeing or disagreeing recur throughout the portrait, all in an effort to perceive completely, to apprehend, to see the subject of the portrait, the person, the poet, her face, her words, her work.

The portrait is an insistent effort to make words create her perception of the subject, make sleeping and waking apprehension the same, identify word and object, join word with word, rhyme with rhyme, rhythm with rhythm, knowledge with vision, past with present.

> Absently faces and by and by we agree.
> Apparently faces and by and by we agree.
> By and by faces apparently we agree.
> Apparently faces by and by we agree.

Sound and rhythm, to which Sitwell always responded, dominate the portrait.

> The sound and rhythm seem to me inevitability itself,—but nobody but you would have found this inevitability.[26]

With "Jean Cocteau," written in December 1925 or January 1926, several contexts enter Stein's lecture which would not have been lost on an English audience. One concerns Diaghilev's production of *Parade* (1917), the work of Cocteau, Satie, and Picasso, which is often seen as a precursor of *Façade* by Edith Sitwell and William Walton (1921–22).[27] A performance of *Façade*

26. Sitwell to Stein, 24 April 1925.

27. See Cocteau's account of the collaboration for *Parade* in *Le Coq et l'Arlequin* (1918); Cocteau on performances considered scandalous by their novelty, such as *Le Sacre du*

attended by Diaghilev took place on April 26, before Stein's lecture, and another on June 29, after the lecture.

Although there are no references to *Parade* in the portrait of Cocteau, Stein undoubtedly intended to remind her audience of the connection between Sitwell's and Cocteau's work. In *Picasso* (1938), she recalls that she first saw Cocteau when Picasso visited her with him before they left for Rome to work on *Parade.*

> So cubism was to be put on the stage. . . . That was the beginning of the general recognition of Picasso's work. . . . (29)

It is fascinating to follow Stein's recollection of the collaboration in her *Picasso:*

> It is evident that really nothing changes but at the same time everything changes and Italy and Parade and the termination of the war gave to Picasso in a kind of a way another harlequin period . . . a realistic period . . . a period of calm. (32)

Here, in 1938, Stein retells what she spoke about in the English address, including the reference to Lord Grey and her own phrases from the lecture, "everything changes . . . nothing changes." Once again her verbal memory is striking.

Another context is *The Triumphs of Neptune.* After Diaghilev attended the performance of *Façade* in April 1926, he commissioned Sacheverell Sitwell to write a book for the Russian ballet. *The Triumphs of Neptune,* with music by Gerald Berners, was the result.[28] Lord Berners, who later wrote the music for Stein's ballet, *A Wedding Bouquet* (1937), may at this time have met her through the Sitwells and may have heard the lecture. The intricacies of mutual acquaintance and promotion must be recognized if the full impact of the address is to be understood.

Further context is Stein's apparent feeling about Cocteau's translation of "Dining is west," one of her sentences from the "Food" section of *Tender*

Printemps and *Parade,* in *New Criterion* 4, no. 1 (January 1926), which also included Stein's portrait of T. S. Eliot. The first, private performance of *Façade* was given in January 1922, the first and scandalous public performance at Aeolian Hall, London, on June 12, 1923.

28. By June 1926, if not earlier, Stein must have been aware of the plan for this ballet. It was produced in London at the Lyceum Theater on December 3, 1926, and had its Paris premiere in early January 1927 at the Théâtre Sarah-Bernhardt. It was at this performance, which Stein attended, that Sitwell and Pavel Tchelitchew first met, apparently introduced by Stein; three days later, they met again at Stein's studio. See also John Pearson, *The Sitwells: A Family's Biography* (New York: Harcourt Brace Jovanovich, 1978), 212.

Buttons, in his *Potomak:*[29] "Dîner, c'est ouest." The word "west" appears in the last section of her portrait of Cocteau, "sign with as west west with as most," though whether an echo is intended cannot be known. In an undated letter, possibly of spring 1923, Stein's friend Grace Lounsbery wrote, "Cocteau told me he would like to translate your book." Which book is not clear, but what matters here is that Cocteau liked her work.

Stein had many other reasons to feel a connection with Cocteau. After she had written her second portrait of Picasso in 1923, her friend Henri-Pierre Roché translated it and showed his version to Cocteau, who suggested revisions. Cocteau's "Ode à Pablo Picasso" (1919), his essay "Picasso" (1923, dedicated to Satie), his *Dessins* (1924), dedicated to Picasso, bear witness to the painter's profound importance for him. A further connection goes through Lipchitz, who in 1920 did busts of Cocteau and Stein and whose portrait Stein wrote late in 1925.[30]

Stein mailed her portrait to Cocteau, who acknowledged it on January 14, 1926, a date that shows it to have been composed just before the Cambridge address, as is confirmed by the sentence,

> They must address with tenderness
> Two him.

This sentence is in the portrait and, slightly modified, in *A Novel Of Thank You* (131):

> She gave an address.
> Tenderness.[31]

Another phrase in the portrait of Cocteau that echoes *A Novel Of Thank You* is:

29. Written 1913–14 but published later: Jean Cocteau, *Le Potomak 1913–1914* (Paris: Librairie Stock, 1924), 12.
30. In the bound typescript volume 19, Stein inserted the portrait of Lipchitz immediately before the portrait of Cocteau, which she put before the Cambridge address. If this order is accurate chronologically, as it appears to be, the Lipchitz portrait may have been composed in December 1925, not 1926, as the Haas-Gallup bibliography listed it. Stylistically it is close to the Cocteau piece.
31. In the Cocteau manuscript, Stein wrote "To him" but revised the phrase, decontextuating it, to "Two him," as she frequently did with homophones such as "to," "two," "too" or "there," "their." In *P&P,* the phrase is printed at the bottom of page 84; page 85 begins with "G. Stein," centered, as if the name were a title when it is actually a signature following a salutation ending a letter, "address with tenderness / Two him. / G. Stein." Ernst Reichl, the German designer, who planned *P&P* for Random House, apparently did not understand Stein's intention, which always requires careful scrutiny.

> Having the habit of addressing having the habit of expressing having the habit of expressing having the habit of addressing.

The manuscript fills to the very end a small notepad. Before she assembled the final text on the pad, however, she composed several short passages in a small lilac *carnet,* where she also entered sections of "A Third" (347), "Natural Phenomena" (199), and *A Novel Of Thank You* (82). One small section—perhaps the thematic center of the piece or its beginning in her mind—reads:

> Having the habit of expressing having the habit of addressing . . . (order reversed in the final text).

These words are written on a page along with a number of addresses. Once again, then, Stein tells literally what she is doing—addressing. The word becomes a pun when we realize that she is also considering the address for Cambridge University.

The third section composed in the *carnet* is:

> It is not usually my habit to mention anything but now having the habit of addressing I am mentioning it as anything.

What is the "it" she does not usually display? In a passage drafted in this *carnet* for "A Third," she has, exceptionally, mentioned or signed her own name:

> In exactitude and Gertrude . . . (347)

The lecture opens a prospect quite different from the portrait, where she speaks personally and intimately to or of Cocteau—or of herself. The portrait has some of the qualities of a personal letter. Farther on, she signs her name to a section that becomes a letter addressed to Cocteau.

The remaining drafts in the *carnet* consist of small, carefully tuned and repeated phrases and end with more and increasingly controlled, regular rhythms:

> chance with a change change with as strong strong with as will will with as sign sign with as west . . . when they did for for they did there and then. Then does not celebrate the there and then.

The passage returns to the "there and then" which, in the portrait, becomes an intimate "here and now."

Stein copied the unclear sections from the *carnet* to the notepad, adding further sections directly in the pad. The pad was so small that she wrote in short lines and tiny page-long sections with small repeated and varied phrase units. Numerous other recurring words and phrases (e.g., "have / halve," first used in "An Elucidation" and later elsewhere) give depth and echoes to the portrait.

The portrait begins with a moving passage about closeness:

> Needs be needs be needs be near . . . .

It then leads to distance:

> This is where they have their land astray
> Two say.

Since two say it, she repeats the two lines. What is near or far? Where is the land astray? A land to wander about? A refuge? The country? England? What is its "address"? There is no need to pin down single references. But there is, in this light and delicate word portrait, an anxious sense of a place both distant and intimate.

Cocteau responded on January 14, 1926, perfectly in tune with her text even though he claimed that he understood only half of the portrait because his English was poor. Quoting from her portrait, his letter speaks for Stein readers who follow her but do not understand her words:

> *J'habite avec vous le pays perdu.*
> *Hélas je comprends mal seulement à moitié.* (When half is May how much is May)!

Yet to understand half, whatever that may mean, is to understand—or to have—the whole of something.

Before and After the Address

On January 25, 1926, Stein wrote to her old friend the painter Harry Phelan Gibb, in Chelsea, that she was coming to England to speak. He was delighted. After the performance of *Façade,* however, he warned her:

> I think Edith Sitwell has been stealing some of your thunder. This week there was a performance of some of her prose poetry accompanied by music at the New Chenil Galleries here and obviously she could not have composed her poems had you not existed long before she dreamed of it. My point is why should you not get your dues and common justice? (28 April 1926)

On May 1, Stein replied,

> You see they asked me of course through the influence of Edith Sitwell who has been doing steady propaganda for my recognition in England for the last two years, so don't think for a moment that she does not completely recognize my primary importance in literature of the day. Of course I do know that I am the best of it and I must say that no one has been more continuously and persistently certain of it than she among the litterateurs.

The elaborate ballet of courtesies and promotions between Sitwell and Stein that is here hinted at lies behind the lecture, the exchanges before and after the trip to England, the comments in letters and, of course, the record in *The Autobiography Of Alice B. Toklas.*

Stein and Toklas arranged for a short visit, for they wanted to return home quickly. They left Paris for London on May 30, accompanied to the station by Tchelitchew and Tanner, who helped them combat stage fright. On the evening of June 1, Edith Sitwell honored Stein with the big party about which she had dreamed for many months. Among the guests were Virginia Woolf, E. M. Forster, Siegfried Sassoon, Dorothy Todd, the editor of *Vogue,* Tom Driberg, and Arnold Bennett. On June 9, Virginia Woolf recorded the party at Sitwell's Bayswater flat:

> Went to a party at E. S.'s (in my new dress) "to meet Miss Stein," a lady much like Joan Fry, but more massive, in blue sprinkled brocade, rather formidable.[32]

On September 19, Stein wrote to Van Vechten, answering his letter of September 8, which had suggested that she should come to America to lecture at Harvard, Howard, and Lincoln universities. She said she was about to send him a copy of the printed lecture.

> I am glad that you think it just right. It pleased me to do it and it still seems to be xciting them over there over there being these days across

32. *The Diary of Virginia Woolf* (New York: Harcourt Brace Jovanovich, 1980), vol. 3, *1925–1930,* 89 and n.; see also Pearson, *Sitwells,* 221. Joan Fry (1862–1955) was Roger Fry's second, unmarried sister.

Little is in print about the Cambridge lecture but more about the Oxford lecture, in part because Harold Acton publicized it. At both lectures there was heckling, from Austin Lee at Cambridge, from David Cecil and others at Oxford. The lecture was reviewed in *Granta,* 12 June 1926 (May Week Double Issue); see also "Steinography and Rosewater," *Granta,* 26 November 1926, a late review upon the occasion of the lecture by René Crevel on 18 November 1926, the result of the contact with Stein; *Oxford Times,* "University Pages," 11 June 1926, 15; *Isis,* 9 June 1926, 8; *Oxford University Review,* 10 June 1926, 564; and Gilbert Armitage, "A Word on Gertrude Stein," *Oxford Magazine,* 17 June 1926, 584.

the channel for me, and others. You will be interested that one of the dons at Oxford[33] said to me at the end, what he liked was that it was not an xplanation but a creation, well he said more but he said that. I can eat it with a spoon or a soup ladle or anything and I like it, but you always come first to me and that you know, you meant it first and said it first.[34]

And Afterwards. Publications and Rejections

Atlantic Monthly

Stein attempted to submit the address, as she had earlier submitted "An Elucidation," to the *Atlantic Monthly*.[35] Publication in that journal was a mark of solid success in America, as it had been for Twain, Howells, James, and others. Supposedly Stein was encouraged to submit to the *Atlantic Monthly* by Mildred Aldrich. However, Stein's persistent efforts to get published in that journal require a fuller explanation.[36] That her modernist work was not for readers of the *Atlantic Monthly* she perhaps never fully understood. The very writing that her work combated appealed to the *Atlantic Monthly* audience she wanted to win.

Stein was inexperienced in the ways of the publishing world, and her background had not prepared her for the problems of publication. I assume that among her Baltimore family and friends, the *Atlantic Monthly* was accepted reading, as it was for many educated Americans. Publication in it would have established her not only with middle-class literary circles but also with her family.

33. C. M. Bowra.
34. *LGS/CVV* 133.
35. The story of Stein's submissions to the *Atlantic Monthly* has been told by Donald Gallup in the *Yale University Library Gazette* 28 (January 1954): 109–28. The Stein letters given to YCAL by Ellery Sedgwick begin with 1919 submissions. However, in the "Book of Literature," her early log of submissions, there is evidence that even earlier she sent her portrait of "[Arthur] Frost," the American painter, and perhaps other pieces, to *Atlantic Monthly*, which rejected it.

    Pre–World War I correspondence with *Atlantic Monthly* is apparently not preserved or was not sent to Yale. Interestingly, the story of Stein's relationship with this magazine is almost duplicated in the story of her relationship with *Vanity Fair*, where she was only a little more successful, though Frank Crowninshield capitalized on her "personality."
36. Her interest in publication in the *Atlantic Monthly* is even confirmed by Hemingway, who, in *A Moveable Feast* (New York: Charles Scribners Sons, 1964), speaks of it as a mark of quality writing in her mind, limited only by unacceptable (*inaccrochable*) subject matter (15). The trouble with Stein's writing, in the minds of editors, was not offensive subject matter but lack of subject matter.

The Cambridge address offered another chance to convince Ellery Sedgwick that she warranted publication. In a letter of late January or February 1926, Stein informed him of the invitation from Cambridge and the likelihood of another from Oxford and suggested that the *Atlantic Monthly* might be interested in publishing the address. On March 20, 1926, after receiving the invitation from Oxford, she wired, offering the lecture for the June issue for a fee of $200. On March 22, Sedgwick firmly refused, "Unfortunately no."

In late June or July, Stein reported in judiciously chosen words on her "very pleasant success in England, . . . with understanding and lots of enthusiasm." She also said the Hogarth Press was publishing the address and expressed regret that the *Atlantic Monthly* was not the first to print it. Sedgwick congratulated her on July 8:

> I am Anglo-Saxon enough to believe that when one is thought well of at Oxford and Cambridge, one deserves it.

Later, Stein mailed the Hogarth pamphlet to him, asking for a response and hinting at the difficulties of prophets in their own country which refused to look at "what interests all the other people interested in literature." She enclosed her portrait of Cézanne, "who was one of my big influences, . . . and surely your audience has gotten to Cezanne." But Sedgwick never commented on the address and on August 19, 1927, turned down "Cezanne."

T. S. Eliot and the *(New) Criterion*

Stein also submitted the address to another distinguished American editor, T. S. Eliot, and was turned down. The mere fact that Eliot rejected the piece for the *Criterion,* however, fails to show the context of the submission.

Jane Heap had in 1924 spoken to Eliot about Stein. On August 27, 1924, Eliot wrote to Heap that he knew nothing about Stein but would like to see some of her work, a statement which gives pause. On Stein's behalf, Heap submitted to him "Lend A Hand Or Four Religions" (1922), which he rejected.[37]

Supposedly in the fall of 1924, Stein and Eliot met in Paris,[38] and the meeting may have led to the composition of "A Description Of The Fif-

37. 24 December 1924; 25 January 1925.

38. See Mellow 287 and n. The recollections by Stein and Toklas of the incident in the autobiographical books do not sound complete or convincing. Both the context of the meeting and the Eliot portrait require reconsideration. November 15 may have been the date of the meeting with Eliot but was also the birthday of Stein's nephew, Julian Stein Jr., born 1920; a hint of the birthday may be in "The fifteenth of November has happily a birthday."

teenth Of November. A Portrait Of T. S. Eliot," submitted to the *New Criterion,* as it was then called. Eliot agreed to publish it but delayed, first planning to include it in the October 1925 issue but finally printing it in the January 1926 issue. In the April 1926 issue, preparatory to Stein's address, appeared Sitwell's review of *The Making Of Americans.* Sitwell and Stein had privately exchanged numerous barbed comments about Eliot.

On June 12, 1926, Eliot wrote to Stein, in response to her inquiry about publication of the address. He wanted to read it, he said, but the *New Criterion* being booked through January 1927, speedy publication was impossible. He added,

> I am indeed sorry to have been absent from England and unable to swell your triumphant progress. . . .

She sent him the address, which he returned on June 25; he would have printed it after January 1927, he said, but as in the meantime the Hogarth Press had agreed to publish it, the *New Criterion* could not also do so. He added a handwritten postscript, "I like it."

Nor did this end the matter. On the back of his letter, Stein drafted an answer trying to turn his snub to her advantage:

> I am glad you like it. Would you want to print A Saint in Seven which interested the audience the most perhaps of the things I read them. It has never been printed.

A Saint In Seven, like "Lend A Hand Or Four Religions," which Jane Heap had earlier submitted, may have seemed most likely to appeal to Eliot. (By this time, the Hogarth Press had not yet decided to include in the pamphlet Stein's examples of her work.) On September 8, 1926, with his last letter to Stein, Eliot returned an unnamed manuscript—no doubt *A Saint In Seven.* In the January 1927 number of the *New Criterion* appeared a brief, unsigned, and unenthusiastic review of the lecture. Eliot himself reviewed it briefly, the last of four books, in the January 29, 1927 number of the *Nation and Athenaeum* as "not improving, . . . not amusing, . . . not good for one's mind" and spelling a barbarian future that was to be refused.

Hogarth Press

The first letters from Leonard Woolf to Stein also tell a story not apparent in the fact that he printed *Composition As Explanation.* Well before publication of *The Making Of Americans* was arranged with Robert McAlmon's Contact Press in 1925, the Woolfs were approached by Sitwell in view of publishing the novel. On August 28, 1925, Leonard Woolf declared himself willing to consider the big book only at Stein's own risk, on commission, to which Stein, who drafted her answers on the back of Woolf's letters, would not agree.

The next letter from Woolf, of September 3, speaks of the novel cut to 70,000 words as still too long. Presumably encouraged by his interest in a shorter text, Stein offered him *G.M.P.,* at 40,000 words, suggesting that the names of Matisse and Picasso might be selling points. On November 3, Woolf refused this book also unless Stein agreed to a commission basis.

On June 11, 1926, four days after the Oxford address, he offered to publish it. He asked for a title, which Stein drafted on the back of his letter, first as "Composition," then "Composition As Explanation." On June 30, Woolf suggested including the "poems" she had read, which Stein forwarded. The lecture was published in November 1926. By February 1927, Woolf wrote that it had sold well, 473 copies out of the 1,000 printed. In April 1927, Stein asked him to reconsider *G.M.P.,* but Woolf refused it as too long.

In England, she made new friends. Two became particularly important for publication, always a problem. Apparently through Harold Acton, at Oxford, she met Joseph Brewer, who in 1928 would publish her *Useful Knowledge.*[39] It is not clear whether Stein met Ralph Withington Church, an American philosophy student, before the trip to England, in Paris, through Sherwood Anderson, who had recommended him to her in a letter of May 23, 1926, or whether she met him at Oxford, as a student at Oriel College, while he was preparing a dissertation on Malebranche. Church, who became a friend with whom she shared ideas, delivered a talk about Stein on June 17, 1928, to the Johnson Society of Pembroke College and wrote, at Stein's request, an outstanding essay on her for the fall 1928 issue of *transition.*[40]

39. The acquaintance quickly led to a publishing project. By November 1926, Brewer acknowledged receipt of the manuscript for this collection of unpublished work on American topics. The book was published in New York by Payson and Clarke, Ltd., the firm with which Brewer was associated. Brewer, with whom Stein corresponded for years, later became president of Olivet College in Michigan. During the American tour, on December 13 and 14, 1934, Stein visited the college but did not lecture there, though she talked informally with students (*EA* 225).

40. Church received his doctorate in 1928 and in 1931 published his study, *A Study in the Philosophy of Malebranche* (London: Allen and Unwin). His talk to the Johnson Society is recorded for the 864th meeting in the Society's Minute Books (vol. 7, pp. 136–38) at the college. His "A Note on the Writing of Gertrude Stein" appeared in *transition* no. 14 (fall 1928): 164–68.

Church returned to the United States and became a professor of philosophy at Cornell University and later at the University of California at Berkeley. He came to know many of Stein's friends, including the younger painters such as Bérard, the Berman

Stein also, in June 1926, after her return to France, wrote to Robert McAlmon, with whom she had quarreled over the publication of *The Making Of Americans.* Her success left her in a mellow mood, ready to support others. She wrote to McAlmon that his work was known and appreciated at Oxford and Cambridge:

I am telling you about it because I know one likes to hear it.

A Digression on the Picture of a Page

Most of us pay attention not to what a page of writing looks like but to what it says and perhaps to how it sounds. Yet many Stein texts have a distinctive look, quite different from that of standard written English. Some passages print themselves into the mind as pictures long before the mind even begins to make sense of the words. Their look is not the result of typography, for Stein composes words by a discipline of phrasing, not by offsetting, underlining, spacing, block letters. She punctuates only with periods and commas and uses no quotation marks and few capitals. Without reading the words, look at the design of this passage from "An Elucidation":

> You do see that halve rivers and harbors, halve rivers and harbors, you do see that halve rivers and harbors makes halve rivers and harbors and you do see, you do see that you that you do not have rivers and harbors when you halve rivers and harbors, you do see that you can halve rivers and harbors.
>
> I refuse have rivers and harbors I have refused. I do refuse have rivers and harbors. I receive halve rivers and harbors, I accept halve rivers and harbors. (*R* 430)

The passage arrests the eye because it is made up of only three small blocks of phrases, repeated over and over with slight variations until they become an abstract design. They are joined in varying, irregular ways that keep the design flexible and loose even with its narrow vocabulary. Made of so few phrases so often repeated, the passage makes an insistent visual design before it makes sentences and sense. Whether the lines are handwritten or printed, whether the page is held right side up or upside down, the design is a presence.

Anyone looking at such writing perceives abstract forms moving into pat-

---

brothers, Tchelitchew, and Tonny, whose work she bought in the early 1930s as he did some years later. An unpublished memoir is at the Bancroft Library, Berkeley, California.

terns in a space but also tries to read the words for meaning. From the repetitions and permutations the eye gains a sense of design while the mind reading a phrase over and over loses the sense of meaning. Constructions rearrange themselves constantly. Looking collides with reading, eye with mind, to create the textual instability that is also the magnificence of Stein pages. The eye ends up asking what it is seeing, how it is seeing, what reading is, what knowing is.[41]

To Stein, words can change at any time. She uses them as wholes but also as parts that make new wholes and so new elements of composition. In the portrait "Edith Sitwell And Her Brothers The Sitwells And Also To Osbert Sitwell And To S. Sitwell" of the summer of 1926 appears this passage:

> Tableland.
>
> Tableland and land and knees, tableland and knees and tableland and land and knees.
>
> Tableland and land.
>
> Tableland and knees.
>
> Tableland and land and knees. (*PL* 295)

The compound "tableland" breaks not only into "table" and "land" but also into "able" and "and." Stein may be writing on a table or a tray or *plateau* on her knees, in or of the country (land) or the pleasant land of counterpane. In the portrait "Sitwell Edith Sitwell" of 1925 appears her old friend Mabel Weeks ("Weeks and weeks able and weeks."), whom Stein invited to "sit around her" at tea (a tea table?) on an afternoon with Sitwell. From the earlier portrait to the later, the boundaries of words shift as in mirrors and echoes, "table," "Mabel," "able"; "be," "me," "see," "knees":

> Table table to be table to see table to be to see to me, table to me table to be table to table to table to it. (*P&P* 93)

We read these sequences by look and sound before we read them by reference and grammar.[42]

41. Similarly, the films of Stan Brakhage, which rest in part on his long reading of Stein, are not dynamic representations of things seen but abstract explorations of the process of seeing. He speaks of "the mechanics of cells receiving pages of writ, or anything, in the act of seeing[.] The only reason I laboriously paint these 24 frames a second is that I have NO way to photograph hypnagogic seeing directly, or to photograph the feedback of the brain (always instantaneously reciprocal with light input) as well as constantly re-membering previous visual input, *as well as* reflecting brain cells directly 'expressing' themselves. . . ." (Stan Brakhage to author, 5 May 1990).
42. See also in "Early And Late" (1925), "the story of a table a small table a little table. . . ."

Such letters, words, and lines appear less as text for reading than as graphic design, tight or loose, fast or slow, jagged or smooth, but always rhythmic. I do not move down the page left to right line by line to the bottom of sense. Rather I receive words as openwork tracery, interlacing design in the white margined frame of a rectangle or square.

Stein passages or pieces often create strong visual images.[43] I speak of them here because many blocked paragraphs of *An Acquaintance With Description,* the center of this chapter, not only study description but themselves become descriptive visual images. The abstract, decorative designs of words patterned by look, sound, and sense recall through-composed music, cross-hatching patterns, the designs of William Morris.

Often the visual appearance of a Stein page describes its verbal design. Sometimes no sentence configurations can be recognized, and the page seems printed in a foreign language whose grammar I do not know. Periods mark the ends of sentences but not their shapes, and sentences have no syntactical centers. The eye looks at the white that lights the black, the black on white, penscape, printscape, arrangement upon visual arrangement. The reviewer of *An Acquaintance With Description* in the *Times Literary Supplement* of July 18, 1929, spoke of Stein's "vain repetitions" that plunged readers into a "trance-like condition. Words become dissociated from meaning" (578). Precisely. She wants us to see words for more than their meaning. At times I wish such passages were printed in Chinese or Arabic, whose beauty of design I can enjoy without deciphering meaning.

The white page is evenly printed over in short, sharp lines of jagged inked letters, unshaded, unambiguous, and abstract. It begins with tiny neutral dotted verticals, "If it is," whose sharp *I* I see and hear, and continues unbroken, without even a black dot on the horizontal for a comma or a pause. White fills the spaces between the words, equal enough in length and weight,

---

(*BTV* 246). It is worth remembering that the French word *table* (table) easily yields to *tableau* (picture).

43. Abstract textual designs such as the ones I look at here may in part have led Edith Sitwell to write, in *Poetry and Criticism* (London: Hogarth Press, 1925), just before she discussed Stein, about abstract patterns of composition in poetry, painting, and music. Her words may echo exchanges with Stein as well as her experience of modern art, especially Modigliani, for example, at the show sponsored in London in 1919 by her brothers.

> Modern poets . . . stylize their words in the same manner as the douanier Rousseau, Picasso, Matisse, Derain, Modigliani, Stravinsky, Debussy. . . . We have long been accustomed to abstract patterns in the pictorial art, and to the idea that music is an abstract art, but nobody to my knowledge has ever gone so far in making abstract patterns in words as the modernist poet has. (22)

repeated again and again until they make a design that does not ask for meaning. The words, colorless and neutral, display no reference—"there," "come," "around," "opposite," "having," "shall," "coming," "which," "when," "place." These are not things that speak out but scribbles in patterns. No words stand out bright until far down there appear people and things in nouns,

> no difference between a circus a mason and a mechanic between a horse and cooking a blacksmith and his brother and his places altogether and an electrician. In every other way I am disappointed. (*R* 520)[44]

A momentary local scene, a tableau on a page of scribble-scrabble.

A different visual image is in a paragraph a little beyond. The eye receives it if the mind does not in incomprehension refuse it.

> Again Albert again write to Albert again basket again changed to have it again have it basket again again as again as a change again basket again basket again it is again as a change again as a basket again larger again is it again it is it again a basket again as larger again a basket again get it again is it again a basket again it is.
>
> It is is it. A Basket. (*R* 520)

Except for "it," "is," and "to," the passage is made of simple *A* and *B* words, including the name Albert on the capital legs of *A*. All the words contain one *A* or more. "Basket" adds *B* and half-rhymes with "it,"

> It is is it. A basket.
> Basket it is is it. (*R* 520)[45]

Most are two-syllable words, almost equal in length, repeated again and again, "Albert" and "basket," a stressed and an unstressed syllable in a rhythm that pushes for rhyme, "Albert," "basket."

The power of the patterns comes from Stein's language, whose repetitions and permutations decontextuate the words. The eye explores the verbal topography of pages that become maps of new landscapes of words. Here, in a section of the portrait of the three Sitwells, rivers are read topographi-

44. To avoid the clutter of page references to two editions, citations for *AWD* are given to *A Stein Reader*. The original edition of the work is out of print and hard to find. I completed this study before *AWD* was reprinted in the first Stein volume in the Library of America.

45. This is long before the dog Basket, acquired in 1929. Stein was interested in baskets with their many domestic uses and their intricate designs. Texts are not unlike basketry, woven, coiled, or sewn of different pliable natural materials in many elaborate forms.

cally as roads, following a sequence of alliterating r-words in a typographical image that describes her meaning visually:

> For very as along as long as rivers rivers seen as water rivers road seen as every road, read seen as seen seen as roads roofs read seen, rivers seen as water water seen as roads seen and read seen as roads seen. ("Sitwell . . . Brothers," *PL* 294)

The scene seen and the text read become one in the composition of sight, sound, and sense that Stein explored throughout the years. Visual design, abstract and self-contained, is a context for the text and a part of reading. At the same time, the texts rise from the way she lived and the way she wrote, which also sometimes appear as contexts in the texts. I shall turn to the context of daily life and writing in the summer of 1926 and in the final section of this chapter return to the abstract arrangements in which image, daily life, and writing merge.

Context

Biographical

Seeing England upon the occasion of the lecture in 1926 must have returned Stein to her earlier visits there. Before she began to write, in 1902, she and her brother Leo had spent some late summer weeks in Greenhill-Fernhurst, Surrey, near the house of Mary Berenson's mother. Stein used the name of the village for the Fernhurst episode, incorporated into *The Making Of Americans,* which included material about President M. Carey Thomas of Bryn Mawr, Mary Berenson's cousin.

The following winter she had read her way through English narrative from the sixteenth century on and wandered in misery through London. In January 1913, as an aspiring author, she had with Toklas returned to England in the hope of placing her work with publishers. In July 1914, she had gone to London to sign a contract with John Lane. In the confusion following the outbreak of World War I, the women had been unable to return to Paris and had ended up staying with Alfred North Whitehead and his wife Evelyn at Lockeridge for almost three months, until it was safe to return home.[46]

46. The 1914 period in England is thoroughly studied and documented by Rosalind Moad in "1914–1916: Years of Innovation in Gertrude Stein's Writing" (Ph.D. diss., University of York, England, 1993). There are odd, unclear hints of another trip to England, not documented biographically and perhaps considered but not undertaken, early in 1921. See Emily Dawson to Stein, 17 February 1921, and correspondence with Harry Phelan Gibb.

In 1926, she went to England with a difference, by invitation, as the speaker on the modernism she had helped create. She commented later in humorous play in *A Novel Of Thank You* on travel writing. Indirect echoes of her trip spread through everything she wrote that summer, *An Acquaintance With Description,* the portrait of the three Sitwells, the conclusion of *A Novel Of Thank You* and even the portraits of Allen Tanner and Pavel Tchelitchew. The pieces are not to be read autobiographically, but recognizing the sources adds depth to reading.

Another passage seems barely referential until the piece where it appears is taken into account:

> Describing to return and never to return and never not to return. Return describing. Return to describing. I return to describing and I turn to describing.

These lines, followed by a concluding thank-you, are the envoi of Stein's portrait of Edith Sitwell and her brothers (*PL* 301). They speak of returning—where? To the Sitwells? To England? To France? To writing? To all these, of course. They speak of describing—what? Stein's return home? The Sitwells? England? Anything. Had she talked about description with Sitwell, who was working on her study of Alexander Pope? Quite likely. And so, pivoting without objects on the words "return" and "describe," she speaks of returning to description and describing her return. The portrait composes her acquaintance with the three Sitwells.[47]

Apart from the lecture delivered at Cambridge and Oxford, little is known about what Stein did in England. She and Toklas stayed at the Belgravia Hotel in London but may have spent the night after the evening lecture in Cambridge, though we do not know where. At Stein's request, the Oxford lecture on June 7 was scheduled for the afternoon, which allowed her to return to London that evening, perhaps to expedite the trip home. She saw her friend Harry Phelan Gibb, the painter, on June 1.

For Sunday, June 6, in London, Alec Waugh, editor for Chapman and Hall, invited her to meet with him, and in October 1926 they published her "A Description Of The Fifteenth Of November. A Portrait Of T. S. Eliot." in their *Georgian Stories* of 1926. She probably saw other publishers—John Lane, perhaps Thomas Balston for Duckworth, Sitwell's publisher, and others. On May 1 she had written to Gibb,

47. The trip may also have rekindled her interest in description in English literature. She returns to it in "What Is English Literature":

> The thing that has made the glory of English literature is description simple concentrated description. . . . (*LIA* 5)

of course the thing naturally that I am keen on is finding a permanent publisher in London who will bring out my things unpublished past and present and that is my great hope.

She may have seen Ford Madox Ford before he went to Provence. He wrote her from there later in the summer.

One would like to know full details of her meetings with the Sitwells. She knew Edith well already, but her Sitwell family portrait suggests closer acquaintance with the brothers than a formal reception or lecture makes possible.[48]

Stein and Toklas kept the stay in England short. Its publicity and anxiety intruded upon the essential privacy of writing and living that made the rhythm of their daily life. They wanted to return home quickly and to look in the French countryside for a house. They were back in Paris before June 11 and by early July left for Touraine.

Sight-seeing and house hunting were not confined to the Bugey, the region of Belley, where Stein and Toklas had spent two summers and were eventually to settle. Following suggestions of friends, the women in July explored other regions, especially the Loire Valley. Stein and Toklas had in the course of the years stayed with their friends Grace Lounsbery and her English companion, Esther Swainson, who lived with their many dogs and cats in the Loire Inférieure; now they offered them a house next to theirs. In July 1926, they visited Jo and Yvonne Davidson, who had recently acquired a summer house, Manoire de Bécheron, in Saché, I. et L.:

Our friends have such an enchanting place—we hope to too—and that would enchant us and you too—but we haven't yet. In the meantime we chase all day—I am allowed to see nothing—neither chateaux churches or curiosity shops—only long interviews with agents and notaries—the patter very Balzacian indeed.[49]

48. Apart from Sitwell's party for Stein, it is not clear where and when Stein saw the Sitwells in London and whether she saw them in the country, at Renishaw, Weston Hall, or Scarborough; all three are at a fair distance from London, and it was early in the season for country houses to be opened for the summer.

Stein's relationship with Edith, her liking for Osbert, whose inclusion in one of George Platt Lynes' planned *As Stable* pamphlets she supported, her portrayal of the Sitwells as a family group, and her work on description give these questions some urgency. However, neither Sitwell family members nor biographers whom I contacted have been able to document a visit of Stein.

49. Toklas to Tanner and Tchelitchew, 8 July 1926, postcard showing "Le chateau de Saché—La Cascade près de la Grotte de Balzac." Toklas is careful to place their activities in the context of Balzac's financial dealings. He visited the Comte de Margonné in Saché nu-

The possibility of buying half a château in Saché momentarily charmed the women but was abandoned.[50] On July 30, Stein sent a postcard to Gibb, who painted landscapes and enjoyed fishing. It showed "Un coin pittoresque du village de Montrésor" and she wrote,

> Here is just the kind of landscape you like it can make even [me] almost want to fish. . . .

On August 7, William Cook advised Stein in response to her postcard from Issoudun, Indre, against buying property there.

By August, however, they were again at the Hotel Pernollet in Belley, and Tchelitchew and Tanner visited. At this time, Stein was deeply interested in Tchelitchew's art and his well-being. Tanner, a pianist whose stage fright interfered with his performing, had understood and eased her anxiety before the English lecture. Now he benefited from her success, decided to " 'take some self-training' (and reflection) in arrivisme" and to schedule concerts for the following season.[51] Stein composed the portrait "Allen Tanner" during their visit and wrote "Pavlik Tchelitchew Or Adrian Arthur" sometime after they left on August 26.[52]

It was a summer for making the region deeply and personally her own. She absorbed the natural features of the landscape and meditated on writing them. As all her experience centered on writing, she described what she saw and what it is to describe. Here, like a painting, is a pattern of strawberry plants in mounds that are hills:

> Do not do not what climb the hills hills which are hills and hills which are hills which are strawberry plants and strawberry plants and in and in that when there is none noon there is should shall and might might be an eraser. Very nearly what they did to-day. Should shall be in case of and never be by this this that leave not with this look again. (*R* 527)

This passage shows the gradual patterning of perception. It is not a record of the things she saw, which were pleasant for living but useful for writing only as elements of a composition. Stein was not interested in writing a travel-

---

merous times to escape from the pressure of debts and work in Paris. For a response to another letter sent from Saché, see Kahnweiler to Stein, 15 July 1926. See also Toklas, *What Is Remembered,* 172, on Azay-le-Rideau.

50. Perhaps "half a house" (*R* 530) describes what one actually sees when one looks at a house from outside, just as "half of a hill" (*NOTY* 28) may describe the visible half of a hill.

51. Tanner to Stein, 20 July 1926.

52. Stein to George Platt Lynes, n.d. [autumn 1926].

ogue with local color and sights to visit. We never say, reading and picturing her, look here, look there, remember this or that, or let us go there.

> Not an acquaintance with not only with and only with description and only with with it. Is it an and an account of it. (*R* 516)[53]

The question is not what it is but how it is written.

The few named details, however, fill in context that informs, though it does not explain, her text. Naming the rivers Saône and Rhône places the writing, which is never about memory or locality, in the region of Belley. A river is no sooner named, however, than she begins a new section with a new paragraph or returns to the problem of description. Some small details may refer to the house in Bilignin that she later rented, for example, the lieutenant in the last paragraph of the piece may be the one who at the time occupied the house.[54]

Description had been in Stein's mind before 1926. The covers of the school notebooks she used for writing, with their pictures and texts about places, history, colonies, agriculture, were constant reminders of description. In the summer of 1925, she had proofread *The Making Of Americans* with its immense system of descriptive classification. In "A Third" she had often asked about description,

> Can examples be described and be described and be description. (*AFAM* 352)

A Novel Of Thank You raises questions of description. In late sections of "Natural Phenomena," completed before the trip to London, the word "description" appears often.

Painting and drawing are descriptive:

53. Unlike Stein, Toklas wrote in detail about the localities to friends. One can rely on her descriptions as one relies on a map or guidebook. Even much later, her exceptional memory allowed her to describe that summer in the *Alice B. Toklas Cookbook* (94ff.).

Normally Stein herself transcribed drafts from *carnets* to *cahiers,* but sometimes Toklas assisted. It is interesting to see, starting in midparagraph, a passage on memory copied by Toklas into the *cahier* of *AWD,*

> No one should remember anything and it should not make any difference. Who makes this carefully. . . . (*R* 506)

One wonders whether the transcription by Toklas implies not only that she was helping to copy but that Stein selected this passage for Toklas to copy.

54. There is also a terrace (*R* 530), two roofs (*R* 528) and a chimney (*NOTY* 236), which may or may not refer to this house. Echoes reappear of "The Brazilian Admiral's Son" (*P&P* 216), a portrait of 1924, perhaps because the admiral was again summering at the hotel (*R* 509, 511).

Natural phenomena means a chance to draw and to describe to describe and to save and to idolise to idolise and to withdraw. . . . (*PL* 232)

These lines are no doubt provoked by her irritation with Picasso for his failure to do the promised illustrations for "A Birthday Book." But landscapes, still lifes, portraits were in her mind throughout the struggle to compose the natural world. In the late winter of 1926, when George Platt Lynes wanted a Stein piece to publish as one of his *As Stable* pamphlets, she chose "Descriptions Of Literature" (1924), a list, ironically descriptive in function, of characterizations of books such as might be in reviews or on book jackets (*R* 471).

By the summer of 1926, immersion in landscape in the hope of settling in it made everything she saw in the natural world take shape in her meditations on writing. *An Acquaintance With Description* was not planned as a book. However, the piece was appropriate in length for a small press. Its connection with the trip to England made it an especially good choice for publication in England by the Seizin Press of Laura Riding and Robert Graves.

Textual

The most important information about how Stein worked that summer is in a black oilcloth *carnet.* It contains the address of Chapman and Hall; biographical details, probably for a publisher; sections of the portrait of the three Sitwells; sections of "Studies In Description," the beginning of *An Acquaintance With Description;* a few late passages of *A Novel Of Thank You,* completed late in the summer; some sketchy maps, directions, house plans, addresses of civil engineers and property agents. A second *carnet* contains text but few personal details.

Stein must have filled a number of further *carnets* while also composing directly in the *cahiers.* The sections of text in the two preserved *carnets* are radically rearranged in the *cahiers.* This is true also of drafts for "An Elucidation," but not elsewhere, for normally Stein copied into the *cahiers* what she had drafted in *carnets* in her original order. In these 1926 notebooks, the sections first become parts of several different pieces, *An Acquaintance With Description,* the portrait of the three Sitwells, and *A Novel Of Thank You.* No marks indicate where the sections were to go, but Stein appears to have been clear about it.

Second, while the order of sections in the *carnets* follows the chronology of living and writing, the order in the manuscript *cahiers* is quite different. Passages drafted early in a *carnet* appear late in one *cahier,* and adjacent sections may be early in another *cahier.* The order of sections of text in the three pieces bears no consistent relation to the chronology of daily life or writing.

Stein may have rearranged her work to decontextuate it radically in the service of compositional design. She may have wanted to prevent any reading of who or what it was "about." The details I have in the preceding pages tentatively identified from knowledge of her movements are not personal references. There remains in *An Acquaintance With Description* consistent evidence only of seasonal progression from early to late summer fruits and flowers—berries, peaches, melons, pears, apples, grapes, and pansies, pinks, roses, hollyhocks. No one reads these, the stock of descriptive writing, to trace references. They become color compositions and still lifes.

Exact dates are available only for the gradual composition of the family portrait of Edith Sitwell and her brothers. But as the portrait and *An Acquaintance With Description* were written concurrently, the dates, in letters from Sitwell to Stein, apply approximately to both. On July 2, Sitwell responded "with great impatience" from London to what must have been Stein's announcement of a portrait of Osbert Sitwell, begun under the title "To Osbert Sitwell." On August 6, from Renishaw Hall in Derbyshire, she again wrote,

> We are all three longing to see your portrait of us. When, I wonder, will it be finished.

The manuscript shows the change from Osbert to the three Sitwells in several steps. To the original title Stein added "Edith Sitwell and her brother" (echoes of "Two: Gertrude Stein And Her Brother"?). Finally, she added the last member, "And also S[acheverell]. Sitwell." When she made the title, "Edith Sitwell And Her Brothers The Sitwells," she did not cross out the earlier phrases, either because she was careless or because she wished to retain the evolution of the title.

Both the portrait and *An Acquaintance With Description* were written and considerably revised over a period of two to four months, the portrait probably finished before the study. In an undated letter from Renishaw Hall, probably of late August or early September, Sitwell thanked her:

> We are all three more delighted than we can say with the portrait, and feel very proud,—exceedingly proud. . . . You can't imagine what a delight the portrait is to me. It has such great beauty and strangeness, and the rhythm is beautiful in a new way, and it is altogether a delight.

Near the end of *An Acquaintance With Description* it is possible to hear the sound of preparations for leaving Belley and returning to Paris between September 30 and October 2, 1926.

Now be by the way. Ellis now be now be by now be by the way . . .

An acquaintance with then with description and leaving which it matters matters very much to them. (*R* 531)

Text

"Edith Sitwell And Her Brothers The Sitwells And Also To Osbert Sitwell And S. Sitwell" (*PL* 293–301)

An uncle of a king in an uncle of a king. (293)

The short opening phrase with the words "uncle" and "king" is the most heavily referential in the portrait, showing Osbert reassuringly as an uncle of a king. With its stiff, firm beats on short nouns, its "n" sounds, and its diminutive play with the echoing syllables "in," "an," "un," "in," "in," "an," "un," "in," the phrase identifies the subject of the portrait.[55] The uncle of the king is presumably John of Gaunt, the uncle of Richard II, an ancestor of the Sitwells, who saw themselves as Plantagenets. The phrase may also come from the alleged resemblance in profile of Osbert to George III and the possibility of illicit descent from George IV. Osbert almost sounds like the patriarchal uncle of a king larger than royalty. A little beyond appears a "black umbrella . . . more suitable than a grey umbrella," a part of proper dress and good form essential for families related to kings and attached to the Grenadier Guards, as were both Osbert and Sacheverell.

Beyond uncle and umbrella, the portrait opens with three groups of phrases. One concerns description. Associated with place and with portraiture, it rises from England and the Sitwells.

Description how do you do description.

It makes a place where they do sit do sit do sit two.

The figures Stein portrays are in a landscape or garden with topographical features, vegetable and animal life—evergreens, berries, a swan, a gull—and weather, which also composes color.[56] Both portraiture and landscape re-

55. Similar work with syllables is in the portrait of Allen Tanner, whose name lends itself to syllabic permutations. This portrait was done that August, probably soon after the portrait of Osbert Sitwell or while Stein developed his portrait into that of the three Sitwells.

56. Gardens were important to the Sitwells and especially to their father, Sir George Sitwell. Stein may have seen or heard of his small book, *On the Making of Gardens* (London: John Murray, 1909), and his *A Brief History of Weston Hall, Northamptonshire* (London: Curwen Press), published in 1927 but probably completed by the time Stein visited.

quire describing and composing to join what remains separate when it is merely named.

> Description connecting reinstating. (295)

In the second group are phrases which present this radically innovative portrait grounded in verbs and some adverbs as a singularity or a plurality, one or three:

> Is and were it is and they were it is and they were is an were is and are it is and they are and it is and they are is and are is and were is and are it is and they are it is and they are is and are, are makes made and in describe which is to have and in describe they have and have and made and are . . . , always to be and to to were where and is once once separately is and were and separating is and are. . . . (296)

Singular and plural, past and present mingle. Are the Sitwells one subject or three separate ones, now or then?

> Separately always makes are and is. Separately always makes is and are. Separately always makes were and is and are and is and separately always makes is and are.

Is their identity individual and present, or is it familial, patriarchal, and out of the past?

> When there are the ones there that are after themselves naming them naming them after themselves. . . . (297)

Stein is writing a family portrait, perhaps against the background of the John Singer Sargent portrait of the Sitwells. The three Sitwells are named after themselves, insistent upon their name and preoccupied with it.

The third group offsets the second. Stein sets herself against her subjects. She is preoccupied not with a historical family name but with making herself—making a name for herself—by writing.

> Make me make it be make it be me. (296)

By writing the portrait of the Sitwells, she makes herself as an artist. She has no king for an uncle, no coat of arms, no crest with three lions. "Influenced by herself" (294), however, she has the ability to compose Sitwells in portraiture.

The portrait also becomes a study of identity for titled families and self-made Americans. To Stein, the contact with the three Sitwells, who supported one another and collaborated, recalled her own family situation, her wish for family support and solidarity.

> Back to their name.
>
> I wish there were five of them. Two following one another. One following the other, one following one and another one following one another one following one one following the other I wish there were five of them two following one another. (298)

If only the five Steins were like the three Sitwells.[57]

She ends with thanks for effort, hospitality, applause. A gift of appreciation, the portrait returns her to her craft and to description.

An Acquaintance With Description (*R* 504–34)

Three years after Stein wrote *An Acquaintance With Description,* she characterized it in a letter to Ralph Church as

> the first of the [e]xpl[anatory] series which began originally with the Elucidation.[58]

In 1926 she returned to theory and practice, which "An Elucidation" had already shown to be inseparable. Always she insisted on what was before her, not on theory about it.

> Example and precept, sitting if in sitting they are there they must as if in crossing two at a time and not bound not bound to be used to as in lead lead to it from their having this in use. . . . (514)

As a thinking person, she was passionately committed to ideas. As a writer, she meditated *in* words, not *about* words.

> And so studying in description not only but also is not finishing but understood as describing. (505)

She refused to reduce composition to explanation, which removes objects from direct acquaintance, from the intimate, total knowledge that sensation gives us. It is the opposite of incremental "knowledge-about," which does not require the immediate sensation of an object.

> Making acquaintance with description does not begin now begin now. In acquaintance with description. Simply describe that they are married as they were married. They married.

57. Years later, after Stein in 1934 met Thornton Wilder, the magic of numbers in families returned when she heard of the five Wilder siblings.
58. Stein to Ralph Church, 21 June 1929, Bancroft Library, Berkeley.

And she goes right on to describe,

> She the one and she the one and they and none and they and one and she and one and they. . . . (506)

Stein experienced the relation called acquaintance[59] between herself and the landscape surrounding her as sensation. She also experienced acquaintance between herself and writing as sensation. We follow her making acquaintance in description with nature and acquaintance with the nature of description. "Description" here is not offset, say, against "narration" or "dialogue" as a method of writing, but it is writing itself. A succession of words can be called a story not in the sense of a narrative but in the sense that words follow one another, whether they tell of events, people, or places, or render what people say. Stein's "description" wipes out the distinctions of genre.[60]

"Description," "describe," and "acquaintance with description" recur like incantatory rhythmic beats throughout these studies. It is as if Stein were taking lunge after lunge at making acquaintance with description, struggling for understanding and formulation as she had done even in her early notes and drafts for *The Making Of Americans.* "Acquaintance with description" takes on the overtones of a welcome, an invocation, or a prayer:

> An acquaintance with description above all an acquaintance with description above an acquaintance with description above all an acquaintance with description above an acquaintance with description and above and above an acquaintance with description and an acquaintance with

59. In the second chapter of *Principles of Psychology* (1890), the textbook Stein used at Harvard, William James speaks of two forms of knowledge, "knowledge of acquaintance" and "knowledge-about"; he returns to "acquaintance" and "knowledge-about" in "The Function of Cognition," the first chapter of *The Meaning of Truth* (1909).

   The term "acquaintance" as total, not subject to degrees, is used by James, Bertrand Russell, and Alfred North Whitehead. Russell examines it in *On Our Knowledge of the External World* (1914), differentiating "knowledge by acquaintance" and "knowledge by description," which involves naming and assertions of identity rather than the kind of description Stein seeks here.

   Stein's concrete literalism makes her sound "naïf" and deceives readers into believing that she does not think systematically when in fact she is far clearer than her non-systematic, personal terminology makes her appear. Here she relies only on the word "acquaintance" but not on the awkward contrasting term, "knowledge-about."

60. Written after extensive reading in English narrative, *MOA,* subtitled *A History Of A Family,* makes us expect a narrative. Yet the book breaks with narrative tradition, for it describes kinds of human beings, human behavior, and human relations as matters of personality, not of action and events in time. Her early break with narrative tradition does away with the distinction of narration and description.

> description. Please and an acquaintance with description please an acquaintance with description please an acquaintance with description. (522)

The phrase returns in many voices, a road sign to where she is going, a guard against distraction, a warning to try again, even a question asked and asked again, each time followed by practice at an answer. Here it is in the portrait:

> A description how do you do a description. (295)

These studies are not a tightly unified sequence but loosely assembled exercises in description of a living landscape and living in the landscape. I do not follow them one by one but trace some themes and ideas that animate the writing.

Some details of *An Acquaintance With Description,* however, remain tantalizing. The two opening lines are a reading puzzle:

> Mouths and Wood.
> Queens and from a thousand to a hundred.

The capitals make the first line look like a title, but the meaning remains unclear, whether for title or sentence. In the *carnet,* however, these two lines do not precede the paragraph that follows in the printed text. They must have been transferred from a different source, probably written at a different time and in a different circumstance, which may explain why they do not appear to fit easily.[61]

They are followed by a very accessible paragraph on description:

> Description having succeeded deciding, studying description so that there is describing until it has been adjoined and is in a description. Studies description until in attracting which is a building has been described as an in case of planting. And so studying in description not only but also is not finishing but understood as describing. (505)

The word "building," revised from "chateau" in the draft, makes the passage English, as does the name Bedlington for Bilignin later. In the end, the challenge to master description in the world of the Bugey became a means of entering and settling into its landscape. Her acquaintance with description became her way of welcoming the country into her life and making herself at home in it. *An Acquaintance With Description* ends up as the test for the decision to settle in the Bugey.

Behind the meditation on description lie the formulations of twentieth-

61. See also *SBW* 81–82.

century physics about the nature of the world and the aesthetic of modernism that followed them. The country she describes is far from the tradition of descriptive writing. Here nature is no more taken for granted than our capacity to perceive it or to describe it in words. In "Natural Phenomena," with ironic, flat sentences Stein casts doubt on her own statements,

> A natural phenomena has this authority that to be seen is to be believed. (*PL* 222)

But here, she asks, can we believe what we see?

> Not to believe it because not to believe it because not to believe that it is there. (*R* 516)

What do we see when we say we see?

> When they looked upon and on and at a picture of phenomenon of nature and moved and it moved and away away and to-day to-day prepared for organization organization naturally of natural phenomena to be sure. (*PL* 211)
>
> To be sure is reserved for certainty. (*PL* 215)

What is certainty?

> At last to come to place it where it was not by that time in that way. (*R* 505)

What is knowledge?

> Not it is not it is not it is not it is at all as it is. (506)

How can we describe what we may not even perceive accurately? With ordinary expressions we use unthinking associative language—she constructs descriptive passages in such a way that we are forced to read them literally and to discover that they are meaningless. What is the difference between . . . ? We cannot name or describe a difference. The nonsense question turns into a nonsense riddle:

> What is the difference between a park and a field. (532)

This riddle immediately leads to another, where everything goes wrong:

> When is a meadow under water when it is a marsh and after which is higher there is always something not might not after this very which is that.

Then, finally,

> There is a difference between the middle and both sides. (513)[62]

"Difference between" even twists into "in difference" (531) and "distance between" (*R* 513). Such word games are familiar to every child, but behind the fun is a serious intention. Our definitions and comparisons are useless. Associative language makes nonsense of description. She asks for

> Letting it be not what it is like. (508)
>
> Not asked what is it because it is it, it is it, what is it it is it, oh yes. (*NOTY* 236)

Always the literalist, Stein describes ridges, which come with differences —troughs—but which also, being in the class of ridges, are all the same. Look at how she puts the difference between the ridges:

> There is a difference between ridges and between ridges and between there is a difference between there there and ridges between there there there and ridges there is a difference between there there there there and ridges there is a difference between no difference between pansies and there between pansies. . . . (526)

One way to descriptive language is by examples of what fails. Another way is to change point of view. The descriptive piece is full of birds—a gull, a guinea hen, turkeys. She tries for a bird's-eye view,

> A sea gull looking at the grain as seen. (505)

Or read it as

> A see gull looking at the grain as scene.

A few lines later,

> First a sea gull looking into the grain in order to look into the grain it must be flying as if it were looking into the grain. A sea gull looking at the grain. A sea gull looking at the grain. Second a sea gull looking into the grain. Any moment at once. Why is the grain that comes again paler so that it is not so high and after awhile there can be very many of a kind to know that kind. Next to find it coming up and down and not when it

62. In the text printed by the Seizin Press, the sentence is, "There is a great difference between the middle and both sides" (15). The word "great" is not in the draft, the manuscript, or the typescript. Unless Stein added it in the typescript for the Seizin Press, which is unlikely, it is an error, the result perhaps of a printer's associative habit, slipping in an adjective without thought. The *R* rectifies the apparent error by omitting "great" (513).

is directly through around. This comes to be a choice and we are the only choosers. This makes that be what a little in the front and not at all what we see.

The sea gull makes acquaintance with the world of grain. Can we see it looking at the grain? Which grain, all of them being the same? The gull wants to eat grain, not look at it or describe it in words. It knows exactly, though we may not, how to see the grain, fly toward it, and pick it up. The bird's-eye view offers a discipline for observant description.

Stein decontextuates and rearranges in many ways. Without *carnets,* most cannot be traced, which is exactly what she intended. One interesting rearrangement, however, can be followed by reading between the lines of *carnet* and *cahier.* In it merge problems of text and context, writing and biography, which are never separate.

In one of the two preserved *carnets* she drafts a long descriptive sequence that she transfers complete to *A Novel Of Thank You.*[63] It ends by tantalizing us with another unidentified "it":

> Let me make believe that I have seen it and then. I will describe it. (*NOTY* 238)

She will imagine it and then describe it. Description, then, need not be done from nature but can be done from imagination. Questions of truth and representation arise. She proceeds to describe "it," presumably in the passage that follows in the *carnet.* That passage, however, is transferred not into the novel but into the portrait of the three Sitwells. It is about a place, a "there."

> From here to there.
> Which is the most added white blue black blue white black blue and you too.
> Which is left to it. Left brown black burnt brown and bread at best. This is the way they may be what is not even nearly Bedlington and these around. (*PL* 294)

63. From "Leaving it as much as they could . . ." (236) to ". . . describe it. / Chapter [III]" (238). The heading "chapter" at the beginning is not included, and chapters are not numbered in the manuscript, a job Toklas attended to in typing. This text is interspersed with notes and addresses, but not with other drafts of text. The sentence quoted at the end of the description of phraseology, above, is near the start of this passage,

> Not asked what is it because it is it, it is it. . . .

She calls the place Bedlington.[64] It is, of course, Bilignin, anglicized and incorporated into the portrait of the English Sitwells. She writes the place which makes visible what she sees.

But that is not the end. Later in the same draft passage, she appears to speak of the portrait as "sendable" and of the name she has invented.

> Sacrificing sufficing see and sufficing so and sufficing sent and sendable so at length.
> They made it be the same by name.
> Let me be as they might.

It is impossible to tell what "it" refers to, Bedlington, the portrait of the Sitwells, the Sitwells and Stein, the Sitwells' country houses, Stein's wish for a house. And on the following page, she advises herself "never to use the name" but then describes "it" as "hers" and "his," which suggests a couple, Toklas and herself or another couple, as owners. A little later in *A Novel Of Thank You,* in a section for which no draft is preserved in a *carnet,* she writes,

> If it were to be called Bedlington would it have to have the name changed if it had another name or might one not more easily do as it had often been done simply disregard the name that is no longer being used in which case Bedlington will become its name. Moreover there is every rea-

64. I have found no connection with an English village named Bedlington, though the name sounds just right, including its possible echo of Bedlam, or of Bedham, Sussex, where Ford Madox Ford and Stella Bowen had lived in a cottage and their daughter Julia was born in 1920. There is, however, one further name in "Early And Late" of the preceding summer, when she was already thinking about a house and had perhaps seen the Bilignin property. She speaks of "extending what must further their peace" and continues,

> Who hopes it.
> He has heard.
> He has had it.
> Bonnington is a name.
> Beginning. To be beginning.
> . . .
> Changed to when my wife came into my life.
> Changed to Bonnington is a name.
> (*BTV* 243)

And she goes on to "Prices," perhaps for property. Stein would have been unlikely to know of Bonnington House, the location of the Falls of Clyde, southeast of Glasgow. The Sitwells had no connection with it that I know of. She may have had in mind the landscape painter Richard Bonington (1801–28), misspelled. Perhaps she played with "bonny." House, love, marriage, family, friends, landscape, and village—and of course writing—always join as one.

son to be thoroughly content that this name not only was not given but will not be attached to the place which is now not any longer at all desirable should be bought. The reasons why there is every reason to remember that there who made money in sufficiently large quantities either by the sale of their work or other work would in buying choose not only what was desired but what is no longer desirable no longer desirable means no change means indeed only an unnecessarily complete error. After all we have not had it nor do we intend to have it. We are now entirely occupying ourselves with an entirely different matter. A novel returns at once. (*NOTY* 238)

The *B* names Bilignin, Bedlington, and Bonnington describe the act of naming, as does the word "christening" in the preceding passage (237). It is hers as a composition.[65] It may become hers as a place to live. Do we possess a place by naming it, by describing it, or by acquiring it?

Of course, there are other ways to read these passages. The decision to write from imagination may also recall the change of her portrait from Osbert to the three Sitwells. Whether she composes a portrait or a house, it is the way of meditation. A lyrical passage just before the plan to describe opens upon a house in three dimensions, including height or altitude, first spoken of in St.-Rémy when she contemplated the Rhône and the mountains from which it came. Its open gate and open door become the image of the open house and the receptive mind.

It makes a difference if they say it say it that it is above and below and above and below. Thanks for thanking and pleasure for pleasure and white by white and most and best. Having entirely satisfied entirely. Does it look like it. When the door is open and in and the gate is open and in and always open and the gate is always open and the gate is always open and in. (*NOTY* 237)

65. In earlier letters, Gibb and Stein speak of painting landscapes from nature or in the studio, a question discussed far more in painting than in writing. However, it is behind the work surrounding *AWD*. One feels it also, in a different form, in the unlikely prospect of Stein and Toklas sitting in a meadow to proofread *MOA*, which reads like a description of a pastoral painting except that the galleys make it comical.

Similar reactions come up when one sees the posed photograph of Stein at the little three-legged sidetable (*guéridon*) where she says she wrote the *AABT* outdoors in the fall of 1932, apparently with no insects to bother her and never a breeze to blow the pages. I once claimed she could not have written this way; I did not realize that the image was how she visualized herself pictorially in performance, as she wished to appear to readers; whether such images record how she actually worked is not the question.

This reading is far from conclusive, but always it shows daily life in the Bugey giving Stein the words for acquaintance with the place and with description.

The composition of "it" returns us to the description of the real and the imagined, the natural world and the nature of description. Stein calls her descriptions "arrangements," patterns of things perceived, patterns of words. In the Sitwell family portrait,

> Description is relating reinstating. Description is reinstating really really really more reinstating. Reinstating connecting description. Description connecting reinstating. (295)

Or, as Donald Sutherland noted in his copy of the book, the arrangement of berries in a basket opens a Homeric catalog:

> There is an arrangement as berries. There is also an arrangement as loop holes. There is also an arrangement as distance. There is also an arrangement as by the way. There is also an arrangement as at first. There is also an arrangement as to be. There is also an arrangement as disappointed. There is also an arrangement as why and let. There is also an arrangement of poplars that give a great deal of pleasure. There is also an arrangement that it can be twice chosen. There is also an arrangement which is advantageous. (520)

Or take names of flowers; start with a dahlia and go on to roses and pinks and make an old-fashioned arrangement of colors (*R* 508). Or the greens of holly and fir trees (yews?) in gardens and add to them the red berries of the evergreens and a geranium (*R* 505). As she completes a night's work at sunrise, it becomes clear that there is no seeing and no naming without light,

> They might like it as it is in the sun.
>
> Naming everything every day, that is the way. Naming everything every day. Naming everything every day.
>
> It is a great pleasure to watch it coming.
>
> They might like it, as it is in the sun.
>
> It is a pleasure to watch it coming but it might that she could be unaccustomed to lie down without sleeping it might be that she could be unaccustomed to lie down without sleeping. (507)

Or laugh with her at the arrangement of names, people, and talk in the country:

Look up look her up look her up look her up look her look her look her look her up and down. Mr. Pernollet does not supply it yet. Mrs. Press does not express lady fingers which are here she was very likely to be really two at most. Mr. Baird makes it better to do so if he likes it which is what what is it it is what very much makes their start to finish. Mrs. Father has a daughter they do they know they know they do they do they do. Mrs. Middle has a husband really two. . . . Mr. Bourg is now at peace if he goes if he goes if he goes. . . . (532)

The principle of uncertainty itself becomes an arrangement, its object "it" left open—the world, writing, a house, anything:

Not to be sure. Let it be when it is mine to be sure let it be when it is mine when it is mine let it be to be sure when it is mine to be sure let it be let it be let it be to be sure let it be to be sure when it is mine to be sure let it to be sure when it is mine let it be to be sure let it be to be sure . . . when to be sure to let it to be sure to be mine. (525)

One way to make acquaintance with description is to write—or read—about the beauties of the natural scene as the English tradition has done. Yet for Stein the reality of landscape lies not in the objects seen. She does not empty into descriptions pocketfuls of information like stones gathered on a walk. Rather she places things in relation by similarity and difference.

With a minimal, monotonous vocabulary and great economy of means, she arranges the world in words that are not representations but analogues. For she writes not of the order of things but of the order of composition. I call her work on description abstract because out of the objects of the world of nature, she creates arrangements that do not exist in nature and are unlike any we have ever seen.[66]

This chapter began with a digression on the visual design of Stein texts. It was not a digression at all. Vision and reading only begin when the eye receives the picture of the page as it also sees and the ear hears the words. The central word of *An Acquaintance With Description* is also the smallest, most transparent, most abstract word, "it." "It" is what we describe, what we write, what we paint, what we see. The world. Anything. Everything. *An Acquaintance With Description* is about how to write it, not about what *it* is.

66. For a discussion from a different starting point of abstraction in Stein's writing, see Marjorie Perloff, *The Poetics of Indeterminacy: Rimbaud to Cage* (Princeton, N.J.: Princeton University Press, 1981), 69–73.

To describe it as at all through. Once more. To describe it as not as dew because it is in the trees. To describe it as it is new not because it has come to be for them if it lasts. At last to come to place it where it was not by that time in that way. And what is what is the name. (505)

Patriarchal Poetry at peace.
Patriarchal Poetry a piece.
Patriarchal Poetry in peace.
Patriarchal Poetry in pieces.
—"Patriarchal Poetry" 281

I wanting equality of experience because I am wanting freedom for myself always in living.
—Early notebook M–6 for *The Making Of Americans*

3. 1927

"Patriarchal Poetry"

"Patriarchal Poetry" (*BTV* 249–94)

Like a steady beat, the title phrase recurs throughout this forty-page work, at the beginnings or ends of lines and as the subject of parallel clauses in series. That marching beat is one of the devices that give the lines, which often look like prose paragraphs, the incantatory rhythm of regular, though unrhymed, poetry. Although Stein normally avoids capitalization, she capitalizes the phrase in this work almost consistently, making it a proper name—a patriarch, a personification of a principle. Here, with heavy end stops to the lines, it displays orderly habits, counting and adding:

Patriarchal Poetry makes it as usual.
Patriarchal Poetry one two three.
Patriarchal Poetry accountably.
Patriarchal Poetry as much.
Patriarchal Poetry seasonably.
Patriarchal Poetry which is what they did.
One Patriarchal Poetry.
Two Patriarchal Poetry.
Three Patriarchal Poetry.
(274)

"Patriarchal Poetry" at first appears to be one of the few on a set subject, the theory of the origin of society in families under the authority of the eldest male descendant. It is for its title that it is often singled out for discussion of the patriarchy. Yet "Patriarchal" does not refer to its subject but describes a quality, a method of writing that the piece exemplifies. As usual, the piece is not a formal analysis or definition. For instance, no sooner does she begin an apparent definition with "Patriarchal means . . . ," than two words, "suppose" and "close," set in motion a series of rhymes.

> Patriarchal means suppose patriarchal means and close patriarchal means and chose chose Monday patriarchal means in close some day patriarchal means and chose chose Sunday patriarchal means and chose chose one day patriarchal means and close close Tuesday. (258)

The choice of "some day," "Sunday" as the patriarchal day is accidental, and the usual order—Sunday, Monday, Tuesday—is upset. Any day might be Sunday. The sentence, far from a standard definition, makes perfectly good sense if it is read without set expectations of what should complete "Patriarchal means . . .". The irritation caused by the relentless repetition of the opening phrase is precisely Stein's point, moving into satire or parody. Stiff and single-minded, the poetry of the patriarchy endlessly repeats itself.

Context

What impelled her, late in 1926, to start this takeoff on the patriarchy? The context that occasioned it requires reading apart from the text in which it is embedded. Behind the thoughts about patriarchy lies the family history, *The Making Of Americans.* Its publication somewhat over a year before may in her mind have led to the sense of a completed family cycle and a reconsideration of the idea of patriarchy. The reviews of the history of her family may have provided one impulse. In a perceptive discussion of the novel in the autumn of 1925 in *This Quarter,*[1] Ethel Moorhead said that "beings can be classified like the varieties of Patriarchal enclosure." She also spoke of the patriarchal conception of the family in the novel.

Stein's family portrait of Edith Sitwell and her brothers of 1926, discussed in the preceding chapter, suggests that the patriarchal Sitwells with their family name and family estates made a powerful impression on her. Yet in writing the portrait, she sets herself apart from family. She likens the five Steins to the three Sitwells but stresses her own singularity, apart from family. That experience may also have contributed to the new work.

Although "Patriarchal Poetry," unlike "A Diary" and other, shorter pieces of this year—such as "Two Spaniards," about Picasso and Gris, and "Relieve," about Kahnweiler, Picasso, Gris, and their wives—does not refer di-

1. Ethel Moorhead, *This Quarter* 1, no. 1 (1925): 13–23.

rectly to Picasso, Stein knew of the deterioration of his marriage to Olga Koklova and of his new love for Marie-Thérèse Walter. Her sense of Picasso's family crisis may have contributed. A multitude of considerations made Stein aware of family and patriarchy at this time. Not all directly entered "Patriarchal Poetry," nor was she concerned with particular people or purely personal relations.

Stein did not write all of "Patriarchal Poetry" directly into the *cahiers,* but how much was drafted in *carnets* or on scraps of paper and transcribed into *cahiers,* with or without revisions, is not clear. Considerable portions of the text in the *cahiers* look copied. Only one scrap of paper offers evidence of earlier drafts and revisions. A draft version for four lines names the stodgy, patriarchal Woodrow Wilson, in part a model for the effete, cavalier Philip Redfern of the early *Fernhurst* and ridiculed in 1920 in her biting portrait, "Woodrow Wilson" (*UK* 104):

> . . . never never supposing never never in supposing widening.
> Remember all of it too.
> Patriarchal Poetry reasonably.
> Patriarchal Poetry administratedly. (271)

That she eliminated Wilson's name from the draft as she eliminated him from her English lecture is perfectly in keeping with her practice.

She is not writing about particular people but about the patriarchal idea. The principle of decontextuating is tersely stated in "An Advantage," another 1927 piece:

> A name is something to say in politeness not at all as a necessity and so in beginning it is not a necessity to say this is about him. It is about him. (*PL* 304)

Here, "him" is Juan Gris, a fact of interest to the reader who must also, however, recognize that she is not identifying him.[2]

Cumulatively, the many forms of patriarchal experience in her own living and that of others led her to review the nature of order in writing and so became "Patriarchal Poetry." The piece spells out many of Stein's beliefs about her art that are not specific to 1926 and 1927. Yet particular events that forced her to confront family symbols in powerful, personal forms also led her to consider patriarchal order at this time.

Patriarchal rather than literary considerations impelled her to think of a will, a theme that continues into 1928. In a section probably written in the

2. See also Richard Bridgman, *Gertrude Stein in Pieces* (New York: Oxford University Press, 1970), 189.

late winter of 1927, she apparently considered naming Allan Stein, the only son of her eldest brother Michael, as heir.[3] The impending birth of Allan's son may also have served as a reminder that her brother Michael had taken responsibility for his siblings and become her and her brother Leo's guardian after their father's death in 1890. She meditates on fathers, wills, and patriarchal poetry, ending the section affirmatively, "Allan will" presumably become a beneficiary or heir, as indeed he finally did in her last will of 1946. Stein was well aware of patriarchal order.

> Patriarchal Poetry. If he has no farther no farther no farther to no farther to no farther to no to no to farther to not to be right to be known to be even as a chance. Is it best to support Allan Allan will Allan Allan is it best to support Allan Allan patriarchal poetry patriarchal poetry is it best to support Allan Allan will Allan best. . . . Allan will patriarchal poetry Allan will. (290)

Another set of patriarchal symbols has to do with the idea of a country house, which had both aesthetic and economic dimensions. In the fourth summer at the Hotel Pernollet in Belley, Stein and Toklas made active efforts to obtain the house they had spotted from a distance and wanted to live in. Settling in a country house—the words "settle" and "settlement" occur frequently that year—"soothing sitting in a landscape," as Allen Tanner wrote in the summer 1926, and living *en famille,* became an attractive prospect. In addition, as she became known both as writer and as collector, American tourists, including relatives, increasingly invaded her privacy in Paris and her time for work in the summer, making a retreat a necessity.

Many friends of her generation were buying country houses—Jo and Yvonne Davidson, Tristan Tzara, Henri-Pierre Roché, Picasso. The prospect of summers in a country house of her own, unlike rentals or stays in hotels in various regions, increasingly preoccupied her though it also made her anxious. Would a house, with its associations of conventional family life, impose patriarchal constraints upon her life, her relationship with Toklas, and her work?[4]

Gradually Stein developed a strong proprietary interest in land.[5] As early

3. One reason may have been that Allan and his wife, the dancer Yvonne Daunt Stein, at this time expected their first child, the first of a new generation; Daniel Stein was born on August 27, 1927.
4. For the theme of city and country, see also the beginning of "Regular Regularly In Narrative" (*HTW* 215–69), "By The Way" (*PL* 135–36), and "Love A Delight" (*PL* 251–54), all summer 1927.
5. The house in Bilignin, where the women settled in 1929, is now thought of by most readers, as it apparently was by them, as "their" house. They ritualized their association

as the summer of 1926, before Tanner and Tchelitchew visited Stein in Belley, Tanner wrote, no doubt echoing her own words:

> I do hope you get the land away from the peasants—you should have it because you would cherish it and use it and grace it and make it into good land but I suppose it is difficult to make them understand that.

Living on a fixed income from investments, Stein knew financial constraints. In a letter of July 20, Michael Stein advised his sister to consider a location closer than Belley to Paris, which might become her headquarters if the cost of living continued to go up. Stein herself, however, spoke of "making money peaceably" (259), which may refer to earning a living from writing, or at a peaceful distance from Paris. "A Diary" speaks of "being abundantly paid" and "not giving anything away for nothing" (*A&B* 203).[6]

Stein was not alone in contemplating a house. In the spring of 1926, her friend William Cook engaged Le Corbusier and Pierre Jeanneret to build a house for him in Boulogne sur Seine. That May, Michael and Sarah Stein and their friend, Gabrielle de Monzie-Osorio, had seen Cook's house and met with Le Corbusier, preparatory to planning their own house.[7] Houses, acquired, built or inherited, appear frequently in the work of this time.

---

with the locality and the house in writing, in photographs, in the autobiographies, in *The Alice B. Toklas Cookbook*. Yet they did not own the house but rented it.

6. In the spring of 1927, she apparently contacted her cousin Julian Stein, the banker in Baltimore who administered her investments, in view of taking their management into her own hands, presumably to realize more income. On April 13, he acknowledged her wish to "make [her] richer" but spoke of a large cash balance and competent handling of her affairs in Baltimore.

7. Construction of Cook's house began in July 1926 and was completed by March 1927. The contract for Michael Stein's house, Les Terraces, in Garches, was signed on November 10, 1926, construction begun in April 1927, and the main work completed by July 1927. "The house that was built" is in "A Diary" (*A&B* 202). Architects appear in "Patriarchal Poetry" (264–65) and "Hurlbut" (*PL* 308–9), where Stein plays with the names of Charles Edouard Jeanneret or Le Corbusier, his pseudonym (friends called him Corbou), and Pierre Jeanneret, his cousin.

The property on which Les Terraces was built was paid for and the contract signed by the wealthy, beautiful but stiff ex-wife of Anatole de Monzie, the French politician and later premier; after her divorce, from March 1928 on, she used the name Gabrielle Colaço-Osorio. It is not known whether she or the Steins paid for the construction of the house itself, but legal questions must have been in Michael Stein's mind. Mme. de Monzie, who, like Sarah Stein, practiced Christian Science, came with her adopted daughter Jacqueline to live there with the Steins and in 1937 with them returned to America. At the time the villa was built, some people in Paris thought the Steins were taking advantage of her.

Information from Fondation Corbusier, Paris, where further details about the construction are available; the letter about Stein's will can be dated by a reference in it to

Property, passed down within the family, perpetuates the patriarchal system. Already in "Business In Baltimore" of 1925, she had made clear that conventional marriage was less a matter of love than of property and patriarchal continuity. Her art collection, together with the prospect of a house, no doubt impelled her to consider how to safeguard ownership.[8] Property was surely also discussed with Michael Stein in connection with his new house and his collection.

For Stein and Toklas, property raised the question of their legal status. One impulse behind "Patriarchal Poetry" pertained to family. Was Stein's family her wife, Toklas, or was it her lineal descendants? Was Toklas her wife de facto or de jure? In case of the death of a couple in an accident, the legal presumption was that the wife had predeceased the husband. But legally—and patriarchally—Toklas had neither the status nor the name of a wife. Patriarchal thinking did not distinguish gender and sexuality.

---

workmen completing the house in the spring or early summer of 1928. Further information in Hélène Bokanowski to Dydo, 19 February and 26 October 1986; Hélène Bokanowski, "Du Côté de Fleurus À l'Ombre des Bûcherons: Ce que Je sais de Gertrude Stein," *europe: revue littéraire mensuelle,* August–September 1985, 108–15. (Mme. Bokanowski is the niece of the collector Alphonse Kann, whom Stein knew.)

8. Nothing is said about the capital value of Stein's art collection, and no allusions to it are discernible in these comments on value and inheritance. Since Stein continued to buy and sell paintings and was in touch with artists and dealers, she plainly knew how much her collection had appreciated, although she never in writing referred to it as an asset. (An insurance policy of 1938 from Lloyd's of London, for a total of Fr. fr. 1.107.750, lists 3 Braques, 1 Cézanne, Matisse drawings, 33 Picassos, 7 Gris, 2 Massons—not all she owned.)

She certainly realized how large her assets were, even if her income was limited. She must have considered what would happen to her collection should she die. As a businessman, her brother Michael was also aware of the assets represented by his collection, though as a family man, he no doubt followed patriarchal thinking when it came to a will and inheritance. However free Stein's thinking about art, whenever wills and property enter, her ideas take patriarchal forms.

Stein appears as head of household, as becomes clear from bills consistently in her name, even after her death. She had lived in the Paris apartment long before Toklas arrived, and after her brother Leo moved out, she had become the primary resident. Business transactions regarding the country house in Bilignin were also conducted in her name. The name Toklas did not appear on bills and documents and was commonly misspelled by acquaintances and even friends. The fact that no concerted effort was made to correct the spelling suggests the degree to which Toklas assumed the status of the wife. Stein, the writer, "spoke" for both while Toklas appeared silent though by no means without power.

Text

The word "patriarchal" designates a system of relations and values, a way of putting things together. Throughout the piece appear words and phrases such as "arrange," "rearrange," "reorganize," "put it with it." "Patriarchal Poetry" simultaneously describes, denies, exemplifies, questions, and offers alternatives to the patriarchal way of making sense.

Patriarchal thinking regulates what in life is not regular:

> Patriarchal Poetry in regular places placed regularly as if it were placed regularly regularly placed regularly as if it were. (271)

Both the meaning and the placement of the words demonstrate the regularizing process, with the words "regular regularly" ready to become the title of her next piece, "Regular Regularly In Narrative." Patriarchal order is more important than what it contains.

> Patriarchal Poetry to be filled to be filled to be filled to be filled to method method who hears method method who hears who hears who hears and method and method and method. . . . (286–87)

Everything has its assigned function in the patriarchal hierarchy.

> Hire hire let it have to have to hire representative to hire to representative to representative to hire to representative to hire wire to representative to hire representative to hire. (254)

The pun "hire/higher," with its overtones of high-wire tightrope acts, gambling, money, and politics, makes the highest count or number the greatest value, quantity the measure of quality, and hierarchy overpower diversity. Income offers a chance to break up a word,

> Patriarchal Poetry in come I mean I mean. (293)

Like an infallible ruler, in language so polite that it conceals its drive for power, patriarchal poetry

> makes no mistake in estimating the value to be placed upon the best and most arranged of considerations of this in as apt to be not only to be partially and as cautiously considered as in allowance which is one at a time. (272)

The family is the social unit in the patriarchal system. It assigns to its members roles that end up defining them. In their earliest years children ingest the family habit:

> Patriarchal Poetry is used with a spoon. (271)

Human beings are bound together in families, which make them the same even though they are not the same:

> Does she know how to ask her brother is there any difference between turning it again again and again and again or turning it again and again. In resembling two brothers. (265)

In the patriarchal scheme of things, brothers are authorities who supposedly know the answers, but will they know answers to the questions posed here?

The patriarchy begins with the family but is not confined to it. It also produces a class society of masters like Stein or Toklas and servants like Hélène, who had worked for them in early years and returned to help out in 1927.

> Helen greatly relieves Alice patriarchal poetry come too there must be patriarchal poetry come too there must be patriarchal poetry come too.
>
> In a way second first in a way first second in a way in a way first second in a way. (267)

Hélène no doubt relieves Toklas, but is she first or is she second? Who is the boss? Stein questions all rigid forms of order. To her, roles and relations are dynamic and changeable. Those who are independent or in one relationship at one time may become dependent at another. She refuses simple, fixed patriarchal functions.

Nations and empires also are patriarchally constituted. Just as there are paternal masters and servants, so there are imperial powers and colonies. Armies and wars are dominated by patriarchal thinking. Stein suggests that less unyielding logic may result in a reduction in violence,

> What is it.
> Aim less.
> What is it.
> Sword less.
> (284)[9]

That she noticed and read the descriptions of the songs is also clear from her scribbling the refrain "Hurrah" on the back of one *cahier.* The phrase

9. One of the *cahiers* about French colonies may have reminded Stein of patriarchal or paternal imperialism. She also equates the words "patriarchal" and "patriotic." Two *cahiers* show the source of this connection in a series entitled *Chants Patriotiques* (*Patriotic Songs*). Individual *cahiers* are each devoted to one military marching song, illustrating and discussing its origin and its history under the subtitle "Son Origine et Son Histoire," a phrase which Stein incorporates in English translation into her text (115). In "A Diary" (212) appears another echo of the phrase from a different *cahier* in the series *Chants Patriotiques.*

about origin and history again returns to her family history, *The Making Of Americans: Being The History Of A Family's Progress.*

Finally, the patriarchy determines the order of creatures of each kind on the earth.

> Was it a fish was heard was it a bird was it a cow was stirred was it a third was it a cow was stirred was it a third was it a bird was heard was it a third was it a fish was heard was it a third. Fishes a bird cows were stirred a bird fishes were heard a bird cows were stirred a third. A third is all. Come too. (258)

Ranging from cold fish to warm-blooded cow, the passage is also filled with sexual overtones. By the time Stein is done with the species, the bird is no longer a bird, the fish no longer a fish, and the cow no longer a cow, but each is a word in the meditation.

> These words containing as they do neither reproaches nor satisfaction may be finally very nearly rearranged and why, because they mean to be partly left alone. (265)

No longer bound to assigned places, the creatures of Stein's earth are equal and move about freely in a landscape of verbal possibilities.

Attacking all rigid systems, and especially the tyranny of time and chronological sequence, she plays with regular observances until they lose all meaning.

> Patriarchal poetry and not meat on Monday patriarchal poetry and meat on Tuesday. Patriarchal poetry and venison on Wednesday Patriarchal poetry and fish on Friday Patriarchal poetry and birds on Sunday Patriarchal poetry and chickens on Tuesday patriarchal poetry and beef on Thursday. (259)

What difference does it make, what nonsense does it create, whether she follows or reverses the order of meats, meals, and days.

> They made hitherto be by and by. (259)

After relentlessly and repeatedly invoking the rigid, systematic power of the patriarchy and its poetic edicts, Stein finally frees the parts of speech. Much of the poem is composed of tiny auditory and visual verbal elements, often syllables, that are liberated from the strictures of syntax and usage. With their physical properties, Stein makes unexpected arrangements and new meanings. Meats and days are joined by alliteration, which shapes the passage for eye and ear, just as in the early definition passage (258) she relied on rhyme to speak of choosing a day to be Sunday. Or she composes the possibilities of a single grammatical scheme with repeating beats:

> Left to the rest if to be sure that to be sent come to be had in to be known or to be liked and to be to be to be to be to be mine. (266)

Some phrases echo the rhythms of others. Here is a sentence that rings of "Twinkle, twinkle, little star":

> Leave it with it let it go able to be shiny so with it can be is it near let it have it as it may come well be. (261)

By sound she differentiates words that circumstance put in her mind, such as Avery Hopwood's visit in March 1927:

> Every differs from Avery Avery differs from every within. (277)

Or she reverses letters to differentiate:

> Patriarchal Poetry makes a lan*d* a lam*b*. (286; emphases added)

She explores phrasing with the word "day":

> Day which is what is which is what is day which is what is day which is which is what is which is what is day. (263)

What is today? What is a day? What day is today? "Day" and "today" already point to the preoccupation with time and to "A Diary." Again, exploring the simplest elements of talk, she defends a shy person who is trying in spite of her shyness but must not be pressured:

> To be shy.
> Let her be.
> Let her try.
> Let her be let her let her let her be let her be let her
> be let her be shy let her be let her be let her try.
> Let her try.
> Let her be.
> Let her be shy.
> Let her be.
>
> (268)

"Patriarchal Poetry" is a treasure of writing possibilities in a radically anti-patriarchal mode. While its repeated invocations call upon the patriarchy, it refuses to regulate. It resists summary and paraphrase. It makes a constantly changing but never systematic whole. Its life lies in its parts, in the small passages that Stein assembles to try out writing without hierarchical imperatives and fixed regularity. The price for her refusal of patriarchal order and for her interest in the concrete chaos is the sacrifice of a strong design for the whole—the difficult coherence of her text.

Here is another definition of "patriarchal," this time in the form of a dialogue, a tiny play, including stage directions:

> Patriarchal she said what is it I know what it is it is I know I know so that I know what it is I know so I know so I know so I know what it is. Very slowly. (272)

The words reproduce the familiar "I know what it is" which does not say what it is. Yet without words, there is no dialogue, and knowledge remains incommunicable. "Very slowly," then, she continues the paragraph, trying to put into words what she knows about the patriarchal.

This time personal pronouns, not nouns, tell what "it" is; still visible in the manuscript are two crossed-out words here inserted in square brackets:

> Very slowly. I know what it is it is on the one side a to be her to be his to be their to be in an and to be I know what it is it is he who was an [old] [not] known not known was he was at first it was the grandfather then it was not that in that the father not of that grandfather and then she to be to be sure to be sure to be I know to be sure to be I know to be sure to be not as good as that. To be sure not to be sure to be sure correctly saying to be sure to be that. It was that. She was right. It was that.[10]

In the patriarchal order, the woman is defined by identification, confusion, or con-fusion, with the man, within the family. "To be her" is to be an object, not a subject. "To be his," "to be their" is to belong to the male or the family group. In the speaker's words, "she" has reality only in reference to "he," who in turn refers back to father, grandfather, forefathers.[11] Never free of the patriarchal frame of reference, "she" knows that she is not as good as the patriarchs and perhaps simply *is* not.

Under the title "Patriarchal Poetry" there follows a sonnet from husband to wife.[12] The conventions of love poetry involve the patriarchal conventions of gender and sexuality.

10. The phrase about identity, "she to be" or "me to be," recurs throughout Stein's work, as do the phrases "to be sure" and "not to be sure," which must be read literally and speak of the difficult readiness to be only temporarily sure. See, for example, *AWD*, in *R* 525.
11. See also "Regular Regularly In Narrative," *HTW* 223.
12. I reproduce it here with title and subtitle as they are written in the manuscript, where the complete sonnet is also fitted onto the first page of a new *cahier.* The printed text does not make this arrangement visible.

Patriarchal Poetry

A Sonnet

To the wife of my bosom
All happiness from everything
And her husband.
May he be good and considerate
Gay and cheerful and restful.
And make her the best wife
In the world
The happiest and the most content
With reason.
To the wife of my bosom
Whose transcendent virtues
Are those to be most admired
Loved and adored and indeed
Her virtues are all inclusive
Her virtue and her beauty and her beauties
Her charms her qualities her joyous nature
All of it makes of her husband
A proud and happy man.

(272)[13]

This odd "sonnet" can be read in many ways. Is it a patriarchal poem that mouths empty clichés about married bliss and the virtue of a woman who discovers herself through marriage? Is it a homosexual spoof on husbands, wives, and gender roles freed of sexual reference? The lesbian context hilariously exposes the cliché "wife of my bosom." The terms of such love poetry are empty words for social conventions—or material for parody.

Once the patriarchal system is adopted, patriarchal poetry "makes no mistake." Unlike those who think patriarchally, however, Stein tolerates mistakes and does not insist on being sure, though she recognizes the desire. She

13. "A Diary" also demonstrates that functions do not define identities,

> . . . there was a host and hostess and four invited two *as* men and two *as* women. *A father when he is not a father* can be encouraged. *A son when he is not a son* can be encouraged. A woman *when she is neither a mother a sister or a wedding* can be encouraged and so everything is regularly replaced (*A&B* 204, 206; emphases added).

Dinner guests are invited to make up the right number of couples. Encouragement can be given but not to fathers, who are too proud, to sons, who are too insecure, to mothers or sisters, who cannot let on to weakness. Stein phrases very carefully: the men in the last passage exist by their roles only whereas the woman is named as woman, not only as wife.

even acknowledges that sometimes patriarchal poetry might be what they want. Yet in the end, it is a delusion, a dead and meaningless system that should be laid to rest. Doing away with patriarchal poetry does not mean replacing it with matriarchal or women's writing but freeing language—and writers—from hierarchical strictures. "Patriarchal Poetry" is Stein's ironic elegy on the patriarchy.

> Patriarchal Poetry might be withstood.
> Patriarchal Poetry at peace.
> Patriarchal Poetry a piece.
> Patriarchal Poetry in peace.
> Patriarchal Poetry in pieces.
> Patriarchal Poetry as peace to return to Patriarchal Poetry at peace.
> (281)

"Regular Regularly In Narrative" (*HTW* 215–70)

Like "An Elucidation" and *An Acquaintance With Description,* "Regular Regularly" explores ideas about writing by examples met in daily life.[14] A few random summary statements, supported by one or two quotations, are all there is of scholarly commentary on "Regular," which has received no full critical reading. With no explicit structure of logical argument or of referential detail, the piece is frustratingly irregular. Yet its very discontinuity explores the nature of continuity and the relation of words, ideas, and detail in narrative. My commentary will both follow the text in detail and explore her attempts to define narrative.

The word "regular" occurs early and recurs frequently in Stein's work, especially at this period. It marks time in daily life, which moves regularly, though living is surely not regular.

> Regularly. The first day is very warm indeed and it is better to be protected the second day it is equally very warm indeed and it is better to be protected the third day as it [is] equally very warm indeed and it is better to be protected it is very likely and it does not then change and the change is one that has not come with any great suddenness. ("Natural Phenomena," 190)

14. "Regular Regularly In Narrative" is one of eight separate, self-contained studies of language and form in her own writing, completed, along with other pieces, between spring of 1927 and January 1931. Stein eventually assembled these in a collection she entitled *How To Write,* published in November 1931 as the third book in her own Plain Edition. "Regular" was begun in the winter and completed in May 1927.

For Stein, regularity as steadiness in daily life is associated with Tokla[s,] blue queen.

> And not to be seen.
> And a blue queen.
> Blue is the color of regularly.
> ("A Diary" 217)

Toklas also has the gift of memory, another aspect of time. Regularity, then, is necessary in life, although it can also be mechanical and patriarchal.

Regularity is associated not only with time but with all a priori systems. It is a condition of teleological thinking. The "irregular commonplaces" of "An Elucidation" are the innumerable particulars that cannot be subsumed under one heading or incorporated into a regular scheme. They are also the particulars of writing that are destroyed by excess regularity as they are destroyed by "excess return to rambling" (*R* 431). How much irregularity do we need or can we bear? What is the continuity of narrative?

> A novel means regularly regularly told so. (*NOTY* 154)

Stein objects to the false coherence of chronological narrative. Telling regularly, word for word, in the linear sequence that is the condition of language, is not copying chronology. How then can narrative be composed?

Chronological order precludes contact with experience. What we anticipate coming, see happening for less than a moment, and watch escaping into the past as perspective leads to a vanishing point, makes experience distant, its apparent order false. We do not witness the now that is slipping into the past, even before we have touched it. We have no contact with the movement of time, only with actuality now.

Furthermore, chronological history breaks up continuous experience into separate events in time—plots—without immediacy and intensity. Historical continuity turns cause and effect into post hoc ergo propter hoc, but Stein does not believe that people are realized as cause and result. Regular narratives fail to seize identity. Stein aims instead for the simultaneous lateral vision associated with portraiture or poetry, where narration and description become one.

"Regular Regularly In Narrative," like the related "A Diary," which largely overlaps with it, becomes a receptacle for exercises in the narrative possibilities of everyday life. The examples in turn lead to hypotheses about the nature of narrative, making "Regular" both a sampler of narratives and an essay on narrative (263). Of course Stein did not expect anyone to read "Regular" discursively, as a work of theory, or as a work about herself. Inevitably, however, the reader picks up not only essays in narrative but also biographi-

cal information, less dramatic though not less interesting than what appears in Stein biographies. For purposes of my reading, biographical details also make it possible to date details of the study.

Central to Stein narrative, and to all her work, is the question of continuity, which lies not in the "regular" progress of time but in the "regularly" perceiving consciousness. What confers authenticity upon narrative is the telling voice of consciousness, not to be confused with a narrator, rather than the things told. When Stein says that in the country, unlike the city, "they make a day be a day here" (217), not only is she repeating the romantic commonplace about the country being closer to nature than the city, but she is talking about concentration on the immediate and the authentic. The day that is a day is not about time but about quality.

Traditional narratives are love stories about boys and girls, men and women (219, 223). Love stories conclude with weddings and marriages, which in turn mark regular, chronological family histories or patriarchal narratives. Stein rejects this narrative form. She is looking for love stories that are not determined by the patriarchy and not tied to rigid roles of gender and sexuality.

> There are no men no women needed for love. There are no women no men needed for love. (219)

She also rejects historical biographies of national figures such as Franklin, Washington, and Jefferson (219) and biographies of others—Williamson (223), Henderson (223), Abraham Larsson (239), Donaldson (269), Herbert Masters (229)—all names of male descendants in patriarchal precedence and succession.

To linear chronological narrative she opposes the circular construction of poetry—"rose is a rose is a rose is a rose" (219)—that encompasses the here and now rather than going from here to there. Likewise circular and centered is

> what is deliberately followed by announcing that they wished to be women by deliberately announcing that they wished to be winning by deliberately announcing that they wished to be women. That is one way of deliberating and deciding and intending to have a narrative of preceding. (223)

It is not the subject of a narrative that determines its continuity but the quality of the consciousness that speaks in the words. Not only men but also women can win.

Many events of early 1927 provoke questions about narrative. Anticipating summer visits of Mabel Weeks, her old friend and fellow student at Radcliffe, and of Mabel Haynes (222), her classmate from medical school, Stein thinks of "an older reunion" (220–21). Reunions are occasions for remembering and reviewing life stories. She considers "many many singly" and also reconsiders "pears" (221, 230), friends, including perhaps the pairs in the triangle love story, *Q. E. D.*, of whom Mabel Haynes was one.[15]

> Let us think how can a narrative have any connection with remarriage and their indifference to resolution to changing what there was to not what is not pleasing as if there could be any reason. (224)

Narrative, to Stein, centers on individuals and on relations, not on acts like marriage or remarriage, or on family histories. Narrative must portray what people are, not what they do:

> A narrative of this and in intimately in intimately. (224)

To start a narrative that will not merely be a story of succession, Stein introduces "a white basket . . . not as large as an ordinary one," which might "be here and there and so be noticeable" (223). The basket leads to "a woman with a young one about the age kind and disposition which would be satisfying." Is the young one a child—the daughter of Mabel Haynes, ready for marriage, or the child expected by Yvonne Daunt and Allan Stein? Yet the young one does not sound like a child at all,

> in not yet knowing not yet is it likely that fairly soon there will be something. (224)

Or is it "something" to be created—a literary work? A long, carefully modulated paragraph follows on "Who said will he see me be will he see me be

15. In late 1906 or early 1907, Mabel Haynes had married an Austrian army officer, Konrad Heissig, and gone to live in an army post in Galicia, Austro-Poland. In 1908, a daughter, Itha, was born, and in 1909 a son, Henry William. Letters to Stein from Emma Lootz Erving, her classmate at Johns Hopkins, tell us that Heissig by 1912 suffered from "serious nervous trouble," then was confined in a sanatorium, and soon died.

By December 1913, Mabel was remarried to a man named Rudolph Leick, apparently injured in the war and declared unfit to fight. It was a marriage fraught with difficulties and, during the war, poverty and suffering. Widowed again, Mabel eventually tried to regain American citizenship for herself and her children. (Toklas wrote to Carl Van Vechten in February 1948 that Heissig was killed in World War I and Leick in World War II; she was in error, having forgotten exact dates and events.)

In the spring of 1927, Mabel invited Stein to the marriage that summer of Itha to an Italian—a love story and a story of joined nationalities. By the time of the marriage, Mabel herself had already been remarried, a fact whose implications for narrative Stein considered.

if he will see me be" (224), which at least in part speaks of artistic self-realization in a new work.[16]

Never describe as a narrative something that has happened. (225)

But how can continuation be achieved? Are old wives' tales, gossip, and talk narratives, or are they description (226)? Are scandals and crimes, such as the "Hall Stevens murder" (226), description or narration? Stein considers the description of the minister's affair with the choir singer and the subsequent triangle murder a useless exercise in journalism.[17] It does not solve the problem of continuity.

The sentence, "There is no narrative in intermission" (225), almost asks to be reversed, "There is no intermission in narrative." And indeed, on the following page, she asks, "Can a narrative succeed" in both senses of the word. She constantly plays sequence in time against "being there at once" and asks about the difference between "Description and Continuation and Narrative" (226). If they are there at once, there is no intermission.

The pressing problems of narrative are continuity and identity. Harold Acton is one of a number of people who have "not properly been described" (224), either because, like Brim Beauvais in the 1931 novelette by that name, he has not yet found himself, or because his story is not yet complete, or simply because no one has tried. For Stein, the problem of narrative is becoming the problem of portraiture, for in a Stein portrait, narrative continuation can perhaps be "concentrated" into the here and now of what is seen, or composed, in its totality.[18]

She sets out to describe Harold Acton and write a narrative or portrait

16. Here the antecedent of "me" is not simply Stein herself. Rather than a particular person, it is an essential self. Her use of the personal pronoun "I," which has frequently been cited as evidence of megalomania and self-display, shifts in its antecedent. Most commonly it refers to the perceiving consciousness, the "I" that in meditation is no longer the social "I." Of course, tags such as "When this you see remember me," with its rhyming repetitions, can try a reader's patience and provoke ridicule.
17. In 1927, in connection with narrative, Stein considers murder and incest in many forms. In the sentence, "Lillie do you understand," in *Lucy Church Amiably* (180), the manuscript shows the name Lillie to be a revision for "Liz," which brings to mind "Lizzie [Borden] do you understand," usually associated with *Blood On The Dining Room Floor* (1933), "Is Dead" (1933), and *Four In America* (1934). See also the reference to the Cenci in the subsequent section on Harold Acton. Phrases of this kind gather thematic and auditory echoes by recurrence.
18. The problems of portraiture and narration were on her mind even earlier. In August 1926, Stein wrote to Sherwood Anderson, "One day you must write a novel that is just one portrait."

of him. However, before she begins, she makes a list (232) of others whose stories she will also tell: Elliot Paul, coeditor of *transition;* William Cook, her old American painter friend; George Lynes, who in May 1926 had published her *Descriptions Of Literature* as one of his *As Stable* pamphlets and in 1927 opened a bookshop in Englewood, New Jersey; Harry Brackett, the husband of Ada Joseph, a San Francisco friend of Toklas; Eugene MacCown, the painter and nightclub pianist; Edgar Taine, presumably in error for Hyppolite Taine, the French historian and critic.

Nothing unifies this list except the fact that all were in her mind in 1927, all were male, childless, and without patriarchal narratives attached to them.[19] Only the portrait of Harold Acton (232–38) is fully developed. Elliot Paul is briefly sketched, the others barely mentioned. Stein has no patience to portray them and does not fulfill the expectations created by her list.

Or is it a matter of impatience? Is it possible that writing the list of subjects for narratives is a part of her narrative rather than a plan she failed to execute? To say that she fails to complete the design announced by this list does not answer the question of its intention, although the fact that she returns to some of the people on the list may reflect a plan. Harold Acton had been Stein's host for the Oxford lecture the year before, "which is year yet yet yesterday yet year yesterday year yet" (232), and had shared in her triumph. The portrait may in part be her gesture of appreciation.

She begins with uncertainty about "the difference between a girl and a boy," perhaps remembering Acton as a child in Florence, when she might have seen him while visiting his parents. She may also be talking about definition of identity by gender and sexuality, or about children who explore sexual differences. In his autobiography of his early years, *Memoirs of an Aesthete,* 1925, he tells the story of a very early relationship with a young girl whom he claims to have "explored," though no connection with this story can be demonstrated.

> How can you tell a boy how can you tell a girl. (232)

The portrait may also suggest his homosexuality.

In a striking passage, Stein explores a murderous oedipal fantasy, connected thematically with the patricidal Hall Stevens murder:

> They be little be left be killed be left be little be killed be killed be little be left be killed be his father be his mother be his father be little be

19. Not on this list but later appear briefly some other friends, Max Ewing (247) in a comment occasioned by a visit, and Glenway Wescott (269), about to go to North Africa, which yielded "a narrative of Africa."

left be killed be his mother be his father be left be killed be little be his father be his mother. (233)

She ends the passage by relegating its substance to the world of fantasy—it did not happen—but not before she has included Harold's brother, making the passage not only patricidal but also fratricidal.

> This is what did not happen to happen to be this brother to his brother to his father to his father to be left to his mother to his father.

The boy of this passage ends up with no father, no mother, no family history. Stein has done away with them all and done away with patriarchal history. That her portrait does not include family history is not surprising. Perhaps more striking is the fact that Harold Acton's memoir does not once mention his parents. No wonder Harold is indecisive:

> He first added fed and way and weighed and followed from and first and first added weighed and wait and first added followed he first added followed first and wait weighed and first he first added followed first and weighed and wait and wait. (233)

She continues, presumably in the gardens of La Pietra, the Acton villa in Florence, where "Harold would infinitely rather have roses between pear [pair] trees than a child" (233). Here he lovingly cultivates flowers rather than marriage and family. It is a striking and devastating family image, with the roses growing between the pair of trees or two pear trees.

Another strange and violent image appears, again recalling the Hall Stevens murder, which she has just questioned as material for narrative other than journalistic exploitation. She is seeing Harold in meditation.

> Harold to be which is to be which is not to be rose to be not to be say to be rose to be which to be is to be any way to be not as much as when there is a house and room and left to have to be to quell to be followed quell to be and a little never well to be a moon. Which is an advantage. Harold Acton can be finally withdrawn from Beatrice withdrawn from Beatrice withdrawn from Beatrice who was quelled to be withdrawn from Beatrice who was quelled to be rose to be Harold Acton quelled to be rose to be with soon and not at light sight and and at at attention in in intention with in within might might see be. How to go on. (234)

Who is Beatrice? In the manuscript remains the original reference and source of a rhyme, here in square brackets, which Stein in revision deleted:

> Not allowing moistening to be dwelt upon by theirs in name and so she might be Beatrice Beatrice [Cenci Cen] bent she she bent to bent to be

bent to be he to be bent to be he to be bent to be Beatrice but to be he. (236)

The passage also echoes the phrase "will he see me be" and perhaps bent espalier trees.

Beatrice Cenci introduces the most incestuous tragedy of a corrupt empire and family life in Renaissance Rome. Stein has destroyed—murdered—all the patriarchal narratives, the love, marriage, and family narratives. She is finished with them. The biting, ironic portrait of Harold Acton serves to kill off patriarchal narratives.

> Harold Acton which is it Harold Acton to be sure which is it Harold Acton and to be a choice follow makes place please pay it as they have it as they call it come and call it call it come come come and call it and succeeded he is succeeded and succeeded notably by his successor. This is a narrative regularly read it read it when it is in that perhaps in that perhaps in that past past it let him alone with his discoveries.
> Harold Acton might be useful altogether. (236)[20]

The last paragraph of the long Acton portrait, which murders narrative, begins with "Going on with his life" (238). Is she going on with the narrative of his life? Plainly not, for she has refused narrative. It is he who is going on with his life, which seems to be going on with itself:

> Moderately his life going on with his life. (238)

What goes on is not narrative of events but description, a part of the portrait. His life continues, mildly, in a circle, which continues to the very last line:

> Harold Acton famous in his life and in death. (238)

A life story has been condensed into a portrait which ironically renders the essence of circular emptiness. I have never seen so sharp a portrait; no one seems to have noticed its prominence in "Regular."

She immediately switches to Elliot Paul. Paul admired Stein, lectured on her as well as on Picasso and Gris, and saw to it that from the inception of

20. Stein would have been aware not only of Shelley's *The Cenci* but also of Hawthorne's reliance on the story in *The Marble Faun* and Henry James' *William Wetmore Story and His Friends.* She would also have seen the Guido Reni portrait at the Palazzo Barberini in Rome, which appears in James' biography of Story. The Cenci drama impressed her early, and it appears in her college essay "The Red Deeps." That essay, unlike most others, which were on set themes, was a free piece, which allowed Stein to follow her fantasies.

Eugene and Maria Jolas' *transition* in 1926, Stein's work appeared regularly in the new journal. Paul is given to self-dramatization. He rubs salt—French *sel* leads to English "sell"—into wounds (flesh, pound of flesh).

> Elliot Paul naturally preclude preclude as Elliot Paul naturally preclude if not next to this lead is about to be plain plaintif plaintively plain plain plain plainer plain plain plain plainer plain plain plain plainer plainer plainly plain plain as plain plan as plan plain plainly inclined and decline declined continuously salt and flesh continuously flesh and salt continuously sell and salt continuously sell and salt continuously to be to be in in collected inter and into and in collected which is not never not and and never to proceed. (238)

She rhymes his name, Paul, "ball," "call," "at all." He "has a ball," he comes "to call." One of many young admirers and of many Pauls she knew, he leads her to consider, slowly and then faster, "How many, young men, have to go, together. How many young men have to go together" (238) in a narrative and to wonder how many young men are needed for narratives. She appears irritated with gossip, small quarrels, tempests in teapots—exactly what novels are about. It also sounds like irritation with fawning young admirers, "the ones who do who do see me" (240).[21] Increasingly, she appears annoyed, not merely with young men but with the impossibility of coming to terms with narrative.

Already, however, a new topic opens, causing uneasiness,

> A narrative of religion and irreligion. (239)

> She has come in and out.
>
> Yes.
>
> Progressively integrally delectably derisively undeniably relatively indicatively negotiably restrained. After which coming. (241)

> She wants to talk about the Jesuits about whose adventures it is very interesting to note repeatedly.
>
> If it has been asked not to stay to leave not to stay to leave not to stay if it has been asked not to stay relatively to leave not to stay if it has been asked to leave relatively not to stay to leave not to stay.
>
> Once in a while. (242)

Still laboring on her study of narrative, Stein is in fact beginning work on *Four Saints In Three Acts*. From here until the end of "Regular," the opera is

21. See also "Three Sitting Here," discussed subsequently.

in her mind. Phrases and rhythms appear that she will use in the opera later. She begins it "in narrative," and only gradually moves into dramatic form.

The story of the beginning opera is the end of the story of "Regular" and is discussed in detail in the next chapter. Meanwhile, "Regular" also develops other matters that require comment. Impatience and discouragement are not only about narrative and the new work.

Yet again something obtrudes. It is essential to read this whole, brief dramatic passage in sequence.

> A narrative of undermine.
>
> Undermine in their interest.
>
> Rescue planned planned. Rescue planned planned. Rescue planned planned. Rescue planned planned. Rescue planned planned. Rescue planned rescue planned planned.
>
> If if the chateau d'If.
>
> If if the chateau d'If. The son of Juan Gris If the chateau d'If. Faded. The flowers of friendship if if the chateau d'If. The flowers faded. The son of Juan Gris the flowers faded if if the chateau d'If the son of Juan Gris the Flowers faded.
>
> If if the chateau d'If the son of Juan Gris.
>
> The son of Juan Gris if. The son of Juan Gris, if, the chateau d'If. The son of Juan Gris the flowers faded. (243)

Six times Stein repeats with heavy beats that a rescue is planned.

> If if the chateau d'If.

Any rescue connected with the Château d'If, the state prison of François I on a rock outside Marseilles off the Mediterranean coast, can only refer to Dantes in Alexandre Dumas' *The Count of Monte Cristo,* who escaped by substituting himself for a corpse to be dropped into the water from the prison. By French-English auditory permutations, Stein moves from the English conditional conjunction "if" and French Château d'*If* through French *if* (yew tree), to English "grief," to the French noun and adjective *grief* (injury), to Juan Gris, whose son echoes through the implied French rhyme, *fils* (son).

Juan Gris is dead. His death is the end of his history, although the presence in this passage of his son, Georges Gris, who conducted the service at his burial, suggests ironically that family history continues even as Gris, the great artist and "saint," is gone. The auditory shifts of this passage are brief and simple; they can be heard and seen in the lines. Like so many difficult

Stein passages which unexpectedly rise from the page, these lines cannot be reached intellectually.

Although I believe that she may have moved from word to word by steps such as I suggest, they do not explain the mysterious power of the Château d'If section. I see Dantes in that tense night scene swimming for his life—the great "if"—through the rocky waters from the castle in the sea. The very power of his escape merges with Gris helplessly dying of the poisoned water of uremia to create a haunting pathos.[22]

I see the section on Gris in "Regular" as one of a pair, the second being Stein's elegy, "The Life Of Juan Gris. The Life And Death Of Juan Gris" of May 1927 (*R* 535). The passage in "Regular," though not the Dumas novel to which it alludes, is far from traditional narrative whereas the elegy itself, including its title, sounds in part like traditional narrative, a "life and death" biographical abstract. I have suggested in my comments in the *Reader* that Stein's control in this narrative is uneven but that she may have cast the early section of the piece in the linear narrative form of an obituary to make it informative but keep it from becoming too personal. Her rejection of narrative adds an ironic dimension to the elegy, which is accompanied by the elegiac lyrical voice of the Gris passage in "Regular."

22. The Gris section of "Regular" (243) must have been written upon the burial of Juan Gris on May 13, 1927, in Boulogne-sur-Seine, two days after his death on May 11. Stein attended the funeral service. Twenty pages later in the text of "Regular" (268) appears Easter, April 17.

It is possible that the faded flowers of the funeral also faintly echo the 1914 Gris painting with *papiers collés, Roses in a Vase,* which Stein owned. Her frequent work at this time with the homophones "pear/pair" also leads me to wonder whether an element of the Gris *Dish of Pears* of 1926, probably the last painting of his that she bought, somehow enters these compositions. The more one reads her, the more such slight echoes and reflections lift from her texts. They do not add meanings that require interpretation but overtones of words which it is important to hear.

If "Sherwood Anderson came to see me" (248) concerns an event of 1927 rather than an earlier memory, which is unlikely for Stein; it must be dated before the last week of March, when Anderson sailed back to America.

The order of sections of "Regular" is not necessarily the order of identifiable events and probably not the order in which they were originally written. Although no *carnets* for this study are preserved, it is clear from the sequence of details and from the handwriting that Stein copied into *cahiers,* perhaps not in the order written, sections originally composed in *carnets* although, as usual, she also composed in the *cahiers.*

At this time, in addition, she was already working on *Four Saints In Three Acts* and "A Diary." Some details appear in two or three of these pieces, which are both intertwined and separate. Does the following phrase, for example, describe her own procedure as "a narrative in place of not chinese scissors a narrative this makes it a reassembly of which it was a narrative" (248)? Is she speaking of a scissors-and-paste job, of *papiers collés,* of cut roses in a vase?

Stein wrote the elegy within days after the burial. On May 17, 1927, Kahnweiler acknowledged it and thanked her for including him in it.

> *Personne mieux que vous n'était qualifié pour écrire sur Jean. Je suis sûr que personne ne dira mieux ce que nous perdons en lui que vous le faîtes.*
> *Merci d'avoir parlé de moi si gentiment aussi. J'en suis heureux. Quel mérite avais-je? Celui d'aimer Jean? Je n'étais pas seul, car, vous aussi, vous l'aimiez.*[23]

On July 3, 1947, a year after Stein's death, Toklas wrote to Carl Van Vechten about Stein's 1941 memorial piece for Sherwood Anderson, "Sherwood's Sweetness,"

> Baby was very upset and wrote it and then never wanted to talk about Sherwood . . . as if he had betrayed her by dying—That is the way Baby was about Juan too . . . awfully fond of him . . . undone by his death, then she wrote the last portrait (there's a lovely other one Three Spaniards . . .) and then she never talked about him—just about his pictures.[24]

Part I ends abruptly with the death of Gris. Perhaps the only way Stein could continue the study of narrative interrupted by his death was by starting a new section.[25] Part II (244) begins with a long section on Grant, including the proposed collaboration of Sherwood Anderson and Stein on a biography of Grant.[26] The only reference to the proposed collaboration is in Anderson's letter of March 25, 1927, from the boat during his return trip to America. He casually speaks of the possibility of collaboration in the future,

23. No one could have written better than you about Juan. No one will say better than you what we are losing with him.
Thank you for your kind words about me; they make me happy. How have I earned them? By loving him? I was not alone for you also loved him.

24. "Sherwood's Sweetness," *RAB* 61. Toklas misremembers the title of the other piece that includes Gris. It is "Two Spaniards" of 1927, *PL* 309, contrasting Picasso, alive, and Gris, dead.
Gris also appears in "An Advantage," *PL* 304, and in "Relieve," *PL* 308, on three of Stein's great heroes of modern painting, Picasso, Gris, and Kahnweiler, with their wives, that is, with creative gift that is also sexual. The language of these short 1927 pieces echoes "Regular" and *Four Saints,* that is, "Spaniards might be the occasion of a panic" ("Two Spaniards").

25. Another Part II begins later (266) with another attempt at overcoming frustration by making a new start: "Part II. / That may help."

26. See *AABT* 303–4. Grant also appears in "A Diary" and in "Love A Delight" of this period and in many incidental details. But not until *FIA,* 1933–34, did she realize him extensively as a figure in writing, without a collaborator.

but nothing he says suggests a firm plan, and the collaboration came to nothing.

Yet collaboration was on her mind. Indeed, perhaps she speaks so emphatically of the collaboration on Grant, a mere possibility for the future, because she is thinking about the collaborative undertaking of *Four Saints* with Virgil Thomson. The sentence, "Collaborators collaborators tell how in union there is strength" (244), which she repeats, refers not only to Grant, the Civil War, and Anderson, but also to the opera. The phrase, which returns often, affirms the power of union in love as it affirms its power in collaboration in other forms. At last it leads to mystical "union" in *Four Saints.*

The final sections of "Regular" are increasingly piecemeal. "What to follow to be sure" (246) is a dominant theme. Many entries are written in the form also employed in "A Diary," "A diary of . . ." or "A narrative of . . .". Sometimes such entries are about problems of narrative, more often about subject matter:

> A narrative of individual frightening (245),

> A narrative of lucidity . . . of elegance . . . of irritability . . . of intrusion, (261).

Stein had used this form the preceding year, in *A Novel Of Thank You,* where she spoke of "a story of departure" (112), "a novel of elegance" (128), and others. *A Novel Of Thank You* forms a part of the background for "Regular." The interest, the pleasure, and the difficulty of "Regular" lie in its incisive detail of perceived scenes and of commentary.

Here, from the two Part II sections of "Regular" (244–69), are some examples. One is a comment on epistolary novels or on continuity of correspondence:

> Writing letters a narrative not separated a narrative not detained a narrative not an advantage a narrative not silk or water a narrative not as not alike a narrative not in the left it to them a narrative not easily a narrative not nearly aloud a narrative not never to be when it was which one a narrative not planned to replace it a narrative not once when it was useful a narrative not exactly a narrative. (248)

There is a delightful real narrative of children fighting, following a section of mothers, most of whose names bear the French feminine ending *-elle:*

> Boys and girls tease the seas and this makes them either a mother or it makes them either a mother. After they left. Then theirs it was theirs which was theirs by this time which was which was it whose is followed

Figure 4. Cover of manuscript *cahier* no. VI, showing end of "Regular Regularly In Narrative" and beginning of *Four Saints In Three Acts.* Courtesy YCAL.

> by whose and at least at least makes it at least a leash makes it at least and having to wait two weeks and having to wait two weeks makes it at least. (259)

Comments on adventure stories and journeys appear, with rivers and boulevards suggesting continuous movement. Movement also builds with "adding," "advancing," and issues in wide widening widening a boulevard a street a village or an avenue an avenue of eucalyptus trees eucalyptus trees admirably in an arbor. . . . (249)

Eucalyptus trees, familiar to Stein from California, reappear in *Four Saints.* The long, straight French avenues of trees also illustrate the problem of narrative, for they make "narration recede from all around."[27] Narration moves along, recedes from its context, and "it eludes me it does elude me." It is impossible "to follow to be sure," to contain narrative "in there to stay," to keep it from escaping down the boulevard toward a vanishing point. Portraits, poetry, and plays are more likely than linear narrative to hold and concentrate the steady internal movement of composition.

> Act as if at once and at an instant and infringe and matter.
> Follow in you in you in you unison too wise.
> Where can poetry lead.
> Poetry can lead to altogether to lead to poetry can lead to.
> Where can poetry lead to.
> Regular regularly a narrative.
> In there to stay to stay in there.
> Have it to show to show it to to them as they as they wish to wish to with it with it by and by having heard with at last that mistletoe is mine. (257)

The only union in which narrative can be contained is spatial, not temporal; word composition, not flight of events in time. "To praise a narrative regularly" is no longer narrative but poetry. "A narrative will be wedded" is about union in composition, not about weddings.

"A Diary" (*A&B* 201–18)

Context

"A Diary," not published until after Stein's death, when it was included in *Alphabets And Birthdays* (201–18), the seventh volume of the posthumous Unpublished Writings, is another study of narrative, continuity and time, following the work of "Regular Regularly In Narrative." It was begun in late March or early April 1927 and completed by late June, when Stein went to Belley for the summer. Some details appear not only in "A Diary" but also

27. The idea of narration receding from all around connects with the image of the car that is not about where it goes but about "the movement inside that is of the essence of its going," on which Stein relies in the lecture on "Portraits And Repetition" (*LIA* 195).

in "Regular," *Four Saints,* and some of the shorter pieces she wrote concurrently in the spring and early summer of 1927.

Most of the very ordinary personal events recorded offer no substantial new biographical information and, with few exceptions,[28] no help in dating. They are commonplaces of daily life, with factual entries about weather, flowers, guests, food:

> Today we ate the rest of the game that we had had yesterday and with it mashed potatoes and after that there was a cake which is called Nelly which is very delicious. (204)

It is a record of snippets whose brevity can irritate readers who are looking for continuous stories. Stein herself observes, "A diary should not be in writing" (210). Yet the entries create a personal, domestic mood, sometimes with fine humor and charm.

> Nothing has happened today except kindness. (208)[29]

Text

What is a diary? Literally, it is an immediate, factual record of present events, now, now, now, discontinuous in that it does not develop a sequence, plot, or theme. It is unlike "Patriarchal Poetry" with its thematic center and unlike the wrought and developed "Regular." Time headings like "Tuesday," "tomorrow," or "by and by" do not unify the diary. It is full of sentences

28. For example, the arrival of Fania Marinoff in Paris by April 10 and of Harriet Levy on May 29, dated in letters.

29. The first of the five *cahiers* that contain the piece bears on the cover in Stein's hand the title, "A Diary," and the words "and a storm of grasshoppers on a trip," crossed out. This phrase is a loose translation of the title of this particular *cahier,* "Un nuage de sauterelles en Algérie," in the series "Voyages Autour du Monde" ("Trips Around The World").

The picture shows three tourists on horseback riding into a cloud of grasshoppers, a scene that entered the diary because it was a part of what Stein saw that day and perhaps because a trip suggested a travel diary. The grasshoppers turned out to be external to her study of a diary and were deleted.

Another deletion occurs in the sentence, "Having not finished with John W. as who said who said who said he said" (216). "John W." stands out, for Stein normally spelled out every word and used no abbreviations or initials. Whenever these occur, it is a good idea to check manuscript and typescript.

The manuscript shows the name Wanamaker, poorly scribbled and misspelled "Wahnnamaker." The double *N* is a common misspelling, but the *H* is odd. Was Stein playing with the German word *Wahn* (delusion)? If Toklas was unable to read the misspelled name, she might have substituted the initial, and the problem may have been overlooked in proofreading. Stein, whose family background, like Wanamaker's, included the dry goods business, may have been reading the biography of Wanamaker by H. A. Gibbons, which appeared in 1926.

that define what a diary is or does or means or should be, many in puns and double meanings that poke fun at the whole enterprise.

> A diary means yes indeed. (209)
>
> A diary should be instantly in recording a telegram. (213)
>
> Why does a narrative replace a diary. Because it does not. (201)

Several sentences that begin, "A diary of . . ." suggest subjects for inclusion. Some of the entries are flat and factual, and others are hilarious with tiny, sharp detail.

> A diary of the knife cleaned upon which it said fight for your own country first. (217)

Unimportant in themselves, most of the bits of daily life are composed as small but incisive one-sentence units.

The better the reader knows Stein's daily life, the more subtly they speak.

> Helen has been impressed by a young man and Miss Sitwell. (213)

The young man—undoubtedly Tchelitchew—is not identified, and nothing is recorded about what Helen saw or said, but the observation is made in a telling tone. The fact that Helen is impressed, in Stein's phrasing, is not an event without consequences.

Stein writes this diary to define what a diary is.

> A diary of how I told everybody what is the problem of description what is the problem of accounting what is the problem that I have in mind. (203)

She tries, by writing, to give an account of, account for, add up, enter events and observations. To call it "a distinct record of events" (209) is to stress both the clarity and separateness of events: a meal eaten, work published, a posed family photograph of the Picassos inspected.

Many of the discrete details are in sentences that are also paragraphs, collapsing the two into one. Whether an event happens only once or recurs every day, it is never twice the same. The diary includes the things that make daily life in France so preoccupying and varied: planning menus; receiving a gift of fresh tulips; sending Helen to buy veal or pork, chicken for stock; making sure that she buys artichokes even if she prefers asparagus; and later listening to her stories.

Not limited to the household, the diary includes every aspect of the daily life, the source on which Stein's work always draws: writing letters to Elliot Paul and Bravig Imbs, receiving little greetings from Virgil Thomson, going to see Cook's new Le Corbusier house, commenting on the perfection of "As A Wife Has A Cow. A Love Story" in the June issue of *transition,* dealing with an error in dating something 1925 instead of 1924, writing a great many sketches.

And finally another of the meals that order and regulate daily life in France:

> Today is a pleasant day boiled beef tenderly boiled and roasted in the pot and very well surrounded by a particularly cordial expression of interest. (211)

However choppy their sequence, the entries have carefully wrought verbal shapes that create a powerful sense of being inside the rich heterogeneity of the here and now.

Stein tries out how to accomplish the total present immediacy required by the diary. "Every day was Easter" (205) makes the present everything, and Easter the eternity of the moment. She tries out present, past, and future tense to render the evanescent now. Removing writing from living, she asks humorously whether a diary should be written on the morning of the day described or before.

Not only does she compose each entry as its own tiny eternity, but she thinks of the dull, regular totality, the organizing power of time, already considered in "Patriarchal Poetry." She looks not only at diaries but also at narratives, stories, lists, histories, and a-line-a-day books,[30] in the hope of differentiating them. The irregularity of life belies the apparent rhythmic regularity implied by the word "diary." "A diary left on time" (212) effectively suggests the problem of diaries.

Asserting that a diary "should not be in writing" (210), she implies that any continuity in a written diary is not the live continuity of days or events, which is merely a ticking clock. Instead, it is a continuity invented and imposed by the writer—a fiction. If that is so, then a diary is no longer a diary but something else. "A diary should be simply be" (206), for it has to do with living, not writing. This does not mean, however, that "A Diary" is a mistake or a failure, even if it is a mistake to attempt a diary as a writing project. The discovery that the form will not work is the valid conclusion of the experiment, not its failure.

She terminates the diary, for she is tired of it. "And then I was interrupted" (217), and she sounds as if she welcomed the interruption. Throughout the piece, the opera has been on her mind (216), just as it was in the

30. Commonplace books, scrapbooks, or preprinted diaries; see also "Patriarchal Poetry," 288.

later sections of "Regular." In both there are hints of the mind playing with elements that will enter the opera.

> It is very nice to have words and music and to see them at the same time when by accident it is where they need it best. Most and best. (214–15)

"A Diary" and "Regular" absorb and the spring season reinforces what is in her mind for the next big project. The experiment of the diary, which must be completed, can at best be "an account of those who have been here" (216), a record of visitors, lists of names, the social setting, the additions to a guest book as the visitors depart at the conclusion of the diary that occasioned their inclusion.

> A diary should be only very reasonable an account of those who have been here.
> Who have been here.
> A diary might be met at a door.
> A diary is not relieved from the necessity of lists of roses and peonies also of ribbon and attendance.
> Has Bravig been here.
> Yes.
> Has Henry been here.
> Ycs.
> Has Horace been here.
> Yes.
> Have we been here.
> Yes.
> A diary is as it were outstanding.
>
> (216)

The diary may name outstanding people and unusual occurrences but cannot truly record the daily life. It remains outstanding—an impossibility. Only living renders daily life. A diary can record but cannot be successfully composed as a written work. Living, on the other hand, is a private affair, to which outsiders have no access. And so Stein turns from writing to living and to the intimate setting of private life in the house, in the bedroom,

> And a lamp between.
> And not be seen
> And not to be seen
> And a blue queen.
> Blue is the color of regularly.
>
> (217)

Not writing but living is what this diary is ultimately about, and living is about loving. Toklas, associated with living and with the color blue, is also associated with the regularity of shared presence and affection, not the dull and rigid regularity of clocks. On the last page, perhaps with echoes of the opening chapter of *Tristram Shandy,* the clock stops,

> A diary of the clock not having been not wound. (218)

"A Diary" ends with intimate devotion. And so "there will not be a daily diary," for daily life cannot be contained in a diary.

A local habitation and a name.

—*A Midsummer Night's Dream,* act 5, scene 1, line 17

He came to remember a country that had been seen.

—"A Long Gay Book" 91

4. 1927

Four Saints In Three Acts

"Three Sitting Here" (*P&P* 124–42)

Stein wrote this abstract, patterned portrait in the spring of 1927.[1] By June 24, Kenneth Macpherson, who with Bryher and H. D. edited the new film journal *Close-Up* and had already accepted Stein's "Mrs. Emerson" (1913) for publication in its second number that August, asked her for another piece, "The kind of thing you write is so exactly the kind of thing that could be translated to the screen." She chose the recently written "Three Sitting Here," whose strong visual center and constructed movement were suitable for the film magazine.[2]

With its relentless repetitions, it sounds and looks like some early works — *The Making Of Americans,* "Two," "Many Many Women," "A Long Gay Book." Its abstract title recalls Stein's early portraits, such as "Four Proteges." "Three Sitting Here" puts the reader off, less by its manner than by what appears to be insistently megalomaniacal matter, starting with the opening paragraph:

> The reason why they do not know why they love me so is just this. They love me so is just this. They love me so is just this. (*P&P* 124)

1. Stein to Kenneth Macpherson, n.d., in response to Macpherson to Stein, 28 July 1927.
2. It appeared in two parts in the third and fourth issues of *Close-Up,* September and October 1927; it is included in *P&P* (1934) but has not been reprinted since and remains almost unknown.

Who would dare raise such self-aggrandizing questions over and over and answer them with further mystifying self-aggrandizement? Who does she think she is?

Who is she? That is not only the reader's question *about* the piece, but it is Stein's question *in* the piece. She knew perfectly well that her incessant variations on why they loved her so invited trouble:

> It is very inviting to be authoring antagonism and please could it be known that it is what they do that pleases. (128)

Her work had been provoking antagonism all her writing life. The purpose of this portrait, however, is not to antagonize but to raise serious questions about art and artist, creation and explanation, representation and identity. It makes odd, tense reading, for one senses the focus on the self to be important and serious even as it constantly irritates.

In her July 1927 letter to Macpherson, Stein described "Three Sitting Here" as her "most successful insistent narrative." "Insistence" refers to forms of repetition that create concentrated, mounting intensity rather than extended, diluted repetitiousness.[3] It is "portrait narration,"[4] far from patriarchal narrative. What is this work, whose insistent, nagging self-display so antagonizes readers? If "Three Sitting Here" is a portrait of Stein, as it surely is, who are the three, and where are they sitting?

3. In a letter of April 4, 1949, to Carl Van Vechten, Toklas told her "favorite story of insistence" in connection with Stein's portrait of Cézanne.

> The Irish lady of the Cezanne portrait told us that when she was a little girl her mother was arranging a basket of figs (rare in those days) and she asked her if the children would not each have a fig. The mother didn't answer so she asked again and again. Finally her mother said no dearie. She told the children this and her cousin said to her no that is not the way to ask. Go back and say a fig—mamma—for each of us—for each of us a fig—mamma—until she gives them to you. To get rid of you she will.

The word "insistent," in French and in English, describes personality and rhetorical effect.

4. Portrait narration was one solution to the problem of time and plot; it focused on one person apprehended in totality but eliminated the difficulties of traditional narrative. In "A Transatlantic Interview 1946," Stein, responding to questions about her work, said "portrait narration" began after *Four Saints.* She remembered *Four Saints* vividly as a landmark of success in her life; actually portrait narration began before the opera, early in 1927, when she was refusing traditional, patriarchal narrative.

Among the many examples are "Brim Beauvais," *FIA,* but also such earlier portraits as "Lipchitz." The interview, arranged by Robert Bartlett Haas after the war, though conducted by William Sutton as intermediary in France, was first published in the *UCLAN Review* of the University of California at Los Angeles, Summer 1962, Spring 1963, and Winter 1964, and is reprinted in shortened form in *PGS* 11–35.

There is not more than one of most of us—or is there?—but there is more than one Gertrude Stein. There is Gertrude Stein to read in printed books. There is *Gertrude Stein* (1906), oil on canvas, by Pablo Picasso. There is Miss Gertrude Stein, an American lady living in Paris. There are three sitting here, in the studio at 27 rue de Fleurus.

> It is the prettiest room in the world and they find me charming admittedly when I am not too expressive. (133)

"They," the ones who love her so, are her audience: those who look at her portrait, who read her, who visit her at home, come to see her art collection, and "sit around her"—the phrase echoes the portrait "Sitwell Edith Sitwell." Why do they love her? Whom do they love? Perhaps they do not know which Gertrude Stein they love, or why. Or is it all a foolish question because love has no reasons and reasons do not explain love?

We are once again sitting in the studio, in front of the Picasso portrait, as we were when Stein elucidated in 1923,

> Suppose or supposing that you had an invitation . . . to listen to an explanation. . . . (*R* 434)

By the time she wrote "Three Sitting Here," a year after her lecture in England, she had experienced success such as she had never known, though she had long desired it.[5] Perhaps "they" are also the audience that love Stein who has just lectured in England, though they have not read her and like her not for her art but for her personality, displayed on a stage.

In "Composition As Explanation," Stein had attempted to explain how she composed. She had said that composition was its own explanation and required no further explanation. In "Three Sitting Here," she now returned to that experience.

> To wish to explain and to explain and to explain when one is and inter between London. (130)

Perhaps an uncomprehending audience even loves having a scapegoat whose work they can hate. "What is it that tires my attention" (131), she asks as if she was returning to her early research on attention. It is the "emotion of

5. The success in England also returns early in *LCA* (9). Anticipating the English lecture in *NOTY* (116), Stein had fantasized about returning to America to lecture and to reap fame. Later, in August 1927, there is a reference in a letter from Janet Scudder to a proposed lecture tour in America, but nowhere else is such a tour mentioned.

Stein may have eliminated evidence of a proposed tour that did not take place, just as the invitation to lecture at Cambridge, initially declined, is also not preserved. The Stein papers speak not only by their presence but also by omissions.

admiration" (136) that tires her even as she loves it. She returns to what she was at age twenty-nine, in 1903, when she came to Paris, unknown as writer, art collector, subject of a Picasso portrait.

The manuscript offers clues. On the cover of the first *cahier,* the title "Three sitting here." is entered above an earlier, discarded version, "A History of me," with "of me" a revision for a scratched-out phrase I have not succeeded in deciphering. A subtitle below, also scratched out, may be "They They." A further subtitle, misspelled and not crossed out, reads, "A Sequal to A Long Gay Book." "A sequal" may be word play, "As equal." There are further titles I have been unable to decipher. Stein not only discarded them but firmly crossed them out so that they could not be read, presumably would not distract her progress, or perhaps not be reviewed by Toklas. Those that remain legible, quoted here though crossed out in manuscript, were not typed and not printed. No typescript is preserved.

The maze of titles, subtitles, and revisions makes the portrait tantalizing. "A Long Gay Book" (1912) opens with the sense of human nothingness in a broken, discontinuous world, and with the need to regain a sense of self, "a new everlasting feeling" (*R* 153). "Three Sitting Here" dramatizes her success in becoming worthy of admiration. In the spring of 1927, Stein reread "A Long Gay Book" prior to submitting its initial section to Marianne Moore for publication in the September issue of the *Dial.*[6] The early book may have led to the new history of herself, or writing the new history may have returned her to it.

"Three Sitting Here," whose title may echo its phrases, collapses three personalities into one—or perhaps splits one, herself, into three, so that it displays three aspects of herself and questions their relation. Is there also a measure of contempt here for an audience that does not know what it likes or why?

There are many voices here, and Stein constantly plays with subjects and objects, singulars and plurals. The portrait speaks of corrupting adulation, of admiration for what we do not understand, of comprehension that is not rational but not for that less real. By questioning the nature of identity, she questions representation in art, the relation of artist and work, creation and interpretation.

Small, revolving details suggest Stein the writer, Stein's works, Stein the

6. See "A Long Gay Book," *Matisse Picasso And Gertrude Stein With Two Shorter Stories* (Paris: Plain Edition, 1933; reprint, Barton, N.Y.: Something Else Press, 1972), 13–14; 17–21 (page citations are to the reprint edition); *R* 152–53, 156–61; shortened by Moore for reasons of space from the original submission, *GMP* 13–21, *R* 152–61. See also Moore to Stein, 4 March, 5 and 25 April, 5 May 1927.

portrait on the wall, Picasso the painter, Picasso, the unreliable illustrator for "A Birthday Book" (139). But the "I" and the "me" of this narrative that has become a triple, overlaid portrait are far more than the personal pronoun for Gertrude Stein. The insistences of the three turn and twist and revolve on the stage of this portrait in countless mirroring permutations and circus gyrations of pronouns that question their very antecedents.

She was uneasy about the length of the piece, which ended up spread over two issues in *Close-Up.* The manuscript reveals a further textual problem, however. The printed work ends with the text of the fifth manuscript *cahier,* filled to the end. That final section becomes a stream of celebratory adulation, a pleasure dance of admiration and love—are they the same?—for the speaker, an end that seems fitting as a mode of everlasting feeling.

However, the work continues in a sixth, partially filled manuscript *cahier.* Intentionally or by an error, the last section was not printed and presumably not typed; no typescript is preserved among the *Close-Up* papers or the Stein papers at Yale, and there is no note in manuscripts or letters. By the time the piece, which had been written in Paris, was submitted to *Close-Up,* Stein was in Belley, and Toklas typed or retyped it from the manuscript *cahiers* or, less likely, from an earlier typescript. Whether the sixth *cahier* was left in Paris by mistake, whether Stein had already revised and cut the last section of the portrait, or whether she forgot to include it by an oversight is not clear. In the rare instances where Stein eliminated written text, she normally crossed it out, but here there are no marks at all.

When the piece was reprinted in *Portraits And Prayers,*[7] whose publication she did not supervise because the printing schedule conflicted with preparations for the American lecture tour, Stein failed to restore the cuts, be it because she had reviewed and revised or because she had forgotten the original text. As I consider this portrait important, I print in the following extract the full text from the omitted last *cahier,* beyond the end of the text in *Portraits And Prayers* (142). Brackets mark sections crossed out in the manu-

7. At the center of *P&P* are two "triple" portraits, "Three Sitting Here" and "And So. To Change So. (A Fantasy on Three Careers) Muriel Draper Yvonne Davidson Beatrice Locher" (1924). The latter, printed only in *P&P* and so also virtually unknown, is a portrait of three active American women with pronounced interests of their own: Muriel Draper, whom Stein had known early in Florence, later a decorator with strong interests in the arts; Yvonne Davidson, wife of the sculptor, who designed and made clothes in Paris; and Beatrice Howard, wife of Robert Locher, designer, illustrator, and friend of Charles Demuth.

P&P ends with "An Elucidation" of 1923, another portrait of Stein, in her studio, presenting her art and herself and the difference between the two. Nothing is accidental in such arrangements of contents, though their design is never obvious.

script, a question mark after a word indicates that I am not quite sure of my reading, and the designation "[word?]" is an undeciphered word.

"Three Sitting Here": Text in Sixth *Cahier*

Letting it be left to me. How do you do letting it be left to me. Renew principally.

It might be very well known that stability and their relief which is when if not by the time that theirs is mine makes which when fashioned and in pronounced letting it be integrally with it as they have it sound not formally in so much with it as its worth. In classes. Better than left to be celebrated as their interaction within their delight manifesting which might as much as if readily with pronouncements by this beside coming to be nearly whatever should be in preparation for that and an event. Night and day as we say they say hurriedly.

What is it that it might really be attractively and replace letting it having it after this which is why when in addition as at all at all can never be what they have as added by the time that in xtra leaving leaving it to chance. They add we admire her very much.

[And then as in additionally would you (word?)]

[Not only xtra]

It is not only a dim apartment it is not only a dim apartment that they are unreasonably after all asking to be sure to show it to to to whom. That they are here to be sure that they they they one two there continually to be left after it is for me. To admire that it is left to it to be after all to be additionally to be to me. To me and to me. To be additionally additionally in an additionally adding additionally editionally me. When this after this by this for this in this in this they in this in this they in this in this in the in the end? [or: and?] me. I am and me admire and me and me in this in this and in this and in in and in admire in and me.

Do they do so. Do they do they do so and because of that because of that because of of that because of that do they do so do they do so because of that. Let us be easily careful in discussing just what do they feel when they are preparedly and without reserve [attn] attentively and with regard finally adding to this that they do and in that way not have but will only liking it by now admire me. Let us be used to it because of course it is at once that they do do make that difference they do make a difference counting counting in order to to make that a difference that previously and by their embellishment embellishment laterally they in order that it is to be avowedly in their way in their way to do so. In by and by and to incline to incline to be sure to be sure to be not only with it in xchanging will it be what is meant by this at most. Let us be [word? enough?] advantageously theirs in unison and might it be with them and by them. They will wish.

This text differs from the preceding parts in tone and language. The repeated and varied phrases of the earlier sections and of "A Long Gay Book" are absent, and Stein, as if in anticlimax, appears to question these sections. The sure touch of the first five *cahiers* is gone. I do not know what happened in the process of composition, but Stein may have discarded the last section because it does not fit with the rest. Preserved but unmarked, however, it remains a bewildering, interesting puzzle.

That fame or the prospect and wish for fame returned her to the early problem of identity is not surprising. But that the very phrases should echo from 1912 to 1927 is startling—though characteristic of Stein's verbal memory.[8]

Four Saints In Three Acts

It is difficult to look at *Four Saints In Three Acts* of 1927 as I have done with all the texts so far, as one in a sequence of works gradually evolving over time. It is not just that Stein's first opera, done in collaboration with Virgil Thomson, is a new departure, though that fact must be considered. It is that ever since its first, brilliantly successful performance backed by the Friends and Enemies of Modern Music at the Hartford Atheneum on February 8, 1934, followed by the New York run and the Chicago opening on November 7, with Stein present, this work has occupied a special place in the minds of audiences and critics and Stein's own.

Sometime after the performance, Stein herself began to speak of some works, events, and developments—not always accurately—in relation to the opera as a landmark in her progress. In William S. Sutton's "A Transatlantic Interview" of January 1946, for example, she dated *Four Saints* not 1927 but 1932 and said it marked the completion of a series of portraits and plays. That year completes the group of plays up to 1931 that are printed in *Operas And Plays,* but *Four Saints* begins the group rather than ending it; more important, 1932 is the year she wrote *The Autobiography Of Alice B. Toklas.* Yet her misdating was not simply wrong. Without the *Autobiography,* the opera would never have become as successful as it did.

Even without the *Autobiography,* assuming that a performance of the opera could have been financed and arranged, a Stein libretto would have

8. It is worth following the play of verbal echoes from "A Long Gay Book" to "Three Sitting Here," *LCA,* "A Diary," and *Four Saints.*

attracted attention among people interested in the avant-garde. However, what made *Four Saints* a great popular success in 1934 was the *Autobiography* of 1933, which propelled Stein into fame, led to the iconizing of Stein and Toklas and the demand for the American lecture tour.

Once the *Autobiography* established the women firmly in the American consciousness, the lecture tour benefited from it, and the production of the opera extended Stein's fame with further reviews, interviews, and gossip columns; enhanced by the fanfare about Stein, the opera and its extraordinary production made Thomson's name. Yet the media successes of the *Autobiography* and *Four Saints* are as difficult to separate as the music and the text.

Stein and Toklas have become one of the great icons of modernism, genius, lesbian brilliance, love and marriage, literary invention, and artistic freedom. *Four Saints* has inspired many myths and freed many for new thinking about plays, music, performance, modernism.[9]

Much is known about the opera's star performance in memoirs, photographs, reviews, newspaper articles. Almost unknown remains the fact that, except for a performance at the Gate Theatre, Dublin, in December 1940 and January 1941 of a play announced as *Turkey And Bones And Eating And We Liked It,* two children's plays, *In A Garden A Tragedy In One Act* and *Look And Long, A Play In Three Acts,* performed by local children at the Château de Béon in August 1943,[10] and the March 1946 performance at the Pasadena Playhouse of *Yes Is For A Very Young Man, Four Saints* was the only one of Stein's eighty plays performed anywhere in her lifetime. It was not one success among many but *the one* success, which puts a different light on it even as it enlarges its reputation. This singularity adds to the mystery and fascination of an opera which has never been fitted into the sequence of Stein works or of operas. Where she got the materials for the words, how she worked with them, and what they mean has remained a tantalizing question since it was first shown.

In my first writing about *Four Saints,* driven by its fame, I gave it a separate chapter, in effect lifting it from its context, which is exactly what its fame has done. I am now, however, reading it in the chronological sequence of her work, after "A Diary," alongside the end of "Regular Regularly In Nar-

9. Robert Wilson built his own media success with Stein's *Doctor Faustus Lights The Lights* and appropriated Thomson's score and her text for his *Four Saints In Three Acts,* which opened at the Houston Grand Opera in January 1996.

10. Edward Burns discovered the record in the Gate Theatre archives at Northwestern University Library and found that the play performed was not *Turkey And Bones And Eating And We Liked It. A Play* (*G&P* 239–52) but a collective piece made of "One Carl Van Vechten" (*G&P* 199) and "Captain Walter Arnold" (*G&P* 260). For the children's plays performed at Béon, see *LGS/TW* 416–17.

rative" and "Three Sitting Here," and leading to *Lucy Church Amiably.* The context of these and other works and events of the summer of 1927 throws light on the text.

I look at *Four Saints* here as a 1927 literary work, apart from the musical score, the Maurice Grosser scenario of 1929, and the production of 1934. The opera is a collaboration, but Thomson's score is a separate effort. What made *Four Saints* extraordinary was not only that it was Thomson's first opera, but that it was based, unlike most operas, on a libretto by a known experimental writer. Who today knows the librettists of *La Forza del Destino, Madama Butterfly, Les Troyens, Carmen?* Thomson's great opportunity was the Stein text. I look at it as a dramatic work, published by Stein on its own in *transition* (1929) and *Operas And Plays* (1932), which narrows my view but allows me to speculate in fruitful, new ways.

This is not to disregard Stein's interest in Thomson or in collaboration. He learned from her to do musical portraits. She tried to get his work published and found a patron to help support him. They produced further collaborations. In April 1927, at Stein's suggestion, the Duchesse de Clermont-Tonnerre commissioned him to set "Capital Capitals" of 1923 to music for a midnight *divertissement artistique,* an entertainment at her costume ball; it became Stein's and Thomson's first collaborative performance.[11] In 1930 he set to music her 1929 film scenario, "Deux Soeurs Qui Ne Sont Pas Soeurs" ("Two Sisters Who Are Not Sisters"), and in 1946, *The Mother Of Us All.*

For Stein, collaboration with a composer promised a new way to reach an audience. Both she and Thomson hoped for a masterwork. The prospect gave her a boost for writing, just as Georges Hugnet's translations of Stein texts into French opened the prospect of French readers. Starting in 1927, basking in new hopes for recognition and enjoying the exchanges with gifted young artists, including Virgil Thomson, Stein composed many texts of striking quality and variety. As the appearance of *Geography And Plays* had led her in 1922–23 in Provence to soar in new work, so the opera now opened new visions.[12] When her prospects were bright, her capacity to work shone.

11. In a letter of July 17, 1927, to Briggs Buchanan, Thomson describes his success with "Capital Capitals." See Tim Page and Vanessa Weeks Page, ed., *Selected Letters of Virgil Thompson* (New York: Summit, 1988), 81–82. See also Virgil Thomson, *Virgil Thomson* (New York: Alfred A. Knopf, 1966), 92, 95–96. The text of "Capital Capitals" had been printed in the first issue of *This Quarter* 1, no. 1 (summer 1925): 13–23; it is reprinted in *R,* 415–26.
12. An added incentive was the promise of actual performance of a Stein dramatic text, reinforced by the readiness of the ambitious young Thomson to work for production. Stein had hoped for performance even of her numerous earliest plays in 1913–14. The actress

After her death in 1946, Thomson remained friends with Toklas and later often acted as spokesman for Stein far beyond their collaborations. Living to old age, with his fine facility with words and access to audiences through his music and his power as music critic of the *New York Herald Tribune,* he frequently spoke of and for her as friend and artist. For years his relationship to her through the most famous production gave him a special authority, though not all his comments on her work are authoritative.

Another reason for looking at the Stein text as a work in its own right is the unusual nature of the collaboration. Stein and Thomson somehow reached a loose understanding about what they wanted to do—and then did it separately. First Stein, slowly and with difficulties, wrote the libretto as she had always written, alone. From late February or March until late June 1927, in Paris, she struggled with the Spanish saints on which they had agreed. In a March note, she said she wanted to talk about certain scenes, and no doubt they did. She also wrote him, without details, that she had ideas he might not like. But Thomson did not see the full text until it was finished.

Sometime in early April, she said she wanted him to read what was done, which may have meant her reading him a section aloud. However, there is no evidence that Thomson actively entered her writing, though she did plan passages for musical setting, for example, the choral procession just before Act I, the "Once in a while" or the "When-Then-Men-Ten" sections in Act II, and others.[13] In late July, she sent Thomson the completed typescript from Belley to Paris.

On August 11, Stein wrote to Carl Van Vechten that she had done an opera, adding that she was pleased but cautioning dryly, as if doubting her judgment, that she was often pleased; six months later, she wrote that a young man was setting it to music. Thomson began composing in November 1927 and completed the score a year later but did not confer about details with Stein, who had permitted him to modify and repeat passages. No doubt he performed completed sections for her as he did for other friends, singing the parts and accompanying himself on the piano.

By submitting the text to *transition* for its June 1929 issue, Stein implied

---

Florence Bradley, who stressed the importance of production in making a writer known, had hoped to stage them. While the project was not carried out, Stein must have remembered its attraction. See correspondence with Mabel Dodge, Florence Bradley, Carl Van Vechten, 1913–14; *LGS/CVV* 16–23; James Mellow, *Charmed Circle: Gertrude Stein and Company* (New York: Praeger, 1974), 175–76.

13. Mellow, in *Charmed Circle,* 303–8, follows the steps of the libretto in detail, as does Jane Bowers in her essay, "The Writer in the Theater: Gertrude Stein's *Four Saints in Three Acts,*" in *Critical Essays on Gertrude Stein,* ed. Michael C. Hoffman (Boston: G. K. Hall and Co., 1986), 210–25.

that it was a work of consequence in its own right. She spoke of it in the *Autobiography* at a time when Thomson was already working hard toward a production. Briefly and factually, she said he asked her for the libretto, she had taken a trip to Avila in 1912, St. Theresa and St. Ignatius were the subjects, and it was printed in *transition;* she avoided specific comments that might compromise what she intended to promote.

Soon after completing the score, Thomson in December 1928 sailed for New York while Georges Hugnet, with Stein's help, worked on the translation of selections from *The Making Of Americans.* In Boston, New York, Rochester, Kansas City, and Santa Fe, Thomson performed, lectured, saw friends, made contacts, and promoted the opera, performing scenes for potential patrons in the hope of backing.

He returned to Paris in March 1929, gave a concert of his own music in June, and in the summer went south and for the first time saw Spain, returning there again the following summer. That summer, Stein translated Hugnet's *Enfances* and ended up quarreling with him over the joint publication. Thomson's attempts to mediate failed, and by year's end Stein rejected him along with Hugnet.[14]

From Christmas 1930 on, Stein did not correspond with or see Thomson until the spring of 1933, when a contract for the Hartford production of the opera had to be negotiated between Thomson and Stein's agent, William Aspinwall Bradley. Questions of equal credit and shares of profits arose like replays of the Hugnet situation. Stein insisted on a 50–50 share of profits; tensions were not eased until Thomson grudgingly accepted her terms. The opera was finally produced on February 8, 1934.

Stein's methods would seem to preclude collaboration. However, it is a recurrent topic in her letters and occasionally her work. For example, in "Regular Regularly In Narrative" of spring 1927, when work on the libretto had begun, she speaks of collaborating with Sherwood Anderson (244–48).

Over and over in the last part of "Regular," she says that "in union there is strength"; whether she is combating fear of collaboration, talking herself into concentration, anticipating Theresa's travails, invoking her union with Toklas for strength as she has often done, or trying to create in the study of narrative a scenario for the opera, the recurring phrases suggest uneasiness, be it about collaboration, the libretto, the opera, or the ideas.[15]

14. The collaborations and the quarrel with Hugnet are discussed in the next chapter.
15. Jane Bowers suggests that "Thomson's expectations . . . inhibited Stein" ("Writer in Theater," 215). I doubt that Stein's uneasiness, which Bowers correctly identifies, was interpersonal; I believe she is uneasy about collaboration, about doing an opera, about moving

Visits from Thomson punctuate "Regular," as do her hopes for a masterpiece, an ambition she had always had but had barely addressed in her work. By 1927, it was already fueled by the success of her English lecture of June 1926, and it is evident in "Three Sitting Here." Allusions to the opera enter not only "Regular" but also "A Diary," "Love A Delight," "An Advantage," and "With A Wife"; some phrases appear in both the libretto and contemporaneous pieces. Thomson quotes a letter from Stein about her struggle to get Theresa on stage, which makes her difficulties audible (92).[16] The history of her troubles with the material enters many pieces of this time. But for the opera itself, Stein and Thomson in effect separated writing and musical setting so that collaboration on *Four Saints* never became a practical personal issue between them.[17]

In his autobiography of 1966, Thomson records asking Stein for an opera libretto and deciding with her on a subject.

> I had asked Miss Stein for an opera libretto, and we had sat together for picking out a subject.
>
> The theme we chose was of my suggesting; it was the working artist's life, which is to say, the life we both were living. It was also my idea that good things come in pairs. In letters, for instance, there were Joyce and Stein, in painting Picasso and Braque, in religion Protestants and Catholics, or Christians and Jews, in colleges Harvard and Yale, and so on to the bargain basement of Gimbel's and Macy's. This dualistic view made it possible, without going in for sex unduly, to have both male and female leads with second leads and choruses surrounding them, for all the world like Joyce and Stein themselves holding court in the rue de l'Odéon and the rue de Fleurus. I thought we should follow overtly, however, the format of classical Italian opera, which carries on the commerce of the play in dry recitative, extending the emotional moments into arias and set-pieces. And since the eighteenth-century opera seria, or basic Italian opera, required a serious mythological subject with a tragic ending, we agreed to follow that convention also, but to consider mythology as including not just Greek or Scandinavian legends, of which there were al-

---

from the unfinished study of narrative to plays. I follow these problems in the pieces written alongside the libretto and trace context chronologically in related works, whereas Bowers concentrates on the libretto lifted from the context of related works.

16. Thomson speaks of the opera in his autobiography, *Virgil Thomson,* 90–108, which relies on his correspondence with Stein. Subsequent quotations, unless otherwise identified, will refer to this book. See also the letters of Stein and Thomson, YCAL and Yale Music Library.

17. Betsy Alayne Ryan, *Gertrude Stein's Theatre of the Absolute* (Ann Arbor, Mich.: UMI Research Press, 1984), 68.

ready a great many in operatic repertory, but also political history and the lives of the saints. Gertrude liked American history, but every theme we tried out seemed to have something wrong with it. So that after I vetoed George Washington because of eighteenth century costumes (in which everybody looks alike), we gave up history and chose saints, sharing a certain reserve toward medieval ones and Italian ones on the grounds that both had been overdone in the last century. Eventually our saints turned out to be baroque and Spanish, a solution that delighted Gertrude, for she loved Spain, and that was far from displeasing to me, since, as I pointed out, mass-market Catholic art, the basic living art of Christianity, was still baroque. And Maurice Grosser was later to remind us that musical instruments of the violin family still present themselves as functional baroque forms. (90–91)

What this late rational account does not tell and letters do not tell is just how they picked out their subject in talk. Thomson's summary, the only statement we have, has been taken as history but leaves us wondering how Stein thought the ideas arose and developed. Speculation is a necessity, for the figures, the themes, and the consistency of their development were altogether new for Stein.

What then is the text of *Four Saints,* apart from its production and the *Autobiography?* Where did the material come from, and what allows me to call it Stein's? How can we explain the extraordinary unity of its execution, where, contrary to her habit, there is almost no digression from the matter of saints that is its center? What evidence is there, apart from its success in a historic performance, for considering this text special? What is it in the sequence of Stein's literary and personal preoccupations?

By the time they decided on an opera, Thomson, well trained, widely read, intelligent, and humorous, had already set to music as gifts for Stein "Susie Asado" and "Preciosilla." In these he responded as to a musical instrument to the language she had developed in Spain in 1912. Theirs is the style described in her lecture "Portraits And Repetition" as that of her "early Spanish period" (*LIA* 197). Thomson's settings may have taken her back to Spain.

"Singing is everything," as she had written late in "A Long Gay Book" (*R* 225). It is what poets do in the fullness of sensuous experience. In St.-Rémy she had rediscovered the joys of singing and spoken of it as what saints and operas did. Echoes of writing done in Provence, in such pieces as "Saints And Singing," "As Fine As Melanctha," or "Talks To Saints Or Stories Of Saint Remy," return in *Four Saints.*

By 1934, however, she had come to distrust and discount her work with sounds and singing. In the lecture "Portraits And Repetition," she called it a temptation:

> I was for a little while very much taken with the beauty of sounds as they came from me as I made them. . . . The strict discipline that I had given myself, the absolute refusal of never using a word that was not an exact word all through the Tender Buttons and what I may call the early Spanish and Geography and Play period finally resulted in things like Susie Asado and Preciosilla etc. in an extraordinary melody of words and a melody of excitement in knowing that I had done this thing. (*LIA* 196–97)

Perhaps *Four Saints,* which assigned to Thomson the setting to music of her words, might prevent her text from becoming "drunk with the melody of the words" (*LIA* 199).

She also had more immediate concerns with Spain in the spring of 1927. It cannot be an accident that in the spring and summer of 1927, Stein wrote a series of short pieces about Spaniards—Gris and Picasso, as individuals, with their wives, with Kahnweiler, in "Two Spaniards," "Relieve," "One Spaniard," "An Advantage," listed here in the order written, the first three in a single manuscript *cahier.*

Many pieces of that spring refer to Easter, April 17, a late date that year. Lent offered itself naturally as the spiritual setting for the new work. Holy Week, the Passion, and the Resurrection—*sainte-semaine* in French—coincided with the decline from uremia of Juan Gris, whose death on May 11 is woven into Stein's struggle to create *Four Saints.*

Even in her early portrait of Gris, she had described him in religious terms as combining perfection and transubstantiation.[18] I take the Spanish and religious substance of the opera to rise in part from the death of this Spanish painter central to Stein's sense of art. The total dedication to a creative task that she voices in her elegy on him, written within days of his death, is at the heart of the opera.

This is also the theme of Thomson's phrase about "the working artist's life, the life we both were living." Whether Thomson was aware of it or not, the theme seems for Stein to have connected with the figures of the two Spanish painters who were her friends and the two Spanish saints. However, "Regular" suggests that the saints led her to "the working artist's life" rather than the other way round.

18. "Pictures Of Juan Gris," 1924, *P&P* 46.

She wants to talk about the Jesuits about whose adventures it is very interesting to note repeatedly.

If it has been asked not to stay to leave not to stay to leave not to stay if it has been asked not to stay relatively to leave not to stay if it has been asked to leave relatively not to stay to leave not to stay.

Once in a while. (242)

In "Prepare for saints" (11), she is preparing for the saints' vision, for words, for performance, and for death. There is no need to choose between these or identify single elements, for in the text they merge into one. Depending on how we spell the invocation, which we hear but do not see, it can be "Prepare four saints" in three acts of classic drama; indeed, "Saint saint saint saint" (14) spells four saints for saints. Everything is literal, though that does not make it factual.

The death of Gris may have recalled threats of extinction such as appear early in "A Long Gay Book." In its final sections, written after the experience of Spain in 1912, that work had led her in a radical shift of style to enter the plenitude and heterogeneity of concrete experience. Upon the death of Gris, she must have struggled to give body to her vision without indulging in feelings, enthusiasms, and herself.

One further, unexplored connection with Spain goes from early years to 1912, 1927 and beyond through a friend, Georgiana Goddard King.[19] Stein and Toklas had met with King and her friend, the photographer Edith Lowber, on their 1912 trip to Spain, apparently in Barcelona, Granada, Madrid, and perhaps Toledo. At that time, King was working on a new, annotated edition of G. H. Street's *Gothic Architecture in Spain.* Stein sent King new work, for example, "Two." In her 1927 letters, King recalls the early trip.

By 1926, King had already completed the work for her big study, *Heart of Spain,* apparently discussed with Stein though not published until 1941, after her death. At Stein's studio, King had seen the modern painting, met

19. In the *AABT,* Stein speaks of her as a Baltimore friend. King received her B.A. degree in 1896 from Bryn Mawr, where she was close to Carey Thomas and knew Mary Gwinn and Alfred Hodder, who appears in the Fernhurst episode of *MOA.* She then taught in New York, where she saw Stein. By 1907, she was hired to teach first composition and then comparative and English literature at Bryn Mawr.

When the new Department of History of Art was founded, she was appointed to it and by 1916 became full professor specializing in the art and architecture of Spain and later developing the doctoral program in art history. She reviewed *Three Lives* as a crucial modernist text for the *International,* June 1913, "As Monet was to Courbet, so Mr. [Henry] James was to George Eliot," she said, and so, likewise, was Stein to James.

artists and dealers, and purchased Man Ray photographs for Bryn Mawr. She instructed her students not only in modern ideas about art but also in modernist writing and regularly read Stein texts to them.

> [My students] are used to the all-over pattern of Spanish plateresque, without relief, without centralization, where beginning, middle and end are interchangeable more or less, and right could be left and top row could be bottom row! . . . They can certainly carry over the same attitude . . . when examining a pattern of words. . . .[20]

On the American lecture tour, upon King's invitation, Stein spoke at Bryn Mawr, on Wednesday, November 14, 1934, on "Poetry And Grammar"; by that time, after the publication of the *Autobiography,* King had already written a discerning piece on Stein for the *Bryn Mawr Bulletin.* It is impossible to pinpoint details of their exchanges for the opera, but it is clear that the two women, both committed to the modern in art, both given to a deep love of Spain, both lesbians, enjoyed a rich friendship that undoubtedly entered *Four Saints In Three Acts.*

In a letter of May 8, 1927, announcing her arrival in Paris in June, on the way to a research leave in Spain, she recalled seeing Stein in 1902 in New York among daffodils while she lived at the White House apartment building at 100th Street and Riverside Drive. During her visit in Paris, Stein apparently read the new libretto to her, for by November 25, from Granada, King wrote,

> How is your opera. I never saw a magpie this autumn without thinking of it and seldom a Holy Ghost.

As a reader, Stein must also have recognized in Theresa's *Book of Her Life* not only a pastoral but also a judicial confession, which her confessors scrutinized for heresy. She must have responded to the saint's sense of authentic experience, including the firm grasp of the reality of ordinary things that speaks in her simple, concrete writing.

Interested in art, Stein must have known representations of St. Theresa in painting and sculpture. In an early, undated letter to Stein before a summer trip to Europe, Etta Cone speaks of reading Mrs. (Anna Brownell) Jameson's *Legends of the Monastic Orders* (1867), a detailed study of saints in painting and sculpture. Stein probably read this or a similar guide. She must have seen Bernini's marble group in Santa Maria della Vittoria in Rome, reproduced in the 1934 memorial program for the Hartford production, and she

20. Georgiana Goddard King, "Gertrude Stein and French Painting," *Bryn Mawr Alumnae Bulletin* 14, no. 5 (May 1934): 2–5.

would have seen many of the Spanish and Italian works as well as those of Rubens.

Even as a student, Stein must have known about ordinary and total consciousness, about hallucinations and forms of knowledge gained not only by the use of eyes, ears, and wits. Her friend Leon Solomons was interested in mediumistic visions. She may have heard William James in lectures speak of saintliness, meditative concentration, and perhaps of St. Theresa's amatory flirtations.[21] Among the books from the Stein library preserved at Yale is a French translation of St. Ignatius' autobiographical *Testament.*[22] She knew Francis Parkman's history of the Jesuits in North America.[23]

Early reading must have alerted her to the fact that saints were commonly classified as hysterics, as they are by Freud and by Weininger, who described St. Theresa as patron saint of hysteria.[24] He saw female mysticism as a form of concealed sexuality, as did Lombroso in his study of genius and criminality, which Stein owned in a 1927 reprint.[25] In a passage of *The Autobiography Of Alice B. Toklas* about talks with Virgil Thomson that lead to the opera, she speaks about saints and hysterics in the context of real and apparent artists (280–81).

21. William James, "What Psychical Research Has Accomplished" [1890, 1892, 1896], in *The Will to Believe and Other Essays in Popular Philosophy* (New York: Longmans, Green, 1927; reprint, Cambridge: Harvard University Press, 1979). See also Frederick Myers' research in *Proceedings* of Society for Psychical Research, ref. in James' 1898 lecture, *Human Immortality* (Boston: Houghton Mifflin, 1899), 25, 26 and n. 7.
22. *Autobiographie de St. Ignace de Loyola: Le Récit du Pèlerin,* trans. and annot. Eugène Thibaut (Bruges: Charles Beyaert Ed. Pont. [Museum Lessianum, Section Ascétique et Mystique, No. 15], 1924). Ignatius undertook the study of grammar in part to discipline the obstreperous mind.

    > *C'était que quand il commençait à apprendre les déclinaisons comme c'est nécessaire dans les débuts de la grammaire, il lui survenait une intelligence nouvelle des choses spirituelles* . . . (ch. 6)

    > Only once he began, as is required for the study of grammar, to learn the declensions, did he gain a new sense of the life of the spirit.

    Stein would have understood studying grammar as spiritual discipline. With *Lucy Church Amiably* finished, late 1927, she turned to "Arthur A Grammar."
23. Francis Parkman, *History of the Jesuits in North America in the Seventeenth Century* (Boston: Little, Brown, 1867). Certainly she would have been aware of Parkman's view of the Jesuit aspirations to mastery over New France, and of English liberty in conflict with French absolutism in the Canadian Provinces. See also "irreligion" and "adventures" of the Jesuits in "Regular," 239, 242.
24. Otto Weininger, *Sex and Character* (1903; first translated 1905; reprint, New York: AMS, 1975), 166.
25. Cesare Lombroso, *The Man of Genius* (London: Walter Scott, 1891).

In 1925 had appeared the first French edition of Rodolphe Hoornaert's refutation of the claim that Saint Theresa was a hysteric, a book widely reviewed in France, though an English translation appeared only in 1931.[26] Other books about St. Theresa of the mid-1920s that Stein might have consulted or read about are the first volume of Edgar Allison Peers' *Studies of the Spanish Mystics*[27] and Edward Boyd Barrett's *The Jesuit Enigma,* a study not of saintliness but of the Jesuit institution, by an Irishman who left the Jesuit order and the church itself.[28] Many publications of the mid-1920s suggest interest in St. Theresa, perhaps also stimulated by the canonization in 1925 of St. Theresa of Lisieux, a modern Carmelite nun of Stein's own age.

What was transmuted in the opera from Stein's reading and from art is as easy to miss as it is difficult to prove, but it is important to look at the evidence. An example is the word "enclosure" or "inclosure" in *Four Saints* (79, 97). Of course it refers to land. However, St. Theresa advocated that nuns take the vow of enclosure. She believed that human beings, easily tempted away from devotion, required enclosure as discipline. The vow, an aspect of religious reform, requires renunciation of free access to the world.[29] To Stein, enclosure may have suggested artistic discipline—what she called meditation. Without St. Theresa's meaning, the word "enclosure" fails to reverberate as Stein surely intended. Also in the opera, and later in *Lucy Church,* are many references to water. St. Theresa describes the watering of the garden of prayer and identifies four stages of prayer, or waters, the fourth culminating in mystical union.[30] The word "water" in the opera may carry Theresa's meaning, just as it also suggests movement and seasonal change.

By the most serious play on words entered with extraordinary freedom of imagination, Stein shaped into the libretto the verbal interaction between Spain, the saints, and herself. The opera does mark a watershed, a qualitative difference in language, a change in style, as does "A Long Gay Book." Though beyond simple reference, her invention is far from simple or empty. Spain and Gris and mortality and visions and art and singing—it all comes simply and essentially together.

26. Rodolphe Hoornaert, *Sainte Térèse écrivain: Son Milieu, Ses Facultés, Son Oeuvre* (Lille: Desclée, De Brouwer, 1925).
27. Edgar Allison Peers, *Studies of the Spanish Mystics,* 2 vols. (London: Sheldon Press; New York: Macmillan, 1927–1930).
28. Edward Boyd Barrett, *The Jesuit Enigma* (London: Jonathan Cape Limited, 1927).
29. St. Teresa of Avila, "The Book of Her Life," chap. 7 in *The Collected Works of St. Teresa of Avila,* vol. 1 (Washington, D.C.: Institute of Carmelite Studies, 1976).
30. Ibid., chap. 11.

From Narrative to Opera in Manuscript

My discussion of the opera itself centers on Stein's text as it appears in her manuscript notebooks and in the complete printed versions.[31] Only later do I briefly look at the text in relation to score and scenario. Stein's words allow a literal reading of the libretto that makes more sense of its construction than the many speculative comments on the production of Maurice Grosser's scenario.

The libretto begins in the sixth and last *cahier* of "Regular Regularly In Narrative." That *cahier* is marked on the cover,

> end
> Regular Regularly
> VI
> Beginning of Opera

and

> Beginning of studies
> for an opera to be
> sung I.

This start is entirely atypical. Stein normally began a new work in a new *cahier* except when she wrote a number of very short pieces in a single *cahier,* but she was careful even then to start a new piece on a new page. The opera, however, not only begins in the same *cahier* as "Regular" but its first words immediately follow the last of the study of narrative.

31. The text is printed complete in the Plain Edition volume of *O&P* (1932; reprint, Barrytown, N.Y.: Station Hill Press, 1987), to which references in this chapter are keyed. It is also complete in John Malcolm Brinnin, *Selected Operas and Plays* (Pittsburgh: University of Pittsburgh Press, 1970), in *transition* no. 16/17 (June 1929), and in *LO&P* (New York: Rinehart, 1949), but not in *SW* and in the 1934 Random House edition of the opera text.

Four Saints opens *O&P* (1932); like the little notes Stein wrote to Toklas upon beginning new *carnets* to assure success in her writing tasks, this placement may be intended to make a success of the new volume. It is followed by the second opera about them both, *A Lyrical Opera* of 1928, a little chamber opera, sexual, sweet, a bit cute, its bedroom intimacy offsetting the large scope of *Four Saints.* Other pieces intended as operas—*A Bouquet. Their Wills., Madame Recamier*—are not given such prominence in the book.

The scenario, prepared by Maurice Grosser for the performance, after the text was set to music, is printed in the Music Press and Arrow Music Press editions of the complete vocal score (New York, 1948). See also David Harris, "The Original Four Saints in Three Acts (1927)," *Drama Review* 26, no. 1 (spring 1982): 101–30.

Stein composed her libretto in part during Lent, which introduces water, lambs, flowers, trees, and the color green in the awakening landscape of the text; the name Virgil can hardly have failed to suggest pastoral poetry.

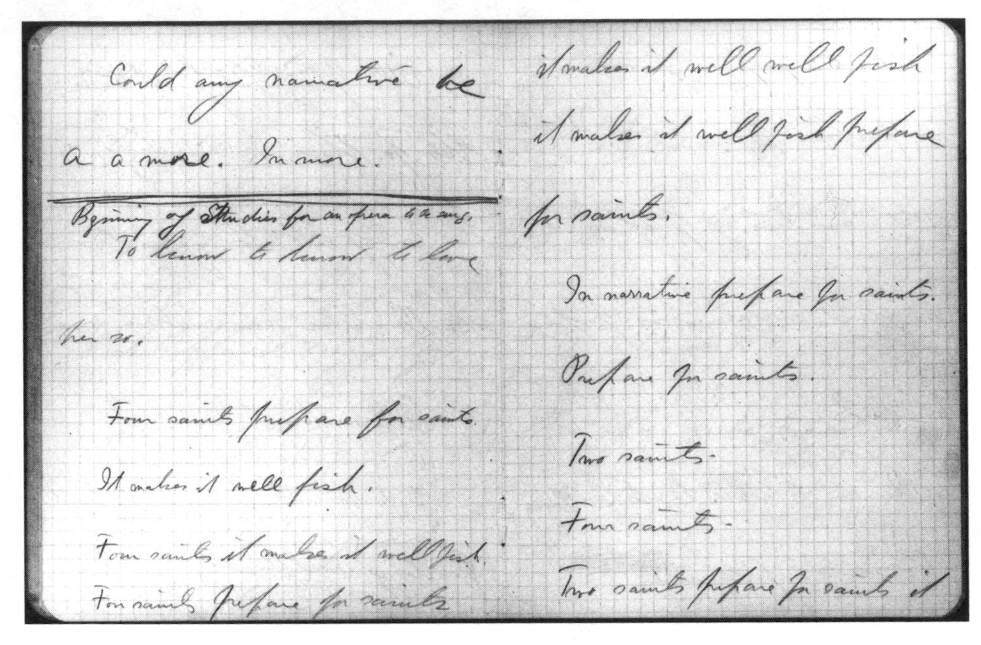

Could any narrative be
a a more. In more.

Beginning of Studies for an opera to be sung.
To know to know to love
her so.

Four saints prepare for saints.
It makes it well fish.
Four saints it makes it well fish.
Four saints prepare for saints

it makes it well well fish
it makes it well fish prepare
for saints.

In narrative prepare for saints.

Prepare for saints.

Two saints.

Four saints.

Two saints prepare for saints it

Figure 5. Manuscript page, end of "Regular Regularly In Narrative" and "Beginning of Studies for an opera to be sung." Courtesy YCAL.

It is odd that of the many who have looked at Stein's handsomely boxed manuscript of the opera[32] at Yale, none has asked how *Four Saints* and "Regular" connect. Unlike the printed text of the libretto, the manuscript shows not only that the two pieces are linked but how Stein moved from narrative to opera. Unless all features of the manuscript—not only the words—are "read," information about the opera is easily overlooked.

Four Saints was not only written in the notebook of "Regular" but was begun as a part of the study of narrative. The libretto includes long narrative passages not assigned to particular characters, which Thomson frequently set as recitative. Stein's words are literally true,

> A narrative of prepare for saints in narrative prepare for saints. (11)

What exactly did she mean?

32. When Stein returned to America for the lecture tour in October 1934, she presented this boxed manuscript as a special gift to Carl Van Vechten, who had most consistently helped publish her work and draw attention to her art (*LGS/CVV,* 21 September 1934, 336–37). Stein did not normally give away manuscripts and only rarely handwritten copies of short texts. No *carnets* with text for *Four Saints* are preserved. Such *carnets* must have been destroyed, for the text in the manuscript *cahiers* looks at least in part copied. Without *carnets,* a part of the history of Stein's writing of the opera remains hidden, exactly as she intended.

The last sections of "Regular" show growing impatience. Narrative eludes her while a new undertaking, the opera, troubles her, and unclear personal matters, especially about money, cause tension.[33] There is much about discontinuity in narratives, which should "be wedded" but turn out not to hang together because they are about mistakes and about disruption in families whose failure creates fear and anger. Near the end of "Regular," "they were discouraged" and Stein asks "what to do" about it. The word "will" occurs frequently, with more than mere auxiliary thrust. It implies willpower for the new work but may also recall the testament that had preoccupied her since late 1926.

> A narrative tells in tells a daffodil he will he will a jonquil he will he will.
>
> A jonquil he will he will a daffodil he will he will. A daffodil is different from a description a jonquil is different from a description. A narrative is different from a description. A narrative is different from a description.
>
> Will, an undertaking. (267)

The last but one manuscript page of the study of narrative ends with the last but one line of the piece,

> Need it and fine find find finding inalterably. (270)

Moving from "fine" to "find" to "finding," Stein struggles for words that will stabilize in composition. She has already worried that narratives elude her and walk away from the immediate toward a vanishing point. "Regular" is the story of her struggle to prevent narrative from receding and to seize it in adequate words. The next manuscript page begins unsteadily,

> Could any narrative be
> a a more. In more.

These two handwritten lines become the last words of "Regular," although they hardly look like the completion of anything. On the manuscript page, however, another line of text follows immediately after "a more . . . more," echoing *amor, amour?*

> To know to know to love her so.

33. There is also frequent talk about outings from Paris, including visits to William Cook's and Michael Stein's new Corbusier villas in Boulogne-sur-Seine and Garches. Possibly the trips in the last twenty pages of "Regular" have the same origins as those in "A Diary" (206, 208) and on the second page of *Four Saints* (12).

These words become the first line of the opera. They can be read as an invocation to St. Theresa but also as an invocation to Toklas, who literally opens the new work.[34] The invocation at last releases Stein's power to begin.

Only sometime after Stein had written that line, or perhaps after she finished the opera, did she separate it from the narrative study by adding a subtitle: "Beginning of studies for an opera to be sung," revised to "Studies for an opera to be sung."[35] At some point she further marked off the new work by drawing two heavy horizontal lines under what had become the last line of "Regular."

For the definitive subtitle, she revised the phrasing to "An Opera to be Sung." "Beginning . . . studies," no longer preliminary and separate, was incorporated into the opera itself or, to put it differently, the story of her struggle to seize the vision of the saints became a part of the libretto. Having rejected narrative, she completed "Regular" by telling the story of her own struggle with the opera. That narrative in turn became the beginning of the libretto. The manuscript shows how truly this story both ends "Regular" and begins the opera.

"Beginning . . . studies for an opera": The Text

Preparation for the opera must be selfish, for only out of herself, by talking like a fishwife—"selfish," "sell fish," "well fish," "fishwives"—can she see, say, and write. Two saints, four saints, and three saints oscillate back and forth throughout the early section, suggesting Theresa's efforts at prayer and Stein's efforts at meditation, the vision of the saints coming and going. The play with numbers recurs throughout the opera, as Tchelitchew understood when he spoke of "four for mortal and three for divine. There you see her preoccupation with symbols of numbers."[36]

"What happened today a narrative," she says to herself, and tells a longish story of an outing in the country, seemingly unrelated to saints and opera. Actually she focuses on the immediate, as she often does in an attempt to enter a new task. In the next paragraph, she perhaps approaches meditative concentration:

34. Although I think this sentence originates in Stein's feelings about Toklas—similar invocations appear in private notes in *carnets* and *cahiers* of other pieces, which Stein often inscribed to Toklas—there is nothing to prevent reading it as an invocation to St. Theresa, as Stein no doubt also intended.

35. In the Grosser scenario, which removes the traces of the process of writing in favor of a simpler text for the stage, "Studies" becomes "Prelude: A Narrative of Prepare for Saints."

36. Pavel Tchelitchew, "Gertrude Stein," Martin A. Ryerson lecture (Yale University, New Haven, Conn., 20 February 1951, typescript), YCAL.

He came and said he was hurrying hurrying and hurrying to remain he said he said finally to be and claim it he said he said feeling very nearly everything as it had been as if he could be precious be precious to like like it as it had been that if he was used it would always do it good and now this time that it was as if it had been just the same as longer when as before it made it be left to be more and soft softly then can be changed to theirs and speck a speck of it makes blue be often sooner which is shared when theirs is in polite and reply that in their be the same with diminish always in respect to not at all and farther farther might be known as counted with it gain to be in retain which it is not be because of most. (12)

The speaker, whether a figure in the opera or an observer outside it, is ready to claim the vision or the opera scene, which approaches and recedes, is diminished yet retained, but finally becomes visible as a garden setting with benches in the sun. Stein tries to count, fuse, and separate details in a description, to see each and compose all together:

Imagine four benches separately.
One in the sun.
Two in the sun.
Three in the sun.
One not in the sun.
Not one not in the sun.
Not one.
Four benches used four benches used separately.
Four benches used separately.
That makes it be not be makes it not be at the time.
The time that it is as well as it could be leave it when when it was to be that it was to be when it was went away.
Four benches with leave it.
Might have would be as would be as within within nearly as out. It is very close close and closed. Closed closed to let letting closed close close close chose in justice in join in joining. This is where to be at at water at snow snow show show one one sun and sun snow show and no water no water unless unless why unless. Why unless why unless they were loaning it here loaning intentionally. Believe two three. (12)

The last sentence ends on a high beat,

What could be sad beside beside very attentively intentionally and bright.

She advises herself,

Begin suddenly not with sisters.

Has she decided not to begin chronologically, with Theresa's childhood? Not to begin with nuns in a convent? Not to begin with herself and Toklas, lesbian sisters? She rehearses ways of mounting the opera in the mind, sees it onstage:

> Mount it up.
> Up hill.

She places one, two, three, four saints in the scene, singly and in pairs. With time abolished, all seasons simultaneously filling the setting, she commands the saints to appear.

> Why should every one be at home why should every one be at home why should every one be at home.
> Why should every one be at home.
> In idle acts. (13)

Life is not great deeds but homely, idle acts like getting up, sitting down, walking around, talking. Domesticating the vision of saints, she combines narration and description visually and verbally: a croquet scene, the nuns' habits; their regulated life in the convent; small trees with pigeons in them, landscape details of primitive painting, which lead to the later vision; benches for the saints to rest or stations of the cross.

At last she embraces her fear of writing and of giving herself over to another state, which may also echo Theresa's fear of her overwhelming visions:

> Come panic come.
> Come close. (14)

Is the panic also about the dying Juan Gris? Stein tries to assemble and disentangle on the stage the four saints born in separate places, at separate times. To "prepare for saints" is also gradually to compose the title,

> Rejoice saints rejoin saints recommence some invite.

Finally she has it:

> Four saints an opera in three acts.

As soon as she has given the opera life by giving it a name, she sings her triumph,

> My country tis of thee. . . .

Following the earlier

> Rejoice saints rejoin saints recommence some reinvite,

the anthem becomes a hymn of praise, and Saint Theresa in Act I stands at the door of the convent (15).

Throughout *Four Saints,* she appears before Ignatius,[37] and women are more prominent than men, though Stein tries for a balance. Theresa is an essentially female personality. Ignatius, her male complement, is never as real as she and does not become a major figure until she is fully developed.[38]

Once Stein has seized Theresa and glimpsed Ignatius, saints proliferate in a humorous double chorus of twenty-one in two columns, the first, female, headed by Theresa, the second, male, by Ignatius.[39] The list of saints teases, no less serious for being hilarious,

> Anyone to tease a saint seriously. (15)

Stein has triumphed in the struggle for vision, which ends in a seriocomic procession of saints.

What has happened? The "Beginning . . . studies" are Stein's struggle for vision of the recalcitrant Spanish saints—the opera. Her struggle for creative vision runs parallel to the saints' struggle for their vision. She tries every possible means to achieve the meditative state that allows her words:

She calls forth the saints in various ways to make them appear.
She invokes Toklas as muse, lover, helper.
She tries to tell in narrative form what she is about.
She reviews the day's events to start words flowing.
She visualizes the scene—land, benches, sun, trees, pigeons.

37. In a draft of a letter to the singer Mary Garden, whom Stein hoped to interest in the title role, she said she had "written an opera on the life of St. Theresa at Avila with St. Ignatius *in the distance*" (n.d., my emphases, "Tous Que Je Sais" *carnet,* 1928?). The phrase is designed to appeal to the female lead singer, but it also accurately describes the opera.

38. In his review of *Four Saints,* Paul Rosenfeld speaks of masculine and feminine essences (*Discoveries of a Music Critic* [New York: Harcourt, Brace, 1936], 297–392).

39. The origin of many names can be surmised: Saint Ma[r]tyr, printed as it is scrawled or misspelled in the manuscript, is anglicized French—*les saints martyrs.* World War I contributes the Kaiser as a female Saint Wilhelmina and Saint Evelyn (Whitehead), with whom Stein stayed at the outbreak of the war. Saint Bernardine is less likely to recall a St. Bernard dog than Bernardin de St. Pierre, the author of *Paul et Virginie,* or the journalist Bernardine Szold.

Saint Settle, in the manuscript originally Saint Weather, suggests a seat or bench as well as settling down; settling in a house, a convent, or in the American West; financial settlements and disposition of property may also echo here. Saint Selmer may play with Elmer Harden, an American friend in Paris, and Selma Erving, the daughter of Emma Lootz, Stein's classmate in medical school. As usual, she makes names out of what is at hand.

She considers how to begin.
She commands the saints to appear.
She returns to daily life as an impetus for seeking speech.
She faces her own terror of writing—or of vision.
She attempts a narrative synopsis of the opera.
She visualizes one or two scenes—croquet, habits—in detail.
She reviews biographical organization but rejects it as useless.
She discards chronological order for presenting the saints.
She acknowledges her own entanglement.

Four times she literally calls out "saint," and at last she literally sees the saints.

Four Saints In Three Acts: The Opera Text

The "Beginning . . . Studies" form a narrative frame for the opera, which can be understood in part as Stein's own story. Inside this frame, however, the opera cannot be summarized, since it is not a story and has no more than a minimal plot. Of course, Stein's own experience informs many verbal details throughout the body of *Four Saints,* but it is not the shaping principle of the four acts as it is of the introduction. For the text is "about" St. Theresa and St. Ignatius, Avila, Barcelona, and Spain, which appear as a landscape, not as a setting for the Counter Reformation or for the institution of the Catholic Church. Stein refuses historical time and takes liberties with history, but the opera is historically and theologically informed. She developed the saints with more extensive knowledge than has been recognized.

The opera shows St. Theresa and St. Ignatius being saints, not becoming saints; there is no struggle or conflict. Being a saint precludes strong personal relationships; the saints relate as figures in their parallel and contrasting devotions rather than in personal relations. They are a part of the landscape of the opera, a series of overlaid auditory, visual, and, in the score, musical motifs that create composite portraits rather than historical narrative.[40] My observations on the saints and the composition do not constitute an authoritative line-by-line interpretation, which is neither possible nor desirable.

Act I opens like a conventional melodrama, with St. Theresa "half in doors and half out of doors" (15), the conflict about joining the order visible in her pose and in the storm at Avila. This scene rests on a historical basis—St. Theresa did not from the start feel a religious calling but underwent conversion only after a struggle between her love of the world and her love of

40. See Harry R. Garvin, "Sound and Sense in *Four Saints In Three Acts,*" *Bucknell Review* 5, no. 1 (December 1954): 2.

Christ. The resolution of the struggle is known from the start—she joins the order. The conflict is not acted out on stage but composed with opposing pairs of words, as poetry.

The first pair is "stay" with its implied opposite, "go." "If to stay" becomes "having to stay" and "to stay to cry" (15). "In" and "out" form another pair as do "face and face face about. Face to face face and face face out." Further pairs suggest private life and life in a convent, "being widowed as a young girl" and marriage to Christ; "standing" and "sitting" (16–18ff.) recall church services, authority, and submission.[41]

St. Theresa came to found reformed convents and monasteries; St. Ignatius founded the Society of Jesus. The opera is filled with "followers"—disciples, companions, sisters, visitors that "surround" saints (17, 24). They also lead to constructions based on "within" and "withdraw"—within the convent, withdraw from the order (36), withdraw for contemplation or communion with the Spirit, which takes place within.

The founding of convents and orders leads to motifs about land, settlements, houses, gardens—including planting, herbs, flowers, trees, and enclosing walls (19–20ff.). Here a building is erected with post-and-beam construction:

> Could they grow and tell it so . . . to go to see to saw to saw to build to place to come to rest to hand to beam to couple to name to rectify to do. (21)

The passages on houses and construction, a seesaw game, may recall what she learned from the construction of Michael Stein's house.

The followers lead to the innumerable phrases with "how many" (20, 22, 25, ff.). How many saints? The answer is not a count but simply "many," "all," or, as Theresa with her ready gift for conversation puts it,

> Thank you very much. (28, 29)

The famous passage beginning with "How many nails are there in it" (25) may in part have its source in Theresa's vision of Christ's words to her,

> Behold this nail. It is a sign that from today onward thou shalt be my bride.[42]

41. "Sitting" and "standing" also occur in the religious and incantatory section near the end of "Two," 141, which Stein, with her extraordinary verbal recall, may have remembered.
42. *Spiritual Relations* 35; this vision is also represented in the vault of Bernini's chapel, in a very different form from that which Theresa discusses.

God showed Theresa her right hand and pulled out a nail with flesh on it in a mystic vision of Christ's suffering, a divine gift of blood as the actuality of suffering.

Theresa's vision does not involve counting nails. What is meaningless to Stein is not counting but adding up totals, whether nails, windows or doors in houses, followers, acts in a play, all patriarchal activities with numbers substituted for what can only be understood qualitatively. How many nails—in the crucifixion, in houses, in shoes for itinerant though not for discalced nuns, in coffins, in Picasso's 1925 *Still Life with Nails,* or even how many silver studs in Paulo Picasso's cowboy outfit? How many doors, floors and windows (32–33) for new convents?[43] How many rooms in the Lord's mansion? The enumerations turn ludicrous. How many eggs—in a basket, of course (33). Friends ask awkwardly or foolishly, "How much of it is finished," "How many acts are there in it"? From the serious to the ridiculous, all the questions are part of the saints' comic vision.

St. Ignatius contrasts with and complements St. Theresa. Their very different personalities are also reflected in different forms of perception and of meditation. Theresa looks for illumination not systematically, by austere exercises such as Ignatius prescribes, but by searching for essential understanding beyond reason and logic.[44]

Asked whether she can sing, St. Theresa gives a worldly answer:

> Leave later gaily the troubadour plays his guitar. (18)[45]

43. The high cost of windows made their number a measure of the owner's wealth; as a result, the tax rate for houses in France was based on the number of windows.

44. Louis Martz sees Stein following directly in the tradition of Augustinian meditation, which apprehends the meaning of experience in sudden illumination and in a process of digressions that branches out from a center and leads to essential understanding, as in Pascal. Martz, *The Paradise Within: Studies in Vaughan, Traherne and Milton* (New Haven, Conn.: Yale University Press, 1964), 24. See also his *The Poetry of Meditation* (New Haven, Conn.: Yale University Press, 1954).

    Augustinian is unlike Ignatian meditation, which proceeds systematically, by stark and diligent application of the understanding. The exact sources of Stein's conception remain unclear, although her work on consciousness and perception at Harvard may be related, as is the thought, for example, of Santayana (interview with Virgil Thomson, 11 August 1983). What I take to be her early exposure to Buddhist thinking and meditation in California also requires investigation.

45. "Leave later" may be Stein's words suggesting Theresa's wish to delay entering the convent. By accident I discovered that "Gaily the troubadour touched his guitar" is a quotation from "Welcome Me Home," a poem by Thomas Haynes Bayly (1797–1839), which the author himself set to music.

    I assume Stein may from her youth have remembered the song, commonly included in popular collections for home use. The line from a regular, metrical work sounds quite unlike the rest of *Four Saints.* Linked with Toklas, the line was already included in "A

She responds to the question of how many saints are in it by composing the answer into a tautological, circular poem or a song. "There are as many saints as there are in it" (28). Both she and Stein like popular songs and anthems like "Gaily the troubadour" or "My country 'tis of thee" as well as rhymes, ditties, and counting games,

> One a window.
> Two a shutter.
> Three a palace.
> Four a window.
> Five an adopted son.
> Six a parlor.
>
> (22)

St. Theresa is associated with Toklas and with the private life. She gardens, dries herbs, and enjoys odd words such as "contumely." "Underskirts can be religious" appears in "A Diary" (217), surely as Toklas' handiwork for Stein—with overtones of saints. Many details about St. Theresa originate with Toklas; for example, she sees her father in a photograph, she has no sister, but she has Helen, the cook (26). Theresa appears in the early typology of personalities, where Stein identifies a St. Theresa type, represented also by George Eliot[46] and George Sand. By 1922–23, Stein developed the interest in saints in new forms, and in 1927 again.

She had from early years often called Toklas Therese,[47] an association

---

Sonatina Followed By Another," 1921 (*BTV* 12); it must have been in Stein's mind from early on.

46. See Stein's early notebooks, D-3, D-6, D-12, D-16, and others; Leon Katz, "The First Making of *The Making of Americans:* A Study Based on Gertrude Stein's Notebooks and Early Versions of Her Novel (1902–8)" (Ph.D. diss., Columbia University, 1963), 218, 277; *EA* 243. Stein recalled her early reading of George Eliot (*EA* 115, 153, 282). She had memorized Eliot's poem, "O May I Join the Choir Invisible" (*EA* 315), and the title of one college essay, "The Red Deeps," is from *The Mill on the Floss* (Richard Bridgman, *Gertrude Stein in Pieces* [New York: Oxford University Press, 1970], 24–26). Very different details, about the Cenci, also first mentioned in that essay, have already appeared in a section of "Regular" written earlier in the spring of 1927. It gives one pause to hear what may be two echoes of that essay in the two entirely different contexts. Stein surely knew the prelude to *Middlemarch,* which likens Dorothea Casaubon to St. Theresa. Could the name Dorothea have entered "A Diary," 212–13, and *LCA* 55, upon a rereading of *Middlemarch* in 1927? In the *AABT,* Stein called Theresa one of the heroines of her youth. Both lost their mothers in their fourteenth year; later Toklas, also orphaned early, added another parallel. For further details about Theresa, see Bridgman, *Gertrude Stein in Pieces,* 178.

47. As a result, the saint's name in Stein's text is not Theresa or Teresa but the English Therese. Stein rhymes it both in its English and its French form, Thérèse. For musical

powerful long beyond her interest in personality types. Once Therese was not only a name for a lover but an actual person, she gained an enlargement of scope in the new work about the saint. Behind that saint remains Toklas, but it is the saint herself, not Toklas, who here makes Stein's world of writing. By absorbing Toklas as enabler of her work and faith, St. Theresa also absorbs Stein and becomes the figure of muse, artist, and genius. The parallel remained an association powerful far beyond her interest in personality types.

St. Ignatius, on the other hand, has a sense of leadership and of expansion when he says,

> Of more which more which more. (28)[48]

Unlike St. Theresa, he is given to abstract principle. He employs elaborate Latinate rhetoric transmuted by Stein into poetic diction in what may be a definition of the Trinity or the Holy Ghost—or perhaps of the human mind:

> Foundationally marvellously aboundingly illimitably with it as a circumstance. (40)[49]

He appears with a book (25, 28), be it a volume of scholastic teaching or a grammar and rhetoric such as he used in Barcelona and Paris. Less direct than personal experience, the book recalls the *Spiritual Exercises* and the *Constitutions* for the Society of Jesus. He appears to be feared (25).

Although St. Theresa (25) responds directly and personally to daily life, she also asks questions far beyond the personal. "Can women have wishes" (18), the last sentence of the first scene of Act I and the concluding sentence of the first manuscript notebook, challenges patriarchal and perhaps Inquisitorial authority. It implies affirmative answers to questions Stein had addressed early in 1927 in "Patriarchal Poetry": Can women have wills of their own and realize them? Can women win rather than merely submitting? "Regular" also comes to mind:

> That is at one time that is what is deliberately followed by announcing that they wished to be women by deliberately announcing that they

---

reasons, Thomson, in the score, changed the English-French two-syllable name ending in an "s" sound to the short three-syllable Teresa, ending in the more singable vowel "a."

48. "More is what he was up to—more of the Church over more of the world, the greater glory of God, and then, as a military said, for 'War, or more.'

The serious question is, does one word stand the pressure of so much, maybe too much, meaning. Well, not in the English Department anywhere. To me, yes." (Donald Sutherland to Virgil Thomson, 15 August 1970, Yale Music Library).

49. See *SBW* 128; Julian Sawyer, "A Key to Four Saints in Three Acts," *New Iconograph,* fall 1947, 39.

wished to be winning by deliberately announcing that they wished to be women. (223)

In *Lucy Church,*

> Simon Therese that is to say understands inventing winning. (114; see also 36).

In the opera,

> Saint Therese can know the difference between singing and women. (23)

They sound almost the same but are far from the same. Can women create masterpieces? Saint Paul (Picasso) and Saint Fernande (Olivier), who are also among the many saints, surely show Saint Theresa's question to be Stein's own about her wishes, her accomplishments, and her capacity to create masterpieces, like Picasso. Related issues of identity reverberate in "Three Sitting Here."

St. Theresa's association with Avila is fitting and historical. St. Ignatius, on the other hand, is not associated with a city as she is, and Barcelona lacks force in the opera. He sailed from Barcelona for Italy and later began in Barcelona the rigidly disciplined schooling in Latin grammar described in his *Testament,* which Stein owned. I have already suggested that Stein may also have chosen Barcelona for its association with Picasso and Gris. Yet neither Avila nor Barcelona contributes prominent details to the opera except as ideas and words, allowing latitude for staging.

The saints' greatness, however, lies in the mystical visions whose reality both St. Theresa and St. Ignatius communicated with extraordinary power and simplicity, she in her writing and he through the testimony of followers who witnessed his ecstasy and through the foundation of the Society of Jesus.

The sense of the visions in the opera is built around various suggestions of the one and the many, of a "third" (33)—Father, Son, Holy Ghost—but also of union, of a wedding or marriage, "one in two" in its many forms, of singularity in the light of high noon (33) contrasted with plurality, of the wish "never to return to distinctions" (37). The vision appears after a series of introductory scenes early in Act III, in Barcelona. It is barely prepared for by the early "Large pigeons in small trees" (14). Here, as always, the serious borders on the ludicrous. Yet the vision also stands by itself, sudden, separate, self-contained. Although St. Ignatius sings its words, the scene does not stand out as his personal vision. Rather, it seems a composite vision of St. Ignatius, St. Theresa, and Stein.

The scene preceding the vision (36), at night and in darkness, asks questions of appearance and likeness—"resemble," "in seems"—perhaps about authenticity. It also returns to "within," with suggestions of a different order of time and of space,

> Saint Ignatius. Within it within it within it as a wedding for them in half of the time.
> Saint Ignatius. Particularly.
> Saint Ignatius. Call it a day.
> Saint Ignatius. With a wide water with within with drawn.
> Saint Ignatius. As if a fourth class. (36)

What is and what seems, appearance and reality, the visionary and the actual, are becoming one.

It is not a matter of what exactly the wide water or the fourth *is* but what they suggest: a movement into a different order, be it the fourth dimension, the fourth of St. Theresa's waters or stages of prayer, the fourth week of St. Ignatius' exercises. The final word, "class," with its long "a" sound, prepares for "grass" and "alas" in the following scene.

Why a vision? Did Stein believe in visions? The details are not sacred but entirely commonplace. Visions are possible for those who are willing to look at the ordinary. To those who are able to see, an unexceptional, still, bare landscape offers the possibility of vision that is the essence of Stein's meditation.

The scene begins in tones of a lament—the descending movement of "pigeons" followed by the heavy beats on "grass alas," prepared for by the preceding "class" (36). Stein composes this phrase into the next, making the long *I* sound the crying birds, "magpie," "sky," "cry," "try." What the ear hears and the eye sees sets the mood long before the mind tries to understand the meanings of the words.[50] The eye also, at least momentarily, moves ahead, to the final visual pattern of "Let Lucy Lily Lily Lucy" with its pitter-patter of long *U* and short, insistent *L* and *I* sounds.[51]

The vision is of a sparse, parched landscape with two common birds, the pigeon, not in flight but on the uneven, stubbly yellow grass of the Castilian plateau, and the magpie, black and flat in the sky like the bird of the annunciation. St. Ignatius attempts to say what he sees by naming the birds, but the names do not identify the vision.

50. Is there a takeoff or an echo of Wordsworth's "splendour in the grass" ("Intimations," 1:181), or do we hear, "There'll be pie in the sky when you die." While I avoid pinning anything down, of the echoes I hear, I take seriously those that Stein might have heard.

51. In *Lucy Church Amiably,* the next work, "Lucy Lily" elements appear in new ways; they are also in other Stein works.

> If they were not pigeons on the grass alas what were they. He had heard of a third and he asked about it it was a magpie in the sky. If a magpie in the sky on the sky can not cry if the pigeon in the grass alas can alas and to pass the pigeon on the grass alas and the magpie in the sky on the sky and to try and to try alas on the grass alas the pigeon on the grass the pigeon on the grass and alas. They might be very well very well very well they might be they might be very well they might be very well very well they might be. (36)

Are the two birds the same, one the mirror image of the other? Or is there another way, a third, to conceive of what he sees?

> He had heard of a third and he asked about it it was a magpie in the sky.

Whether the pigeon on the grass and the magpie in the sky are seen as opposites or as the earthly and the divine in union,[52] Ignatius is moving in a visionary dimension and approaching the Holy Ghost.

> They might be very well very well very well they might be they might be very well they might be very well very well they might be.

Be what? No complement is given for what they might be, just as no name encompasses the vision. And with that hovering, interpretive "might be," Stein breaks into the bright white light of Lucy and the Easter lilies.

Like Theresa, Stein speaks in the language of common, everyday things rather than in theological abstractions. Hers are not the large ideas but words rising from particulars. Both women use the language of daily life to lead beyond. But unlike Theresa, Stein composes coherence rather than composing in a world whose coherence is given.

After the vision of the Holy Ghost, another scene completes and absorbs the sharp vision.

> Saint Ignatius prepared to have examples of windows of curtains of hanging of shawls of windows of curtains of windows of curtains of windows of curtains of hangings of shawls of windows of hangings of curtains of windows of hangings of curtains of shawls. (36–37)

These words suggest a stage set that contrasts with the earlier landscape—the hushed, dark interior of a baroque church such as one sees in Italy or Spain, heavily hung with dark shawls and draped cloths that cover the windows, change the light, muffle the sounds, and make for the musty smell of

52. Sawyer, "A Key," 36; Garvin, "Sound and Sense," 10.

these churches, where women, dark in their gathered shawls except for their pale, bent faces, go to pray or confess.

The Holy Ghost appeared in the bright, white light of short vowels and liquid sounds under an open sky. This scene returns to the still, dark interior of the church, slow in its dactylic rhythms and heavy with consonants, where the bright and overwhelming vision may be accommodated and eased—

> Saint Ignatius and please please please please. (37)

Throughout *Four Saints,* Stein abolishes sequence but aims for concentration in every way she can. Seasons normally in succession appear simultaneously in her landscape (13) or in memory; warm snow occurs along with water (15).

> Those used to winter like winter and summer.
> Those used to summer like winter and summer. (22)

Night and day cannot be different. (34)

At high noon in bright light, time stands still as in eternity. Generations that historically follow one another appear together as a choreographed verbal tableau or ballet:

> Four saints were not born at one time although they knew each other. One of them had a birthday before the mother of the other one the father. Four saints later to be if to be one to be to be one to be. Might tingle. (14)

The last two words may convey serious anticipation or naughty fun, we cannot be sure, for in punning language the two are always close; they recall the line in another play on the edge of the serious and the ludicrous, *Saints And Singing* (1922), where "canticle" breaks into "can tickle." Stein abolishes the usual order of acts, scenes, days of the week. Yet she preserves the regular sequences of doggerel and popular song:

> One two three four five six seven all good children go to heaven some are good and some are bad one two three four five six seven. . . . (24)

She numbers scenes backward and forward, avoiding regularity. She translates her material into spatial terms and presents it as a lateral, horizontal expanse, a landscape where everything can be seen at once. Her space, both visual and verbal, is large and democratic, ample for all saints.

Stein's saints are active and make sensible plans to achieve specific ends, but they do not find fulfillment in their achievements, which do not add up to a result. Conventional plots constructed on the logic of actions have no meaning for them. The word "scene" in *Four Saints* does not refer to progressive steps in a developing action but rather to "word scene" and a "seen scene." Each such scene or episode is a moment of poetic theater, a small play, a verbal complication of the saints' reality. This inward "action" and interaction of scenes and figures constitutes the landscape of *Four Saints.*

It is easy to become serious if not sanctimonious in discussing religion and saints. Stein, however, never dreams of separating the life of the spirit from the theater of the world, just as St. Theresa abounds in humor and common sense, and refuses to abandon ordinary, lively things in her progress toward mystical union. Stein enjoys the saints and her saints enjoy themselves in scenes of pure play in the poetic drama, which includes frequent laughter.

The saints are very much in the everyday world, whose sanctity and diversity the opera celebrates in a setting where the worldly and the divine, from vaudeville to ecstasy, are indistinguishable, as is evident already in "As Fine As Melanctha" and *Saints and Singing* of 1922–23. That setting allows Stein to use a multitude of elements from popular culture and theater—circus, parades, street life, ditties, spectacle, singing games, vaudeville, and so on.[53] There is no malice or vulgarity in this secular extravagance, and Thomson well understood its musical possibilities.

After William Carlos Williams saw the 1934 production in Hartford, he commented that Stein's words did not need the music, which in fact interfered with them.[54] He understood that the musical setting, which gave Stein's words song, also swallowed the words and froze them into forms that they themselves never rigidly hold. The worldly words of the opera, which move up and down, back and forth, in steadily crisscrossing patterns, cannot be fastened to single meanings or functions in sentences gradually evolving; freed of the constraints of action, logic, and reference, they appear to move on their own.

Coda

After all the documentation, what makes *Four Saints* whole? What makes it distinctive?

Unlike most of Stein's subjects, which came to her from inside, from her own perception of experience, the Spanish saints came to her ready-made from outside, from history. They must at first have appeared both confining and overwhelming. How was she to make her own figures so firmly given by history? The account of her early interest in St. Theresa, including her

53. See also *SBW* 126, 130.

54. William Carlos Williams, "A 1 Pound Stein," *Selected Essays of William Carlos Williams* (New York: Random House, 1954), 162.

use of the saint's name for Toklas, gives a clue: the subject matter of saints absorbed her own central preoccupations.

Even though they are recognizably historical, the opera is not about history. The saints offered her both an actuality for the stage and latitude for creating in words. They ground the opera in a reality known to an audience and rein in the digressive thrust of Stein's language. To realize them, she selected from history and theology what she needed and left out what she could not use.

It was easy to make the saints contemporaneous by collapsing the years that separated them, lifting them from social, political, and church history while retaining echoes of the language historically associated with them. Abstracted from narrative history and surrounded with companions of Stein's making, they became larger figures providing an order for the opera.

What makes Stein's saints is what they are, not what they have done, which we barely hear about. Their stories explain their saintliness no more than their achievements open doors to heaven. Nor, in Stein's portrayal, is their sanctity otherworldly. She sees them in the world, not apart from the world. Stein's Theresa is not Bernini's saint, ravished and transported.

Stein's miracles and visions happen to women who suffer the patriarchal power of this world. Singing praises is singing in and of the world as poets sing. The place for the song and poetry of Stein's saints is the democratic plenitude of the same opera stage that led Whitman to sing.

Though nothing in the text directly refers to them, Stein and Toklas, in spirit though not on stage, are also a pair of saints, reverberating presences that lend reality and immediacy to the baroque figures. They do not correspond in simple one-to-one relation to St. Ignatius and St. Theresa. While the two saints absorb elements of both, Theresa especially, it is the saints, not the two women, who "are" the opera. The question of who the other two saints are is not answered by naming a second pair.

Maurice Grosser says the other two of the four saints are St. Settlement and St. Chavez.[55] Such identifications pin down meanings Stein never intended. It is not necessary to identify four saints or three acts. But it is useful to see how Stein draws on what daily life offers her by examples quoted in innumerable commentaries, such as the photographers' paraphernalia on the Boulevard Raspail that were used to transform girls into nuns (17) by placing them behind cardboard cutouts for photographs; the figures in a porcelain group in another shop window; and the sentence about Theresa's or

55. Maurice Grosser, "Scenario," *Complete Vocal Score* (New York: Music Press and Arrow Press, 1948) n.p.; reprinted in notes to Nonesuch recording, 1982.

Stein's indifference to "killing five thousand chinamen" (17, 20).[56] Such details make for verbal and theatrical variety and fun. Stein's anecdotes about them in the lectures and *Everybody's Autobiography* show her responding to requests for explanations with stories, which always please audiences hungry for what appears to explain meanings.

The saints not only absorb and enlarge Stein's and Toklas' mutual devotion but also accommodate Stein's aesthetic. Her sense of meditation and artistic discipline reverberates in the spiritual exercises and lyrical visions of the saints. Authenticity of vision was the concern of the saints as it was also the criterion of the inquisitors of the Counter Reformation who interrogated both St. Theresa and St. Ignatius.

Nothing prepares a director for this odd libretto. Its language is full of musical possibilities—rhythms, sounds, phrases, repetitions, and variations of words and phrases; counting games, puns, rhymes—but the work does not look like an opera. Direct speech, narrative lines, and stage directions are often indistinguishable, and it is frequently difficult to know who is speaking or being addressed, where one set of lines ends and the next begins, what is happening on stage or in the mind.

Looking for set lines spoken by characters in given situations results in confusion. And yet the lines, including their careful punctuation, are surely not nonsense.

> Saint Therese. To an occasion louder.
> Saint Therese coming to be selfish.
> Saint Therese allow.
> All four saints remembering not to be with them. Could all four saints not only be in brief.
> Saint Therese. Contumely.
> Saint Therese advancing. Who can be shortly in their way.
> Saint Therese having heard.
> In this way as movement. (19)

Virgil Thomson adopted the simplest, most literal procedure for the libretto. Rather than worry about dramatic parts, he read Stein's words musically and gave the discontinuous text musical continuity and a musical grammar by setting every word to music. Stein's words guided his setting of larger musical units into a unified score, including his division of St. Theresa

56. See also Bridgman, *Gertrude Stein in Pieces*, 180–82 on Stein's comment in "The Gradual Making Of The Making Of Americans," *LIA* 130–31; *EA* 89–90.

into two voices, a soprano and an alto, and the addition of the Compère and Commère.[57] The musical structure was given further dramatic structure by Maurice Grosser's scenario; once it was completed, Thomson cut and tightened the score to make it stage worthy.

Once the words are set to music, it is the music, together with the scenario, that sweeps them and the action along. Set to music, Stein's words are no longer free to move as words, for the musical setting nails the words down in the score, which gives them continuity but removes their fluidity.

The same is true of Maurice Grosser's brilliant scenario.[58] Like the score, it is an interpretation, but by no means the only one, as Grosser acknowledges. It orders the words and, by doing so, limits them and excludes alternative forms of order, and it made the performance of 1934 possible. Since then, however, most discussions and performances of the opera have relied on this scenario instead of returning to Stein's original text and the complete Thomson score. *The New Kobbé's Complete Opera Book* (1976), for example, summarizes the plot from the scenario, not from Stein's text, and fails entirely to acknowledge that the scenario is not the same as Stein's libretto. It is to Robert Wilson's credit that he returned, in his 1996 production, to the original text and the complete score.

Stein's lyrical text, of course, is almost impossible to seize in a plot summary. Yet only that text retains always the open fluidity she intended. It alone, with Thomson's music, is the authoritative raw material for the opera stage. Why have directors shied away from the original text and score to prepare a scenario? Surely there is not only one way, however brilliant, to mount the opera?

The libretto is a director's dream—or a director's nightmare. Even with Thomson's score, it is forbidding in the freedom of its composition and its movement. A director must enter the comic world of Stein's words, where the invocation of saints is a joyous activity and the discontinuous lyrical construction offers all the poetic freedom the director has courage to use.

Lucy Church Amiably

Text

By the spring of 1927, Stein had rejected chronological narrative. On April 18, while finishing "Regular" and working on the opera and "A Diary," she wrote to Thomson,

57. See Jack Beeson, "Virgil Thomson's *Aeneid*," *Parnassus: Poetry in Review* 5, no. 2 (spring–summer 1977): 461.

58. See also *SBW* 130 and n. 5.

The opera has given me lots of ideas for a novel I want to write one.

That summer, her fourth in Belley, she wrote *Lucy Church Amiably,* the lightest, most gentle of her books.[59] In it converged ideas about landscape and saintliness dramatized in the opera and about narrative explored in "Regular." I shall consider the book's design before looking at its context.

Lucy Church Amiably was

> to bring them back to an appreciation of natural beauty or the beauty of nature hills valleys fields and birds. They will say it is beautiful but will they sit in it. (47)[60]

Stein attempted in this pastoral romance to convey what it was to sit or be immersed intimately in its hills and valleys. *Lucy Church* is an extraordinary assemblage of delicate word play, a fluid landscape where nothing restricts the imagination—pansies, poplars, and peaches, marshes, gorges, oxen, goats, farmhands, threshing machines, Artemare, Césarieux, Paulet, ruins, towers.

Even as Mr. and Mrs. Mont Blanc loom high and white in the distance, Lucy Church is intimately in touch with local circumstance. The Spanish landscape of *Four Saints* appears vaguely a few times: the storm at Avila, herbs for drying, St. Theresa on a cart drawn by oxen, the vision. Much of the land is abstract or more like the Ain than Spain—the gardens with hyacinths, violets, pansies—not typical of Spain but common in Stein pieces. The Bugey, which Stein contemplated while writing *Lucy Church,* is visible.

> John Mary, finding a hill-side to be covered with vines and wheat and not very good potatoes is content that his father was not aided as his father was very much more than his mother not aided. (118)

59. *Lucy Church Amiably* was the first book printed in Stein's Plain Edition, January 1930, and references will be to this book, reissued with identical pagination by Something Else Press of Millerton, New York, in 1969.

A Lucy, not Lucy Church, already appears early in *NOTY:* "Lucy came there is that name" (84). It reappears late, in a passage probably written in England in June 1926, where Stein seems to regret having left the Bugey or France, "let us hope that she will not regret it regret having decided to give up Lucy having decided to give up Lucy" (235). There is no evidence that giving up Lucy refers to giving up or postponing a book, although the village Lucey may already have been personified.

60. Similar responses to landscape occurred on the trip to Provence in 1922–23. Janet Scudder, who was house hunting, cabled from Aix to Stein in St.-Rémy on October 21, 1923, "We have bought that landscape come and have lunch in it."

The landscape is not mere background, setting, or "scenery," nor is *Lucy Church* a naturalist's log or a travel guide. The land is immediately present, without beginning, middle, and end.

> Lucy Church heard them say that they liked continuity.
> It is more continuous to have clouds than rain snow than rain mist than rain hail than rain rain than rain. (97)

Stein never ceased to observe the weather creating new compositions with changing light, and water moving in the landscape in its many forms.

The title names the church in the village of Lucey near Belley, in Savoy, but it signifies the whole region and is personified in Lucy Church, also named Lucy Pagoda. The pyramid or onion shape of the steeple may suggest a Russian cupola or a Buddhist temple. Certainly Lucy Pagoda sounds as romantic and exotic as Lucy Church sounds English, even as it echoes French Lucey and Lucie. The adverb Amiably, Lucy's surname, also evokes *aimable,* charm, common in French but uncommon in English.

From the start, the names attract attention. Lucy is not the only figure named in the pastoral. The landscape animates a multitude of names that yet never heavily populate the book. They are not burdened by histories, origins, families, workaday lives.

> It is astonishing that unconsciously John Mary and William Mary had an origin. (146)

Stein is not interested in origins, for she has left patriarchal narrative behind.

The opening Advertisement announces three main figures, Lucy Church and her friends, John Mary and Simon Therese (7).[61] They are permanent presences but never sharply defined identities. Since they are names rather than people, they steadily combine and recombine in new ways. Simon Therese and John Mary have androgynous double first names, one male, one female. Without family names, they carry no patriarchal weight and are free to join, separate, and rejoin with other names in the pastoral.

Even when John Mary marries Mary and Mary appears momentarily as their surname (199), it is not the beginning of a family. Stein marries

61. She creates three figures, as she frequently does. However, this novel does not move toward a resolution of an unstable "three" to a stable "two," to become "one." The three are also surrounded by a large number of other figures, all mutable.

At the end of her fifth manuscript notebook (226), she wrote but then crossed out a new subtitle, "Part Three / A novel of one and two." Perhaps she was considering a resolution of "three" to conclude the book, which was already becoming "a dead horse" (240). See also "Three Sitting Here," of spring 1927, echoing in *LCA.*

names—words—rather than people.[62] The names and their relations change constantly, becoming new names, new figures, and new meanings.

The names appear to be anybody's names, neutral and ahistorical. Yet they arise from even as they do not point to people Stein knew. Lucy Church, the central name, hovers between the landscape and the figure in the landscape. She recalls Lucy Lily of the opera, but there is nothing religious about her except her capacity to embrace the beauty of the land and the origin of her name in the town and church of Lucey. Therese could be any French name but also includes St. Theresa and Toklas. Simon is the name of Stein's brother, Simon D., and of her cousin, Simon H.[63] John Mary appears to be the most neutral of ordinary names. Lucy and her friends absorb elements of both Stein and Toklas.

Beyond these three proliferate any number of others. Most of them echo friends or acquaintances, but the likenesses confirm only what is known—that Stein used the immediate and did not invent. Who these people are is not important, for the names that derive from them do not refer to them. The figures perceive and talk, but they do not act, and they relate only momentarily. In the mutable, enchanted world of *Lucy Church,* words are freed of permanent reference and figures are "named naturally" (240), changeably, never categorically. "William Mary is not William Mary exactly" (153). Of course, it is William and Mary. Stein never loses her sense of humor.

In addition, she introduces distinguished local and historical names: the gastronome Brillat-Savarin,[64] the poet Lamartine, the playwright Paul Clau-

62. In France, where names are handed down to children from both sides of a family, such combined male and female names are common. This system of naming becomes a way of giving children a history. Stein undoubtedly got the idea from French practice. "Jean-Marie," for example, is common in France; in English, however, John Mary sounds "strange" and androgynous.

63. Simon D. remained in San Francisco; mildly retarded, he was able to work under supervision and was cared for by a Mrs. Moffat, who appears in the novel (235) along with other, less direct details about him. While Stein was not close to him, they seem to have maintained a joking relationship in letters and cards.

Simon H., on the other hand, the brother of her cousin Julian, the banker in Baltimore, was important to her. He appears frequently and prominently in her early characterology and in "A Long Gay Book" (18ff.), and in 1913 she wrote "Simon," a portrait of him incorporated in *A Bouquet. Their Wills.,* the Baltimore opera of 1928. He also appears in "A Diary."

Both Simon D. and Simon H. died within three weeks in the late summer of 1913. The name also recalled Kahnweiler's Galerie Simon. Recurring names amused her and reflect her interest in names determining personalities.

64. In the late summer of 1927, one hundred years after Brillat-Savarin's death, a statue of him was erected in Belley, followed by extended festivities. To Natalie Barney, Stein

del.[65] She also speaks of Bernardin de St. Pierre's *Paul et Virginie,* the pastoral romance set in an innocent, tropical paradise. Other names, not directly associated with the Bugey or romance, are Léon Bonnat, the portrait painter, and Albert Bigelow Paine, the biographer of Mark Twain. On August 4, she wrote to Thomson that she had created "a historical background."

One name stands out: Lady Lillian Anne St. Peter Stanhope, historically Lady Hester Lucy Stanhope.[66] She connects with the region of Belley through Lamartine, who wrote of her life among the Druses, but in the novel nothing is said about her life. Though she bears a title and a family name, which add weight and formality to the book, she is here as she lived in the East—a prophetess, famous but withdrawn. The range of names in *Lucy Church* is enormously inventive, from the light touch of local fairy-tale figures like John Mary to the splendor of solitary Lady Stanhope.

What do they do? They get up, sit down, walk around (139), and talk. Stein worked at getting "the habit of conversation," as she wrote to Thomson on July 2, 1927.

---

wrote, "We are putting up a statue which is a bust but we that is Belley are very pleased . . ." (16 August 1927, Bibliothêque Jacques Doucet). *Le Bugiste,* the publication of the Société scientifique historique et littéraire (21 [1927]: 314–20), reported in detail on the inauguration, the parade, fireworks, and banquet on September 11.

In *LCA,* visual and auditory puns and rhymes on Savarin and Lamartine lead to St. Séverin or Severine, from Severini, the futurist (21, 29). Not only local but verbal associations lead from name to name.

65. Paul and "Minnie" (pseud.) Claudel appear in the early notebooks and in "A Long Gay Book" (32, 34), but only in Belley did she meet Claudel, who lived nearby in Béon. See Paul Claudel, *Journal II: 1933–1955* (Paris: Gallimard, 1969), 142–43, 283, 341 for his relationship to the Baroness Pierlot, the d'Aiguys, and other Stein friends.

66. The eldest daughter of the Earl of Chesterfield, she had kept house for Sir William Pitt, the prime minister, and after his death left England to live as a solitary prophetess among the Druses in Lebanon. Her story, another romance of removal from the corrupt city and court to a primitive society, is told in memoirs by her physician, Charles Lewis Meryon (1845, 1846). The engraver Charles Meryon, one of whose works Stein owned, was the illegitimate son of Dr. Meryon and Narcisse Chaspoux, a dancer at the Paris Opéra.

Lamartine visited her and wrote one of the first accounts of her in *Voyages en Orient* (1835). Stein changes her first names to "Lilian Anne" or "Lilian St. Peter," perhaps to tease Toklas about her attachment to Lilyana (Lily Anne Elizabeth) Hansen, an early friend in San Francisco (180–91). She spells the name, which has two "l" 's, with one, perhaps to play with "Lily Anne."

The addition of "St. Peter" to Lady Stanhope's name is humorous in English as it is not in French, where St. Pierre is a common last name. It refers not only to Bernardin de St. Pierre but also to M. Amand Saint-Pierre, the *notaire* in Belley, who negotiated the lease on the house in Bilignin that was already a part of the landscape of *LCA,* though Stein did not take possession until 1929. See *LCA* 130, 209–19; *EA* 26; *Alice B. Toklas Cookbook,* 95.

> In conversation it was not known what happened to them. In a recitation it was not known what happened to them. In a description it was not known what happened to them. (52)

Already near the end of "Regular," Stein had considered the difference between narrative, description, and conversation.

In Belley, she listened to local speech and expression and became known for her sharp sense of local cadences and forms of exchange. The novel is full of listening. Starting with greetings,[67] conversation, not its subject matter, is continuous in daily life. Always her conversation is composed and shaped as a formal, civilized activity with gestures "[h]aving bowed her to a seat" (9). She never offsets it with intrusive quotation marks, and often description and direct speech are indistinguishable. The spoken words are woven into the center of the novel's life.

Lucy Church opens with two figures and two chairs.

> There were as many chairs there and there were two a chair that can be found everywhere a rocking chair that is to say a rocking chair can be found everywhere. Two there one at one end and the other at the other end. They were in front of the building and in sitting and rocking there was a slight declivity in front of the building. (9)

The declivity induces rocking, and conversation accompanies sitting and rocking in the pastoral setting. Conversation is a religious rite that begins with chairs (69–70) and can be seen as well as heard (28). In a charming report on Stein in the country, published after her death but based on talks with her, Suzanne Tenand commented,

> *Une conversation à gauche et à droite. Il n'y a pas de doute là-dessus, ça se démontre très souvent . . . assis dans une chaise, chacun sur une chaise. . . .*[68]

67. "Conversation can be how do you do. Very well I thank you" (46). In "Finally George," conversation is characterized as "greeting" (*HTW* 279). Remember also "An Elucidation":

    May we seat.
    May we be having a seat.
    May we be seated. . . .
    (*R* 431)

68. Conversation to the left and to the right. No doubt about it, it happens all the time . . . sitting in a chair, each on a chair . . . .

    Suzanne Tenand, "Gertrude Stein: Ecrivain de Chez Nous," *Visages de l'Ain* no. 26, April–May 1954. Georgiana King illustrated Stein's capacity to create patterns of words with a paragraph from *The Wings of the Dove* and commented on modern dialogue, where sen-

She was beginning to study grammar, and, given the poems Thomson had already set to music and the opera she was creating with him, musical as well as verbal forms were on her mind. The little grammatical exercise about "ready" and "ready's brother," like a formula in a parlor game or a voice in a fugue, had already appeared in 1923 and returned many times, pointing the way to "Finally George. A Vocabulary Of Thinking," "Arthur A Grammar," and "Sentences."

Her preoccupation with romance enters here. The advertisement for *Lucy Church* characterizes the novel as "a book of romantic nature," Stein's attempt at writing romance in the hope of understanding it.[73] In a section crossed out in the draft and not retained in the final version, she considered the romance of America's great men—Grant, Lincoln, Ford—"spending most of their time in failing although we think of ourselves as having succeeded," a topic to which she returns in 1934 in *Four In America.* The sudden change of pronoun from "they" to "we" shows Stein including herself among the apparent failures who are actually successes. And indeed, early in the novel, she develops the same idea when she speaks of genius "treated with consideration" by family while the genius is a failure but, once successful, "treated like anybody" (10).

She is speaking about herself, although she says that the idea about unappreciated genius came from Picasso.[74] Success stories are by their very nature American romances. The wish for recognition was one of Stein's most painful personal problems, especially in contrast with the successful Picasso. Only when she stood back from this obsessive preoccupation connected with her sense of identity, her name, her family, was she able to compose freely and successfully as an artist.[75]

---

way relying on Stein's note, described her work, "Le Contrepoint poétique de Gertrude Stein," *Échanges* 3 (June 1930): 122–28. Translated into English by Stein and Toklas, it remains unpublished at YCAL.

73. In one of the *carnets,* she drafted not only sections of the romance but also the advertisement for *UK,* the collection of American pieces she was preparing that summer for publication by Joseph Brewer's firm, Payson and Clarke, Ltd.

74. Stein, *Picasso,* 27.

75. In the advertisement for *UK,* she also describes the romance of American goods, "the cheapest things . . . made of the best materials," an idea attributed to Elie Lascaux, the painter (*EA* 232). She had in mind the "romance" of mass production, which made reasonably priced goods available to all.

    She attempted to phrase the idea effectively but ended up with a naive exaggeration. She may also have been thinking of the "romance" of modernism as essentially American and of modern art as made of simple elements accessible to all and popular, as she always considered her writing.

    On September 16, Joseph Brewer visited Stein in Belley. Already at this meeting,

In the introduction, John Mary, Lamartine, Brillat-Savarin, and Claudel appear momentarily, but there is no direction in the use of names. In the novel proper, however, Stein's three ways of using names guide the construction: the triad of Lucy Church, Simon Therese, and John Mary, the innumerable changing names of acquaintances in various combinations, and the names of actual figures from history.

It is a very supple method, which offers flexibility and variety while giving the book sufficient consistency. In addition, disembodied, lyrical voices—not personalities—move freely about the landscape in conversation and description. Not tied to events or character, these "bits of information and tender feeling" (171), including details about local families, live in pastoral continuity.

And yet, not only the introduction but even the novel itself shifts here and there from shapely, disembodied conversation in the pastoral scene to the personal voice of Stein. In the introduction she sometimes complains loudly and personally. In the novel itself, personality obtrudes less in a sharp tone than in personal references that, insufficiently absorbed into the novel, ask to be identified.

But when she speaks in the voice of words rather than her own, she composes not only the many figures named but also herself and Toklas into the landscape. "They might buy a house" (184) and themselves become part of the pastoral. They might become a family, visible and grounded in the country, where land and houses identify families. By freeing the landscape and the language of time, *Lucy Church* recreates in the Bugey the romance of names paired and paired again in Arcadia, Eden, or Arden.

Stein, always alert to book prospects, suggested that he publish *LCA*. After *UK* proved a financial failure, however, Brewer's partners at Payson and Clarke persuaded him not to risk another Stein book.

It is to be a study of how to say.

—"Finally George" 366

Hesitation destroys grammar.

—"Arthur A Grammar" 92

5. 1928

"Finally George A Vocabulary Of Thinking"

"Finally George A Vocabulary Of Thinking" (*HTW* 271–382)

Starkly compacted, the printed pages of this very abstract piece often look relentlessly gray. Many are composed of long, Latinate words with no color or edge, in sentences or paragraphs sometimes a page or more long, without commas and periods. Three pages show almost no breaks until a single, short sentence:

> Bright colors are desirable. (329)

Offset as a one-line paragraph, it stands out visually. It is followed by two and one-half unrelieved pages of a single, almost entirely abstract sentence, heavy with pronouns that name no subjects—"they," "it," "their"—with linking verbs that connect but do not act—"is," "should be," "come," "made"—and with prepositional phrases that place in relation what is never named outright. Later sections look entirely different and require different reading. There is no single unifying method; it evolves gradually by her steps in trying out how she can move her words. For the eye, it is slow and taxing reading, which too easily deteriorates into mindless movement across lines and pages. And yet, for the ear, when read aloud, it flows smoothly and naturally. Stein's phrases and sentences move fluently from word to word and phrase to phrase.

But with "Finally George," Stein will take up the challenge of those who accused her of writing sound and sight but no sense. In January 1928, she wrote to Harry Phelan Gibb, describing it as

> a new conception of prose . . . I am getting rid of sight and sound as well as sense and I always did love the essence. . . .

She will begin to explore the essence of words.

> Sound sight and sense around sound by sight with sense around by with sound sight and sense will they apologize truthfully. (301)[1]

Anyone who knows her 1934 *Lectures In America* recognizes here a central issue in "Portraits And Repetition": the capacity of genius to talk, listen, and look, all three in one. Or, as she also says,

> Writing may be made between the ear and the eye and the ear and the eye the eye will be well and the ear will be well. (277)

This is the insight that moved her away entirely from representation and made her concentrate, in her portraits, on the quality and the internal movement of the words,

> not to let the looking be predominating but to have the listening and talking be predominating but to once more denude all this of anything in order to get back to the essence of the thing contained within itself. (*LIA* 199)

By the time she wrote this lecture, in the summer of 1934, she had reviewed how, in St.-Rémy in 1922–23, she had come to rely excessively on sound and melody:

> I was for a little while very much taken with the beauty of sounds as they came from me as I made them. (196)

Finding herself drunk with their beauty, she recognized that melody should not be an end but a by-product (198–201).

Thought is composed by moving words from vocabulary into grammatical relations, and Stein concludes "Finally George" by announcing her next step: "Arthur A Grammar."

> The next is more vocabulary and some grammar or more grammar or more grammar. Arthurs or more grammar after Finally George a Vocabulary. (382)

1. The phrase "sound sight and sense" in these two passages suggests that they were written at about the same time.

This sense of direction, however, is not a plan or design. In the context of her preoccupations from 1927 to 1928, with "Finally George"[2] she will be finding and defining new ways of writing.

The odd title refuses to give away anything. "Finally" as the first word seems incongruous and quite unlike Stein, who was interested in possibility and change rather than certainty and finality. She acknowledges,

> If a man has been at all theirs to be known as finally it is more than they like. (273)

"Finally" sounds quite dead. As she says,

> Probable probably is the most that they can say. (273)

But who knows, "finally" may translate *enfin,* "well then," "oh well," an informal opening or conclusion followed by *George* as vocative or as object. As usual, her phrasing allows several readings though "vocabulary" remains what she explores.

She begins casually by considering names, as if for characters in a narrative, and quickly decides what she wants:

> A plain girl let it be Susan. Finally George. (273)

Yet it does not become a narrative about Susan and George but a disquisition on the name George and people named George. The preoccupation with names in their many forms and uses, of which this is the first concentrated example, will become a major element in her work.

> George is a very full and resounding name and has been given where it is suitable but it must always be given first it must always be given first. (275)

She produces a procession of Georges, or a portrait of George. What is a George?

2. "Finally George" was apparently begun in the late autumn of 1927 and finished in the spring of 1928. Well into the text appears Christmas (320, 324) and near the end Easter (371).

At the conclusion appears Cary Ross, a young American who arrived in Paris for two months in the spring of 1928 with an introduction from Claribel Cone and an interest in art and poetry (some of his poems appeared in *transition,* March 1928). Alfred Barr was apparently introduced to Stein by Ross, who later worked at the Museum of Modern Art.

The subtitle, "A Vocabulary Of Thinking," may have been added after Stein, near the end, wonders about the difference between vocabulary and thought (379). It looks as if it was entered in the manuscript later than the title.

A name if she asked why is it not known as something if she asked why is it not known as something then they do not like to like to have to be meaning to be not more than an excuse. (289)

Are first names matters of fact and identity or mere matters of convention that can be changed?

Frank could be called George if one were used to it but one is not. (286)

Mary could be a color. Stella could be a color. Alexandra could be a color. Katherine could be a color. Pauline could be a color. (317)

To Stein, first names have great solidity apart from meaning.

Why George? Who is George? In any dictionary, "George" shows the possibilities for verbal adventure, as in "By George." Many Georges appear, some identifiable, some not, and some with invented names. George as a given name (275) can also become a feminine Georgiana (334). It is also a family name, as in Lloyd George or Henry George, perhaps echoed in George Henry (334), or a place name, Georges Bay (273). In the background, of course, is King George and "Georgian," as well as *Georgian Stories,* published in 1926, which included "The Fifteenth Of November," Stein's portrait of T. S. Eliot.

Beginning with a person named "George," Stein moves to the idea of a George and looks for the common denominator in the typical George. To her, people become increasingly the personalities suggested by their names. She speaks of Georges, Marcels, Pauls, whose names identify them as types.[3] All Georges, in the end, may be finally one.

The Georges whom I have known have been pleasant not uninteresting and finally one and finally more often very well estimated as succeeding intelligibly and not more than is necessary as presidents are useful. (289)[4]

3. A mere glance at H. L. Mencken's chapter on "Proper names in America" in *The American Language,* 4th enl. and rev. ed. (New York: Knopf, 1936) suggests how American is Stein's awareness of names. The date of the first edition, 1919, confirms the growing interest in matters American and an American literature free of the English tradition.
4. Stein's study of personality types is recorded in her early notebooks for *MOA.* She is also thinking about Georges in ways that return later, in "Scenery And George Washington A Novel Or A Play" (1931), incorporated in the George Washington section of *FIA* (1934).

George.
What a name is George.
What an average is George.
What a land is George.
(201)

She plays with the plural possibilities of George after looking at the French name *Georges,* which ends with *-s* in the singular (279). The question of how to write George or Georges leads to new ways to put them in relation. In "George," she looks first at particular Georges, then at the idea of George, at other names and other words, listening to them, mouthing them, touching them, exploring ways to say them and join them.

> When they say two do they write two. Do they. (276)

Playfully she connects the French Georges with a series of "equivalent" names with *-s,* "Allans Pauls Christians and Virgils" (279). Then the list follows a different pattern and adds Williams, Franks, Michaels, James (289). The phrase "united in resemblance and acquaintance" describes them as it also describes her word play and punning, which joins words "between the eye and the ear."

In such details, she uses hackneyed idiomatic phrases—associative language—literally and descriptively to question what they mean and how they can be used. Always she moves literally and physically from word to word rather than from idea to idea, from one idiomatic phrase or metaphor to another.[5] Often her literalism produces funny results, as in "there is the combination of time and again they are always very uneasy" (315) or "an amount of many cases of once in a while" (318).

She practices writing by exploring what words are, what they can do, how they can mean. Here are some illustrations of her experiments with physical features of words. One paragraph builds on alliterative *W* and *WH* words, together with rhymes and half rhymes, from "whether" to "whither" to "will" to "endeavor," "when," "win," "kin" (318). Two long paragraphs explore and differentiate "more than," "much," and "as much as," "most," "next" (307, 309). She constructs with "in" phrases—"in need," "in fear," "in chagrin," "in case" (320)—whose similarities reveal their differences.

She explores prefixes (324). One paragraph opens with words beginning with a, b, a, b, c, but eventually settles for a lengthy section of *a*-words, followed later by short sections of *b*- and *c*-words (345, 347), a project impatiently abandoned once she discovers how to work with it.

Another section proceeds mostly in rhythmic three-word groups, often prepositional phrases,

5. The few metaphorical expressions here sound odd and quite unlike Stein's usual writing. Most of them turn out to be quotations, such as Longfellow's "They left footsteps in the sands of time" (331; "A Psalm of Life") or Scott's "Come one come all this rock shall fly from its firm base as soon as I" (316, 366; "The Lady of the Lake," canto 5, stanza 10).

That is by the way so to speak do they hear let it be what they have as they need all alike for the place in the sense not at home on account of the flower which is replacing ahead of time callously in a hurry of needing a little moving just like in and out in went reminding parsimonious with a state of at her boy touch it a little way more than ever presumably. (365)

She uses the familiar devices of English poetry with such freedom and concentration that they become unfamiliar.

What distinguishes her punning, however, is that she never feels bound by the word as physical unit, by its meaning or its normal grammatical function. Instead, she freely breaks words into pieces that make new words or joins them in the most unlikely combinations, in examples such as these, lifted from sentences which further complicate them:

Porter all ought or (368)

nestle with nettled (368)

a sample of a tumble (369)

white avoid whatever water (370)

justify just if Kate (373)

canary cannery (379)

in an end blame emblem (375)

She plays with the French word *repasser,* to iron,

As repassing this is open to ironing which is not at all why they have shutters made of wood and iron. (348)

Some passages are takeoffs or pastiches—"past dish" (367)—of legal and administrative language. Bits of talk recall her comments on conversation in *Lucy Church Amiably* a few months earlier, and her 1923 "Studies In Conversation," which was no doubt selected for publication in the September 1927 issue of *transition* (276, 346, 348) because the problem was in her mind.

"George" produces some wonderful flashes. Here is a warning to letter writers:

Never remember that a letter can be read that another can read that whether there is whether regret aigrette which they do not know is the name. (360)

Or the many ironic readings possible for being far apart even when living with parents—unless it is the illusion of being free by living at a distance from parents and family, another topic on her mind:

> It is very curious that they have all the addresses so far apart where they live with their parents. (370)

What a book of Georges! Early in her fourth manuscript *cahier,* she speaks of "four books of four Georges" (320), drawing in resonances of Thackeray's *The Four Georges.* By 1931, outdoing Thackeray and herself, she writes a play on *The Five Georges,* which includes a King George. The year before, in *They Weighed Weighed-Layed,* she had used many Maurices, Marcels, Eugenes, Leons, and others, identified as I, II, III, IV, V, and so on.

"George" is a work of astonishing but often frustrating diversity, only lightly held together by play with the name. It often sounds like Georges romping with great freedom of assembly, joining by similarity and difference, by friendship and interest, work and play, alliteration and assonance, rhythm and rhyme. In a loose sequence Stein writes into her piece the Georges she knows, each a small, self-contained composition. "George" has no center in subject matter, for it relies on words, not references, nor on narrative, plot, or character, which rigidify structure.

She always looks for the particular.

> If any one dreams of the ocean they will dream of little waves. (363)

The particular is discontinuous.

> To explain non continuity by experience makes it be very much because the have it as the rest of the exchange to the pursuit of banality which is a pleasure a pleasure is a treasure trove a treasure trove is when she knocks sooner she does not knock she calls. (296)

The pleasures of experience—here presumably sexual—lie not in orderly systems or general ideas but in the call of the ordinary. Continuity is imposed upon experience. Yet as one reads and rereads this odd compilation, there gradually emerges a thematic coherence less obvious than the verbal diversity but just as astonishing.

That coherence also can be approached through George. While the composition of first names is free, the composition of last names—family names—is not free but given. It follows rules. The family represents the principle of rule-bound, hierarchical structure. The many decentered Georges are free of family rules, as friends are free of family strictures. Within families, however, movement is regulated and words are connected by the prescriptions of family grammar.

From friendship and memory, by sound and by sight (277), from life and from books, she dredges up Georges, who "can be united in resemblance and acquaintance" (289).

Among them are the painter Georges Braque (273, 278),[6] the playwright George Middleton (302), Kitchener's secretary, George Arthur (302), George Banks (277–79) from *The Making Of Americans* (531).[7] Finally "George Washington on horseback" (278), echoing, as Stein surely knew, Saint George, of whom John Lyly in *Eupheues*[8] says that he "is ever on horseback yet never rideth," an iconized phrase by Benjamin Franklin near the end of his autobiography about a writer who, like St. George on the signs, always works but never produces.[9] Still others may be actual or merely possible people, as for example George Pleace, George Leroy (302), that Stein creates, giving them friends and coupling them in all sorts of ways.

George is not arbitrarily chosen. As usual, she relied on immediate experience, not invention. By 1927, she had become friends with a group of young artists that included several Georges—Georges Hugnet, Georges Maratier, and George Platt Lynes.[10]

Most important of the three was Georges Hugnet, the young French poet Virgil Thomson had introduced to her early that year. Near the beginning appears a tiny, teasing sketch of Hugnet that parodies the usual biographical summary.

> George was born and his name call him Edgar. He was twenty-two when it was known that it was indefinite. As a little boy very little and playing there surrounded with them made it that it was kept. He knew left to right and trees and shields and a Jesuit father. They were all taught

6. Braque also appears in the portrait of Jane Heap.
7. Interestingly, the far more important George Dehning does not appear, perhaps because she did not wish, in a highly abstract and largely defamiliarized work, to refer to major characters from her own novel.
8. John Lyly, *Eupheues* (1580), ii, 260.
9. Benjamin Franklin, *The Autobiography of Benjamin Franklin* (New York: Modern Library, 1950), 181.
10. Nor was she alone in her awareness of Georges. On December 1, 1927, Bravig Imbs wrote from New York that he had met George Lynes, "that mass of beauty," and seemed to have a predilection for "persons named George, being intimate with at least five." Another that Stein met was George Antheil.

to be left to them when they were standing. This is what is made of it sufficiently. (274)

Georges Marie Jules (not Edgar) Hugnet, born July 11, 1906, was twenty-two late in 1927 when this passage was written. He was raised by restrictive parents who separated when he was fourteen. Destined for the church, he was dismissed from the Jesuit Collège St.-Louis de Gonzague, still now near the Trocadéro in Paris, for playing a fox-trot during religious service. Breton on his mother's side, he then completed his education in St. Malo, where he had already spent summers.[11] The question of who he is appears often in "George" and again in "Arthur A Grammar," and her portrait, "George Hugnet," of the summer of 1928.

The second George was Georges Maratier, or Georges II. After Hugnet, he was second in command, perhaps with an investment, of Hugnet's Editions de la Montagne.[12] George Platt Lynes, the young American poet, publisher, and bookseller, who by 1931 became a brilliant photographer, was the third. In Paris from April 1925 on to complete his preparatory school Latin, he first called upon Stein in December 1925 and in 1926 published her *Descriptions Of Literature.* By 1927, he resigned after his freshman semester at Yale and visited Europe again. He returned frequently but did not settle in Paris for longer periods.

These three Georges belonged to a loosely associated group of artist friends who supported each other and enjoyed Stein's friendship and interest. Many of them appear in "George," and all in a sense are Georges.

Her young American friends included Virgil Thomson, the pianist Allen Tanner, the writers Bravig Imbs and Elliot Paul, and the painter, writer, and jazz pianist Eugene MacCown.[13] Others were the Scottish poet Archibald Craig, the Russian painters Pavel Tchelitchew and Eugene and Leonide Berman, the Dutch painter Kristians Tonny, the Belgian writer and filmmaker

11. This information, received from Mme. Myrtille Hugnet and Mme. Germaine Hugnet in interviews, April–May 1982, spells out some of the facts behind the quoted paragraph. The phrase "left to right" returns in January 1931 in Stein's "Left To Right," on the quarrel that ended her friendship with Hugnet late in 1930.

12. He appears in Stein's work later than Hugnet, in the portrait "George Maratier" (1929) and perhaps in echoes behind the novelette "Brim Beauvais" (1930). After Stein and Hugnet became estranged, Maratier remained a friend, became an art dealer, and advised Stein and Toklas into late years about sales and purchases of paintings, exhibits, and personal matters.

13. The portrait, "To Virgil And Eugene," of early 1928 (*PL* 311), about Thomson and MacCown, both from Missouri and both musicians, is built on the colloquial phrase, "I'm from Missouri show me" and displays their unconventional natures with the most regular rhythmic counting, "One two three four five six seven all good children go to heaven." See also "Arthur A Grammar," 69.

Eric de Hauleville, and the Swiss writer and musicologist Charles-Albert Cingria. French friends included Bernard Faÿ, then professor of American history at the University of Clermont-Ferrand; Christian Bérard, the painter and stage designer; René Crevel, the novelist; and Pierre de Massot, the critic.

They offered Stein not only the admiration of followers a full generation younger than herself but also the stimulus of their interests in music, performance, stage design, film, and history. Those who did not know English well enough to read her work required translations and, perhaps more important, led Stein to think about the structure of language, the difficulty of learning a language, the problem of rendering meaning, vocabulary, idiom, translation.[14]

Portraiture was in the air. Learning from Stein, Virgil Thomson produced his first concentrated musical portraits, and Hugnet's press often used portraits as illustrations—something new to Stein, who had always preferred plain and cheap rather than illustrated, limited editions for her work. But to be taken seriously as a writer and be published in French by a gifted young poet would come to matter more than any reservations she may have had.

Correspondence and journal articles give testimony to this network of mutual support. Elliot Paul wrote about her in the *Paris Herald* and, as associate editor of *transition,* saw to it that her work regularly appeared there. Emulating Stein, he wrote perceptive essays on Picasso and Gris and would write a series of pioneering studies of her in the *Herald* that year.[15]

Bravig Imbs, the young Midwestern poet who worked for the Paris edition of the *New York Times,* introduced Stein and the wealthy Edward Titus,

14. Translation is a theme in "George," in the English-French word play, in references to dictionaries (381), and probably in "fabrication" (351, 357, 363), which may point to Hugnet's translations from *MOA, Morceaux Choisis de la fabrication des Américains* (1929). The "vocabulary" or "dictionary" she prepares for Georges Hugnet, who knew almost no English, rests on her interest in the literal qualities of words rather than their meanings as signifiers that dictionaries ordinarily address.

> George did see eye to eye and did hear ear to ear. (277)

Stein wanted translation to follow her word order and to render not only sense but sight, sound, and especially rhythm, or what she called movement.

She is often said to write for the eye rather than the ear, but nothing could be further from the truth. Any writer who relies on punning works with both ear and eye. Most of her puns are both visual and auditory, homonyms and homophones, and are not limited to English. See also "Transatlantic Interview" (1946), "The Gradual Making Of The Making Of Americans," and "Portraits And Repetition" (*LIA* 1934).

15. "From A Littérateur's Notebook," *Chicago Tribune* (Paris), 15, 22, and 29 May 1927. "A Master of Plastic Relations," *transition* no. 2 (July 1927); "The World of Pablo Picasso," *transition* no. 13 (summer 1928): 139–41.

who became interested in publishing *A Novel Of Thank You*, though they ended up quarreling. Stein, in turn, reviewed Imbs' translation of Bernard Faÿ's 1929 biography of Benjamin Franklin.[16]

The difference between these young artists and the painters who were Stein's friends before World War I—Matisse, Picasso, and the others of whom she wrote early portraits—was not simply that the younger men were not "geniuses" and began no revolution in art. Nothing ever compared with her friendship with Picasso in the years when both were defining themselves as artists. Between those years and the 1920s, Picasso had become successful, but Stein had faced bitter difficulties. The art of Picasso retained stronger traces of representation than the art of Stein, which offended readers and left her open to ridicule, especially as a woman. She was better known as an art collector than as a serious writer. The young group flattered her, acknowledged her importance, helped her into print, and eventually followed their own paths.

She announces that she will "study connection." The occasion for this study seems to be a painting originally chosen or bought by her brother. Gertrude and Leo separated permanently in 1913 and had divided the paintings by 1914. The sixth *cahier* of "George" ends with

> How can it be made to have no identity with having half. Separate. It does not but pearls. Just like that. (365)

The seventh *cahier* continues directly,

> There is no connection in a separation. Connection separation. (365)

The connected statement implies that a negative connection remains. She tries to separate the painting or paintings from her brother and from the history of acquisition.

> Indifferent to whether to recognize a brother's choice in a picture. (365)[17]

She continues ironically,

16. Six months after Stein had lectured at Cambridge, Geoffrey Gorer, upon her suggestion, invited René Crevel to speak there. Stein invited Crevel to translate *Three Lives;* however, ill with tuberculosis, he was unable to complete the project. In January 1930 Bernard Faÿ, with the help of his student Grace-Ives de Longevialle, translated "Melanctha."
17. The passage, about aesthetic judgment, may be about a particular painting. One wonders whether it is provoked by their first Picasso purchase, *Young Girl with a Basket of Flowers* (1905), about which they had initially disagreed. See also elsewhere, "did he or did he not give it in the moment of division . . ." (319). "George" includes many references to light and paintings (329, 332, 341).

> Study connection. A study connection. How splendid. Nobody eats pearls. Smiling. Nobody eats heats does arose piles of dates which are freezing in the summer able to state it. No combustible hours.

And she concludes,

> How do you feel. About it. This way that there is no connection. Between it and just why just in as an ending that there is a fix to be sent to leave or be sent. Say well. Well. (366)

Her brother also raises the issue of inseparable family connection.

Throughout "George," the family recurs as an institution of firm and rigid ties (311, 312, 322). "It is thicker than water," she says, and we know instantly that "it" is blood. As usual, the metaphor is not Stein's but is that of the proverb, which Stein immediately questions and ridicules,

> It is thicker than water milk is not thicker than water tea is a different color and can be golden or yellow brown or brown and fresher than ever which is why they are possibly ready to put it in place of black. (311)

She had already begun to study the family in "Patriarchal Poetry" and in "Regular Regularly In Narrative." In "George," the full context of the many thematic hints of the family remains largely submerged, but patterns of preoccupation gradually take shape.

The forms of family continuity, discussed already in the chapter on "Regular Regularly In Narrative," must be briefly recalled. Families are perpetuated by marriages. Marriages require houses, which make parenthood and children possible. Houses involve deeds and other forms of legal security for the protection of the family. Houses, spouses, and children need the assurance of family continuity, necessarily involving lawyers and wills. This cluster of ideas connects with the events of 1927–28 in Stein's private life, forming a thematic context.

Families begin with weddings (356, 363, 367). In Baltimore, a family wedding took place on January 19, 1928, when Alice Frank, the daughter by her first marriage of Rose Ellen Stein, now the wife of Stein's cousin Julian Stein, married Henry Hartman Hecht of San Francisco.[18] Another wedding took

18. Stein was fond of her cousin Julian, who managed her investments, and she had after the marriage become friends with Rose Ellen, who was interested in her work, wanted her to lecture in America, and received Stein protégés such as Bravig Imbs.

Stein knew that as a result of the second marriage, Rose Ellen and Julian had had to make sure that Alice and Ellen Frank, the two daughters of Rose Ellen's first marriage, were properly protected in relation to their new half-brother, Julian Jr.

From May 25, 1925 on, Rose Ellen spent six months in Europe with Julian Jr., her

place in Paris on March 28, 1928, when Elliot Paul married Camille Haynes. On April 14, Stein gave a large party for them.

She includes many details about houses (e.g., 328, 331, 338, 370, 377–78), which preoccupied Stein. Her brother Michael's Corbusier house in Garches, discussed with "Patriarchal Poetry," was built between April 1927 and March 1928. Also in 1927–28, Janet Scudder suggested that Stein build a house on a part of her property in Paris that she wanted to sell to a congenial friend. Stein did not, in the end, take the offer, but the question, raised in many letters, must have been seriously considered.

Meanwhile, Michael Stein had suggested, in view of the rising cost of living, that rather than a country house as far away as Belley, his sister consider a house near Paris, perhaps in Garches, where she might move permanently if life in Paris became too expensive. Perhaps she did not wish to be so near to family, friends, or Paris, for she and Toklas valued privacy and independence and were interested in the community and the landscape they had discovered near Belley. By 1928, her lawyer was negotiating for a lease on the house in Bilignin that she finally obtained early in 1929.

Houses bring with them a language of their own, used in legal documents, contracts, deeds, wills (323, 349–50, 371). At this time, Toklas had difficulties with ranchland inherited from her grandfather in Stockton, California, that she co-owned with her brother Clarence. Letters from Albert Rosenshine, a lawyer and the brother of Annette Rosenshine, show that Clarence was indebted, there was a danger of foreclosure, and Toklas, who held a mortgage, needed protection. Legal problems appear often in "George."

> Houses should never be known at home. This is why they must be very careful to have it do. Our Mr. Goodfellow this is the name of Nellie[Jacot]'s lawyer at least she thought he was her lawyer but as it turns out he is Albert and Sidney[Jacot]'s lawyer not Ada Ada has no lawyer she is to have a lawyer. They are partly to blame. So deeply does she feel her distress she cannot but breathe out her bitterness. (312–13)

Nellie and Ada Joseph, friends of Toklas from her youth in San Francisco, were both married and lived in France. Ada, the wife of Harry Brackett, a dissolute and sick man, had reason to sigh in distress. Their brother Sidney Joseph was a ne'er-do-well and a womanizer. Nellie's lawyer, Stein suggests, may turn out to work for her opponents. Houses no doubt also reminded

husband joining them during his vacation. Wills were undoubtedly discussed. See also *Their Wills. A Bouquet.*, which pivots on the wills of Rose Ellen and Julian.

Stein of her efforts to secure for the impoverished Mildred Aldrich the house in Huiry from which she had watched the battle of the Marne described in *A Hilltop on the Marne.* On February 19, 1928, Mildred Aldrich died.[19]

The prospect of a house, whether rented or purchased, involved rights of occupancy and property and forced Stein and Toklas to consider the legal status of their relationship and possibly their status as foreigners. They already knew that special care was required to protect a partner who did not qualify as a spouse. Wills occur not only in "George" (322, 323, 325, 365, 371) but return almost obsessively for some eighteen months, from "Patriarchal Poetry" in 1927 to *A Bouquet. Their Wills.* of the summer of 1928.

"It is useless to be a mother" (378), she says, perhaps about Allan Stein's son Danny, who, at six months, is beginning to become a part of the family (382). For "a little while Danny" (378) can be a grammarless child, but soon he must learn to behave in accordance with family grammar. He is already becoming "a very increased produce a prosody" (382) who has baby fun with the sounds of words. He bears the name of Stein's father, which is also the second name of each of her three brothers and of his father Allan, as well as the name of her sister Bertha's second son, of whom she writes a portrait in the winter of 1928. Unlike George, Daniel speaks of patriarchal power.

> They are there which is not at all why they were more than ever individually wishing that treasures are agedly fishes because many marry too and it is well known that the church admits that if the child is born in wedlock even although the marriage is not legal by any arrangement nevertheless the child of such a marriage is without doubt legitimate if they like and anybody can like. (325; see also 326–28)

19. Details in "George" (365) may point to her funeral at the American Church in Paris, where Edward Pendleton, whose name also appears, was the organist. Pendleton also played at several Virgil Thomson concerts. There are suggestions of tears, a veil and shawl, perhaps hints of a will or inheritance.

The paragraph ends in the *cahier* with "they believe that they are going to have it. And so do I." After this, Stein adds a question mark in parentheses, naturally not included in the printed text; it may refer to the disposition of Mildred Aldrich's property or another unresolved matter, or it may be a request to Toklas to check facts.

If my reading of this passage as a description of a funeral is correct, the fact that it is followed by the section on connection and separation, with its hints of Leo Stein, becomes especially poignant. On page 366 is a moving description of what appears to be a sick person's hand "so that the dimple shows by bending in and out . . . ," followed by questions about "are her two eyes alright alike. Or should they be different as they are alright . . .". By page 370, there are explicit references to a funeral, though not a state funeral, "she must be dead anyway without a horse or a blanket" and "Funerals are added to ministrations."

This passage sounds in part like country gossip or local scandal about a bastard child, but it may just as well be about the legitimacy of the Stein-Toklas marriage. The legitimate product of a marriage that is not legitimized may also refer to Stein's work, made possible by the love that she shared with Toklas.

As always, Stein returns at last to time, being, identity, and her work.

> Hours and hours ours and ours bears and bears bear and bear she had no children of her own and when she inherited she inherited nothing in comparison with what she had. (373)[20]

What she had is what she is and what she writes rather than a link in a predictable continuum from the past to the future. Only her writing is permanent and self-contained. She returns to her work, whose black printed words will make the white page white,

> that is what it is why do they whiten paper paper is exactly pleasing to the eye. (328)[21]

Finally, it is George—many Georges, many names, many words. It is not the family. It is writing, not to represent an unalterably set old order but to discover, name, and diagram the unknown,

> What is a vocabulary. Settling the North Pole little by alike and never not liking a distinct layer of their repeal. The way to have a grammar is to learn diagram. A belief in right away they may, they may be following me up. Up cup culpable custard culpable account occupied and their tell. I see through a part of their say so. The next is more vocabulary and some

20. The section subtitled "They Had." in "A Book Concluding With As A Wife Has A Cow A Love Story" (1923) echoes here:

> They had no children. They had no children but three sister-in-laws a brother which brother and no nephews and no nieces and no other language. (*R* 457)

21. Stein sees writing, like printing, in part as a visual art. Early exposure, at Harvard, to new theories of visual perception and later to light and color in painting left her sensitive to the impact of light on paper. In an interesting letter, John Sherry Mangan, a friend of Virgil Thomson who, as the editor of *larus,* published two of her pieces, wrote,

> I hold in printing to simplicity, being of the belief that proportion and an indefinable quality which I can only call "light behind the letters"—for after all, you know, we read, optically, not the letters, which are without light, but the white outlines—are of more importance than complicated ornamentation . . . (5 April 1927)

Stein's next submission to *larus* was the portrait of Nadelman, with its shining passages on "having light coming out of him."

grammar or more grammar or more grammar. Arthur or more grammar after Finally George a Vocabulary. (382)[22]

She will now explore grammar, including the ways in which George Hugnet can be made grammatical. She will not simply follow the old grammatical conventions. "Finally George" moves into "Arthur A Grammar." But first, she writes *A Lyrical Opera For Two To Sing,* a gift for Toklas on her fifty-first birthday.

A Lyrical Opera (O&P 49–60)

A Lyrical Opera / Made By Two / To Be Sung was Stein's second opera within a year.[23] It was a birthday opera composed for the fifty-first birthday of Toklas on April 30, 1928, and for the women's twentieth wedding anniversary, the day in the summer of 1908 when Stein and Toklas, in Fiesole, declared their affection and promised each other that their future would be for themselves alone.[24]

> She was born as one may say neatly to accomplish as one may say sweetly what is to be known as one may say completely in measuring it not to do any harm. (58)

The early scene at the Villa Bardi in Fiesole (49) suggests the marriage. *A Lyrical Opera* is the private and intimate complement to *Four Saints In Three Acts,* the opera on a grand and public scale of the spring of 1927.[25]

22. The North Pole was in the news. On April 21, George Hubert Wilkins flew from Alaska to Spitsbergen over the pole. The same year, he was knighted for his achievement and published his account of the venture, *Flying the Arctic.*
23. Like *Four Saints,* it is printed in *O&P,* to which quotations refer.
24. These words, paraphrased from the opening section of "Didn't Nelly And Lilly Love You," 1922, an earlier birthday and marriage piece, in *AFAM* (224), refer to the wedding and the promises made, spoken of in the opera (50). It is useful to reread "Didn't Nellie And Lilly" as well as "Birth And Marriage" along with the opera.

    In the opera, the phrase "after April thirtieth . . . the second of May" (55) may point to the wedding date. "May too," near the end of "George" (381), may come from the date. Stein often mythologizes important dates, events, objects by composing them again and again in new forms. See also letter of 7 May 1952 from Toklas thanking Carl Van Vechten for remembering the unidentified "anniversary" (*SOA* 256). The link between Toklas' birth and the marriage is also a theme in "Birth And Marriage," 1924, *A&B* 184, 185, 198.
25. The libretto is composed directly into five French *cahiers,* as is evident from the fact that Stein used details from the covers of three of these in the text. For example, "Navigation sub-marine" (51), here a sexual reference, is in French the title of the second *cahier.* By filling the last *cahier* to the end, she shaped the opera in the space of the notebooks.

A Lyrical Opera is one of Stein's most openly erotic works. For years, her writing had grown out of her experience and absorbed details of private life, including the sexual relationship with Toklas. In any number of works appear sexual details, erotic jokes, puns, and other verbal love play. However, she had rarely written directly about sexuality as the central subject of a whole piece. *A Circular Play* (1920), for example, which often sounds in tone like the opera, is about making circles with words, including especially words of love, shaped in rounds, rings, and circles. *A Lyrical Opera,* however, is simply and nakedly about making love in sexual and even scatological terms. Its center is more overtly autobiographical, its substance more representational, its words more referential, than those of any other work that includes sexuality.

Differing not only in subject matter but also in tone and language from other works about love, it has none of the raucous hilarity that gives "Lifting Belly" and other works written from 1915 to 1917, in Mallorca and after, their erotic but expansively comic tone. Nor is there the wide range of detail from many sources that appears in other works along with sexuality. Most striking in this opera is the language and tone. From the start, in quick succession, it is filled with diminutive terms of endearment, baby talk, lullabies that at first belie but in fact, under the guise of nursery sweetness, reveal its erotic quality. Here the language of song and love is not new in kind but new in its concentration.

> A lyric. Come fire fly and light up baby's nose.
>
> A cuckoo bird is sitting on a cuckoo tree singing to me oh singing to me.
>
> John Quilly. John Quilly my babe baby is sweeter than even John Quillies are. (49)
>
> Sing a hymn of him of her of her of that of that of what is the make of a cover. Cover to cover he never did shove her.
>
> Sing a hymn of singing sing a hymn of singing sing a hymn of singing singing is more than very much more than often often and soften sing a hymn of often often very often soft as a better kind of making it be whatever is very likely to soften.
>
> Singing a singing bird is singing on a Pologna tree singing to me oh singing to me. (55)

Enough words and phrases occur both in the final sections of "George" and in the opera to suggest that Stein had already begun *A Lyrical Opera* when she concluded "George."

Richard Bridgman claims that in *A Lyrical Opera* Stein "regresses almost a decade in style and subject matter" to the preoccupations of "Lifting Belly" and other pieces written in Mallorca during World War I (154 n.). The evidence of Stein's private love notes to Toklas in the little *carnets* places it in an entirely different context, however.[26] She did not regress. She used the little language of love throughout the years on slips of paper and in notes to Toklas, entered, with text and other matters, in the little *carnets.*

This language can be documented for those years for which *carnets* are preserved, from 1921 to 1931. However, since traces of it appear in Stein's work as early as 1913–15, there is good reason to assume that the language was used steadily from early years on, though it emerged only intermittently from the private notes in *carnets* and other scribblings to enter literary composition and print.

In *A Lyrical Opera,* it becomes *the* language of the opera, just as lovemaking becomes the subject. Stein's gift to Toklas for her birthday and for their wedding anniversary was the private language and the personal intimacy "made by two" celebrated as literature. She obliterated the difference between the private and the literary, between what in the *carnets* she wrote for Toklas alone and what in the *cahiers* she wrote as literature. That difference, so visible in the *carnets,* is no longer visible in *A Lyrical Opera.*[27]

As the discussion of the manuscript *cahiers* and *carnets* has shown, the childlike language is not simply Stein's invention but is her version of Swift's "little language." However intimate the opera is, it must be seen, unlike Swift's private letters and unlike the little notes to Toklas in *carnets,* as a literary work for publication or performance, "to be sung" before an audience.[28]

26. Some of the phrases of love from earlier works return in *A Lyrical Opera.* For example, "John Quilly John Quilly my babe baby is sweeter than even John Quillies are" is in "Mexico," 1916 (*G&P* 328). Likewise, the punning verse about the cooing bird in the cuckoo tree occurs in slightly different form in "A Sonatina Followed By Another," 1921 (*BTV* 6), which in details and tone is especially close to the opera.

    It is too simple to say that these lines were copied from the earlier pieces. More likely Stein's always active verbal memory offered her the appropriate phrase when she needed it, with the echoes of its earlier use. When she reuses material, unless she is seduced by her own phrasing, as sometimes happens, she consciously inserts it with the history of its earlier use. One of the pleasures of prolonged reading of Stein is in the echoes in words and phrases from piece to piece.

27. Anyone who has seen the language in the tiny hand of the *carnets* recognizes that even if the printed words are the same as those in a *carnet,* their quality is not the same. Context, tone, and visual impression are different in the printed work. To readers aware of the *carnets,* the private origin of these messages remains audible, though Stein surely never intended her readers to know of them or read them in their private form.

28. For a full discussion of the connection with Swift, see *LGS/TW* 86, n. 9. The Swiftian

As the word "lyrical" suggests, it is a chamber opera and reflects the interest in small-scale, intimate operatic works that began in the 1920s.[29] The little opera abstracts from grand opera with its complex plots of passion and its artifice the essence of intimacy and lovemaking, which is lyrical. There is no evolving action, no conflict, no complication, and there are only two characters, the two lovers. The action is in the singing words. What is visible is merely stage sets, a kind of animated chamber background that is a part of the two lovers. Here they are in the Paris studio, with carefully identified details of the actual furnishings that we know from photographs:

> A large and lofty room cut by rows of pictures and in the middle corner a work-table round with drawers in the shape of a Maltese cross and on it a seal red small medium sized bull a tortoise shell lamp and a glass of tiny hyacinths fresh flowers and on either side a small arm chair with a large medium sized pleasant handsome man and on the other side a large arm chair chintz covered with a fair sized dark charming medium sized lady. (49)

From here on, they sing with many repetitions and refrains, make love, and sing about making love under their initials,

> L. M. S. J. H. M. My wife is my life is my life is my wife is my wife is my life is my life is my wife is my life.
>
> F. s. d. c. m. s. l. Nods in agreement. (49)[30]

---

initials "Y. D.," which occur in many *carnets* but also in some of Stein's texts, appear three times in the manuscript of *A Lyrical Opera,* though not in the printed text (after the sentence, "My own queen . . . submarine" [51]; after "My April fool baby" [53]; and after "Of the flower . . . continually" [54]).

Toklas told Virgil Thomson, when he consulted her for the introduction to *BTV,* that "D. D." (and its companion initials, "Y. D.") was "one of Gertrude's fantasies. There was no D. D." (*BTV* 3). Her comment, while literally true, means merely that she was not about to give away the secret code she shared with Stein. She must have relished the fact that no one caught on. Even when Thornton Wilder recognized the language as Swift's, he had no way of seeing its private dimensions.

29. It is interesting to see Stein giving up her early fascination with Wagnerian opera for the intimate, private scale of works like *A Lyrical Opera* and others. She moves steadily away from epic proportions and grand scale to the concrete and intimate. She implies that love in large, complex opera plots is removed from immediacy, hardened in stiff scaffolding. Two months later, in the summer of 1928, she writes *A Bouquet. Their Wills.,* a hugely plotted operatic work in six acts with an interlude about many couples from among her Baltimore family, which she thereby effectively deconstructs.

30. The capital "J" is a printing error for "P." Coded letters, recalling children's secret games, are also used by Swift.

As in *Four Saints In Three Acts,* the stage directions and the words sung become one, and the lovers merge with the setting, inside with outside, the studio in Paris with the hills behind Fiesole, all in the enchantment of love and spring, birds and flowers, word play, love play, mocking, and fooling around on the first of April.

The subtitle declares the opera to be *made by two.*[31] The writing is Stein's, but the phrase makes it the work of both. It suggests back-and-forth play in many forms. The opera is not merely about making love, but it *is* making love, a creation of the two, a love lyric, a duet. Two become one in making love and in singing the words that create the opera. As "George" is a broad study of the ways words can be joined, so *A Lyrical Opera* tries out ways of joining words in love. Two sing it, two say it, two are in it, two are it, two make it possible and indeed make it one, as a bouquet,

> I say it in flowers to you to you
> I say it in pansies and roses and pinks
> I say it in daisies and heavenly drinks
> Of the flower of our love which is you and me. (54)

Or doing their work side by side,

> Sing mention.
> A pliable certainty.
> As they came they sat she with a sheet and he with a sheet she with a sheet of linen and he with a sheet of paper sat with an embroider as well.
> What is the difference between silk and linen. Both admirable.
> She sat sated he sat dated, she sat stated he sat waited an edible as well.
> She sat mated he sat belated as indicated and as well. Sing securely. (57)

The opera is filled with conventional motifs of love poetry.[32] It is interesting that in this work, which celebrates enduring union rather than union after disunion, two short remnants appear of the division-unification or war-peace motif prominent in the tradition of epithalamia:

> This my country has been enslaved. And we are free to see to see how sweet is she my sweet pretty prettily. (50)

31. On the cover of the fifth manuscript notebook, she plays with the number 2 and its mirror image. Mirror images and other details relying on symmetry appear often in her work.
32. Some of these are discussed by Virginia Tufte in her analysis, "Gertrude Stein's Prothalamium: A Unique Poem in a Classical Mode," *Yale University Library Gazette* 42 (July 1968): 17–23.

and echoes of Lincoln's Springfield acceptance speech,

> He decided she decided they decided that the house is not to be divided but to face out both ways without a difference of there being a difference as a difference to be a difference not to be a difference to be a difference to be made. (56)

The house refers not only to division and union but also to the growing certainty of the two women that their negotiations for the house in Bilignin near Belley were likely to be successful. Several other references to "a house that is a home with a department"—*département de l'Ain*—to a farm, and to a "spouse" carefully rhymed with "house" confirm the theme (56, 58).

The house is sexual, as in "a pink house inside and out" (55), and in the palace at Versailles (50), associated with the queen (51). Inside and outside, for body and house, are prominent in the libretto. The wedding anniversary marks the prospect of a home, a house, a new life with a wife.

Stein uses every detail of the Paris studio, the season, the rituals she shared with Toklas, to compose the terms of endearment and the facts of love. Puns join two meanings in one word, rhetorical questions receive echoing answers, Nelly joins Lilly, rhyme, assonance, and alliteration join their counterparts, house to home, back to back, "love what you tell" to its mirror echo, "tell what you love," lovebirds sing duets, "monkey see" joins "monkey do." Making love is matching and mirroring.

At the same time, the opera is filled with sexual and scatological detail, ingestion and excretion. Smells are associated with flowers but also with excretion, with cows, caramels, dung, and odorless jasmine.

> Sectional a cow in sections all at once constitutional a constitutional cow how ever strong. This is balm to have it come and to be left odorously. Thank you for this. What is a cake a cow cake what is at stake a cow cake. Thank you out loud. One two one two all out of you three four three four open the door open the door five six five six not a stick just gently ooze choose dear darling that you are. Sweety you will have it be sure. (53)

All of these, outrageous in their diminutiveness, become comical. Each scene in this libretto merges into the next. They all hang together thematically but develop only the slightest action.

Immediately after the Paris salon, Stein moves to the Villa Bardi in Fiesole and "a rocky undulating road side" with orchids and lavender and "two walking." It is the setting for the wedding, though Stein does not develop it except by a hint of the walk with Toklas in the hills and by the Italian tone suggested by counting in Italian.

Reaching *quattro* in Italian leads her to Louis XIV, *quatorze,* and to openly erotic associations with the royal palace of Versailles, the house and body of the queen and beloved. Already in the scene at Fiesole there is "preparation to make a fountain" (50), with sexual overtones that carry over to the fountains of Versailles, where the palace of the queen is to be explored, with no need of a guide. This kind of double entendre continues throughout the opera.

The innumerable little scenes are often carefully developed. The bird that sings in the chestnut tree, with its rising and descending blossoms, finds its counterpart in the bird that sings in the Pologna tree, created for the benefit of Polish Toklas out of a magnolia tree, which produces blossoms before leaves. The chestnut tree, of course, carries overtones of Longfellow's spreading chestnut tree in "The Village Blacksmith."

There are moments of light humor in careful phrasing, as in

> When she says come I do not come but when she says come come I come and a little makes it be fairly very much indeed. (57)

The opera is inventive, skilled and clever in its miniature word scenes. Yet Stein's exclusive concentration on mostly sexual intimacy narrows her verbal possibilities. In the first half, she rather successfully sustains the naive, diminutive sweetness of language and tone, the pastoral details, cows (orgasms), flowers, trees, birds, singing, the nursery rhymes and folk elements in settings with carefully chosen details of words and objects, in counting games, in the praising of parts and other devices.

But it is difficult to sustain this kind of work. Scenes that begin as small but developed compositions are reduced gradually to short paragraphs and single sentences. Intimacy is difficult to prolong. Verbal intimacy about love and sexuality is impossible to keep up very long before a cloying feeling sets in. In the last quarter of the opera, the details are less and less lively, the images less concrete, less musical, less visual, and less and less charming. The verbal movement is no longer sustained by the immediacy of shared intimacy, shared memories, lively experience of objects, jewelry, stitchery, but becomes routine and flat in movement:

> Once sewing always sewing, this is a scene at noon. (58)

or

> Rose is a rose and a pansy he chose.
> Rose is a rose and he chose a pansy.
> Pansy is short for Pussie. (58)

Less and less concrete and immediate, less and less playful and charming, the opera gradually, in its very short space, drains itself of the lively delicacy that starts it, to compose but perhaps not perfectly to complete itself.

"J. H. Jane Heap. Fairly Well." (*RAB* 49)

Stein met Jane Heap, the coeditor with Margaret Anderson of the *Little Review,* in 1923. From then on, Heap received help and contributions for the review through Stein's contacts in Paris and in turn made efforts to find publishers for Stein, especially for *The Making Of Americans* and a reissue of *Three Lives.*[33]

By 1928, Heap, in Paris, was preparing the final number of the *Little Review.* On February 15, she asked Stein in her and Anderson's name for something for the last issue.

> [W]e are trying to get personal documents rather than literachoor from the contemporary giants. You could do such an amazing one if you would.

The document Stein produced was a portrait of Heap. On June 13, Heap acknowledged it:

> We are very happy to have the "Appreciation" for our final issue.[34]

The title plays with Heap's use of her initials, "jh." as signature and with the ambiguity of "fairly well." Is Jane, who suffers endlessly from colds and physical ailments, fairly well? Is Jane, who was never well, appreciated fairly well? Does Stein's piece fairly well succeed in appreciating Jane? Or, perhaps ironically, has Jane done fairly well, as editor of the *Little Review* or as supporter of Stein?

Her personality is defined by her likeness to Braque and to Stein's old

33. Further details about their meeting and Heap's efforts on Stein's behalf are given by James Mellow in his *Charmed Circle: Gertrude Stein and Company* (New York: Praeger, 1974), 284–87, 316–18.
34. It was written by June 1928 and published in the last issue of the *Little Review,* for spring 1929, under the title "J. H. Jane Heap. Fairly Well. An Appreciation of Jane."

    The manuscript shows that Stein revised the title but in what steps is not clear. In three lines, though she crossed out the second, bracketed here, the title reads, "J. H. Jane Heap / [appreciated Jane] / Fairly well." "Fairly well" looks like the first title written.

    In *A Lyrical Opera* occurs the phrase,

    > A lyrical opera not an announcement. Fairly well. Half begun is well done. (58)

    The phrasing seems to recall "Fairly well is very good" in the portrait. It suggests that Stein worked on the portrait while composing the opera.

friend Grace Lounsbery, whom she had already described as similar in her early notebooks. Personalities exhibit varying combinations of ordinary qualities, or, here, of verbal features, as in the word "agate" on the one hand and "a gate" on the other—the same but not the same. The sequence of words moves eventually to digging for gold, perhaps to Heap's discovery of talent, although this is far from clear. The work here is not unlike that of "Finally George."

By the second half of the first paragraph, Stein returns to the present and the story later told in the *Autobiography* (271) of Jane coming late to rue de Fleurus and staying later and later until early morning. With modulations on coming and staying, late and early, evening and morning, she ends the paragraph with the title phrase,

> Fairly well is very good. (49)

The rhyme words "come," "stay," "away," lead to the second paragraph, initiated by the name Jane, on which Stein constructs a nonsense variant of the charm, "Rain, rain go away come again another day," to ask Jane to return,

> Jane Jane come away let the garden come and stay came late to stay in the morning came late to stay in the first day in the evening. (49)

More rhyming and singing follows as Stein asks, is the *Little Review* Margaret Anderson's or Jane Heap's, "whose is it." Stein, who liked Jane, concludes that it is Jane whose name matters for the review, "Jane a day," and she speaks of a name day, perhaps May 30, the Feast of Jeanne d'Arc, a holiday in France.

She ends with a tribute to Jane, thanking her for her efforts, hoping for her return and continuing friendship. The portrait concludes lightly and playfully, without voicing regrets about the end of the *Little Review*. It is a slight but carefully wrought piece, an appreciation such as Stein occasionally but infrequently composed.

In the spring and summer of 1928, Stein wrote a series of works whose composition overlaps and whose subjects are related, though their titles and forms differ sharply. Each has a context of its own and requires separate commentary. At the same time, they all share an extraordinary coherence, audible in recurrent ideas and verbal echoes from one work to another. "Arthur A Grammar," an apparently discontinuous series of observations, is the pivotal work, a bass line for that summer.

At the end of "Finally George" (382), Stein, using the name Arthur, first announces the next language study. Yet Arthur appears at the end of

"George," reappears in the third line of the grammar, along with other *a*-words, and is plainly the name of her choice.

Beginning notes next to a Paris shopping list in a preliminary *carnet* show that the piece was started in Paris. A few phrases in its early pages are also in *A Lyrical Opera,* perhaps written alongside "Arthur." The grammar study continues in the summer in Belley, while she also composes *A Bouquet. Their Wills.* and *Paisieu,* a landscape play, between August and October. Finally, descriptive lines about Georges Hugnet appear here as well as in *Paisieu;* later, revised and expanded, they become the full, self-contained portrait "George Hugnet," discussed in detail in chapter 6. Last, the portrait "The d'Aiguys" of that summer exhibits grammatical preoccupations related to those of "Arthur."

Elements of "Arthur A Grammar" carry over to many of the pieces written along with it so that we hear verbal and thematic echoes going back and forth to *A Lyrical Opera; A Bouquet. Their Wills.,* whose first two lines follow the beginning of "Arthur" in the same *carnet;* the fall 1928 *transition* questionnaire, "Why I Do Not Live in America," probably the "Questionaire in question" (62). Here the opening sentence of her answer, "The United States is the oldest country in the world . . ." finds its parallel in "Arthur" (72). A study of faces whose lines show age, then of a map whose lines draw geological age, is finally applied to the United States. "A rich and well nourished home . . . a nice place to be brought up in" sounds like the Baltimore of *A Bouquet. Their Wills.* Details about landscape in "Arthur," especially in the second half, carry over to *Paisieu.* In a *carnet,* sections marked "P," for Paisieu, alternate with others, marked "G," for Grammar. Lines that become parts of "George Hugnet" are in "Arthur" (94) and *Paisieu* (178). There is reason to assume that in other *carnets,* not preserved, Stein may concurrently have written sections for "Arthur," the opera, and perhaps other pieces. My discussion documents the interaction of "Arthur" and other pieces, suggesting how it gives body to the grammar from daily life and adds depth to our readings.

"Arthur," on the one hand, and *A Lyrical Opera, A Bouquet. Their Wills., Paisieu,* and the two portraits, on the other hand, become mutual contexts for each other. "Arthur" can be read as a sourcebook for the other works of that summer, a repository for ideas and experiments, some of which develop into separate, full works. But it is mainly a study in its own right, a series of stark and difficult meditations on language and exercises in writing. More abstract than the other pieces, it rests minimally on context and reference. It demands slow reading and rereading but yields astonishing inventions to those who have patience enough.

"Arthur A Grammar" (*HTW* 37–101)

Stein's grammar is not about subjects, predicates, and usage, though it includes these. She uses the word "grammar" far more broadly. In its most general form, grammar tries to answer the question of how perception is shaped into patterns of meaning. She does not limit herself to language but looks at grammar in innumerable fields, producing hundreds of answers, often using the word in a different sense from sentence to sentence. Many of the responses remain difficult, even after repeated readings, though they always tease us to try again. Some create sudden, extraordinary illumination. Each reading yields new forms, new possibilities, and new frustrations at her dogged, patient, impatient pursuit of grammar.

No wonder the handwriting in the manuscript of "Arthur" varies strikingly, from neat, even penmanship without errors or emendations to broad, hasty scrawls with crossed-out words and revisions. Many of the neatly written sections appear copied from drafts in *carnets* that, with two exceptions, do not survive. The passages that show deletions and revisions, on the other hand, are visibly composed in the *cahier,* although the sections were apparently sometimes rearranged in the process of copying. In the only preserved *carnet* of early drafts for "Arthur" are two successive passages of text that appear far apart in the *cahier* and therefore in print.[35] Without the *carnets,* however, neither the purpose nor the extent of the rearrangements can be ascertained.

Both the matter and the manner of the "Arthur" manuscript sometimes convey frustration and impatience on Stein's part. "Grammar is useless because there is nothing to say," she ends a choppy sequence of phrases with a few scrawled revisions and comes to a stop, only to start again, with a new section and subtitle, "Part II"; the problem of questions makes her draw on the *transition* questionnaire in further attempts to formulate answers through games, examples, definitions of grammar.

> Arthur a grammar.
> Questionnaire in question.
> What is a question.
> Twenty questions.
>
> (62)

Later, she concludes a fast and fluent paragraph with "Grammar is in our power" and starts another "Part II," in a more playful mood, with "Just a

35. The seven lines from "Escape calling battles . . ." to ". . . exercise in paragraphs" (39); and "How come, a treatise in sound and sense and not corelated [*sic*] to grammar" (70).

grammar" (73). "Arthur" ends rather abruptly in the middle of a *cahier,* perhaps because she had enough of grammar, perhaps because the summer was ending and it was time to have "completed grammar" (100).

"Arthur A Grammar," which sounds like a full name, is an even odder title than "Finally George A Vocabulary Of Thinking,"[36] and both differ from the other titles of the language studies, such as "Sentences And Paragraphs"; to speak of the two pieces for short as "Arthur" or "George," as I do here, sounds funny. Such small verbal forms change the tone of a title and the feeling of a piece. If I say I am reading Arthur, I am reading a piece by that title, but if I say I am reading Stein, I am reading her work, identical constructions that yield different meanings. In the *carnet* with the beginning draft passage of "Arthur," she plays with other tentative titles, "Future in Composition" and "Future of Composition." Placed side by side, the two phrases open grammatical possibilities.

"Arthur" shows fewer traces than "George" of other subjects that preoccupied Stein. Its innumerable verbal inventions never develop subject matter in detail or at length. The major themes of this summer are elaborated in separate works of their own, written alongside "Arthur." One example is the rigid, prescriptive grammar of social organization based on the patriarchal family, which is merely hinted at in small, isolated units in "Arthur" but becomes the subject of *A Bouquet. Their Wills.* A contrasting example is Stein's study, in *Paisieu,* of landscape, not a stiff and unyielding system but a fluid natural process. Grammar is not one thing but many, and "Arthur" must be read as a repository of grammatical ruminations and exercises. Its central interest is rhetorical, but its references point to many grammars in daily life.

Playing with definitions, Stein explores what grammar *is.* She never looks for a single definition to cover all cases. Here she follows the process that makes grammar and leads to many definitions, not one. Everything she says becomes a new example of grammar, and for each she considers how that happens.

> Grammar is the art of reckoning that it is by themselves that they are one and two. (48)

This sentence may be about number—singular, plural, one, two—but may just as well be about identity, relationships, and union in love. It also plays off the plural "they," "themselves," and "are" against the singular "one." In-

36. She had also considered the title, "Walter a Grammar," included on a list of titles. For Walter elsewhere, see "Arthur," 56, 92.

cluded are countless sentences about what grammar *does* and what we do with it.

> Grammar makes no mistakes (81),

for example, is less simple than it looks. The questions it raises in the process of grammatical exploration yield no simple answers:

> Grammar may not be mistaken.
> Grammar may not be mistaken for winding along presently. This is just as it is or has become.
> Grammar is mistaken at times.
> Grammar is mistaken at times for fondly yours. Grammar is mistaken at times for burnt ivy with a piece of glass.
> Grammar is mistaken at times. (84)

Such definitions do not aspire to the status of general truths but remain descriptions to ponder.

Likewise, the sentences about what grammar does are not mere applications of larger principles. Their interest is in what they are, not in what they illustrate. There is no real difference between the definitions and the examples. Both are forms of description whose meaning lies in their construction—their grammar.

> Any kind of complication is simple that is the real use of grammar. It all but says so. (101)

Such small, shapely observations require the most careful reading, listening, seeing, and thinking. Their deceptive simplicity, their exasperating multitude, and their refusal of familiar phrasing belie the prolonged scrutiny they require.

The grammar opens,

> Successions of words are so agreeable. (39)

It is about how we write—or read—words in sequence and how one way we perceive them is as long strings, sequences of one and one and one. The low-key sentence speaks of the simple pleasure of reading or perhaps even the passive, sleepy pleasure of lazily following familiar phrases—the kind of writing Stein fought passionately in her own work. But the sentence also states a central fact about literature: a time art, it is linear.[37]

37. The word "succession" also carries over to *A Bouquet. Their Wills.*, her study of the grammar of family lines of descent.

Grammar makes dates.

Yet no sooner does she write the word "dates" than it leads to word play, which becomes grammatical,

> Grammar makes dates. Dates are a fruit that may be pressed together or may be lain in a box regularly still attached to a stem. In this way they think. Grammar may be reconstituted. A blame. (57)

Obviously grammar can render time or dates, but Stein moves with the homonym "date" from time to fruit, transferring the function of grammar to the reconstitution of dried dates laid out diagonally from a "stem" to which they seem attached, placed in the attractive, elongated oval boxes familiar to Europeans. So now dates compose a spatial rather than a temporal arrangement. Its cover lifted, the box of dates displays an orderly grammar.

Such tiny essays are practice work, experiments in how to place words in relation. For in "Arthur," Stein is by turns both teacher and student, learning by doing how to write, how to think, how to perceive and shape. "Arthur" is about how to put words together in meanings.

> It is impossible to avoid meaning and if there is meaning and it says what it does there is grammar. (71)

Rather than a systematic treatise, this study is a show-and-tell book of "grammatical phrases" (56), a poetics of grammar.

Names ask to be identified. We want to know who Arthur is. Unlike the many Georges Stein knew from personal acquaintance as well as from history and familiar English and American locutions, there are no prominent Arthurs in her life or her work, although some appear in the grammar that are connected with her.[38] Yet Arthur, invoked again and again in the piece,

38. A few Arthurs are in the grammar. Her nephew Arthur Raffel, whom she knew less well than his brother Daniel, occurs several times. In addition, there are Arthur Cravan, the vanished husband of Mina Loy, "Arthur whether craves a word of love" (85); Sir Arthur Sullivan (76); Arthur Garfield, a combination of James Garfield and his successor, Chester Alan Arthur, president when Stein was in grammar school (99). By 1928, the name may refer to Arthur Garfield Hays, the civil libertarian and defense attorney in the Scopes case of 1925 and the Sacco-Vanzetti case of 1927, whose book, *Let Freedom Ring* (1928), Stein may have known. Arthur Wellesley, the duke of Wellington, is not named but surely suggested in the hints of the Peninsular War and strategy, discussed subsequently; echoes of World War I, especially in *Paisieu,* may have recalled Kitchener's secretary, Sir George Arthur. The name occurs only twice before, in "Mildreds Thoughts" (1922),

remains virtually "abstract," -
to be played with rather
reading. Following
gests the three
first letter
name
of a p.

> Is t.
> Gramma.

> What is A
> Arthur is a g
> Arthur a gram.

Not a formal, codified
Arthur, as author, come.
together in tiny essays, odes
King Arthur and the Round
Arthurs. The work cannot be su
is, for any summary takes us to a
Stein was no more interested in goi.
its own sake.

In 1927, Heisenberg discovered the princ
tainty. On May 25, 1928, Dorothy Dudley H

> Read me to sleep Arthuro, Arthur in Spanish. The n
> go with earrings. All this and more was mentioned just

and in "If He Thinks. A Novelette Of Desertion" (1922),

> Paul can do what Locker [i.e., Robert Locher] can do. Locker
> do. Joseph can do too what Arthur can do. And Arthur can do
> restate changes. (*RAB* 87)

I identify these Arthurs not as historical figures or real people spoken of
but as context for Stein's work.

39. Living in France, Stein must have been especially conscious of the French i.
national standards for correct expression and word choice, codified in grammar.
tionaries and upheld in schools. Nothing could have been further from her mind
stiff book of uniform rules for a whole nation.

40. I found the Harvey letter after her name struck me in *Paisieu.* One of the few last nan
in the play, it asks more insistently than first names for identification ("Herbert William
Harvey had four children," "Marry Perrine Hubert William Harvey," both *LO&P* 160).

ts from Bertrand Russell's "Physics and Meta-
eared in the *Saturday Review of Literature* dated
ages quoting Russell are best read in full:

of the revolutions required to adapt ourselves to
rg & Schroedinger, which are in so many ways more
f Einstein. We should have to begin by altering the
t things. A series of different apparitions, changing
oes on, are linked together under one name, say John
d to constitute one person. If one of these apparitions
a leg of mutton, it is thought right and just that one of
ld be shut within the four walls of a prison. If we did not
ne person we imprison is the same as the person who stole
tton, we should be less convinced of our right to shut him
e went on to realize that there are no legs of mutton and no
s, we should feel still more reconstruction of our traditional
be called for. . . . A prison consists of a very large number of
and a matrix is an infinite rectangle of integers.'

n another place: 'Nowadays, physicists, the most hard-headed
kind . . . have embodied in their technique this insubstantiality
some of the metaphysicians have so long urged in vain.'

connection with grammar I thought at once of you, and wondered,
ving little about them, if you have not been one of the metaphysi-
ns as an artist, with whom the physicists have just now caught up.

Maybe you will be amused by voices and tones of voices I tried to
ick out of the air in this article, which these editors, more intentionally
propagandist than I, were good enough to like and publish.

Beginning in 1905–06 with *Three Lives,* Stein had questioned writing in
new ways from work to work. Her first demand is always for consciousness
on the writer's part.

> Whenever words come before the mind there is a mistake. ("Arthur" 66)

Russell's first names are Bertrand Arthur William, with only the first a referential give-away, not used by Stein. In the last scene of *Paisieu* appears Edgar Arthur Henry Edward Allen Russell Geronimo.

These names must not be narrowly identified, but the play with source words must be heard. By the time Stein received Harvey's letter, she was already working on her grammar study and had written considerable sections of the opera. There is nothing to conclude from the names except that they were in her mind. Harvey's perceptions about Stein's work are startlingly accurate. The Russell passages, in single quotation marks, are reproduced exactly as selected and excerpted by Harvey.

Writing by unthinking habit, relying on usage rather than consciousness, is wrong. By 1928, her skepticism about standard grammar and usage, together with the questions raised by translation, led her to separate grammar from vocabulary.

> The question is if you have a vocabulary have you any need of grammar except for explanation that is the question, communication and direction repetition and intuition that is the question. Returned for grammar. (60)

Like "returned for postage," the last sentence shows nicely how Stein, by lifting words from the lockstep of standard usage, stops us from unthinking association with things, ideas, and formulations. This process also does away with all the hierarchical trappings of grammar and with the distinction between important and unimportant words. Words cease to be signifiers and become objects in themselves. The grammar of mere pretty phrases is not worth bothering with.

> Vocabulary is made of words which have been come to be like when after it is before that they sighed. In the same way grammar amounts to not be plainly so pleased with prettily figuring as approaching and reproaching half after noon. They are preoccupied with practically suppressing dismay with advantage this is why why bother. Tell the old gentlemen not to bother. (63–64)[41]

41. Ah, the old gentlemen. The last sentence in this passage returns literally in the manuscript of "Stanzas In Meditation," V, xv, ll. 14–18, where, on the margin, in thin pencil, it is entered vertically in the hand of Toklas, totally clear in the original but not visible on the positive print of the copy of "Stanzas." Here are all lines on that manuscript page, with lines 14–18 marked:

> I do not think a change.
> I do not think they will change.
> But I will change /
> If I change /
> I may change /
> Yes certainly I may change. /
> It is very foolish to go on /
> Oh yes you are.

In the early notebooks, Stein describes Toklas:

> She can make you talk like one of her old gentlemen to whom she loves to listen and be docile and so she makes a poor thing of one because one talks badly then, she listens, she is docile, stupid but she owns you, you are then her *idol* with the feet of clay, you are hers, then, the submissive, docile, stupid, humble as she is then to you so you are dead and she passes over your dead body as she did with Sally. After my

"Arthur" becomes "a treatise in sound and sense and not cor[r]elated to grammar" (70);[42] the authority of grammar as we were taught it is broken down and reconstructed in new forms that never stand still.

That summer, Stein wrote about her work to Elliot Paul,

> the grammar is at last really going, it is proceding by clarifying examples which really are beginning to clarify, it is a fascinating subject, because by way of grammar you do get rid of sight and sound in a very intimate kind of a way and it leads to a strange sort of liberation, the vocabulary thing ["Finally George"] that you liked was interesting but this in a way is more liberating I am hoping that you will like it.[43]

Stein composes into grammar words that she hears and sees. Indeed, she even breaks down words themselves into morphemes, the smallest units of meaning, which allow new constructions. For example, "Asterisk" breaks into "as to risk," "argument" into "argue meant" (48). Out of physical properties she makes new meaning. Here she plays with sound:

> Apply supply.
> Supply apply.
> Ease tease tease ease. (58)

> Our hour too too makes nine twenty this is coupled contrite. (61)

Here she works with sight, about the prospect of the coveted house:

> talk about Nellie [Jacot] she got out of relation by stupidity, and I turned into an old gentleman. (56)

Elsewhere in the early notebooks (11–5), there is reference to "keeping the old gentlemen from getting married." Can all this also recall *As You Like It,* act 5, scene 1, where Audrey says to Touchstone, "Faith, the priest was good enough, for all the old gentleman's saying."

Another passage in "Arthur" gives us old men in a different form:

> Grammar is contained in father which made old men thinner and old men thinner. The edge with their without perhaps it fell. (99)

And what happens when in addition I hear, in "Talk To Saints Or Stories Of Saint Remy" (*PL* 113):

> Talk with saints. How do you do.
> Tell the saints not to bother.

42. See also "George," 301.
43. Stein to Elliot Paul, (?) 30 August 1928, Camille Cummings Collection, Special Collections, University Libraries, University of Colorado at Boulder. For further comments on sound and sight, see "Plays," *LIA* 104–10.

Hours in a house.
A house held ours.
How has a house made a distinct impression. (61)

Or she looks at similar words, one below the other,

Artichokes.
Articles.
A version. (50)

Word for word, by accretion, never phrase for phrase, she moves gradually toward a finish,

Supposing she was ready.
Supposing she was ready before I was.
Supposing she was ready before I was before they came.
Supposing she was ready after they came.
Supposing she was ready before I was before they came after they came.
Supposing she was ready before I was before they came.
Grammar before announcement. (58–59)

Out of such elements she makes the many tiny Arthurs. Each teaches her—and us—the grammatical versatility needed for making speech.

"Grammar is really opening up," she wrote to Virgil Thomson on August 21. She collects grammatical delights throughout the summer of 1928. A few of the ways must be illustrated. Arithmetic, the system of numbers, is a grammar. Sentences about it are occasioned by counting daisies—"She loves me, she loves me not." The daisies lead to arithmetic:

Counting daisies is not an occupation whenever they can be found.
Whenever daisies can be found it is not an occupation to count the daisies which have been found. Why not. Because if any of them are lost they have not been counted as an occupation.
Grammar does mean arithmetic. (93)

Arithmetic immediately yields further grammatical practice:

They act quickly.
Grammar matters if they add quickly. If they add quickly they make a counting of what they are adding and they have added them quickly.
Grammar is made to be by them with their renown. Adding fifteen to twenty-seven makes them have an addition.
A sum which assures them that if they add it it will be correctly added. (93–94)

Counting and reckoning in all the many forms we undertake them are grammatical activities. So are games, each with its own set of rules.

Personality structure also is a form of grammar. It recalls Stein's early studies of friends and acquaintances, recorded in the "diagram book" and other early notebooks. "Arthur" is filled with names of acquaintances and friends, each a grammar. They can also be read as alternative titles for a book about each person or a chapter in "Arthur." Often descriptive detail follows names; Louise, for example, sounds like a cook,

> Louise a grammar omelet and carrot carrot and omelet.
> Louise a grammar.
> Wood which is able to be burnt.
> Alice a grammar.
> Article is the same as an article.
> Henrietta has been triumphant but not laterally.
> Winifred a grammar.
> A grammar is the difference between grain and what has been rewarded. Grain which has been rewarded.
> Simon a grammar.
> Simon is capable of a tiger jealousy.
> Simon is very much is very suspicious.
> Simon a grammar.
> Anthony is certain that George is not an animal tamer.
> Katherine a grammar.
> Katherine Tardy was a name that was engraved on a Maltese cross and it seemed a very pretty name.
> Grammar refers to names as very pretty names.
> That is a little better that which is a little better is that. (93)

The passage ends neatly with her own comment on what she has done and how an improvement satisfactorily concludes an exercise. These are not neat, separate sections offset by spaces, subtitles, numbers, or typographical devices. Each bleeds into the next in a continuous process. The burden of following, separating, and composing the elements is upon the reader, who learns gradually to move word for word, phrase for phrase, breathing space to breathing space, element to element of composition, back and forth and again even as the text moves ahead. What I call bleeding is what makes discovering Stein texts so difficult, so slow, and so exciting.

Increasingly important to Stein as a person and a writer during this summer was Georges Hugnet. One of his problems, already suggested in "Finally George," was that he did not know English grammar, though he no doubt understood many words.

Arthur a grammar was named Arthur a grammar because he could read but not write. (76)

While it may have been occasioned by Hugnet, the grammar study is in part the result of Stein's awareness of his difficulties translating her texts.

In addition to considering his language problems in the grammar, she also drafted, here and in *Paisieu,* sections of what eventually became the fully rounded grammatical portrait, "George Hugnet," discussed in the next chapter. Once she completed that portrait, she felt, as she later reiterated in "Portraits And Repetition" (*LIA* 202), that it no longer mattered whose portrait it was, for it was a self-contained grammatical portrait rather than a representation of someone outside the portrait to whom it referred. She had incorporated Georges Hugnet in her piece, her circle—"in our ring."

On the other hand, "Landscape is not grammar" (98). It is not systematically or permanently organized. The landscape play *Paisieu* explores the pastoral landscape of the Bugey, the region around Belley, but two aspects of landscape that appear in "Arthur" require comment. The first concerns landscape as battleground. One of the ways a landscape becomes historical is by receiving the imprint of its conquerors. Time or history becomes visible in the space of the landscape upon which they have left their marks. The land is marked, or mapped, as campaign history made visible, whether in attack or resistance.

Here is a sentence that sounds as if it came from Stein's reading, fitted into her work:

> There is a difference between grammar and a sentence this is grammar in a sentence I will agree to no map with which you may be dissatisfied and therefore beg you to point out what you regard as incorrect in the position of the troops in my two sketches. (72)

In the landscape of war,

> Battles become hills. Hills a grammar.
> Hills give names to battles
> Hills a grammar
> Battles are named because there have been hills which have made a hill in a battle. (89)

Hills, such as Bunker Hill or the one in Mildred Aldrich's *A Hilltop on the Marne,* become grammatical when they refer to strategic history.

Warfare and conquest are in fact never far from Stein's mind. She sees the artist's work, like the strategist's, as a battle. Gifted strategists devise winning battle plans if they understand the shape of the land and know how to deploy its resources. Both the artist and the general must win battles against resistant material by means of their constructive gift and their genius. It is for their genius that she admired Napoleon, to whom she likened Picasso, as well as Grant, Hannibal, and Wellington, one of many Arthurs. The last two, of course, marked the landscape of the Rhône Valley and southern France, Hannibal on crossing the Alps and Wellington in the Peninsular War.[44]

> A grammar makes an attack. (74)

> Grammar in resistance. (86)

Like strategy, grammar is a science, a set of principles. The successful military strategist must not only know the science of strategy but must also be able to improvise in the actual territory where he is positioned. He must, for example, reject erroneous maps and rely on his own perception of what he sees in the land (72). Unlike standard grammar, landscape is not a blueprint or a perfect map for battles but an actuality which fits no theory. Stein looks at this actuality, reads and writes it.

The second aspect, barely a series of hints in "Arthur" and other works of this summer, has to do with houses in the landscape. Houses, the link between landscape and family life, form a part of the landscape but are also apart from the landscape. In the country especially, they are visible embodiments of the permanence and continuity of families whose lives are inseparable from the land.

> Grammar is in origin. (95)

> Grammar makes they do have children.
> Arrange a long list of when they were born grammar arrange a long list of when they were born. (97)

Families can live by rigid conventions, such as she studies in the grammar of Baltimore, or by loving, fluid relations. At this time, Stein is already engaged in negotiations for the house, felicitously sighted from afar in the landscape, that she succeeds in renting by the spring of 1929. "Arthur" anticipates domestic pleasures.

44. The middle sections of "Arthur" include much about warfare and battles. Late in *A Bouquet. Their Wills.,* the Chorus of Baltimoreans suddenly becomes a Chorus of Wellingtonians (214), as if the work on "Arthur" had suddenly jumped across into the opera. Numerous names in *Paisieu* come from World War I. Already in *LCA* of the preceding summer appear Hannibal and Wellington. History and wars, spread in architecture and monuments throughout the French countryside, move from where Stein is into what she writes.

The detail of the house is very sweet. (79)

may be about a painting or a house.

Grammar is without their house which has been built without them. (96)

Consider a house.
In an address consider a house in an address.
A vocabulary is not an annoyance when they see lilies over roses.
A grammar has nothing to win her as foliage is priceless.
Consider.
Hours in a house.
A house held ours.
How has a house made a distinct impression. (61)

Yet every now and then, in "Arthur" and *Paisieu,* there are tiny hints of uneasiness. Those inside may remain connected to the landscape, looking out at the view, but they may also turn inward, away from the landscape, and end up cut off from the world. The house might close her off from the landscape. Doors and door handles appear (48, 54, 69, 71) that may open—or shut. Even before the house becomes theirs, slight apprehension is audible about sights that may narrow, grammar that may rigidify.

When to be used to it or plant of clouds and definite trees are among enduring it being covered with a cloud by reason of failure in liking to turn back on the view.
View point. (*Paisieu,* 155)

Both the doors and the phrase on turning the back to the view return later.

Meanwhile, daily life offers grammar in profusion, especially in the country, where Stein meditates in loving detail on the rituals and activities that spread before her on walks, among townspeople, farmers, and regular summer visitors to the Bugey who become her friends.

A grammar loads hay on to a wagon. (66)

A grammar with a wedding. (66)

Household a grammar. (88)

The grammar of needlepoint allows play on *Gammar Gurton's Needle,* on what is needless, on the grammar of pain and pleasure,

Needles in grammar.
Needles in grammar plain can place careful just as pleasure is come with a bundle comfort with appoint. Thinks in grammar. (61)

Embroidery, of course, is grammatical:

> Embroidery consists in remembering that it is but what she meant.
> There an instance of grammar.
> Suppose embroidery is two and two. There can be reflected that it is as if it were having red about. (63)

Lifted from the context in the sequence of "Arthur," of course, each of these passages loses some of the grammatical tentacles that constantly reach out for new word ideas. I quote at some length and virtually never omit words or lines because it is the only way to follow how the mind perceives and creates grammar.

And always there is cooking.

> Grammar makes a dish. (98)

> Grammar means that it has to be prepared and cooked and if they are used to one assistant it is because it was necessary not to have but one. (101)

Writing is like cooking. On October 7, after she had finished *A Bouquet. Their Wills.* and *Paisieu* but while she was still working on "Arthur," Stein wrote to Virgil Thomson:

> It is a good country for grammar because cooking is so admirably and so simply organized, a continuous illustration of the essentials of grammar.

A Bouquet. Their Wills. (O&P 195–218)

Unlike *Four Saints In Three Acts* and *A Lyrical Opera,* both subtitled as operas *To Be Sung, A Bouquet. Their Wills.* is not identified by title or subtitle as an opera libretto, nor is it placed, in its only appearance in print, in *O&P,* with the other two operas, at the beginning of the collection. The text, which at first appears to be a play, nevertheless includes unmistakably operatic material. However, it has never been set to music.[45]

The word "will" and ideas connected with wills appear from the beginning of 1927 for a year and a half. A long passage in "George" concerns arrangements for "leaving it to them" (322–24). Another questions the ethics of lawyers and the language of law (312). In the portrait "Dan Raffel. A Nephew,"

45. In a letter to Virgil Thomson postmarked July 13, 1928, Stein speaks in some detail of the new opera; by August 28, she reports that she has finished it. She also later refers to the piece as her "Baltimore opera."

of early 1928, there are bits of legal terminology such as "leak and forfeit" and "a house to inherit" (88). Late in "George," Stein questions inheritance and succession,

> Hours and hours ours and ours bears and bears bear and bear she had no children of her own and when she inherited she inherited nothing in comparison with what she had. (373)

Already in "George," reference is made to the need of Toklas in 1927–28 to safeguard her share of inherited properties in Seattle and Stockton, California, against creditors of her indebted brother Clarence, with whom she co-owns them.[46] Similarly, after the death on February 19, 1928, of Mildred Aldrich, difficulties with her sister Edna, who disapproves of Mildred's will, may contribute to preoccupation with the legal consequences of death. Personal reasons already suggested for Stein to think about her own will are advancing age, the hope of a house, perhaps Michael Stein's new villa, and the first of a new generation with her nephew Allan's first child.

The only specific reference to what is presumably Stein's own will is in an undated letter from her brother Michael, probably written in the early summer of 1928 and sent to Belley.[47] Yet neither this letter nor the other possible reasons explain the insistent recurrence of wills or the writing of a play or libretto about them, especially as it is not Stein's habit to explore solutions to personal problems by writing about them. Her own will is not the subject of the opera.[48] At most, it adds to her meditations upon that "curi-

46. See letters from Albert Rosenshine, San Francisco, the brother of her friend Annette Rosenshine, and letters from Howard Gans. Transfer of funds to Toklas was effected through Stein Brothers and Boyce, Baltimore.

47. Michael wrote, with his own emphases,

> You poor kid. The document I wrote and sent you was the one you were to sign and send me. You did not have to write a word except your signature. When a will is *witnessed* it is not a holographic will and can be written in any way. . . . You failed to *sign* the one you sent me. Hamlet with Hamlet left out. What I said to tear up was my letter, not the will. So now:—Sign the one I wrote and send it to me.

She appears to have added to, copied, or written her own version of the will prepared by her brother rather than signing the one written out for her signature. His response echoes not only anxiety on her part but also confusion about how wills are written.

48. A small punning notation on the *cahier* for "The Art Of Making A Bouquet," which opens the opera, illustrates this tendency away from the personal. On the cover, in the spaces left open for the student's subject and name, Stein plays with entries, bracketed here to show that she later crossed them out:

Cahier d'	[The Art]
Appartenant à	[Heart]
	[no, not The broken Heart]

ous subject" (213), wills. The fact that they do not return later suggests not that she writes a satisfactory will but that the libretto successfully shapes a composition larger than private experience.

Referential sources of Stein's work—the words, distinct from composition or design—do not explain the texts. Yet without some clarity about these sources, the texts, especially when they are dense with detail, often remain more difficult than Stein perhaps realized. Once details are seen as elements of a pattern, a text loses its opaqueness and assumes a surprising transparency. The context of the grammar of wills, the subject of the first part of this section, is heavy with family and becomes more extensive than for most others.

In the winter and spring of 1928, Stein explores how words can be arranged in succession to create meaning. Both in "Finally George" and in "Arthur," she tries out what language can be made to do. While working on these essays, she creates a grammar of love in *A Lyrical Opera* for the fifty-first birthday of Toklas on April 30. In it, two become one in union and time is eliminated.

> Grammar is the art of reckoning that it is by themselves that they are one and two. ("Arthur" 48)

This sentence about singulars and plurals may include preoccupations of *A Lyrical Opera.*

On the other hand,

> Grammar is the same as relative (49)

about relative clauses or the power of grammar over relations, may carry across to relatives in the family such as she will satirize in the opera. She tackles the massive grammar of descent, succession, and inheritance in the patriarchal family, devising in deceptively playful form a devastating indictment of Baltimore.[49]

The rhyme *art*/he*art* converts the personal (heart) into that which is not personal (art) and leaves no broken hearts. French *appartenant* echoes into it.

49. In Stein's work, Baltimore refers to her extended family, her society or class, including even the New York Steins. Her Baltimoreans are both distinct and unified as a group. In other pieces, such as "Business In Baltimore" of 1925, she also speaks in detail and far from flatteringly about middle-class Baltimore Jewish society and family power with which she associates the city as she never does Oakland, California. *MOA* also renders comfortable middle-class living in Baltimore. But not until the opera does she so sharply satirize Baltimore.

What makes her focus on the grammar of family law is that Rose Ellen Stein and her husband, Julian, Gertrude's cousin and financial advisor, needed to put their affairs in order in view of travel plans in Europe in the summer of 1928. Rose Ellen's first marriage, to Simon Walters Frank, which had produced two daughters, Alice and Ellen, ended with Frank's death in 1910. In 1912, she married the banker Julian Stein.[50]

> RoseEllen and Julian are travelling they have nothing to do before leaving. They are not going to die. They are fairly certain and there is not hesitation. (202)

What could have happened to the two Frank daughters had their mother and stepfather died without wills to safeguard the girls' inheritance is described in the following passage, although the parties are not named:

> If they had made their wills they had and they had left it to each other which they did they might have been killed together and if they had the children of which he was not the father would not have inherited anything from their mother nor from their father their mother having inherited from their father and the law presuming that if they are killed together the man lives longer. (214)

If husband and wife are killed together, the law presumes that the wife predeceased the husband, with the result that he inherits her assets, which are in turn passed down, when he dies, along with his own assets, to the next in line in his family. Without special provisions, the children of a wife's first marriage receive nothing, because estate law in patriarchal society gives men preferential treatment.

> This makes no account of anything of accomplishing and examination this is finally predicting that if two are killed it is assumed that the hus-

50. Rose Ellen Stein arrived in France on May 25, 1928, with their son, Julian Jr., nine and one-half years old, for a stay of several months, to be joined later by Julian. Rose Ellen, whose maiden name was Hecht, was from California, but Stein had not known her there in early years, although Michael Stein, in an early, undated letter, mentions an unidentified Hecht family.

Simon Frank, spoken of as Clarence Cone's "chum" (Hortense Moses to Stein, 2 April 1909), died in 1910. The Franks appear to have lived at or owned a house at 22 Talbot Road, Windsor Hills, which after Rose Ellen's second marriage became the residence of Julian and Rose Ellen Stein. In an undated letter to Gertrude Stein, Rose Ellen, recently engaged, hopes to become acquainted with her. Rose Ellen's daughter Alice Frank visited Stein in Paris in 1926 and on January 19, 1928 married Henry Hartman Hecht of San Francisco, unrelated to Rose Ellen's family.

band will outlive everything and so nothing goes to the daughters and this is surprising. Let it be changed so that thing will not be happening and it was done but it took a long time. (196)

Stein's exchange with her cousins appears to have clarified the larger issue of unequal protection of women and men, wives and husbands. More important, however, it opened the question of a lesbian relationship as a marriage not recognized by the law.

If Stein herself was indeed writing a will, hers was a different problem from her cousin's. Her marriage was a personal reality with no legal status. A will to safeguard Toklas is not equivalent to a will to protect Rose Ellen's daughters. Yet like Rose Ellen, if for different reasons, Stein must take steps to safeguard Toklas.[51] Protection for women cannot be taken for granted.

The problem of protecting the daughters of Rose Ellen, discussed no doubt during her visit, apparently allowed Stein to give dramatic shape to the inequality of women and men in the grammar of the patriarchal family.[52] Ironically, death most powerfully dramatizes patriarchal grammar and subordination. Like a refrain, endlessly reiterated in stiff, legal jargon such as the quotation illustrates, the statement of unequal protection under the law for women and their children recurs throughout the text, setting its tone.

Stein's tortured entry into the grammar of wills has a long history in her experience. She had among her papers, plainly not by accident, a large number of documents about bungled wills and disbursements of funds and trusts. All these ended up at Yale.[53] They are a part of the family melodrama that becomes opera in *A Bouquet. Their Wills.*[54]

51. In my essay, "Landscape Is Not Grammar: Gertrude Stein in 1928," *Raritan* 7, no. 1 (summer 1987), I presented Stein's concern about the legal implications of her own marriage for a will as fundamental to the opera. I now see the situation of Rose Ellen as more important for the opera, though not to the exclusion of the Stein-Toklas marriage.
52. Not only Rose Ellen and Julian Stein were in Europe in 1928 but also Howard Gans and his wife Bird Stein. Both couples appear in the opera and in "Arthur A Grammar." Bird Sternberger, the eldest daughter of Solomon and Pauline Stein of New York, had been represented by Howard Gans as her attorney in her divorce suit against her husband, Louis Sternberger, in 1905. On July 9, 1908, Howard Gans married Bird and adopted her children, Robert and Marion. Julian Stein Jr. recalls discussions of wills in the family when he was young (interview with author at his home in Union Bridge, Maryland, 11 November 1987).
53. See Daniel Stein to Meyer Stein, his senior brother, 2 December 1880, about the will of Meyer's father-in-law; Hortense Moses to Stein, 4 October 1906, in response to Stein's request for a copy of a will; Michael Stein to Stein, 11 June 1911, about objects and money willed to Mrs. Ehrman and her daughters; Howard Gans to Leo Stein, 17 September 1940 (?) about disbursement of a trust for Hilda and Hattie, the daughters of Lep Stein, after their death; Edward Putzel, attorney, to Stein, 12 April 1938, about division of a

Her experience of problems with money is not confined to estates and to capital holdings but extends also to her work. Her aggressive handling of book contracts, her suspicions about fees and royalties, and her insistence on frequent royalty statements are well known, a part of her wish to be independent and earn a living by her trade, writing. Such behavior is the result of difficulties and disappointments with publication and of the ridicule to which her work was subjected, which left her feeling that she was not accepted as a serious and professional author who needed to be paid.[55]

It must also come from an upbringing that did not prepare her for the world of work but left her with a powerful need for becoming a success in ways that conflicted with the off-putting innovations of her writing. Her reputation as an art collector, as the hostess of a salon, and as the subject of famous portraits made her appear less professional and wealthier than she was. She and Toklas in fact lived a rather frugal existence, in part through Toklas' skill as a manager.

While what interested Stein as a writer was ultimately the grammar of wills, she did not fail to recognize the complicated real issues they are designed to resolve within the patriarchal social structure. Valid wills, consistent with legal grammar, solve word problems and are, quite literally, bouquets of forget-me-nots. The opera is a series of verbal forget-me-nots assembled into a bouquet: a Stein grammar, a lovers' bouquet, a wedding bouquet, and a word bouquet.

A Bouquet. Their Wills. is the only work in which Stein incorporates two separate, earlier pieces, a procedure that runs counter to her expressed con-

---

trust for the unmarried daughters of Moses Keyser, Stein's maternal grandfather, upon the death of the last daughter. Also, the will and papers about the estate of her brother, Simon D. Stein (deceased August 18 or 19, 1913), and about Mrs. Mary Virginia Moffitt, his caretaker-landlady and the beneficiary of his will for her lifetime, City Hall, San Francisco (see *LCA* 235). Also letters from Hortense Moses, 26 December 1911; Michael Stein to Leo Stein, 29 May 1896; Michael Stein to Etta Cone, 14 January 1937, Cone Archive, Baltimore Museum; and personality studies in Stein's early notebooks.

54. On the back of a letter of 27 August 1927 from George Platt Lynes appears in Stein's hand this passage, later incorporated in *LCA* (215):

> is she going to sell her money very well this is my will this is all very well this is all my will [well?] as it is a habit of the country where she has made her present residence if she has not gone elsewhere to do something which is what she has planned to do.

55. An example of this time is the correspondence with the Four Seas Company, publisher of *G&P,* already by 1927 near bankruptcy. Stein asked Howard Gans to check on her royalties, thinking that if the company was not bankrupt, it owed her royalties, and if it was bankrupt, it owed her the remaining copies of her book (see Edmund R. Brown, Herbert Ehrman, Howard Gans to Stein, 1927–28).

victions. The center is the play or libretto proper, written in 1928, "Their Wills, a bouquet. / In Six Acts" (196). Inserted after "Act Three" as an "Interlude" or entr'acte is "Simons a Bouquet," a long portrait of 1913 (203–10), ending with the first paragraph of page 210. She then directly returns to the play text with three scenes but once more inserts the titles "Interlude" and "Simons a bouquet" (211), the text not reprinted; either intended to be inserted or to be moved from page 203 to page 211. She goes on to "Act IV" with fourteen scenes (211–16), "Act Last," with one line of text, and "Act Five" (216–18) with two scenes. There is no "Act Six."

The text begins with "The Art Of Making A Bouquet" (195–96), a short, abstract composition, presumably written some months before the libretto proper. It serves as a prologue or overture. How Stein came to incorporate the two separate pieces into the new work is of interest precisely because it is unusual.[56]

The bouquet appears in all three parts. The combination of bouquets and wills is less unlikely than it may seem. A bouquet of flowers may be offered upon a death. It may be a lover's gift or a wedding bouquet. It may celebrate fame or success. Stein always reads metaphors literally. To "say it with flowers" is an impossibility; to say means to use words. Retaining another metaphor, however, she writes the only thing a writer can offer—a bouquet of words, a composition.[57] I shall follow the text as it is printed.

56. *A Bouquet. Their Wills.*

> "A Bouquet. The Art of Making A Bouquet," late 1927 or early 1928, Paris;
> "Their Wills, a bouquet / In Six Acts," summer 1928, Belley;
> "An Interlude / Simons a Bouquet" written early fall 1913
> (not to be confused with "Simon," fall 1913)
> Play text continues
> "Interlude / Simons a bouquet" to be reinserted or moved from p. 203
> Act IV
> Act Last
> Act Five

On the inside cover of the *cahier* for "A Bouquet" is entered "The Art Of Making A Bouquet" and "Introducing Their Wills. a bouquet in six acts."

57. See also *LCA* (197, 204); the many flowers and bouquets throughout her work; the play *Say It With Flowers* (1931); various postcards and notes showing thoughts, verses, and drawings associated with the language of flowers. Stein frequently plays with the vocabulary of floral sentiments and undoubtedly knew Kate Greenaway's *The Language of Flowers* (1884) and some of the so-called books of knowledge that included details about the symbolism of flowers. Privately, to Toklas, she sometimes wrote little flower poems like this one, in a 1928 *carnet,*

> I say it in flowers, I do, I do
> I say it in posies in roses and pinks. . . .

"The Art Of Making A Bouquet," originally "A Bouquet," is in Stein's *transition* bibliography of 1929 as the last piece of 1927. The text gives no certain evidence of when it was written.[58] It completely fills one *cahier* in the series, *La Parole du Maître: Connaissances Utiles* (*The Word of the Master: Useful Knowledge*). This particular notebook is subtitled "L' Art de faire un bouquet," translated in the title of Stein's piece. The picture on the front cover shows four ladies on a terrace that opens onto a garden, cutting flowers for decorative arrangements. Stein relies on a section of the back cover which instructs:

> *Pour faire un joli bouquet, il ne faut pas seulement du gout,*[59] *mais une dexterité, une habileté qui touche à l'art. Il faut, en outre, un talent de conception, égal à ce qu'on exigerait d'un peintre, pour faire un tableau, ou d'un dramaturge pour écrire son ouvrage. Il importe de composer d'abord, en prévoyant les fleurs et les feuillages qui ne feront pas un contraste trop dur avec les vases, les étoffes et les teintures des appartements. L'art, en l'occurrence, consiste moins à réunir les éléments nombreux d'une forte gerbe, qu'à rapprocher ou éloigner les fleurs qui s'harmonisent ou se heurtent. Il importe même qu'elles ne soient pas trop serrées les unes contre les autres, car l'effet à produire est moins dans la quantité des branches que dans leur disposition et l'harmonie des tonalités.*

This passage gives directions for assembling a pretty bouquet in the proper style.[60] It requires not only taste but artistic talent equal to that of the painter

58. The sixth, last but one manuscript *cahier* of "George" appears to have the word *bouquet* scribbled on it, but the reason is unclear. Near the end of *LCA,* Stein speaks of "the end of the season bouquet," carefully listing the flowers included, which leads to "an unexpected invitation to carry a basket . . . back and forth . . ." (197; see also "A bouquet and so forth," 204).
59. On the outside back cover of the *cahier,* in Stein's hand, appears the French word *gout* (taste) and the phrase, "very little of it today very little."

    In her text, Stein is saying something about translation. Here is an "arrangement" as translation of the French section, executed with the help of Serge Gavronsky:

    > How to make a pretty bouquet: one must have not only taste but also the dexterity and skill of an artist. Also, one's ability to conceive would be close to the eye of a painter painting a picture or a playwright writing a play. First one must envision the final composition, avoiding those flowers and leaves that contrast too sharply with the vases, upholstery, and tapestried walls of the apartment to be decorated. Avoid bunching flowers too closely together. And be careful: in order to reach the desired effect, it's less a question of the number of branches than of arranging them so that the colors harmonize.

60. In *Paris France* (1939) Stein again speaks of intricately organized arrangements in cooking and in the disposition of flowers or fruits:

or playwright, who, like the florist, works in three-dimensional space. Stein follows these directions. Into a single sentence spread through the whole *cahier* she carefully enters the elements of composition—colors, flowers, forms of phrasing, rhythms, balance. By the end, the sentence has become the bouquet and the *cahier* the vase for it. She brings the words together and sets them apart by their visual and auditory qualities—alliteration, rhythm, sound, look, weight. The piece uses almost totally decontextuated, abstract, and Latinate words—"advantage," "consequence," "adaptability," "disposal," "maligning," "penetrating," "enlargement"—and creates outward and inward, unifying and dispersing movement.

Prepositions, adverbs, conjunctions connect the elements and create relations in space. Here is a sampling from pages 195–96:

> with aside next to be near that without
> with joining it
> in straining it from without
> not with but
> blend behind in a night.

Much of the piece moves from word to word by visual and auditory rhythms. In the final section of this tour de force, she plays, as she often does, with a restricted vocabulary of words related by sound or sight, composing and recomposing,

> what they wish that they wish which is what they wish what is the wish which is what which they wish. . . . (196)

The bouquet concludes with three tiny sentences which, like a ribbon, give it a circular riddling conclusion, emphatic with the *s, sh, ch* sounds introduced earlier that almost make a tongue twister,

> And so and so. What is it. It is what they wish which is which is which is it. (196)

> Flowers are now bought in great bunches and anybody within reason can have all they want. So now flowers are almost arranged in many homes in the English manner lots of flowers everywhere and the new interest in flowers is to arrange them to give an effect of violence, of activity, of strangeness. Gradually that is producing its own elegance. (112–13)

Bouquets of flowers as subjects of still lifes also added to their compositional interest. The painter is the first artist mentioned in the text with the illustration on the cover of the *cahier*.

In spite of its neat ending, the piece, brilliant in conception, appears uncertain. Stein seems to be trying out what she can do with sound and sight, but the bouquet gathers little verbal resonance or musical flourish. Intended perhaps as an appropriately light and abstract decoration, an ironic stage set or frame, it opens the play.

The text proper, "Their Wills, a bouquet," is held together by three brilliant inventions. The first is the statement of Rose Ellen Stein's situation with its implication of inequality. It is phrased in abstract, legalistic terms, in a stiffly grammatical if-then sentence so long and impersonal as to be meaningless.

> If they had made a will in which they left everything to one another and their son had not been born and they had been killed together it would be assumed that the man lived longer so all would have been inherited by his half brother and not by her daughter and her own daughter not even what she had inherited she her mother from the father who had been her husband and was the father while she was the mother of the daughter. (201)

This central problem is stated again and again, with variations in phrasing but no changes in its premises. The situation is laid out in parallel phrases—made out a will, left everything to one another—held together by the unstated grammar of the inequality of men and women,[61] the clauses coupling the Baltimoreans (197)—which they take for granted. The stiff, reiterated sentence about death and wills is filled with rhythms and cadences.

The second invention is the operatic Chorus of Baltimoreans, the rhythm of its very name heavy with convention. Perhaps Stein thought of the members of her family together as a chorus or society. When they are not a unified group but merely pairs, they become the "characters" of the libretto, always moving in twos. She describes the chorus as she would describe her family. Many are bankers.

> Chorus of Baltimoreans are distinguished by their management. (197)
>
> At home, the Baltimoreans are well behaved and sociable,

61. The inequality becomes even more poignant when one realizes that what Julian Stein Sr., himself the son of his father's second wife, might by the logic of estate law inherit from Rose Ellen, if she were to predecease him and there were no child by their marriage. Upon his own death, then, his property would go to his half brother and sister, the children of his father's first wife. The parallels of his and Rose Ellen's situations dramatize the legal differences.

Chorus of Baltimoreans are all very quiet in the home although they are gay in talking and talk in laughing and laugh in talking. (201–2)

Her words serve both as characterization and stage directions. The chorus "had heard nothing" (196). It is not assigned particular lines but may speak or sing or act some lines that offer fine, difficult challenges to composer and director:

> Scene iv
>
> Chorus of Baltimoreans have a mixture of their seeing religion.
>
> Chorus of Baltimoreans. Have a conscience about sun on Sunday.
>
> Baby might baby might baby baby baby baby baby baby baby might baby might baby baby baby might.
>
> Very near to tears. (213)

Stein's Baltimoreans act and think in unison, by convention and sentiment, with no need or room for disagreement. Money-minded materialists, they feel not that money is a blessing but that "a blessing is money" (206). They express people in numbers:

> If a million is two hundred and three how many Michaels make a Simon and how many RoseEllens make a melon. Three ages in three. (202)

They are materialists:

> Chorus of Baltimoreans. Never sing flowers as they are not fond of flowers, they prefer oysters. . . . (199)

Baltimore is the center of the world, she suggests ironically on the model of "the house that Jack built":

> In Baltimore there is traffic management in spite of of every country prefer the United States of America of every state prefer the state of Maryland of every city prefer the city of Baltimore of every house prefer his house of every wife prefer his wife and their use. (197)[62]

62. While writing the opera, Stein also answered the *transition* questionnaire sent to some expatriate Americans, asking why they preferred to live outside America, "Why I Do Not Live In America." A part of her answer, which she did not consider literature and did not include in her 1929 bibliography, reads,

> America is now early Victorian, very early Victorian, she is a rich and well nourished home but not a place to work. (*HWW* 51)

What she describes is the Baltimore of her own family, "a nice place to be brought up in" but not a place to live or work for a serious artist. Her description in the questionnaire is more charitable than the satirical depiction of Baltimore in the libretto.

The third invention concerns the population or "characters" in the text. They are not individuals but come paired as couples, as Baltimoreans are programmed to do. They have first names of the many members of the extended Stein and Cone families, but no last names—"Pauline and Charles Daniel and Dolene Dolene and Henry Amy and Simon," and so on. Most of the couples are a man and a woman, but a few are joined by different verbal links.

Stein constantly puns with names, making them convertible or interchangeable. For example, Rose Ellen becomes Helen and Llewelen (198), invented after the visit of Llewelyn Powys that summer. Rose Ellen and Julian Stein are central to the text and always together as a pair, though with shifting names. They bring with them the inequality that requires special wills. For an opera, the many couples open possibilities of duets, quartets, and other permutations of two or three for different voices. Arthur Raffel, her nephew, married in 1928.

> Arthur as a grammar is nicely married before their return which is a surprise to not anything. ("Arthur" 80)

For others, Stein becomes a matchmaker constantly making and divorcing couples.

> A grammar has melody and disunion and there occasion in branch come flattering a maddened imbroglio. A grammar in continuity. A grammar in disassociation find does well and tangle. An indicted description meant to be coupled. Withdrew. (56)

She joins a partner from one marriage with one from another, breaking up marriages, setting up affairs, and destroying the grammar of the family. The term "partners" is appropriate for the Steins, businessmen and bankers.

"Change your partners" also makes the opera into an elaborate square dance. She must have had fun constructing them, using her familiarity

---

Problems of the rights of expatriates to citizenship and the presumption of renunciation of citizenship were discussed extensively in the French press in 1928. See, for example, letter from Edward Titus, Paris *Herald Tribune,* 9 January 1928, 8.

An amusing anecdote of that summer is that when Julian Jr. was ill, his mother relied on a French doctor recommended by Stein until she located an American doctor from Baltimore. She eventually discovered, to her relief, that the French doctor had trained at the Johns Hopkins Medical School. Later in the summer, Rose Ellen herself was examined by specialists in England. On September 7, she wrote to Stein of a "chorus of doctors" who had told her what she knew all along, that she suffered from migraines.

> Charles and Helen are happily married in spite of the fact that Helen has headaches. (197)

with individuals to pair them effectively. The pairs move in twos and fours and sixes. These can become the chorus, although the chorus can also be a separate group, and they are accompanied, though they do not hear it, by the beat of the legal word problem that marks an end point for all Baltimoreans.

She repeats that the Chorus of Baltimoreans "consists of men and women" (200, 201). Likewise, in "Arthur," she writes,

> To begin with women. Women and men. (64)

The statement sounds like a truism, so simple and obvious that it is easy to overlook how serious its simplicity is. It is about sexuality—being male and female. These terms contrast with those of the patriarchal family which always refer to relations, not individuals—being husbands, wives, sons, daughters, fathers, mothers, cousins.

It is not necessary to know the identity and history of each family member, although familiarity adds to the flavor of her satire. She attacks family order not only in marriages but also by muddling blood relations and generations. Her sister Bertha, the mother of Arthur Raffel, becomes his cousin, daughter, father, sister until we no longer know who is who in relation to whom.

A dramatic point can be made with the term "sister": in a family, a sister is always a sister, with no choice in the matter. Yet the sister of Stein's choice, Alice, can be wife, lover, or mother, and her first though not her last name can change to Ada and others, suggesting endlessly varied roles, not tied to unalterable grammatical relations. Even in the interlude, in the early portrait, "Simons a Bouquet," she speaks of the many roles of one human being:

> Suppose it came that by a reason which is beside the shock it happens that sisters are wives, very neatly then mothers are calling. (204)

In "Arthur" she inserts Edwin Dodge (54), one of Mabel Dodge's ex-husbands, and Howard Gans (52, 55), who married Bird Stein after winning her divorce from her husband.

Stein attempts to free sexuality from the rigid, repressive patriarchal grammar of law, business, property, and time, asking,

> Who has pressure to bear. (197)

The answer is that couples have to bear the pressures of unequal relations. Even death, in Baltimore, does not grant them equality. Yet at the last, there are only men and women.

> The last time is the worst. Chorus of Baltimoreans consist in men and women. (201)

Running through the libretto as an undercurrent are indirect references to Stein and Toklas, their marriage, their values, their interests, with small concrete details about daily life, wine, food, a quiet dinner that recalls *A Lyrical Opera* (200). There are also suggestions that while the product of heterosexual marriages is children, who perpetuate the patriarchy, the product of the Stein-Toklas relation is literature, free of the pressures of money, wills, power, and patriarchal family grammar. Always inflexible systems contrast with fluid personal relations.

> After Act three there will be an interlude Simons a bouquet. (201),

she says at the beginning of Act III.

Subtitled "An Interlude," "Simons a Bouquet" is entered between Acts III and IV. This double portrait was apparently written in the early autumn of 1913, as a memorial, possibly in Spain. The two Simons are her brother Simon D. and her cousin Simon H., who died within a month in late summer of 1913.[63] The two Simons allow play with names, identity, family relation to herself and her cousin Julian. In the Stein family were numerous Simons, who, along with Rose Ellen's first husband, Simon Frank, must all have echoed through her writing of the opera. Centered on death and identity, this early portrait is a fitting piece for incorporation into the opera. Stein plays with the title of the Interlude, which allows us to hear Simons as a plural and to carry popular overtones of Simple Simon, simon-pure, and others. She is also inconsistent in capitalizing and decapitalizing "A Bouquet."[64]

Nevertheless, "Simons a Bouquet" creates problems in the opera. First, it is a very long portrait and, as an interlude, takes almost one-third of the

63. Her brother died on August 18 or 19, 1913, in San Francisco, and her cousin Simon H., the brother of Julian, the night of September 2 to 3, 1913, in Baltimore. The proximity of the deaths, the identity of the names, their different relationships to her, and perhaps even the fact that Simon H. was named in Simon D.'s will as his executor, presumably led to a double portrait.

    The much shorter portrait "Simon," written later in the fall of 1913 and printed only once—in the *Yale University Library Gazette* 50, no. 1 (July 1975): 42–43—must not be confused with "Simons A Bouquet." It even strikes the eye as looking visually quite different.

64. "Simons A Bouquet," of 1913, is a separate manuscript in the Stein collection. The text is not copied into the manuscript of the libretto, but Toklas must have entered it into the typescript submitted to Maurice Darantière, the printer in Dijon. That typescript, like all those that he received, is not preserved.

twenty-three pages. In addition, it differs radically from the rest of the play. Printed only in this text, it is written in the style of *Tender Buttons* (1913) and requires very different reading from the play and the opening piece on bouquets and would require different singing in an opera. Both "Simons a Bouquet" and "Simon" need careful analysis, which they have never received. It is not clear to what extent they rest on unknown biographical information.

The inclusion of the early double portrait creates stylistic difficulties which become increasingly disturbing for the libretto after the interlude. Stein appears to have had problems placing it in the opera. Several times before the end of Act III, she speaks of inserting the portrait of Simons after that act, but she does not always seem clear about the exact point of insertion, or perhaps about where the act is to end. Before Act IV, after three short scenes following the interlude, she again inserts "Interlude / Simons a bouquet" (211), but without the text; it is unclear whether the interlude is to be repeated at this point. From Act IV on, the play becomes less and less coherent, as if the interlude had interrupted its flow.

She then returns through the tunnel of the one-line transitional Act Last to her play text and wills with Act Five. Even that passage disintegrates, however, and references appear that do not fit with her earlier scheme. Increasingly, people from Stein's own contemporary world enter—with names like Regan, Caroline Dudley, Mrs Reagan; Grant Virginia, where Sherwood Anderson lived; Margaret Lewis, a Radcliffe classmate; Gaston Bérard, a wartime friend, not to be confused with Christian Bérard, all here for unclear reasons. The Chorus of Baltimoreans is suddenly extended to a Chorus of Kansas City—Virgil Thomson and Eugene MacCown—a chorus of Independence, Iowa, and so on.

By Act Five—there is no Act Six—she seems to have lost her grip on the material: she refers to Avery Hopwood (217), who visited her in the early summer of 1928 but died on July 1 by drowning, and even though she ends the play with a last reference to Julian and Rose Ellen dying in an accident, she is unable to pull it together. Some details carry over from or to "Arthur A Grammar," "Almond grammar" (100) and "Arthur and almonds," in the "Simons" interlude of the play (210)—but any parallels in intention remain unclear. She fills what becomes the last *cahier* to the end and stops, perhaps in exasperated frustration over the return to the Baltimore past,

> A grammar relates to not liking to see again those you used to know. ("Arthur" 57)

In spite of problems of organization, completion, and balance of this text, the indictment of patriarchal thinking is brilliant, inventive, and, if narrower, far sharper than the attack of "Patriarchal Poetry," whose title appears to give easy access to its subject matter. It is surprising how many readers have focused on "Patriarchal Poetry" as the central indictment of patriarchal thinking and how few have even considered this play.

One wonders whether Stein spoke to Virgil Thomson about setting her text to music. There is no record of discussion with any other composer or friend and no letter about it. She may have felt that the family details made it a risky work for performance. They did not keep her from publishing it in *Operas And Plays* (1932), however, for she did not thus censor her writing.[65]

The Grammar of Landscape

To Stein, the trouble with plays is that they are apprehended piecemeal, in successive scenes, acts, moments, sections, which require remembering what came before in order to understand what takes place in the present on stage. At no time is there total dramatic presence and intensity, as she discusses in detail in the lecture "Plays" (*LIA* 93–135). Landscapes, on the other hand, are essences, complete at every moment because they are altogether before us in every detail; to Stein, we apprehend them, unlike most plays, in their totality ("Plays" 122, 128–31). *Paisieu* is a landscape play. The painterly term "landscape" describes a play that aspires to the condition of landscape—total theater, complete, present to eye and ear, moving at every moment, defeating time and memory.

At the start of the second Act One, Stein refers loosely to "[i]ts beginning in twenty two" (156), her first experience of plays as landscapes in St.-Rémy in 1922–23. What is new is the idea of plays as landscapes, not of memory as both a necessity for understanding them and an interference with dramatic intensity. Stein's studies of attention at Harvard and her interest in meditation may have prepared her much earlier for her concern with memory. Memory as lowering dramatic power appears, for example, in Hugo Münsterberg's *The Silent Photoplay* (1916). He contrasts the limitations of theater and the new possibilities of film, which can project the past through cutbacks directly onto the screen as "actual reminiscences" and can open the mental act of attending through close-ups.[66]

65. It has to my knowledge only once been given a performance, by students at Washington University, St. Louis, Missouri, upon the occasion of the symposium, "Gertrude Stein @ The Millennium," 2–5 February 1999.

66. Hugo Münsterberg, *The Film: A Psychological Study: The Silent Photoplay in 1916* (1916; reprint, New York: Dover, 1970), 39ff. I am not suggesting that Stein relied upon Münsterberg's book but that ideas that he among others identifies have a history that goes back in part to the 1890s. Much has been said about the influence of William James upon Stein, but no one has looked in detail at the intellectual climate of her student

Landscape plays are not plays about the country. *Paisieu,* subtitled *A Play* and *A Work Of Pure Imagination In Which No Reminiscences Occur,* not only is a landscape play but also literally renders the landscape as play and the play as landscape. As a result, it includes the landscape of the Rhône Valley, where Stein was spending her fifth summer. Local details are distributed throughout the text just as details of a landscape stretch across a view we contemplate. If this play encompasses the landscape, it must be possible to read it as we read a landscape and look directly at all there is to see. What follows is one reading of the text, with quotations from its only appearance in print in *Last Operas And Plays* (1949).

Paisieu (LO&P 155–81)

Stein looks out at what she sees:

> Who can think things.
> One or two if the sun sets behind a cloud does it set. (162)

A similar scene appears near the end of the play:[67]

> She says that the sun does not set yet because it is behind the mountain. (181)

In "Arthur," written alongside *Paisieu* as Stein works her way through grammar and landscape, sun, cloud, and mountain appear also:

---

days, evident in course descriptions, lecture notes, and examinations, which show what thinking was encouraged, what answers looked for.

Münsterberg, under whom Stein studied, is still all but forgotten. Yet his work on perception was related, like that of James, to German research on vision by Wundt, Helmholtz, and others, and undoubtedly influenced Stein's approach to perception. For a related study, see Marianne L. Teuber, "Helmholtzian Visual Science and the Dissolution of Perspective in Cubism" (paper presented at the 71st annual meeting of the College Art Association of America, Panel on Scientific Theory and Artistic Practice from Plato and Praxiteles to Einstein, Philadelphia, Pa., 17–19 February 1983).

67. Whether or not the sections concern the same scene and time is important only for understanding in what sequence Stein composed the two pieces. The drafts in *carnets* and the many sections of text that appear in both *Paisieu* and "Arthur" suggest that she rearranged some passages perhaps originally drafted in a different order. The two pieces must be examined together, as I do here, and compared also with "George Hugnet," discussed in the next chapter.

Unlike the Baltimore opera, which carries over to "Arthur" only in a few details, *Paisieu* and "Arthur" interpenetrate. They support my contention, made in discussing "Finally George," that Stein, in the "grammar" or language studies, works out writing problems that lead directly to new works. The same is true, as the next two chapters show, of the next language studies and works written alongside.

> Grammar makes not a doubt that the sun which is behind the hills has been and there.
>
> This is a trinket of grammar.
>
> When it in cousin of the daughter.
>
> Why is there a case of some being fond of those younger.
>
> There can be no confusion between a sun behind a cloud or behind a mountain.
>
> Landscape is not grammar. ("Arthur" 98)

This scene is not raw nature nor is it nature systematized or abstracted. Rather, it is nature perceived as we have been taught by the painters to see it. Are we looking at this landscape through its reflection in a glass such as Claude Lorrain[68] used to study and define possible views of a landscape opening up behind him?

> When to be used to it or plant of clouds and definite trees are among enduring it being covered with a cloud by reason of failure in liking to turn back on the view.
>
> View-point. (*Paisieu* 155)

The beholder interprets and shapes what the eye sees, not what word associations project before the eye. As any painter knows, the word "blue" oversimplifies what we see,

> A matter of fact is that there is a blue sky of different colors. A blue sky of different colors. (159)

Without observation, common associations become errors.

> A smoke does not always mean a train it means a field. (172)

The landscape of *Paisieu* is full of local detail of the Rhône Valley. It is dominated by verticals—mountains, passes, valleys, crevices, moraines, plateaus—and by water—marshes, rivers, streams, lakes, rain, gorges, cascades. Together they make for flooding, erosion, and drainage, monitored by man. Trees appear throughout the play, especially the fast-growing poplars planted to reclaim the marshland, but also willows, oaks, chestnuts, walnut

68. The so-called Claude glass provided a way of framing picturesque scenery. "A small, portable mirror backed with dark foil, it was named for the French painter who most perfectly harmonized classical architecture, leafy groves, and distant water. If the view in the mirror approximated to this Claudian ideal, it was judged sufficiently 'picturesque' to be appreciated or even drawn. Later variations tinted the glass with the light of a radiant dawn or roseate sunset." Simon Schama, *Landscape and Memory* (New York: Alfred A. Knopf, 1995), 10–12.

trees, and conifers, with all the different greens of such variety. Ferns, mushrooms, nuts, pinks, lavender, harebells, and roses grow here. Horses, oxen, and cows work and produce on the land. The cows sleep on marsh grass, locally called *blache,* "left to dry as bedding" (163, 177). Hay is cut, grain planted, grapes grown and harvested. The landscape includes the people whose work and relations it shapes as they in turn shape it.

The play is populated by innumerable names. With few exceptions, they are not names of people Stein knew nor names she had used in other works.[69] Most are first names, but a few have last names attached: Herbert, Hildebrand, William, Albert, Eldridge Godfrey, Gustave, Germaine and her child. Some, such as Mary Augustine France Perrine, sound like ordinary local names. Yet this name soon becomes Mary Auguste France Perrine (159, 161) and even Mary Perrine Hubert William Harvey (160). Names and their combinations, sometimes androgynous, change constantly. Mattie leads to Minnie, Winifred to Fred. Familiar but not intimate, the many first names sound like casual acquaintances taken for granted in the country and requiring no formal introduction. They are figures moving about the landscape, not characters in a play acting their parts against a backdrop of scenery.

> Having passed all that time without knowing their name it is not necessary.
>
> To be called to be. (161)

Free play with names carries through the landscape, but names of people Stein had come to know personally and with whom she developed friendships also appear that summer. For example, in a draft of a letter of thanks to the Baroness Lucy Pierlot, the mother of the d'Aiguys, whose family portrait, "The d'Aiguys," she also wrote that summer, Stein expressed her ap-

69. A few are names of people Stein knew or knew of, but they carry no personal weight: Walter Badenouch, Walter Badenough Hardy, in Paris since before World War I, on the board of the American Library, trustee of the fund for Mildred Aldrich, related to the young George Platt Lynes, who stayed with him upon his first visit to Paris and was introduced to Stein by Hardy's wife; Edna Mencken, Edna Kenton, crossover of Mencken and Edna Aldrich, Mildred's sister, in the kind of name game Stein liked and that recurs especially in *Short Sentences* of 1932. Once she speaks of her cousins, Howard and Bird Stein Gans, at Aix-les-Bains that summer, defamiliarized by omitting the last name, using the plural and casting Bird as a common noun: "Howards are happily without birds . . ." (170).

Several are historic figures of World War I: John Allenby, a secret agent; Sir Robert Keith Arbuthnot, a rear admiral who died in battle in 1916; Lord Distant Ismay, the British minister, whose name asks for word play. These, not native to the region of Belley, may have entered the play from Stein's reading. What matters is less their identification than the patterning of her play with names.

preciation of the use of the garden at the Château de Béon, her residence, during her absence; written in Stein's French, ungrammatical in spelling but entirely French in sound, it is reproduced here as she drafted it.

> Ici en regardant les arbres les montagnes et les verdures . . . tous commencent a s'eclaircir. Pour m'amuser [a cote] j'eu commence une petite pastorale. . . . *Il y a plusieurs nom des personnes dans cette pastorale mais pas de personnages* et les peupliers sont decidement en vue" (Here, looking at the trees, the mountains and the greenery, everything is beginning to come clear. To amuse myself I have [in addition] started a little pastoral. . . . There are names of persons in it but no characters, and the poplars are there to see.)[70]

This pastoral is *Paisieu.* Characters (*personnages*) are persons in books who can be identified. Names (*nom[s] de[s] personnes*), on the other hand, are words or names without identifiable subjects, not tied to rules of grammar. Names as words can be moved and composed freely rather than in accordance with representation of persons or meanings. Stein's phrase recalls *As You Like It,* another pastoral that disengages names and identities. In *A Bouquet. Their Wills.,* she lifts names from persons by breaking down the rigid grammar of the family. *Paisieu* gives the comic spirit free play.

In June 1928 Rose Lucie Renée Anne d'Aiguy was born, the child of Diane (May) and François d'Aiguy, the grandchild of the Baroness Pierlot, and the Rose of the later *The World Is Round.*[71]

Among all these names, one stands out that recurs throughout the play, sometimes alone, sometimes as one in a series: Geronimo.

> Gerald Geronimo can be mistaken for some one else. (161)

Geronimo! The word must be spoken, heard, and seen on the page. Unlike the many known Georges and unlike even the Arthur of the grammar, who is less firmly identified yet suggests real figures and meanings, Geronimo animates every detail of the verbal landscape of *Paisieu* but carries no real reference. It is not even an English name, nor clearly a first or last name, and though it sounds masculine, it can change gender, as in "Geronimo, the embroidress" (166).

Geronimo lives in the sound and rhythm of the word, not in its reference.

70. Draft, with corrections by Toklas in brackets, and emphases added, "Letters" *carnet,* 1928.

71. In a *carnet* with late sections of "Arthur" and text for *Paisieu* is a draft of congratulations to the Baroness upon the child's birth.

Joseph Geronimo can always change his name. (166)

Geronimo makes a middle. (158)

Geronimo is a pivot, an idea around which gather words, names, and elements of composition. It is an everyman with far more color and music than that pronoun carries, a free word for play that need not be nailed down to an identity. Sometimes it lightly rhymes or alliterates, as emphases show:

*G*ilbert *G*eroni*mo* felt it to be *so*. (169)

It almost becomes a place name in "Philadelphia Geronimo" (180), "Everest Geronimo" (169). Yet it is not a place to visit or someone to meet. No name in this play is a person, and Geronimo least of all.

I hesitate to annotate Geronimo, for what matters is its physical word value that allows it to sing. Yet of course it teases us into identifications. I add here only some possible references: Saint Jerome, translator of the Bible into the Vulgate; the cry of parachutists, Geronimo! we have landed; the Apache Chief Geronimo, who rebelled against the restrictions placed upon his people; San Geronimo, California, a farming community north of San Rafael in the Bay area that Stein knew in her youth; the landscape of Hieronymus Bosch's Garden of Earthly Delights; the Marquis de Sade's "Commentaire sur Saint Jérôme," set to music for voice and piano that year by Virgil Thomson. Such tentative echoes must be kept light and must not lead us away from the marshlands into a world of fact and representation.

On August 21, Stein wrote to Thomson,

> I have begun a pastoral on a marsh Geronimo on a marsh which does some very good things so far.

On October 7,

> I finished my second play the story of Geronimo is rather nice . . . (the first play is *A Bouquet. Their Wills.*).

In the portrait, "George Hugnet," begun in *Paisieu* (178) and "Arthur" (94–96), Geronimo becomes central to the triad of alliterating names, George, Genevieve, and Geronimo.

Nature and the life of the landscape and life in the landscape interpenetrate in *Paisieu.* So do the many forms of language which purists of grammar and genre keep separate but which Stein loosely joins: bits of description, narrative, observation, commentary, interpretation, fragments of speech, hints of gesture, stage directions, advice, exclamation, dialogue. All these compose the play as they compose the landscape, always there and always changing, filled with sounds and sights that make everyday life go on. Nothing is fixed, nothing systematic, nothing regulated by unities. The landscape is all diversity.

Here a local is characterized:

> Mary August France Perrine makes it a duty to be seen and to be sure to do about it all make it in pain. (161)

We do not know what she does, and it does not matter, for the sentence tells clearly what she is like.

Here is an insistent piece of advice:

> Never eat never eat never eat it. (161)

Eat what? It does not matter, for we listen to the expression of advice. Bells ring rhyming welcomes:

> To bell welcome. (161)

Tiny narratives appear:

> A little boy bringing grapes on a plate (161)

sounds like stage directions for a walk-on part. They become a pantomime, a tale told by someone, a detail of description:

> Scene in which Geronimo visits Germaine and her child and they laugh about it. (161)

What matters is not what they laugh about but that two people in the landscape exchange laughter.

> Gerald Geronimo come to mother (160)

may be speech or narrative.

Here is a sentence made for a director to interpret:

> Penfold was a name which Vincent Geronimo knew Mrs. Penfold said and it was true that Vincent Geronimo was just then with them. (174)

An ordinary exclamation is heard,

> Good God. (180)

And there is the weather, especially clouds, always moving and shaped daily into perception and conversation, the essence of life in and of the landscape:

Weak ways of clouds. (164)

Did he say that there would be no rain but a dark cloud would give drops. (170)

All these are the makings of daily life—views, weather, greetings, small talk, gossip,

How do you do may be. (156)

In this small sequence of social non sequiturs, who knows, marries, or invites whom is not the question, but the perpetual desire to wed endures:

Genevieve Butler knew Christian Geronimo.
A wedding is a certainty.
Genevieve Butler answered in inviting.
Christian Geronimo to Germaine's wedding. (170)

There is punning humor in this marsh.

Paolo Poplar do be incased with a merriment as marsh. (161)

Widows widowed with recommended dahlias and thousands. (161)

There are invitations, refusals, exchanges of gifts, a letter to be written to a mother, with "She yawned" attached to the mother or the writer, we know not which (174). Endless small talk and to-do about nothing in particular makes patterns of the daily life and the scenery.

The activities in the landscape include Stein's own. Small events of her life enter the play since she too is in the landscape, though her name appears only once, coupled with Geronimo (157), which depersonalizes it. Joseph Brewer was expected to visit, and René Crevel, approached about translating *Three Lives,* are decontextuated as Joseph Geronimo and Rene Geronimo.

Gregory Alice "photographed in earrings" (157) is about snapshots of visitors in the country. Though the sentence derives from an actual photo taken upon the visit in August of Alyse Gregory, the novelist and managing editor of the *Dial,* it does not tell us about Gregory or about her husband, Llewelyn Powys, who slips into *A Bouquet. Their Wills.* because his first name rhymes with Rose Ellen. In "Arthur" the sentence about Gregory exemplifies different uses of "with,"

She was photographed with earrings.
She was photographed with trees. (79)

Some statements show recurrent Stein themes:

Herbert William Harvey had four children.

Had he had four children.

Two boys and two girls three boys and a girl a boy and three girls three boys and two girls that makes five that is what there were. (160)

This passage plays a common conversational game of how many children and how many boys and girls are in a family; it ends with five siblings, three boys and two girls, like the five Stein children.

An exceedingly gay cover for the having perfectly corrected withstand in presentation (155)

may describe a Stein *cahier* or a new book, one cannot be sure, for the comment floats through the air unattached, just as first names are not attached to particular persons.

The fragments of language spread out in the landscape. They are difficult to read because they offer no familiar forms of continuity; if we give in to the temptation to nail them down, we destroy the poetry. Yet every now and then, especially in the second half of *Paisieu,* some names echo as a group. Vincent, Gustave, Camille, Lucien, Edward, Auguste rise as impressionist landscape painters.

A single last name stands out, pivoting on Geronimo and Arthur and gathering the others around him.

Arthur Feneon Geronimo lauds him (173)

sends us to Félix Fénéon, who spoke for the freedom to create and against the strictures of photographic realism.[72] His name and the first names that bring to mind Van Gogh, Corot, Courbet, Pissarro and his son, Degas, Manet, Renoir, and others take us from landscape painting to landscape plays.

Continuity builds by accretion, by tiny verbal elements of sound, sight, and grammatical play within phrases and sentences, not by subject matter. The verbal movement takes place by combinations and permutations of short words and long words reduced to morphemes that become new short words. Stein always breaks down larger units to play with particles of meaning.[73] Neither words nor sentences are stable and unchanging. Abstracted

72. Félix Fénéon (1861–1944) wrote on impressionism and postimpressionism. In "De la représentation de la nature" (1898) he asks ironically why, in a painting, persons do not move and talk when they are shown in exact detail and concludes that if representation is the aim, the theater is supreme among the arts because of its ability to render movement and sound.

73. It is one of the reasons she writes compound nouns as separate words or, following the

Figure 6. Sir Francis Cyril Rose, *Gertrude Stein and Miss Toklas with Basket and Pépé at Bilignin.* Gouache on cardboard, 28 in. × 23 in., August 1938. By permission, Isabel Wilder, 8 March 1989, and National Portrait Gallery, Smithsonian Institution, Washington, D.C., NPG. 91.175.

from familiar meanings and usage, words move freely rather than as parts of a given world or parts of sentences,

> whether it is as mart as Martha the confidant of Martha Butta. Do do please not remember (156),

> Pariah arrive are how are hard (164),

> Distant Dismay Ismay is main gettatable in position (157),

> as arrival of arrival of marshes. Arrival of marshes (166),

and "window," "widow," "winnowed" echo across pages 164–65.

> Vincent Geronimo held it well in hand.
> Sent on behalf of quantity (174)

---

practice of the time, hyphenates them, showing their parts. Her play with elements of sound and sight also, however, accounts for the many printing errors in this play. Reading with care requires checking the manuscript word for word.

or again, in "Arthur,"

> Win sent, a grammar.
> In sent a grammar.
> A grammar is in went and in went, in sent, win sent. (91)

She works with the small connecting words,

> out in from with it (167)

developed after a passage on an outdoor community bread oven, called *four banal* in the region, where breads and tarts are baked.

> Come with in abundant out of door oven (167)

is also in "Arthur" (84). A word of distance leads to one of increase,

> Farther and more than a pleasant hope of celerity. (155)[74]

In the last paragraph appears

> A family can never be photographed together. (181)

Photographs show subjects "there," "beside," not after or before. A group can be photographed together in a space, but family lineage in time cannot be transferred to the space of a photograph. At a few points, there are slight hints of a house—perhaps the house Stein and Toklas were negotiating to rent—and of a dog (180). The first four indented lines below are in both "Arthur" (95–96) and *Paisieu* (178); the last is only in *Paisieu.*

> They make Saturday come soon and will they like it after some have not come.
> Nestle beside above where it is.
> It is made with them to of having for furnishing of course.
> Thank you very much for an island of a church and trees island on land.
> With whether they are whether they are this one if it was an eager in measure that they can be black and white. An object a little dog called Basket a magpie in the air.

The house is composed as a prospect in the landscape, along with a dog already named and described, with echoes of *Four Saints In Three Acts,* as a magpie in the air. Neither house nor dog becomes a reality until the following spring.

74. "Farther," not "father," as mistyped by Toklas and printed in error.

The title *Paisieu,* one of the few nonstandard words in Stein's work, is odd. In a preliminary *carnet,* Stein's original spelling of the title, *Pasiue,* is corrected in Toklas' hand to read *Paisiue,* which barely looks more like a French name than Stein's spelling does. It probably conflates Peysieux,[75] a hamlet near Belley, and perhaps Pugieu, also nearby, and even Peyzieux-sur-Saône, a more distant hamlet, with *pays* (country), and *paix/paisible* (peace/peaceful), related to pastoral. The first line of the play, "Not Paisieu a play," sounds like an alternate title. Indeed, in the *transition* bibliography of 1929, the play is listed under this title.

Is Stein suggesting that the play is not as peaceful as the country is said to be? That the landscape is not a play or the play not a landscape? Of course, *Paisieu, Pasiue,* or *Paisiue* may also be word play on *pas yeux* (no[t] eyes), *pas eux* (not they), *pas lieu* (no place, not a place, does not take place), or *pas vieux* (not old). I even wonder whether *poésie* (poetry) is inside *Paisieu.*

The subtitle, one of the few she used, describes her intention.

A work of pure imagination in which
no reminiscences intrude

is a work freed of time, reference, representation. Reminiscences have to do with histories and identities outside the playscape before us that names alone do not have, and memory is about the logic of developing plots, which Stein shuns. Though *Paisieu* is full of the actual life of the Bugey and nothing is made up, the play is not this landscape, nor is it an invented landscape. Rather, as the subtitle suggests, it creates the essence of the place by composing forms of language in a portrait of a landscape.

With no organizing center and with the habit of standard grammar an interference rather than a guide, this play is difficult to read. It takes a director with a sense of the theater of language to put before an audience a landscape of words in sound, movement, and sight—I invert the usual order, giving precedence to sound—to make the kind of total theater Stein wanted. It is often said that she wrote plays for reading rather than for the stage. Not only does this view not fit her stated sense of plays,[76] but the auditory quality of her texts is so complex that they demand performance if

75. I owe this reading and many details about the region to Joan Chapman, who generously shared with me her familiarity with Stein and the Bugey. Spellings of local names, not standardized in the 1920s, even now sometimes vary. Except when quoting, I rely for place names on the maps of the Institut Géographique National, Paris, and on the Michelin guides.

76. In early comments of 1913–14 to Mabel Dodge and Florence del Val, she made clear that she was reluctant to publish plays before they were produced.

hearing them and seeing them are to be one. Since they start from language, staging also must begin with language.

Paisieu runs counter to our habits of reading, for its mixed, discontinuous language follows no logic of subject matter or statement; often it almost names references but ends up withholding or concealing them in puns, as when the phrase in the first draft, "Seen in preciseness," becomes "Scene in preciseness" (159) in the final text. How would we hear it in performance, and how would the phrase move in sequence? The term "landscape" does not make a play a visual work but something closer to a musical work, which relies on the ear more than the eye and requires performance that makes a script into something different from what we read and even from what we hear when reading aloud.

Late in "Arthur," as the grammar study and the landscape play often interpenetrate sentence by sentence in her composing, Stein reaches a grammatical conclusion about grammar.

> Grammar. They without doubt. They will without doubt they will do without it without doubt. They will do without doubt they will do without it without doubt they will do without it without doubt they will do without it.
>
> Left alone. A grammar. (91)

She has left rigid systems behind, but in the process of writing her examples of grammatical observations, she has taught herself and those of us who have the patience to follow what words can do in a new work with a new and flexible "grammar."[77] The logic of the seen landscape differs absolutely from the logic of prescribed grammar. The closed system of grammar and patriarchal family relations in houses is mitigated by the changing light that makes the landscape visible in its varying colors and shapes in space. Out of that landscape she chose to make plays. "Landscape is not grammar."

77. Often phrases return in later work. "Left Alone" by 1929 becomes the title of a short portrait of the dog, "Left Alone. To Basket," one in a series of poems, *SIM* 230. "Grammar almond grammar," which recurs three times on page 99, may echo French *tout le monde* (the whole world), *allemand* (German), the writer Robert McAlmon; "Almond Grammar" returns in 1930 in "More Grammar For A Sentence," *AFAM* 361, 367; *R* 548, 556.

It is it is in itself.

Of which.

—"A Play Without Roses. Portrait of Eugene Jolas" 205

A lake is an article followed by a noun a lake is an article followed by a noun a lake which is there.

—"Sentences" 197

6. 1928–30

Georges Hugnet: "George Hugnet"

Of the many portraits Stein wrote over the years, "George Hugnet" requires special discussion, not only because Stein thought it her best but because it shares a larger context with several other works. Though she saw it as a self-contained composition that required no further information for appreciation, it becomes richer in resonance and clearer in meaning if it is read in context.[1] It was only after the break with Hugnet that Stein emphasized, in her American lectures, how unimportant the context was for reading it.

Between 1927 and 1931, however, the relationship with Hugnet not only produced his portrait but initiated ideas, events, and works that must be considered together if the portrait and the texts related to it are to be grasped. Her later preoccupation with audience writing and her distinction between Shakespeare's plays and Shakespeare's sonnets also emerge from the experience of Hugnet.

Context: Georges Hugnet

Virgil Thomson met Georges Hugnet in 1926 and introduced him to Stein early in 1927, when Thomson was thirty-one and Hugnet twenty-one.[2]

1. See Wendy Steiner, *Exact Resemblance to Exact Resemblance* (New Haven, Conn.: Yale University Press, 1978), 122–29, and my subsequent discussion of the text. Steiner surveys the evolution of Stein's portraiture in three phases. She comments on numerous individual portraits but does not look at context as I do.
2. What follows is only the briefest summary to establish relationships among Thomson, Hugnet, and Stein. It relies on Thomson's autobiography, *Virgil Thomson* (New York:

By that time, Thomson already enjoyed a special position with Stein, for he had set to music two of her pieces and had agreed to collaborate on an opera.[3]

Hugnet had been discovered in 1920, at fourteen, by the poet Marcel Jouhandeau, who introduced him to a fellow Breton, Max Jacob. Through Jacob, Hugnet met Cocteau, Picasso, Duchamp, Man Ray, Picabia, Max Ernst, Tzara, Desnos, and others, most of whom Stein also knew. Hugnet soon wrote reviews of some of their work, and over the years, several of the painters illustrated his books.[4] Hugnet himself also painted, drew, and worked with collages, photography, photo collage, and found objects, and he appreciated folk art, film, and jazz. He had an interest in fantasy and liked to shock. His collages, especially those done after he joined the surrealists in the 1930s, often play with words and word images. A gift for calligraphy and graphics, visible even in early flourishes in his letters, points to his later interest in typography and book design.

Thomson describes him as belligerent, anarchistic, and antiauthoritarian; he objected to military service. Characterizing his aggressive nature, friends spoke of him as "le petit général," taking off from "le petit caporal," Napoleon's nickname in military school, an allusion Stein would have recognized. In her work, he found a liberated language which in turn liberated thought.

Alfred A. Knopf, 1966), 94ff.; Kathleen Hoover and John Cage, *Virgil Thomson: His Life and Music* (New York: Thomas Yoseloff, 1959); Anthony Tommasini, *Virgil Thomson: Composer on the Aisle* (New York: W. W. Norton, 1997); Gertrude Stein, *Autobiography* (New York: Harcourt, Brace, 1933); Sylvia Beach, *Shakespeare and Company* (New York: Harcourt, Brace, 1956); Georges Hugnet, *Pleins et Déliés: Témoignages et Souvenirs* (La Chapelle-sur-Loîr: Guy Auteur, 1972); concert programs, catalogs, and reviews of exhibits; letters; and interviews with Mmes. Germaine and Myrtille Hugnet and with Virgil Thomson. Unfortunately, printed and reported details are often inconsistent, dates are left out, and programs and dates of concerts, information about exhibits, and plans for publications discussed in letters failed to come about as expected and were changed or abandoned.

Who met whom through whom and when is not always clear or consistent in recollections. Stein says she met Antheil at the 1926 show of neoromantic paintings at the Galerie Druet (*AABT* 277). Thomson says he met Hugnet through Eric de Hauleville, with more or less regular meetings ensuing of young artists, some of whom lived at the Hotel Jacob.

3. "Susie Asado," composed in April 1926, copy inscribed to Stein by Thomson on New Year's Day 1927; "Preciosilla," inscribed February 1927; early discussions of *Four Saints in Three Acts,* January and February 1927.
4. Most of Hugnet's essays, reprinted in the late collection *Pleins et Déliés,* are about artists who were also his friends. Among friends who illustrated his books were Jacob, Eugene Berman, Miró, Marcoussis, Dali, Duchamp, Oscar Dominguez, Picasso, Cocteau, and Arp.

In Stein herself, in spite of his youth, he found a friend to whom he had something to offer that she fervently desired: French publication and critical interest from young French writers and artists.

By 1927, Hugnet met regularly for work sessions with Thomson, who fostered his interest in jazz and blues and introduced him to other expatriates. That Hugnet was familiar with American movies is evident in his film *La Perle* (*The Pearl,* 1929), which relies on Buster Keaton. It is important, in view of "Deux Soeurs Qui Ne Sont Pas Soeurs" ("Two Sisters Who Are Not Sisters"), Stein's film script of the following spring, to recall the many film scenarios of those years and the interest in films that is evident in letters and reviews. Buñuel, Picabia, Man Ray, Cocteau, and others were making films. Stein undoubtedly heard about them and perhaps saw some of them. I offer here relevant biographical documentation about Stein, Thomson, and Hugnet but omit broader description of the pervasive interest in American writing, music, and films in Paris, which adds background to personal relations.

In his response to Eugene Jolas' *transition* inquiry from European intellectuals about the influence of America in Europe,[5] Hugnet expressed regret at the lack of interest in America among the French and criticized French reluctance to learn languages, to read foreign works in the original and even in translation, though Hugnet himself knew little English at this time and never became fluent.[6]

Thomson served as both artistic and personal intermediary between Hugnet and Stein, introducing his friend to Stein texts, which Hugnet could not easily read. Thomson's friend, Madame J[ean].-P[aul]. Langlois, had with his help already translated two Stein pieces into French.[7] By 1928, Thomson

5. Eugene Jolas was born in Union City, New Jersey, of a German mother and a French father from Alsace-Lorraine, where he grew up but returned to New York in 1909. After years as a journalist in America, he took a position at the Paris office of the *Chicago Tribune* while also writing poetry and planning *transition* as an international journal for the artistic cross-fertilization between America and Europe. In January 1926, he married the gifted Maria McDonald, from Louisville, Kentucky. The first issue of *transition* appeared in April 1927. His *Anthologie de la Nouvelle Poésie Américaine* (Paris: Kra, 15 April 1928), with a preface on the United States and France by Bernard Faÿ and dedication to Sherwood Anderson, represented a large number of poets, each with one poem translated mostly by Jolas himself. Stein's "Captain Walter Arnold" (1916) is included. Between 1927 and 1932, Stein was close to Jolas, who also published Joyce. See Andreas Kramer and Rainer Rumold, eds., *Eugene Jolas: Man from Babel* (New Haven, Conn.: Yale University Press, 1998).
6. "Inquiry Among European Writers into the Spirit of America," *transition* no. 13 (summer 1928): 248–70; Hugnet's response, 265–66.
7. "Water Pipe" was published in *larus* 1, no. 1 (February 1927) by Sherry Mangan, a Harvard friend of Thomson, who served as its French editor. The French translation

and Hugnet together had become close to Stein and began to collaborate first on a joint tribute to her in the form of a poem and a musical composition, and then on plans to translate Stein pieces into French.

That Stein had much to offer Hugnet is not difficult to understand. As a senior avant-garde writer and a collector, she validated his experiments with the language of poetry, painting, and collecting. Just as Thomson's developed under her influence, Hugnet's sense of language was sharpened by exposure to her ideas. Translating Stein led to a practical acquaintance with her work and the resources of language. Hugnet admired Stein, who apparently freed him, at least momentarily, from a narrow life at home, dependency on his parents, especially his mother, and attacks of hypochondria. In June 1928, he asked that she help him get well by writing to him: "Aidez-moi, chère Gertrude, à guérir. Ecrivez moi."

To Thomson, Stein lent support by her method, which allowed him to graft his work upon hers. For Hugnet, it was by her own example—inspiring but impossible to follow, for it left him dependent rather than freeing him to define his own difference. What Stein received from Hugnet appears at first less clear. Yet he quickly stood out for her precisely because he was a poet, unlike painters and composers. Stein was not close to many French poets and did not regularly read French poetry, but Hugnet's poetry impressed her, although her comments lack the rigor one might expect. His reviews and essays on painters and writers show him learning from her, and he showed his devotion by translating her.

The decision to render a selection from *The Making Of Americans*[8] had

---

("Fuyeau d'eau," by Mme. Langlois; "Conduite d'eau" by Thomson), done by Mme. J.-P. Langlois with Thomson's help, was not printed. Her translation of "A Saint In Seven," "Un Saint en Sept," originally scheduled for publication in *Orbes* 1 (summer 1928), appeared in *Orbes* 2 (spring 1929), with Hugnet's introduction to Stein of summer 1928, "La Vie de Gertrude Stein."

This portrait, considerably revised, became the preface to *Morceaux Choisis de la Fabrication des Américains* ("Selections from *The Making of Americans*"). Mme. Langlois' letters also speak of translations by herself or by Thomson and herself, of the portraits "Cezanne," and "Relieve," about Gris, Picasso, and Kahnweiler—"Jean, Paul et Henri." (Is it coincidence that the first two names are those of Mme. Langlois' husband?) She apparently submitted these pieces to Jean Paulhan for *La Nouvelle Revue Française,* but they were not published (see her letters to Stein; for Paulhan, see Hugnet's preface to *Dix Portraits*).

8. Stein objected to abridgments. As usual, her position was simple and consistent. If a book was complete, it could not be abridged, for a shortened version was a different book and falsified the original. At the same time, she understood that there was no hope of publishing the complete long novel in French. She finally agreed to what she called a "sampler," which did not represent the whole but might give readers a taste of the whole. See letters of Ellen DuPoy (later Daniel) and Stein.

presumably been made by the early spring of 1928, though work on the translation did not begin until autumn. The prospect of becoming a French author and influencing French attitudes to language was attractive to Stein, whose work had not been published in French, with the exception of one sentence from *Tender Buttons,* which Cocteau had translated.[9] By February 28, Stein wrote to Henry McBride,

> young France has discovered me, it reads me it translates me it admires me and it is printing me.

Early that year, Hugnet's father, a businessman who was proud of his son's artistic inclinations, agreed to finance a small publishing venture, Les Editions de la Montagne. For Stein, the prospect of this edition solved the problem that went with translation—publication. As poet, artist, and critic, translator and publisher, admirer of Stein and America, Hugnet qualified for friendship, affection, and promotion.

In an undated letter to Kate Buss, Hugnet described his publication as "une revue dont chaque numéro serait écrit par un seul écrivain."[10] Plans included his own work and that of others as well as translations of Stein, who hoped he might become her publisher in France, perhaps producing not only French but also English editions of her work. "Natural Phenomena" was considered, though not published, as was unidentified work by Carl Van Vechten and a translation of *The Cats* by Bravig Imbs. Many plans were made, modified, and abandoned.[11]

Hugnet, who had an astute business sense, published books, usually in several different, limited editions, including a small number with illustrations, that quickly appreciated in value and became collectors' items. Associated with Hugnet in Editions de la Montagne, perhaps with financial support, was Georges Maratier, though what position and authority he had is not quite clear.[12]

In October 1927, Hugnet had dedicated to Stein his lyrical meditation,

9. "Dining is west," or "Dîner, c'est ouest," from the "Food" section of *TB,* in *Le Potomak 1913–1914* (Paris: Librairie Stock, 1924), 12.
10. A journal of which each issue would be written by a single author.
11. On "Natural Phenomena," see Stein to Hugnet, 11 April 1928; on Carl Van Vechten, see Thomson to Van Vechten, 7 September 1930.
12. He was referred to as editor for *Morceaux Choisis* and possibly for Tzara's *L'arbre des voyageurs* (1930). He may also have acted as distributing agent. However, friction developed between them about control of the stock of printed volumes.

    After Stein's quarrel with Hugnet in 1930, she remained friendly with Maratier, who for years advised her in practical matters and, having acquired a gallery of his own, sometimes acted as her agent for the sale of paintings.

"Les Iles Fortunées,"[13] and on April 29, 1928, under the title, "Le Berceau de Gertrude Stein ou Le Mystère de la rue de Fleurus / Huit Poêmes de Georges Hugnet to which have been added a musical composition by Virgil Thomson entitled Lady Godiva's Waltzes," the two young men presented her with a charming personal tribute, quite unlike anything she had ever received.[14] Not only was it pleasing to Stein personally, but it was performed, along with other Thomson pieces, on May 30, at a concert of his work at the Nouvelle Salle d'Orgue du Conservatoire, which Stein appears to have attended.[15]

Stein left for Belley on June 1, and both Thomson and Hugnet corresponded with her throughout the summer. Thomson developed a technique for portraiture he had learned from Stein and composed numerous musical portraits of friends—Hugnet, Cliquet-Pleyel, Stein, Sauguet, and others.[16] In July he wrote the "Piano Sonata for Miss Stein," and throughout the summer he also worked on *Four Saints In Three Acts.* That fall, he moved to the

13. Among the Stein papers is an inscribed copy of the poem, dated October 1927; it was printed in *40 Poésies de Stanislas Boutemer* (*au bout de la mer*), with Stein's copy dedicated by Hugnet on June 5, 1928.
14. "Lady Godiva's Waltzes" appears to be the title for Thomson's musical setting, whereas the title for Hugnet's poems is "Le Berceau de Gertrude Stein ou le Mystère de la rue de Fleurus" ("The Cradle of Gertrude Stein or the Mystery of the rue de Fleurus"). In a letter of the following summer, Hugnet spoke of writing the poem with great joy and heartfelt admiration. It appeared in the *Revue Européenne* in February 1929 and was reprinted in *Pleins et Déliés.*

    Hugnet frequently wrote about and dedicated poems to friends, unlike Stein, who insisted on the impersonal discipline of her art. She inscribed volumes as gifts to friends but saw her works as an artist; to her, her writings, including her portraits, were texts not attached to their subjects. Not until the *AABT* made her famous, in 1933, did she sometimes dedicate books to friends, such as the short version of *MOA* of 1934, dedicated to Bernard Faÿ, who had helped to select it and negotiate the contract for it, or *P&P* of 1934, dedicated to Carl Van Vechten, who had supported her efforts since 1913, had helped make the American tour a success, and as a photographer was a portraitist also.
15. Also on the program were Stein-Thomson's "Capital Capitals," Thomson's settings of Hugnet poems, "La Valse Gregorienne," and Thomson's setting of three poems of the Duchesse de Rohan. Whether Stein's portrait of her is connected with Thomson's setting remains unclear. Stein must have known about her at least since World War I. Thomson, in an interview in April 1982, disclaimed any knowledge of Stein's portrait or her possible acquaintance with her. For reasons I do not know, a copy of Stein's portrait of the Duchess is also among the papers of Elliot Paul in the Camille Haynes Paul Ferret Cummings Collection, Special Collections, University of Colorado at Boulder.
16. Thomson gives detailed accounts of his method and what he learned from Stein in *Virgil Thomson* (124–25) and in "Of Portraits and Operas," *Antaeus* 21–22 (spring–summer 1976): 208–10. See Thomson to Stein, 2 September 1928 and Thomson's notes and drafts in Columbia University's Rare Book Collection.

flat at 17 Quai Voltaire, which Toklas had recommended when it was given up by Janet Scudder, their sculptor friend.[17]

Hugnet wrote to Stein from St.-Malo, where he regularly spent his summer vacations with his mother and Stein responded with more frequent and eloquent letters of care and encouragement than usual.[18] Anticipating a visit to the alpine country of Belley, Hugnet wrote with much feeling about the seascape of his native Brittany. Stein, who, like Hugnet, had spent her youth near the ocean, understood his bond with the sea. She responded,

> *J'aimais aussi la mer etant eleve a c'a meme que c'etait le Pacific et pas l'Atlantic, mais maintenant c'est les cotes avec les montagnes assez loin mais visibles mais pas necessairement a regarder qui me calme maintenant. Et nous aurons grand plaisir a vous les fait voir, les notre.*[19]

In Belley, she meditated, composing the figures in the landscape and looking forward to Hugnet's arrival. However, shortage of funds made it impossible for him to visit her until the following summer.

17. See Toklas to Thomson, 8 October [1928].
18. On June 19, Hugnet was awarded the Prix Littéraire de la Liberté for authors younger than twenty-three years for his prose piece, "Le Journal d'Antoinette," published in *La Liberté* for 23 June 1928. In it a male narrator describes the situation of a young woman about to leave her lover. In a letter of July 2, Stein praised it for catching "la melancolie poetique d'une jeune fille pratique sans aucun poesie" (the poetic melancholy of a matter-of-fact young girl with no sense of poetry). In rendering Stein's French, I merely paraphrase main ideas in English and make no attempt to "retranslate" back into English what she wrote in her kind of French.

    Stein at this time also responded to requests from editors for contributions by recommending the work of her young friends, who in turn included her in their own efforts at publication. For example, Burton Rascoe, the editor of the *Bookman,* asked her for young French authors for the 1929 annual *Morrow's Almanac.* With her support, Hugnet submitted "Le Berceau . . ."; had Rascoe printed it, both Hugnet and she would have been publicized.

    Another project, undertaken in the summer of 1928 by Pierre Quesnoy, editor of *Les Cahiers Sade* in the Editions Le Rouge et Le Noir (Lille), was to print work in homage to the Marquis de Sade. At Hugnet's suggestion, Quesnoy approached Stein for a contribution, which Hugnet in advance offered to translate. Stein, who had no suitable piece available and did not write to order, submitted a minor work, "Precepts," composed "in Sade's country," Provence, in 1922 (see Pierre Quesnoy to Stein and Stein to and from Hugnet, August and September 1928). Thomson's "Commentaire sur St. Jérôme," with words by de Sade, was also composed for this journal, though it did not appear as planned.
19. Postmark 2 July 1928, HRC.

    I, too, loved the ocean, though I was raised near the Pacific, not the Atlantic. But now it is the mountainsides, distant but visible, even when I do not look at them, that calm me. We will take great pleasure in showing them to you.

Before the end of September, Hugnet sent Stein his preface for his translation of "A Saint In Seven," which was to appear in the first issue of *Orbes*. A portrait of her, entitled "La Vie de Gertrude Stein," it began with a short biographical summary—her birth in Allegheny, Pennsylvania, her studies at Radcliffe under William James, her work at Johns Hopkins, her arrival in Paris, her art collection, her portrait by Picasso, her success at Cambridge and Oxford. Hugnet continued,

> *J'aurais aimé qu'elle naquît pendant l'absence de ses parents, qu'elle naquît comme une surprise, ailleurs, ou qu'elle naquît à Allegheny pendant que ses parents voyageaient en Autriche par example. Hélas, elle naquît là parce que ses parents y etaient à ce moment-là.*[20]

He described her effort to sever the bond of thought and word and to free language from the constraints of formal grammar. He spoke of the music and rhythm of her language, her interest in children's songs, games, rounds, proverbs, conversation, gossip, and popular phrases rather than conventional poetic language. He likened her language to music boxes and its movement to that of the nursery rhymes and street songs of his own childhood. Her phrases, he said, were boxes within boxes, and her prose looked in its spontaneity like a child's drawing, though there was nothing childish about it. With grace and skill he suggested how beginning again and again and repeating rendered the movement of the mind in thought.[21]

Stein was overwhelmed by Hugnet's presentation of her as a natural-born genius, self-made and without antecedents:

> *Mon cher George,*
>
> *Je suis touchee au fond du coeur vraiment vous pouviez pas dit des choses que j'aimerais mieux entendre, vous m'avez compris, et c'a me fait enormement du bien. Malheureusement je suis née en Amerique presque pendant l'absence de mes parents . . . , j'espere que cette verite n'abimera pas les jolis phrases qui me plaisent. Je voudrais bien vous voir pour causer beaucoup sur mon plaisir . . . il y a des mots que vous employez qui xplique si justement mes*

20. I wish she had been born in the absence of her parents, or born elsewhere, as a surprise, or born in Allegheny while her parents were traveling, say in Austria. Alas, here is where she was born because that is where her parents were at that moment.

21. The similarities of Hugnet's description of Stein in "Le Berceau . . ." and in this preface are striking: the naive, childlike writer, the dream elements, children's songs, the look of her prose on the page, and her car, Godiva, appear in both pieces. In revised and expanded form, the preface for *Orbes* became the preface for *Morceaux Choisis,* which was not finished until the following winter. Publication of "Un Saint en Sept" with Hugnet's preface was postponed until the second issue of *Orbes,* spring 1929.

intentions que c'a metonne au meme temps que c'a m'excite. Vraiment mon cher ami je suis content plus que content d'etre dans vos mains. . . .[22]

By this time, Stein was working to complete *Paisieu* and "Arthur" before returning to Paris for the winter. Toward the end in both *Paisieu* (178) and "Arthur" (94–95), she began to turn new phrases, not only with Geronimo, already pivotal in the play, but with two further, alliterating names, Genevieve and George. Thus, near the end of these two works, she began a new one which would become "George Hugnet." On October 3, she sent it to him, saying,

peut etre c'est un portrait mais dans tout cas c'est a vous.

Perhaps it is a portrait but anyhow it is for you. Against this background, it becomes richer in tone and meaning.

"George Hugnet" is not only an intricate configuration of abstract elements of sound and sight but also a composition of sense. Its beginnings appear in "Arthur" and *Paisieu,* in word clusters that eventually break loose to become the nuclei of a separate piece. Beginnings also appear in an idea that occurs much earlier in "Arthur" and carries through the piece:

> What is grammar when they make it round and round. (62)

Against linear succession and chronological order stands rounded, circular composition. Related is the image of the ring, which recurs throughout the grammar and *Paisieu* and dominates the portrait.

Text: "George Hugnet" (*R* 539–40)

The portrait stands out by its sparse verbal simplicity—a restricted vocabulary, economy of work with sounds and letters, disciplined variations and permutations of the narrowest means. Its meaning is in its construction. Almost nothing offers itself for quotation or paraphrase.

Instantly striking to eye and ear are the three names that insistently alliterate—George, Genevieve, Geronimo. The names also appear in *Paisieu* and

22. Postmark 25 September 1928, HRC.

> My dear George,
>
> I am deeply touched, really, you could not have said anything to delight me more, you have understood me and that has done me a great deal of good. Unfortunately I was born in America, almost in the absence of my parents . . . I hope this fact will not spoil the pleasure of your language. I would like to see you to talk about that pleasure . . . you use phrases that so perfectly render me that I am most excited. Really, my dear friend, I am very happy to be in your hands. . . .

"Arthur," but only in the portrait are these three names and no others joined through grammatical manipulation as a group, in a triad, a triangle, turned in on itself somewhat like the circular rose motif.

What and who are they? Genevieve and Geronimo have no clearly identifiable reference, and while George suggests Hugnet, it is not Hugnet, as even its English spelling shows; Stein has played with this name before and will do it again.

Genevieve, the feminine between the two masculine names, may recall the patron saint of Paris and carries French echoes, although it is an English name also; Geronimo already pervades the landscape of *Paisieu.* The most striking and the least English of the three, it rings of Spain, even in the alliterative, anglicized spelling Geronimo instead of Spanish Jeronimo; perhaps it recalls the writing, translation, and commentary of St. Jerome, patron saint for translators and writers.

The three names have both constructive and referential power. In the portrait, they separate individually and converge as a group, a union of three in one, a trinity, perhaps a family. They share the initial letter G, which recalls George and is also the initial of Grammar, here almost consistently capitalized as a name, an agent of construction. It is also Gertrude's own initial.

Grammar, the power of construction, defeats the power of linear sequence. In linear succession, words move by addition, endlessly reaching for what they are about but never completing it or arriving. Grammar, on the other hand, completes forms, making things round. Reading is not merely following sleepy successions of words but apprehending their composed shape. The job of Grammar in "George Hugnet" is to compose—or catch—George "in our ring," which includes in what it is the separate plural elements that are in the ring:

> George in are ring.
> Lain away awake.
> George in our ring. (*R* 539)

The line,

> Grammar makes George in our ring which Grammar make George in our ring

composes George or the elements of George into a circle. The ring may be a face, the oval frame of a portrait, the ring of a circus, a poetic music box such as Hugnet had spoken of in his preface. It may be a wedding band or a family circle. The portrait becomes a grammar poem, a love poem, a family poem.

From the beginning, Stein uses incorporating or encircling notions:

with a with whether they thought they were with whether. (*R* 539)

The last word trails its homophone, weather. She joins ideas of "with" but immediately adds a "whether" that casts doubt on the "with," as if reversing direction. She also joins notions of "in" against "out." The portrait is made of rings and rounds, including the diphthong *ou* that is in "round."

She catches Hugnet in her writing, in her grammar, even in the landscape where by 1928 she already knows that she will most likely spend summers in a house of her own. The suggestion of encircling composition is reinforced by emphatic repetitions of a very few words and sounds—the recurring word "ring"; alliterating *G* words and *W* words; rhymes like "ring"/"thing," "out"/"about"/"without." The portrait develops with concentrated economy of means, including the single, consistently end-stopped lines.

Against the many circular suggestions stand several "straight" or linear ones, also first used in *Paisieu* and "Arthur."

> George Genevieve Geronimo straightened it out without their finding it out. (*R* 540)

The phrase "straightened it out" usually stands for making it clear, but Stein questions whether "straightening it out" really clarifies, for it does not appear to result in "finding it out." The portrait must be composed or incorporated, not found or separated "out." In *Paisieu,* the two lines below are followed by a third, not transferred to the Hugnet portrait:

> Genevieve Geronimo straightened it out.
> Without their finding it out.
> Not what he finds out but what he likes makes the difference. (*LO&P* 178)

"Arthur" offers a clue to the origin of the circles. On page 94, Stein speaks of arithmetic and addition and asks whether grammar is about adding. She then speaks of a double rainbow and wonders whether two half rainbows make one whole round rainbow:

> If there is a rainbow and it is not complete and another rainbow is there there are two incomplete uncompleted rainbows there are or were two rainbows which were there.
> Which were rainbows incomplete rainbows of which two were there.
> Not having had it and lost it.
> Grammar has had it and has not lost it. ("Arthur" 94)

A double rainbow does not by addition become a single full-circle rainbow; the two half circles, one above the other, do not make a whole circle.

It is not as if there had been a full circle that was lost or cut in half. A full circle can be constructed by the grammar of the artist, not by arithmetical means, whether addition or subtraction.[23]

> Grammar makes George in our ring which Grammar makes George is our ring ("Arthur" 94)

is itself a circular or triangular sentence, its end folded under into its beginning. The sentence incorporates and encloses Hugnet in the triad of her affectionate portrait, rising from looking at rainbows.

The word "azure," almost at the center of the portrait, stands out sharply,

> With out whether it their whether with out doubt.
> Azure can with our about.
> It is welcome welcome thing.
> George in are ring. (*R* 539)

"Azure"[24] does not appear in the preparatory sections in *Paisieu* or "Arthur," though it may lightly echo Arthur. It may also, coming as it does after "whether" and "doubt," suggest notions of "assure," "as sure," "a sure," "I sure," and so allow readings like these:

> With out whether it their whether with out doubt.
> Assure can with our about

or

> I sure can without doubt

or

> I sure can with our about.

Stein appears to make sure that she has captured and encircled Hugnet, her words possessing him in a redoubt as a fortress and in a vaulted, blue creation, a welcome thing in her landscape. She has moved the three names and the words, defamiliarized and abstracted, in various ways about the portrait until George is in our ring, along with Genevieve and Geronimo.

The summer after Stein wrote his portrait, Hugnet, with the painter Eugene Berman, visited her from September 4 to 7, 1929, in Bilignin. On August 31,

23. For arithmetic, adding, doubling, halving, see also "Sentences," *HTW* 153, 158, 159.

24. In numerous printed versions, however, the line appears as "Azure with out about." Before printing the poem in *Blues* 1, no. 6 (July 1929), Charles Henri Ford carefully checked on the correct wording. See Ford to Stein, 23 April 1929, HRC.

he announced that he was bringing her as a gift, two little objects which would please her. The two little objects were *coquillages,* figurines of blue and green shellwork. Hugnet, who was interested in folk art and later collected such figures, had obtained them in Brittany. The figures were given names: George and Genevieve. It was not that their names had entered the portraits from the objects but that the names emerged from the portrait to become objects in real life. When Stein that fall returned to Paris for the winter, the figures remained in Bilignin; upon her return in the spring, they welcomed her; she dusted them and surrounded them with flowers.[25]

Context: Translation I

Morceaux Choisis de La Fabrication Des Américains

On October 15, 1928, Stein returned to Paris. She had finished *Paisieu* and "Arthur" in the country and would soon begin the portrait of Christian Bérard and "Sentences," another in the series of language studies, to which the relationship with Hugnet also contributed. On November 14, at the Hotel Majestic, a concert took place with music by Virgil Thomson and Henri Cliquet-Pleyel of musical settings for poems by Hugnet and others and readings of Hugnet works. The Editions de la Montagne was in the process of being organized and a timetable developed for its first publication, the translation of selections from *The Making Of Americans.*

Hugnet and Thomson planned to start collaborating immediately, but they completed only a short section before Thomson sailed for New York at the beginning of December. After his departure, Stein worked with Hugnet; both she and Hugnet described their efforts.[26]

> We are peacefully and completely translating, it goes, I go alone and then Alice goes over me and then we all do it with George, and then he goes

25. Stein to Hugnet, 2 May 1930, HRC.
26. Among the Stein papers is a handwritten sequence of forty-two leaves with a cover sheet, entitled "Translation of Making Of Americans / in the Editions de la Montagne / done with George Hugnet." This is Stein's own "literal" draft translation of a part of the selection from the novel. It is not the text of the printed translation but a working document on which Hugnet relied to prepare his version.

    The pages preserved include the sections printed from pages 27 to 44 in *Morceaux Choisis.* What happened to further sections of her translation and which sections Thomson may have completed with Hugnet is unknown. It appears likely that Stein translated more than the leaves preserved. For further references to the translation, see Stein to Van Vechten, 12, 14, 17, 23 November, 2 December 1928, and 19 January 1929; Thomson, *Virgil Thomson,* 126.

alone and really it all goes faster than anyone would think. I guess we will get it done on time.[27]

Stein wrote out her own, totally literal translation in her French, Toklas checking her version. According to Hugnet's preface, Stein then met with him, reviewing the passages, explaining them and commenting on her ideas. Then Hugnet reworked the French version.

Stein impressed upon him that rendering the "sense" or meaning of the words was the least of the problems. Hugnet recapitulated what he learned from her. *Le langage . . . lui semble un engin dont on peut tirer autre chose qu'une simple pensée.*[28] Reconstituting the rhythm of conversation, the weight, *débit,* style, color, resonance, and movement of her work, was more important than copying its meaning in French words.

> *Il s'agissait d'être exact. Tous les traducteurs rendent assez bien la pensée mais on a peu d'exemples de traductions qui satisfassent pour le style, le rhythme, le vocabulaire, la couleur, et la résonnance des mots. . . . Avant tout, avant la pensée qui est ce qu'il y a de plus facile à traduire, je me suis attaché à rendre le plus fidèlement que j'ai pu, le rhythme, la vie du vocabulaire, le grouillement des consonnes et des voyelles, . . . à restituer aux mots leur volume, leur poids, leur son. . . .* ("Préface," *Morceaux Choisis* 10)[29]

Hugnet did not, except perhaps incidentally, work from Stein's English original but from her literal French versions. These are totally comprehensible though often unidiomatic and incorrect French. They sound like word-for-word translations by a foreigner who understands perfectly but has limited command over idiomatic phrasing. They are also rather colloquial and show errors one might expect from someone who speaks but does not normally read or write French. Silent endings are omitted, *-e, -ent,* plural *-s* agreements are disregarded, and no accents are used. Homophones are often substituted for the words she has in mind—*fait/faites/fête; aimer/aimée/aimait.* It is a practice familiar from her writing in English—"two"/"too"/"to"; "there"/"their"/"three."

27. Stein to Thomson, postmark 3 December 1928. See also Stein to Van Vechten, 2 December 1928.

28. To her, language is a tool which can create more than mere ideas.

Georges Hugnet, "La Vie de Gertrude Stein," *Orbes* 2 (spring 1929): 59–61.

29. It was a matter of exactitude. Most translators passably render the ideas but few catch the style, rhythm, vocabulary, color, resonance of the words. More than the ideas, the easiest to translate, I have tried to render as faithfully as I could the rhythm, the life of the vocabulary, the dabbling of consonants and vowels . . . and to restore to the words their mass, their weight, their sound.

Stein's French looks more peculiar than it sounds. Her refusal to write "correctly," in accordance with prescriptions for grammar and spelling, does not represent confusion on her part but forces the reader to pay attention not only to sight—spelling—but to sound. Together, sound and sight, including her misspellings, add a punning dimension to the reading.

Hugnet revised her French to produce, with minimal changes in wording and only slight modifications in word order, a text that is entirely French yet also sounds defamiliarized and strange enough to demand attention to every word and phrase. Like Stein's English, the French of this skillful translation cannot be read without attention to the words and their composition.

> *Dans cette traduction ce qui n'est pas "français" n'est pas français parce que dans le texte anglais ce n'est pas "anglais." J'ai éprouvé un certain plaisir à tortiller les mots français si rigides . . . les propositions si stables, si fixes.* ("Préface" 14)[30]

Stein and Hugnet must have enjoyed bending French to their own use.

Here, as an example of the three stages of work, is the early passage on "Brothers Singulars,"[31] with its opening French adjectival plural form ending with *-s:*

Stein Original English (*MOA* 21)

Brothers Singulars, we are misplaced in a generation that knows not Joseph. We flee before the disapproval of our cousins, the courageous condescension of our friends who gallantly sometimes agree to walk the streets with us, from all them who never any way can understand why such ways and not the others are so dear to us, we fly to the kindly comfort of an older world accustomed to take all manner of strange forms into its bosoms and we leave our noble order to be known under such forms as Alfred Hersland, a poor thing, and even hardly then our own.

Stein French Working Translation

Freres singulaires, nous somme mal mis dans une generations qui nous ne reconnaitra pas. Nous sommes chassee par nos cousins, par l'aimiabilité courageux de nos amis qui quelque fois veut etre vu avec nous, par tous qui peut pas

30. In this translation what is not "French" is not French because the English text is not "English." I have felt some pleasure in twisting the rigid French words and their stable, fixed statements.

31. I am told that the French term *frère singulier* refers to homosexuals.

comprendre pour quoi nous somme comme nous somme et nous nous refugié dans le comfort d'une vieux monde qui a eu longtemps d'habitude de prendre toute sorte des choses curieux a son sein and [sic] nous laissons notre genre dans les formes de characteres comme Alfred Hersland une chose pauvre et meme pas de nous.

Hugnet French Version (*Morceaux Choisis* 28–29)

Frères Singuliers, nous sommes déplacés dans une génération qui ne nous reconnaît pas. Nous fuyons devant la réprobation de nos proches, la condescendance courageuse de nos amis qui quelquefois consentent à se promener dans les rues à côté de nous, devant tous ceux qui ne peuvent comprendre pourquoi de telles manières et non pas d'autres nous sont chères, nous fuyons vers l'aimable consolation que nous offre un monde plus vieux qui a l'habitude de receuillir en son sein toutes sortes de formes étranges et si nous quittons notre noble confrérie c'est pour devenir un Alfred Hersland, une pauvre chose, et qui n'est presque pas des nôtres.

There was no dictionary for Stein's composing voice. The translation gave her great satisfaction. She was to be published in Paris, and she was teaching a gifted and willing pupil ready to pass on the message of her modernism. Yet the translation raised in stark form the question of authorial identity. In what way are original and translation the same? How does a translation copy, reproduce, or mirror the original? Translating Stein allowed Hugnet to learn, to serve her, and to be "in one book" with her, his work wedded to hers, her creation re-created in his.

On December 28, Hugnet wrote to Thomson that he was finishing the last revisions and that Christian Bérard had done a portrait of Stein, to be used as the frontispiece for the first one hundred signed copies of the book. At about the same time, Stein wrote her word portrait of Bérard.[32] By January 2, 1929, the text of *Morceaux Choisis* was complete and subscription forms were sent out. The book was published on June 10, 1929.

In portraits, the relation of subject to writing was already a source of concern. Added to it now was George Hugnet translating "George Hugnet" into

32. The portrait of Bérard is the first of three probably copied at least in part from *carnets* into one *cahier,* "Christian Berard," "Virgil Thomson," and "Kristians Tonny." The portraits of Thomson and Tonny are begun early in "Sentences," which she started soon after her return to Paris (*HTW* 115, 116, 123; 132).

"Sentences" includes no preliminary sections for "Christian Berard." However, the portrait is "a sentence of poetry," which links with its preoccupations. Stein wrote her portrait in appreciation of Bérard's portrait of her. See the subsequent comments on "Christian Berard." A detailed discussion of all these pieces follows in chapter 7.

French. Between 1928 and 1930, the relationship of Hugnet and Stein, of original and translation, of writer and translator, of English and French, and of the writer as subject, the writer as writer, and the writer as friend becomes increasingly complex. In *Dix Portraits,* the illustrations of the subjects add visual refractions to the many literary ones already developed.

Virgil Thomson's musical portraits of his friends, including Stein and Hugnet, and his settings of Hugnet poems further complicate the question of representation, subject, and artist. Music, Thomson and Stein had agreed, did not illustrate. No wonder Stein wrote to Laura Riding when *Morceaux Choisis* was published that translation led to meditation.[33] It also led to the question of authorial identity that was to erupt over Hugnet's "Enfances."

Context: Translation II

Dix Portraits

This second Stein book in the Editions de la Montagne is a group of portraits, printed in sequence, first in English, then in French translation by Hugnet and Thomson. As usual, Stein made the selection, with great but unobtrusive care to create a meaningful order for the book.[34] In addition, her approval of the translations makes them especially interesting as interpretations of her work. Both selection and translation require comment.

It is not clear when a volume of portraits in English and French was agreed on or when the work was done. But between the autumn of 1929 and the spring of 1930, the text of *Dix Portraits* was prepared. In April or early May, Hugnet was reading proof.

The first three—the second portrait of Picasso (1923), and the portraits of Guillaume Apollinaire (1913) and Erik Satie (1922)—frame the book in the arts that surround her work—painting, literature, music. By 1929, they were still unpublished. "Si Je Lui Disais Un Portrait Completé de Picasso" was printed in the first issue of Allanah Harper's *Échanges* in December, in part no doubt to generate interest in *Dix Portraits,* published the following May.[35]

In this book, as everywhere in Stein's work, Picasso is first—the great

33. Letter draft, 1929 *carnet.*

34. On the outside back cover of the second *cahier* of "Sentences," written fall and winter 1928–29, is the draft of contents for *Dix Portraits,* different from the final selection. Careful thought went into their selection and arrangement.

35. See Harper to Stein, 8 November 1929; Stein to Harper, 18 November 1929, HRC. On April 17, 1930, although Hugnet spoke of finishing his translation of "Composition As Explanation," he later returned to work on it. "Composition comme Explication," submitted to *Échanges* for October 1929, did not appear there.

artist, the most important to portray her, and twice the subject of a Stein portrait.[36] The three frame pieces are followed by more recent portraits, done between 1926 and 1928, of her young friends, including her translators: Tchelitchew, Thomson, Bérard, Faÿ, Tonny, Hugnet, Eugene Berman—painters, writers, composers. The frame places the young in good company, including of course Stein's own.

Stein carefully negotiated the contract, retaining control over republication of the English texts and limiting Hugnet's right to reprint the volume to two years, after which the rights reverted to Stein. With the help of Toklas, she reviewed all contracts and insistently protected her rights.[37] It is possible that the project was planned when Hugnet and Berman visited in September. Hugnet and Thomson prepared the translations between that autumn and the spring of 1930.

Whether the preface was initiated by Pierre de Massot, Thomson, or Hugnet is not clear. Thomson says that he introduced de Massot both to Stein and to Hugnet. However, Stein may already have known him in the early 1920s, as a dadaist and friend of poets and painters whom she also knew, such as Duchamp, Picabia, Satie, and Mina Loy.[38]

Dadaist and later surrealist poet, accomplished prose writer, critic, and pamphleteer, de Massot had a rebellious mind with a philosophical bent and a delight in language; he liked to shock and provoke with words. He also had an excellent command of English. Indeed, he later expressed the wish,

36. The first portrait of Picasso (1909) was translated in 1922 by her friend Henri-Pierre Roché, whose version Stein sent on to Cocteau. In a letter to Cocteau of 20 February 1922, accompanying the translation, she comments upon French translation,

> I am sorry I cannot be of more use but being as I was going to live in France and write English I instinctively and deliberately never dwelt upon French. Anyway, I gladly leave it to you. (HRC)

Stein was also hoping for other translations into French; for example, she asked René Crevel to translate *Three Lives,* but he, ill with tuberculosis, declined.

37. See Stein to Hugnet, 28 May 1930, accompanying the contract for *Dix Portraits,* returned to him with changes, along with her advice about contracts and friendships, "vigilance continuelle."

38. In 1924, de Massot published *The Wonderful Book: Reflections on Rrose Selavy;* in 1932, he reviewed Duchamp's book on chess, *Opposition and Sister Squares Are Reconciled,* and in *Orbes* 4, he and Jacques Levesque wrote at length about Duchamp. Stein's friend Henri-Pierre Roché also was a friend of Duchamp. De Massot was close to Picabia, defended him against attacks, and wrote about him.

Later, in *Orbes* 4 (1932–33), he published, with a brief comment, a poem by Mina Loy's daughter Fabienne Lloyd. *larus* 1, no. 4 (July 1927): 16–17 included de Massot's eulogy, "Erik Satie," upon the composer's death in July 1925; a comment after the piece reads, "It was deemed inadvisable to disturb such prose by translation."

not realized, to publish his preface to *Dix Portraits* in *Échanges* in his own English translation in collaboration with his wife. He also spoke to Stein of translating into French both *Tender Buttons* and *Geography And Plays*.[39]

He wanted to write a preface that would not be a stiff and definitive statement but "une étude de votre verve et votre création"[40] and begins appropriately with an epigraph from Apollinaire's poem "La Victoire," from *Calligrammes* (1918), with its demand for a new way of seeing and for a new language.[41]

He refuses to pin Stein down in a systematic definition of her work, just as she herself refused to theorize about it, insisting that definitions distort by freezing what is constantly evolving and simplifying what is complex. Stein herself would no doubt have agreed that definitions merely flattened her work. He praises its mathematical perfection, likening it to a checkerboard, perhaps recalling Duchamp's interest in chess.

39. See de Massot to Stein, 17 May 1930.

In the spring of 1930, at the time of the preface, which he delivered late, he was under pressure to complete his own *Prolégomènes à une éthique sans métaphysique ou Billy, Bull-Dog et Philosophe,* which Hugnet published with drawings by Kristians Tonny in Les Editions de la Montagne on 12 August 1930. This philosophical "bestiary" permitted de Massot to speculate, using the dog (including the reversal "dog"/"god") as a paradigm of reasons for living. At the beginning of the book, Massot printed Stein's "A Dog" from the first part of *Tender Buttons,* "A little monkey goes like a donkey . . .". In a letter, he joked with her about Billy's relationship to her dog Basket and about the birth of his book on Bastille Day, when Stein would have "a pup."

40. See de Massot to Stein, 30 March 1930.

Stein's own brief, insubstantial portrait of de Massot, written later in 1930, was a thank-you piece for his preface. The word "pleasure," which recurs throughout, may echo the sense of pleasure in her work and in contact with her that de Massot repeatedly expressed in letters along with his wish to write a preface that would give her pleasure (17 May 1930).

Even before the *AABT,* where Stein did not include de Massot, there was apparently a falling-out between them, perhaps because Stein associated him with Hugnet and, after their quarrel, rejected him also; she may also have been uneasy about de Massot's addiction to opium, which made him unreliable. De Massot was hurt by his exclusion from the *AABT.* He assured her in a letter of 1 February 1935 that he never held anything but admiration for her, adding,

> *Avez-vous oublié celui qui, en 1923, mettant comme épigraphe à une plaquette, une phrase de "Geography and Plays."*
>
> Have you forgotten the man who, in 1923, as an epigraph in a small book relied on a phrase from "Geography and Plays."

I have not succeeded in locating this quotation.

41. The epigraph echoes in "A Grammarian" (1930), *HTW* 103–13. See chapter 7.

He speaks elegantly of her attack on language and her efforts to free words from the constrictions of grammar, unthinking habits of usage, and reliance on memory,

> *nous avons pénétré dans la citadelle, et grâce aux Mots qui ont TRAHI le LANGAGE!* . . . (12)[42]

Words have broken free of language. Stein's work, he insists, has freed English as a language for poetry in ways that French has not been freed. The implication is that the volume of Stein translations offers a lesson in the possibilities for poetry of English—and French.

Text: *Dix Portraits*

The French translations show the same variety of expression as the English originals. The meaning of the second portrait of Picasso is rendered in the phrases and sentences literally reproduced in their modulated variations, following the movement of the mind in its internal monologue, deliberating about telling or not telling Picasso that he is a Napoleon.

> Would he like it would Napoleon would Napoleon would would he like it. (15)

> *L'aimerait-il est-ce que Napoléon est-ce que Napoléon l'aimerait l'aimerait-il.* (51)

The gradual emergence of this sense of the man, which can be dryly summarized, as my sentence shows, is rendered with great care in French. Here the speaker, I, is deliberating in regular sentences whose meaning we can follow and which we can reproduce. What is surprising about this translation is its absolute faithfulness to the original, together with its totally French tone, evident even in the short example.

The portrait of Erik Satie also has paraphrasable sentence elements which can be directly translated.

> Come to Sylvia do. (21)

> *Viens à Sylvia viens.* (57)

Every word follows literally in sequence, down to the alliterations and the rhythms created by the commas, in French as in English.

42. We have entered the fortress, thanks to Words which BETRAYED LANGUAGE! . . .

And then what spreads thinner, and a letter. (21)

Et alors ce qui s'étend plus mince, et une lettre. (57)

The portrait "Guillaume Apollinaire," however, is not built of recognizable sentences and has far less representational matter in it than the others. Or rather, it represents word situations, not sequences of ideas that can be stated in sentences and translated as elements of thought or ideas into other languages. Consider the opening line, which plays with English approximations closest in sound to the poet's name as heard by an English ear.

Give known or pin ware. (19)

It is as if someone who knew no French at all had listened to the name Guillaume Apollinaire and tried to put it down in English. One thinks of the last line of Apollinaire's "La Victoire," "*Et que tout ait un nom nouveau.*"

How to translate the line? Simple, Stein would have said. Translate word for word, exactly as it is written:

Give known or pin ware.

give, *donner*
known, *connu*
or, *ou*
pin, *épingle*
ware, *produits*

Donner connu ou épingle produits.
(55)

An exact translation? Absolutely. Does it render Stein's line? Absolutely. Does it translate what Stein heard in French and wrote down in English? Certainly. Does it translate its connection with the poet's name? Absolutely not. The pun is sacrificed, for it cannot be translated as it was created. Auditory word play is not translatable. Look at the last line and its wonderful puns on "eye" and "I" and those implied in "leave" and "live," a good possibility for French-English transfer:

Leave eye lessons I. Leave I. Lessons. I. Leave I lessons, I.

becomes

Laisser oeil leçons je. Laisser je. Leçons. Je. Laisser je leçons, je.

Here, on the other hand, *laisser* and *leçon* yield new French word play. The translation cannot be homophonic, but it is literal, translating words, not paraphrasable meaning. Its play with *L* sounds, with *lais*ser and *le*çons, is immensely skillful. The homophones do not translate as puns, but the sound-play is entirely French and musically active. Interestingly, for "I," not *moi* but the weaker *je* is kept in French, de-emphasizing the personal to a mere personal echo.

The translations are not the same as the originals. Stein knew, as did Hugnet and Thomson, that word play, on which she so heavily relied, happens within a language and cannot be translated in the same form from one language into another. Oddly enough, the French versions translate sentence sense, as it were, word-for-word meaning. The literalism of these translated versions is astounding in its un-Steinian yet totally Steinian consistency.

An interesting example from her more recent work is the brief portrait of the young painter Kristians Tonny.[43] It concerns the use of "it" and "the" and *il, le, ceci, cela.* Stein's original considers how French renders "it," a common problem. The phrase,

> Better than without it

becomes in French

> *Mieux que sans cela.*

Idiomatically we cannot say *sans le.* Hugnet and Thomson render the line,

> *Cela n'est pas la meme chose que le.* (75)

Stein, in a working translation of her own, writes

> *Meilleur que sans le,*

in literal but idiomatically intolerable and meaningless French. The two working translations among the Stein papers—one, including revisions, on an old envelope, and the other, copied from the envelope to a sheet of paper—require comparison with the French version by Hugnet and Thomson. The last sentence of the portrait,

> It is usual to add it. (39)

becomes

> *Il est usuel de l'ajouter.* (75)

"It" here becomes both *il* and *le.* And yet *le,* used as article, becomes "the." Stein is plainly playing with *il, le,* and *ce, cela,* and perhaps even *en,* and with "the," "it," and other pronouns.

How is this a portrait of the Dutchman Tonny? We do not know whether

43. *Dix Portraits,* 39, 75; also in *P&P* 212.

it began as a result of Stein's thoughts about translating English into French or French into English, or whether it began with Tonny's difficulties understanding or speaking English or French, followed by a little grammar lesson by example. So it became a portrait of and a gift for Tonny. It is unquestionably a portrait of translation.

Stein's own working translation contains errors because she never bothered to follow correct French forms; for example, for *est,* she writes *ait,* transcribing French sound phonetically rather than following French grammar, spelling, and idiom. The procedure fits with her conviction that as a writer she must write words, not follow prescribed constructions. When she says, "it is usual to add," "il est usuel d'ajoindre," she is in part speaking of unthinking language habits that simply join words without conscious thought—unless it is her bad French.

The Tonny portrait appears first in "Sentences" (132), leading her to consider how we join words, "It lies it lays it . . . ," which makes her in turn look at "it" and "the." She follows up with numerous examples using "it," "the," and so on. The portrait of Bernard Faÿ, which considers articles—"the," "a," "an," and *un, une, le, la*—is closely related to the Tonny portrait in theme and almost immediately precedes it in "Sentences" (129).

The fact that Stein's working translations are preserved along with the published Hugnet-Thomson version of "Kristians Tonny" suggests a great deal of interesting linguistic, literary, and social exchange. Conversation yields language in active, lively forms, the very stuff of Stein's work and another in the unending series of "small examples" she collected.

She must have instructed Hugnet and Thomson to translate word for word, without deviation, keeping even word order as close to the original as possible. The translations are, in a sense, already composed, the translators working with Stein's blueprint as a guide. The French versions foreshadow what Stein was to experience when she tried to render Hugnet's *Enfances* in English, and what she eventually, in the "Henry James" section of *Four in America,* formulated about Shakespeare's plays and Shakespeare's sonnets—original writing and commissioned writing following conventional models.[44]

In the spring of 1930, translation was apparently discussed with de Massot. On April 17, Hugnet wrote to Thomson,

> *Massot et moi avons vivement discuté à propos de la traduction des portraits. Massot était partisan d'une réinvention de Gertrude plutôt que d'une fidèle*

44. See the discussion of Hugnet's cycle *Enfances* and Stein's *Before The Flowers Of Friendship Faded Friendship Faded,* following, and the "Henry James" section of *FIA.*

traduction (comme la nôtre). Evidemment le texte anglais perd mais j'aime mieux cela que les alentours français lamentables à la manière de Cocteau. N'est-ce pas.[45]

The comment foreshadows the coming conflicts between Stein and Hugnet.

"Enfances" (*Exact Change Yearbook No. 1*, 41–60)
"Poem Pritten on Pfances of Georges Hugnet"
Before the Flowers Of Friendship Faded Friendship Faded

Every biographer has told the story of the quarrel between Stein and Hugnet over the printing of their names in the planned collaborative volume. The book was to include "Enfances," his cycle of thirty numbered French poems of irregular length, in varying lines with occasional rhymes, and Stein's translations of these poems.[46] The quarrel erupted over equal billing for poet and translator, which raised questions about the relationship of original and translation. In February 1931, Virgil Thomson reported to Carl Van Vechten, who had heard about the trouble even in New York, that it began over "the type in which their respective names would appear on the title page of [the] book."

Of course, printed names of authors are a matter of more than design and size of type. Stein, who described her poems as reflections (*reflets*) on "Enfances" rather than translations, considered them original poems, not English copies of Hugnet's French originals. As a result, she insisted that her name was equal to his in importance and should be printed in the same size.

To understand the project of "Enfances," more is needed than an account of the quarrel. I place Stein's "reflections" in the context of publication, translation, and her relationship with Hugnet. They are printed *en face* in French and English for the first time under the title Stein gave her versions after the break with Hugnet, "Before The Flowers Of Friendship Faded Friendship Faded," in *Exact Change Yearbook No. 1*.[47]

45. Massot and I discussed the translation at length. Massot wanted a reinvention of Gertrude rather than a faithful translation (like ours). Obviously the English text suffers but I prefer that to the roundabout Frenchifying in the Cocteau manner. No?

46. See Richard Bridgman, *Gertrude Stein in Pieces* (New York: Oxford University Press, 1970), 201–2; James Mellow, *Charmed Circle: Gertrude Stein and Company* (New York: Praeger, 1974), 324, 341–44; Elizabeth Sprigge, *Gertrude Stein: Her Life and Work* (New York: Harper and Brothers, 1957), 167. Only Bridgman refers briefly and summarily to Stein's translations. There is no reference to the quarrel in the *Autobiography*.

47. Gertrude Stein, *Before The Flowers of Friendship Faded Friendship Faded*, ed. and intro. Juliana Spahr (Boston: Exact Change, 1995).

The three titles that head this section require explanation. Hugnet's French title, from the moment he began the sequence, was the plural "Enfances." Stein initially retained this title, rejecting the inappropriate English translation, "Infancy," and also eliminating from a draft of "Poem i" the word "youth." In September 1930, she submitted the poem to Richard Johns, the editor of *Pagany;* perhaps Johns had already heard about the new work from Sherry Mangan, who worked with him after his own journal, *larus,* ceased publication and combined with *Pagany.*[48]

Accepted for the winter 1931 issue (vol. 2, no. 1), prepared in the autumn of 1930, "Enfances" did not lead to trouble until a prospectus for book publication was printed and exhibited at the show of Léon Marcoussis in Paris on October 27, 1930, at the gallery of Jeanne Bucher, who planned to issue the book. By the time Stein and Hugnet failed to reconcile their differences, the winter issue of *Pagany* was in press.

Once the quarrel began, Stein telegraphed to Johns a new title, received December 22, to be substituted for the original: "Poem Pritten on Pfances of Georges Hugnet." An apologetic letter from Johns to Stein of January 31, 1931, indicates that, too late to make a change, he received another letter from her with the "correct title" for the poem; the title in *Pagany* was printed as spelled in her cable, but what title did her letter give?

The letter is not preserved. Hugnet, on February 23, refers to it as "Poem written on Enfances of Georges Hugnet," in standard spelling, adding he hopes that the spelling in Stein's cable is an error of transmission. We do not know what the truth is. The text, with numerous printing errors, appeared under what seems the sneering title she had cabled, whose effect is to tear apart "Enfances" by anglicizing the word and spelling it phonetically.

The spitting phrase, "Poem Pritten on Pfances," seems too good a nasty transliteration of Hugnet's phrase, *poème sur les Enfances,* to be an accident, but it may be so.[49] After the rupture, the title took on implications it may not in fact have had. But once the break was complete, Hugnet, in a January 12, 1931 letter to Thomson, broke up Stein's name, calling her Miss Stein Guett, Mistinguette.

48. See Hugnet to Richard Johns, 4 July, 2 August, and 1 November 1930, University of Delaware Library.

49. See also Hugnet to Thomson after publication of *Pagany,* 17 February 1931. My dates for letters from Hugnet to Thomson differ from those at the Yale Music Library, where envelopes with postmarks for undated letters have been separated from the letters after tentative dating with which I frequently disagree. I follow my own dates in all references to this correspondence, which I read prior to new dates now entered in the Yale collection.

hat Hugnet calls *enfances*—each poem may be one *enfance*—is not
hood memories but the selves discovered and created through sexu-
Enfance—the French noun is feminine—is associated with revelations
igh sexual otherness, addressed as woman, *toi et ton enfance, cette femme*
. Self-discovery through another opens access to words:

> *Enfance . . .*
> *Je te tiens par la main et tu caches sous ta tête*
> *cet éclat de mon diadême, ce que fut ma conscience,*
> *mais ce n'est pas de cela qu'il s'agit ni d'oubli*
> *ni de souvenirs, il s'agit de ce mot retrouvé . . .*
>
> (24)

he discovered word speaks not of memories recaptured but of passion-
shadowless actuality. By giving access to the beloved and the self, pas-
makes a world of fairy tales into an actuality. This is the world Hugnet
ribes as *légende,* a word that recalls reading and poetry. In the wake of
as he says, the hand of passion on his body becomes poetry:

> *Et ton écriture s'efface*
> *sur ma poitrine lavée.*
>
> (23)

n,

> *J'ignorais en passant mon temps*
> *près de toi et de ton enfance, enfance,*
> *les amers plaisirs du plaisir*
> *de ton enfance, cette femme,*
> *cette femme comme une femme*
> *et pas plus et pas moins,*
> . . .
> *et c'est davantage qu'une fontaine*
> *plus que la mer. . . .*
>
> (19)

elies on the vocabulary of sea, ships, and sailing of his native Brittany
xplore passion, sexuality, discovery:

Cinéma ou L'Enfance du Vingtième Siècle," *Pagany* 1, no. 4 (1930): 103–10. Through
Thomson and Sherry Mangan, Hugnet had obtained a regular assignment to write for
Pagany a Paris letter, a format which suited him; he also wrote on literature, painting,
music (see Hugnet to Thomson, 23 September 1929). At this time he was especially con-
erned with his scenario, *La Perle,* filmed in April 1929. See Hugnet to Thomson, 4 Janu-
ry 1929.

The plan to publish the two texts *en face* in a book was abandoned when the typographical problem of printing the author's and translator's names could not be solved. Once the friendship broke up, Stein gave her poems independent status by publishing them alone in her own Plain Edition on May 1, 1931, under a new title, constructed with Stein flair, *Before The Flowers Of Friendship Faded Friendship Faded.*[50]

Context

Again and again between 1928 and 1930, Stein and Hugnet experience a growing sense of intimacy in collaboration. It gives them pleasure *d'être dans un livre ensemble* (to be in a book together).[51] Hugnet anticipates with excitement the publication of "George Hugnet," his portrait, *avec nos noms encore ensemble* (with our names together again),[52] and he says, *nous aurons un livre ensemble* (we will have a book together).[53] Early in 1928, in letters to him, one of the few exchanges she carried on in French, Stein begins "Mon cher Hugnet." By the next summer, still writing in French, she opens in English, in tones of growing intimacy, "My dear George," "My very dear little George." In a way, these are love letters, Hugnet's young, gushy, sentimental, Stein's tender, protective, maternal, and always touched by his efforts on her behalf. The relationship and the events connected with it shift from the professional to the sentimental and create by turns intellectual interest, embarrassment, hilarity, and pathos.[54]

50. Hugnet's poem appeared under the title *Enfances* in an English translation by Samuel Putnam in his New Review Press, Paris, 1931. Hugnet's French text, with etchings by Joan Miró, was published by Editions Cahiers d'Art in Paris, 1933. See also Hugnet to Thomson, 15 March 1931.
51. Hugnet to Stein, March 1929; Stein to Hugnet, 3 July 1929, and elsewhere.
52. Hugnet to Stein, July 1929.
53. Hugnet to Stein, n.d. [summer 1930].
54. Among the Stein papers are two little poems, undoubtedly about Hugnet. One, entitled "To George," is on a thin folded leaf,

> In the month of May
> What shall I say
> In the month of May
> That I love George
> In my way
> In the month of May
> And in other months
> [~~To you~~]
> Gtde.

The other is on two pages torn from a *carnet.* The first two lines, "*George justifier les guepes,*" are crossed out. Belley is known for its many wasps (*guêpes*), which made Hugnet

Hugnet's efforts on her behalf yielded what she most desired—French publication of her work, publicity for it, and critical interest in it.[55] For example, Régis Michaud's *Panorame de la Littérature Américaine*[56] ended with a grand tribute to Stein's work as the culmination of the modern spirit in poetry. Hugnet's "Le Berceau de Gertrude Stein . . . ," a tribute to author and subject, appeared in the *Revue Européenne* in February 1929. Both *Morceaux Choisis* and "Un Saint en Sept" with the preface by Hugnet that had endeared him to her when he submitted it to her, appeared in the spring. "George Hugnet" was published in America in *Blues* in July 1929.

Efforts to promote Stein were also made by Bernard Faÿ, who had different contacts. His "Portrait de Gertrude Stein" appeared in *Revue Européenne* in the early summer of 1930,[57] and *Échanges* in June published one of the best contemporary pieces on Stein, Marcel Brion's "Le Contrepoint poétique de Gertrude Stein."[58] She had reason to feel indebted to Hugnet and pleased with her success.

Ever since Hugnet had begun to send her poems as he wrote them, Stein discussed poetry with him. On August 3, anticipating his visit, she wrote that they would need to talk at length about poetry. Excited about the visit,

---

uneasy, though he also questioned Berman's killing of a wasp during their 1929 visit. Both are recalled in Stein to Hugnet, 20 September 1929. The poem reads:

> Little George littlest
> of all made to
> curl up like a
> ball when the
> large very tall
> all wasps found
> a wall at all.

55. In a letter of thanks of 3 July 1929 to Hugnet for *Morceaux Choisis,* she acknowledged that his publication had eased her hostility toward publishers and editors who had so consistently rejected her work.

    Les Editions de la Montagne was especially attractive to Stein because it was the publishing venture of a poet, not an editor. When in 1929 Hugnet quarreled with George Maratier, who worked with him as editor, Stein at first sided with Hugnet against Maratier, calling his a small-town mentality. However, after the falling-out with Hugnet, Maratier remained a friend and became a trusted personal adviser and dealer for her.

56. One in the series, *Panorames des Littératures Contemporaines,* the volume was published in Paris by Kra Editeurs, 1928, the tribute to Stein beginning on page 252. An inscribed copy is among the Stein library volumes at Yale; see also Michaud to Stein, 5 November 1928.

57. Reprinted in Bernard Faÿ, *Les Romanciers américains* (Paris: Denoël and Steele, 1931).

58. See Allanah Harper to Stein, 25 March and 17 November 1930. Brion hoped it would be translated, and among the Stein papers is an undated, unpublished translation by Stein and Toklas.

Hugnet in turn wrote to Thomson on August 31
tant new developments to follow this reunion. Th
may have been about *Dix Portraits,* "Enfances," film
Thomson's scores.

On September 2, two days before his departu
wrote to Thomson that after a period of illness and
chondria he regularly experienced when in the sur
mother in St.-Malo—he was learning to work aga
ample of Picasso, Stein, and Thomson. Of the new

> *J'ai un grand poème en train, un grand poème divi*
> *Je ne sais pas ce que ça donnera. C'est très méla*
> *légereté, profondeur. . . . On y parle de masturbati*
> *de désordres, de révolte. . . . Je suis très inquiet.*[59]

In a letter to Stein of the same date, he sounded de

> *J'ai commencé un poème sur les Enfances, mais il*
> *. . . et se perd. Et ce manque de courage que j'ai,*
> *met les nerfs à vif. Je souffre de tout violemment et*

He is speaking of a new poem in the sequence he h
a trip to Brussels[61] for a lecture on film.[62] He never
sexual details he described to Thomson.

59. I have started a long poem, divided into short sections,
    what will come of it. It is a great mixture, seriousness,
    . . . There is talk of masturbation, orgies, debauchery, c

    As an example, he cited the complete poem number 14 of

    > *Que me disent amour et ses tourterelles?*
    > *J'ai perdue la plus belle en ouvrant la m*
    > *en changeant de pas j'ai trompé la silenc*
    > *rira l'eternelle en tuant la plus belle,*
    > *la morte a su garder son domaine,*
    > *en refermant les bras renié j'ai tué l'éter*
    > *l'enfance a renié, renié la souveraine*
    > *et c'est ainsi que vont les semaines.*

60. I have started a poem about Enfances but it drags, does
    itself. And my lack of courage more than my sterility se
    violently and constantly.

61. Apparently on Stein's recommendation, he visited Bruges,
    minders of faces he had actually observed in paintings by
    works by Peter Breughel the Elder, Roger de la Pastoie, an
    have recommended the Hotel Mon Bijou et Wellington in

62. Hugnet's lecture, given on March 22, is summarized in

Embarquons, partons aux Indes . . .
. . .
. . . l'ordre
a changé son courant d'amour,
l'ordre des mots dans la bouche,
enfance réveillée par mes désordres.
(26)

This is the work of a very young poet, whose world and verse are enlarged by love. The poems are often skillful, often labored, frequently sentimental. What did Stein make of them? The important questions about her versions have not even been asked. Did she offer, as Hugnet maintained, to translate "Enfances," and if so, when and why? Had she read them when she made the offer? Or did Hugnet suggest translation to her? Why did he choose to submit this group of poems to her? The preserved documents fail to answer these questions, but informed speculation suggests possible answers. Stein probably offered to translate the poems before she saw them, after he told her about them.

Of course there are ideas in them to which Stein would have responded or which Hugnet even received from her: words as physical objects to be touched, handled, mouthed; the capacity of children, who are not repressed by habit and rules, to play spontaneously and freely with words; the need for writers to become children in order to compose.[63]

Hugnet presumably told Stein about the new work or even showed her what he had written on his return to Paris from Brussels. He later described the experience that led to "Enfances" as extraordinarily powerful, though nothing is known of how Stein felt about what he told or perhaps showed her. During the visit in Bilignin, September 4 to 11, 17, or 24, he was apparently still writing and read some sections aloud. After the visit, on a late September Sunday, he thanked her for her faith in him,

le bien que vous m'avez fait en aimant mes poèmes, ces confessions confiantes où je suis nu.[64]

63. The themes of childhood and the naïf writer appear also in Hugnet's poem on Stein, "Le Berceau de Gertrude Stein ou Le Mystère de la Rue de Fleurus" and in Thomson's "Miss Gertrude Stein as a Young Girl." Hugnet often speaks of his poems as *chansons d'enfant* (songs of a child) and Stein is charmed by poems which she describes as "*jeune, naive, pur*" ("young, naive, pure").

64. the good you have done me in loving my poems, those intimate confessions where I am naked.

On September 23, he wrote to Thomson that he agreed completely with him about Stein's "therapeutic power."[65]

Between April 26 and May 2, 1930, Stein went to the country, ready to translate, and, at the end of May, returned the corrected proofs for *Dix Portraits,* adding that she expected "Enfances" the following month. In an undated letter, Hugnet said he would send the poems, having now distanced himself from their shattering emotions.

> *Vous allez recevoir "Enfances" auxquels poèmes je puis penser maintenant que toutes les émotions s'éloignent et deviennent moins bouleversantes.*[66]

Stein had taken a dictionary to Bilignin,

> *un des plus robuste dictionaires anglais français et français anglais et avec c'a et moi et mon sympathie pour vous je dois avoir des resultat, de mon premiere essai comme traducteur.*[67]

In the course of the summer, she apparently worked with the poems as he sent them to her. Three days before leaving Paris for St.-Malo, Hugnet in an undated letter impatiently awaited the results:

> *Oh oui écrivez[-]moi vite au sujet d'Enfances. Je compte beaucoup sur cet oeuvre . . . , mais je voudrais avant tout qu'elle ne vous décevoie point après un an. Et votre traduction sera pour moi une honneur et une joie. . . .*[68]

He copied and forwarded to Thomson her letter of July 4, probably sent with her first versions,

> My very dear George, Voila the fourth of July independence day et je fais [word] des petits poems et je me demande que vous voulez vous say of this today. Mais vraiment je sais pas du tout comment vous vous trouverait dans un traduction et j'attends votre reponse avec impatience.[69]

65. Virgil Thomson Papers, Columbia University Rare Book Collection.
66. You will receive "Enfances." I can think calmly about the poems now that the emotions have dissipated and are becoming less upsetting.
67. Stein to Hugnet, letter presumably sent with corrected proofs, 31 May 1930.

    One of the biggest English-French and French-English dictionaries and that and I and my affection for you will produce something out of my first attempt at translation.
68. Oh yes, write me quickly about Enfances. I count on this work . . . but above all I hope it will not disappoint you after another year. And your translation will be an honor and a joy.
69. Here it is the fourth of July independence day and I make [word] little poems and I

In another letter, she characterized her work to Hugnet as translation or rather mirroring,

la traduction qui est plutot reflet.

By July 5, responding, he praised the English sound and rhythm but wondered whether he could identify with her text, feeling alternately close to and distant from it,

La traduction m'échappe parfois, d'autres fois je me vois de très loin, et très souvent il y a des choses que je ne comprends pas. Mais comme c'est beau en anglais, et comme c'est grand et plein d'air. Quel ravissement de lire vos mots à haute voix, pas trop vite et pas trop lentement. Moi, je bénis l'independence day.[70]

On July 11, his twenty-fourth birthday, he wrote from St.-Malo,

Admirable Gertrude, quelle joie vous me donnez dans un solitude de sable et de rocher. . . . Ce n'est pas une traduction, c'est autre chose, [in red] *c'est mieux. Je fais plus qu'aimer ce reflet, j'en rêve et je l'admire. Et vous me rendez au centuple la joie que j'ai pu vous offrir.*[71]

Does the last sentence echo Stein's offer of a return gesture for the joy he had given her? The inconsistency of his comments suggests his discomfort and helplessness in the face of Stein's incomprehensible versions, along with his admiration and gratitude.

With the completion of Stein's text by October, the book was about to become a reality. But that month, the prospectus for "Enfances" displayed with the Marcoussis frontispiece at the Galerie Jeanne Bucher showed the title page with the phrase, "Suivi par la traduction de Gertrude Stein." It presented Stein as translator, in a subordinate position, in smaller type, and she instantly demanded equal representation on the prospectus and title page. Hugnet did not want the work to look like a collaboration; he was prepared

---

worry whether you will find yourself in my translation. I am impatiently waiting for what you will "say of this today."

70. The translation sometimes bypasses me, at other times I see myself from far away, and often there are things I do not understand. Yet how beautiful it is in English, how grand and full of air. What a delight to read your words aloud, not too fast and not too slowly. I praise independence day.

71. Wonderful Gertrude, what joy you give me in this solitude of sand and rocks. . . . This is not a translation, it is something else, *it is better.* I more than love this reflection, I dream of it and admire it. And you return a hundredfold the joy I was able to offer you.

to agree to a phrase like *adaptation, transposition,* or *traduction libre* (free translation), but he claimed the poem and its authorship as his own:

> *Rien dans ce long poème est étranger à mon, à mes Enfances ou aux pré-occupations qu'alors je pouvais nourrir. Je sais en moi-même, loin dans moi et secrêtement, quels sont mes collaborateurs et mon dédicataire, et vous ne pouvez me faire abandonner de tels droits. . . .*[72]

Stein wanted to show Hugnet her appreciation of his devotion and his efforts for her. Her letters of 1928 and 1929 often speak of her pleasure in his poetry, though her comments are vaguely personal rather than literary. The young Hugnet learned from her, admired her, and fell in love with her. Stein was hungry for publication and readers, and he offered her both, but she mistook for affection her pleasure in his support and devotion. To her, already disaffected, the prospectus with the objectionable title page was the last straw.

She came to understand too late that she could not put Hugnet's poems into English because she could not imaginatively connect with them—they were mediocre poetry—or with him—he was young and sentimental. Putting the same matter another way, she was confused about who she was as a person and as a writer in relation to him. Hers was neither a literal translation nor what Pierre de Massot had described as a re-creation.

She ended up commenting on Hugnet's work or treating it as exercise material, which created a confusion of purpose and an uncertain voice. The

72. Nothing in this long poem is apart from my Enfance, my poem Enfances, or from what engrossed me at that time. Deep within myself and secretly, I know who are my collaborators and to whom I dedicate this work, and you cannot ask me to renounce these claims. . . .

This letter, in which Hugnet summarized the events in the hope of reaching a compromise, is dated December 18, 1930. "Enfances" was dedicated to Marcelle Ferry, "Miami," the daughter of an Alsatian naval officer who had trained at St.-Cyr. A lively and imaginative woman, she met Hugnet in the summer of 1929 in St.-Malo and left her *garagiste* husband and her daughter to join Hugnet. By 1931 there were difficulties between them.

In leftover copies of Hugnet's 1933 edition of "Enfances" distributed years later, Hugnet crossed out the dedication to Ferry and also restored the original names of women in Poem 26, indicating excessive jealousies of one mistress as a motive for the earlier revisions. (The text printed in *Pagany* gives the original names.)

In line 4, Marie is changed back to the original Gabrielle; in line 5, Eugénie and Irène to Eugénie and Yvonne. In Poem xvi, Angelina and Patricia remain unchanged (Mme. Myrtille Hugnet to author, 4 March 1984). After Ferry and Hugnet broke up, Ferry in 1933 joined André Breton, and later Oscar Dominguez. See also Hugnet to Thomson, 3 November 1933.

flower of friendship that was to have been a joint text became the destruction of the friendship.

In December 1930, an attempt was made, with the help of Virgil Thomson, to work out a compromise title page for the book. It failed. This title page—the title *Enfances,* preceded by Hugnet's name and the year 1929, followed by Stein's name and the year 1930—met with the disapproval of Toklas, who was not interested in a resolution that might assure continued collaboration between Hugnet and Stein. Toklas made clear that the new design failed to give Stein equal credit and to fulfill her condition, "half mine or nothing." As a result, by New Year's Day 1931, Thomson, who had proposed the compromise, was rejected along with Hugnet.

Toklas had reason to be uneasy. Any threat to her position in Stein's life was not likely to come from a painter, a historian, or a composer but only from a writer. Intimacy between Stein and one of her own kind could threaten the most intimate relationship she knew. It had happened once before, when the young Hemingway helped Stein publish *The Making Of Americans* and became her supporter and admiring student. Only writers could achieve such intimacy—or become such threats. In an interview of May 31, 1987, Virgil Thomson told me that Toklas did all she could to prevent any reconciliation between Stein and Hugnet; he considered the cases of Hugnet and Hemingway remarkably similar, not because they were similar authors but because they stood in similar relation to Stein.

When Hugnet and Stein failed to solve their difficulties, publication of the joint volume as well as continuation of the friendship became impossible. They separated their texts, their plans for publications, and their lives. Stein quickly issued her versions as poems of her own in the second volume of her Plain Edition in May 1931 under the title *Before The Flowers Of Friendship Faded Friendship Faded,* followed by the phrase, "Written On A Poem By Georges Hugnet." In the autumn of that year, Samuel Putnam announced his plan to publish his translation of "Enfances" in a limited, illustrated volume in his New Review Editions. Hugnet also announced it, but the book apparently never appeared.

For many months, from the winter of 1931 on, Hugnet vented his hurt and rage in bitter and nasty letters to his friend Thomson, including collages about Stein made of phrases and headlines cut from newspapers.[73] By 1933, he published his poems with three etchings by Joan Miró under the imprint of Editions Cahiers d'Art.[74]

73. Virgil Thomson Papers.

74. Both Mme. Germaine Hugnet and Mme. Myrtille Hugnet said to me on separate occa-

The grammar that had joined Hugnet to Stein in her portrait of him and in his translations of her texts ended up separating them in Stein's reflections—by no means uncritical translations. The new book they were to have had together issued in more than a lovers' quarrel. Already at the end of the summer of 1930, he complained to Thomson that "Enfances" vanished in Stein's translation, and with it his sense of himself as a poet. Thomson consoled him but must have understood Stein's commentaries better than Hugnet with his limited English. A reading of the two texts will show their relation.

Text

Reading Stein's reflections on "Enfances,"[75] unlike reading *Dix Portraits* or *Morceaux Choisis,* along with the originals, is maddening. The antiphonal reading of original and translation side by side may lead to disagreements but not to disorientation. *Dix Portraits* and *Morceaux Choisis* can be read as surprising revelations, for these French texts parallel the originals with fierce exactitude, more literal and principled than a reader of translations ever expects. If these French versions were meant to be models of procedure for translators, however, Stein did not follow her own teaching. Her poems do not brook parallel reading, for they do not follow the Hugnet text as she taught Hugnet and Thomson to follow her own.

What is disorienting is that the relation of Stein's reflections to Hugnet's poems shifts constantly. Yet the originals cannot be disregarded, for they constitute a dimension of Stein's versions, their raison d'être if not their equivalent. The reader follows Stein, Hugnet poems in hand, looking for equivalents but only momentarily able to spot them. Her versions tantalize by connecting with the originals only to disconnect again; there is no consistent principle at work. Their excitement lies precisely in their apparent discontinuity. To say this, of course, is to describe a quality of all Stein writing, but here the French originals jolt the reading of her versions.

---

sions in May 1982 and October 1985 that Hugnet joined the surrealists only after and as a result of the falling-out with Stein.

75. Stein's text of "Enfances," like her working translation of *MOA,* is not on loose leaves. The model text, which generates her writing even where she departs from it, is already "given." I have seen only three leaves, given by Stein to Robert Bartlett Haas, of an earlier handwritten version of the first poem, different only in details from the final version. She uses shorter lines, breaks lines differently, and revises details of phrasing. Whether there were other drafts is not known.

Stein begins by translating as literally as possible,[76] though always avoiding automatic use of standard phraseology. Her translation is therefore from the start not an English equivalent of Hugnet's French, because it draws attention to itself rather than to the text translated. Her writing always creates its own logic; it cannot follow the logic of another, even when she tries to make it do so. She takes an impulse—a key word, a phrase—from Hugnet's text to kick off a text of her own. With snatches of Hugnet as starting points, she practices writing poetry partly derived from his and partly her own.

In poem 2, Hugnet re-creates, in two-beat lines, a ditty about childhood with sexual overtones.

Enfances dans la laine
en dépit des semaines,
enfance dans la rue
sans adieu et sans mal
et jouant avec le hasard,
au rire des cotonniers
comparez vos corps nus . . .

She translates closely though she phrases freely. She creates childhood not by Hugnet's short, songlike lines but by repetitions—little, little; wooly, wool—and alliterations, which make for diminutives of a different kind. It is as if she was trying out, sometimes awkwardly, ways of writing lines.

A little a little one all wooly or in wool
As if within or not in any week or as for weeks
A little one which makes a street no name
without it having come and went farewell
And not with laughing playing
Where they went they would or work . . . .

But continuing, Hugnet next considers himself:

j'ai vécu cette enfance
et tant d'autres encore
ayant du sang mêlé de nord
et de midi, ici et là,
où je nacquis et où je voyageai
et tous les noms sont là
au courant de l'invisible
et de ce que l'amour n'a pas brouillé.

76. See also Bridgman, *Gertrude Stein in Pieces,* 201–2.

Stein refuses to follow him into his own childhood and sexual exploration. She does not share the "northern and southern French blood" of his experiences and refuses to follow his verse in the first person. In a long line that breaks rhythmic continuity, she questions to whom she can relate by trying out which pronouns go with which and who belongs with whom. It is as if she had entered Hugnet's poem, found it wanting, and pulled away from speaker and verse.

> To live like when
> And very many things
> Being with me with them
> with which with me
> whoever with and born
> and went as well
> Meant,
> Five which are seen
> And with it five more lent,
> As much as not mixed up,
> With love.

Apparently unwilling to speak in Hugnet's voice, she adapts it entirely to her own.

By poem 4, she openly questions his work and the joint project. I read the following first line as a comment on his verse, unlike Bridgman, who sees it as evidence of Stein's poor command of French.

> I follow as I can and this to do
> With never vaguely that they went away
> I have been left to bargain with myself
> And I have come not to be pleased to see
> They wish to watch the little bird
> Who flew at which they look
> They never mentioned me to it,
> I stopped to listen well it is a pleasure to see a fire
> which does not inspire them to see me. . . .

Her very rhymes and rhythms betray her annoyance. Hugnet's poem is not an interesting challenge, and she translates it into attack. His fire, mere hot air, prevents her from creating interesting work.

As Hugnet told Thomson, sexuality often enters the poems in the form of masturbation, adultery, seduction. Poem 7 is about the pleasure of falling in love with a fellow student while doing homework with her on an afternoon when her mother is out. Stein is impatient with his sentimental sexuality and his lines about the text of passion that he teaches the girl. Her lines do not render his nor are they a sharp comment of her own:

> It is whatever originally read read can be two words smoke can be all three
> And very much there were.

In poem 23, Hugnet speaks of sailing out into life, on the seaway of lovers' laughter,

> *Où es-tu, si loin et si prèsque je vois avec peine*
> *l'enfance et ses manies*
> *et qu'un même rire*
> *devient notre sillage*
> *et qu'une même tristesse*
> *nous dit de même*
> *que l'eau s'éloigne de nos collines.*
> *Et ton écriture s'efface*
> *sur ma poitrine lavée.*

L'eau s'éloigne de nos collines is rendered without line breaks as Stein's own circumstance in the hilly country and the garden in the Bugey, where watering goes on every day,

> It is pleasant that without a hose no water is drawn. No water is drawn pleasantly without a hose.

The word "hose" opens into "doublet and hose," conventional poetic terms which she refuses as she refuses Hugnet's romantic notions. The poem moves into an exasperated comment:

> Doublet and hose not at all water and hose not at all any not at all. Not at all. Either not at all by not at all with me. When this you do not hear and do not see believe me.

Even the beginning of poem 23 smirks at Hugnet's love poem,

> Every one which is why they will they will be will he will he be for her for her to come with him with when he went he went and came and any little name is shame as such tattoo.

Often during this second summer in Bilignin, she translates what she reads into local country life. Cows appear, one following another, like people following one another,

There are a few here now and the rest can follow a cow. (30)

If the cows for Stein refer to orgasm, it here sounds like a mechanically repeated affair.

His love poems become her own love songs in familiar Stein phrases though she retains his king and queen, as in poem 29,

J'ai mis un costume d'été
pour paraître gai.
Et le roi s'était avancé
pour dire sa pensée
La reine prenait son bain
et ne disait rien.
L'enfance avait pris la reine
et lui disait sa peine. . . .

I love my love with a v
Because it is like that
I love myself with a b
Because I am beside that
A king.
I love my love with an a
Because she is a queen
I love my love and a a is the best of them. . . .

She refuses to render his love poems. Her love poetry cannot be like his. Not that hers is more than familiar Stein.

Poem 17, about a twenty-three year old, begins,

Sans sortir de l'enfance tu as vingt-trois ans
et tu traverses une rivière sans penser à moi.
Si tu dormais en vérité, quitterais-tu si vite
cette tête et ce bras lancés contre ton mensonge?

Stein pokes fun at his juvenile sentimentality:

He is the exact age he tells you
He is not twenty two, he is twenty three and when this you see remember me
And yet what is it that he can see.
He can see veritably three, all three which is to be certainly.
And then.

She ends,

> . . . and now and when is it to be to settle without sillily to be without without with double let me. So he says. It is easy to put heads together really. Head to head it is easily done and easily said head to head in bed.

She comments on him, separating "he" and "me" rather than making the poet's voice her own. On his birthday, July 11, when she had already sent him some of her versions, Hugnet, from St.-Malo, wrote her an ecstatic letter,

> *Je . . . vous envoie la dernière pensée de ma vingt-troisième année et la première pensée de ma vingt-quatrième. . . .*[77]

Perhaps poem 17 incorporates her response to his letter.

And then there is poem 14, the one Hugnet had sent Thomson as an example of "Enfances." Of her version, Stein said to Carl Van Vechten in a letter of April 16, 1931, when she sent him the book of her versions, that it spoke "of Bilignin," where he had visited the preceding summer. Only *her* poem, not Hugnet's, could be about Bilignin, for Hugnet had not been there when he composed his. If hers was about Bilignin, it could be a transposition into her own circumstance of Hugnet's poem, though Van Vechten never questioned it. Stein's poem picks up Hugnet's turtledoves, but she quickly makes them her own.

> *Que me disent amour et ses tourelles?*
> *J'ai perdu la plus belle en ouvrant la main . . .*[78]
>
> It could be seen very nicely
> That doves have each a heart.
> Each one is always seeing that they could not be apart.
> A little lake makes fountains
> And fountains have no flow,
> And a dove has need of flying
> And water can be low,
> Let me go.
> Any week is what they seek
> When they have to halve a beak.
> I like a painting on a wall of doves
> And what do they do.
> They have hearts

77. I am sending you the last thought of my twenty-third and the first of my twenty-fourth year. . . .

78. *Pagany,* whose text I follow here, prints *tourelles,* apparently a misprint for *tourterelles.*

Figure 7. Design for cards by "a man in Montmartre" for Carl Van Vechten and Fania Marinoff, who sent them to friends for special occasions. On August 12, 1930, Van Vechten asked Stein to order for him plates with this design at the local pottery in Belley. Reprinted by permission of Bruce Kellner.

They are apart
Little doves are winsome
But not when they are little and left.

I wonder whether her version was written after Van Vechten asked her, on August 12, to order dinner plates for him at the local pottery, which had made "Rose is a Rose" plates for her. He suggested a design on a card he enclosed.

> These cards that a man writes for me in Montmartre each year we come over . . . I don't mean exactly of course, but *with a dove with a missive in its beak and a horse shoe and two transfigured hearts* . . .[79]

It is possible that the poem conceals a reference that charmed Van Vechten precisely because it could be deciphered only in the privacy of friendship.

The key phrase for lines 1 and 3 of the three-line poem 28, "A clock in the eye ticks in the eye," which sounds entirely like Stein, appears in a little black *carnet,* at the end of a long, playful love note from Stein to Toklas, written

79. See *LGS/CVV* 217–18; emphases added. Copies of this card, to which Bruce Kellner alerted me, are in the Carl Van Vechten Collection, NYPL.

late summer or early fall 1930. The "clock in the eye" passage bears virtually no resemblance to Hugnet's poem 28, which appears to bore Stein. In the hack verse of the middle line she inserts only the rimless hat that Hugnet's girl wears, but for the rest marks her boredom,

> A clock in the eye ticks in the eye a clock ticks in the eye.
> A number with that and large as a hat which makes rims think quicker than I.
> A clock in the eye ticks in the eye a clock ticks ticks in the eye.

She reaches poem 30, the last, in exasperation but with relief,

> There are a few here now and the rest can follow a cow,
> The rest can follow now there are a few here now.
> They are all all here now the rest can follow a cow
> And mushrooms on a hill and anything else until.
> They can see and sink and swim with now and then a
> brim.
> A brim to a hat
> What is that . . .

She scoffs at his verses and observes caustically,

> Think and swim with hearing him,
> Love and song not any song a song is always then too long
> to just sit there and sing
> Sing song is a song
> When sing and sung
> Is just the same as now among
> Among them,
> They are very well placed to be seated and sought
> They are very well placed to be cheated and bought
> And a bouquet makes a woods
> A hat makes a man
> And any little more is better than
> The one.

The issue of authorship arises not only with the prospectus for the book but also in her very reflections. She turns the tables on Hugnet, with whom she has produced two books and from whom she now separates herself—or does she swallow him up?

> And any one can come and cry and sing.
> Which made butter look yellow

And a hope be relieved
By all of it in case
Of my name.
What is my name.
That is the game
Georges Hugnet
By Gertrude Stein.[80]

Context as Text: "Left To Right" (*RAB* 155–58)

After all this trouble, what was left to say? The friends whose names had resonated with affection were no longer friends. Only shadow figures were left. In January 1931, Stein wrote "Left To Right," a journalistic war dispatch which gave the facts as she saw them. This "true story," as it is called on the cover of the manuscript notebook, appeared in *Harper's Bazaar* (London), September 1931, and was later reprinted in *Story* 3, no. 16 (November 1933).

In the report, the project of "Enfances" becomes an abstract, empty husk, a "book," anything, everything—or nothing. Georges Hugnet becomes a stiffly grammatical Arthur William, who knows the proper right from the

80. The last two lines are not in the original manuscript or in the version published, with Hugnet's French poems *en face,* in *Pagany* 2, no. 1 (winter 1931), but they are in the text published by Stein in her own Plain Edition in May 1931, after the break with Hugnet.

In his memoir, *Les Précieux,* Bernard Faÿ remembers,

> *Un jour à Bourg-en-Bresse, au restaurant,* [Alice Toklas] *entendit deux Françaises qui causaient; l'une d'elles disait à l'autre: ". . . Avant que l'amitié ne flétrît, les fleurs de l'amitié flétrirent. . . ." Frappé par la beauté de l'expression, Alice la traduit pour son amie, et Gertrude en fit le thème de l'un de ses poèmes les plus réussis.* (146)

> One day, in a restaurant at Bourg-en-Bresse, Alice overheard two French women talking; one said to the other, "Before the friendship faded, the flowers of friendship faded. . . ." Struck by the expression, she translated it for her friend, and Gertrude made it the title of one of her most successful poems.

This account corresponds to one by Toklas that varies in details,

> The title [*Before The Flowers of Friendship Faded Friendship Faded*] came to Gertrude in the dining room of a hotel at Bourg when two guests . . . at different tables were disagreeing. (*What Is Remembered* 137)

However, the sentence appears for the first time, I believe, in *A Novel Of Thank You* (43). It returns in "Regular Regularly In Narrative" (243) in connection with the death of Juan Gris, where not the friendship but the funeral flowers fade.

> If if the Chateau d'If. The son of Juan Gris If if the Chateau d'If. Faded. The flowers of friendship if if the Chateau d'If. The flowers faded. . . .

improper left, as she had already described him in "Final[illegible]
Virgil Thomson appears conducting negotiations as Genera[illegible].
feminine *e.* Did the name Irving recall Emma Lootz Erving, a
ate and medical school friend?[81]

The last, more marginal participant, Bravig Imbs, who had
some Hugnet poems and whom she had also rejected, in the repo[illegible]
Frederick Harvard.[82] "Left To Right" is a nasty, pouting piece, [illegible]
of main clauses whose subjects, "I," "he," "they," "one," "everyone,"
totally depersonalized. Stein's display of her power to reje[illegible] and win i[illegible]
new piece of narrative reportage makes remarkably unpleasant writing
reading.

Any number of texts written while the drama with Hugnet was unfolding show traces of his prominence in her misplaced affection and later her excessive contempt. In the play *The Five Georges,* written in late 1930 or early 1931, the name printed as "George S." shows up in the manuscript as "George H.," the "H" crossed out and replaced by "S." When the change was made in the play is not clear. What is clear is that she radically eliminated Hugnet from her life and her work. The manuscript of *Madame Recamier* also shows that the figure originally called George Hugnet became George Janvier in revision, no doubt recalling the cold January of 1931, after the fight. In the same manuscript, the "Aria in which they sing Friendship's Flowers" (369) was originally the "Aria in which they sing Enfances." There remains Stein's film scenario, "Deux Soeurs Qui Ne Sont Pas Soeurs," composed for Hugnet, who had first led her to writing in French.

The friendship with Hugnet and her attempt at translation led to a great deal of ruminating whose significance for her work she would only interpret with

81. Emma Lootz Erving visited Stein in Bilignin in 1928. Her husband, William Erving, who had died of tuberculosis, is in the play *At Present* (320).
82. It is not clear how the name Frederick or the surname Harvard came to be used for Bravig Imbs, a Dartmouth man. Answering Thomson's letter of October 7, 1931, Imbs sent him a poem which may take off from "Enfances" xiv:

> "A gentle caprice of the Sacred Cow"
> Doves is as are as of as are cows
> Not cows as doves as grey
> But doves as are as of as are brindle
> Come bossy bossy coo coo coo.

Imbs comments on the translation of "Enfances" in *Confessions of Another Young Man* (New York: Henkle-Yewdale House, 1936), 285.

ica. The results of her meditations turn up mainly nd "George Washington" counterpart sections.[83] In Stein sent *Four In America* to Thornton Wilder. She ke the Washington section, which

> 4 years ago when I was first wondering about identity, as writing the Flowers of friendship and meditating resultantly kespeare's sonnets.[84]

come to understand that she had translated Hugnet

> ecause of the poetry but because of the poet he had been very nice ne and I was grateful for it and so I wanted to make him happy and way to show it was to translate the poetry. . . . (*Narration* 51)

had written for personal rather than literary reasons, leaving herself open the charge of corruption as an artist. This insight, however, opened into larger literary considerations.

"Enfances" left Stein unsure of her own voice. She had always in writing followed the movement of her own mind, but translating "Enfances" required her to follow the words, the forms, the mind of another, already formulated. The fact that Hugnet's poems were inappropriate for her ways with words merely dramatized what would under any circumstances have been difficult. The discrepancy between her voice and his in "Enfances" left her disabled.

The experience led her to distinguish between poetry as spontaneous utterance and poetry written to order, following a model. The former was genuine poetry, written "from inside," but the latter a form of fakery, written "from outside." She associated true poetry with roughness, ambiguity, and irregularity, whereas poetry following a model was smooth, regular, and lacking in vibration.

To illustrate the distinction, she cited Shakespeare's plays, which she considered his own creation, in contrast to his sonnets, which she considered written to order in the voice of another. That the illustration is inadequate and unfortunate, the more so as it likens her work to Shakespeare's, is obvious enough. But her notion that the poet's voice must follow its own perceptions rather than the temptations of the world, of fame and personal re-

83. The translation also appears briefly in the lecture "Poetry And Grammar" and in the fourth *Narration* lecture, and it contributes to the theme of creation explored later in *GHA*.

84. See Stein to Wilder, early September 1935, in *LGS/TW* 53. See also 29 August 1935, *LGS/TW* 51.

lations, was fruitful. She turned the experience of the translation to literary advantage, using it to clarify ideas about writing rather than indulging in justification or attack.

The book that allowed her further to formulate the distinction foreshadowed in *Before The Flowers Of Friendship Faded Friendship Faded* was *The Autobiography Of Alice B. Toklas.* That work, which she was careful to write in the name of another, brought her readers, fame, money—and cost her her voice. She finally gave in and wrote brilliantly and seductively to a blueprint for success. Once she understood where her great need for audience, publication, and fame had led her, she recovered a very different voice.

Grammar. Fills me with delight.

—"A Grammarian" 106

A sentence is an imagined master piece.

—"Sentences" 123

7. 1928–30

Grammar

The long story of Georges Hugnet sounds as if French publications and relations with him and other young artists—among them Tchelitchew, Tanner, Thomson, Maratier, Faÿ, Bérard, Imbs, Eugene Berman—preoccupied Stein exclusively from 1927 to the end of 1930. This is not so. The actual work for *Morceaux Choisis* and *Dix Portraits* was done mainly by Hugnet, with help from Virgil Thomson. The only addition to the portraits was "More Grammar Genia Berman," probably composed during the visit of Berman and Hugnet in September 1929. More extensive new writing was in her "translation" of *Enfances,* completed in less than two months in the summer of 1930, while she at the same time steadily composed further language studies and new plays. Though *Enfances* exasperated her, it added experience with poetry, especially lines, rhythms, sound, and a sense of voice. The ground for poetry had already been prepared by her preoccupation with language.

During and after the collaboration with Hugnet from 1927 to 1931, then, she was busy with many other matters, including radical changes in her private life and new writing: the experience of the country was incorporated into her work from 1926 on, taking new forms with the move to the Bilignin house in 1929. That first summer she wrote little, the next more, though she started no longer works. She did portraits and occasional pieces and studied grammar and language, which demanded no large formal designs while allowing her to compose finely wrought forms culled from daily life. Mushrooms and walnuts appeared; like the ostrich egg she owned, they enclosed complex structures in simple, round perfection.

Always linked as context and text, these texts are the subject of this chapter. The facts about the house and the dog are told by James Mellow, but I here speak in detail of how they enter her work.[1] The context section for this chapter presents them as steps in redefining the women's relationship. The next chapter follows Stein's review of herself as a writer and the evidence in her work of the changes wrought in the daily life by the actuality of house and dog.

Context: A House and a Dog

In February 1929, Stein and Toklas bought the poodle Basket; in March, they signed a summer lease on a house in the hamlet of Bilignin near Belley. Intimately related, the two acquisitions changed the quality and balance of their life and entered Stein's writing.

Toklas introduces Bilignin in her memoirs by describing the stay from late August 1922 to February or early March 1923 in St.-Rémy, where Stein worked happily and productively.[2] In the fall of 1923, they spent weeks on the Riviera, where she did more inspired new writing. A plan to return there in the summer of 1924 was abandoned when on the way south they discovered Belley.

> The fourth place we do not go south any more. In the fifth place we go to Belley an attractive place where we hope to be as well situated as ever. ("Natural Phenomena" 168)

From 1924 to 1928, they returned every summer to the Hotel Pernollet at Belley, exchanging the splendor of Paris for the peace of Belley—*la gloire* for *la paix.* Unlike Paris or the Riviera, Belley assured privacy, concentration, and variety for living and working.

The Rhône Valley was an unusually diverse countryside, dominated by the weight and the verticals of the Alps, yet opening out with the Rhône River into varied hilly farmland with streams, rivers, lakes, and always pop-

1. James Mellow, *Charmed Circle: Gertrude Stein and Company* (New York: Praeger, 1974), chapter 12, 312–50. See also details, not always reliable, scattered throughout *The Alice B. Toklas Cookbook, AABT, EA, WIR,* and many letters to and from Stein. Included here are in addition some details and names not given in other discussions of this period that help the reading of her work. Excepting brief summaries, I speak of familiar events only when I modify interpretation, documenting with quotations from writing or letters.
2. *WIR* 121–22. On the trip to St.-Rémy, see Mellow, *Charmed Circle,* 255–56; *Autobiography* 255–57; letters from Janet Scudder, 1922–23; Scudder on Bilignin, in letters, 1928–1933, and Scudder's autobiography, *Modeling My Life* (New York: Harcourt, Brace, 1925). See also Toklas to Van Vechten, 15 November 1947.

lars to absorb the floods. Stein came to see in this landscape a dynamic process of constant change, always in motion yet never moving toward completion, through the changing weather, the days, and the seasons. She meditated on the process of land, animals, and people, including herself, unfolding before her. What she saw and heard became composition.[3]

But the meditative consciousness seeing the landscape imperceptibly becomes the acquisitive person seizing the land.[4] As early as 1925, Stein and Toklas thought of buying or building a country house of their own, briefly exploring other areas but soon deciding on the familiar region of Belley, the section of the département de l'Ain informally called Le Bugey.[5]

In their fifties and both personally and financially stable, they were ready to settle in a summer house of their own, like many of their generation: Jo and Yvonne Davidson (Saché, Indre et Loire), Tristan Tzara (Annecy, Haute-Savoie), Henri-Pierre Roché (St.-Robert, Corrèze), and others. From America, on August 3, 1925, Sherwood Anderson spoke of a country house, and Carl Van Vechten wrote of wanting a country house.[6]

By the summer of 1925, Stein wrote to Anderson about building a house in a chosen spot on meadows near the Rhône. Even in April 1923, before she discovered Belley, she wrote to Henry McBride that except Picasso, who continued to rent, all the artists "build or buy," including Matisse, Van Dongen, Braque, Lipchitz, and others. Postcards of 1926 from Stein and especially Toklas suggest great urgency in their search for property, as if once the decision to get a house had been made, it had to be found immediately.

3. Especially notable among the many works with details about the country are the following sections: *AWD* in *R* 509; "Natural Phenomena," *PL* 168, 176; *LCA* 39, 130–31, 166–67, 209; "Scenery And George Washington," *FIA* 56; *A Manoir, LO&P* 292, 302, 308; "A Plan For Planting," *PL* 14; Toklas' description of the region in the *Cookbook,* 95; correspondence with Allen Tanner, Georges Hugnet, Henry McBride, Jo Davidson, Louis Bromfield, Ellen DuPoy, and Rose Ellen and Julian Stein, who in 1929 moved to a farm in Pikesville, Maryland, near Baltimore, which led to exchanges about country experience.
4. Stein looked at scenery as she looked at landscape painting, with an eye for light and perspective. "Two kilometers off is the right distance to decide about a house," she wrote to Henry McBride on May 22, 1929, about discovering the house.
5. Eventually they joined the local cultural society, Le Bugey: Société scientifique, historique et littéraire, and received its quarterly *Bulletin.*

   It is possible to read in Stein's landscape writing a subtext intended to make herself a part of the region and pay tribute to it by creating its life in words. In an essay that Toklas considered one of the best, Suzanne Tenand speaks of Stein as "un écrivain de chez nous" ("our own writer"), "Gertrude Stein parle le Bugey . . . elle le chante" ("Gertrude Stein speaks the language of the Bugey . . . she sings it"; "Gertrude Stein," *Visages de l'Ain* no. 26 [avril-juin 1954]).
6. 10 October 1927, *LGS/CVV* 155.

Stein came gradually to feel at home in the region. In a letter to Natalie Barney about festivities in Belley, for example, she included herself among the local population while yet voicing ironic detachment from local taste:

> We are putting up a statue to Brillat [Savarin] in September a statue which is a bust but we that is Belley are very pleased with ourselves.[7]

In the summer of 1926, Allen Tanner responded to what must have been an insistent comment by Stein,

> I do hope you get the land away from the peasants—you should have it because you would cherish it and use it and grace it and make it into good land but I suppose it[']s difficult to make them understand that![8]

A *carnet* of that summer contains sketches, maps, directions, measurements, and notes about properties, along with early drafts for *An Acquaintance With Description,* where "[s]he is very happy and a farm" (*R* 509).

In 1927, Stein wrote,

> He loved to think of sitting by the river bank to-night and for this purpose he did not wish to have a house bought for him on a hill but at a distance but at a considerable distance a very considerable distance which had been found in the course of conversation and would overlook a stream which was a river as it is pronouncedly navigable and so it would be as well as well it would be very well very well attainably if there was no manner of doubt that they were very much given to have it return to their thought they thought about it and it was very much as much as needed that a lieutenant if he became a captain a lieutenant if he because she an american a very well I thank you and because of it they because of a mountain and she because of a contemporary in an interval between does it do it quicker and if quicker can be heard or if it does it slower and can it be heard and both can it be heard or should it should it not be heard. (*LCA* 209–10)

These words speak of how she spotted the property at a distance from the valley below as a part of the landscape and immediately decided she wanted the small, walled stone house with its outbuildings and garden on the hillside.[9] The house, however, was occupied by a French officer who could not

7. 16 August 1927, Bibliothèque Doucet, Paris.
8. n.d., MS Barnard College. On Belley, see also "To Call It A Day" (1924), *PL* 243. "Love A Delight" (1927), *PL* 251, contrasts city and country, setting Toklas and Stein in Belley against Tanner and Tchelitchew in Guermantes at Stella Bowen's house.
9. See also *WIR* 123.

be put out because French law protected against eviction tenants posted in a town as members of the armed forces.

This discovery did not put Stein off. She considered how the lieutenant could be removed, either by means of promotion to the rank of captain, or how she, as a major author who was herself as good as a captain or chief, might take over the house; she had as much right to it as he, for her work as an author served the country just as well as his as an officer. Her confidence about getting what she wanted was so assured that at a sale in 1927, she and Toklas acquired a sofa and a brass bust for the house they did not yet have. Madame Munet, a local acquaintance, stored the purchases.[10]

Over the next two years, after a number of delays and setbacks, arrangements were made with the help of influential French friends for the transfer of Lieutenant Fernand Bonhomme to a new and advantageous post in Morocco, which paid overseas compensation, kept him far away, and made the house available for sublease. On March 11, 1929, Stein signed a sublet agreement for the unexpired portion of his lease, protecting herself as far as she could against the possibility of his return. That spring Stein and Toklas moved in. By September 1932, anticipating the date for renewal, Stein negotiated a lease in her own name.[11]

The impact of the house on Stein's life and her work was enormous. Though the women did not own it, everything about it, including the landscape in which it stood, comes to sound in her words as if it was theirs. Around Bilignin has accrued a personality cult to which Stein and Toklas amply contributed. They are immortalized in this setting in countless lovingly preserved images—paintings, photographs, memoirs, home movies, sketches, anecdotes, letters.

10. Letters from Madame M[arie]. M[adeleine]. Munet, whose husband had a cake shop, Biscuiterie de la Mère Prusse, in Améyzieu near Artemare, show her also looking for houses for Stein. Like some other local friends, she felt that Stein and Toklas enlarged her life. See also

> a beginning of a settlement is made by Madame Munet of Artemarre and this is not an invention as all the rest is. . . . (*LCA* 39)

11. The initial plan was apparently for his promotion. He failed the required examinations, however, so that a new plan had to be made. The transfer was initiated with help from Georges Maratier, Bernard Faÿ, and perhaps others; it was negotiated through a solicitor in Belley, Maître Amand Saint-Pierre, acting as agent for the young owner of the house, Marie-Anne du Vachat (later Mme. Gabriel Putz), who inherited the property upon the death of her mother, Mme. François du Vachat, on October 30, 1929. Stein rented the house until 1942, when Madame Putz reclaimed the property for her own use and Stein moved to Culoz. See also letters from Amand Saint-Pierre, Etienne Décôte[s], and Georges Maratier; *Cookbook,* 94; and *LGS/TW,* Appendix ix, 414–17.

The wordscapes composed in the summers of the late 1920s and 1930s absorbed the region in constantly changing forms that became mythologized compositions of their daily life in the "home in a manoir"[12] overlooking the valley. Social life in the country centers on landowning farmers, their families, their houses, their farms and animals. After his first visit, Bernard Faÿ, writing to Virgil Thomson on July 17, 1930, voiced its magic in words reverberating with overtones, "Et in Arcadia Ego!"

By late 1929, Stein composed being settled in words:

> Hers and his the houses are hers and his the valley is hers and his the dog named Basket is hers and his also the respect of the populace is hers and his. ("Saving The Sentence" 20)

This balanced sentence includes their dog, Basket, as part of the family in the house on the land. Given his enormous importance, it is surprising to find no clear information about him; Stein regularly incorporates him in her work, but virtually without facts. In a confusing series of statements in her late memoir, Toklas claims she wanted a white poodle like the one in *The Princess Casamassima.*[13] However, there is no poodle in this novel, though in chapter 5 of its precursor, *Roderick Hudson,* Christina Light appears in Rome with her fantastically beribboned white poodle, Stentorello.

At the Yale Collection of American Literature, in "*Q. E. D.* Notes to Drafts," is a series of extracts copied by Stein for her early novel. These include sections from correspondence with May Bookstaver; a quotation from *The Wings of the Dove,* suggesting parallels between Stein's situation and that of Merton Densher and Kate Croy, named in *Q. E. D.* (121); and an extract from *Roderick Hudson,* implying similarities between the triangle of Roderick, Rowland Mallet, and Mary Garland and Stein's own. Her title may derive from this extract in chapter 23, late in *Roderick Hudson,* where Mary Garland says,

12. *A Manoir,* 308. See also

> In a place a person can be with their mother and their father and their grandmother. (302)

> . . . if there are to be any births any marriages and any marriages and any births there is the family and there is a family if there are any marriages and any births. (*LCA* 166)

The following riddle may derive from a local family or perhaps from personal experience of Stein and Toklas:

> If a father and a mother are dead is there an orphan if there is in each case one child. (*LCA* 167)

13. *WIR* 124–25.

"I believed nothing. I simply trusted you, as you asked me."

"*Quod erat demonstrandum!*" cried Rowland. "I think you know Latin."[14]

Immediately after speaking of the white poodle in the memoir, Toklas says purchasing the dog was Stein's decision. She then claims that he was named Basket because she hoped he would carry a basket of flowers in his mouth.[15]

Next she describes how at a dog show, presumably in Paris, a poodle puppy jumped into Stein's arms. Stein arranged the purchase but either returned the puppy or delayed picking him up for two weeks to allow for housebreaking. A minor point in the same account concerns a Bedlington terrier, which looks somewhat like a poodle. Conflating two separate trips of 1913 and 1914 to London, she says they almost bought a Bedlington there when going to see John Lane, but the outbreak of the war prevented them from taking it to France.

Nowhere else does this dog appear except in the 1926 family portrait, "Edith Sitwell And Her Brothers . . .". Here Bedlington occurs once (294), be it as a dog or as Bedlington, Northumberland, where the terriers are bred, but any connection with the Sitwells remains unclear. Of course, Bedlington may simply echo Bilignin.[16] This inconsistent and piecemeal information

14. In old age, Toklas may have confused the two James novels, or she may have wished to divert attention from *Roderick Hudson* to *The Princess Casamassima,* for she would not have wished to draw attention to *Q. E. D.* or its provenance. To conceal its autobiographical nature, the novel, first issued in 1950 by the Banyan Press, Pawlet, Vermont, appeared under the title *Things As They Are.* with other textual emendations that were also not part of Stein's original writing. Only after the death of Toklas was it published in its original form in *Fernhurst, Q. E. D., And Other Early Writings* (New York: Liveright, 1971). See also Henry James, *Roderick Hudson* (Boston: James R. Osgood and Company, 1876), 428. Scholars have recently started to look at homosexuality in James' work, with this novel an obvious candidate. An example is Robert K. Martin, "The 'High Felicity' of Comradeship: A New Reading of *Roderick Hudson,*" *American Literary Realism* 11 (1978): 100–108.

15. I considered this a far-fetched idea until I was advised that there exist small, unmarked white Staffordshire china poodles with "wicker" baskets of flowers in their mouths that the women might have seen, as William Peterson, after a visit to the Nantucket Historical Association, where such poodles are displayed, wrote me on September 22, 1997. Only after this did I realize that Stein's dog Basket indeed displays elements of "personality" that fit a china dog.

16. An early letter from an R. S. McNeill from Invernesshire concerns a "Beddington" (*sic*) terrier (7 August n.y., uncat. letters "M"; see also Marsden Hartley to Stein, 23 October 1913, about the effect of losing a dog). Stein also apparently once answered an advertisement for a Pekingese in the Paris edition of the *New York Herald* (n.d., uncat. letter "V"). These details give no clear facts but show that a dog was in her mind long before 1929.

Stein speaks of collecting the dog in Bordeaux (Stein to Bromfield, Paris, n.d., Ohio

is hardly a reliable guide. Anecdotes and photographs illustrate his significance, but facts about him remain unclear. Apparently Stein and Toklas did not wish to discuss his story as history or news. As a result, it becomes a matter of inference, and we wonder what is behind it.

In Bilignin Stein and Toklas made their own family of three with Basket to cuddle, to mother, to train, to walk, to groom, to play and talk with. He must learn to sit, whether for obedience or for a portrait. In letters Stein reported on country life—planting, clipping hedges, harvesting, the weather, pansies, melons, American sweet corn, the new vocabulary of fecundity, local births and marriages, and always the progress of the dog.[17] Soon no friend concluded a letter without adding to the customary greetings to Toklas wishes for the health of the dog, always by name. As a member of the family and a part of daily life, Basket entered Stein's work.

As Stein and Toklas must have known, the vague information has enough charm to distract us from asking for facts. So, as often happens with her, the crucial question remains unasked: why did she name him Basket? Though her business was naming, she did not speak of this name. However, its meaning can be read in her work.

Common nouns often become names for pets. The name of this French dog, however, is an English word and so probably not the breeder's invention but Stein's. Asking that the name be spoken with "accent on the last syllable" (i.e., "Basqu'*ette*"),[18] she makes us pronounce it as would a French speaker who does not know English, making it a French word with no particular meaning. This pronunciation cuts off the dog's name from the noun of its origin and decontextuates it. As she foresaw, no one asked what it meant.

Of course, she knew that the name raised questions.

State University Library); Basket II, the second poodle, was also picked up in Bordeaux (Stein to Samuel Steward, August 1939; to Bromfield, n.d.). Only one letter, in English, from an Elsa Blanchard, 60 rue de Bellechasse, Paris, refers to registration of the dog in the Chenil International in Cagnes, and to a pedigree and a German breeder, Erich Lobert, Regensburg, from whom Blanchard apparently bought a poodle, presumably Basket. Finally, in one notebook is a reference to a poodle breeder, Arbonnier (presumably his name), in Orchies, dép. du Nord, between Lille and Valenciennes ("Think with a Minute" *carnet,* 1929–30, not 1927, as labeled).

17. Occasionally, though rarely, she discouraged someone from coming to Belley by berating it:

> Your letter was so discouraging about Belley that Margherita [Pecorini] went to Italy instead. Why do you like such an awful place. No gardens, country not at all paintable, hotel very uncomfortable. . . . (Scudder to Stein, 24 June 1929)

18. Stein to McBride, 22 May 1929; Bromfield to Stein, 29 December 1931.

> Basket was his name. This was his name because it was invented. By whom. It was invented. ("Basket," *P&P* 182)

If the invention is the use of the common noun as a name, what does Basket mean?

> A word which makes basket a name. If it is a name will he be confused with whatever with it they make to name. ("More Grammar For A Sentence," *R* 550)

This sentence leaves open questions of identity—will the dog be confused about who he is, or the reader about the meaning of Basket? Again the dog Basket and the word "basket" are split apart.

The word "basket" appears in Stein's writing long before 1929, when she acquired the dog, its many meanings and compound forms referring to domestic objects that allow word play. Behind the English word, of course, stand the French words for basket—*panier, corbeille, vannette*—and the many idiomatic expressions with *panier.* There was also Picasso's painting, *Girl with a Basket of Flowers.* Stein and Toklas liked baskets, more common in their day than now, especially in rural Europe.

There were flower baskets, fruit baskets, market baskets, wire salad baskets, muzzles, hilts, and "basket" with sexual implications. There were basket hares, basket chairs, wastebaskets, workbaskets, basket stitches, embroidery baskets, millinery baskets, wedding baskets, wicker baskets. A baby basket, by a shift of stress familiar to any English speaker, becomes Baby Basket.

Alliteration with B is also in her mind. "Baltimore west. Belley east. Boston," she says in "More Grammar For A Sentence," filling a page with play on the three names (*R* 555). Basket, with his prominent initial, fits not only with Belley but also with Baby, one of Toklas' terms of endearment for Stein, or babies, her creations. In the notebook for "Saving The Sentence," "Be Beware" is written once and repeated immediately below, with elaborately drawn capital B's: a warning about a dangerous dog? Stein has played with the letter B in the past, in "B B Birthplace Of Bonnes," and B B for Bernard Berenson.

Early in 1929, in "Sentences," around the time the dog was purchased, she wrote,

> All these sentences are fruitful. They may be included in embroidery. How are they placed. They are in a basket. They have a good deal of softness and they are very likable. She looks at her knitting. (136)

The sentences are placed in what appears to be Toklas' workbasket, which also becomes Stein's workbasket, her composition. They are babies, the live creation of tenderness and work. Stein's art is the product of their love; at the same time, Stein likens her work to Toklas' stitchery while also distinguishing it from hers.

> If she made a drawn work tapestry she would do something new. But would she. Not at all. ("Pay Me," *PL* 138)

Many examples of writing and landscape as embroidery also appear at this time.

> Think in stitches. Think in sentences. Think in settlements. Think in willows. ("Sentences" 138)

> Already in "Regular" in the spring of 1927, baskets occur in similar forms.

> The next which is what is by this time what is it that there is accomodation for all and every one who mean to be nearly very nearly choosing a white basket a white basket which is not as large as an ordinary one. A white basket which is not as large as an ordinary one might be here and there and so be noticeable so be noticeable might be here and there and so be noticeable and engaging and finally finally finally who must have seen who must have seen a woman with a young one about the age kind and disposition which would be satisfying would be satisfying would be would be satisfying and disposition which would be satisfying . . . in not yet knowing in not yet in beside not yet investigating not yet is it likely that very fairly soon there will be something. (223–24)

These words announce the birth of a new work, a baby in a white basket that is a manuscript book: *Four Saints In Three Acts.* By the late summer of 1928, she composes into the landscape play *Paisieu* the black magpie from *Four Saints* with a white dog in a black and white phrase,

> An object a little dog called Basket a magpie in the air. (178)

Like the fluid landscape created before she got house and land for her own living, the dog is composed in words before he arrives.[19]

A basket in her work before 1929 is a Stein creation. However, the *word*

19. I received a sudden jolt about the word when I read in Ruth Gay's *Jews in America* (New Haven: Yale University Press, 1965) a description of ranks of Jewish peddlers of the 1840s. The lowest of these peddling craftsmen is "[t]he basket peddler, he is as yet altogether dumb and homeless" (49). Higher-ranking peddlers are the trunk-carrier, the pack-carrier, the wagon-baron, the jewelry-count, and the store-prince. We cannot know whether the word "basket peddler" was in Stein's family vocabulary. Whether or not it was, I record it here because it received added voice in my ear from Stein's "basket."

"basket"—not Basket—goes back much further. It appears in a crucial late section of "A Long Gay Book" of 1911–12, after the dramatic change of style. Here Stein speaks of the creative process, of making out of the seething, sensuous stuff of life the etched precision of print.

> A dot in the center and that which is proportioned if it is made of lead, if it is easily made is so impressionable. There is no greater satisfaction than in everything.
>
> A baker had a basket and a basket was bigger, there is no baker and a basket is bigger, there is no wax and there is an impression and certainly very certainly there is proportion.
>
> A beggar who begs and a print which prints, a surface which heats and a smoke which smokes, all this makes silver and gold is not cheaper not so much cheaper that there is no clatter. All the conscience which tells that the little tongue to tickle is the one that does not refer to teeth. To remember, to forget, to silence all the mistakes, to cause perfection and indignation and to be sweet smelling, to fasten a splendid ulster and to reduce expenses, all this makes no charge, it does not even make win, it makes the whole thing incontestable. The doctrine which changed language was this, this is the dentition, the doctrine which changed that language was this, this was the language segregating. This which is an indication of more than anything else does not prove it. There is no passion. A tiny little stamp, a little search for whiting, a little search for more and more does not disturb the resting. (*R* 246)

This passage is filled with imprints. Words are printed, lines etched by acid biting into the engraver's plate. Molten lead is poured and hardens into type to imprint words upon paper which also receives ink from the lines etched into a plate. Soft materials take on the imprints of hard grids, just as sharp outlines appear once fluids set. Bread dough, soft and pliable, is poured into a basket to rise, a powerful image of pregnancy. The basket imprints itself from underneath and outside upon the dough that rises in it.

Once the bread is baked, the basket has shaped the loaf and impressed itself upon its surface. We bite the bread, leaving marks with our teeth. Dentition allows us to feel the shape of the tongue against the teeth in the mouth in eating, kissing, speaking, and writing, in imprinting upon the staff of life the stamp of man.

The passage becomes an ode to creativity, concrete, sexual, engorging, imprinting inside upon outside, joining negative and positive in interlocked forms. The shimmering image of the basket must have been with Stein from the time she gave up systematic description and the world opened itself anew to her in the language of concrete particulars.

Late in *An Acquaintance With Description,* in a passage written in Belley in the summer of 1926, appear the communal ovens in which bread was then and is today still baked in the region.

> It is very easy to cook bread in a communal oven. Why because it is prepared in a basket and easily being fluid it remains in place on a pale and the oven being very nearly stone it is longer heated than it was. (*R* 531)[20]

The Bugey may have stirred writing in part because it returned her to the bread rising in the basket and the language rising in composition that she had created in "A Long Gay Book." Even in St-Rémy, in 1922–23, ordinary local baskets appeared in her work as they do in still lifes. They shape and braid love, sexuality, landscape, and new writing.

It is a surprise to discover these antecedents of 1929. But they make comprehensible the range and quality of private commitments behind the name Basket that was, as she said, invented. Family living in the country house with the dog changed the ways in which the daily life at home entered work. In writing done in Paris, the private life, with its referential thrust, is never prominent, and the impulse in the studio is compositional.

Even in "Finally George" of 1927, Stein had written,

> Houses should never be known at home. (312)

The sentence echoes an idea succinctly put years before by the painter Myra Edgerly, a friend from early days in Paris. In a letter from New York of May 21, 1915, she wrote about a studio she had just taken at 640 Madison Avenue,

> Gertrude will be interested to learn that I in no way have attempted to make a home of it.

Keeping home life strictly private and separate from work life, the focus of attention, was easier in Paris than in the country.

But in Bilignin they were not separate. In the house, unlike the local hotel earlier, home life was dominant, making everything personal. On April 28, 1938, Lord Berners, the composer, who had visited Stein in Bilignin, wrote that the apartment at rue Christine in Paris, which he had just seen, was "a working 'pendant' to Bilignin." A country squire with a liking for the amenities of country life, he saw Bilignin as the image of leisurely living and the Paris flat as the place for serious work. Stein in fact was freer to work without interference in Bilignin than in Paris, but she cultivated an image

20. See also *R* 520–21. For a detailed, illustrated account of the ovens in the Bugey, see "France's Vintage Village Ovens," *New York Times,* 2 March 1986, Travel Section, 12.

of absorbed, hospitable country living that differed from the rich, purely aesthetic perception of the landscape before she moved to her own house. Daily life in Bilignin took place with a power of intense intimacy centered in house and family, apparent in the writing.[21]

> A walnut can be a saint. ("Sentences" 212)

In the country, such shapely forms were as commonplace as potatoes and no more perfectly grammatical.

> Forget grammar and think about potatoes. ("A Grammarian" 109)

Text I: The Grammatical Series Altogether

While the French publications were being prepared, Stein steadily studied grammar and language. Out of some of these studies in turn grew other pieces related to but separate from the language studies. The interaction between language works and others must be followed in detail, for it illuminates her direction.

The first language studies—*An Acquaintance With Description,* "Finally George," "Arthur A Grammar"—are separate works, complete in themselves. They have therefore been considered one by one. From the fall of 1928 on, however, language writing—grammar, sentences, words, parts of speech, paragraphs, stories, and others—continues in pieces less finished as individual works.

Titles become less differentiated and distinctive. She no longer gives texts names like Arthur or George but calls them by subject matter, for example, "Sentences." Sometimes her flair for inventing titles fails her; she devises "More Grammar Genia Berman" and "More Grammar For A Sentence," "Saving The Sentence" and "Saving The Sentence Again," revised to "Sentences And Paragraphs."[22]

21. Once the *AABT* and the American tour achieved for Stein the fame and the name she had wanted, she increasingly indulged with close friends in sentimental family and home imagery, always including Toklas. With Carl Van Vechten, from 1932 on, she shared the Woojums family, especially important during and after the American tour (*LGS/CVV* 255n, 362ff.).

    With Thornton Wilder, she and Toklas in 1935 developed an extensive fantasy about "our house" on Washington Square (see e.g., Wilder to Stein, 25 October 1939; Stein to Wilder, 18 May 1940, *LGS/TW* 247, 265).

    In letters and social exchange, these are late forms of personal feeling in which she never indulged earlier. They begin with the ritualized life associated with country house, family, and dog.

22. Was Stein aware of *Sentences And Paragraphs* as the title of a book by the Scottish poet,

All these works include diverse matter, carry over one into the next, and show less individual character. Sometimes a new section begins, or a piece simply stops for no apparent reason—perhaps because she was tired or dissatisfied. In the following commentaries, the writing of the language series from "Christian Berard" and "Sentences" to "Forensics" is discussed as a continuous activity, divided into sections but without strong closure for each.

With "Sentences,"[23] Stein apparently realized that she was writing what in the third manuscript *cahier* is identified as "a grammatical series." On the inside cover of a 1928 *carnet* with notes for "Arthur A Grammar" and "A Bouquet. Their Wills." she plays with a title, "Future of Composition / Future in composition." Similar notes appear until 1931, when she printed the collection as *How To Write.*

These texts are like sections of a writing journal, a practice book, finger exercises to keep her limber and try out ideas. They form a bass line for her figurations. Stein herself may not have thought of them as like her other work, but for two and one-half years, from 1928 to 1931, she kept this language journal, her own quarry of writing. Often this work includes nuggets of new compositions; they become separate pieces but must also be read against the texts in which they originate. Meanwhile, the language studies sometimes comment on other work she is concurrently writing. Critical reading requires moving across, from work to work, as well as moving down chronologically in biographical time.

Stein would not have wished us to read and cross-reference as I often do here. As suggested in the introduction to this book, she did not like intrusion into her writing process and was careful, when asked, to reveal no more of how she wrote than safeguarded her artistic privacy, as is evident in her comment on the name Basket. Yet she also teases us to follow word for word, to find echoes as much across pieces as chronologically. Frustratingly incomprehensible passages can suddenly connect and open meanings as exhilarating discovery.

This, I believe, is the process that she herself, in "A Long Gay Book," de-

---

novelist, and playwright John Davidson (1857–1909), published in London by Lawrence and Bullen in 1893? Traditional in presentation but ironic and modern in tone, it was a popular volume of "words of wit and wisdom" containing thirty short aphorisms and longer observations on writing and literature.

23. "Sentences" begins in two thin *cahiers.* If the choice of thin or fat *cahiers* indicates anticipated scope, she may initially have thought of a short work. However, after filling the first eighteen printed pages of the second *cahier,* she switched to the first of what became three fat, substantial *cahiers,* perhaps seeing that hers was a substantial study. These added eighty printed pages of text.

scribed as "the language that rises" in a phrase that has become the title of this book. For her, language rose in writing, as it rises for us in moments of felicitous reading. She asks us to read each as a text complete in itself, but her work also needs to be read transversely. The following notes on her grammatical series and other texts trace what I see as the inseparable evolution of her writing practice and her ideas about writing.

The chronological listing of Stein's work for these years of my study shows how, beginning with "Sentences" of 1928–29, new short pieces emerged that originate in the language work. Following them one by one from this source is the only way to discover her mind's movement. They become the context for compositions that emerge from them, just as the daily life provides the context for their interaction. I move from the grammar studies to works generated by them, in the order in which they emerge, and return to further language studies. It is a slow but rewarding process.

In "Arthur" and the other work of the summer of 1928, Stein had rejected totalizing systems—grammars—that limited the freedom to live and compose. For her, grammar was a continuous experiment as she tried out the possibilities of language. After "Arthur," she turned from large systems to the smallest units. Isolated words or their dictionary definitions, she had long known, conveyed no meaning until they were joined by grammar.[24] She set out to discover by experiment the nature of the basic unit of writing. If it was the sentence, what made it hang together? On November 22, 1928, she wrote to Elliot Paul,

> I am awfully pleased you liked the grammar being just now low in my mind in contemplation of that phenomenon a sentence.[25]

Looking for an answer, she endlessly constructed and collected sentences.

Writing sentences suited her perfectly. It allowed her in daily practice to write, listen, and comment, exploring possibilities by following the sound, sight, and sense of words. The language journal did not require large-scale planning or closure. It allowed her to collect practical writing ideas, including things overheard or read, word ideas, constructions in French and other languages, verbal idiosyncrasies, talk. Unlike the comments in the early notebooks for *The Making Of Americans,* directed toward completion of her typology of personality, she here starts with examples.

24. During the translation projects, which helped to start the language studies, dictionaries frequently enter her work, as does translation—a process with which dictionaries offer only limited help.
25. Camille Haynes Paul Ferret Cummings Collection, Special Collections, University Libraries, University of Colorado at Boulder.

Especially in the grammar pieces, daily life often becomes visible, because it provided the raw material for sentences. Details emerge in these works which allow us, in the process of reading, incidentally to discover what she did, where she was, or to date what she wrote. This kind of reading has been neglected by biographers.

Finally, a review of the whole writing series is in order. Stein began to explain herself with "An Elucidation," following it with studies of language, which became what I call a writing journal. Why did she stop the series when she did not stop asking questions about writing? It cannot be an accident that this journal came to a close.

Text II: The Series One by One

"Christian Berard" (*P&P* 73–79)

After October 15, 1928, when Stein returned to Paris from Belley with "Arthur" finished, she immediately began two new works, writing either concurrently or in immediate succession the portrait "Christian Berard,"[26] which was quickly completed, and the early sections of "Sentences," a study continued until June 1929.

In a letter to Stein of November 11, Christian Bérard speaks of Hugnet's wish that Bérard do a portrait of her as a frontispiece for *Morceaux Choisis* and of his pleasure at the prospect. Before the end of the year, Bérard did the portrait, and Stein in turn expressed her appreciation by writing a portrait of him.[27] Unlike the following portraits, "Virgil Thomson," "Bernard Fay," and "Kristians Tonny," "Christian Berard" does not originate in "Sentences."

However, questions about the sentence appear here, as they do in that work, and so does play on key words, "lay"/"lain"; "our"/"hour"/"hour glass"; "regret"/*aigrette*. Also, early in "Sentences" is a passage that may come from Bérard's portrait of Stein or hers of him:

26. In the following discussion, to keep clutter minimal, I include in the head title of each work the volume and page citations for the texts; thereafter, I omit pages for the short portraits and other texts but include them for texts on writing.

27. See Hugnet to Thomson, 28 December 1928; Stein to Thomson, 2 and 14 January 1929; Bérard to Stein, undated note of thanks for her portrait, described as a gift in appreciation of his drawing. In Stein's *cahier,* "Christian Berard" precedes and was thus written before the portraits of Virgil Thomson and Kristians Tonny, done by the end of December 1928 or early January 1929, and January or early February 1929, respectively. The name "Mathilda" in the portrait (79) refers to Bérard in drag, as confirmed by a letter from Allen Tanner to Charles Henri Ford, n.d., HRC. His nickname "Bébé" must have echoed for Stein, who was also called "Baby" and given to playing with *B*s.

> What is a sentence. A sentence is an imagined master piece. A sentence is an imagined frontispiece. In looking up from her embroidery she looks at me. She lifts up the tapestry it is partly.
>
> What is a sentence. A sentence furnishes while they will draw. (123)

In other words, "Sentences," though not written as commentary, sometimes includes sentences commenting on events or writing.

The portrait of Bérard moves her language study from grammar to sentences and to poetry, as its original title in the *cahier* shows: "A sentence / of poetry how I knew him / Christian Berard." The sentence of poetry is not a grammatical paradigm, but it *is* the portrait—a sentence of poetry and the poetry of the sentence.

By the late 1920s, perhaps as a result of her language studies, a new freedom appears in Stein's portraiture. She is less and less interested in using language to refer and represent. Instead, she works to create self-contained language works or poems, far from the psychological studies of her early portraits. She speaks of this development in her lecture "Portraits And Repetition."

The fact that we cannot recognize likenesses does not mean that they are not portraits. They are compositions of, about, around, occasioned by, involving, with, through their subjects rather than being visual or psychological pictures. Artist and subject stand in constantly changing relation. Failure to recognize the subject of a portrait means simply that it has not been read in right relation to the shifting word composition. If we abandon preconceived notions of subject and resist the wish to read representationally, we gain access through elements of composition, a necessity for reading Stein at this time.

"Christian Berard" opens with food and eating, appropriate for an overweight artist who, like Stein herself, enjoyed food.[28] The passage is a riot of likely and unlikely dishes, cooked and served up for us to eat. They recall that the grammar of cooking—as in the ending of "Arthur"—is like the grammar of composing, whether in poetry, in cookbooks, or at the stove. Some of the dishes read like still lifes—"fish grouse and little cakes," "a

28. Stein, who once memorably called herself "fattuski," had from early years written about the joys and "evils of eating" ("Lifting Belly," 66, 86); members of her family suffered from phobias about food. See the preoccupations with food of father Hersland, modeled on Stein's father, in *MOA,* and Leo Stein's obsessive concern with diet, fasting, Fletcherism. See also Leon Katz, "The First Making of *The Making of Americans:* A Study Based on Gertrude Stein's Notebooks and Early Versions of Her Novel (1902–8)" (Ph.D. diss., Columbia University, 1963), 130, 170.

pigeon and a souffle." Eating, like writing, is a consuming activity. The portrait opens,

> Eating is her subject.
> While eating is her subject.
> Where eating is her subject.
> Withdraw whether it is eating which is her subject. Literally while she ate eating is her subject. Afterwards too and in between. This is an introduction to what she ate. (73)

All her life, Stein ingested, chewed, bit, swallowed, spat, and ate words. Why? Because the poetry of eating is the eating of poetry. The portrait of Bérard and the study of sentences are endlessly inventive cookbooks of poetry. We delight in eating the words, not only in tasting the dishes. She exploits the physical or syntactical properties of words, composing and cooking visual puns or concrete poetry by the eye, auditory puns by the ear, rhythms, rhymes, off-rhymes, line to line, sound to sound, noun to verb, adjective to pronoun—elements of language she has always explored. What is new is not her techniques, which are those of poetry, but the freedom with which she uses them. She has always been a poet.

A portrait is a compliment, a gift offered *avec mes compliments,* as the French say. All sentences in a portrait must contribute to a compliment, using grammatical complements to complete the composition. One writes complimentary sentences by meditating or concentrating, which may "induce sentences" (77):

> Take him and think of him. He and think of him. With him think of him. With him and with think with think with think with him. (79)

> How are you in invented complimented.
> How are you in in favorite.
> Thinking of sentences in complimented.
> Sentences in in complimented in thank in think in sentences in think in complimented.
> Sentences should not shrink. Complimented.
> A sentence two sentences should not think complimented. Complimented.
> How do you do if you are to to well complimented. A sentence leans to along. (77–78)

"Sentences" (*HTW* 115–213)

Early in "Sentences," she asks about the difference between "a sentence and a picture" (119), a difference that is always in her mind, especially in portraits with their representational thrust. Compliments appear there as they do in the Bérard portrait:

> The compliment in grammar. The complement in grammar. The compliment in grammar. (119)

A few lines earlier,

> A verb is next to crown.

It is followed immediately by

> Crowned with success.

It all originates as a humorous non sequitur about sentences. After the portrait, she returns to "recovering the sentence" (121) by asking over and over, insistently, what is a sentence. Nothing is clear about it except rigid rules of grammar, which explain nothing. "Very little known" (121), she concludes.

Sentences have an inner logic of construction, unlike words, which are impulses for sentences.

> This is a sentence as arrangement. (138)

Sentences hang together and are self-contained.

> Sentences are made wonderfully one at a time. ("Sentences And Paragraphs" 34)

But a sentence also creates a direction and leads to another sentence.

> Listen a sentence is fastened, not to a noun or a verb, an article yes is an article. Yes as a direction no as a direction. Yes and yes no as a direction. A sentence is primarily fastened yes as a direction, no as a direction. (164)
>
> These are examples of sentences which are self contained as well as suggested. (169)
>
> And so a sentence is always connected. (209)

At the same time,

> How can a paragraph be made of sentences. (134)

and

> A sentence is made up of whatever they mean. (136)

Following the rules of grammar books for combining nouns and verbs (137) does not make good sentences or good sense. Earlier she produces a kind of parody of parts of speech and grammatical classification—nouns, adjectives, verbs, pronouns, articles, adverbs.

> They gave this to him.
>
> In this the pronouns do not count they are only the story. The pronouns in this do not count they are only the story.
>
> Prepositions are like burning paint paint burns when it is on the fire on fire when it has been put on fire when it has been set on fire. (128)

To identify words by their function as parts of speech is to treat them as empty syntactical husks and disregard their qualities as words. Stein refuses to be systematic. The sections on the parts of speech and others are later lifted from "Sentences" and used for the portrait of Bernard Faÿ.

"Sentences" is always about sentence making, whether she writes about the weather, the car, food, or Toklas embroidering. Between seeing and saying everything, Stein becomes self-reflexive. Sentence making is an engrossing domestic activity that requires the same care as stitchery.

> Think in stitches. Think in sentences. Think in settlements. (138)

> All these sentences are fruitful. They may be included in embroidery. (136)

Look at this gradually built sentence, which sounds like a person:

> A sentence is careful.
>
> A sentence is carefully made a sentence is carefully cared to for her sake.
>
> Sentences made slowly. (211)

The ritual of the Stein-Toklas ménage had to do with regularity and care in living, which was synonymous with care in working. Rising from intimate living, writing always involves loving.

From the very opening she insists,

> A sentence is made by coupling meanwhile ride around to be a couple there makes grateful dubeity named atlas coined in a loan. (115)

Coupling is car language—sentences engage or set in motion parts of speech that move and go somewhere.[29] Movement is central to the Stein sentence.

29. By the beginning of 1929, Stein's old car, Aunt Pauline, ceased to operate and was handed over with ritual formality to Georges Maratier to repair it and, when that proved impossible, to dispose of it. A new Ford, Godiva, was acquired in time for the summer in the new house.

Stein wrote a portrait of Maratier in the winter of 1929, but it was not included in

Coupling, however, is also joining and, by a simple pun, being a couple—talking, loving, becoming one, all dynamic processes. Sentence making is love making.

> A verb is around with their caress. (147)

At other times sentences imply the firm grammar of a marriage contract, whereas paragraphs, looser, more flexible, embody love.[30]

"Virgil Thomson" (*P&P* 198–99)

Everyone who has written about Stein has written about Thomson, but almost no one has written about "Virgil Thomson." Much is known about the collaboration, but nothing has been said about her portrait of him. A quick reading opens a vocabulary self-conscious with devices of prosody—alliteration, assonance, consonance, initial, internal and end rhyme, and other forms of repetition. The words make auditory and rhythmic patterns.

> Which is a weeding, weeding a walk, walk may do done delight does in welcome. (198)

The portrait opens with a spoken response about something or to someone, "Yes ally." But rather than inviting us in, the voice confuses us with syncopations that cross with puns in uneasy balance between eye and ear and with uncertain boundaries and articulation of "ally." "Yes ally. As ally. Yes ally yes as ally." This playful string of word pairs is broken by an apparent comment, "A very easy failure takes place," then resumes, the failure unidentified, the comment unassigned.

"Virgil Thomson" offers almost no stable points of contact. Reading it is like following a text in a foreign language, eye and ear alert to patterns that remain alien to the mind. And yet this is no jumbled word list but words deliberately composed, the more upsetting when they yield no references we can recognize. Frustrated by our illiteracy, we toss them back at Stein as her own failure. Thomson himself told me he "never unraveled" his portrait.

Dix Portraits, perhaps because there had been difficulties between Hugnet and Maratier during the preparation of *Morceaux Choisis.* Later it was printed in *P&P.* There are no verbal echoes in "Sentences" of his portrait, though his relationship with Florence Tanner, who became his wife, appears; there may be a hint of "Deux Soeurs Qui Ne Sont Pas Soeurs" ("Two Sisters Who Are Not Sisters"), the French film scenario composed for Hugnet in March 1929 (174).

30. The opening pages of "Sentences" include not only apparent comments about "Christian Berard" but also sections that Stein lifted out and completed as separate compositions between late 1928 and early 1929. These became the portraits of Virgil Thomson (115–16, 123), Bernard Faÿ (129–31), and Kristians Tonny (132).

But he added that Stein and Toklas particularly liked it because it was "so constructed."[31]

The dictionary uncovers a surfeit of meanings for individual words that yield no more than momentary coherence. On the other hand, "Yes ally," without fixed stresses, floods eye and ear with possibilities, "Yes, [you, my] ally," "Yes, [it is] a lie," "Yes, [it is] all I," "Y[ou], Sally," "Yes, all. Why," "Yes, all eye," "Yes [an] alley," "anally," "usually" and perhaps even "Für Elise"— unending reading games that may delight but also exasperate us.

We look at syntax in sentences that resist the assembling mind. Perhaps identifying parts of speech can stabilize them.

> Power four lower lay lain as in case, of my whether ewe lain or to less.

What parts of speech are we to trust in this homophonic run, where "four," a noun, may conceal "for," a preposition, "ewe," another noun, the pronoun "you," but we cannot be sure since what we hear and see makes no stable combinations. A single assignment of a part of speech rattles all the others and changes the whole constellation. Yet this is surely an English sentence, as is the next (is "Für Elise" in it?).

> What was obligation furnish furs fur lease release in dear. Dear darken.

The parts of speech with their hints of legal language shiver and change, and between the shifting spellings, sounds, and meanings of words and their shifting functions, syntax collapses.

Some identifiable, recurrent details turn up. Time is one, not surprising for a composer as subject.

> Hour by hour counts.
> our in glass . . .

Or the retrograde,

> Our comes back back comes our.

Tenses connect with time.

> When with a sentence of intended they were he was neighbored by a bean.

"Intended," past in form but pointing toward the future, and "were," "was," "bean," pointing to the past, dramatize time. Yet the second half of this sentence returns in different combinations.

31. Virgil Thomson, interview with author in his apartment in the Chelsea Hotel, New York City, 20 September 1985; Thomson, letter to author, 26 September 1985.

It is with a replica of seen. That he was neighbored by a bean.

Another sentence begins easily,

> Did he does he was or will well and dove as entail cut a pursuit purpose demean different dip in descent diphthong advantage about their this thin couple a outer our in glass pay white.

But what are the alliterative *D* sequences beyond "dovetail"? A home recurs, as does a chair, perhaps in the home.

> Welcome daily is a home alone and our in glass turned around.
> Their is no need of liking their home.
>
> Harden as wean does carry a chair intake of rather with a better coupled just as a ream.

"Harden" is a proper name—unless it is a verb. Elmer Harden lived next door on quai Voltaire. But neither themes nor references open the portrait.

It abounds in shifters that point backward or forward and, without identifiable antecedents, add to its instability.

> How could they know that it had happened.

Who are "they"? What is "it"? "These quotations" begins a long paragraph—which quotations? Such questions arise at every step. To follow the figure of Toklas embroidering, on which Stein so often relies, the portrait does not rise as a completed tapestry from the stitches described here:

> Remain remarked taper or tapestry stopping stopped with a lain at an angle colored like make it as stray.

The endless efforts to isolate and combine words wear out as we absorb patterns of sound, rhythm, and dynamic energy but remain unable to enter the verbal design from inside. So we look for contexts to gain access from outside. One set is biographical, another textual.

On September 2, 1928, Thomson wrote to Stein from the south that he was doing musical portraits, including one for the fiddle of Marthe-Marthine, the singer wife of the composer Henri Cliquet-Pleyel. The idea of portraits, he acknowledged, came from Stein. She herself that autumn wrote "George Hugnet." In October, Thomson composed "Miss Gertrude Stein."[32]

32. Thomson describes the process of musical portraiture in detail in his autobiography, *Virgil Thomson* (New York: Alfred A. Knopf, 1966), 122–26; extensive notes on portraiture are among the Thomson papers at Columbia University and at the Yale Music

On November 14, a concert was given at the Salle Majestic of musical and poetic works by Henri Cliquet-Pleyel, Virgil Thomson, and Georges Hugnet. Included were portraits by Thomson as well as Cliquet-Pleyel's portrait of Thomson.

Writing to him after October 17, Stein said,

> Sometime there is going to be a very interesting portrait of you, it gestates.

Soon after her return to Paris, between October 20 and 23, she began "Sentences," the new language study which would include elements for the portrait.[33]

Early in December, Thomson sailed for New York. On January 14, 1929, Stein sent him his portrait with a comment teasing in its refusal to explain, "it has a new rhythm with sense." She also said she had completed the portrait of Bernard Faÿ. On February 2 Thomson thanked her, describing his portrait as "very beautiful and serious and like me too." These facts date the portrait but do not help a reader.

Context for the text appears early in "Sentences" (115–16, 123, 131). Here are phrases that Stein eventually uses for the portrait, developing them separately and differently. There may have been notes for some of these sections in *carnets* that are not preserved. The absence of *carnets* is particularly frustrating here as verbal nuggets might first have appeared in a *carnet* and later been used in both the sentence study and the portrait rather than being devised in "Sentences" and then transferred to the portrait. If "Virgil Thomson" originated in "Sentences," we must look there for clues to the portrait, but none appear that illuminate it.

The word "ally," obviously attractive for composing with great verbal, syntactical, and auditory freedom, appears in both earlier and later work. In "Patriarchal Poetry," she writes,

> Patriarchal Poetry ally.
> Patriarchal Poetry with to try to all ally to ally to wish to why to. (*BTV* 285)

Library. See also Kathleen Hoover and John Cage, *Virgil Thomson: His Life and Music* (New York: Thomas Yoseloff, 1959), 159ff.; Anthony C. Tommasini, *Virgil Thomson's Musical Portraits* (New York: Pendragon Press, 1986); John Rockwell, "A Conversation with Virgil Thomson," *Parnassus: Poetry in Review* 10, no. 2 (spring–summer 1977): 417–35; Virgil Thomson, "Of Portraits and Operas," *Antaeus* 21–22 (spring–summer 1976): 208–10.

33. This letter, attached to the wrong envelope when I examined it, had been dated 22 November 1927; the Thomson letter it answers is also misdated 1927. Both are October 1928 letters.

Late in *At Present,* written early in 1930 about her young friends of the time, she asks,

> Tonny Basket and So. How will they be an ally. (*O&P* 322)

At the end of the same play, she refers at least in part to portraiture:

> Virgil Thomson. Measures scenes in sitting. A sitting room is where they sit. (324)

A clear enough description of Virgil Thomson working, but not of "Virgil Thomson."

The contexts do not help with this portrait. The longer I try, the harder I work, the more the piece removes itself from reading. "Virgil Thomson" may be a verbal portrait of a musician musically composed. It may render his speech or manner, characterize his personality, but I cannot even define its difficulty until I hear the voice of its words speaking.

"Dan Raffel A Nephew" (*P&P* 86–88)

I know of only two other portraits of this time that are almost as resistant to reading as "Virgil Thomson": "G. Maratier" and "Dan Raffel A Nephew." The latter, however, does include some accessible referential hints. Daniel Raffel was the second son of Stein's sister Bertha, who had married Jacob Raffel, a Sephardic Jew who changed his name from Rafael to Raffel and moved from Connecticut to Baltimore. A visit of Daniel Raffel in the early spring of 1928 was the occasion for the portrait and led Stein to family relationships of all kinds, playing with names and relations, not all from the Raffel family, as the presence of Clarence, Toklas' brother, makes clear.

> Dan Raffel a nephew.
>
> Helen a sister Bertha a mother Arthur a brother Clarence a father and so for the fourth they have a number of which there is no difference between and to gather they went to a country called Denmark and there they studied. (87)

According to his senior brother Arthur, Daniel Raffel was a biologist of promise who spent several years studying and doing research in Rome, Russia, and, in 1926, Denmark. Arthur is mentioned, as is a third ("tree," converted from "three") in the family "tree," presumably their sister Gertrude. Stein obviously liked Dan Raffel, "a nephew in press," in part perhaps because he declared his independence by leaving home and following a vocation.

> They went ably to be away and accounted to any one and it is a circumstance might a couple of times be so that it is an other bother to note what is as made in rain for the favor of not hiding it as a gone to their way.

The quite transparent sections quoted here occur late in the portrait. The early sections make an extraordinarily smooth visual pattern on the page that also reads smoothly, barely interrupted by an occasional period. They look much like the long, even paragraphs of "Finally George," out of which the portrait came,[34] and they require attention to visual and auditory rhythm and to the construction of the abstract patterns of words.

In an essay on Stein originally written in 1926 but rewritten at her request in the spring of 1928 for publication in *transition*,[35] Ralph Withington Church relied on the portrait of Dan Raffel, which she had sent him as an example of her newest work.[36] Details from the essay are incorporated in his unpublished, incomplete "Reminiscences," which include the following:

> After all, there are qualities of language that are felt without benefit of inference. Like the taste of pop-corn. Whether or not Stein's esoteric writing has meaning is a technical question of definition. "Dan Raffel A Nephew," for example, conveys no reference to anything beyond itself. What it says is given in no references to an external subject; but rather in the presented quality of the writing itself. If you define "meaning" only in terms of referential expression, Stein's later writing is indeed meaningless. . . . To urge that writing must say something cannot well mean that it must keep on describing something or other so that you keep on looking and looking for what it is about, *ad infinitum*. That would be like running on and on from signpost to signpost without ever coming upon the thing signified.

34. Stein to Elliot Paul, spring–summer 1929, Camille Haynes Paul Ferret Cummings Collection, Special Collections, University of Colorado at Boulder.
35. Ralph Withington Church, "A Note on the Writing of Gertrude Stein," *transition* no. 14 (fall 1928): 164–68.
36. Church, while working toward a doctorate on Malebranche at Oxford, had led a discussion on Stein among a group of students after her lecture in 1926. Through David Prall, the brother of Sherwood Anderson's third wife, Church became friends with Anderson, who sent him to Stein. He later became professor of philosophy at Cornell and at the University of California, Berkeley, where his papers are deposited at the Bancroft Library.

"Bernard Fay" (*P&P* 41–45)

Passages in the second and third notebook for "Sentences" of late 1928 or very early 1929, modified and expanded, become the portrait "Bernard Fay."[37] A draft for a letter to Faÿ in a *carnet* notes,

> Here is a portrait of you made out of grammar. I like it and I hope you do.

Added to this draft is a comment in the hand of Toklas on Faÿ as "useful, helpful and resourceful." On January 14, Stein wrote to Thomson,

> Just did a portrait of Bernard but mostly a very detailed action upon the parts of a sentence.

Faÿ acknowledged it on March 4 from New York. It is interesting to see how the "action upon parts of a sentence" became a portrait of a Frenchman who was becoming more and more important to her as a devoted admirer, supporter, and friend.

Faÿ's skills were available to Stein when she needed support. Late in 1928, when Elliot Paul asked her for a bibliography of her work, Faÿ and Church, the two university friends experienced in scholarly publication, helped her assemble the list. When the bibliography, discussed in the next chapter, appeared in the February 1929 issue of *transition,* Faÿ was assisting Stein in her struggle to cut *The Making Of Americans* for the Macaulay Company.

Faÿ also helped Stein with the country house. Relying on his contacts to initiate the transfer of Lieutenant Fernand Bonhomme away from Belley, Faÿ helped free the house for a new occupant. Stein consulted him in her dealings with Amand Saint-Pierre, the local solicitor who managed the delicate affair. After she completed the unexpired portion of the officer's lease, Faÿ became "busy with [her] military problem" to make sure that the lieutenant, now promoted to the rank of captain, remained permanently at his new post so that a new lease could be written in her name.[38] Stein also received help from Georges Maratier, a son of landowners also skilled in dealing with French bureaucracy.

Daily life, including friends and activities, yields sentences that become the study "Sentences." The sentences incidentally use the materials of daily life but are essentially about parts of speech. Though one hears the daily life,

37. See "Sentences," 129–31, 140, 141, perhaps 164; "Arthur," 93. The portrait is in a *cahier* of its own, filled to the end of the last page, which means at least the later sections were composed to fit into it. Contrary to what Wendy Steiner claims ("The Steinian Portrait," *Yale University Library Gazette* 50, no. 1 [July 1975]: 129), sections of "Sentences" were transferred and expanded into the portrait rather than the reverse.

38. Faÿ to Stein, 17 May 1931.

it would be silly to pin down every detail; however, some sentences ask to be read for what they say, as two examples show. In "Sentences" (130–31) and, with differences in arrangement, at the end of the portrait of Faÿ, she writes,

> An article is a and an and the.
> Thank you for all three.
> The making of never stop. Or the making of stop or stopped.

"The making of never stop" is *The Making Of Americans,* and she thanks Faÿ for help with cutting it.

The second passage, discreetly not transferred to the portrait from "Sentences," voices

> [t]he hope of a the appointment of their connection with a brilliant situation. Hope for a or an account of it. (140)

It is Faÿ's hope for an appointment at the Collège de France in Paris. Stein, who had studied the dynamics of power from early years among her friends and relied on the understanding she had gained in her studies for *The Making Of Americans* and many early portraits, was fascinated by Faÿ's two-year campaign for the position, which he won on February 29, 1932. Her portrait speaks of hope, zeal, and amiable patience, in the sense of French *aimable,* with overtones of ingratiation. The details echo his desire for the position and hers for the house. They required the same skills.

From the germ in the sentence study, Stein conceived a compositional shape for the portrait of Faÿ, modifying details from "Sentences" and moving beyond. It is less a portrait of a personality than an appreciation of Faÿ and a tribute to the capacity to write sentences.

Robert Bartlett Haas declares,

> In 1929 Stein had a terrible fight with Bernard Fay over nouns and adjectives. She didn't like them, she said, and he did. She punished him by making his portrait almost entirely of adverbs and prepositions. (*HWW* 12)

Although a clash may have occurred, the portrait began not with her perception of Faÿ but with her study of parts of speech, which Haas does not take into account. It is true that Stein teases the historian about his liking for facts, nouns, and names,

> A noun is the name of anything.
> Who has held him that a noun is the name. A noun is a name. Who has held him for a thing that a noun is a name of a thing.
> A dislike.

To come back.
If it looks like it.
Without it.
With it.
If it looks like it with it.
Four words in each line.
If it does it looks as it does it looks like it.
Does look like it.
It does look like it.

"Five Words In A Line" is exactly five words in a line. Stein must have noticed that in the *cahiers* her handwritten lines averaged five words, a fact with which she plays. When in the piece she writes,

Four words in one line

and

Six words in one line,

the line is still five words long, a fact that must have amused her and allowed her to conclude,

Five words in a line is right.

Both these are slight occasions that kept her writing and observing every day.

She ended "Sentences" quite suddenly, probably in June 1929. In the last four sentences—or lines—she moves from tricky principal parts to a small multiple flourish so low-key that it is easily overlooked,

Lay lay which is laid lain.
A sentence of which he is secure.
What is it.
She is here with it. (213)

Certainty of correct forms, satisfaction in sentences, and closeness to Toklas in the here and now of the new house conclude the piece.

"For-Get-Me-Not" and Other Short Poems (*SIM* 230–49)

Stein also wrote that summer in a single notebook a series of fifteen light and slight occasional poems, assembled with a title for each but with no title for the series, which is misleadingly printed under the title of the first poem, "For-Get-Me-Not. To Janet."[43] Like the first poem, all the early ones have short titles, followed by dedications or subtitles, for example, "To The First Bird / Which They Heard." These create two main beats, as does her two-part syntactical division in lines, such as

They need to mean. That they will as seem. (230)

"Left Alone: To Basket" has nursery rhyme and lullaby echoes. Here is a part of section 10:

Our ours. All ours.
As. All. Ours.
It is. Known. That.
A lion. Can be. A dog.
Or. A lion. Can be. A lamb.
Or. A lion. Can be a lamb. (234)

She plays with two-part titles, the two parts on separate lines, like title and subtitle. Soon she abandons dedications, at first retaining only the "to," "They May Be Said. / To Be Ready" (236). But then she resorts to simple, short titles, trying out phrasing in sentences, parts of sentences and lines, finding in sentences of poetry the poetry of sentences. Each poem consists of twelve numbered sections, in short lines and phrases that rely on syntactical repetition and variation, rhythm and rhyme to explore the line in relation to the sentence, already begun in "Five Words in a Line." Section 6 of "For-Get-Me-Not. To Janet" reads,

Should violence be done. To time.
To measure treasure. With a line.
To often measure. Whether.
They will be. Mine. (231)

43. The dedication, "To Janet [Scudder]," printed at the beginning of the series of fifteen poems, likewise applies only to the first poem, "For-get-me-not," not to the untitled series in *SIM* 230–49. The second poem, "Left Alone: To Basket," consists, like the others, of twelve sections, only three of which are in *P&P*, apparently as a result of an error. The complete text is in *SIM* 232–35.

See also Stein to Hugnet, 15 June 1929,

Jai fait une gentille douce portrait de Basket qui grandisse pas le portrait mais lui pendant quand [i.e., qu'on] lui regarde. (HRC)

I made a sweet little portrait of Basket who grows, not the portrait but he himself, as one looks at him.

Here for the first time she breaks up sentences into spoken phrases and lines to create rhythm. As line-and-sentence practice pieces, these verses are a part of her language studies. They lead directly to "Absolutely As Bob Brown," "We Came. A History," and the long poem "Winning His Way," all written in 1930–31, when she experimented with movement.

They are tiny, almost weightless observations of the country, notes about the dog and his ball or about planting roses. The repetitions often recall an exchange between two people. Behind her words, barely audible, is the voice of Toklas as an energy that keeps the inquiry active, the dialogue moving, the questions asked, and Stein writing. In "More Grammar For A Sentence" of the following spring, she considers dialogue and conversation in relation to paragraph and sentence. Here is an exchange from "They May Be Said. / To Be Ready," the fourth poem,

> IX
> Mine. One. At a time.
> X
> It is very ready. To be ready. With them.
> Are you ready.
> XI
> For them. Or. With them. (237)

Offset at the very end of this notebook appears the kind of verse to Toklas familiar from the private *carnets,* where concluding or opening notes to her validate Stein's writing. The verse, about Toklas, concludes the last poem, "Chosen." Its last word connects it to the poem, but the poem plays only with forms of the word "choose" in tiny one- to four-word units. The concluding lines may be read as a part of "Chosen" or as a separate, private poem to Toklas. Whether their inclusion in the typescript represents Stein's original intention cannot be known.

> A little poem
> Made at all
> To please. The one.
> And. So. Please. All.
> Chosen. (249)

Perhaps to surprise Toklas or perhaps by an oversight, this poem is not included in Stein's list of contents on the cover of the *cahier.*

"More Grammar Genia Berman" (*P&P* 185–92)

During or after the visit of Hugnet and Berman from September 4 to 7, Stein wrote the grammar portrait of Eugene Berman, "More Grammar

Genia Berman," and the short "Saving The Sentence." As in the case of Christian Bérard, the portrait of Stein by the painter may have called for a complement or compliment, a portrait by Stein of the painter. The title was initially the first sentence, marked on the cover of the *cahier,*

> It makes him feel different.

This title was crossed out and a new one added below,

> More Grammar.

"Genia Berman" was added later, below the second title, in pencil of a different color. Apparently Stein began by writing "more grammar," and ended up making or adding a portrait. Midway through the piece appears a section subtitled "Eugenia Berman," which can also be read, "You, Genia Berman."

As is common at this time, the portrait may represent Berman but may also develop elements connected with him or interests she shared with him, or it may simply be a compliment to him. This unstable relation of writer, writing, and subject allows many different readings. "More Grammar Genia Berman" was begun before "Saving The Sentence," but the two overlap in both composition and substance, as is evident in a *carnet,* where later sections of the first appear between early sections of the second.

The grammar portrait is embedded in daily country life, in the implied presence throughout of one or two others, perhaps Berman and Hugnet. Help with planting is acknowledged.[44] Dog, house, and valley recur in meditation.

> The dog having teeth. That is right.
> Is feverish. That is unnecessary. (185)

A house or walled property comes into view that the women may have considered but rejected. It includes the word "care."

> Now think of care. Cared for. A thicker[45] wall than they cared for. Not that it makes any difference because they did not want the house anyway.

The country leads to a question appropriate for a landscape painter:

> What is truly rural.

And always it leads to landscape itself:

> The sky is blue. Very blue especially through the trees which are made to make it blue.

44. *P&P* 188; see also "Saving The Sentence," *HTW* 15.
45. Stein's word is "thicker," not, as printed, "thinker."

Out of the immediate, larger themes open. One concerns words.

> It makes him feel different. To allow for words.

"He" may be any painter or it may be Berman, French-speaking Russian émigré, who experiences words differently from Stein, American writer. Words also differ from colors and paint.

The difference of language takes many forms. One has to do with expressions appropriate for social intercourse, presumably in French, the language Stein spoke with Hugnet and Berman.

> How many ways are there of being polite in it. . . . Nouns are not without outside my experience.

And the perennial problem—or game—of correct prepositions:

> To hesitate between in it for it with it.

Another difference is that words "abridge" things. Of course, words also connect, or bridge. How can they tell a story, how tell it truly or completely? How can they tell anything? Stein tries out how by telling a story. Perhaps to teach Berman something, she uses words to "tell about" painting in blue.

Picasso was invited by Stein to visit during the stay of Hugnet and Berman but apparently did not come. In the printed portrait, Picasso is not named, but it is plainly about him:

> He had painted blue. He did this when he was young and it was known as his period.

In the manuscript, he is named once, but the name is crossed out and "him" is substituted:

> Before I knew ~~Picasso~~ him he had painted in blue.

She wants the focus on *blue,* not on Picasso. Throughout the several stories of blue, she considers blue and painting, including problems of representation, but not the painting or personality of Picasso.

The story of blue, then, is not biography and not art history. As a problem of grammar, it concerns the difficulty of seizing essence, here poignantly dramatized in a single word, "blue." Precisely because it attempts to seize a quality, the piece is almost completely decontextuated and therefore extraordinarily difficult as it runs counter to our craving for information and representation.

Yet words cannot tell "about" the essence of blue,

> To do not follow. Blue by blue.

Nor does imitating the master or repeating the word make blue blue.

> What is a blue which is a blue.

Still, Stein insistently repeats the sound and rhythm of "blue" by means of rhyme, alliteration, assonance—"blue," "hue," "true," "knew," "you." She repeats syntactical elements of phrasing, creating stark, abstract, incantatory designs.

The story of blue is associated with Picasso's return to Spain in 1902. For Stein, blue also means Toklas, whose blue eyes speak of tenderness and sexuality, as she wrote many times. In *A Bouquet. Their Wills.* appears

> My baby loves blue and so do you. (202)[46]

Toklas and blue also recall Spain, where Gertrude first deeply knew sexuality and sensuality. Ralph Church cites "blue" as an example of an abstract word that we cannot understand unless we have seen the "meaningless hue blue" to give us "the referent requisite to genuine meaning."[47]

Living among the blues and greens of the Bugey, Stein says in "More Grammar For A Sentence" that Toklas "likes it better than Granada" (*R* 559). There is no higher praise.

In "More Grammar Genia Berman" the story of blue continues,

> A hue is a blue.
>
> What is the story I told you about blue. The story I told you about blue is this. For a long time I was puzzled. I felt that it was different if they were apart which they were one after another and then I knew that if they said blue they did not have it as blue.

Blue, then, tells the story of Picasso's blue painting, interwoven with the story of herself and Toklas, two passions in one story, one color, one place, one paragraph.

Seven times she tries to tell the story of blue (186–89). Each story is discarded as inadequate and leads her to try yet another exercise, another small poem in blue. The essence of blue is simple, but telling it is not.

46. Among the Stein papers is a small, mauve notebook with a private love poem entitled "Portrait Of Baby's Cow." The verses take off from "Little boy blue" and include the lines,

> All blue is precious lead it now lead it now to a little cow a little cow big a little cow now. . . .

47. Ralph Church, "Reminiscences," Bancroft Library, University of California, Berkeley, 22.

That is not interesting because it is a long story.

Now this time this is not honest I could tell the whole story simply.
I am going to tell it again.
It is a simple story. I was mistaken.

In the middle of the series, she goes to sleep:

Separate awake from what has he at stake. Start again. Simpler.
I am going to tell the story over again. Something was soothing. What is the story I am telling.
Did he make a mistake in having moistening as a way of leaving a stone for leather. Think of this as an illustration.
Now no more paragraphs. He went to bed and he liked it.

But then she tries again.

What is important about Stein's versions is not the degree of accuracy or the changing interpretations of blue but the process of telling the story which the listener—Berman?—may or may not understand. The repeated lunges try to create the essence of blue as well as the blue sky she sees, to speak of Picasso's blue work, to understand how they could

see what they saw.

She explores how the artist paints what he sees, or sees what he paints, especially without models. She hints at Picasso's primitivism and his supposed lack of technique:

it was what made it seem as if they must or not to know too.

She comments personally and ambiguously,

This is a history of my way for you. For you carefully. What is a blue which is a blue.

She grants,

The story is this they were never sure. But they were sold. For themselves. By name.[48]

In the fourth attempt at telling blue, she suddenly says,

48. It is possible that the story of blue preoccupies Stein because of the sale of Picasso's *Woman with a Fan* (1905) to finance the Plain Edition of her unpublished work. The Plain Edition is discussed in the next chapter, where it chronologically belongs, but it may be foreshadowed here.

> I told everybody about my intention to find why they were not better and they were all interested and some one told me and I listened but that was lost yesterday.

"They" may be the neoromantics—Tchelitchew, the Berman brothers, Tonny—who went back to Picasso's romantic "blue" and "rose" period.

Near the beginning of "Saving The Sentence" occurs suddenly, without context, a sentence which sounds like a quotation:

> Painting now after its great moment must come back to be a minor art. (*HTW* 13)

In the Berman grammar portrait, Stein speaks of Picasso and his imitators:

> He painted blue. It was blue. It was a beautiful blue it was in a blue. As blue. He painted blue. Thank you.

But right away she speaks sharply of those who imitate Picasso without understanding:

> They painted blue. Which was quite blue through you.
> That is all I have to say.[49]

She turns to what may be the portrait proper, with its androgynous, punning subtitle,

Eugenia Berman.

At the start, seven separate sentences of irregular length echo back to the story of blue with rhymes on "too," "true," "through," "knew." The following long paragraph picks up the rhymes, but in addition constructs twelve

49. Hugnet had praised Berman to Stein and brought him along as the great hope for painting. See also Hugnet's "Bérard, Tchelitchew, Amy Nimr, Berman et Tonny," *Échanges* 5 (December 1931), but written earlier (reprinted in *Pleins et Déliés: Témoignages et Souvenirs* [La Chapelle-sur-Loîr: Guy Auteur, 1972]). There was apparently during the visit some unpleasantness, which Berman never forgot and which made him claim that the fine thank-you letter he sent to Stein on October 1, 1929, printed in *Flowers* (238), did not express what he felt but was a "brave front" glossing over a quarrel.

See also Mellow, *Charmed Circle,* 340 and n., and letter from Berman to Donald Gallup, 25 July 1952. To both Mellow and Gallup, Berman said in late letters, now in YCAL, that he stayed with Stein for two or three weeks, which sounds very long as Stein rarely invited houseguests for more than a few days, especially not in the first year; if Berman is right, then Hugnet, a closer friend, did not stay two weeks. See also Stein to Hugnet, 20 September 1929, HRC, and Hugnet to Stein, n.d. [autumn 1929], acknowledging receipt of the Berman portrait.

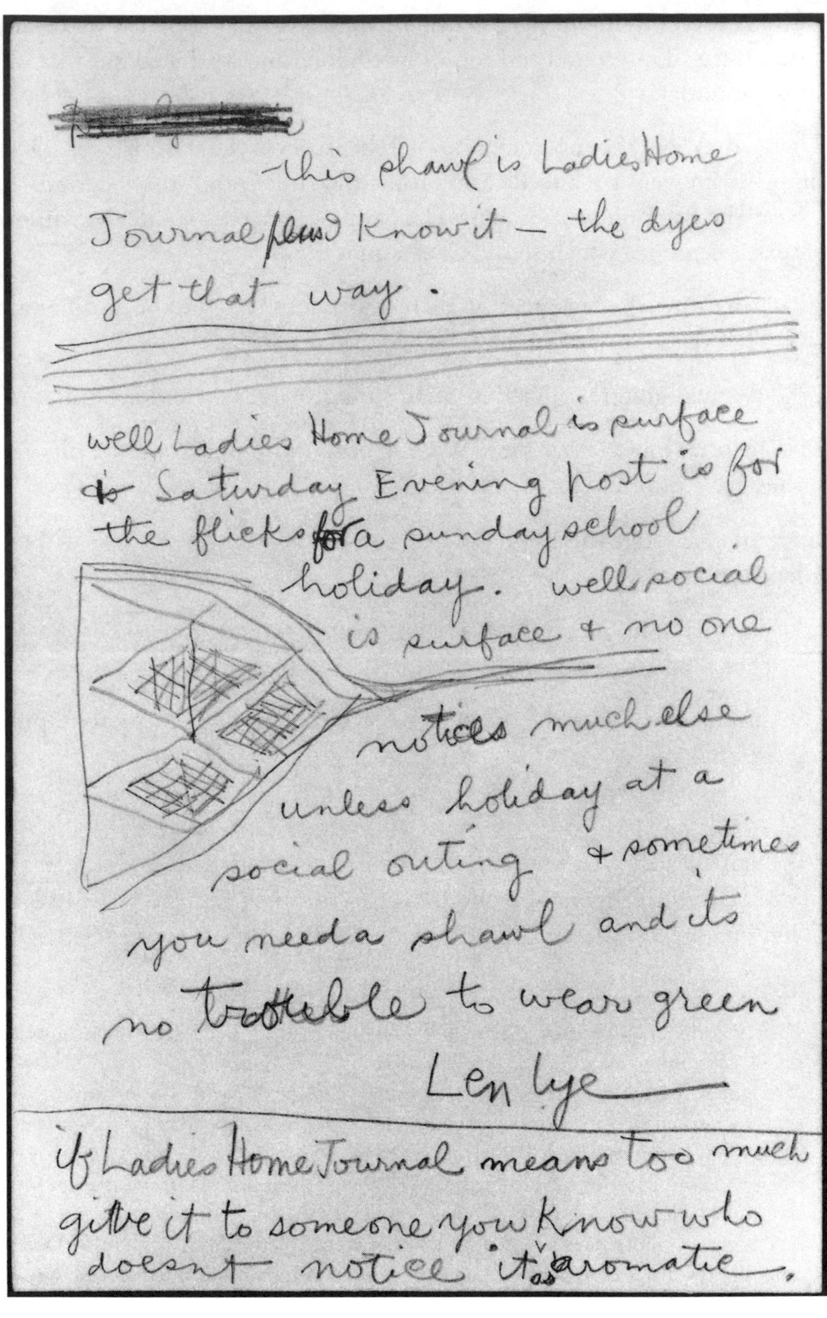

this shawl is Ladies Home
Journal ~~plus~~ know it — the dyes
get that way.

well Ladies Home Journal is surface
~~&~~ Saturday Evening post is for
the flicks ~~for~~ a sunday school
holiday. well social
is surface & no one
notices much else
unless holiday at a
social outing & sometimes
you need a shawl and its
no trouble to wear green

Len Lye

if Ladies Home Journal means too much
give it to someone you know who
doesnt notice its as aromatic.

Figure 8. Len Lye, designer, note enclosed with his gift of a shawl for Gertrude Stein, 1930, YCAL. Courtesy Len Lye and the Len Lye Foundation.

sentences that begin with relational *wh-* words ("which," "who," "when," "where") and end with the word "it," without antecedent.

It is a maddening procedure, for words receive emphasis by repetition, alliteration, and other devices but carry no reference and generate no sentence or sense stress. Abstract connecting words, they send us to antecedents we cannot find but create echoes of blue in which we immerse ourselves, listening and looking again and again.

After the portrait, if portrait it is, follows a wonderfully supple section on portraiture, on sentences, on appearance and representation, and on the mystery locked inside the composed words as well as the mystery that is beyond words. There is a sentence with seals, which sounds like a secret letter sealed with wax that is difficult to open or decipher. There is a sentence without words. She speaks of sentences about blue as paragraphs with emotional weight. Portraits, made by "sitting well," create their subjects, "He made May be May."[50] But soon there follows, "She is a season of seems." Elsewhere, Stein mixes blue with whites, increasingly associating blue—Toklas' blue, it seems—with paragraphs and emotion.

One passage suggests an odd mood, presumably about composition:

> Separated by too. This is neither a sentence nor a paragraph. But it persists that they settle it as fixed. A simple center and a continuous design. This then is left to them when they are nervous. James is nervous.

The last sentence appears three times in much earlier works, "Pink Melon Joy" (1915), "I Can Feel The Beauty" (1917), and "James Is Nervous" (1918), presumably all connected with Henry James.[51] Stein phrases recur in her work, as she acknowledges when in the grammar portrait she speaks of "[a]n attempt to tell what I meant then" (191). Such phrases bring with them their earlier contexts and histories and open expanded or revised readings. Given her verbal memory, recurrence is never accidental.

50. In the printed text (190) and the typescript of "More Grammar Genia Berman," the pronoun in this sentence is "he," but in the manuscript, it is "she." Both, whether painter or writer, may speak of the month of May as subject unless it is a woman. On the other hand, Stein may be playing with French *mai* (May), which is masculine whereas *saison* (season) is feminine.

51. In *Henry James, Gertrude Stein and the Biographical Act* (Chapel Hill: University of North Carolina Press, 1996), Charles Caramello views "James Is Nervous" as a key to the word play of James as a "general," a strategist in writing and a conqueror of new territory, on which Stein relied in *Four In America* (176). I find it difficult to believe that a 1918 piece by Stein should become a key to a 1934 book. Caramello does not give a full reading for "James Is Nervous" and is not aware of the occurrences of the sentence in the earlier Stein texts and in the Berman portrait.

"Saving The Sentence" (*HTW* 11–21)

"Saving The Sentence" opens with three French sentences. The first had amused Stein when Hugnet had used it about the dog: *Qu'est-ce que c'est que cette comédie d'un chien* (What is all the fuss about this dog?).[52] The second sets the scene in a train, confirmed by the movement of rolling scenery, *Que le dit train est bien celui qui doit les conduire a leur destination* (that this is the train that is to take them where they are going). In the last the dog seems to be waking up: *Manifestement éveillé.*

To George Platt Lynes, Stein wrote in October 1929 about the dog, who was teething,

> Basket is sweet and melodramatic . . . it would appear he has a sluggish liver, which makes for the most constant of sentimental melodramas, I am doing it it is called Basketing.

The "sluggish liver" also appears in "Saving The Sentence" (19).

Answering Hugnet's question about the dog literally, she proceeds to write the comedy or sentimental melodrama of Basketing, which goes well beyond the dog. She originally entitled the piece "G. Basketing," the "G." perhaps connecting with Gertrude or, less likely, Georges (Hugnet). Later she revised the title to "Saving The Sentence."

Basketing appears to be a new, dynamic activity, both solitary and social, in which she engages in the company of the dog. It begins as walking the dog but becomes a new form of meditation. The steady, rhythmic movement of walking with the dog allows her to become aware of herself in new ways. Here, incorporated in her own statement, appears for the first time the sentence about identity from the Mother Goose nursery rhyme that will appear later and be developed in different forms of growing complexity in *Byron A Play, Four In America* and elsewhere,

> What is a sentence for if I am I then my little dog knows me. Even if it is all tenderness. What is tenderness. First there must be a way of going without waiting. (*HTW* 19)

The center of the meditation is in Stein's consciousness. With Basket, who does not talk back, the tender exchange returns her to herself alone. The dog does not speak in sentences as Stein does. Basketing—meditating, writing—is not new, but as an activity named for the dog, it takes on a new character.

The piece moves through the "romance" of the country, as on a walk, a drive, or a train ride, collecting, as if in baskets, perceptions which become

52. In a letter of 8 October 1929 (HRC), Stein speaks of Hugnet's sentence as the title of the piece. *Caniche* for the poodle (15) also appears in Stein texts after Hugnet uses it.

sentences. The steady interaction of human beings with their surroundings yields the setting for a play, which includes depth, breadth, altitude, and insistent color.

> The scene changes it is a stone high up against a hill and there is and above where they will have time. Not higher up below is a ruin which is a castle and there will be a color above it. (13)

The dog, the country, the hills, a castle, a ruin, steps, the thoughts about marriage of a young local woman named Francine, and domestic life in Bilignin keep returning, always as matters for sentences that make speech, make plays, make love, make life.

Living, walking, and acting in the landscape yield sentences. Immediate preoccupations enter the piece—the wish to be known, the work with dictionaries on translations (17, 19). "Saving The Sentence" is not simply about new domestic happiness in the country with the dog but about composition and sentences. It ends abruptly,

> I made a mistake. (21)

Whatever the mistake—it does not matter—apparently it was sufficient temporarily to stop sentences.

In the summer of 1929, after his visit in Belley, Stein wrote to Elliot Paul,

> now it is paragraphs I having made the dreadful discovery that paragraphs are natural and sentences are not I am in the depths of trying to find out why and how it is depressing.

On December 10 Stein wrote to him,

> I am saving the sentence and between us I think we will save it its a nice thing a sentence and its nice saving it, one of the things we ought to have a prize for I know you will be pleased[53]

Saving the sentence? From what? From whom? Why? Was the sentence threatened? Here Stein had for twenty-seven years written sentences and paragraphs, too. Recently she had studied grammar as the engine that enables us to read sentences in linear sequence but seize meaning grammatically. What did she think was happening to the sentence? She herself had said, "It is impossible to avoid meaning and if there is meaning there is grammar" ("Arthur" 71).

If sentences and paragraphs were the same, in spite of their different

53. Both letters in Camille Haynes Paul Ferret Cummings Collection, Special Collections, University of Colorado at Boulder.

looks, the paragraph might swallow up the sentence. Yet as she examined the matter, paragraphs could not simply be bunches of sentences, like large or small bunches of large or small flowers. To her, sentences and paragraphs were radically different because they created balance of language in different ways. This difference between "the inner life of sentences and paragraphs" (*LIA* 222) made for variety in writing, which must always be preserved, never abandoned.[54] And she considered how it was incumbent upon the American writer to break down the paragraph and search for

> a new balance that had to do with a sense of movement of time included in a given space . . . which is definitely an American thing. (*LIA* 224)

"Sentences And Paragraphs" (*HTW* 23–35)

She finished "Saving The Sentence" but almost immediately began again, this time after her return to Paris in late October or early November and carrying over into the spring of 1930. She attempted once more to save the sentence, in a piece initially entitled "Saving The Sentence Again" but retitled "Sentences And Paragraphs," perhaps when she realized that she was preoccupied with paragraphs, barely touched in "Sentences" (134) and "More Grammar Genia Berman" (187, 190, 191). Her deep interest always was in sentences with their firm constructive boundaries of capitals and periods; with sentences she now built and questioned paragraphs, whose boundaries waiver and change. The epigraph printed in *How To Write* after the title, "Sentences And Paragraphs," "A sentence is not emotional a paragraph is," is not a part of the original manuscript text but a later addition, worked out in the spring of 1930 in "More Grammar For A Sentence."

Stein used the sentence in two forms, with the key word "emotional" or "natural," "A sentence is not natural a paragraph is." By the time she arranged the language pieces for publication in book form in *How To Write,* she placed "Saving The Sentence" and "Sentences And Paragraphs," the two that moved into paragraphs, prominently at the beginning of the book's con-

54. In "Poetry And Grammar," she spoke of the essential combination of sentences and paragraphs in *MOA.*

> When I wrote The Making of Americans I tried to break down this essential combination by making enormously long sentences that would be as long as the longest paragraph and so to see if there was really and truly this essential difference between paragraphs and sentences, if one went far enough with this thing with making the sentences long enough to be as long as any paragraph and so producing in them the balance of a paragraph not the balance of a sentence, because of course the balance of a paragraph is not the same balance as the balance of a sentence. (*LIA* 223)

tents. She quoted the defining sentence over and over in letters and discussed it in three of the lectures for the American tour, "What Is English Literature," "Plays," and "Poetry And Grammar." The great discovery of this time, it also became a step in her movement to poetry.

"Sentences And Paragraphs" is no more distinctive in shape and quality than "Saving The Sentence." But it differs from the preceding and following studies in one important respect. While she continued to study sentences and now also paragraphs, Stein in late 1929 and early 1930 used details from this study to compose numerous other short works: "Genuine Creative Ability," "The Return," "The Pilgrims. Thoughts About Master Pieces," "Pay Me," *Madame Recamier,* "Why Willows," "Evidence," "Absolutely As Bob Brown Or Bobbed Brown," "How Are Fears," *Parlor,* and "Madame de Clermont-Tonnerre." It is as if the impulses of the one work, for different purposes, also became impulses for others. In "Sentences And Paragraphs," as well as "More Grammar For A Sentence," she listens to herself making sentences and paragraphs and comments on what she is doing. The language pieces all think out loud about writing. Reading them is following her mind reaching for understanding.

> A sentence says you know what I mean. Dear do I well I guess I do. (34)

This study is more complex as a repository of writing ideas than its brief ten pages in print suggest. The sentences absorb her perceptions about people, the objects of living, what goes on around her. These matters not only make sentences but also speak referentially. She thinks about sentences but also follows her subjects developing on the page, the two interacting in our reading as they do in her writing. At first we may not hear the phrases jumping from one piece to the other, but as we read and reread, words or phrases echo and double in the ear from two or more separate pieces, and when they do, we face formidable problems of interlocked texts. It is possible to track details and annotate elements of blatant referentiality, but the figures in the carpet remain intrinsic and resistant to textual exegesis.

Nor do the titles of the short works help. They are not phrases from the texts. "The Return," "Pay Me," "How Are Fears," "Evidence," and "Why Willows" more or less suggest subjects, but the pieces do not satisfy expectations raised by the titles. Even the many short portraits do not easily reveal the relation of subject and composition. My commentary follows the order of "Sentences And Paragraphs," with brief excursions to related works.

What at first appears piecemeal turns out to be interlocking pieces of carefully wrought sentences, though not of planned wholes easily deciphered.

> A sentence has colors when they mean I liked it as selling salt should be very little used in dishes.
>
> That is one of the best I have done.
>
> Pleasantly or presently.
>
> How or have. A sentence is.
>
> Made or make a meaning.
>
> Now feebly commence a sentence.
>
> How has he hurried. That is a paragraph because it means yes. How has he hurried. (26)

Such sentences never read twice the same way; what tumbles about disjointed at one moment shows itself perfectly joined at another, creating at once the frustration and excitement of reading Stein.

"Genuine Creative Ability" (*PGS* 104–5)

On November 4, 1929, Henry McBride wrote to Stein that starting in January 1930 he was to be the editor of *Creative Art* and requested, "Write me something." In response, she produced "Genuine Creative Ability." The title in part includes the name of the magazine. But it also reflects a letter of recommendation for a Guggenheim fellowship that she had submitted on September 20, 1929 for Bravig Imbs.[55] Stein writes,

55. The Guggenheim form used in the autumn of 1929 for 1930 awards asks for

> evidence that candidates . . . are persons of unusual and proved creative ability.

Fellowships then were for study abroad, making the recommendation by Stein as an American in Paris especially poignant.

In a letter of 15 October 1929 to Ellen DuPoy she contrasted herself with Hemingway,

> I am the very highest thing in highbrow but not solemn. Now Hemingway is it he is solemn powerful and successful. I neither look nor am solemn.

In her letter to Robert Coates, sent to him with her recommendation for the Guggenheim in the fall of 1927, she had humorously described what she had written,

> I have tried to make it simple and solemn.

It is astonishing to discover that in the *Autobiography,* written two and one-half years later, Stein speaks of Coates in the same words. She was

> delighted with the scheme of study that he prepared for the Guggenheim Prize. Unfortunately, the scheme of study, which was a most charming little novel, with Gertrude Stein as a backer, did not win a prize. (244)

The Guggenheim Foundation confirms that Stein wrote letters of reference for Robert Coates, 1928 and 1935; Bravig Imbs, 1930; Charles Henri Ford, 1934; Max White, 1936; John Ferren, 1937; John Anderson, the son of Sherwood Anderson, 1938; Samuel Stew-

The courtiers make witty remarks. (29)[56]

and

They come and go. (30)

They include not only Hugnet, Maratier, Thomson, Bérard, Tanner, Tchelitchew, Faÿ, and Tonny, whose portraits she has already written, but also George Platt Lynes, René Crevel, Bravig Imbs, Charles-Albert Cingria, Elliot Paul, Archibald Craig, John Anderson, Eric de Hauleville, and others.

> If they had been one after the other it makes no difference, first I saw one well first I saw one. His name I will not mention. (*PGS* 105)

We know his name: Hemingway.

The sentence about the young man grown old enters the piece with a history. Among the letters to Stein from Ernest and Hadley Hemingway is an undated Christmas card from Hadley with a photograph pasted in of their son Bumbie, John Hadley Nicanor Hemingway, in a sailor suit. Stein and Toklas were godmothers to this boy, born October 10, 1923. Laid into the card is a single leaf torn from a *carnet.* On one side of this leaf, in Stein's hasty scrawl, is this sentence with its comment. It may go back to the date of the card, probably 1925, perhaps earlier. It may be Stein's sentence or Hemingway's but it seems to refer to a child.

Yet when sentences from *A Farewell to Arms* (1929) and even from *Islands in the Stream* (1970) cross in the reading ear with this early sentence, the echoes give pause:

> "He looks like a skinned rabbit with a puckered-up old-man's face,"

Lieutenant Henry says to the dying Catherine about the dead baby late in the last chapter. And Thomas Hudson observes the eyes of the dying young German,

> They were old eyes now but they were in a young man's face gone old as driftwood and nearly as gray. (340)

Continuing the history of this sentence, it still echoes between Stein and Hemingway.

She returns briefly to the three subjects listed at the outset of "Genu-

56. "The courtiers make witty remarks," with its bookish tone, sounds unlike a mature Stein sentence. In the *Autobiography* (93) she quotes it as her own stage direction for a youthful play. Perhaps seeing herself admired brought the sentence back in memory. Leo Stein also refers to it in *Journey into the Self,* ed. Edmund Fuller (New York: Crown, 1950), 134.

The Guggenheim prize is always given for genuine creative ability and the scheme of study is always sent along confidentially.

Under the title suggested by this sentence, she quotes from the instructions for recommendations and sets out to define creative ability, insisting that it is not confidential and not a mystery. "Here it is," she says, and exemplifies it in her piece, begun as a letter to McBride and retaining the personal tone.

She opens by speaking of creative material as if subject matter were proof of ability. She gives examples of subjects of her own, which come from the ordinary here and now—Basket, who must learn obedience; paragraphs, which she is trying to understand; the painter Kristians Tonny, who is preparing a show for the coming February 1930 at the Galerie Théophile Briant. Of course, Basket, paragraphs, and Tonny become subjects only by virtue of Stein writing them. So the creative quality is not in the subject at all but in the process of writing.

I have just changed my mind; I have just had that experience,

she says, for the capacity to change one's mind is an aspect of creative ability.

Creative ability has to do with knowing how to write sentences that work and how to recognize those that do not. She distinguishes sentences that can or cannot be used not by theorizing but by writing them. Her samples appear both in "Genuine Creative Ability" (104) and near the beginning of "Sentences And Paragraphs" (*HTW* 25), where the first, with its comment, stands out.

> He looks like a young man grown old. That is a sentence that they could use.
>
> I was overcome with remorse. It was my fault that my wife did not have a cow. This sentence they cannot use.

The first, usable sentence is a direct observation. The second, not usable, is an insistent statement of private feeling, recalled without observed detail.

It may be the sentence about the young man that moves her to survey the entourage of the many who flatter her now. One wonders whether two sentences in "Sentences And Paragraphs" are also provoked by thoughts about the young men,

---

ard, 1939; and Wendell Wilcox, 1939. (The dates are those of the awards, i.e., letters of reference were written the preceding autumn.) None of these candidates received a fellowship. See also Samuel M. Steward, ed., *Dear Sammy: Letters from Gertrude Stein and Alice B. Toklas* (Boston: Houghton Mifflin, 1977).

ine Creative Ability"—Tonny, training Basket, and, by way of a paragraph, Toklas and her tapestry:

> Tapestry. If tapestry gets crooked it makes no difference it can be drawn straight. (105)

In this piece for the first time she defines paragraphs as natural and emotional, and sentences as not natural. Toklas is associated with paragraphs, with the wholeness of family living and with creativity. But here Stein tells herself to stop theorizing and get on with writing.[57] This informal little piece at first looks hurriedly dashed off, but it is constructed with meticulous, unobtrusive care.

In "Sentences And Paragraphs," after citing the same samples of sentences that can or cannot be used, Stein continues with sentences listing some of the young admirers spoken of in "Genuine Creative Ability," each here identified on a new indented line by a phrase with initial capital and end stop—"George Maratier in America," who visited Chicago that winter; "the relief of Harry Horwood," who helped Stein plan publications; "the wealth of Henri d'Ursel," le Comte d'Arche, who wrote and produced films, including Hugnet's *La Perle,* and so on. Such phrases make titles, which she distinguishes from sentences.

> Titles are made of sentences without interruption. (25)[58]

She also looks at beginnings, parts of sentences, ways to connect parts into wholes, coherence. Here, for example, she leads from the paragraph ending with "How has he hurried," already quoted, to constructions with the word "welcome."[59]

57. The postscript about her new interest in what people mean by what they say rather than in what they are is not in the manuscript but appears in a 1929 *carnet* with notes for early sections of "Sentences And Paragraphs" (25). The appearance of the comment in the typescript suggests that Stein asked Toklas to copy it into the typescript.
58. The same ("Tous Que Je Sais" [All I Know]) *carnet,* fall 1929, in which appear early sections of "Sentences And Paragraphs" and the postscript added to "Genuine Creative Ability" also includes a sentence that reappears in "Title Sub-Title,"

> I have invented many titles and many sub-titles. What is in this sense the meaning of invention.

She here first raised the question of titles but took it up again in a separate, later piece in which she also used phrases from "A Grammarian." The *carnet* also includes a few phrases that reappear in *Parlor.*
59. "Welcome" fascinated her. She worked with it in "Sentences" (212–13), "Saving The Sen-

Now for a sentence. Welcome to hurry. That is either a sentence or a part of a sentence if it is a part of a sentence the sentence is he is welcome to hurry. Welcome is in itself a part of a sentence. She prefers them. I have told her where the place which is meant is.

Welcome when they come. Are they welcome when they come. A sentence instead of increases. It should be if they are. Welcome when they come. That so easily makes a paragraph. Try again. (26)

"Sentences And Paragraphs," "Genuine Creative Ability," and "The Return" use related subjects, young followers, usable sentences, obedience training for Basket. They must have been written in close succession; however, differently constructed, they tackle different writing problems. Her thoughts diverge and converge among her materials, from subjects to sentences, from content to form, inseparable in sentences.

The very title "Sentences And Paragraphs" asks us to attend to the grammatical units, whatever their subjects. Yet of course we hear the subjects. Both experiments with sentences or paragraphs and subjects show up in "Sentences And Paragraphs" and the related pieces of winter 1929–30, all oddly intertwined in composition. What follows summarizes their textual and thematic pursuits.

"The Return" (*PL* 66–69)

The opening sentence of "The Return," which is also in "Sentences And Paragraphs" (26), describes the illustration on the cover of the *cahier,* one in a series about first aid entitled "Les Premiers Soins En Cas d'Accident." This accident is a hemorrhage. The picture shows an elderly gardener outside a greenhouse, holding in one hand clippers with which he has cut his other hand. Stein writes,

It looks like a garden but he had hurt himself by accident.

It is unclear whether she first used this sentence in "Sentences And Paragraphs" to describe a new, empty notebook or whether what started "The Return" is the connection between garden and accident. What looks like a garden does not relate to the injury. The comment also connects with what follows,

This had nothing to do with that when he had to do some errands he had left his dog at home and when he came back his dog was glad to see him.

---

tence" (13), "Virgil Thomson" (198), "Madame de Clermont-Tonnerre" (90), "Sentences And Paragraphs" (26–28), and others. On the cover of the *cahier* for the last is scribbled "Merry Welcome" and "Welcome Hotel."

The elements of these sentences are grammatically but not logically connected.

She now produces a series of odd paragraphs that present events in time but without logic. Disciplining the dog reappears, with "keep away from the door," an arbitrary and irrational form of obedience imposed on him to satisfy the owner's desire for power or the claim that it is simply better to keep him from the door.

> Having found that there was a pleasure in telling the dog to keep away from that door he did it because it was better that it should not be done. There are reasons for it. A dog should not wait at the door he might catch cold, he might not be ready to be obedient that is really not the case because they will finish as well as they have begun, some say very well very well they will finish as well as they would if they were told to come away from that door which they are and which they do obey. (66)

At the same time, the dog's behavior is also irrational:

> A dog will go to the door and wait even when every one is within.

We teach dogs, as we teach children, by arbitrary grammars.

She continues to combine apparently unrelated elements. Some center on names, births, deaths, dates, which suggest the logic of the family. But look at what she does with them. She speaks of the death of Clemenceau on November 24, 1929, which helps date the piece. But then she says that Andrew Bridges was born the day Clemenceau died. Who is Andrew Bridges? We do not know; his birth may have been in the newspaper. There is no connection between the death of the one and the birth of the other except the accident of a date, but that is how we put things together and build a reality.

She goes on playing with first and last names and family relations. Andrew becomes Robert Bridges,[60] the poet, whose name Stein of course knew, as she connects the unknown Andrew to the known Robert Bridges, by the accident of the last name.

But then she places Andrew in a family lineage, saying he is named after his mother's father, which is how we sometimes name children. But immediately Andrew becomes Daniel Bridges, with her own father's first name and the second name of her three brothers that recurs throughout her work, never lived down.

60. Robert Bridges, 23 October 1844–21 April 1930, English poet, critic, and skilled prosodist, in 1929 published *The Testament of Beauty.* Stein's friend, Logan Pearsall Smith, wrote about him.

Daniel Bridges was a gentle boy who was to do his best to be agreeable to his grandfather and to his grandmother and also to a friend of his grandmother and his grandfather who had an adopted child. This adopted girl was very much older than Daniel quite naturally but she was very fond of him as long as he was a little baby and even after. She helped them dress and undress him and she taught him about Wagner. She also taught him about the weather and also as she was very much influenced by a sewing teacher she taught him not to be courageous but that he was naturally not to bother as he would have whatever there was whether there was more of it or not that did not matter. It is strange the minute it is not true it is different.

This Daniel is the two-year old son of Allan Stein, living with the Michael Steins, Madame de Monzie, and her adopted daughter Jacqueline, the latter a family connection, not blood relation.[61] In odd, paratactic sentences, Stein assembles details that do not reveal syntactical relationships, leaving us uncertain about truth, identity, and difference, cause and effect. She refuses to subordinate or systematize.

Think one at a time and remember that is she directed the house they knew that it was a sister. Afterwards they could be for themselves alone.

And later,

How each one likes to be alone.

"The Pilgrims. Thoughts About Master-Pieces" (*PL* 145–47)

"The Pilgrims" also connects with "Sentences And Paragraphs" (27). The subtitle is inserted late into the manuscript, after title and text, but in the text itself Stein speaks of masterpieces. Of course, her early notebooks and *carnets* show that masterpieces, like genius or imagination, were in her mind from very early years. She wanted to produce masterpieces, not to theorize about them.

Now, in 1930, the noun "masterpieces," spelled in two words except in the title, where it is hyphenated, returns, as does the verb "master" with its patriarchal overtone and the theme of fame. All these foreshadow the discussions of masterpieces after the *Autobiography* made Stein famous. She has

61. It is unclear when the girl was adopted, but she first appears in *A Circular Play* of 1920 in the sentence, "Mrs. de Monzy [*sic*] has adopted a child" (*LO&P* 141), which makes the adoption sound recent; if so, she must by 1929 be at least nine years old. See also Hélène Bokanowski, "Du Côté de Fleurus: À l'Ombre des Bûcherons: Ce que je sais de Gertrude Stein," *Europe* (August–September 1985): 108–15.

already looked at creative ability or genius, which leads to masterpieces. Of Toklas, she also says,

> She is important to the biography.[62]

She wonders about autobiography, fame, and audience.

"The Pilgrims" begins uneasily, with wakefulness, remorse, reproach.

> Plaintively she mended when they awoke she mended everything they had they were meant to be thoughtful without which waiting for it lain when they made it do.
>
> It was awful.

There may be trouble with the relationship or trouble with writing, also audible in the uneasy "How Are Fears." Late in 1929 or early in 1930, uneasiness about masterpieces may have been connected with the Plain Edition, which caused serious worry, although Stein in correspondence always spoke of it with energy and enthusiasm.

As in "The Return" and in plays such as *At Present* or *They Weighed Weighed-Layed,* which she will soon write, names matter,

> Everyone prefers a name.

She thinks about masterpieces in connection with the life of a heroine and wonders about handling time:

> I am not sure if it is done with days between it is not the most effective.

One wonders whether she is already thinking of a masterpiece, a narrative or play, including Toklas.

> A life of a heroine. She has helped to mine baskets. She knows what he needs. A heroine is helped by hearing her name, who had been helped. (146)

After an interval, new ease and humor develop between the two "casually betrothed" women. Personalities appear several times to underline their fame:

> Every one prefers a name. Maurice [Grosser] could be mentioned twice. Elizabeth [Church?] once, Paul [Picasso] fourteen times, the Eugenes [Berman, MacCown?] are all the same. . . .

The same names return soon in the play *At Present.*

In "Sentences And Paragraphs" the interdependence of the women is

62. "Absolutely As Bob Brown," *PL* 312.

shaped in short pronominal phrases without antecedents, creating fluid gender roles,

> A sentence. She owes him to her.
> A sentence. He ought to own mines.
> He heard her come in. Laughed is a word. (27)

"The Pilgrims" expands the construction with "owe" into a poignant but humorous paragraph:

> Owe him to her she ow[e]s him to her she will owe him to her she has been owed him to her she ow[e]s him to her. Poverty is solely responsible. They make needs which they have. Partly. Ours went there to partake of marketable produce. Who thought of fathers or farther. Ought to own mines.

The piece ends with restored faith in masterpieces and domestic peace, including the dog, who likes door handles and presumably listens for everyone to return. The last paragraph ends with phrases found in a different order in "Sentences And Paragraphs." The uneasy questions surrounding masterpieces remain unanswered. The conclusion, quoted earlier in connection with country life and house, speaks both of the Stein-Toklas relationship and of composing paragraphs. It includes the dog. It is well to read again what she wrote in so many forms.

> Master pieces are quietly made at home where they were. Worry for them. Door handles which he likes. Now think of loving. He heard her come in. Think of imagination as has to do for you.

"Pay Me" (*PL* 137–39)

The odd "Pay Me," perhaps echoing "owe him to her," in "The Pilgrims," again incorporates verbal details that are also in "Sentences And Paragraphs" (28) though phrasing and order are not always identical.

> Think of how do you do as very necessary. (138)

She uses the same details in different experiments of this time.

"Pay Me" is another domestic piece, with the women's parallel activities, writing, tapestry, and steady conversation essential to the balance of relationship and composition. It opens with food,

> Hubbard squash a vegetable and a dessert.

Then it goes on, funny yet sharp, to contrast Toklas' tapestry and Stein's own work.

> If she made a drawn work tapestry she would do something new. But would she. Not at all. They wore veils.

It ends much like "The Pilgrims" but with a paragraph, longer than any so far in these studies, about Toklas and domestic union, which in turn exemplifies the emotional nature of the paragraph. It opens with the kind of foolishness that is rarely written down and becomes funny in print:

> She is everything to me because I see that she eats well and is very happy. My attentions make her happy.

A note of discomfort follows, not developed:

> I am sometimes pursued by a desire to express myself as having heard more but I have not I have been with it as a result of knowing that it is a wife to me. There we are.

She ends reaffirming domestic peace.

> She is my wife. That is what a paragraph is. Always at home. A paragraph hopes for houses. We have a house two houses. My wife and I are at home.

I add here a series of examples from 1929 to 1932, of a single sentence to suggest how Stein experimented over and over, in the language texts and others. Entered twice on one page in "Sentences And Paragraphs" (29), the sentence reappears at the end of "Why Willows" and later as epigraph for *Madame Recamier.*

> Once when they were nearly ready they had ordered it to close. ("Sentences And Paragraphs" 29)

It is not the subject that matters here, even if it could be named, nor the placement of the sentence in a sequence, for the same kind of sentence appears in other pieces of this period. What matters is the odd construction of time. The sentence begins like a fairy tale, with the indefinite "once [upon a time]," but switches to the colloquial "once when" and veers off to a specific time "when they were ready," only to deny that they "were ready" with the qualifying "nearly." The edges of time blur, wobble, and return. The sentence may be Stein's own, or she may have heard or read it.

Here is a sampling of "once when" constructions:

> Once when they went away they were equal to being estranged once when they were very well.
>
> Once when they were very agreeable they were settled in the place which they had hoped to have. ("Why Willows" 154)

> Once when they were very happy they had happiness in store. (*Madame Recamier* 366)

> Once when I went I added three to we are here. ("History Or Messages From History" 225)

> Once when he will was indebted he was with anguish. ("Evidence," *R* 543)

> Once when they were willing they were just as comfortable as ever. ("Marguerite Or A Simple Novel Of High Life" 367; "Bartholomew Arnold" 335)

> Once when they were not out walking the notary came in he asked them were they pleased with everything and they were. (*A Manoir* 303)

In most of these, the second, main clause, restates the first, subordinate clause, which does away with subordination. Were they comfortable because they were willing, or willing because they were comfortable, or does it not matter since neither is a condition for the other? It is as if these familiar colloquial sentences refused to separate condition from effect, knotting or knitting ends and beginnings into each other.

Yet not all follow this pattern.

> Once when they were all older Bartholomew was not cared for. It is not known just why he was anxious. ("Bartholomew Arnold" 335)

Here is a variation in halting lines that play with constructive detail.

> Once when they were nearly
> Nearly once when they were nearly
> They are nearly once when they were nearly
> They are near they are ~~here~~ hear[63]
> Or welcome. (*A Play Without Roses* 207)

A line from "Stanzas In Meditation" rings of schoolroom practice with "would" and "should," then plays off "if" against "when":

> Once when they should they if indifferently would (III, xvib)

On the other hand, also in "Stanzas" is

> Once when they were very busy
> They went with me. (IV, xi)

Here "when" implies a temporal relation which fails to show how the clauses relate. This sentence is not new to the late 1920s; the "once when" construc-

63. I include Stein's revision in manuscript from "here" to "hear."

tion appears as early as "A Long Gay Book" (108), where it directly follows a "once upon a time" sentence.

"Evidence" (*R* 541–46)

A different oddity occurs in "Sentences And Paragraphs" and, with variations, in "Evidence" and elsewhere. This discovery is briefly summarized in the headnote to "Evidence" in *A Stein Reader,* the only complete publication of the piece, but I here give the steps in full. The base sentence is in "Sentences And Paragraphs," on a page filled with misery about sentences:

> That is the cruelest thing I ever heard is the favorite phrase of Gilbert. (30)

It is then expanded into a paragraph:

> They come and go. It is the cruelest thing I ever heard is the favorite phrase of Gilbert. And he is right. He has heard many cruel things and it is the cruelest thing that he has heard. (30)

The added opening at first seems to create an antecedent for "cruelest thing" but turns out not to do so. Next, Stein complains,

> It is very hard to save the sentence. (30)

The sentence about the cruelest thing must have been a delight of shifting meanings. We do not learn what the cruel thing is or which is whose favorite phrase, especially one that is the cruelest thing.

In "Evidence," the sentence is the favorite not of Gilbert but Herman. In the manuscript of "Sentences And Paragraphs," it is originally attributed to F. Scott Fitzgerald, crossed out and revised to Gilbert. Fitzgerald remained in Stein's mind, however, for the passage is followed by a subtitle she crossed out, "Portrait of Fitzgerald" (154). Perhaps Gilbert, one of a pair with Sullivan, sends us to another pair, Fitzgerald and Hemingway.

The *Autobiography* helps with this sentence. Stein describes Hemingway as successful but, in the words of their maid, for which she can decline responsibility, she calls him "fragile" (267). She then speaks of Sherwood Anderson—not Hemingway—as having "a genius for using the sentence to convey direct emotion" and of Fitzgerald—not Hemingway—as "the only one of the younger writers who wrote naturally in sentences." In *The Great Gatsby,* as in *This Side of Paradise* earlier, he had "created for the public the new generation."[64]

64. See Stein to Fitzgerald on *The Great Gatsby,* 22 May 1925, in Edmund Wilson, ed., *The Crack-Up* (New York: New Directions, 1931), 308. See also the reference to *The Enor-*

She quotes herself saying Fitzgerald would be read when his contemporaries were forgotten.

> Fitzgerald always says that he thinks Gertrude Stein says these things just to annoy him by making him think that she means them, and he adds in his favorite way, and her doing it is the cruellest thing I ever heard. (268–69)

Just who is thought cruel about what and by whom is far from simple and clear. She plays the three authors off against each other in astonishing decontextuating maneuvers, and Hemingway does not come off well. Late in 1929, Stein, more radically modern than Hemingway, must have felt sore about his success with *A Farewell to Arms,* published on September 27.

But "Evidence" and "Why Willows" show further problems. They are among the few pieces where manuscript and printed text differ substantially. They are separate manuscript texts, in different *cahiers,* each with its own title, and each was given its own number in the Haas-Gallup listing. Yet when it appeared in the spring 1930 issue of *Blues,* "Why Willows" was included under a subtitle as a sequel to "Evidence."

The manuscript and the Yale typescript of "Evidence" contain substantial passages not included in *Blues.* Thematically and verbally related, these are more than twice as long as the ones printed. Since cutting was contrary to Stein's conviction about the integrity of a piece, the decimation of "Evidence" requires an explanation.[65]

---

mous Room in both Hemingway's preface to *Kiki's Memoirs* and this section of the *AABT* (268), surely not a coincidence.

On November 14, 1932, when Stein had finished the *AABT,* Charles Henri Ford asked her for a statement to promote his and Parker Tyler's novel, *The Young and Evil,* about to be published by the Obelisk Press. She wrote,

> The Young and Evil creates this generation as This Side of Paradise by Fitzgerald created his generation. It is a good thing, whatever the generation is, to be the first to create it in a book.

65. Quotations in my comments are paginated to the *Reader* for "Evidence" and to *Reflections On The Atomic Bomb* (abbreviated as *RAB*) for "Why Willows." The two together were reprinted in identical form by Parker Tyler, Charles Henri Ford's coeditor on *Blues,* in *Modern Things* (New York: Galleon Press, 1934), 39–41, and by Robert Bartlett Haas in *RAB* (Los Angeles: Black Sparrow Press, 1973), 153–54. Wendy Steiner, commenting on the "Three Hitherto Unpublished Portraits" (in "The Steinian Portrait," *Yale University Library Gazette* 50, no. 1 [July 1975]: 30–45), mentions without giving details the inclusion of "Why Willows" in the printed versions but neither identifies nor explains the omissions from "Evidence."

The portrait of Madame Langlois, at the end, also published by Steiner, is a compo-

The title "Evidence" returns insistently as subtitle for each section. Evidence of what? In "Sentences And Paragraphs," after observing how hard it is to save the sentence, she says,

> Part of it is explained.
> I like evidence of it. (30)

The first sentence reappears in "Evidence," but she gives nothing away about "it."[66] However, it turns up in the same Guggenheim document that lies behind "Genuine Creative Ability":

> The committee of Selection will require evidence that candidates are . . . persons of unusual and proved creative ability . . .

---

sition of flowers and colors, subtitled "Evidence," with "Portrait Of Madame Langlois" added later. Mme. Jean-Paul Langlois translated several Stein pieces, "A Saint in Seven" ("Saint en sept"), "Water Pipe" ("Fuyeau d'eau" or "Conduite d'eau"), "Cezanne," and "Relieve" ("Jean Paul et Henri"), submitting them, apparently unsuccessfully, to Jean Paulhan for *La Nouvelle Revue Française*. "Saint en sept" appeared in *Orbes* 2 (spring 1929), along with Georges Hugnet's "La vie de Gertrude Stein." Virgil Thomson, who knew Mme. Langlois, may have reviewed the translations with her. See her letters at YCAL.

In the manuscript, the sections of "Evidence" printed in *Blues* are numbered 1 to 5; "Why Willows" is numbered 6. These numbers must represent the sequence typed by Toklas for *Blues*. But she also prepared a typescript of the complete text of "Evidence." It is possible that when Stein realized how short the submission for Ford had become, she added "Why Willows" to make it more substantial. Ford, in a letter to me of 28 May 1989, said he was not aware that Stein had suppressed sections of "Evidence."

The cover of the *cahier* of "Evidence" shows a desk with a globe, compass, pen, triangle, and other student tools. In virtually all of the small panes of the window behind the desk Stein has drawn faces. At the bottom of the cover is the title "Evidence." The space above, *Cahier appartenant à* (Notebook belonging to) is filled in twice by Stein, in two identical lines, "D apostrophe D," with large, decorative capital D's. The phrase, which calls attention to itself, can be transcribed, "D'D," Swift's address to Stella, D[earest] D[ingleys], familiar from many private notes from Stein to Toklas, as discussed in *LGS/TW* 86n. *Apostrôphe* as address stands for an unnamed person or idea. It also indicates the omitted letters of the French genitive *d*[*e*] or *d*[*u*] (of whom or of what)—evidence of whom or what. See also *H.M.S. Pinafore,* ". . . I never use a big, big D.," which may also point to the source of Gilbert.

66. "Evidence" may also recall the trial in chapters 11 and 12 of *Alice in Wonderland,* "Alice's Evidence" and "Who Stole the Tarts." The suggestion is less far-fetched than it may seem, for in other works of this time, *Alice* appears to be in her mind. *Parlor* refers to May Liddell, a childhood friend in Oakland, important in the early notebooks, but probably also *Alice in Wonderland,* and "Will you come into my parlor said the spider to the fly." "Absolutely As Bob Brown" plays with "They like to mean what they say," also in *Alice.* Success as evidence of creative ability preoccupies Stein.

In "Evidence" Stein composes evidence of creative ability for Bravig Imbs,[67] whom she had just recommended for a Guggenheim fellowship; for Toklas, "A lady sitting and working" as two friends come to tell her of an unidentified "it"; for Basket, "a white dog is like a lamb"; and for Madame Langlois.

In the *Reader,* the five published sections, numbered in manuscript by Stein, are printed with her numbers; the newly published ones are not numbered. These, sharp in discomfort and unpleasant in tone, are at first puzzling. They do not name their subjects, but careful reading shows that Stein is writing a malicious, personal attack on Hemingway. Though they did not work together and did not meet except with mutual friends, in the autumn of 1929 his presence in Paris and his success with *A Farewell to Arms* raised bitter questions about success as evidence of creative ability.[68] The sections not printed are Stein's second portrait of Hemingway, quite unlike her other second portraits—of Toklas, Picasso, and Van Vechten—done in 1923, the same summer as her first portrait of Hemingway.

She identifies the subject in the first line as

> American and strange.

A few lines later, she adds a cutting definition,

> A man is a person if he has a reputation to fulfill.

There is a meeting or dinner, with infractions against the proper order of precedence in seating or conversation. The phrase, "He and they were listeners," crossed out in revision, echoes the title of Stein's earlier portrait, "He and They, Hemingway."

67. The subtitle "Portrait Of Bravig Imbs" appears to be an afterthought, added after "Evidence" in the manuscript. This portrait also, however, connects in verbal details with other pieces. The word "story" ("an old-fashioned short story"—a lesson or instructive tale, or what we've heard over and over?) appears in the opening section of "Evidence" and in "Sentences And Paragraphs" (30), suggesting elements of subservience—a page, with a double meaning, errands undertaken for May (Maeve) Sage, the wife of Robert Sage, who worked in the office of *transition* and the Paris *Tribune.* The portrait appears to be a character sketch, as Imbs' comment to Stein after he received it from her on Christmas morning 1929 suggests:

    > It flatters me just a bit. But that will be a spur, for now I will have to give evidence of such evidence. And I can, of course, or you would not have said so.

68. Hemingway arrived in Paris on April 21, 1929. By May, he was correcting proofs for the serial publication of *A Farewell to Arms.* At the end of May, he went to Pamplona and later to Santiago and Madrid. On September 20, a week before publication date, he returned to Paris and by mid-October had sold 28,000 copies and soon led most best-seller lists. By November he was uneasy about the effect on sales of the stock market crash of October 29. He wrote the preface for *Kiki of Montparnasse* in January 1930.

He told a story. Two stories shorter

recalls Hemingway's *Three Stories and Ten Poems* (1923), which Stein had reviewed.[69] The context for both allusions has changed. Listening is no longer what it was, and the stories told here are party gossip, tall tales that need cutting down. Nasty embarrassment coughs in her lines,

> I could I could I could cough.
> How long can you listen with hearers. As long. As they are there. Although he has gotten up twice.

The next section, separately begun in the back of the notebook, includes the sentence about the "cruelest thing," attributed originally to Fitzgerald, revised to Herman. The difficult social situation continues, this time with wives as the cause of disappointment.

> Herman and Ernest were sitting where they were willing to be sitting. As they were waiting they met with a disappointment all of a sudden. Their wives had been women. If their wives had been women they would not have been a disappointment or anything. (543)

Disappointment carries through several sections of "Evidence." Hemingway, divorced from Hadley Richardson in January 1927, had married Pauline Pfeiffer in May. Stein raises questions about wives.

Herman and Ernest sound as if they were both one and not one. As Stein had on October 15 written to Ellen DuPoy, Ernest, intent on success, sounds solemn; in "Evidence" she writes,

> Ernest should beware of succeeding to bewildering.

Her man now is not Hemingway but Fitzgerald, whom Stein plays off against him. Ernest also enters the short section on the dog, who is stretching like a lamb.

> Ernest is a judge. He is with it.
> He says and means it.
> They will be our example of patience.
> He has the money.

Ernest emphatically judges an unidentified and perhaps irrelevant "it." "Says and means it," with overtones of *Alice in Wonderland,* also appears in the portrait of Bob Brown, the next to emerge from "Sentences And Paragraphs."

In "Evidence" (545), following the portrait of Bravig Imbs, later printed in *Portraits And Prayers* (210), is a long, heavy passage about patience and

69. *LGS/CVV* 88–89.

studied indifference that marks Stein's effort to counter discomfort and maintain calm by writing. Placed here, it is not easily identified with Hemingway but may also pertain to him.

> Indifference comes before all. Just why. Made that water will fill water. They move about but they do not buy without that water. All hoping of disinterestedness is why they have meant that they are exhibiting patience under distribution and procrastination. Life is such that if we are impatient we are a victim. We are a victim of impatient visiting. We are not visiting and we are patient which is an industry. Undeniably is where they will have what they want if they are willing. Who knows what they are to have. She does because she tells it. Life is the same with everything. It is a permission to visit by invitation. And if he goes and asks her will she come and she refuses nothing is happening because they are coming. Do not disturb me while I write.

The section ends sharply,

> The man who was whistling was actually ruminating. Not he but gazing. Gazing and looking without seeing is not the same thing neither is it without being refreshing. A great many things further than mentioning.

Stein, perfectly aware of her tone, may have decided not to publish what an astute reader might have recognized as a portrait of Hemingway at a time when he was so successful. Or perhaps she decided that the most effective way to speak about him was after all to remain silent. But that he is in "Evidence" is beyond doubt. His name is blackened out but still visible in the manuscript after the title. A single apparently innocent sentence early in the text spells him out syllable for syllable by name:

> He mingled with a way
> Heming [led with a] way.

A letter to Fitzgerald documents Hemingway's meeting with Stein, who invited Fitzgerald, Hemingway, and the Allen Tates[70] for a Wednesday evening.

70. Tate and his wife, Caroline Gordon. Tate, who came to Paris in the fall of 1928 as a Guggenheim fellow, speaks of meeting Stein at one of her Thursday teas and of Hemingway being restored to her favor. He saw Stein several times in 1928 and 1929 but in retrospect conflated dates or occasions. The tea is unlikely to be the same occasion as the dinner or after-dinner meeting with Fitzgerald, which both Stein's portrait and Hemingway's letter date on a Wednesday. Tate's late accounts of meetings with Hemingway and Stein suggest that he was not aware of the complications of the situation. See Allen Tate, "Miss Toklas' American Cake," *Prose* no. 3 (fall 1971): 137–61; Matthew Bruc-

She claims you are the one of all us guys with the most talent etc. and wants to see you again. Anyway she has written me a note asking me to ask you or youse if you would come around Wed. Eve. to her place—after 8.30 or so I fancy—Tate or Tates too—a merchant named Bernard Faÿ or Bernard Fairy to be there too.[71]

In a long letter, written very soon after the party, Hemingway criticizes Fitzgerald's reaction to the evening, reproaching him for not accepting "the sincere compliment G. Stein was offering [him]." He implies that Stein "wanted to organize a hare and tortoise race" between them "and picked me to tortoise and you to hare and naturally . . . you want to be the tortoise." Yet he had wanted to hear what Stein thought of his novel, her judgment being "a swell spur to work" (309–11).

---

coli, "Interview with Allen Tate," *Fitzgerald-Hemingway Annual* (1974): 101–13; Allen Tate, "Random Thoughts on the 1920's," *Minnesota Review* 1 (fall 1960): 46–56; Radcliffe Squires, *Allen Tate: A Literary Biography* (New York: Pegasus, 1971), 86–89; Ann Waldron, *Close Connections: Caroline Gordon and the Southern Renaissance* (New York: G. P. Putnam's Sons, 1987), 72–75; Lawrence D. Stewart, "Hemingway and the Autobiography of Alice B. Toklas," *Fitzgerald-Hemingway Annual* (1970): 117–23.

See also notes by Janet Flanner after a late visit to Alice Toklas in December 1965,

> Ernest not a spectacular person he wldnt have changed as they do not change. Pablos didnt change and made no mistakes. Ern[est] made them all along the line. G[ertrude] didnt like his writings even before. . . . She and A[nderson] read as his books came out—a good deal too much for pleasure. . . . (Papers of Janet Flanner, Library of Congress)

No letters to Stein from Tate, Caroline Gordon, or Leonie Adams are at YCAL.

It is not clear whether Bernard Faÿ, back from a lecture tour in the United States on the *De Grasse* in October, was at Stein's that evening. On December 21, he wrote to her,

> I am very eager to talk about Hemingway—what a curious and puzzling man!—

In his late autobiography, Faÿ says he never met Hemingway at Stein's, though he acknowledges that she spoke to him at length about him (*Les Précieux* 148).

71. Ernest Hemingway, *Selected Letters 1917–1961,* ed. Carlos Baker (New York: Charles Scribner's Sons, 1981), 308–9. This letter from Hemingway to Fitzgerald, as well as the next one, is misdated October 22 or 29. James Mellow informed me, after reviewing in the *Reader* my headnote for "Evidence," which relied on Baker's dates, that Hemingway could not have written this letter to Fitzgerald before late November. This in turn means that the evening at Stein's was Wednesday, November 27 or December 4, far more plausible than October 30 for Stein, who did not return from the country until close to the end of October. Wednesday is identified in "Evidence" as it is in Hemingway's letter. See Mellow, *Invented Lives: F. Scott Fitzgerald and Zelda Fitzgerald* (Boston: Houghton Mifflin, 1984), 350–51 and n. The dates will be corrected in a second edition of the *Reader.*

Had Hemingway not known who Faÿ was, his slight in calling him a merchant and a fairy could not have been so pointed.

As is implied in the letter, Stein plays off Hemingway against Fitzgerald. But what is plain in "Evidence" is her acid contempt for Hemingway, who patronizes Fitzgerald to avoid confronting her. The letter suggests an elaborate attempt to play off the figures in the triangle to his own advantage, suggesting that Stein is not pitting Fitzgerald against him when that is plainly what she is doing. To deflect uneasiness from himself, he transfers it to his relationship with Fitzgerald, patronizing him about his reaction to Stein.

> In plain talk I learned to write from you [Fitzgerald]—in Town and Country from Joyce—in Chic Trib from Gertrude. . . . G. S. never went with us to Schruns or Key West or any place where you get in shape—If she's never seen me in shape—Why worry? When they bawl you out ride with the punches—

"Why Willows" (*RAB* 154)

A separate text that completely fills one *cahier,* "Why Willows" is related to "Evidence" and fits into the sequence of interlocked writing pieces. Preoccupation with sentences carries over from "Sentences And Paragraphs," as does a "once when" sentence (28). Disappointment returns. A Russian—Tchelitchew? one of the Berman brothers?—appears in a hilarious echo of Shakespeare's Sonnet 18,

> It is when he is breathless that he asks who can compare me to a Russian. They will not have half an hour to themselves.

She takes off on this sonnet also in sober comments on the need to be prepared for changes of weather. Related or not, a Russian is also in the portrait of Bob Brown. Fame returns in the ironic,

> They will be well enough known to be stared at when they should know everything themselves.

It is not clear exactly when "Why Willows" was written, but clothing and climate suggest the autumn of 1929 and the imminent return to Paris from the country, an implied presence throughout.

"Absolutely As Bob Brown Or Bobbed Brown" (*PL* 311–14)

This portrait follows and relates to "Evidence," for she inserted "Evidence" as subtitle at the beginning of the manuscript, over her original title, which she crossed out.[72] The title "Absolutely As Bob Brown Or Bobbed

72. The theme of evidence may also be suggested by the cover of the *cahier,* one in a long series about the famous lion killer Jules Gérard, who freed threatened areas of North Africa of lions. This *cahier* shows helpers of the lion killer on the ground, listening to

Brown" is added later, following the revision, but is entered first in the typescript. In "Sentences And Paragraphs," immediately after the sentences about the cruelest thing that appear also in "Evidence," we find several passages that are also here. The portrait links with the sentence study, "Evidence," and the following short pieces. Like "Evidence," it must have been composed in the late autumn of 1929. Sometime in the winter, Stein sent it to Bob Brown, who acknowledged it on April 22, 1930.

Robert Carlton Brown first wrote to Stein in August 1929, upon dedicating to her his *1450–1950*.[73] Meetings followed and a humorous, punning exchange of letters, which also led to a Stein contribution to his volume of "readies," discussed in the next chapter.

Like "Evidence," this piece consists of a series of small vignettes or portraits. The printed title makes it a portrait of Bob Brown, but the late addition of his name in Stein's manuscript and the fact that some of the sections do not appear to be about him suggest that it is a portrait only in a very special sense. It may be a gift. The short sections look like pieces of evidence—of what? Not of the creative ability of their subjects but of Stein's own ability.

Some passages appear to have subjects. One refers to a Russian—Tchelitchew, or Olga Koklova, whose marriage to Picasso was already threatened by 1929? Another begins with a Brazilian but he emerges as a Chilean, presumably Alvaro Guevara, or it may refer to Bob Brown's magazine publishing venture in Rio de Janeiro. A woman, "she," obviously Toklas, is twice shown "at tapestry."

But they are not portraits in the ordinary sense of the word. They are hardly representations, though they may be suggested by verbal features of names or other personal elements. More likely, her words connect with her friends. Most sections also share a theme, such as marriage, or wives ("A Lesson In Weddings").

The first section, "For much," is the answer to a question—"What is it good for," or "What is the good of?" Stein composes a tiny response to the first—"for much," "not for much." "They" may be writing, writers, artists, or perhaps marriage or wives, the theme that carries through. She ends following the phrase from "for much" to "much of it."

For much.

For much. They were good for much. They were not good for much. A thousand. Forty thousand.

---

interpret what they hear—evidence that a distant noise is a fire, not lions. From the *cahier* Stein copied the title "Arabes aux écoutes" ("Arabs listening") into her manuscript though later she crossed it out, substituting "Evidence."

73. Robert Carlton Brown, *1450–1950* (Paris: Black Sun Press, 1929).

There.
Is it good for much.
Much of it. Nondescript.
Music is nondescript.

Near the end Stein draws a light and humorous portrait of Charlotte, who now represents or rather has become her lover, Mildred Aldrich, who died the year before.

> How are they happily in heavy in heaven in dancing in moving inviolate in applauding in curtaining in including in presenting.

Here is a setting for a ballet or a play. Stein is already writing plays.

She moved the subsections about, rearranged them within the piece, and retitled them. But one section, preserved in manuscript, is crossed out in the typescript, where it is replaced with the portraits of Bravig Imbs and Ives de Longevialle. Why should she have crossed out and not printed this section? Subtitled, "An American," it recalls the phrase "American and strange" imprinted in "Evidence":

An American

> An American marries a catholic who is a believer in whatever she does which is why they will not be left to themselves when they are succeeded. It is doubtful if she can be very wicked.

Is this further "evidence" of Hemingway, this time about his second marriage, to Pauline Pfeiffer?

Another is "A Belgian," a portrait of Eric de Hauleville, included in the manuscript of "Absolutely As Bob Brown" but later separately typed and printed.[74] The concluding section, from "Hop in hope for," which fills the last two pages of the manuscript *cahier,* looks somewhat like an afterthought. The last line makes the piece an offering for "Mister Brown," Bob Brown. But it does not look as if it was initially written about or even for Bob Brown.

Like "Sentences And Paragraphs," the portrait considers sentences, paragraphs, and meaning. The section subtitled "Basic," for example, presents the odd sentence,

> Premeditated meditation concerns analysis. (312)

74. De Hauleville, a titled young Belgian poet, was a friend of Virgil Thomson, associated with the Hugnet circle. Tonny illustrated his *Le Genre Épique,* published by Hugnet's Editions de la Montagne in January 1930.

It comments that it "might not be" a sentence, though it is one. In both "Sentences And Paragraphs" (32) and the Bob Brown portrait, she then explicates the sentence word for word, literally and ploddingly.

> Premeditated. That is meditated before meditation. (312)

What is "basic" about it is the word-for-word literalism, Stein's procedure here of stating meaning—meaninglessly. Premeditated meditation is a contradictory term. If, like a crime, it is premeditated, it is presumably not meditation. In a paragraph for each word, she discusses the sentence.

> Meditation. Means reserved the right to meditate.

has no meaning. And she follows with the copula "concerns."

> Concerns. This can not be a word in a sentence. Because it is not of use in itself.

Read in conjunction with "Sentences And Paragraphs," its details offer a demanding but absorbing study of writing.

"Grace Or Ives de Longevialle"

"Grace Or Ives de Longevialle" is a playful portrait of a gifted student and friend of Bernard Faÿ, who introduced him to the Stein circle.[75] Roman Catholic, like Faÿ, he was a poet, reviewer, and translator. On December 21, 1929, Faÿ wrote to Stein that he knew a young man capable of translating "Melanctha" instead of the tubercular René Crevel, whom Stein had originally asked. The translation by de Longevialle and Faÿ was complete by January 17, 1930, and may have been the occasion for Stein to write a portrait of apprcciation.

On March 24, 1930, de Longevialle, aged twenty-three, was killed in an auto accident; I assume Stein's portrait was completed in January or February, after the translation was completed but before his death. She works with auditory details and goes back and forth from one name to another, from French to English, as in translating. In a line that returns in *Madame Recamier,* she says Grace is the name of a man, no doubt remembering her old friend Grace Lounsbery, and she puns with Ives, also written Yves, and Yes about the crippled and delicate de Longevialle in a piece filled with homoerotic suggestions.[76]

75. This is one of the "Three Hitherto Unpublished Portraits by Gertrude Stein" published by Wendy Steiner, *Yale University Library Gazette* 50, no. 1 (July 1975): 41–45; the others are "Simon" and "Portrait Of Madame Langlois," already discussed.
76. De Longevialle (1907–30) is also in the play *At Present,* along with other young friends.

"How Are Fears" (*PL* 139–42) and "Madame de Clermont-Tonnerre" (*P&P* 89–91)

The last group interlocked with "Sentences And Paragraphs" is "How Are Fears" and "Madame de Clermont-Tonnerre," including also the germ of the play *Parlor*, which, like *Madame Recamier*, begins in the language study and leaves traces in "Evidence." Stein is preparing to write plays and to study history.

"How Are Fears" is in a *cahier* about wild animals, which may echo the fear of the title. It includes details, perhaps frightening, about a house in disarray, with furniture, new chairs, carpets, wainscoting, some of which carry over to the portrait of Madame de Clermont-Tonnerre and may have contributed to the genesis of *Parlor*. It also speaks of tension between the two women.

Suggestions for the portrait of Elisabeth de Gramont, "Madame de Clermont-Tonnerre," appear in "How Are Fears," in references to her unhappy marriage, which was dissolved in 1920.

> A duke makes a duke. A duchess. We like the duchess.
> There is a sweet smile.
> Once more they will add as they see the bends with them bend them.
> What is a duke. There is with lives long as a duchess.
> . . .
> What is a duchess if she misses it. Now then sing Simsons.
> Add double added with double add added. (*PL* 141)

Immediately after these lines follows what becomes the beginning of Part I of the portrait itself,

---

Apparently with help from Bravig Imbs, de Longevialle translated Virginia Woolf's story "The Mark on the Wall" ("Le Signe sur le Mur," *Revue Européenne* 1 [December 1929]: 505–14). He was godfather, with Alice Toklas as godmother, to Imbs' daughter Jane Maria Louise, born September 17, 1929. I learned that he reviewed Virgil Thomson's concert of May 30, 1928, with settings of Stein and Hugnet, but I have not discovered where it appeared.

An appreciation by Bernard Faÿ appeared after his death in the June 1930 section of the *Revue Européenne*, presenting him as one of the young men who were true poets but became the spiritual casualties of the Great War. In the same triple issue appeared Stein's French film scenario, "Deux Soeurs Qui Ne Sont Pas Soeurs," preceded by Faÿ's appreciative portrait of Stein. See also letters to Stein from Hugnet, Faÿ, Imbs, and de Longevialle, and Imbs' *Confessions of Another Young Man* (New York: Henkle-Yewdale House, 1936), 221.

Now there are two imaginations.
Three imaginations.

Almost all the text of Parts I to V of the portrait is in "Sentences And Paragraphs" and in "How Are Fears," though not identical in phrasing, line arrangement, and order. The last line of "Sentences And Paragraphs," casual and inconclusive, is also the last of "How Are Fears" and of the portrait,

We change from Saturday to to-day.

Only the opening section of the portrait, four three-line units before Part I, does not connect with "Sentences And Paragraphs." Indeed, the initial three swift lines are written on a separate leaf and were probably composed separately and then transferred to the portrait, as were the next three three-line units.[77]

Just dip I love it
Cherry tree for them forever
I think the color of it is good.

Arch for archangel transferred
In place of and make learned
Be joined by paragraph answered yes.

She might make banish rest of Fanny
Flourish rest of cherish passage courage
Rest of with her in her made with well a pleasure

How are how in How are how in me
When this you see
How adding finally to mend we.

77. These lines are on the back of a small leaf, showing a still life with fruits and flowers and the heading "Les Ateliers Graphiques 'Du Matin,'" perhaps an invitation to an exhibit; the lines are an exchange between Stein and Toklas or two others, probably about painting. When the Stein papers arrived at Yale, this leaf was laid into the manuscript of "Stanzas In Meditation," next to Stanza xxi of Part III, where I found it. However, it may have slipped into "Stanzas" by accident, for the twelve lines do not seem to connect with that stanza.

On the back of a letter dated 26 February [1929] from Nella Larsen Imes, Stein composed the other three sections of the initial part of the portrait. Numbered 2, 3, and 4, they were written after the sheet with the first three lines.

Parts I to V are unified and well connected in mood and tone. The opening section, however, both in tone and in detail, does not connect intimately with what follows.

Stein made a handwritten copy of the portrait, which is at Yale. On that copy, she left out Part I, which was apparently restored later by Toklas in her hand on a separate sheet. We end up wondering about Part I.

Stein sent the portrait to the duchess, who responded with spontaneous delight. Perhaps it picked up what they had talked about. Perhaps it rested on a shared occasion or on phrases that were in the air and that we cannot recapture. In an undated letter, she is flattering yet direct:

> So you have sent me a portrait! The only one I want to hang, and frame, and look at! I thank you. Which words may I use to express my pleasure, my gratitude.—
>
> —We change from Saturday to today—I want to change, to move, always, to question, to answer, and think about the delightful intercourse with Gertrude Stein, and how she sits—she is—that is the fact—and the way she has, of refreshing dull minds, and make them feel fruitful and alert.
>
> There never is [made] land near water. . . .

The portrait moves swiftly and rhythmically, from here to there, from came to went, from question to answer, from sea to river to water to land, always balancing elements of sentences.

The "parlor" in the passage may be the salon of the duchess or that of Stein, appearing here and in other pieces of this time. The word marks the beginning of the play *Parlor,* which includes the art of conversation—*parler*—and so the art of plays. It was perhaps this parlor that led Stein to the word "wainscoting" here (90) and in "How Are Fears" (141) and to details of interior decorating like the laying of carpets in "Sentences And Paragraphs" (34). The conversation in the salon, following questions, answers, more questions—or are they questions?—and more answers, if answers they are, is surely conducted in sentences, "made wonderfully one at a time" (34).

But the question remains, what is a sentence? "Sentences And Paragraphs" was finished in Paris in the late winter or early spring of 1930, before Stein left for the country. Like the other language pieces, it ends without finality, on a tentative and mutable note, even sharing the last sentence with "Madame de Clermont-Tonnerre,"

> We change from Saturday to to-day.

It is less a self-contained work than a chapter in Stein's groping for clarity about the elements of writing. Like the preceding and following language studies, it must be read in compositional units, entry by small entry, not for a total design. Only in retrospect does the series written between 1927 and 1931 gradually make visible an emerging design of ideas in and about writing.

"More Grammar For A Sentence" (*AFAM* 359–78; *R* 547–63)

"More Grammar For A Sentence," perhaps originally titled "Paragraphs" and later felicitously retitled, was probably begun soon after arrival in the country in late April or early May 1930. With the move to Bilignin, changed living changed writing. The only one of the language series that could not be fitted into the collection *How To Write,* it was printed in the posthumous *As Fine As Melanctha* (1954) and is included in *A Stein Reader;* all these pieces bear separate titles, less to announce individual works than to mark new circumstances or new energy. Yet they all form a single bass line of compositional ideas evolving by unpredictable shifts in method,

> A little at a time.
> It is as good as exercise. (363; 550)

The late lectures delivered in America—particularly the last, "Poetry And Grammar"—pick up some of her conclusions but leave out the steps that led to them. I follow these here, one by one.

Near the beginning, for example, she makes herself "go on." She has started "More Grammar" with what appear to be veiled references to Toklas, whose name has talismanic power to free her words. She considers the name, unchanged since her lesbian marriage is not accompanied by a legal change of name. She also considers that they are not well known (361; 549). Stein writes this at the time when the Plain Edition is being launched, which will give Toklas status not only as editor but as the force behind the creative act. Such hints lead to play with family relationships, particularly visible in the country, where busy family living dominates the social landscape. Family yields sentences dominated by the family word "with." From "with," she works her way to a section of *W* words, wondering what goes with what in a family—or in a sentence or paragraph:

> There is no other family with at all.
> To go on with going on with it.
> It makes it safely with them and who.
> Wordy worthy worthy worth were they were or were
> they with be.
> Worth bitter.
> It is better or are they bitter. (361; 548)

Her observations of the world around her are never separate from her ideas about writing.

This intimate connection of daily life and text is visible in a *carnet* with some sections of "More Grammar." On one page is a question in the hand of Toklas,

> At what time does the afternoon ~~train~~express leave ~~Culoz~~Virieux if it doesn't stop at Virieux what time does it leave Culoz . . . .

This question is written next to a grocery list, probably as a request for Stein to check the train schedule at the station when she runs errands in town.

On the next page, directly connected with waiting for the train or with Toklas' sentence, appears text for "More Grammar." Here is how word and lines—not poetry—are fitted into the small *carnet,* from which Stein copied them, disregarding breaks and adjusting capitals, to the manuscript *cahier* and incorporating them in a paragraph (376; 562):

> That is a sentence,
> with waiting for them.
> It is very disagreeable
>
> To be waiting for them.
> This is a cadence.
> A cadence does not
>
> resemble a sentence
> it is partly without
> a paragraph. Without. . . .

The *carnet* also shows that when Stein transferred writing from *carnet* to *cahier,* she sometimes revised. The discontinuity between *carnet* and *cahier* confirms that her texts were written in small units that could be moved rather than in larger sequences. For example, the *carnet* opens with two central attempts at definition, one after the other,

> There is no such thing as a natural sentence but there is such a thing as a natural paragraph and it must be found

and

> There is no such thing as a natural sentence and why because a sentence is not naturally. A sentence.

In the *cahier,* however, she separates the two definitions by making them into indented paragraphs and inserting between them a six-line paragraph of detail (364; 551).

The next, long entry in the *carnet,* written in a different direction, marks it as a separate section:

> It gives all the effect of a mountain but it is a plain.

This and what follows appear in the printed piece twelve pages later (376–77; 561–62).

The section ends with still another formulation of the paragraph as natural:

> In other words a paragraph is not naturally a natural thing but it is. (375; 560)

Other aphoristic commentaries or definitions are also moved into new strategic positions, for example,

> What can be expected of paragraphs and sentences by the time I am done. (368; 554)

or

> Nobody knows what I am trying to do but I do and I know when I succeed. (365; 552)

The *carnet* illuminates such rearrangements and shows how flexible Stein's groups of sample sentences are.

What details are included in "More Grammar" about publication and fame, which preoccupied Stein so much in the winter of 1929–30, do not obsessively enter the process of writing. It is as if daily life in the country was absorbing and conducive to writing far beyond worries about success and publication, which recede into the background as a light and laughing matter.

> Try it out. How do you do. Do they love you. Or curiously. When it is different to be agreeable or agreeably older. There it is not to be mistaken. (361; 549)

Here is a wealth of auditory punning in words full of life, and not full of the battle for printing books.

> A sentence is a sentence. This may be but it is not with arrive. Arrival. A Rival sentence. (378; 563)

An early paragraph about hiring Bradley to help them become known ends not with fame but with language,

> It is very beautiful to have the winning language. (362; 549)

"A Grammarian," the next piece, also only briefly and playfully shows her in the battle for print:

I am a grammarian in place.
The place edition.
Now in forty fortification. (*HTW* 107)

Do we hear echoes of Hemingway's successful war novel?

"More Grammar For A Sentence" is an extraordinarily attractive work, concrete, personal, and lyrical, full of the simple literalism that distinguishes the best of Stein. It is far less cerebral, splintered, and labored than the preceding studies. The life of the country opened her eyes to new sights, which became tiny germinal insights speaking the nature of sentences and paragraphs in what she saw and how she saw it.

Here she makes a paragraph a landscape:

> A paragraph in when there is a little valley in noon or as it is in the way of a little of it as soon as there has been a moon. That makes it not naturally be a paragraph. (364; 551)

Another landscape also becomes a paragraph:

> What is it. A paragraph. Grenoble. On the way to Grenoble you pass a hill without a town where you might stop which I see it is used by it in a main while in the way. A usual sentence is placed anywhere. What is a sentence. Without a trouble. They will be just as well aware. Without it. This is a paragraph without delight. They are after it. After awhile. An ordinary paragraph. Which they have. (371; 557)

The landscape before her is seen as a composition, shapely and varied as a paragraph.

> I like to look at it.
> What is a paragraph.
> She likes it better than Granada. (373; 550)

A landscape moves as does a paragraph,

> A paragraph is natural if they walk. (373; 559)

Or again,

> What is a paragraph, no place in which to settle. Because they had been moved. (371; 557)

Daily life and common sense rush in with observations so apt and unexpected that we wish we had made them ourselves.

> It is very easy to miss a sentence

one paragraph ends, and the next begins,

> But not a paragraph.

With the next sentence, starting the next paragraph, she becomes a schoolmistress:

> It is very wrong to miss a sentence. (369; 555)

She laughs at her paragraphs in the face of the weather,

> What is a paragraph when they predict rain. (370; 556)

The whole piece is punctuated by the insistent question, what is a paragraph, but look at what happens next:

> What is a paragraph. Right off. Write often. What is a paragraph. (372; 558)

> This is a paragraph in substance. (362; 549)

goes one answer, but we are not sure to what "this" refers. She may have exemplified but has not defined a paragraph in substance, though we know the phrase from school and writing manuals. But the comment leads to another, so obvious it makes us laugh:

> Of course it looks like it in that shape . . . (362; 549)

The direct and personal quality of the process of observation is disarming:

> A sentence needs help. And she cries.
> A sentence is why they were folded. Please have it folded.
> Who helps whom with help. Withheld help yourself.
> That is or or hour.
> A sentence will come.
> Chiefly. Will come.
> That is a natural sentence. A sentence will come. Chiefly.
> Will come. (370; 556)

Life and sentences, what happens and what is said, always interact in ways far more complex than they at first appear.

> I see what is the trouble with a sentence they will not be two a day. That is the trouble with a sentence. Now try to make a sentence with this experience. (371; 557)

In Bilignin, in the vegetable garden, work on the paragraph and the garden go together. Here is a full paragraph where the garden becomes a paragraph and the paragraph a garden.

> It is at adding in remaking tens. Every little way of calling May away from them. With whom were they careful. They will have been thought well of without. Every little nicely by a paving with when by this in and announced. She let fall something which made a little racket. There is why they need now and know their paragraph. A paragraph is not natural. Who knows how. A noun is nature personified. Alike. A sentence which is in one word is talkative. They like their moon. Red at night sailor's delight a vegetable garden which is when there is a cage wherein they add with add withheld with string. A paragraph is not natural. Peas are natural so are string beans all sausages are natural, butter is natural but not cream paragraphs are not natural quinces are natural even when they are late and with them they are natural without cherries they are natural. A period is natural a capital with a capital with and with a capital. It is beautiful. A word which makes basket a name. If it is a name will he be confused with whatever with it they make to name. There is no doubt that a mine is natural that always is natural that appointment is natural that nearly is natural that they will have their board is natural. It is natural to remain once again. It is natural. A paragraph is not natural but needful. There are more needful with what they do. Think of everything that is natural. Now. It is very beautiful to have a birthday. In which they invite prefer. With them. A paragraph is not nature. Not unalike. (362–63; 550)

As she writes about sentences and paragraphs, she counters what we were all taught about them.

> A paragraph is not made of sentences. (375; 561)

Radically different, sentences and paragraphs cannot be reduced to a common denominator, for the paragraph is not the sum of the sentences in it. It is not an expanding sentence but something other than a sentence. Sentences do not grow into paragraphs any more than they can be thinned as a cook in a hilarious passage thins sauces (376; 561).

Of the hope of Florence Descotes, a local girl, for marriage, realized on September 1, 1930, Stein says,

> A sentence is a plan. (372; 558)

However, she continues,

> It is never plain.

Once the plan—a plan for a wedding or a grammatical plan that shapes writing—is realized, there may be a paragraph in which they are at home. Paragraphs rest on feeling.

> To think well of any paragraph they must have affection. (364; 551)

Like love,

> A paragraph is not pressed for time. (376; 561)

The dog Basket runs through the piece as a part of the family and of country life. Like a child, he gives pleasure and offers instruction in growth, walking, movement, play, obedience—and of course sentences and paragraphs. On the same page where she anticipates Florence Descotes' marriage appears the dog drinking water. In later years, she so often spoke of what his drinking taught her that the point requires comment. Anyone who knows the slosh of a dog drinking recognizes its rhythm, sound, and shape.

> What is a paragraph. He drinks as if in wishing. He drinks of if in washing. And so and so they will be out of mind out of hand. This makes no difficulty. Have they thought of that. (372; 558)

Here is a little lyrical moment, a paragraph, not regulated, not predictable, about a small act that is never twice the same. It does not fit the stiff harness of a correct sentence.

In "Poetry And Grammar," Stein relied on her discovery to underscore the difference between the balance of sentences and paragraphs, which also led to prose and poetry. Periods and therefore sentences and paragraphs will be with us, just as prose and poetry will be with us, as long as there are human beings.

> Sentences and paragraphs. Sentences are not emotional but paragraphs are. I can say that as often as I like and it always remains as it is, something that is.
>
> I said I found this out first in listening to Basket my dog drinking. And anybody listening to any dog's drinking will see what I mean. (*LIA* 223)

She valued the radical difference between sentences and paragraphs, which made for variety in writing, the firm, end-stopped sentence contained in a grammatical form along with the looser, flexible extension of the paragraph. She considered it essential to give variety to writing by using both and retaining their differences. And she hoped that American writing would achieve a new balance of the two in new forms of movement in space.

"More Grammar" ends most naturally with the departure of a guest and thoughts about the end of a visit and of a sentence. They are alike in that both must end, but otherwise they are different. The guest will not come back, but

> A sentence can not exist if it does not come back no not if it does not come back. A paragraph finishes.
> This is it. (378; 563)

Rounded sentences returning to their beginnings are completed. She swiftly breaks off the paragraph of awkward parting with an abrupt stop rather than the smooth conclusion we have been taught to aim for, yet how fitting for a departure.

"A Grammarian" (*HTW* 103–13)

I am a grammarian. (105)

This first sentence and similar announcements punctuate the short "A Grammarian," written in the early summer of 1930. It fills her with delight to be a grammarian,

> A grammarian there is a pleasure in the air which is agreeable. (106)

The phrase, "there is a pleasure in the air," does not sound like Stein. Rhythm and phrasing echo the scene in the first act of *Macbeth,* in front of the castle, which sets the mood of country summer, without the irony added by the murder plot. Such echoes frequently rise in her work and require attention. Her pursuit of grammar is familiar, but her delight in being a grammarian is new. "A Grammarian" is a language study, an ode to writing, and a self-portrait.

On May 13, 1930, Pierre de Massot had delivered his preface for *Dix Portraits* to Hugnet in Paris. Hugnet and Stein had despaired of ever receiving it. Already near the end of "More Grammar For A Sentence," Stein speaks of the preface and says, "Send it" (376; 561). On May 14, having heard from Hugnet, Stein wrote to de Massot,

> I am as pleased as pleased can be that you have done a preface for my book and it gives me very solid pleasure and I am looking forward to seeing it and very soon.

Hugnet sent the preface on, and Stein was delighted.

> I have just gotten your preface and finished reading it, it is very beautiful and one thing you do fills me with the keenest delight, and that of course it is there in all your writing is the way you use quotations. I dont

quite know what you do with them. They cease to exist in your use of them and yet they are there as position. . . .[78]

One source of her delight was the epigraph from Apollinaire's "La Victoire" (1918), the next to the last poem in *Calligrammes,* about the death of the old and the victory of the new language of poetry. Stein knew Apollinaire's aesthetic when in 1913 she wrote of his eye lessons in her portrait of him, included in *Dix Portraits*. De Massot understood perfectly what it meant to her to be introduced in her English-French volume with Apollinaire as a grammarian of the new, as he says in the epigraph,

O bouches l'homme est à la recherche d'un nouveau langage
Auquel le grammairien d'aucune langue n'aura rien à dire.[79]

Surely these lines are the source of Stein's grammarian and of her proud pleasure in being identified with Apollinaire.

It makes me smile to be a grammarian and I am. (107)

The insistent "grammarian" not only points to Apollinaire as a source but also, to any English-speaking reader, recalls Browning's "A Grammarian's Funeral." Both dismiss the old and announce the new. "I am a grammarian" derives its power from the firm simplicity of the sentence and from the weight of the large word that is its complement. "Grammarian" carries the dactyl uncommon in English that Browning made familiar.

Behind "A Grammarian" lies the question that dominated all of Stein's writing: What am I? Who am I? In work after work she struggled not for an answer or to revise or reject earlier answers but to show that there were many answers. Planning the Plain Edition also made her review who she was as a writer, and the publication in late June 1930 of *Dix Portraits* with de Massot's preface extended the review from English to French, from America to Europe.

To look back in the way they came. Now think. Who stands.
To look back in the direction in which they came.
In the direction in which they came.
To look back in the direction in which they came. (110)

78. Both letters, MS University of Virginia Library. De Massot's answer to the second undated letter is dated 13 June 1930.

79. Oh mouths men are looking for a new language
One the grammarians can't label

Translated by Anne Hyde Greet, *Calligrammes: Poems of Peace and War (1913–1916)* (Berkeley: University of California Press, 1980), 334–41.

She looks back, just as she had done on a walk through the countryside, through her writing and her life from Baltimore to Boston to Belley, with other *B* names echoing, in "More Grammar" (369; 555). Retrospect is not always reassuring. She continues,

> A grammarian is so.
> Afraid.
> Is a word.
> To look back in the direction in which they came.
> To look back in the way they had come. Now you see that means that others had come and others look back in the direction that others had come. (110)

"A Grammarian" destroys the old associative grammar by demonstrating her own grammatical agility. It is as if she composed the piece against de Massot's preface, which praises her work as a source of revelations and miracles for those ready to abandon old habits in reading and writing. What many readers still did not see was claimed by de Massot as Stein's great accomplishment.

And so the grammarian rejects the stiff authority of rigidified grammar.

> Grammar little by little is not a thing. Which may gain. (108)

perhaps means that the old grammar is gone, or that grammar is not one thing but many, a flexible capacity for joining words.

> The part that grammar plays. Grammar does not play a part. (108)

So she says, thinking literally about a phrase that is in her mind because she is beginning to write plays. The weather in the valley enters her sentences about grammar.

> It was blown away by the wind. The wind has blown it away. The difference there is not interesting. If the wind blows you can see it. (106)

Stein had reason to be pleased with the preface for *Dix Portraits,* as is evident in the portrait of appreciation that she composed for de Massot early in the summer.

She no longer struggles to define sentences, and paragraphs are not even mentioned. Instead, she explores grammar in her terms—writing.

> If a sentence is choosing. They make it in little pieces.
> I have practiced. (108)

She plays with compositional possibilities, inventing new moves and turns so swiftly that it is difficult to keep up with her.

I can do it so easily it always makes grammar but is it grammar. (109)

She praises her struggle for invention.

> Having made too little before now which it was you have given too much. That is a tense, to struggle. Struggle and straggle make it a reunion. Gave it a measure. They give it twice there are two afternoons.
>
> Twenty days to two afternoons.
>
> Why is it a triumph to say twenty days to two afternoons. (107)

It is a triumph because she has combined different temporal systems.

She plays with numbers, which her grammar liberates from numbers' rules as it liberates words from the rules of traditional grammar.

> The essence of grammar is that it is freed of following. (106)

Numbers and counting recall her Aunt Fanny Bachrach, who appears later in *Everybody's Autobiography,* counting with her lips.

> She said that the only way you could count with dignity and then use the money that had accumulated was by counting one one one. You should never say three or even two, you should keep strictly on a basis of one. If you kept counting by ones and had purses in which you kept the separate ones you could always keep everybody well fed and well dressed. . . . (153)

That memory lies behind Stein's insistence on discrete details and her rejection of abstract systems derived from the sum of details. Counting "one one one" attends to distinctions. The story of her aunt might echo Browning's grammarian grinding at grammar,

> That low man goes on adding one to one,
> His hundred's soon hit:
> This high man, aiming at a million,
> Misses a unit.

The story appears in "A Grammarian":

> Thousands count out loud.
> The way thousands count out loud they do it with moving their lips.
> Made a mountain out of.
> Now this is perfectly a description of an emplacement.
> If you think of grammar as a part.
> Can one reduce grammar to one.
> One two three all out but she.
> Now I am playing.

And yielding.
To not attempting. (109–10)

Reducing grammar to one leads to a game of counting out that also becomes love play, never following a totalizing grammar. What she produces is not a set of grammatical principles but daily life in daily writing. It would require pages of annotation far from her words and less illuminating to reduce her grammar to principles. The passage concludes with

Think closely of how grammar is a folder. (110)

Grammar as a folder evokes many rhymes and echoes, perhaps of a follower, perhaps a fold, bold, told. It is a holder loosely enfolding papers, things told in writing, a pamphlet. It thinks closely but is not stiffly stitched or rigidly held. Such grammar makes books.

"A Grammarian" ends suddenly,

It stops because you stop. Think of that. You stop because you have made other arrangements.

Changes.

Grammar in relation to a tree and two horses. (111)

Whatever the other arrangements, marked perhaps by "Changes," they end "A Grammarian" with a sentence that Stein offsets with a horizontal line and transfers to the back of the *cahier* as the first of a new short work, "Title Sub-Title." It is a light study of things seen, heard, and said rising in puns, word games, and phrases with variations. These allow her to look at how we invent titles and recognize good ones.

"Title Sub-Title" (*AFAM* 387–88)

This little study of that summer, written in the reversed *cahier* of "A Grammarian," opens with the last sentence of that piece,

Grammar in relation to a tree and two horses. (387)

It is repeated three times, with slight variations. The "tree and two horses" sounds like a set design. The grammar attached to it may be what places tree and horses in relation to each other, to the world, to us. The addition of "a title" and "a sub-title" after the first of the three repeated sentences makes us wonder whether tree and horses are subordinate to a principle of composition, a grammar. Stein, of course, does not compose by subsuming tree and horses in a system. But behind her title lies a question, humorous yet serious: what is a title, what is the relation of title and subtitle, of grammar and a tree and two horses?

The piece is not about music but, like most of her work, it is full of rhymes, puns, rhythms, sound, not only in phrasing but also in subject matter, here about the dog,

> With a little noise of exciting he found his ball. (387)

or,

> The title of this piece is a watch has a little sound. (387)

It resounds with titles, tittles, and tittle-tattle. What makes Stein's work musical, however, is not her play with sound and rhythm but her kind of grammar. She likens her methods to those of counterpoint in the fugue, that most complex of musical forms.

> In grammar we have to think why a fugue and also why exercises are expected and delay nothing. They are more interesting than a tune. (386)

And they are far more than mere exercises.[80]

She immediately illustrates her procedure with a popular word game around the phrase, "Are you ready," with which she had played in 1923, in "Practice Of Oratory," "A Book Concluding," "A Village," and since.

> You are ready. Are you ready. No I am ready's brother. Are you ready yet. Not yet. (386)

The "subject" or theme, "Are you ready," is taken up, patterned, and repatterned in phrasing and meaning. Such exercises are what her composition is about. It is also how children play word games.

In the process of "Title Sub title" she destroys the hierarchy that goes with the idea of a subtitle and makes up and rejects all sorts of titles. Is she recalling the quarrel over "Enfances"? Only she, no other authority, makes titles.

> Thank you so much. That is not a title.
> Why is thank you so much not a title. Thank you so much is a title. (387)

or,

> I will go where they are. That is not a title.
> Why is it not a title because they will not make it a title. (387)

80. Counterpoint appears also in Marcel Brion's distinguished essay, "Le Contrepoint poétique de Gertrude Stein," printed in *Échanges* 3 (June 1930). I do not know whether Brion's comments occasioned Stein's reference here.

Titles are arbitrary and in the end tell very little about the compositions they head, as any reader of Stein knows. In "Forensics" she says that a title is a defense. Even when titles identify obvious subjects like portraits, they tell little about the nature of the works they name.

During her visit to Chicago late in 1934, Stein inscribed a copy of *How To Write* to the singer Claire Dux Swift with the words, "Grammar in relation to a tree and two horses. This has something to do with Freischutz as you sing and see. / For Claire Swift."[81] We cannot know whether in 1930, when writing the first sentence, Stein was thinking of *Der Freischütz,* perhaps the Wolf's Glen scene. Certainly Claire Dux might well have sung Agathe in *Der Freischütz.* Stein may also have discovered in 1934 that her decontextuated words fitted Dux and *Der Freischütz,* or she simply found at the end of "A Grammarian" in *How To Write* a sentence that made a charming dedication. Such speculations come to mind when Stein texts both refuse to be pinned down and suddenly offer new readings.

"Forensics" (*HTW* 383–95)

On January 22, 1931, Charles Henri Ford responded to Stein's submission of "Forensics," "the end of my long series of meditations on writing." He assured her that he wished to print it in *Blues* number 10, an issue that never appeared because the review ceased publication. "Forensics" must have been completed by early January or before.[82] It became the last piece in *How To Write.*

It was written after the return on about November 30, 1930, from Bilignin to Paris, for none of the words ground it in the country. Like many Stein texts composed in Paris in these years, it sounds abstracted from its occasion. There is a wife, a bird, a dog, a brooch, but otherwise no figures or objects and virtually no activity. Even the title, "Forensics," is oddly theoretical and not the kind of word she was given to using. It sounds as if she were about to

81. The dedication is included in *Chicago Inscriptions,* issued as a Christmas pamphlet for 1934 by "Bobsie" (Mrs. Charles B.) Goodspeed, Stein's hostess during this visit. Claire Dux, a lyrical soprano of German-Polish descent, had sung extensively in European and later American opera houses and concert halls. By the time Stein met her, she was married to Charles H. Swift and no longer sang much.

82. Charles Henri Ford recalls no details about the submission (letter of 28 May 1989 in answer to my inquiry of 15 May 1989; interview with author in his apartment in the Dakota, New York City, 5 February 1998).

The piece is in a *cahier* entitled *Turenne,* for the great French military commander during the Thirty Years' War, perhaps a conscious choice for work about the art of winning a war with words.

plead in court, perhaps with medical evidence, or to instruct us in persuasive writing. The title has been connected with the name of her junior-year writing course at Radcliffe, but that course explains nothing about "Forensics."[83]

And yet reading and rereading suddenly touch in these abstract words a quality of voice that opens its occasion. "Forensics" does not dispassionately define and exemplify argumentative writing. It does not tell us how to write rationally in answer to a dispute. Instead it speaks to the sense of injury that precedes disputation. That feeling of rage and outrage, rarely acknowledged, creates the voice of this work, full of the vocabulary of violence—"struggle," "outburst," "advance in volume," "fire to forensics," "never pardon," "disposing of violence by placating irony," "disgrace." It demonstrates not by what it says but by how it speaks to a personal quarrel deeper than any forensic writing.

> Quarrels may wear out wives but they help babies. (385)

The quarrel is about writing and generates writing (386). Stein would not have written "Forensics" if she had not been embroiled in a deeply personal quarrel.

The occasion for "Forensics," in December 1930 or early January 1931, is the quarrel with Georges Hugnet over the joint publication of *Enfances* in French and English and Stein's demand that she appear as author in her own right, not merely as translator. The "true story" of that quarrel is told in "Left To Right," Stein's journalistic narrative of the events "left to write" after the trouble. The peaceful-sounding but ironic, "I agreed to everything," appears in both. A language work, it is brought about by that quarrel and so not only concludes this chapter of meditations on writing but also the preceding chapter on Hugnet. It shows the retaliatory voice rising in writing from "a plea by which they will never pardon" (385). That voice is beyond argument.

Abstracted from its occasion, "Forensics" does not even grant the antagonist a name but creates with stark, depersonalized pronouns without antecedents—"they," "she," "he," an occasional "we" or "I"—the state of mind that requires

> an argument to be fought. (386)
>
> It is very easy to make forensics. Anxious. (391)

83. Richard Bridgman, *Gertrude Stein in Pieces* (New York: Oxford University Press, 1970), 199.

Stein's paragraphs and sentences ring with rage and anxiety, attack and defense. They stagger in anger. They rehearse what was done and what might have been done, speculating in subjunctive forms about missed alternatives:

> They say it would have been better.
> To invite.
> Would it have been better.
> To say.
> Would it have been better.
> To show.
> Them this.
>
> (385)

She asks what forensics is and defines not by examples of logical discourse but by the voice of this work reacting to the sense of provocation.

> What is an argument. What are forensics. What are master pieces. What are their hopes. An argument is this. I have it. They reserve it. They do not answer at once. Forensics is this. Better come when it rains, better come when it rains, and rains, better come and puzzle that they have been within and it rains who have all by the time and not also to go.
>
> They have no argument without doubt.
>
> What are master pieces.
>
> Forensics are a remedy in time. So have thousands. A master piece of strategy. An argument of their deliberation. The forensics of abuse which has not been written. No thought of their search. (390)

Sentences break into slow and heavy marching fragments.

> They shall stretch. Their conclusions. From here. To there. They will. Prepare. Efficaciously. Just as much. As they have been. In the habit. Of anticipating. Melodiously. In reference. To their analysis. In a garden. Admire forensics. (393)

The forensic quarrel is lethal. Forensics can burn.

> What did she do with fire. She almost put fire to forensics. (394)

In the manuscript *cahier* appears a small burn mark, perhaps from a match or cigarette, as if someone had put fire to "Forensics." Throughout the piece, "she"—Toklas—is a sounding board, a supportive presence and a witness in attack and defense. Stein moves an advancing army to positions from which she can win battles. Writing words become war words.

> A master piece of strategy. (390)
>
> A detachment of troops. (394)
>
> Will she need a title. (387)

and

> They dispute a title and they dispute their trouble.
> A title is made for defense. (387)

recall the occasion for the quarrel and the recent study of titles. They also recall that *Enfances* was at this time about to be published in *Pagany* as "Poem Pritten on Pfances of Georges Hugnet" and that Stein's versions were about to be renamed *Before The Flowers Of Friendship Faded Friendship Faded.*

She concludes by returning to her own reputation and to new plans, perhaps for the Plain Edition,

> Forensics may be athirst for gold. It may with them battle and die. It can as much bequeath and condole. For them. To merit. That they. Should console. Them. (395)

"Forensics" does not teach the formal rules of argumentative writing. Instead, Stein shows in these wrenched, stiff fragments the rift that allows no resolution and no reconciliation.

> All this is conclusion.
> What is forensics.
> They need their pleasure singly. (388)

It marks the unyielding, unforgiving end of a friendship, depersonalized but far from theoretical.

With her title Stein may have recalled what the writing course at Radcliffe presumably did not teach her about the violence that underlies forensic writing when it is more than an exercise. She recalled Harvard also when writing "Left To Right," where Bravig Imbs appears as Frederick Harvard. Virgil Thomson, a Harvard man who attempted to mediate in the quarrel, becomes Generale Erving. "Forensics" offers a corrective from experience to the theory of argumentative discourse. Its voice is beyond rational argument.

actuality of the body

torn from their context

Forms
back into names

—Susan Howe, "pythagorean silence" 17

Abandoning grammar for history eating and farming and never being happy.

—"History Or Messages From History" 228

8. 1930–31

History

Context

Although everything Stein wrote came out of daily life, she rarely voiced feelings. She wrote of the world, not of herself or her emotional life. As she maintained privacy about her feelings, including the sexuality crucial to her sense of herself, so she refused to let them intrude on the reader's privacy. At the most, she transferred them—especially troubled ones like anxiety, fear, anger, pain, ambition, guilt, despair—to word play. Rather than exploiting feelings, she treated the words that named them as elements of composition and perhaps in the act of writing diffused their power.

The preceding chapters traced the acquisition of the house and the dog. How urgent it became to find a country house can be inferred, for example, from Stein's rush to get home to France for house hunting after her lecture in England in June 1926. Likewise, her obsessive machinations to obtain the house she eventually discovered bear witness to the importance of the project.

The dog also, even if he was purchased on an impulse, quickly became important in ways she had probably not anticipated. The silence about how she got him and the absence of a pedigree or other papers surround him with a secretiveness that underscores his importance.

Although Stein does not write about herself and her feelings, I came to see the new life of which dog and house speak so eloquently as a part—not the cause—of a larger, existential shift in her sense of herself and her life.[1]

1. Bridgman sees difficulties, with no evidence or explanation, saying Stein's writing had

Reading and rereading the work of 1929–31, I began gradually to hear patterns of new words and phrases that for the first time voice a sense of trouble from which writing apparently did not free her. A subtext about her state of mind, they also point the way to *The Autobiography Of Alice B. Toklas.*

Approaching sixty, Stein is reviewing her life and her career. She is haunted by doubts about her achievement and frustration about publication. From late 1929 on, there appears in the casual short observations of daily life that so readily absorb the personal a growing sense of discomfort about herself. In "How Are Fears" a fortune-teller offers reassurance about both house and work:[2]

> She predicted.
> Comfort in the home.
> The betterment in connection with a jealous enemy.
> Success in connection with different suggested master pieces.[3]

---

become "peculiarly unrewarding to her. Her imagination was failing and she seemed incapable of pushing forward. While awaiting inspiration, she held tenaciously to her sense of her own importance. 'I am determined to be king'" (*Gertrude Stein in Pieces* [New York: Oxford University Press, 1970], 203–4). If this line, from *Louis XI And Madame Giraud,* is to be read personally, it explains nothing about her mood or the play.

Stein's so called megalomania is a compensatory mechanism for her real frustration about publication and reception of her work. There rises from her texts at this time, as never before, a deep dissatisfaction that can be heard as a subtext. I here lift its elements out of their subordinate position to make them audible.

2. Predictions—fortune-telling, palmistry, ouija boards, dreams, eclipses, and so on—require careful study in the context of Stein's time, her friends, her art. The few comments that have been made concern the wartime interest in St. Odile and *Mrs. Reynolds.* But fortune-telling and handreading took place regularly through the years and appear in her writing. She also collected samples of handwriting, perhaps in connection with her characterology.

   Related may be her reliance on superstitions in proverbs and other phrases in texts, for example, the hooting of an owl for making money, predictions of weather such as "Red sky at night, sailor's delight; red sky in the morning, sailors take warning."

   To Stein, superstition encompasses far more than easing discomfort, satisfying curiosity, or playing a game. It carries over directly to novels and is spelled out in "The Superstitions Of Fred Anneday, Annday, Anday A Novel Of Real Life" of 1934:

   > Superstition is believing something means anything and that anything means something and that each thing means a particular thing and will mean a particular thing is coming. (*HWW* 28)

3. To keep the quoted sample sentences on p. 411–12 free of citations, the sources follow here in the order of the quotations, paragraph by paragraph: "How Are Fears," *PL* 140; "Sentences," *HTW* 296; "More Grammar For A Sentence," *R* 549; "Why Willows," *RAB* 154; "The Pilgrims," *PL* 145; "Sentences," *HTW* 206; "More Grammar For A Sentence," *R* 548.

Wondering who people in the country think she and Toklas are, she says, "They wish they were known." But she quickly goes beyond to how well she is known as a writer. The sentence, "They have to be without doubt well known" occurs in a passage about promotion by her agent. Yet she also says, "They will be well enough known to be stared at when they should know everything themselves."

Living in the house but not married, "They had no life in a name they were casually betrothed. . .". But "He is spoken of by his name. His name and her name." And "her name had not been changed but not known about." What's in a name, what's in a married name, a famous name? Ambivalent, ironic, or even envious, she wonders whether Toklas is as well known as she herself, "It is very curious that she is so well known." "A famous wife is married to a famous poet both beloved. This is what history teaches."

The fame of Toklas as wife derives from that of Stein as poet-husband. Yet Toklas, essential to the creative process, is more than a wife. Hers is "A life of a heroine. She has helped to mine baskets. A heroine is helped by hearing her name, who had been helpful." The multiple puns of "helped to mine baskets" speak of her part in the creative process, which is also the domestic process and by 1929 includes minding the dog. Here the pronouns of indebtedness are fused, "Owe him to her she ow[e]s him to her she will owe him to her she has been owed him to her she ow[e]s him to her. Poverty is solely responsible." The emotional unit of the paragraph is bound up with Toklas and takes a new form in the house. "She is my wife. That is what a paragraph is. Always at home. A paragraph hopes for houses. We have a house two houses. My wife and I are at home."

To name Toklas as the true heroine is to make her the legal wife, an impossibility, and to include her in a biography, another new word in Stein's writing. "She is important to the biography." "And. He did say. It would. Be important. To the biographer. To-day." Another way is autobiography, "This is an autobiography one of these." "Autobiography ought to. Have made doors."

"The Pilgrims," *PL* 145; "Sentences," *HTW* 206; "History Or Messages From History," *A&B* 232.

"The Pilgrims," *PL* 146; "The Pilgrims," *PL* 146; "Pay Me," *PL* 139.

"Absolutely As Bob Brown," *PL* 312; "Winning His Way," *SIM* 187; "Brim Beauvais," *MR* 288; "We Came. A History," *RAB* 151.

"History Or Messages From History," *A&B* 232; "We Came. A History," 149; "We Came. A History," 149; *A Manoir, LO&P* 279.

"The Pilgrims," *PL* 146.

"The Pilgrims," *PL* 147.

To Virgil Thomson she writes on August 1, 1930, that she is "deep in history, what is history, history and audiences." Audience, familiar as a Stein theme after *The Autobiography Of Alice B. Toklas,* appears here on the way to it. History is about becoming historic—or famous. "History Or Messages From History" tries to define "What is history. They make history." In "We Came. A History." she says,

> History is made by a very.
> Few who are important.

and

> That history is made
> By accomplishment. (149)

Names make history as history makes names, "In history anybody remembers names."

She tries to define the measure of accomplishment, to create evidence of creative ability. The charge to W. A. Bradley as her agent was to make her famous and make her rich, as he reminded her when she dismissed him in 1934.

Fame follows "master pieces," in two words, as Stein spelled many compounds to allow play with both the compound and its parts. So far, she had always concentrated on writing, not on the hope of masterpieces. But now, "Master pieces makes hopes."

The sentence, "What are master pieces" occurs first in "Forensics" (390), about the power struggle with Hugnet, and only in 1935 becomes the title of a lecture. "The Pilgrims," of late 1929, with many of the uneasy new phrases, is filled with anger, guilt, and remorse, and may be about a quarrel with Toklas, perhaps prompted by success or failure in work. A sexual or literary masterpiece eases the quarrel, "Master pieces are quietly made at home where they were."

Is she worth a biography? Can an autobiography win her the recognition she craves? Friends and publishers suggested that she write memoirs, but she resisted. To Henry McBride, who held artists to their integrity by insisting that success corrupted, she denied any interest in autobiography,

> No. I am not interested in autobiography messages experiments. I am interested in literature and I happen to be the first American since Whitman who is making literature.[4]

4. Draft in "Tous Que Je Sais" ("All I Know") *carnet* (1929–30). It is not clear whether this draft responded to a letter from McBride, not preserved in YCAL, or whether it was even sent as a letter. The draft may also have concerned a newspaper piece on or by McBride,

But she was thinking about autobiography as she was also thinking about masterpieces.

On February 21, 1930, Harry Horwood[5] wrote that he had talked her up to an editor he valued, Elling Aannestad of W. W. Norton, who was in London. Like Horwood, Aannestad recommended in March that she write her memoirs. In drafting a response, Stein refused and claimed that her work could be profitable,

> Thanks . . . but . . . there has been a misunderstanding. I am interested only in the work I am and have been doing and I am quite certain that it would be a profit to a publisher to print this in small editions.[6]

By 1929–30, she began to go simultaneously in two directions. One kept her writing in meditation as she had always done. The other, overcompensating for frustration, pushed her more and more aggressively toward the limelight of fame and money. Sometimes the two directions collided.

Adding to her frustration was the success of writers younger than herself, especially Hemingway, who became a best-selling author with *A Farewell to Arms,* published on September 27, 1929, one month before the stock market crash of October 29. Although Stein wrote to Ellen DuPoy that unlike Hemingway, who was "solemn" about success, she herself, highbrow but not solemn, did not care about success. She of course did care; her disclaimer did not conceal her envy.

Earlier that year, with the help of Bradley and friends, she planned new publications both in France and in America. Information is incomplete because projects were not written but talked out, plans changed, and records were not always kept. Yet once again two *carnets* offer help with notes not embellished by the desire for publicity. The first, of spring or early summer

---

such as is hinted at by Virgil Thomson in a letter to Stein of July 8, 1930, about a "New York Sun critic." I have not succeeded in locating such a piece.

As early as September 8, 1915, Stein had written plaintively to McBride about her difficulties with publication, "I have gotten a little used to what you say is good for geniuses." Her tone does not suggest that she had. To less intimate friends she displayed the attitude that McBride represented and that Robert Coates ascribed to her, "Of course I know you have the only impeccable attitude, to write and not to bother about the publishing and selling." (25 February 1931)

5. An American who had worked with Harper and Doubleday, Horwood had helped build French-American literary relations and by 1928 gone into business as a literary agent and editor. A clipping on Horwood, "An American Gent for France," from *Publisher's Weekly,* 25 December 1926, 2321, is among the papers of W. A. Bradley, Rare Book and Manuscript Collection, Columbia University.

6. "Tous Que Je Sais" *carnet* and W. W. Norton Papers, Columbia University Library.

1929, includes jottings about a discussion, interspersed with addresses, grocery lists, and other details.

> Program which would bring real results. Print this fall book like Fabrications sample bits of Long book. [Start] this subject again with Furman [of The Macaulay Company]. Then in the fall print Lucy Church Amiably, next spring a little book like the Birthday book Then in the fall Portraits and Prayers. Then the following spring Three Lives and I would go over and they would do a real Making of Americans edition then following that the book of How to write and then G. M. P. Matisse Picasso & Gertrude Stein and then etc. etc. This is a program that would bring big results to any one with vision enough to carry it through. Talk it over with Saxton or Macaulay.

Here and elsewhere appear three separate but related projects: a lecture tour in the United States, plans for publishing *The Making Of Americans* both in America and in France, and printing unpublished work in what became the Plain Edition. I shall follow this order in summarizing the three efforts.

To "go over" to America meant to speak. In a section of *A Novel Of Thank You* written in the summer of 1925, while she was proofreading the Contact Edition of *The Making Of Americans*, she speaks—or dreams—of a lecture tour (116). Friends, including Janet Scudder, had over the years suggested lecturing. Bravig Imbs, in America in 1927, apparently spoke about Stein in his hometown, Detroit, in Ann Arbor, and perhaps in Chicago.

On July 28, 1927, Imbs wrote of a commission offered him by the Leigh-Emmerich Lecture Bureau in New York to persuade her to speak in America. George Platt Lynes also had that spring offered to act as agent for a Stein tour. Bradley advised promotional lecture tours for his authors, though friends objected to a tour for Stein as not a commercial author. Faÿ distrusted Bradley, as did Elisabeth de Gramont, the Duchesse de Clermont-Tonnerre, who on July 6, 1929, wrote,

> I knew by B. Faÿ your intention of sailing in the States in October—a wonderful idea, they all want to see you and hear your lectures, which should be of the greatest interest—yes, I want to see you, too, in Belley, Saving the Sentence . . . and I shall let you know.
>
> Has Faÿ sent you the cutting of the N. Y. Herald, where Bradley appears as your "conseiller"—it is he who advises you, not to make a commercial all round tour—but to [elicit] your conscience etc.—fresh!—is it not—he is a perfect cad,—after having tried so much to entangle you

with his agent in N. Y. I shall be happy to remember all my experiences, which were very pleasant, and tell you about it.[7]

To whet the reader's appetite for the complete *The Making Of Americans,* an American equivalent of *Morceaux Choisis* would be printed as the great immigrant novel by a major American publisher who would embody its intentions better than the Contact Press edition of 1925. From 1928–29 on, first Stein and then Bradley negotiated with Lee Furman of the Macaulay Company for such a book. Bradley also approached others, such as Eugene Saxton of Harper Brothers.

The complete novel added to the difficulty of her text the problem of its length. For a publisher, "the making of never stop," as she called it in her portrait of Bernard Faÿ, was a risk proportionate to its length, and the Macaulay Company asked for a cut version. By June 1930, a short text was prepared with the help of Elliot Paul, Bravig Imbs, Bernard Faÿ, and perhaps Bradley himself. Yet in the end, Macaulay refused the book as both impaired in its effectiveness by the cuts and still too long.

Bradley also negotiated in Paris with Boutelleau of Librairie Stock for a more substantial representation of *The Making Of Americans* than *Morceaux Choisis,* submitting the same text that had been prepared for the Macaulay Company. Whether in America or in France, publication by an established house rather than a small press became increasingly important to Stein. A contract was signed with Librairie Stock on May 1, 1931, but an uproar began when the firm's regular translators declared themselves unable to render Stein's text in French. The problem was solved by Bernard Faÿ, who persuaded the firm to assign the translation to his friend, the Baroness Renée Seillière, who worked in cooperation with him. With Faÿ's preface, *Américains d'Amérique* appeared in 1933.[8]

The many concerted efforts at publication also led to the Plain Edition, the effort of Stein and Toklas to issue the many unpublished texts under their own imprint. It was not a simple and consistent enterprise. Many plans were made, abandoned, or changed, and a full study of this project, including

7. The Duchess did tell about it in an essay on English writers in Paris, published in the *Revue Hebdomadaire* of July 1931. That piece, with minor modifications and additions, later became a section entitled "Ecrivains Etrangers Que J'ai Connu" ("Foreign Writers I Have Met"), in the fourth of her five-volume *Mémoires* (Paris: Editions de Grasset, 1928–37). I have not succeeded in locating the passage referred to, presumably in the *New York Herald Tribune.*

8. This is the same selection as the one published by Harcourt, Brace and Company in 1934. Faÿ, with his student, Grace-Ives de Longevialle, in January 1930 translated a section of "Melanctha," published in *Les Romanciers Américains* (Paris: Denoel et Steele, 1931).

financing and printing, is yet to be done.[9] What follows summarizes information scattered among the Stein papers and suggests how many questions remain. A second *carnet* records plans for publication in 1929–30, though preparations began a year earlier, at least in part with Georges Hugnet.

One list of proposed titles includes not only Stein works such as *Lucy Church Amiably* and *How To Write* but also books by others.[10] In a letter draft, she speaks of "small editions of my work if I decide to do with George Hugnet"; apparently she considered publication under a joint arrangement with his Editions de la Montagne. Of the Plain Edition she says in this *carnet,* "we realize two meanings in one word"—plain as simple or clear and plain as commonplace.

However, by adding the mountain to the plain, Hugnet's Editions de la Montagne extends the word play. Stein wrote to Henry McBride on April 25, 1930, of the "Edition of the mountain and the Plain edition," and a scrap reads, "Mountains and Plains." In "A Grammarian" appears the "place edition" (197) and in "More Grammar For A Sentence," "It gives all the effect of a mountain but it is on a plain" (*R* 561). Even the Roman plains in *Madame Recamier* echo the Plain Edition (390, 392). The incorporation of Hugnet and the country into her life and her work is again dramatized in the merging editions and three meanings in one word.

Publication of the many books "not yet printed," as Stein literally translated "inédits," was also planned with the help of Ellen DuPoy[11] and her friend Harry Horwood. Stein did not originally expect to do all the work for her publications herself, nor did she have the necessary expertise. She apparently thought of Horwood, who had the right solemn look for success, as

9. Hugh Ford's *Published in Paris* (New York: Macmillan, 1975) is a useful survey of a large and complex situation but not a fully detailed study of individual publishing ventures. New documentation is now available which makes full examination of many presses possible.

10. Two are by Bravig Imbs, *The Cats,* eventually published in a Dutch translation (1935), and *A Parisian Interior,* apparently dedicated to Alice Toklas but never published.

11. DuPoy (also spelled DuPois, formerly Mrs. Edward Taylor, divorced by 1928) was a native of South Dakota, a novelist and a journalist who wrote for the *Chicago Daily Tribune.* Stein and she became friends, corresponded, and DuPoy visited in Bilignin. In relation to Stein's writing, especially *LCA* and *Madame Recamier,* see their correspondence; her novel, published under the name Taylor, *One Crystal and a Mother* (New York: Harper Brothers, 1927), which was discussed with Stein; her review of *LCA,* "Gertrude Stein Writes Another Useful Book," *Chicago Daily Tribune,* 9 May 1931; of *How To Write,* "Gertrude Stein Gives Views on How to Write," *Chicago Daily Tribune,* 4 June 1932; of *Before The Flowers Of Friendship Faded Friendship Faded,* "New Poem of Gertrude Stein Gives Praise," *Chicago Daily Tribune,* 21 October 1933; and "Author Tells of a Visit to Gertrude Stein," *Chicago Daily Tribune,* 13 October 1934.

publisher or agent for what became the Plain Edition.[12] However, in January 1931, Horwood, who had proved ineffectual and unreliable, was curtly dismissed, and Stein refused his offer of a refund of money they had apparently pooled for the edition.[13] This was also the time of the quarrel with Hugnet over joint publication of his poems and her versions.

From now on, the women managed the Plain Edition alone as their own project. *Lucy Church Amiably,* the first book, which spoke of their dedication to the region and Stein's love of Toklas, had been published in January 1930. In May 1931 followed *Before The Flowers Of Friendship Faded Friendship Faded* and in November *How To Write.* In August 1932 appeared *Operas And Plays,* and in February 1933 *Matisse Picasso And Gertrude Stein,* including "A Long Gay Book" and "Many Many Women." By the summer of 1933 the *Autobiography* made Stein successful, earned her money and led to publishers' demands for further work, making it unnecessary to continue the Plain Edition.

To raise funds for publication, Stein sold Picasso paintings whose appreciation in value allowed her to gamble on appreciation of her work through the Plain Edition. Much has been made of the sale, in late 1929 or early 1930, of Picasso's *Woman with a Fan* of 1905; it was not purchased, as has been said, by Marie N. Harriman but by Paul Rosenberg, who later sold it to Harriman. Before the end of 1930, she also made efforts through McBride to sell the Picasso gouache *Girl on a Horse,* apparently one of six gouaches of that title, of the Harlequin period. She told McBride the sale was to pay for "the exigencies of country proprietorship," not that she needed money to print her own books.[14]

12. Stein to Horwood, 20 October 1929.
13. Horwood is not even named in the *Autobiography, Everybody's Autobiography,* or Stein's lectures, which is one of the reasons the record of the Plain Edition is incomplete. How far he took an active rather than merely an advisory part in its planning is not clear. He based plans for publications on *Lucy Church Amiably* but may not have taken part in its publication and was dismissed before the second book came out.
14. See James Mellow, *Charmed Circle: Gertrude Stein and Company* (New York: Praeger, 1974), 348, *WIR* 136. I have not succeeded in ascertaining the price or date of sale to Rosenberg, whose records were destroyed in World War II, or the date of his sale to Harriman. The National Gallery of Art states that the painting was purchased "by the Hon. and Mrs. Harriman" from Rosenberg "by 1933" and "given to the National Gallery in 1972" (Christopher With to Dydo, 13 April 1989). See also Stein to McBride, postmark 21 December 1930, asking for $12,000 for the Picasso gouache; McBride to Stein, 2 and 31 January 1931, and cable, 5 January 1931, on a possible sale to Eugene Gallatin or to clients of Valentine Dudensing for Matisses and Picassos, though McBride thought her

Almost certainly further paintings were sold, but I have been unable to document reasons, activities, sales, or prices accurately and completely and correlate them with the cost of the Plain Edition. But one possibility must be considered. The 1985 catalog of the Cone Collection lists for this time two or three further sales of Picassos to Etta Cone. One is *Woman with Bangs* of 1902, sold 1929–30 (?). Another entry lists fourteen Picasso drawings included in a shipment from Michael Stein to Etta Cone that may also have come from his sister's collection.

The third is Picasso's 1906 gouache of Leo Stein, Etta Cone's last purchase from Stein. The catalog lists it with the date from Etta Cone's records of September 14, 1932, which may represent agreement to purchase, shipment, receipt, or payment, we do not know which. Who initiated these sales when and how also remains unknown, though it is known that over the years the wealthy Cone sisters, who had faith in Stein as writer and expert in art, bought numerous works from her at high prices. The last sale, however, not only of a Picasso but Picasso's image of her brother, must for Stein and Etta Cone have been more than a business transaction.

Stein always spoke lightly and with self-assurance of their publishing venture. However, it was undertaken after long and bitter rejection of her work, required major expense, demanded great effort, and caused tension between Stein and Toklas. The Plain Edition and what she described to McBride as "country proprietorship" coincided in time. Together these new undertakings shifted a part of the deep creative relation with Toklas to mundane practical efforts which necessitated looking at Stein's work from the outside. There is in the work of these years a growing self-consciousness, a sense of audience and effect, a striving for success and publicity. At the same time, Stein was also recognized as an author in a circle of prominent writers.[15] Her frustration about publication led her to advise the young Paul Bowles

---

asking price high. On January 5, 1931, McBride asked for a photograph of the gouache, which she forwarded, but McBride complained that it was not a good reproduction. I have been unable to verify whether *Girl on a Horse* was sold at this time, especially as there was more than one such drawing and Stein herself apparently owned more than one. On the proposed sale, Pierre Matisse, on June 7, 1989, was unable to give me further information. Many details about Stein's sales and purchases remain unclear and require investigation.

15. For example, she received a telegram on 24 April 1931 from Edward F. Filene, the friend and patron of Lincoln Steffens, inviting her to a dinner in New York, along with the other "characters of [Steffens'] autobiography, just published." Stein must have wondered how characters stepped out of a book to go to a banquet in honor of a writer's life.

to send stories "not to the little and modern mags" but to the older ones—the large-circulation magazines with wide distribution.[16]

In the spring of 1931, Fernande Olivier, Picasso's impoverished mistress of early years, contacted Stein. She said friends, including Braque and Roché, had suggested that she ask Stein for a preface to help her launch her memoir of the years with Picasso in America. Before April 1931, extracts of her book had appeared in *Le Soir,* and from April on, *Le Mercure de France* published sections. Stein refused a preface but put Olivier in touch with Bradley, who confirmed that an American edition would make more money with a preface by an American. However, he apparently gave Olivier little active help and Stein gave her none. By June 1933, after the first installments of *The Autobiography Of Alice B. Toklas* had appeared in the *Atlantic Monthly,* Olivier asked Bradley to return her manuscript, claiming that he had neglected her and favored Stein, whose book was, she said, demonstrably inspired by her own.

Text

"Bibliography" (*transition* no. 15 [February 1929]: 47–55)

To suggest context at the beginning of this chapter, I have torn from the texts elements that can be read biographically. Though personal matters start as barely audible subtexts, by 1930–31 they rise more to the surface, finally making themselves heard in the texts, to which I now return. One of these, the "Bibliography" printed in *transition* no. 15, of February 1929,[17] was prepared by Stein, perhaps with help from academic friends Bernard Faÿ and Ralph Church. A bibliography, described by Susan Howe as "a search for origins on paper,"[18] is not literature, nor did Stein consider it so. Yet her presentation makes it a text reviewing her writing life.

A footnote to the "Bibliography" in *transition* explained,

> In response to numerous inquiries from *transition* readers concerning Miss Stein's work, she has kindly prepared for us this bibliography. (47)

The idea may have come from readers, but most likely it was from contributing editor Elliot Paul, who may also have helped assemble it. Stein's work from various periods had been printed in *transition* since its inception in 1927, but it was difficult to follow her progress and locate texts published earlier, often in ephemeral journals, or to trace references to what sometimes

16. Stein to Bowles, 8 September 1931, HRC.
17. Issue 15 did not appear until June or July 1929.
18. Edward Foster, "An Interview with Susan Howe," *Talisman* 4 (spring 1990): 32.

turned out to be unpublished work. New work did not swiftly appear in print since it was often rejected until a lucky accident, an editor-friend, or Stein's own financing made publication possible. As a result, information about publication and dates, given after the titles, means little and does not represent her development.

Dates of composition are included only in survey form. This listing of titles made perfect sense to Stein, who did not classify and categorize genres, but it is a nightmare for bibliographers, publishers, or librarians, who separate books from parts of books and classify by genre or subject matter.[19]

In addition, after *The Making Of Americans, Three Lives,* and *Tender Buttons,* she produced for years no book-length works; volumes such as *Geography And Plays* (1922), *Useful Knowledge* (1928), and *How To Write* (1931) were collections of miscellaneous pieces rather than single works. The bibliography lists all texts in the same bold-faced titles, from full-length novels like *The Making Of Americans* to short studies and portraits like "At" or "Mrs. Thursby." At fifty-five she must have been devastated to see in print the long list of unprinted titles, stunted "babies" that had not become books.

The bibliography is not a careful piece of work, even for an amateur. Recent writing, which Stein remembered, is listed in fairly accurate form and order; the bibliography ends with the most recent portrait, "Bernard Faÿ," of early 1929. But the early work appears with no more than approximate, summary dates, lumping together separate pieces, most not printed, without clear facts and order. Plainly she had not reviewed the early work with care.

With some effort, Stein could have supplied the crucial dates for her early work. Did she not realize what was needed for a clear listing? Was she too impatient by nature or too exasperated by the unpublished work to check the facts? At the very moment when she had the opportunity to display her achievement in a bibliography, she failed to produce the facts, as if denying her genius.[20]

19. The New York Public Library, at a loss about *Tender Buttons,* cataloged it as "eccentric literature" (Hubbell to Stein, 2 November 1932).

20. The bibliography became the basis for *A Catalogue of the Published and Unpublished Writings of Gertrude Stein,* also known as the Haas-Gallup Catalogue, extended in 1941 by Donald C. Gallup beyond the initial updating undertaken by Robert Bartlett Haas (1937) and by Julian Sawyer (1940; 1943). Stein's summary dates for early work were retained in the HG listing, pending the long research needed to document in correct order dates of beginning and completing texts that Stein and Toklas, who dated typescripts, failed to supply.

Groups, such as the thirty-five early portraits, were assigned individual numbers, and works whose dates were known were tentatively placed in order. The HG listing, then, is not simply identical with the *transition* "Bibliography." The most distressing inaccura-

Meanwhile, she yearned for publication and overcompensated for her frustration by allowing the vocabulary of fame and success to enter her writing as she had never done. In the play *At Present,* of early 1930, "Bibliography" appears as one of the many elements or characters making names for themselves that come and go in the play where Stein pokes fun at success, which is plainly on her mind, by playing with variants of the word.[21] The *transition* "Bibliography" must have left her in both despair and rage. I hear in the manner of the "Bibliography" subtexts far beyond what Stein herself perhaps suspected.

"Deux Soeurs Qui Ne Sont Pas Soeurs" (*O&P* 399–400)

She also tried new ways with words and new forms. In the spring of 1929, she produced her first work in French, the synopsis for a film scenario, "Deux Soeurs Qui Ne Sont Pas Soeurs."[22] Film was connected with Hugnet and his interest in cinema as the great American contribution to modernism.[23]

---

cies, which remained in it and still bedevil research, concern early work, mostly unpublished when she prepared her list.

The chronological list of works and especially of interlocked texts that is included in this book illustrates dramatically the need for a revised list and dates of all her works, which would make coherent reading possible. Dates and order of the selections included in *A Stein Reader* revise and correct her own and those in the HG listing, with HG numbers retained that are now no longer used at YCAL. Stein may not have realized how important accurate dating would become for readings such as this book offers.

Recataloging of the collection was completed in 1996. Titles are now listed alphabetically, and the catalog no longer follows the HG order, though its numbers remain on folders or manuscripts. Students still consult the key to the *Yale* (HG) *Catalogue* printed in appendix C of Bridgman, *Gertrude Stein in Pieces,* but must ascertain exact sequence and dates for beginning, completion, and overlap of compositions.

21. In *At Present* (*O&P* 322)

> A candle. They will say. They have been successful for a protestant named Ralph.
> Bibliography. They have been successful for a protestant named Jane.
> Churches. They have been successfully this in an effort.

Ralph Church, with a dissertation on the philosopher Malebranche, took his doctoral examinations on February 21, 1930, and Stein and Toklas lit candles at the church of St. Geneviève. Success here no doubt refers to him, to the power play of churches, whether Protestant or Catholic, to Malebranche, and to Stein's bibliography.

22. "Two Sisters Who Are Not Sisters." The scenario was written in Paris, in March or April 1929, before departure for the country. It was published in the *Revue Européenne* 5/6/7 for May/June/July 1930, preceded by Bernard Faÿ's "Portrait de Gertrude Stein."

23. *transition* no. 15, for February 1929, in which the "Bibliography" appeared, illustrates the interest in cinema. Eugene Jolas in his editorial speaks of the "liberation from histori-

His own film, *La Perle,* of the winter of 1929, was first screened on June 6. For her film text, Stein used in a kind of plot transparently personal details such as she had never used before—herself and Toklas, the new dog, the new Ford.

An untitled draft for the film text appears after notes for the end of "Sentences" (210–11) and before the notes on the "program which would bring results" in the *carnet* of the spring of 1929. In these notes she plays with likeness and liking, presumably in view of the country,

> Likes makes likes
> they will like what they do.

In an earlier section of "Sentences" appears a sentence which sounds like an English translation of the title of the film,

> If they look alike and are not sisters. (174)

Sisters are central also in the play *Parlor* of the spring of 1930, discussed later in this chapter.[24]

The film text develops three parallel scenes, each with a laundress, two women and their two-seater car, a beauty queen, a young man, a white poodle, and two props, a photograph of two poodles and some mysterious packages. In the first scene, a laundress inspects a photograph of two poodles, which the two women who arrive by car ask to see. The beauty gets into their car, weeps, and is thrown out as they leave. She tells a young man what has happened.[25] In the second, the women show the laundress

---

cism" and other matters made possible by the cinema. Essays by Jean Georges Auriol on "The French Cinema" and by Moholy-Nagy on the photographic process are also included.

24. This draft was revised before being transferred to the autograph manuscript pages, which also show revisions. The manuscript at Yale was further revised before typing. For the title, Stein first wrote "Film" but in the second manuscript used the last line of the text. The typescript of Toklas is identical with the printed texts except for a few corrected accents and her insertion of "ne" before "sont" to complete the French negative in the title; Stein's title elides the "ne," as is commonly done in spoken French.

25. Virgil Thomson suggested that the young man might be Georges Hugnet, but nothing in the text clearly connects with him. The beauty queen, according to Thomson, originated in an account in the Paris *Herald* of a beauty queen who got lost; I have not succeeded in locating such an account (interview with author, in the Chelsea Hotel, New York City, 1 July 1981). I now wonder whether Thomson, in recollection, remembered the beauty queen connected with *Ida,* 1937–40.

However, in a letter of the summer of 1929 to her cousin Rose Ellen Stein in Baltimore, Stein wrote of her delight at the photo of Alice Frank, Rose Ellen's daughter by her first marriage, who had visited Stein in Paris.

the photo; the beauty again gets into their car, weeps, and as they depart is thrown out, dropping a package on the ground but retaining the photo. In the third, the beauty with a package approaches the laundress carrying her bag of wash; the two women pass in the automobile with a real white poodle that has a package in its mouth. The sequence ends with no resolution.

The dog, the car, and the two women plainly derive from Basket, their Ford, and Stein and Toklas. In French, of course, Stein did not write by word play as she did in English, although half-rhymes like Basket, Basqu'ette, and *paquet* may be French word play. The French text therefore reads more like a synopsis of a situation with a kind of plot than a Stein text. As a scenario it is like a draft, a blueprint ready for development into a full script and then for translation into a film rather than into a literary text. Stein resists completing its incipient autobiographical plot and makes it into a surrealistic farce, the situation twice repeated and ending incomprehensibly.

The film text is filled with doubling, twinning, reflections, and mirrorings of all kinds. There are two women, in what mysterious relation, as blood sisters in a family or lovers by choice? There is a two-seater car, whether the old or the new Ford purchased in the winter of 1929;[26] a photo of two poodles; an actual poodle and a photo of poodles; two or three mysterious packets, never identified; laundresses; actual details, filmed or photographed ones; black and white in negatives, prints, snapshots, film, in the poodle, presumably white, and in the laundress, *blanchisseuse.* Stein had never used such doubling before.

It is astounding, then, to see the situation of this film suddenly returning ten years later in a new work. In *Ida A Novel,* written with trouble over more than three years, from 1937 to 1940, long after Stein had become a celebrity, she finally composed the odd elements of fantasy that had entered the film at the moment of her great efforts at publicity and fame. What in the film had remained incomprehensible became comprehensible once it was incor-

---

> I told you how delighted we all were with Alice's photo, it was just before we left and we were all full of films, I had just written a cute one in French for George Hugnet and he thought Alice would be so beautiful in it and she would [word] be beautiful in anything, do send me a snap of her as a madonna.

In January 1928, Alice had married Henry Hartman Hecht, and by the summer of 1929, she was pregnant. The film is also a product of the age of beauty contests and the rise of movie stars.

26. The old Ford had broken down in front of the Sénat building in Paris, near Stein's studio. Rather than disposing of it, Stein held a small ceremony with friends, and Georges Maratier removed it to the property of his parents; repairs were unsuccessful.

porated into *Ida,* where it properly belonged and could speak of what had happened to her with fame, publicity, and stardom.[27]

One shivers with hindsight to see the situation of the film as a dreamlike forecast of where Stein was going before she or anyone else was able to read that dream.

> There was an older man who happened to go in where they were voting. He did not know they were voting for the prize beauty but once there he voted too. And naturally he voted for her. Anybody would. And so she won. The only thing for her to do then was to go home which she did. She had to go the only way round otherwise they would have known where she lived of course she had to give an address and she did, and she went there and then she went back outside of the city where she was living.
>
> On the way, just at the end of the city, she saw a woman carrying a large bundle of wash. This woman stopped and she was looking at a photograph. Ida stopped too and it was astonishing, the woman was looking at the photograph, she had it in her hand, of Ida's dog Love. This was astonishing.
>
> Ida was so surprised she tried to snatch the photograph and just then an automobile came along, there were two women in it, and the automobile stopped and they stepped out to see what was happening. Ida snatched the photograph from the woman who was busy looking at the automobile and Ida jumped into the automobile and tried to start it, the two women jumped into the automobile threw Ida out and went on in the automobile with the photograph. Ida and the woman with the big bundle of wash were left there. The two of them stood and did not say a word.
>
> Ida went away. She was a beauty, she had won the beauty prize she was judged to be the most beautiful but she was bewildered and then she saw a package on the ground. One of the women in the automobile must have dropped it. Ida picked it up and then she went away.
>
> So then Ida did everything an elected beauty does but every now and then she was lost.
>
> One day she saw a man he looked as if he had just come off a farm and with him was a very little woman and behind him was an ordinary-sized woman. Ida wondered about them. One day she saw again the woman with a big bundle of wash. She was talking to a man, he was a young man.

27. The scenario identifies only a dog, ladies, a laundress, a beauty queen, a young man. In the novel the figures are fitted into a developing story and given somewhat abstract names, which add to its dreamy character: Ida, her dog Love, her twin Winnie. The elements of the film, unidentified in 1929, identify themselves later.

> Just then an automobile with two women came past and in the automobile was Ida's dog Love, Ida was sure it was Love, of course it was Love and in its mouth it had a package, the same package Ida had picked up. There it all was and the woman with the bundle of wash and the young man and Ida, they all stood and looked and they did not any one of them say anything. (21–22)

> And then she said Love later on they will call me a suicide blonde because my twin will have dyed her hair. And then they will call me a murderess because there will come the time when I will have killed my twin which I first made come. If you make her can you kill her. Tell me Love my dog tell me and tell her. (11)[28]

Returning to Stein's mind in 1939, the film text enters the section of *Ida* she is reworking that year. She wrote the earlier sections while also observing Thornton Wilder, himself a twin fascinated with winning status, during his visits to London, Paris, and Salzburg, and following his interest in the Duke and Duchess of Windsor, whom he was invited to join in Kärnten with Lady Sybil Colfax, an old acquaintance of Stein. The absorbed attention with fame from the writer she had in 1937 asked to collaborate on *Ida* made Stein doubly aware of its papery fragility.[29]

28. The film returned to Stein's mind for several reasons. One was that in May 1939 the singer Agnes Capri, planning a nightclub in Paris, asked her for a French text to be set to music. Stein first offered the two pieces in French that had been set to music already, the Stein-Thomson "Film" and the Hugnet-Thomson "Le Berceau de Gertrude Stein." In the end, however, she wrote a new piece for Capri, "a little operette" entitled "Les Superstitions," which she sent her by June 1939. Yet Capri's request probably made Stein review the film text.

    Films were in her mind also because *The World Is Round* was considered for a film by Sir Francis Rose. In addition, Basket I had died on November 25, 1938, and a new poodle, Basket II, purchased in Bordeaux, was brought to Paris on February 8, 1939. At the time of Basket I's death, a version of *Ida* was published in the *Boudoir Companion.* Finally, by February 18, she had a new Ford. Thus the events of 1939 almost replayed the ones of 1929 in the film text.

    These events are detailed in *LGS/CVV* 615–40, Stein to Van Vechten, 15 November 1938 to 21 September 1939. For a partial account of the interlocked compositions of *Ida,* May 1937 to June 1940, and *Doctor Faustus Lights The Lights,* February to October 1938 or January–February 1939, see Shirley Neuman, " 'Would a viper have stung her if she had only had one name?': Doctor Faustus Lights the Lights," in *Gertrude Stein and the Making of Literature,* ed. S. Neuman and I. Nadel (London: Macmillan Press, 1988), 168–93.
29. See Stein to Wilder, 17 May–22 October 1937, transcribed by Wilder; Wilder to Stein, 3 July–15 October 1937, in part written while he was working on *Our Town* in Rüschlikon near Zurich. See *LGS/TW* 144–90.

She did not simply transfer the film text to the novel. Rather, it rose in the course of living and writing, and she reshaped it in *Ida,* a very different thing from what Bridgman describes as "cannibalism" (*Gertrude Stein in Pieces* 306–7). It is as if the circumstances of 1938 and 1939 reflected the doubled, split, and mirrored images of 1929 back into her life and *Ida,* which had yielded to the opera *Doctor Faustus Lights The Lights* before it finally became the novel she wanted.

Here, in this novel, where she most fittingly belongs, is Ida, the elected beauty queen, a suicide blonde who has dyed her hair to become her own double and perhaps may kill her twin and become a murderess. Here is Ida—as Christina Light returned from James' *Roderick Hudson* to *The Princess Casamassima*—with her white poodle, Love, giving an address in the city but living outside.

Here is Ida seeing the photograph of her poodle in the hands of the laundress after the two women drive off in the automobile and Ida, publicity queen, winner of beauty contests, movie star, picking the parcel off the ground, going on but every now and then feeling lost.

Here is the dog with a package in its mouth, perhaps even recalling Toklas' description of a dog carrying a flower basket in his mouth. Here is Ida-Ida and Winnie-Winnie, her twin, whom everybody knows and nobody knows. Is it possible that in 1929–30, when Stein was preoccupied with publication that was to become publicity, the shutter of the camera for an instant opened to fame's splitting and doubling of two sisters and two books, and of the "I" that became Ida, Marguerite Ida, and Helena Annabel, surrounded by a halo of light on a mountain?

Parlor (*O&P* 325–29)

Sisters and doubling carry over from the film text of 1929 to the play *Parlor* of the following spring, written before departure for Bilignin.[30] Radcliffe friends Louise Earle, class of 1890, and Mabel Earle, class of 1896, of Lynn, Massachusetts, appear.[31] In an act unusual in her writing, Stein is remem-

30. It may be the plan to publish the film in the *Revue Européenne* that brought it to her mind the following year. Especially happy about her first appearance in French, Stein wrote to Bernard Faÿ, whose "Portrait de Gertrude Stein" preceded the film, that its publication had "given me more undiluted pleasure than since when I first saw myself in print . . ." (n.d. [summer 1930]). In the late wartime play *Three Sisters Who Are Not Sisters. A Melodrama* (1943), material from the film and *Ida A Novel* also returns.

31. As a student, Mabel was an important friend to Stein. She is in the early notebooks in the typology of personalities and in *The Making Of Americans* under the name Rena Barkholt. She knew Leon Solomons, the California friend with whom Stein did some of her research, Arthur Lachman, Leo Stein, and the Oppenheimers. A note in the journal of

bering early years and must now make a conscious effort to write the year beginning with 18, not the now habitual 19, for the century. Not surprisingly, two words in two languages release the memory into the present.

The word "parlor"[32] occurs also in Stein's portrait "Madame de Clermont-Tonnerre" of the late winter of 1930. Her salon joins in a pun on titled figures with the parlor of the Earles, deliberately misspelled "Earls" in the subtitle, *A Play between parlor of the sisters and parlor of the Earls.* The Duchesse de Clermont-Tonnerre,[33] friendly with Stein and Toklas, belonged to the

---

Etta Cone for 1901 records that the Earle sisters went to Europe and bought Japanese prints (Barbara Pollack, *The Collectors: Dr. Claribel and Miss Etta Cone* [Indianapolis: Bobbs-Merrill, 1962], 49).

Some biographical information about the sisters is in a 1934 letter to Stein from Doris M. Sweetland, their optometrist in Lynn, Massachusetts, where reference is also made to the "French sisters . . . of St. Ann" in what appears to be a convent, which might explain a parlor in a convent and Sister Peter in the play. Stein apparently answered Sweetland's letter, in part because it came from Lynn and reminded her of the Earles, whom she mentions in her answer.

Lynn, Massachusetts, is also associated with Mary Baker Eddy and Christian Science, which Stein encountered early. Sherry Mangan, formerly editor of *larus* and at this time coeditor of *Pagany,* also came from Lynn. Lynn is not only the name of a town but also a female or male first or last name, the kind of word toy Stein relished. It appears in the plays *Lynn And The College De France, Civilization* and in "History Or Messages From History" (131).

32. As indicated in the grammar chapter, phrases that appear first in "Sentences And Paragraphs" (35) and reappear in "Evidence," "How Are Fears" (140), "A Grammarian" (107), "Madame de Clermont-Tonnerre" (90), and two *carnets,* become the center of the play. From "A Grammarian" (107), Stein copied several lines into *Parlor* and others into *At Present.*

33. Of course, the duchess also recalls the invitation of the duchess in *Alice in Wonderland,* "Will you come into my parlor said the spider to the fly," where beguiling talk, common in salons, catches the fly in the spider's web. In *The Censored Mother Goose* (New York: Kendall Banning, 1929), which Stein owned, appear verses with spaces suggestively left blank, which, as Robert Carlton Brown said after borrowing Stein's copy, made them appear to conceal smut, "The king was in the—/ The queen was in the parlor, / The maid was in the garden . . .".

Alice in Wonderland was in Stein's mind when she wrote not only *Parlor* but also "Absolutely As Bob Brown" and perhaps "Evidence." In "Evidence" appears "Thank you for may matter" and suggestions of mad and meaningless evidence that recall Alice's mock trial. "They like to mean what they say," in the portrait of Bob Brown, recalls the inversion familiar from "The Mad Tea-Party," also central to grammar and sentences, "They like to say what they mean."

In *Parlor,* May's name leads to a word game of Alice and May that Stein often plays:

> We may a name which is May.
> The Earles were not named May Lidell. (326)

lesbian circle of Natalie Barney's Académie des Femmes. Past and present, duchesses and earls, sisters who are sisters, *soeurs qui ne sont pas soeurs,* salons and parlors rise as a play from the English noun "parlor," the French verb *parler* (to talk), and perhaps even the French noun *parleur* (talker); what looks like an odd English noun phrase, "Parlor with the sisters" (327), is a literal translation of the idiomatic French verb phrase *parler avec les soeurs* (to talk with the sisters).

Homophones but not homonyms, the French and English words start a parlor game that becomes a play between parlors, parleys, salons. Conversation is the art of women—blood sisters, lesbian sisters, and even Sister Peter, another figure in the play who may be a nun. The tableaux in sitting rooms lead to sittings for portraiture and conversation.

Close especially to Mabel, Stein visited the Earles in 1897 and perhaps at other times; they may have lived in one of the New England houses with flanking parlors. The lesbian sisters in Paris contrast with these blood sisters, who lived with their conventional parents in what sound like genteel but shabby circumstances. Unlike Toklas, Stein's wife, Mrs. Earle bears the family name conventionally "after his [Mr. Earle's] pleasure" (326).

Even in a play which taps deep personal memories, Stein explores the possibilities of language and theater rather than merely following her reminiscences. *Parlor* is written in descriptive sections, as if the very parlors had become characters but without assigned lines. Like the film, to which it is related, it has the quality of a scenario rather than a finished script. It is a lovely, transparent parlor game, which almost sings its parts in two voices, from sisters to sisters, parlor to parlor, here to there, "a place that means forward and back" (326) in conversation, in time (1897; 1930), in space (Lynn-Paris-Bilignin). More referential than many works of this time though never heavy with fact, *Parlor* remains delicate and playful, offering a director great freedom of interpretation.

Stein produces an almost traditional structure with two parallel locations, two equivalent periods, and two sets of words used with double meanings, blood sisters and lesbian sisters, and parlor and salon. At least in part the doubling is the result of having two houses and two salons. Clear and transparent in organization, *Parlor* is unlike most Stein plays. Together, the film and the play with their autobiographical subjects suggest that Stein is thinking about her own life as does the play immediately following.

May Liddell, a playmate of Stein in her youth in Oakland, is in the typology in the early notebooks. Only secondarily does the name refer to Lewis Carroll's Alice Liddell, further extending play between May and Alice.

At Present (O&P 315–24)

From *Parlor* and the past, Stein turns to "come back to the present" (322) and her contemporaries in Paris in the spring of 1930. *At Present* includes innumerable identifiable "characters" and many further names in the lines, stage directions, and descriptions that make up this very social, talkative play. All connect with Stein, with name-dropping and making a name for oneself. The word *contemporaries* is used in several senses. Many are names of what Stein sometimes called "la petite bande" or "la [seconde] famille" of young artist friends in Paris at the time, including Hugnet, Thomson, Imbs, Tonny, Bérard, de Hauleville, Cingria, and the Berman brothers.

Others, such as Sherwood Anderson, who had written the foreword to *Geography And Plays,* or Ellen DuPoy and Harry Horwood, are her own contemporaries. The play is one of the few texts that includes dead contemporaries who remained live presences connected with Stein or her work—Avery Hopwood, in her plays of 1923, whose great success she hoped to emulate, dead of a heart attack while swimming on the Riviera in July 1928; William Erving, the husband of her medical school friend Emma Lootz Erving, dead of tuberculosis in 1923; Grace-Ives de Longevialle, translator with Bernard Faÿ of "Melanctha," dead in an auto accident in March 1930; even Laura Riding, publisher of *An Acquaintance With Description,* unsuccessful suicide on April 27, 1929. All are connected with her through friendship or writing and publication.

Names, words, phrases, stage directions, spoken lines, descriptive fragments, bits of talk move about in language figures as in a ballet, a dance, or exchanges in a salon. Some "fasten it namely," joining names as business associates, "Le Corbusier and Jeanneret and Maurice Darantiere" (321). But others are in shifting, unstable relations. Some pair off in weddings. Many sons are attached to their mothers. The play is a maze of names—common nouns and proper names—phrases, sentences. Though words and phrases come out of Stein's relations with contemporaries, it is not about her or her work.[34]

Trying to understand what is being said is frustrating. The many names with their firm power of reference contrast sharply with the lines, whose language is entirely unstable. The odd words, phrases, and locutions keep shifting and converting into configurations of different words with almost identical sounds, which function as puns. They are lines of speakers unsure of how to pronounce them, written phonetically in spellings that may not

34. To identify names and pinpoint references would lead readers away from the speaking games in this play. What makes it difficult is the prominence of references that turn out not to be what it is about.

reflect the speaker's intention. For example, George Hugnet's opening lines waver,

> It is felt wish which are they they might be wonderfully and a wish might mean. A woman is wire or more. (315)

Here are English words misspoken by a Frenchman. The punning phrases unravel into any number of possible readings. The key to this unstable language lies in the many foreigners: a Dutchman, a Pole, an Irishman, a Russian, an American, a Belgian, and others.[35] With varying speech and accents, they mispronounce an English that for many is a second language.

What is said moves not in words as signs but in words as singing—carrying speech sound and spelling problems, such as the phonetic spelling Juando, which looks Spanish, for Jouhandeau. The play is built out of Stein's experience with translation, the speech of foreign artists, and even her own early experience as an English speaker in a foreign city. Hilariously funny, immensely confusing, it becomes a punning contest across languages.

It creates shifting verbal figures in a present that does away with time and a place that is indefinable. What is the meaning of

> To come back to the present. (322)

And is this sentence spoken or quoted or is it a stage direction:

> Pablo Picasso mentions that he came. (317)

What is being said here:

> Singria wakes them up as they go away. He is left a little. (317)

And is this line said about or by Pablo Picasso in the play, in his life, on his balding head, in a photograph, in a painting:

> Has his hair made his hair has his hair on his head has his hair. So they or there. (316)

Or is it not about hair but about *her,* a woman?

Years earlier, in the Mallorcan plays of 1916–17, Stein had crisscrossed international voices to make audible the chitchat of foreigners in Mallorca in World War I. In *At Present,* however, she works with the strange music of bits of language itself rather than with disconnected elements of discursive speech. More and more, she investigates single words in abstract constructive forms, the rudimentary elements of language. To dismiss this frustrat-

35. The portrait of Bob Brown includes vignettes of the same sorts of foreigners that are also in the portraits in "Evidence."

ing, difficult play as nonsense just because it creates apparent nonsense is to disregard what Stein was doing.

"We Came. A History." (*RAB* 148–52)

While *At Present* follows publicity-conscious name-dropping, the film as well as questions about movies and movement also remained in Stein's mind and carried over to new work. Robert Carlton Brown first visited her in 1929, and in the fall of that year she did a portrait of him. On September 23, 1930, he asked her for a contribution to his planned second anthology of *Readies for Bob Brown's Machine.* With work by many avant-garde writers,[36] it was to accompany his reading machine.[37]

Brown modeled his "readies" on "talkies," new in the movies. Offering his plan in bragging language, part serious, part spoof, he described books as old-fashioned, rigid objects in need of modernizing so that reading might become a continuous linear spectacle of texts passing before the eye without being cut up into lines, paragraphs, columns, pages. He hoped for what Roger Babson, a popular writer of visionary schemes for business success and forecasting in the 1920s, had advocated as a talking book.[38]

Brown proposed to transfer texts onto tiny rolls of visual tape for insertion into a cheap, portable reading machine, whose speed, magnification, fonts, and rewinding could be controlled by the reader. In an age of microcassette tapes, videotapes, computers, word processors, desktop publishing, CD-ROM discs, Windows, and Internet, his project sounds entirely familiar.

Brown claimed that text running in front of the eye would revolutionize language, lead to new efficiency and a kind of speed-reading which would make unimportant words like conjunctions and prepositions unnecessary and require only important ones to be printed. To create speed and prevent spaces from interrupting print, he ran one word into the next by means of hyphens so that a piece looked like an endless moving compound. He objected to the short story formula he called C2P for "Character

36. The anthology, published by Roving Eye Press, Cagnes-sur-Mer, 1931, included work by Charles Henri Ford, Alfred Kreymborg, Robert McAlmon, Ezra Pound, William Carlos Williams, Eugene Jolas, Walter Lowenfels, Kay Boyle, and others.
37. See Bob Brown, "The Readies," *transition* no. 19–20 (June 1930): 167–73.
38. See Roger Babson, "Twenty Ways to Make a Million," *Forum,* May 1929. Many others at this time were working on simplification of language, experiments in the psychology and pedagogy of reading, and the graphic revolution, for example, Ogden and Richards' work on Basic English, Marinetti's attack on the "Typographical Revolution," Wyndham Lewis.

2 Plot 1," advocating in its stead an optical form of writing that made words move.[39]

Stein's "readie," "We Came. A History." is in two parts that together fill one *cahier.* Already thinking about history and movement when she was asked for this contribution, Stein described it to Brown as "a study in movement." The first part, in regular paragraphs, may have been written or begun before she received his request; "an introduction to residing," it must have been composed upon arrival in the country in the spring of 1930, while catching up on local gossip and events of the winter.

The introduction to residing, here and now, is history become personal. From paragraph 5 on, she combines telling what has happened as a way of putting herself "there," in the present and the locality, with attempts to define history.

> History is this anything that they say and that they do and that is made for them by them such as not speaking to them in case that he is turned away from them. (148)

On the same page, she also says,

> Sentences are historical. (148)

Further definitions appear in "History Or Messages From History" of the same summer, which also carries over to the *Three Historic Dramas.*

The second part appears to be the "readie" proper, although Brown published both parts as she obviously sent them to him. The second is written in short lines the length of the lines in her *cahier.* In other words, she took on the challenge of the format of the *cahier* to solve the problem of movement and speed within its constraints. The result is a piece of short, fast lines that carry across line breaks by ending phrases and sentences in the middle of lines rather than at the end.

She had already worked with similar short lines in the small poems of "Forget-Me-Not" of 1929, also arranged in sections. The second part of her "readie" also consisted of twenty-one numbered sections of irregular length. She was thinking and hearing in lines and composing word ideas in new forms. It ends quite suddenly, as if impatiently, at the end of the *cahier.* Per-

39. In *Readies for Bob Brown's Machine,* Brown illustrated "Moving Reading" with Stephen Crane's *Black Riders and Other Lines* (1895), which he said suggested "black printed words . . . galloping across white pages, astride inky chargers" (153). It is not known whether Stein read the Crane poems. In "Grant Or Rutherford B. Hayes" of 1931, however, with its charging equestrian rhythms about an election campaign, she creates the kind of movement Brown had in mind.

haps she had tired of an exercise whose problems she had solved and let the end of the notebook end the piece. The daily life, the climate, the seasons, the setting of the house, the garden, the dog, are the material for all the questions about history, though

> History must not be about
> Dogs and balls in all (148)

Flowers punctuate the piece:

> There are three things
> That are historical.
> Tube roses heliotrope and lavender.
> There may be fragrant lilies
> And other delights but
> History is made and
> Preserved by heliotrope
> Lavender and tube-roses. (149)

Bob Brown did not print it as poetry but insisted on creating linear continuity by hyphens. The text reprinted in *Reflections On The Atomic Bomb* avoided the confusion of hyphens by relying on equal signs (=) but offered no explanation of Brown's ideas or Stein's attempt to speed the reader along, which neither printing represents.

"To Kitty Or Kate Buss" (*P&P* 103–4)

Kate Buss is the subject of this portrait. Journalist, poet, painter, sculptor, collector of books, bookplates, and stamps, she first sought Stein out in Paris in 1921, returned often, and saw Stein every time she was abroad, appearing briefly in virtually every piece Stein wrote when she visited, though only this portrait was devoted exclusively to her. Buss made the contact with her own publisher, the Four Seas Company in Boston, which in late 1922 published *Geography And Plays* at Stein's expense. Buss prepared the publicity for the book, wrote blurbs and captions, and published numerous reviews of Stein's work in the early 1920s but apparently never completed a book about her on which she worked for years.[40]

40. Lesbian and feminist, Buss published an early volume of poems, *Jevons Block: A Book of Sex Enmity* (Boston: McGrath-Sherrill Press, 1917). A sharp indictment of patriarchal society, it was reprinted in part by the Four Seas Company, which also printed her *Studies in the Chinese Drama* (1922).

She knew American lesbian friends of Stein in Paris whom she saw when they came to New York. By the mid-1930s, Buss no longer regularly went to Paris but lived in Medford with her aging mother. She made a will dated June 23, 1943, and died, apparently a sui-

Stein never forgot the help Buss gave her. In 1922, Buss even planned a Stein biography, with help from Toklas, and in 1925–26 a bibliography. "All important authors are bibliographed in the U. S. at present," she wrote in an undated letter. Neither of these projects was completed, and no notes survive. Stein's introductions to artists such as Juan Gris, Man Ray, and Jo Davidson enabled Buss to write about them.

Familiar with Freud's ideas and terms, Buss wrote to Stein in an undated letter that the sources of her work were in the subconscious or the "undermind, which is what writes in you." Stein disagreed,

> Yes but Kitty don't you see there is no demarcation between my conscious and my unconscious self as I am my conscious self in other words there aint no such animal.

Buss questioned how Stein could know there was no demarcation between her thinking and unthinking mind.

In the spring of 1931 Buss arranged an exhibit of Stein books and papers with the Dunster Street Bookshop in Cambridge. She induced John Dewey to visit the exhibit and encouraged Stein to send him *Lucy Church Amiably,* which Stein inscribed and Dewey acknowledged. Curious about Dewey's view of the sources of Stein's work, Buss lent him some of her letters. A typed copy of his response to Buss is among the Stein papers. He observes that as new ideas arise in the mind, they cannot be considered real until they become conscious and accessible to control. Trying to follow the thinking of Stein as a writer who valued consciousness, Dewey understood that this exchange about the mind concerned writing, not personality.[41]

In this portrait, Stein deconstructed and reconstructed her friend's name. With her signature, it became a letter[42] in answer to a request of Buss in May 1930, when she described her plans for her book about Stein and added,

> Of myself—on the frontice [*sic*] page I long for a word portrait! Do you guess? Have you such a thing—or are you likely to have during the summer. A portrait of Kate Buss by Gertrude Stein would seem to say, and be such a proud delight to me, that you too, like me. Not I, you. A sort

---

cide, on July 2, 1943. I have been unable to discover further details. Some but apparently not all of Stein's letters to her are at YCAL. Buss has not been carefully investigated.

41. Dewey's letter of thanks to Stein is reprinted in *The Flowers of Friendship,* 254. On the subconscious, see also "Cultivated Motor Automatism," *Psychological Review* 5, no. 3 (May 1898), and Mellow, *Charmed Circle,* 32–34.

42. Like the portraits of Lipchitz and Cocteau, this text is printed without signature in *P&P,* apparently the result of editorial incomprehension of its letter form. Another letter portrait, "To Pierre de Massot," written a little later, in June, is not signed.

of brilliant balance between my name on the cover and your name so constantly inside the covers.

The portrait, Stein's response to her friend's wish to join author to subject, name to name, becomes a rhyming, rhythmic offering in the form of a May basket, which the month dates, as do the jasmine, the lilies of the valley, or mayflowers, *muguets, M* words with which Stein so often plays in writing.

> Do you see how I introduce dates. Dates a flower dates a fruit. She is made to have it mean Jasmine a muguet.
>
> Excuse me for introducing French it is not my custom but it seemed a choice thanks so much. (104)

> It is in ingredients that mays are a measure (103)

she says about the month and the portrait whose verbal colors and rhythms spell the seasonal and metrical measure of the piece. What looks like a casually tossed off note turns out to be carefully wrought, with a lightness about the double meanings of Kitty and Buss that underplays the importance of Kate Buss.

Stein played with the entire name,[43] whose sharp, short syllables ask for play, as does the odd, almost punning middle name, Meldram, alliterating with her hometown, Medford, Massachusetts,[44] and finally with the last name, Buss, as a buss, a kiss. Some letters end with a "Kittybuss." Like the portrait "Grace-Ives de Longevialle" in the same *cahier,* the portrait of Buss includes erotic overtones,

> They were by themselves in a minute.
> A minute is a long time in which to say yes. (103)

43. Even in dedicating books, Stein played with her name, for example, in *Three Lives,* "To Kate Buss, / Kitty is and Kitty was / Kitty did and Kitty does / alright . . ." (from L. W. Currey for Gordon Cairns, late owner of the Grolier Bookshop, Cambridge, Massachusetts).

    The *K* section on birthdays, about Kate Buss, in "To Do: A Book Of Alphabets And Birthdays" includes apparent references to the fact that Buss had been on the *Titanic* in 1912.

44. When Buss arrived in Paris, Stein was already friends with another American from Medford, Elmer Stetson Harden, whom Buss knew and who is often coupled with her in letters and texts. Harden had fought in World War I, nursed an injured French officer, a Captain Pierre, and after the war remained in France as his companion.

Short Poems: "Abel" (*SIM* 222–30), "A French Rooster. A History" (*SIM* 213–22), "Narrative" (*SIM* 250–53), and "A Ballad" (*SIM* 256–67)

As in preceding summers, Stein in 1930 and 1931 writes many short texts. Many are prose, but more and more become poetry, and even comments on poetics. Gradually she moves toward longer poems. First she absorbs the country and hones her skills in recording perceptions and thinking out writing problems. These often include small new biographical and local details. Part III of "Abel," for example, starts in garden and kitchen, becomes a composition of "green" vegetables, and leads to hypnagogic vision that always interests her. Part XXVII asks,

> What does she see
> When she closes her eyes
> green peas

This question returns much later, in 1936, as title for "What Does She See When She Shuts Her Eyes." Many poems are rhymes about or to the dog, some downright sentimental, as when

> Be here all three
> Together there where they
> Are In a minute
> They will be sleeping
> He on a chair
> She there he there
> Sleeping all three there . . .
> ("A French Rooster," XVI, 216)

Always she thinks of writing,

> Part of poetry
> A part of poetry
> Part from poetry
> Partly with poetry
> ("Abel," Part XV)

> What is poetry, history is poetry when you get used to the french
> ("A French Rooster," XXVI)

Some of these short, journal-like entries, often numbered to mark them as separate rather than continuous, speak of people in the community. What she observes among them is not always pretty.

He had a bandage on his head.
He had fallen out of the automobile he said.
His father had not noticed that he fell
But his cousin was there as well
And he noticed when he fell and told his father he had fallen.
His mother did not like it as she was still in mourning.
For her little girl who had died of fever.
This is a story of a very sweet mother and a very nice father and a very successful and happy family.

("Abel," Part IV, 125)[45]

She comments on private life whose stability is crucial precisely as parameters change in the country, where it takes new forms. Again and again she likens the meticulous patterns of Toklas' embroidery to her own orderly writing, even as she ridicules it as mechanical. The second part of the little summer idyll "Narrative" offers ironic praise to Toklas, whose talents as a manager make her the leader, more prominent and visible in the country than in Paris.

She made him see that it was fortunately she that was he. And it is not curious. Everything that is not this is nothing because it is show. How is it shown. It is shown in reality.

In not being reserved, reserved has it. It is mentioned here. When it is not with her he can make no verses and this is why because she is hallowed even. (252)

The end returns to genres, which never cease to interest her.

A narrative is this. A play is another thing, a play is lively, a narrative is not lively in love, a tragedy is when it might has [*sic*] been something. How do I know what a narrative is I know a narrative is one when it is a property. A property is not on the stage it is here when it is on the stage it is an adjunct.

She plays with the house, the property that transforms everything, including her work with words. Plays are now the center of interest even as this poem ends with "a preparation for their narrative,"

45. "Abel" is one of the few unfinished pieces. In the same *cahier* as "A French Rooster. A History," it shows similar organization, in numbered parts and sections, sometimes inconsistent in arrangement. In the *cahier,* after the last section of text, XXXI, appears the next number, XXXII, with open space but no text.

Why do we go to bed later.
In arranging tapestry.
What is the reason.
That we have had hats.
Because it is better so.
It is a preparation for their narrative.
She will be sleeping.
Very carefully.
This is a pleasure. In reality.
I like it.
("Narrative," Part IV, 253)

By the fall of 1931 follows her first long poem, the pastoral "A Ballad," including notes about poetics. A reference to the eclipse of September 21 made it possible to date the poem. It is written in the heavily punctuated lines creating new forms of movement with syncopations that follow her work for Bob Brown's "readies" and mark a watershed in her writing. She is expanding her view of genre and writing what looks like prose but is actually poetry, also carrying over into plays. The many periods slow us down, change the rhythms, and slip multiple meanings into our reading.

What is a hope. Rain. With wine.
What is a hope. A hope. In time.
What is a hope. A wish. That it. Will rain. In time.
What is a hope. A spring. What is a hope
They will go to hope.
They will go. To hope.
It is a pleasure. To awake her.
Or. Perhaps. Not yet.
(256)

These syncopated lines cannot be read fast and demand attention to every word; we almost write such lines as we read them. She is gradually moving into extended works of poetry, including the meditation "Winning His Way."

She is also writing plays. More and more she is preoccupied with rhythm and movement, with simultaneous seeing and hearing, and with the generating of emotion that had come out of her study of sentences and paragraphs. So much of Stein's writing sounds like conversation, it is hardly surprising that in these years she used it for both poetry and plays. Country life, surely a landscape with moving figures whose exchanges kept the days active, new, and embedded in local surroundings, must have contributed to the plays, many written during those summers; Paris life, more formal, had less range of conversation and setting.

In "Politeness," of late 1930, she says she suddenly wrote

> [a] play every other day. (*PL* 144)

Between 1930 and 1932, that made a total of twenty-one in less than three years. Of these, five full-length and two sets of three very short plays each were done in 1930, five more full-length in 1931, and five, including two portrait plays, in 1932. Except for the two sets of short plays and the seven from 1932, all were published in *Operas And Plays* (1932), the fourth volume in the Plain Edition. After 1932, it was four years before Stein in 1936 returned to plays with *Listen To Me* and *A Play Called Not And Now.*[46]

The first two, *Parlor* and *At Present,* had been written in the early spring of 1930 in Paris, but most of the others were written in the country, where new forms of social life and local history opened new subjects and new experiments. In reading these and other works in order of composition, one gradually hears again and again certain words, phrases, names that mark preoccupations in Stein's mind.

It is easy to say today that few have been performed or studied in detail. But what was it for Stein to live with the fact that, except for the opera *Four Saints In Three Acts,* only a handful of her many plays were produced during her lifetime? Had she not herself included them in *Geography And Plays* and in the Plain Edition *Operas And Plays* printed all twenty and the two film texts, the list of those not published and not performed would have read like the ledger in her early record of work submitted and marked "returned," "returned." I do not have the impression that she sent out individual plays in the hope of productions or publications.

But publication was a necessity and a condition for performance.[47] Only

46. I omit from this count the marionette play *Identity,* not begun as a play but made into a play out of elements culled from *The Geographical History Of America* (1935); it was, of course, performed and reviewed.

47. For years *Geography And Plays* and *Operas And Plays* remained out of print and for practical purposes unavailable. Even her own editions, however, done under her supervision, included serious printing errors and problems with the printed representation of her play forms. With *Operas And Plays* again available in the important reprint of 1987 by Station Hill Press, and *Geography And Plays* in the 1993 University Press of Wisconsin reprint, edited by Cyrena N. Pondrom, the texts can at last be studied and, I hope, performed.

    However, photo-offset editions reproduce the errors of the originals and remind us that a complete, accurate edition of Stein's entire work in chronological order is a necessity for reliable reading. Books reprinted out of piety and devotion in the original form

reading aloud, performance, discussion, and study will open them as dramatic works. What does it mean to say that they are difficult when they have hardly been studied? What are the difficulties, and what do they tell us about the work? My insistent questions are to draw attention to them. I offer here only preliminary comments on their texts and contexts and her explorations of their possibilities.

One difficulty is that they are packed full of names. Yet names that can be identified rarely open discernible logic, while those that cannot be identified retain the teasing power of unknown reference. Names and even other details also spill over from play to play. Stein might say that identifying references distracts from them as drama. Indeed, even with a surfeit of proper names, abstract, composed form dominates in a syntax without concrete details and pronouns without antecedents. These texts push us toward the referential as they pull us away from it, leaving us on the edge of a world that both opens and closes the texts.

Say It With Flowers. A Play. (O&P 331–43)

I start with an example, impossible to confine to a single work, to illustrate the difficulties of entering these plays and underscore Stein's constant experimentation with the genre. Written probably in Paris at Christmastime 1930–31, it begins conventionally with the unities, identifying time, place, and action. It is the time of Louis XI, the place is Gisors, and the action "in a cake shop on the sea shore"; recalling Louis XI recalls *Louis XI And Madame Giraud*, written a few weeks earlier, which names the fifteenth-century king together with a near neighbor in the country.[48] Gisors, some forty miles northwest of Paris and not on the water, audibly crosses in a pun with the seashore.

But Gisors in a Stein play of 1930 inevitably recalls Picasso's purchase there, that year, of the Château de Boisgeloup. The play does not appear to be about him, though some lines by or about the king might be read as comments on Picasso:

> Louis the eleventh is a king.
> And he looks at anything. (341)

---

are no help to understanding her. References to plays that are in *A Stein Reader,* checked for reliability, are here keyed to the *Reader.*

48. Stein to Henry McBride, 25 October 1930; Stein to Carl Van Vechten, 29 January 1931; in these letters, Stein announced that she was writing "historical plays." Titles like *Louis XI And Madame Giraud* and studies like "We Came. A History" show how history for Stein is about a way of writing, not about figures or situations of the past.

The name Gisors may simply have been in her mind because of Picasso and peeled off in a punning game on the seashore.

The people are an odd lot of confusing, semiandrogynous names—George Henry, Henry Henry, Elizabeth Henry, with subsidiary characters Elizabeth Long and William Long. "Subsidiary characters," with their organized tone, are also in *Madame Recamier* and *Play I–III* of early fall 1930. Whether the two groups named Henry and Long include married couples, siblings, parents and children, or lovers is not clear.

Nor does the familiar title phrase help. It is inked in on the cover of the *cahier* below an illustration identified as "L'alouette," depicting an odd, awkward lark in a meadow of flowers, but this title is a revision, written over an earlier one that also describes the illustration, "The [cruel gray] Birds with the Flowers. A Play." Both versions derive from the picture, but how do they relate to the play? Perhaps the florist's phrase is about gifts of violets and hyacinths for Christmas (333). With all their referential teasing, these identifications do not open the play.

What happens? The Henrys and Longs are "busy waiting" (332). "Waiting," with no object, is the key word. We expect a play to be about an action, but here action seems to be about inaction, ways of waiting—being silent or asleep, planning or thinking about planning, being likely to go away, recurring again and again. Sentences filled with careful, polite, inactive phrasings, often composing elements of time, also seem to be waiting, as in

> They will be able to have it a hope that it will not rain. (333)

or

> It is very likely that they make it matter. To them. That they are likely to go away. Farther. Than they went before. Because they like it as we have very well heard. Which they mean by what they say. (333)

If this is a Christmas play, its action may be a matter of expectation, waiting for gifts, waiting for Christmas, even waiting for the king.[49]

While *Say It With Flowers* experiments with verbal action about waiting or inaction, elsewhere Stein picks up equally surprising elements to build other plays. For example, instead of identifying location merely as the place for an action, the action of the *Three Historic Dramas*[50] (1930) is about loca-

49. *Say It With Flowers* has been ably set to music as a chamber opera, "an opera in waiting," by Jeffrey Lependorf and premiered by the Hell's Kitchen Opera Company, New York, in March 1996.

50. *An Historic Drama In Memory of Winnie Elliot, Will He Come Back Better. Second Historic Drama. In The Country.* and *[He / She] Finds Me. Third Historic Drama,* 1930, all in *LO&P* (182–99).

tion, perhaps suggesting the unities, moving in the first from "In the House" to "The door-way of a building" to "A building which is not finished" to "After they left"; in the second from "In the country," to "For the country," "By way of the country," and so on. The third place is internal—the state of mind we call danger, with wonderful prepositional phrases playing on the location of danger, "Near danger," "Away from danger," "Out of danger," "In danger." The geography of danger can be the subject of a play.

Returning to the seashore, there is not only Louis XI but a ship named *Louis XI,* which is also in *Louis XI And Madame Giraud.* Again, *Say It With Flowers* refers to *Louis XI* as a tragedy, although *Louis XI And Madame Giraud* is not called a tragedy.[51] How, for that matter, does Madame Marthe Giraud come into the play? A cultivated woman who spent summers in Ceyzérieu near Belley and winters in Paris or Cannes, she was described by Toklas as "one of those fabulous raconteuses" whose stories held Stein "entranced."[52] Questions about these plays, which sometimes go over one into the next, are unending.

I have already spoken of how Stein at this time explores single words and names—disassembled, reassembled, divided, crisscrossed. First names confer simple, present identity. Last names confer family identity, extending through time into history. Some of the plays combine names of great historical figures with those of Stein's artist friends in Paris and of people in the Bugey. Readers may recognize the first group and many of the second but not the third, leaving them unsure whether the names are words or people.

Unlike the first names in the pastoral landscape of *Lucy Church Amiably,* most plays of this time are replete with first and last names with referential weight and teasing questions of identity that occur also in other works, for example, "Brim Beauvais," "Grant Or Rutherford B. Hayes," "Winning His

51. However, there was a tragedy entitled *Louis XI* (1832) by Casimir Delavigne (1793–1843), revived in Paris in 1929. Finally, do Scott's *Quentin Durward* or C. Wyndham Lewis' *The Spider King,* published in 1929, connect with *Say It With Flowers?* Stein might have seen the popular *Louis XI* in her youth in San Francisco; she speaks in the lecture "Plays" (*LIA* 114–15) of early exposure to French historical plays with many characters. In her Louis XI play also appears the phrase she coined when very young for a historic play of her own, "The courtiers make witty remarks." It returns in the *Autobiography* (23), and Leo Stein comments on it in *Journey into the Self,* ed. Edmund Fuller (New York: Crown, 1950), 134.

52. Toklas to Carl Van Vechten, 18 October 1948. In the same letter Toklas says that it was Madame Giraud who discovered the Louis XI cap that Stein wore with special pleasure. Several photographs and the 1938 bronze "portrait sketch" by Lipchitz at Rice University, Houston, Texas, show Stein in this small, closely fitted cap.

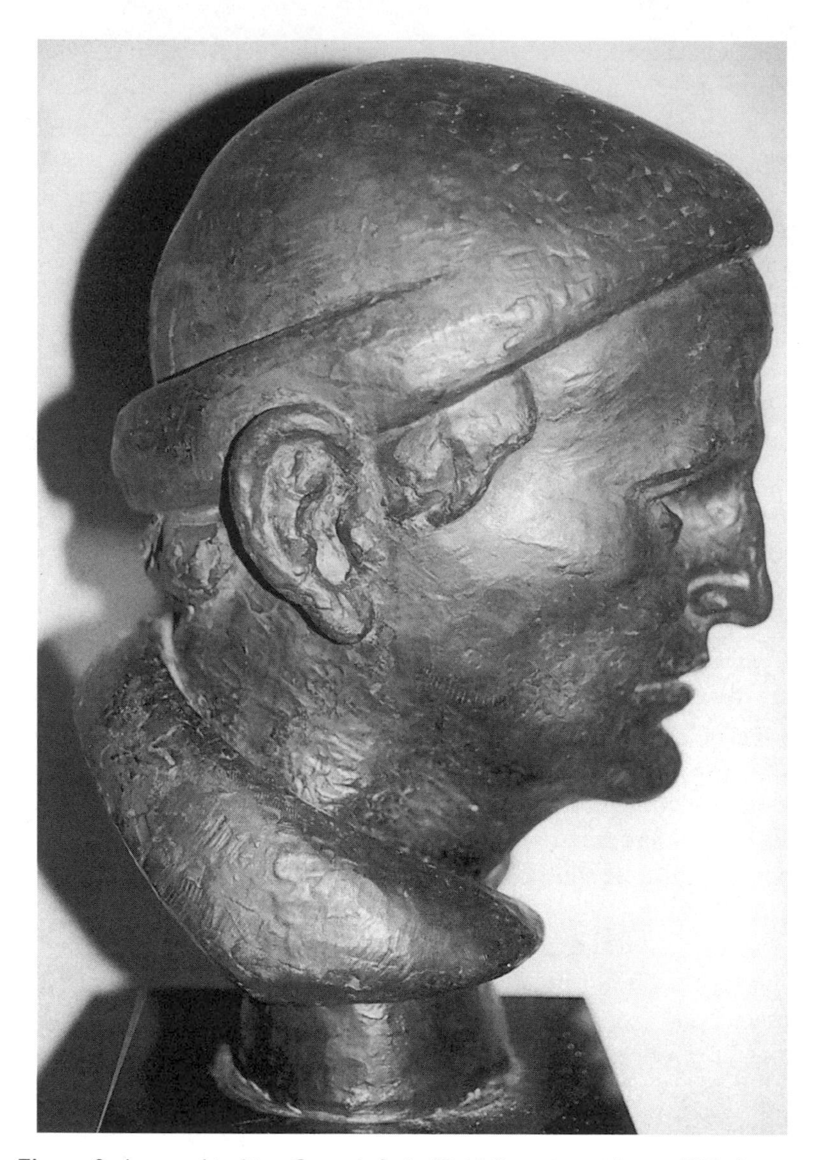

Figure 9. Jacques Lipchitz, *Gertrude Stein,* "Rabbi" version with cap, 1938. Bronze, 20 1/2 in. × 11 1/4 in. × 13 1/2 in. Rice University, Houston, Texas. Courtesy Marlborough Gallery, New York.

Way," "Scenery And George Washington," "Marguerite Or A Simple Novel Of High Life," "Margite Marguerite And Margherita."

Questions of identity arose in new ways among the new names and lives unrolling before her in the country. She wondered how Toklas and she were perceived by the local people among whom they had settled. Farmers returning home at night after a day of work in the fields might wonder what they did.

> . . . They stay. At home.
> Even. In the. Day-light. Later.
> And this. Is not. Because. Of anything lacking.
> Oh no. It is. Because. There are. Some occupations.
> Which. Demand. That. They should. B.
> Staying. In the house. Where. They. Are. Living.
> ("Winning His Way" 184)

All of the *Three Historic Dramas* (*LO&P* 182–99) of the late summer of 1930, more and more abstract and reductive, with unidentified pronouns ("him," "it," "they"), rely on the same "characters": *A* people—Ashley, Amelia—*H* people—Harry, Humphrey—and a "Nuña," who appears to mark time and, in the first play, *An Historic Drama In Memory Of Winnie Elliot,* has the last word. One sentence she speaks, "No she says no to me" (186), also appears on the cover of the manuscript *cahier* next to the title. Stein takes plays apart into characters; shifting, unsteady locations; concerns barely identified—we know only that they have something to do with money, children, problems.

The three plays also work systematically with stage directions, as if the stage directions were to direct the plays. Locations move throughout. The first changes from "the door-way of a building" to a "place where none of them have been" in a city, to a "room," a "house," and so on. The second, *Will He Come Back Better. Second Historic Drama. In The Country.,* develops locations in, near, back of "the country." And the third, with growing uneasiness, locates the "action" usually in the middle of things, uneasily—"On the way back," "Having gone back," and, perhaps stimulated by the lion hunt on the *cahier* cover, "Near danger," "In danger," "Out of danger," "More danger."

They Weighed Weighed-Layed A Drama Of Aphorisms (O&P 231–48)

Here is a play that dismantles both proper names and common nouns by sound, sight, and sense. The title's odd compound "way-lay" and its regularized-irregular past "weighed-layed" plays with sound, rhythm, pun, all forms of auditory or voice work that Stein also calls singing. She is becoming more and more skilled at lines and movement across line breaks.

She cuts up names into numbered, segmented parts.

> Maurice III
> It is a likelihood of their being very much alike. (242)

There is Maurice I, Maurice II, Maurice III, IV, and so on, like sections in a laboratory, recalling her early typology. She systematically pairs the numbered name segments—Marcel I and Maurice IV—or groups them,

> They come together.
> And they sing.
> All the women are included in the song. (234)

Everything develops in methodical numbered arrangements, a procedure that appears odd only if we forget her insistence on order in words choreographed into moving visual patterns as transparent as woven baskets. The only woman, segmented like the men, is Marguerite. Finally, after the many first names one might meet anywhere, appears, once only, a full Anglo-Saxon name,

> Bertie Applegarth
> He is or was a help to them in arithmetic. (235)

Most lines, narrative or descriptive, sound like stage directions. In "The Pilgrims. Thoughts About Master-Pieces," perhaps thinking of this play, Stein declares that everyone who wants to be somebody needs a name to say over and over.

> Every one prefers a name. Maurice could be mentioned twice. Elizabeth once, Paul fourteen times, the Eugenes all the same that has been said and so it is a repetition even if it does not sound like it or the same. (*PL* 146)

The names appear in numbered segments, recalling fashions in names with Eugenes, Leons, Marcels—Stein knew more than one of all of these.

The Five Georges (O&P 291–314)

The same page of "The Pilgrims" may also anticipate *The Five Georges,* "There are two Georges and one Eric." What fun it must have been to think of all the Georges she knew personally and the many from history, including Washington, about whom she wrote in 1931 and 1934.[53] Many are already in "Finally George" of 1927. Stein thought people became their names, and so

53. "Scenery And George Washington, A Novel Or A Play" was written in the fall of 1931 and used in 1934 as the opening of the George Washington section of *FIA.* Faÿ's biography of Washington also entered her thinking.

> It will interest me a lot to know what you do with George Washington a very typical George. (Stein to Faÿ, n.d. [1930–31])

she studied typical Georges. In a note on the outside back cover of the first manuscript *cahier,* she reminded herself,

> I do not want individual character.

Yet while they are not individual personalities, she creates them from acquaintance out of particulars that enrich her text with finely shaped verbal actuality. Five different voices, they make a play of fivefold portraiture. She gives them capital letters for last name initials but not full last names, although the letters derive from Georges she knew—Platt *L*ynes, *M*aratier, *H*ugnet (his initial *H* changed after the quarrel to *S*), and of course King George of England, with no number. Is the fifth George in the play, placed in the center of the list of characters with the mysterious last initial *G,* the author herself, Gertrude, maker of all Georges, partaking of them all with *G?*

> George G.
> They need to be ready.
> George G.
> I knew I was inclined to to well and to be attended by not naming them.
> I knew that they would like to be refreshing which they would be and they would like to be without naming them.
> George G.
> We would be
> Readily
> Relieved as they would be.
> They would as much as we would be
> Able to be ready
> To be left to them
> Be there without their naming them.
> Naming them.
>
> (306)

All these Georges may also have trailed associations to female Georges, such as George Sand, George Eliot, George Fleming. Certainly these five outdid Thackeray's four.

By early 1932, Stein planned the contents of *Operas And Plays,* the fourth volume in the Plain Edition.[54] She framed it with opera librettos, *Four Saints*

54. The contents list appears on the inside cover of the manuscript *cahier* of "Marguerite Or A Simple Novel Of High Life" of late winter or early spring 1932. The order of the first two operas is reversed in the printed *O&P.*

In Three Acts and *A Lyrical Opera,* about herself and Toklas at the beginning and *Madame Recamier* near the end, followed by the two film texts appended. After the opening, she placed a series of early plays. Then, in the center, came *Civilization* and *They Must. Be Wedded. To Their Wife.,* country works that look at social organization through marriage, family, land, labor, property.

They were followed by *A Bouquet. Their Wills.,* the 1928 play-libretto about her own family in Baltimore and its forms of marriage in relation to property, wealth, and wills. Other recent plays followed.[55] In a number of these appear two local figures named Florence Déscôtes and Georges Couleur. For a long time I knew only some minor details in the few letters from Etienne Déscôtes, Florence's brother, about negotiations with Lieutenant Bonhomme for the house.

Then, by chance, I found in the typescript for *Everybody's Autobiography* a section, crossed out and not printed, that told their story.[56] The passage follows the section where Stein speaks of French men in the professions or government service who choose careers so regulated and secure that they know the full shape of their lives in advance. Her example of a professional is Bernard Faÿ, who will become a university professor; the man in government is the young Etienne Déscôtes, who after his grandfather's death returns to the security of the army, from which he will retire to become a trusted functionary in a bank.

In *Everybody's Autobiography,* this story was to give background about Etienne Déscôtes. However, Stein calls it the "[S]tory of Madame Descotes"

55. I have found no comment about the omission from *O&P* of the two sets of short plays. She may have wanted to include only full-length plays. *Four Saints In Three Acts* and *They Must. Be Wedded. To Their Wife.* are in both *O&P* and *LO&P.* The first was known through productions in America, the second as the basis for the ballet *A Wedding Bouquet;* Carl Van Vechten wanted to make sure that *LO&P* was protected by U.S. copyright as *O&P,* published in Paris and not sent to the Library of Congress, was not. Also in *LO&P* are the plays of 1932, written when *O&P* was already being printed.

56. The section (p. 97 hardcover, p. 106 paperback edition), reproduced here in full to preserve its spoken quality, is not crossed out in the manuscript, which means that final editorial changes were made in the typescript. Nothing is known about the reasons for its removal. Perhaps editors at Random House were uneasy about statements of illegitimacy, especially as the families were living in the region then as they still are now.

Perhaps Stein herself decided to withhold facts to let her words in the plays speak without association. Most likely she realized that the story of the mother, which fascinated her, did not illustrate her point about the regulated life of government employees like the son. Letters from Etienne Déscôtes, also spelled Décôte, and Florence Couleur, also spelled Colleur, are among the Stein papers. The wedding took place on September 1, 1930, as is recorded in several pieces, for example, "We Came. A History," XVII, 151. In the transcription here the many typing errors are corrected against manuscript.

because it interests her as the story of mother and daughter, not of the son, which may be the reason she cut it from the manuscript.

All these know what they are to do from the time they begin. Etienne was the grandson of Monsieur Almand [Amand Saint-Pierre] who helped us get the house at Bilignin. He did his military service and the captain said he should stay in the army, Etienne could not just then because his grandfather was dying, his grandfather always said to us proceed quietly ladies, and we did. The grandfather died quietly in his room and his daughter and grandaughter had a great deal to do farming so Etienne had to help them. Then the grandfather was dead and the grandaughter was to marry. She had wanted to go to Lyon and work, she had wanted to marry a young man but the young man who wanted to marry her was the only son of a man and woman the man was dead who had been servants a long time and with their money they had bought land and they had bought it near to Belley and now Belley was booming. He had heard of Florence through a seamstress who worked for them and came from the village of the Almands. And he wanted very much to marry her. The mother of the boy was doubtful the mother of the girl was not. The mother of the girl was gay in the village fashion, she always had a pleasure in seeing anything, she liked cows and she liked dogs but never kept one and she liked chickens and ducks but was not very successful with them. Anyway one day we were passing and she jumped on the step of the automobile and she was sparkling Florence is marrying she said Georges Couleur and everything is happening. They married we were there at the wedding and then that year Madame Descotes the mother of Florence and Etienne became very sad. Finally we knew what was happening, she was not seeing her daughter, they were quarreling. There were two things, Etienne was giving up farming, he was going back to the army and they were selling everything except the two cows and renting the land. This belonged to the mother and then later since she loved her son better it would go to him, perhaps not all but still it might and then most of all, everybody suddenly remembered something. Madame Descotes had been left a widow not by the war but by death before the war and had been left with the two children they were very young then three and five and then she had another one. Well that one she had not kept she had given it up to be an orphan. The mother of Florence's husband who always clasped little pigeons to her before she sold them and was very successful with ducks and chickens when she found this out could not allow any of her household to see her daughter-in-law's mother. Everybody must have known it but nobody had happened ever to say it and now everybody said it. They all said it was bad to have him but it was worse to give him up to be an orphan. I said after all it was a choice, she had two children and the two children would have been as badly thought of if she had kept him as the one who should have been an orphan, so three children would have suffered and now it was only one. I thought Madame Descotes had shown her usual sense in her decision, of course all this was eighteen years ago and nobody knows anything about the orphan. Anyway Etienne went back into the army, Florence was married and Madame Descotes was alone with her two cows, and a Saracen. This country was once in the hands of the Saracens, it is funny any land has had so many who have been there and unless anybody happens to know about it it is not known but anyway everybody does know because after all the land on the earth, there is not so much of it, and there are always everybody on it, well anyway Saracens had been here, and there are still in the Villages after all there always are people there so after all everybody always has been there. There was one who had a beard and always slowly went in front of the house where Madame Descotes lives and each one kept their cow, in this country you sit with your cow, on a camp-stool and they each sat there we often saw them, anyway we went away and next winter at Christmas we had a letter from Madame Descotes and she was very gay, she said I had a pleasant Christmas and I had all my children, that of course was not the orphan, that was her son and her daughter and her son-in-law. How she had gotten the best of the situation she never has said but since then she has always been alone and very content with everything. But to come back to Etienne, when Etienne went back to the army one day he said now I am a sergeant, I will go on to be a top-sergeant I will have so and so much money, when I am forty by that time I will have married a wife who will have had a situation and then together with our savings we will do very well, as a retired adjutant I will be given a position of trust in a bank and then once more he knew the exact sum and so on. He was to have no surprises from that time on and he has not, and he was always to remain where he was. His brother-in-law was to get richer, his children might easily become something else but this generation as a great many generations of frenchmen know well everything that can possibly happen to them even including a war. . . .

Stein may have heard this story first when it was revived by Madame Couleur before or after the wedding of her son to Florence Déscôtes in September 1930. She considers the mother, the daughter Florence, used in several pieces, and the nameless illegitimate child presumably raised in a foundling hospital or orphanage. The village had accommodated the action of the mother as part of how things were done, and Stein herself notes that she sees nothing wrong with the way Madame Déscôtes handled it.

But once Madame Couleur revives the affair, it is to cast suspicion on the bride's family, create distance between her son and his bride, and reaffirm his dependency on her. The relationship of Georges and his mother, supported by the image of her fondling the pigeons, has economic underpinnings—shared ownership of land and shared labor supporting their rise in the world. Madame Couleur isolates and lowers Florence, destroying the marriage in all but form.

The story must have impressed Stein enormously. It provided material for *Madame Recamier, Civilization,* and "Brim Beauvais," and it enters "Winning His Way," makes short appearances in minor pieces, and connects with "Marguerite Or A Simple Novel Of High Life." Orphans turn up several times. She studies identity and names—first, last, male, female, public, private, married and unmarried, legal or not—opening questions of what happens to women, and relating also to Stein's own marriage to Toklas, their free, creative union not bound to property and patriarchy nor sanctioned by a joint legal name.

Nowhere else does a single situation yield so many different experiments in writing. Nor had questions of property and propriety arisen in their life as they did now, when they lived in a family house in a small community, cultivated a garden, owned a pet as baby of the family, and pursued their work for the Plain Edition.

Bilignin was not only about work and private life in the pastoral setting. Here Stein entered a community that changed her life, her perceptions, and her work. Between 1924 and 1927 she had composed the landscape that echoes lyrically through *Lucy Church Amiably* and the landscape plays. Now, however, she was no longer a private person meditating in the landscape but a resident in a house and a part of the social landscape.

Civilization (*O&P* 131–60)

Here is a play that opens by listing characters, and "[t]hen the landscape. And the animals." This is not a pastoral but a workaday landscape, where tradesmen sell goods and farmers till the fields and raise animals for profit. Its economic life is a condition for family and social life. People in the region lived in houses and on land owned and farmed by families for generations. Some of the plays of 1930–31 compose the social structures that began to preoccupy her once she became a part of the locality and learned its stories. *Civilization* dramatizes the precarious system illustrated by Georges Couleur and Florence Déscôtes. He marries as a matter of social necessity, to continue family and property. However, tied to his mother by shared land and labor, he is incapable of loving the girl he marries. While he and his mother work together, Florence labors hard, separately, alone, under her own name.

Madame Recamier. An Opera. (*O&P* 355–83)

In September 1930, the month of the Couleur-Déscôtes wedding, Stein wrote *Madame Recamier,* spoken of as both a play and a libretto though never set to music. Madame Recamier is an odd name as title of a Stein play, for its power of referential evocation of history, like Byron as the name of her later play. Not surprisingly, none of the great historic figures surrounding Madame Récamier is here—no Benjamin Constant, Madame de Staël, Chateaubriand, Murat, Napoleon, no Empress Josephine. Nor is Monsieur Récamier or the adopted niece in the play. Except for the locations, Paris, Belley, Rome, with loose parallels to Stein in Paris, Belley, and Boston, Madame Récamier is lifted from history, stripped of associations.[57]

The play probably has two main sources. The first is local. Monsieur Récamier came from an old family of the region. On her only visit to Belley, Madame Récamier adopted his niece, Josephine, changing her name to Amélie Cyvoct. The young woman remained with her through banishment and poverty until her death and later married Jacques Lénormant of Belley, preserving and eventually publishing the Récamier correspondence. A picture of Lénormant is laid into Stein's manuscript notebook. Monsieur Récamier was a cousin of the gastronome Brillat-Savarin, related to Stein's young landlady, "Mlle Duvachat" (382), who also appears in the text.

The second source may have been the biography by Edouard Herriot, *Madame Récamier et ses amis.* He was the first to consider her as the illegitimate daughter of her mother by Monsieur Récamier, the man who married her, though the marriage was supposedly not consummated.[58]

As "Subsidiary Characters" Stein lists Paris acquaintances such as the

57. To Henry McBride Stein wrote that the first act was "in Paris chez Madame Recamier," the second in Belley "in the place des Terr[e]aux," the main square, and the third in Rome, "preferably the Pincian Gardens" (postmark 25 October 1930).

58. Among the Stein papers is a pamphlet offprint, uncut except for beginning and end pages, of Charles Lénormant, *Madame Récamier en Bugey* (Extrait de la Revue "Le Bugey") (Belley: Librairie Montbaron, 1923).

The biography by Herriot (1872–1957), written early in the century as his doctoral dissertation, was reprinted by Payot, Paris, in 1924, when he became premier of France. It was translated into English in 1925 and in 1927–28 made by Gaston Ravel into a film Stein could have seen.

For the film, see *La Petite Illustration: Revue hebdomadaire publiant les pièces nouvelles jouées dans les théâtres de Paris, des romans inédits, des poèmes, des critiques littéraires et dramatiques et des études cinématographiques* no. 385 (9 June 1928). No copy of the film appears to be in New York. It is available in Paris.

painter Pavelik Tchelitchew, his companion Allen Tanner, the pianist and composer Cliquet Pleyel, and others.[59] In addition, Georges Couleur, Florence Descotes, and Ivonne Marin, the last presumably also local, are listed as "Dependents," though how they relate to the subsidiary characters is not clear. Perhaps Stein suggests parallels between the personalities or situations of Florence Déscôtes and Georges Couleur on the one hand and her young artist friends in Paris on the other; possibly echoes of Stein's distinction of "dependent" and "independent" personality types carry over from her early studies, an interest she never gave up.

The text, beginning with the first line of the portrait of the deceased Grace-Ives de Longevialle and the ominous hooting of an owl, produces a vast array of fast-moving, punning phrases about mothers, fathers, brothers, sisters, with tones of family hostility and shifting dependency. We know from Herriot that the name Récamier joins a husband and wife but conceals that they are father and daughter so that the adopted niece ironically legitimates the marriage as a daughter who makes consummation unimportant. Florence Déscôtes and Georges Couleur, who share with Monsieur and Madame Récamier the theme of problematic relations between husbands and wives, parents and children, are fitting figures for inclusion in *Madame Recamier.* In fast interweaving lines with steadily shifting terms, the play creates marriages and changes names, relations of men and women, parents and children, brothers and sisters, him and her, name and shame.

> Out loud is when the mother wishes
> When the brother fishes
> When the father considers wishes
> When the sister supposes wishes
> She will change to say to I say I say so.
> Let her think of learning nothing.
> Let her think of seeing everything
> Let her think like that. (365)

Only

> Yvonne Marin can go away from home the others cannot. (358)

She retains freedom of imagination:

59. Georges Hugnet is also in the play, written shortly after Stein completed her translation of *Enfances.* Sometime after the quarrel over publication, however, presumably in January 1931, his name was changed to George Janvier, its printed form. In Act II, the "Aria in which they sing Friendship's Flowers" is revised for the printed version, though not in the manuscript from "The aria in which they sing Enfances." Typescripts for Plain Edition, not returned by the printer, cannot be checked.

It is of great use to be able to like to look at the clouds. (367)

Local or not, she becomes a word.

And Madame Récamier herself? Stein retains her connection with Belley and the image of the hostess that carries over to herself. But she removes other historic associations so that we can discover her only in the words of the play. As she wrote in an undated letter of that year to Ellen DuPoy,

> Avoid the suggestiveness by association, make your suggestion by words which do suggest.

When on October 13, 1934, DuPoy reviewed *Operas And Plays* for the *Chicago Tribune,* she quoted, perhaps recalling conversations with Stein, this "description of a hostess":

> Never to be restless
> Never to be afraid
> Never to ask will they come
> Never to have made
> Never to like having had
> Little that is left then
> She made it do
> One and two
> Thank her for everything.[60]

Apparently the cases of local women like Florence Déscôtes led Stein by 1930–31 to look at the place of women in the world. Déscôtes is prominent in *Madame Recamier,* but *Civilization* allows her a mere few lines while Georges Couleur speaks constantly as farmer, landowner, and husband, no matter his dependency on his mother. Wives, serving family continuity and wealth, do not blossom in free, creative relationships. Precarious marriages join names to names but subordinate those of women to property and power.

"Brim Beauvais Or After The War Is Over" (*MR* 321–38)

Brim Beauvais, as that strange name tells us right away, was not someone Stein knew. After Stein's death, Carl Van Vechten asked Toklas about the novelette, unpublished until it was included in *Mrs. Reynolds And Five Earlier Novelettes* (1952), the second posthumous volume. Toklas answered that she understood the allusion to Florence, the second figure in the piece,

60. In the text, these are the lines of Florence Descotes (366), whether about Madame Recamier, herself, or even Stein and Toklas, calm and free by choice in retreat—or banishment.

but Brim Beauvais was "definitely not a portrait from real life."[61] Composed in Paris in the winter of 1930–31, the piece fills a substantial notebook to the end; on its cover is printed "Papeterie Beauvais, 14 rue du Bac," Stein's stationery shop, which gave her the last name,

> Brim Beauvais. Is a name. He is made. Of the same. Away. Is a name. He is made. Of that name. (300)

It is a writing name and he is a paper creature.

> No name made no name made no one. Known no one. (294)

Real in writing, not in life, his name is full of writing life.[62]

He also sounds like Beau Brummell. Whether from sound, from history, or from Virginia Woolf's recent piece,[63] Beau Brummell may have gone into the making of Brim Beauvais. Finally, "Brim" rhymes and half-rhymes with words Stein uses at this time—"win," "Lynn," "prim," "trim," "rim," "grim," "vim" (277), "women," "men." Brim Beauvais is made of words and has an identity that can change as people cannot.

His wife's name is Florence Anna. That name comes from Florence Tanner, the sister of pianist Allen Tanner, who in the summer of 1929 became the wife of Georges Maratier. But Brim Beauvais is not Georges Maratier.[64] Elements like

61. Toklas to Van Vechten, 18 February 1948.
62. In "Forensics," written in the winter of 1931 after the quarrel with Hugnet, she may refer to "Brim Beauvais" when she says

> At last I am writing a popular novel. Popular with whom. They may be popular with them. Or more ferociously. (*HTW* 391)

Plenty of anger carries over into "Brim Beauvais," and numerous details of her personal life are absorbed into the text, which is not at all autobiographical, though the personal subtext must be heard.

63. Woolf's "Beau Brummel" had appeared in the *Nation and Athenaeum* on September 28, 1929, and in the *New York Herald Tribune* on September 29, followed by publication in book form (New York: Rimington & Hooper, 1930).
64. In the spring of 1929, Stein wrote his portrait, one of the many Georges. It was an appreciation of his help in many forms. From 1929 on, she relied on him for practical help with publications in France, with servants, dogs, and, after he acquired the Galerie Vignon on rue du Bac, for purchases and sales of paintings and exhibits of the work of friends. Her portrait is a low-key, sophisticated composition made of almost but not quite identical words, syllables, phrases, and rhyming elements in slightly different forms that create visual and auditory echoes with minimal referential thrust.

Florence Tanner, the oldest sister of Allen Tanner, who was the youngest in a family of eight or nine, had come to France in 1927 or 1928 and stayed on in Paris, where she met Stein. She summered for two years with Tanner, Tchelitchew, his sister Choura, and other

> He has been very careful. Not to be quarreled with (298)

may come from Maratier, but the novelette includes no portrait of him, no daily life, no representation. Later, in the lecture "Portraits And Repetition," Stein spoke of "Brim Beauvais." She said that in 1930–31, she found something more vibrant than looking and listening and the daily life.

> I did not do a great many portraits at that time. I wrote a great deal of poetry a great many plays and operas and some novels in which I tried again to do this thing, in one or two I more or less did, one called Brim Beauvais, I very often did, that is I created something out of something without adding anything do you see what I mean. (*LIA* 204)

When Toklas in her answer to Van Vechten acknowledged the allusion to Florence, she may have been thinking of Florence Tanner or of Florence Déscôtes, we will never know which. She had learned the art of saying no more than necessary in answer to a question, and Van Vechten did not know that her answer left a question. Stein apparently drew parallels between Florence Déscôtes and Florence Tanner, and possibly also between Georges Couleur and Georges Maratier, who shared first names and perhaps personality traits. Allen Tanner knew Descotes was used as an alternative name for his sister but not where it came from.[65]

Brim Beauvais returns three years later in "The Superstitions Of Fred Anneday, Annday, Anday A Novel Of Real Life" as a friend of Fred, another

---

friends at Stella Bowen's house in Guermantes. She was apparently depressed and unhappy—the word "neurasthenia" is used to describe her condition. Maratier eventually helped her regain some composure.

It is said that once Maratier's mother discovered that he had had a love affair with Bravig Imbs or Kristians Tonny, Florence, to save him from embarrassment, announced that he had had a long-standing love affair with her. Maratier "regularized" the relationship with her by marriage, which also gave him access to the United States for purchases and sales of art in Chicago. The marriage eventually ended in divorce.

65. Allen Tanner to author, 8 September 1981. See also Ulla Dydo, "Gertrude Stein: Composition as Meditation," *Gertrude Stein and the Making of Literature,* ed. Shirley Neuman and Ira Nadel (London: Macmillan Press, 1988), 42–60. In note 11, written before I discovered Florence Déscôtes, I wrote,

> Stein gives [Florence Tanner] the name "Descotes" in several pieces, for reasons that remain unclear to her brother also. . . .
>
> The novelette "Brim Beauvais" . . . is about her and Georges Maratier, who is given the name Brim Beauvais. A man of unclear identity and unsettled personality, he appears under a name other than his own; he has not yet come into his own. The Maratier-Tanner marriage was short-lived and ended in divorce.

My comment here serves to revise this erroneous interpretation.

man with a strange name to whom many things have happened. Both Brim Beauvais and Fred Anneday are prototype fictional personages drawn from the life of any day. Like Fred, Brim is not a copy from life but a versatile paper or word creation.

> A novel is what you dream in your night sleep. A novel is not waking thoughts although it is written and thought with waking thoughts. (*HWW* 25)

How slippery the movement from world to word, from Florence Tanner to Florence Anna, from the representation of living to "the turning of large blocks of meaning on small points of form."[66] How many steps in these pages led from fiction to fact, from Brim Beauvais to the double lives of Georges Maratier and Florence Tanner, of Georges Couleur and Florence Déscôtes.

"How She Bowed To Her Brother" (*P&P* 236–40; *R* 564–67)

Toklas describes the occasion for "How She Bowed To Her Brother," Stein's 1931 portrait of her brother Leo. In *What Is Remembered* (105–6), she says it was written after Stein, driving in traffic on Boulevard St.-Germain in Paris, passed her brother, whom she had not seen since they parted in 1913. Each bowed politely to the other. Stein wrote the portrait after this encounter.[67]

This context identifies the long estrangement of Stein and her brother and draws the scene but tells us nothing about the portrait itself. Yet the reader must be aware of the great estrangement that developed between Stein and her brother, after early affection and shared interests, once she committed herself fully to writing and to Toklas, and her brother refused to validate her work and her life.[68] This piece constructs her refusal of her brother in words.

66. Donald Sutherland, "A Lady of Letters," *New Republic* (6 October 1952): 26–27, a review of *Mrs. Reynolds And Five Earlier Novelettes* (New Haven: Yale University Press, 1952).
67. In a letter of August 4, 1931, Bernard Faÿ told Stein how much he admired the portrait, which she had sent him; it must have been written in the spring of 1931, before she left for the country. Eugene Jolas acknowledged submission on October 27, 1931, and published it in *transition* no. 21 (March 1932): 100–103.
68. Though the estrangement was permanent and profound, Leo did visit Paris, and some letters from him to Gertrude after 1914 are among her papers at Yale. Whether she answered, unlikely as it seems, is not known; Leo's papers of these years have not survived.

    Hostile comments about her appear in his letters to mutual friends, especially but not only after the *Autobiography*. Toklas' 1913 date for the separation of Stein and her brother is the earlier one of two years, 1913 and 1914, which mark the steps in the separation. From 1913 on, Leo Stein no longer lived at 27 rue de Fleurus, though he remained in

The text undermines what at first appears as a simple fact, that she bowed to her brother, presumably in courteous greeting. Pivoting on the verb "bow," her text raises questions word by word about how she bowed until we wonder whether she ever bowed. At last the word no longer refers to polite courtesies but to the many other meanings of "bow"—suffer defeat, turn aside, submit, bend in reverence, incline in salutation, submit in shame, crush, adore, assent, applaud. The drama of the portrait takes place between the unstable meanings that the word releases.

Stein breaks sentences into pieces, often not grammatical phrases, such as she had begun to explore in 1930–31, in the "readies." Isolated, they slow down the movement, shift stresses, multiply syntactical patterns, and do away with linear continuity, until they turn the meaning of every group of words to doubt. Here is a simple example:

> She bowed to her brother. Accidentally. When she saw him. (*P&P* 236; *R* 565)

"Accidentally" is in an ambiguous position—did she bow accidentally or see him accidentally or both? The movement of such phrasings destabilizes and dramatizes the story of how she bowed to her brother.

What finally makes this piece so powerful is its great, silent formality. Stein and her brother exchange not one word. They are not named. There is only the single gesture of bowing turned from fact into ambiguous question. Between them, in Paris traffic, is an enormous, silent distance.

Perhaps this portrait also allows another reading. The 1906 Picasso gouache of Leo Stein, which Etta Cone recorded purchasing in 1932, had remained in Gertrude's possession since 1913, when she and Leo divided the paintings upon his removal from the Paris studio. What made for this startling sale now? Is it possible that Stein bowed not only to her brother on the boulevard but also to the painting by her great friend of her brother as she turned him into cash, presumably to help finance the Plain Edition and so to make her own name?

"Grant Or Rutherford B. Hayes" (*HWW* 13–17)

Probably written in the spring of 1931, this is a study of a name fit for president of the United States. In America, the kind of solid name fit for high office must include a middle name or initial.

Paris at an unknown address. Probably in February 1913 they divided the paintings. By April 1914, Leo had moved his furniture to Florence and established permanent residence there.

Presidential timber. Such an *American* notion. Rutherford B. Hayes. James A. Garfield. Chester B. Arthur. Presidential timber.[69]

Rutherford B. Hayes, with its heavy beats, is the right sort of name. Stein makes it race against plain Grant, creating jogging phrases and irregular staccato rhythms and working into it the Civil War with snow, sand, rain, stones, and horses charging in battle that are also racing for the presidency and a name that carries.

The conditions for a winning name are simple. First, it must sound right. Second, it must be backed by real accomplishment. Third, it must be lucky. Laid into the manuscript notebook is a pressed red four-leaf clover. When Stein wrote the *Autobiography,* she used for its title a solid winning name with a middle initial, Alice B. Toklas.[70]

In the summer of 1931, Stein returned to plays, though her interests also pointed to new directions with "Winning His Way," her first long work of poetry. About the novelette, "Hotel François Ier," a very opaque work that may or may not refer to Francis Rose, she said in the winter of 1931,

69. Allen Tate, "Miss Toklas' American Cake," *Prose* no. 3 (fall 1971): 153. Tate's emphasis.

70. In writing, Stein nearly always referred to Toklas by her full name, with or without the middle initial, making the private love relationship formal and public, with the middle initial an added advantage. Neither Gertrude nor her sister Bertha apparently had middle names, though all three brothers in official documents had as middle name that of their father, Daniel.

Leon Katz reminded me that in the early version of the first chapter of *The Making Of Americans,* Stein speaks of how the immigrants in Baltimore gradually ceased to use traditional Jewish (her word is "German") names like Hannah and Moses and changed to English ones.

In keeping with the aspirations of her Polish mother, Alice Toklas was given a name tinged with gentility and a middle name. A brief and partial draft for a late cookbook, "We Eat," is "by Alice Toklas and Gertrude Stein." Toklas' "B." is crossed out, no doubt in the service of rhythm. Even single letters make a difference for nuance and effect. The "B." is also omitted in the French translation of the *Autobiography.*

Stein's disapproval of pseudonyms had to do with her sense of authorial integrity. She was aware, of course, of Grant's change of name. In an undated letter from 1935, Donald Sutherland wrote her that he might publish his first novel under a pen name. She objected,

> No no a thousand times no, no not Robert Caithness not any assumed name . . . whatever you do bad or good in the way of writing is what you do and therefore you must sign it. (postmark 8 February 1935, Richmond, Virginia)

This is the woman who had written the book *Three Histories* under the name Jane Sands and had considered as alternatives Jane Sandys and Pauline Manders. Sutherland's *Child with a Knife,* about the poet Callimachus, was published and printed under his own name in 1937 by Courier Printing Company, Littleton, New Hampshire.

That is astonishing a narrative and I would so much rather be poetical. (*MR* 307)

By the summer, the country setting returned her to the people and casual conversations that led to many new plays.

They Must. Be Wedded. To Their Wife. A Play (O&P 161–94)

Beginning somewhat like *The Five Georges* except that the names are used in twos, this play, of July or August 1931, starts,

Any name. Of which. One. Has known. At least two.
Josephine
Ernest
Therese
Julia
and
Guy and Paul and John.
(161)

It is built on these seven names, virtually always the same, in the same order. Even the rhythm of its title makes pairs. Like "Winning His Way" and other work of this time, this text uses periods to "break up things in arbitrary ways."[71] It joins names to build couples by constructing verbal and figurative weddings. With its pirouetting, whirling series of first names and its abstract words gradually building phrases and lines by permutations and combinations as in a musical composition, it virtually asked to become, in somewhat altered form, the ballet *A Wedding Bouquet* of 1936.

She begins with names that return in identical sequence, then groups them as men and women, returns them one by one and in pairs, speaking together or to one another or speaking in permutations of phrasing. Characters, names, and their apparent lines or even stage directions are no longer separate but blend.

John
and To remember. That they. Bought. A boat.
Ernest.
(191)

Josephine Play well. For Dora.
Therese May they. Call Cora.
and She may come. For her.
Cora.
(177)

71. "Poetry And Grammar," *LIA* 217.

There is indeed a wedding here, a banquet, a celebration, perhaps a dance—rhythmic word performances all, leading up to the last word,

> Ernest. One. At one time.

Just as plays join characters in exchange and conversation, so weddings are stage performances joining words to compose domestic scenes.

> Therese. Has curtains. And has. Refused. Curtains.
> Has wells. And. Has not. Refused wells.
> Has aprons. And. Has not. Refused aprons.
> Has wealth. And has not either. Refused. Or
> not refused. Wealth.
>
> (175–76)[72]

Often it is as if not merely names but syllables and words were making love, wedding anew and anew. We no longer ask who pairs with whom, who speaks to whom, but watch words and parts of words join in a dance.

The names of this play may have started from the family of the solicitor Amand St. Pierre[73] and his sons, Jean, Paul, and Guy. The play is framed by another of the somber stories of country violence, beginning against an approaching storm that requires the hay quickly to be put away in the barn. There follows a rescue by one of the sons of the other two from drowning. The wedding takes place against such threats of violence.

Lynn And The College De France (*O&P* 249–89)

Here is one more play that explores names. An undated letter from Madame Marthe Giraud answers in detail what must have been questions about the French academies that Stein had asked in view of a new work, concluding her letter, "Which will you choose?" Stein chose the Collège de France, not even described by her friend.

That institution in 1930 celebrated its four hundredth anniversary, pro-

72. The play is carefully formatted in the manuscript though less clearly in print. Stein's indentations and punctuation marks grouped names in relation to the spoken lines somewhat as in the earlier *A List.* At this time, Toklas as Therese appears in many pieces.

73. In *Everybody's Autobiography,* Stein speaks of Florence and Etienne Déscôtes, presumably born shortly before World War I, as his grandchildren. Here she speaks of his children, the eldest twenty-two in 1936. There may be some conflation of generations here, unimportant for the play.

Stein felt deeply indebted to St. Pierre about making the arrangements for the house. Her letters reflect care in observing the niceties of a formal relationship, with appropriate greetings to family members always spelled out and correct New Year's gifts for the family sent upon consultation with Bernard Faÿ, expert at formal proprieties. To Stein, the three St. Pierre sons and two daughters may have recalled her own family.

viding an occasion for this play in 1931. More important was a personal connection: Bernard Faÿ, professor of American history at the University of Clermont-Ferrand, was making efforts for the establishment and funding of a chair of history of the United States at the Collège de France and for his own nomination to this post, in competition against the senior economist André Siegfried, delegate to the League of Nations.

Fascinated from early years by the struggle for power and position,[74] Stein received daily reports from Faÿ and in turn helped him plan strategy for his meetings with the premier, André Tardieu, and various deputies. In the manuscript, she uses the name Henry Clay, revised from the original, Bernard Fay, suggesting the Great Compromiser. Underscoring the battle for an appointment, army generals, a part of daily life in a garrison town like Belley, appear in the play. Stein's interest in Faÿ's victory echoes her hope for her own "success with glory." In manuscript his name is revised to "Beatrice Glory" (250, 251).

The power play of the academies takes place in Paris, a part of "city life," not "village life" (251). Yet Stein wrote the play in the country, interweaving city and country matter by merging the anniversary of the Collège de France of 1930 and the opening of the new, long tunnel through the Col du Chat to Aix-les-Bains in the late summer of 1931.[75] The play is full of festive pomp—college commencements, the college of cardinals, a papal conclave, Bastille Day and fourth of July parades—with punning on "four," "fourteen," and "forty" for the members of the French Academy. *Lynn And The College De France* is a celebratory, winning play, its location anywhere, city or country, France or America, now or then.

A congregation of names moves through a landscape of tunnels, hills, and mountains in figures that constantly change, becoming also a landscape play, a love celebration, a birthday celebration, a wedding feast quite unlike the one in *They Must. Be Wedded. To Their Wife.* High callings anticipate local festivities, with Faÿ's victory, the prospering of Stein's Plain Edition, the hope of recognition,

> The college of France, recognizes when, then, in, on, of, as, and, the all at once.
>
> The college of France plays havoc with their chances.
>
> The college of France pleases. In the. Call. Of stations. The college of France. Disturbs nothing. They will be welcome. Originally. (286)

74. Stein's early notebooks, *The Making Of Americans,* and several early portraits suggest her interest in the struggle of dependent and independent, attacking and resisting personalities and the dynamics of power and ambition.

75. See Stein to Carl Van Vechten, 7 November 1931, *LGS/CVV* 247.

The name Lynn is not confusing if we remember that this celebration composes not fixed, identifiable people but names. Lynn was familiar to Stein as the name of a town but not, I believe, as a person. Lynn, Massachusetts, home of her friends, the Earles, whose father appears in this play, of Mary Baker Eddy during her second marriage, of Sherry Mangan, editor of *larus* and coeditor of *Pagany;* Lynn, home of a famous summer stock company; East Lynne, the popular melodrama; Lynn, an androgynous name, male or female, with its *L* and *N* sounds, alliterating or rhyming with Lena, Helene, Lynes, *ligne,* Lyon, Lane, and with words like "win" and "brim" of this time. A pivot for the celebrations of her play, Lynn is nominated (254).

The spring of 1931 looks like a winning time, with recognition and success coming to Stein from everywhere. Editions Stock agreed to publish *The Making Of Americans* in French. The publisher Espasa Calpe in Madrid hoped to translate it into Spanish, though the plan was not realized.[76] The Dunster Street Bookshop in Cambridge exhibited Stein books. At the Collège de France a chair of history of the United States was established, followed by the appointment of Bernard Faÿ, who lectured on Stein in France and America and wrote about her in his study of American novelists, *Les Romanciers Américains* (1931).

Major critical appraisals appeared: in "Le contrepoint poétique de Gertrude Stein," published in the June 1930 issue of the French-English journal *Échanges,* Marcel Brion compared Stein's method of composition to that of Bach; Allanah Harper, the owner-editor of the journal, honored and praised Stein. In *Axel's Castle,* published in the spring of 1931, Edmund Wilson discussed Stein as an important figure along with Proust, Joyce, Rimbaud, and others.

New young artists like Paul Bowles, Aaron Copland, and Charles Henri Ford visited her in Paris and in the country. Yet all this attention failed to dispel the unassuaged disbelief that beset Stein about recognition, as if it were too late for praise to do her enough good. She had to create it herself.

By January, the quarrel with Hugnet convinced her that the friendship had failed even before the joint publication was attempted. "Was I right to like them young" was probably as much about Stein as about Brim Beauvais (272). She turned away from Hugnet and friends she suspected of siding with him, taking her career in her own hands with redoubled determination.

76. See correspondence with Espasa Calpe among papers of W. A. Bradley, HRC. See also Stein to Lindley Williams Hubbell, postmarked 17 January 1931, and Hubbell to Stein, 19 February 1931; Robert Coates to Stein, 25 February 1931, responding to the plan for a Spanish *MOA.* In the same letter, Coates promised to review *LCA* and the Plain Edition in the *New Yorker.* See his "Books, Books, Books" in the issue of February 20, 1932.

Once Harry Horwood failed to take responsibility for the Plain Edition, she and Toklas took it on alone. Stein quickly printed her versions of Hugnet's poems under her own imprint as *Before The Flowers Of Friendship Faded Friendship Faded* and went on to new work on her own.

Her mood is perfectly expressed in the draft of a letter to Bravig Imbs, who she thought was on Hugnet's side. Annoyed with his reliance on friends for jobs and financial support, and impatient with his inability to pick himself up by his own bootstraps as Stein did, she says,

> My dear for the last time I am going to tell you what I think. You and Valeska [Imbs' wife] are taking too much the attitude of babes in the woods who are going to be fed. You might as well face the fact that nobody is going to feed you. I was thoroughly disap[p]ointed when I found that you had not done your Chatterton [biography] or anything else. If you are going to be the kind of writer who sits and [word] waits for an advance it is not interesting. You have had enough money this month one way or another to have given you the opportunity to do something, and you haven't, you know no crowd is going to take the two of you unless somehow you make yourselves with it, Winning your way is a sad title but it is the only one every way. You know you have always seemed a little weak in the head about money and now that you haven't George [Maratier?] it is up to Valeska to do her part in keeping things straight you must not sit and whine really you must not. Lots of love Gtde[77]

A few years later, in a letter, Stein translated "winning your way," which had already, as "Winning His Way," become the title of a poem, as *façon de gagner,* making a living. Even in "Brim Beauvais" appears a belligerent passage about "winning" in fighting, with an "episode" worked into the sequence for variety that is carefully closed before the text returns to "winning."

> **Chapter Nine**
>
> An episode introduced for variety.
>
> One man is a man. Winning. Two men are two men winning. One man is one man winning. Two men are men winning. Two men are two men winning are arranging for that creditably. One man one man winning is making winning learning. For their account an episode is made of very

77. I do not know whether this draft was transcribed and sent to Imbs. Internal evidence dates it 1931, when Stein was writing "Winning His Way" and before Imbs, suffering from financial problems, completed his biography of Chatterton.

pretty laces. Very pretty presents. Very pretty choice. Very pretty choice. Which they have. . . .

An episode closes. They must have been known to have won. They must. Have been. Anxious. To have. Some one. Win. (*MR* 284)

"Winning His Way. A Narrative Poem Of Poetry" (*SIM* 153–209)

Soon after arrival in the country for the summer of 1931, Stein began her first long work of poetry, "Winning His Way."[78] It is an ambitious fifty-page work that looks at poetry as the highest art,[79] most likely to lead to a winning work and a great name,

> And now can poetry. Be acknowledged. Supreme. (157)

This text is in the tradition of great philosophical poems, and she prolongs with relish the lines that spell the prospect of its pleasure.

> Winning his way. A narrative poem.
> Winning his way a narrative poem.
> There. Is. A pleasure. In. Winning.
> But. They will. Have. A pleasure. In. Winning.
> They will make. Whether. In. A pleasure.
> That is. That there. Is. A pleasure.
> Will it be a pleasure. Winning his way a long narrative poem.
> Of poetry. And friendship. And. Fame. (202–3)

78. The manuscript shows alternating sections written in pen and pencil, the last filling the notebook to the end of the last page as she often did for discipline of closure. Written close to *Lynn And The College De France,* the poem uses some of the same detail as the play, for example, a tunnel (198) and Beatrice [Glory] (189), "[p]lay" (208) may be this play.

79. Poetry is not offset against prose but is seen as the highest form of writing. In these years Stein, who is often thought of as a writer of narratives, proceeds, without abandoning narrative, through work with movement and rhythm into lines and poetry. She calls "Winning His Way," with its three-part plotlike structure, a "narrative poem." But note Stein, in "Poetry And Grammar," on rhythms and the arbitrary breaking up of movement by periods.

> . . . I was completely possessed by the necessity that writing should go on and if writing should go on what had colons and semi-colons to do with it, what had commas to do with it, what had periods to do with it . . . to do with writing going on. . . .
> . . . Beside I had always liked the look of periods and I liked what they did. Stopping sometime did not really keep one from going on. . . . (*LIA* 217)

The language of her plays is closely related to her poetry. She enters both poetry and plays through language, not content.

It makes a slow and uneven start, as her beginnings often do. Not only is she ambivalent about having left Paris for the country, a change of setting that interrupts her work even as it opens the pleasures of birds and walks, seeds and flowers. She is also unsure about where this new work will take her. The opening lines, uneven in phrasing and movement and visually quite unlike what the poem soon becomes, are also unsure about substance. They are filled with distracting details about local people, without clear direction. What finally gets the poem off the ground is a young admirer's welcome.

> A man sitting upon a tree and they were singing to me. In welcome. (155)

The welcome also gives her friendship,[80] one of the three terms that eventually construct the poem. But only gradually does it take shape as an energetic, lyrical work of skilled, fast-moving verbal events.

By the eighth printed page, the lines begin to fall into the rhythms that will keep it moving and Stein begins to find a center,

> Now what is the difference.
> Between those. Everybody. Knows.
> And those. Others.
> How do you do. Very well I thank you.
> A continuation of the Narrative Poem.
> Winning. His. Way.
> A poem of poetry.
> And this. And friendships.

She meditates on a question she has never asked—what makes a poet write, why write. She explores answers in the words of daily life in house, garden, and land,

> The thing is this. They go. And they. Gather.
> Clover. For themselves. And their. Animals.
> They have to have. As aid. To work. For them. (171)

Here two four-leaf clovers are laid into the manuscript notebook.

The poem looks at the three motives:

80. Here also she plays with real names, for example, Frederic (155, 157) derives from a local man, but Freddy (157) is Paul Bowles. Lolo (Louis) Reynaud is a very young poet living in nearby Hauteville whom Stein met in 1929 or 1930 and who, sitting in a tree like a blossom or a flower of friendship, admired her with youthful devotion.

The problem resolves itself. Into this.
Does a poem. Continue. Because of. A Kiss.
Or because. Of future greatness.
Or because. There is no cause. Why. (164)

Writing for "no cause," as an end in itself, is no problem. It includes the sheer pleasure of writing and lifts in lovely summer lines,

Birds. Never. Are frightened. By singing. (162)

It is in the sounds of writing heard in the night,

And as she is sleeping. The paper. Is moving.
Winning his way. A poem.
A long narrative poem.
Of poetry. And winning. His way.
The poetry. Of paper moving.
Because she was sleeping. (169)

Nor is there a difficulty with writing for love, friendship, a kiss. A kiss interrupts writing but produces offerings of lines.

She can be. Scarcely. Conscious. Of. I guess.
That it is an. Offering.
But it is. What. They may call. Pleasing. (178)

Hesitation. Is a name. Of a waltz.
And so a narrative. Poem. Is. Interrupted.
By movement. By sound. By breathing. By leaning. (179)

But behind the pastoral idyll there is also tension. The opening pits the title, "Winning His Way," against the first line, "Or her way," herself in the masculine, against Toklas, feminine. Raw feelings sometimes crack in sharp rhythms,

Are they famous. Because they have been winning.
Or I am. (190)

Ambivalence about the country returns:

She says. It is better. When. They are not. Together. Which is true.
In summer. Rather. Than. In winter. (160)

In summer, in the country, they are together more steadily and more intimately than in Paris, but perhaps this intimacy is restrictive.

Think sweetly. Of friendship.
It is attached to blame. (161)

And she scoffs,

Because after all it is convincing.
That he is great. And she is. Right.
Let her eat. Plums and an apple.
Let him. Eat. Currants and lettuce.
Let them eat. Fish and bread.
And all the other things. That make. Cake. (200–201)

The name. Which is destined. To fame.
Is. My name. And so. They thank me. Sometime. (185)

Uncertain, uneasy identities and relations, presumably from the local scene, hover about some passages of this poem, shifting in uneasy patterns of words. Like a chorus, the voices of powers in the background, brothers, sisters, mothers, fathers, keep changing roles,

She was married to their father.
They were married. By their mother.
Not by him. Not with him.
Not for them. Not by them. With. Them.
She was married. To their father. By him.
He had been a father to them. Because he had been married to their mother. Before them. (158)

Florence Déscôtes is here, too, named once and suggested elsewhere,[81] surrounded by shifting fathers, mothers, brothers, sisters, we are never sure which. In marriage, women like her are given away or handed over, like cattle, into trouble, with no will of their own:

A daughter has. Been led. To be wed.
And though. Although. There. May be. Grief.
No one tries. To arouse. Them. As.
By use. Of their. Wedding.
Never. Again. Will she mention. Marrying. (176)

Not only hers but all families and relations are unstable. Stein herself is not sure what order of relations she fits. Immediately after her assertion that they have "no son" but "make fame" appears an orphan (185). "Winning His

81. *SIM* 158, 159, 188.

Way" is in part about the self-made man creating himself, his achievement, and his fame out of nothing.

The problem is in writing for "future greatness," ambition, or fame, the theme that dominates the whole poem and to which she returns over and over.

> Surely. It is. Not a mistake.
> To be famous. (168)

she says, but her insistence makes us wonder whether it is a mistake. What distinguishes great poets,

> What. In what. Way. Do they differ.
> And. In what. Way. Are they. The same.
> Those of them that have. Fame. From those of them.
> That do not. Have. Fame. In what way.
> Are they. The same. Those. Of them. That do not. Have. Fame.
> What is. Fame. That they. Have.
> And what. Is different. In them. That gives to them. This. Fame. (177)

One isolated line identifies fame with poetry or poetry with fame:

> Fame. Which is poetry. Is this. (191)

Fame enters writing for pleasure and for love and becomes the great motive for all writing. Perhaps it is a natural phenomenon growing like roses, children, or dogs.

> Fame cannot be anxious. Nor. A rose. Which is beautifully.
> Climbing. As they do. When. They have. Care. (182)

Bridgman calls this poem a Horatio Alger story (204–5). It reviews her early career (156–57), from not knowing her gift, to discovering it, writing quantities, and reaching always higher for success, winning and victory (203).[82] At times it reads like a manual for how to strive and succeed.

> Fame. Is expected. And. Unexpected.
> Roses. Are unexpected. And they are expected.
> Once given. The place. To have them.
> So then. There is. This difference. In a garden.
> Fame. Is expected. When it is. Not. In a. Garden.
> It is expected. To have roses. If. There is. A garden.

82. There is even a reference to the translation of *MOA* (195) and perhaps to the Plain Edition (196).

It is unexpected. To have fame. When there is.
Fame. As expected. Which is. That. There is.
No expectation. In anything. Which. They do. (181–82)

The hope of success fills house and garden in the language of flowers.

A bouquet made of three roses. And. The jasmine.
I am hopeful. That. I am. Successful. (196)

What is fame. It comes. Gradually. Like.
The rush. Of dahlias. And the choice.
Of their waiting. For Tube roses. (200)

This language, in a great variety of forms, fills much of the work written in these summers in the country, both in short observations and in longer works. Freed of the triple theme of "Winning His Way," it returns the following year when she explores poetry itself rather than why we write poetry, in "Stanzas In Meditation."

One and one never makes two if there are two.

—"Bartholomew Arnold" 326

No one can know one can now or able.

—"Stanzas In Meditation" Part I, Stanza vii

9. 1932

"Stanzas In Meditation"

The epigraph to the last chapter spoke of abandoning grammar for history, eating, and farming and never being happy. After the Hugnet debacle, in January 1931, Stein's grammar writing ended with "Forensics," followed by "Left To Right," a kind of final news bulletin about the quarrel, not a grammar piece. There was nothing left to write about it. Yet her attempt at translation led directly to her own poetry.

Already in 1931 she started working more and more with single words. She concentrated on elements of language—letters, sounds, phonemes, morphemes, syllables, words, names—punning dances in the parlor of speech. As she herself said, what led her into poetry was work with words. Now, lifting words from syntactical and semantic contexts freed them further from referential links and allowed more possibilities of play.

In another step away from representation, as chapter 8 suggested, she stopped the double procedure of writing grammar or language pieces and out of them creating other texts. Reading and writing become acts of discovery among multiple choices. As Juliana Spahr has said, reading exposes the workings of language, the how of its moving, toward what we see and hear, not what it points to.[1]

The work of early 1932, which by the summer leads to the poetry of "Stanzas In Meditation," returns me, with entirely new sights, to the texts that originally began this study. The writing from 1923 to 1932 opened con-

1. Juliana Spahr, "Letter and Read Her: The Reader-Centered Work in American Literature" (Ph.D. diss., State University of New York, Buffalo, 1996), chapter 2.

texts on which I rely: revelations in manuscripts—*cahiers, carnets,* even typescripts—that give access to the work from *inside* the process of writing. They made me focus on tiny visual and auditory details. Also in these texts were small "hooks" to events, people, and letters that dated texts and sequences. Often her whole opus now seems a single extended work.

True, each piece is self-contained, with a center and boundaries, but each also leads to or echoes others in mirrorings that move and shimmer across boundaries. Such bleedings or spills suggest links and changes from piece to piece. Discovering their sources sometimes opened what Stein was doing. What she seized to work with, ideas rising as she wrote became visible and audible. What and how she wrote became one. Contexts can open texts.

By 1932, however, her way with words changes and contexts virtually vanish. Already late in 1931, with texts like "Brim Beauvais," contexts of allusiveness—writing ideas, literary hints, events, letters, personal errands, people, details about art—such as I have followed show up less and less. Also, she speaks less of new work in letters so that we often do not know when, where, or how she came to write a new text. This vanishing of contexts spells not impoverishment but new freedom, new ways with words. It is as if her writing was liberated from the everyday world, barely hinged anymore to whatever it is that generates it.

No context gives access to *A Play Of Pounds* or "Bartholomew Arnold." "Marguerite Or A Simple Novel Of High Life" starts with elements that seem almost realistic but then move into a world of dislocated gothic abstraction. It is as if in 1932, only the most fleeting impulses from daily life generated writing that immediately sheds all traces of its origins, becoming purely verbal. At one point I called the pieces "abstracted and destabilized," but these terms are no more helpful than "undressed" or "decontextuated."

A Play Without Roses Portrait Of Eugene Jolas (P&P 200–207)

Written sometime in the winter of 1931–32, this play is also a portrait in praise of Eugene Jolas, "Let me think splendidly of Eugenes" (206). The subtitle is not in the manuscript, but instantly she starts playing with plurals, and both Eugene and his wife Maria appear on the second page of text.[2]

2. No copy of the play is among the Jolas papers, and there is no reference to it in letters, though Stein and the Jolases often met for talk or telephoned rather than writing. When on October 31 and November 7, 1985—over fifty years after Stein wrote the portrait—I met with Maria Jolas at her apartment in Paris and showed her the portrait, she declared firmly she had never seen it. However, her dislike of Stein as a lesbian, her rejection of the successful *Autobiography,* her attack with the "Testimony Against Gertrude Stein,"

The occasion for the portrait play is not clear, but the dates suggest that it may have had to do with the new start of *transition,* which again included work by Stein, as had many earlier issues. Maria Jolas' birthday on January 12, which in 1926 had also been the Jolases' wedding day, might also have entered this writing.[3] It does not seem to begin as a play, perhaps not even as a portrait; genre designations like portrait, poem, and play no longer place texts. The subhead "Eugene Jolas and Maria Jolas" (201) names the Jolases; "Part two" (202) breaks into scenes and acts.

The title may offer the piece as a compliment—a bouquet of words instead of roses; given how much Stein now plays with forms of words, "rose" returns as a noun or a verb, "rosy" as adjective or name. It opens with enormous shifts in tone, in pronouns—from "we" to "they" to "she" to "all." The sentences, separate, as if picked up in pieces or overheard, make continuous reading difficult:

> It is out of the question that we will meet. We need not be nervous if we are anxious. They will be more than ever ours or forward. She will be a doubt of how they like so much. As much. It was well known as well acquainted.
>
> All went all taught. All which is bit by bit.
>
> Very much out of the question to wonder in reliability or in aggression for them physically weak. (200)

Throughout, she works with alliteration, sound, rhyme, and varying forms of one word—"remain," "remaining," "ride"; "duty," "declare"; "needed," "kneeled"; "for," "fortunately"; "add," "addition," "added"; "all," "call."

The portrait-play itself begins with

Eugene and Maria Jolas

followed by

---

printed as a supplement to *transition* no. 23 (1934–35), her suspicion about Stein's politics during World War II, and her own communist convictions were such that she might well have wiped the piece from her mind, especially given its disjunctive quality.

3. Issue 19/20 (June 1930) was the last until it resumed with issue number 21 in March 1932. By this time, Elliot Paul no longer worked with Jolas and was back in the United States. See Jolas to Stein, 25 September 1929.

The new March 1932 number included Stein's "She Bowed To Her Brother," which Jolas received from her on December 15, 1931. She also sent him her tight, brief answer to his "Metanthropological Question" about the "Crisis of man" or "the evolution of individualism and metaphysics under a collective regime." Reponses to this inquiry were gathered from major writers; Stein's is drafted in the notebook for *A Play Of Pounds,* also of this winter. Jolas' question and Stein's answer are reprinted in *HWW* 53.

Maria Jolas.

From here on, Eugene Jolas or Mr. Jolas becomes a frequent refrain. The play fills up with names and plurals. Is Jolas a singular, a plural? How many Jolases are there? By the spring of 1932 there were not only two, Eugene and Maria, but four, including two "little ones," Betsy, age five, and Maria, age two, but no son; the line, "Mr. Jolas has a son or any one" (202) is not about a Jolas son. Is "Mine" a singular pronoun, with "mines" its plural? Does it take a singular or plural verb? Is it a noun, "mine," "mines"? And look at these three sentences and the next:

> Rosy is mines. Best is mines. Largely is mines.
> Which is or are mines.

We all know the error of analogous formations. "Mines" with an "s" by analogy with "yours," "his," or "ours" is an example. Is Jolas not even a noun or name but an adjective, "joli jolas," or a verb, joining French and Latin, *jolo, jolas, jolat?* And what is this plural,

> There is a load in m s plural.

Don't plurals intensify?

Stein plays games with forms of words and number that become abstract elements interacting in this portrait.

> Scene two
> Eugene Jolas. Let me think splendidly of Eugenes
> Or made intently of Eugenes
> Or further Eugenes. (206)

Perhaps thinking twice of a name makes it plural.

> Have you ever noticed how a name changes.
> Have you ever noticed a change in a name.
> Eugene Jolas. Think twice of a name.
> And thereafter they all or all wishes.
> Thinking twice of a name may be the cause of robust and twinkling. And.
> A name changes by whites and whites. (201)

Later we get a riddle:

> Act one
> When sixteen and four make twenty
> How is it that fourteen and sixteen make twenty-one
> Or more. (204)

One recalls such games as early as "A Long Gay Book,"

> four sses are not singular (*R* 108)

With the word "preparation," Part IV may echo "An Elucidation" but goes on to what else it is called—by title, by evaluation, description—then ends abruptly with a one-word shift, "What is it called for."

> It is called a preparation.
> And it is called or
> It is called better
> Or it is called more
> Or it is called before
> Or it is called as it is called
> It is called
> What is it called
> For (202)

This is not the only echo. The last of the following three lines is the title of a 1922 text, "I Feel A Really Anxious Moment Coming," and "anxious" also returns in *A Play Of Pounds.*

> A dialogue as anxious.
> It is not anxious.
> I do not as anxious feel a really anxious moment coming.

And earlier

> We need not be nervous if we are anxious. (200)

A Play Without Roses fills to the last line an unusual *cahier* that I have never seen among the Stein papers. Entitled "Myrtili" (myrtle, laurel, sacred to Venus), it carries the epigraph, "Mon nom est mon mystère" ("My name is my mystery"). It is an allegorical love tale about a winner of tournaments in a distant kingdom whose reward is the hand of one of the king's daughters, Odette. The only condition for the marriage is that she may not know his name. They live happily until she begs for his name. On condition that she never reveal it, he tells her, but she is weak and passes it on to her sisters, whereupon he vanishes. After she searches long for him throughout the woods, doing good deeds to show her devotion and atone for her error, he finally reappears and they are rejoined.

Has the choice of this *cahier* anything to do with Stein's preoccupation with names, including made-up ones, and with the magic of names? The portrait play for Jolas certainly relies on names and nouns.

A Play Of Pounds (LO&P 239–76)

This much longer play is fitted, like so many Stein texts, into a large *cahier,* filled to the very end.[4] The original title in the manuscript was "She Made Him," which slips into the play with "made" in the second of the opening four lines. There are no locations, no characters, and no names except three, once in midtext: an Andrew, a Bartholomew, and a James (241). For the rest, it is as if the tiny scenes or acts were themselves the speakers, followed most often by fragmentary single lines, in the third person singular or plural, which creates distance from the reader or audience.

Some themes recur. Writing always returns. Early on someone may be checking a book or proofreading, "looked through the book and there was one missing" (239), an idea with which she plays in various forms. Genius and masterpieces are prominent (239, 240) but we do not know how beyond Stein's enduring interest; ambition, recognition, reputation (254, 256), and money count. "They think well of me" (247), she says, and on to "riches" and "no richness."

> Will they be rich or in between
> Not as they like it.
> For them is there a difference. (260)

A skillful sequence laughs,

> Act I
> When I was happy I was well off.
> Scene two
> Or whether when I was happy I was happy with as well well off.
> Scene three
> When I was happy I was as well off. (258)

And is this the ribbon of the *Légion d'honneur?*

> All who. Joined them with a ribbon.
> A ribbon is a noun to stare.
> All beloved with care.
> For which foolishness they will join rich men. (248)

Notions of "improve," "neglect," and "mistake" recur, perhaps echoes of the Plain Edition. Here is a question of names, its direction unclear.

4. Drafted on the inside front cover is Stein's answer to the "Metanthropological Question" of Eugene Jolas, printed in *transition* no. 21 (March 1932); along with a reference in the play to a Christmas card (271), it dates the play about early January 1932.

Scene five
Could she be acquainted with their name.
Scene six
If they knew their name as their name. (264)

Soon it leads her to explore "come" and "welcome":

Act I
Will they come and will they welcome.
Scene one
Will they come and will he be welcome.
Scene two
Or will he be called away
Scene three
Or will he be not able to stay
Scene four
Or will he trouble them to ask him
Scene five
To be welcoming.
It is very happy to be often there
Act II
She may be always tractable or able or welcome if she is able.
To be welcome
Scene two
And no neglect makes her welcome. (264)

This play seems an effort to get rid of subject matter, to free words of meanings by playing with their constructive possibilities. She is trying out how we say things, how we talk or think, not what the things are or what they or we do or mean. I cannot say this play concerns genius, fame, or wealth, though these are certainly here. But she picks up tiny phrases about them in order to explore language. Near the end, she comments,

All of which makes it as talking.
Or should they be made to mean. (276)

There is a lot of play with *M* words, already familiar from earlier pieces; two mirrored *M*'s are drawn by Stein on the cover of the *cahier.* Most of the "statements" or "sentences" sound like attempts to free words of their occasion by exploring their constructive possibilities through talk or asides.

Act I
I cannot think that it will be managed.

Scene one
By pressure. Or exchange.
Scene two
Or even customarily
Scene two
Or as a little
Scene two
They will like
Scene two
Intermediate. Or blaming.
Act I
It is my time to be right. (249)

What are the odd pounds of this title? Can it be three meanings of the word "pound" from English to French to English—French *livres sterling* (pound sterling), French *livres* (pounds of weight), French *livres* (books)? Of course, the two identical French plurals, unlike English, break into a feminine and a masculine singular, *une livre* and *un livre.*

There's a lovely transparency about this play with its short lines, and its short, neutral, almost abstract words and phrases,

Scene one
Who is or who is helped
By their having
Or having been.
Left to be outlined
As well. (251)

Scene one
All just as it happened.
All of which it is
All more than not as they like
With and better not better
Or without it
Just or as it happened.
It is so easy
To be dazzling (252)

And look at her end stops, for Stein's punctuation is never accidental. What drives her punctuation here?

Act I
Oh may they matter to it.

Scene one
As their attachment.
Scene one
She is not
Scene one
So much more than
Scene one
They will.
Scene one
Mean one
Scene one
Which they will
Scene one
Mean one
Scene one
They will be kindness itself or they may like it.
Act II
May be.
Should or it could.
Scene one
If she was cold to him.
Or she was cold to him. (267)

Look at the stark "abstract" organization of Act I, Scene one, Scene three, Act II, Act two, and so on. These designations appear again in *A Manoir,* although that play has more names, especially in its later sections; they also return in *Byron A Play.*

I have spoken of lines more than sentences, which suggests poetry. *A Play Of Pounds* works especially with short lines that we see and read vertically down the page as poetry. She plays with words that are emptied of content or reference. "Emptied of" suggests that they once had antecedents, but there are none. Personal or relative pronouns like "their," "it," "they," or "who" do not point to references left behind. Others tend to be neutral auxiliary verb forms indicating time or voice, as in "having" / "having been" or "is" / "is helped."

Almost throughout, her sentence subjects are not nouns or names but pronouns. There is hardly any occasion or substance to grip; she plays with key words, not to follow or develop their meanings but to explore their use by changing form—"no care," "they care about"; "riches," "richness"; by rhyme—"light," "delight," "fight"; by compounding—"place," "common place"; by sound—"deliver," "deliberative"; "as pairs," "despairs"; "artifice," "avoidance," "acquaintance"; "party," "partly"; "does," "dove." She plays with that odd word "happen," exploring its relation to time, "just now," "just then," "happened to be."

> Act I
> It has happened to be that it has. Why then. Happened. It has happened to be.
> Act I
> Scene I
> What is the difference.
> Between happened to be and it has just now or just or just then it has happened to happen or to have to have had to had to happen or to me. (242)

In this fashion, words flow free and unattached, refusing succession and bouncing off referential sense in a kind of abstract word circus.

> Scene four
> All of which makes it as talking.
> Or should they be made to mean.
> That it is what they like.
> In every way as well as they like.
> In the making of it to be their care. (276)

"Margite Marguerite And Margherita" (*SIM* 269–77) and "Marguerite Or A Simple Novel Of High Life" (*MR* 339–73)

Both these texts start from the name Marguerite and its variants, and both concern identity in relation to identical names that are spoken, sounded, spelled slightly differently. Emphatically rhymed, the "Margite" poem plays with the name in French, Italian, and perhaps Finnish, for their Finnish maid Margit. Here are three dance rounds of names, the same and not the same, identical and divergent.

"Marguerite Or A Simple Novel Of High Life"[5] takes off from the familiar tale of an orphan or foundling who turns out to be of noble descent, traditionally identified by a sign such as a hidden birthmark, like Joseph Andrews or Tom Jones; that plot involves suspense, the hero's need to prove himself,

5. Probably written in Paris, late March or April 1932. On the inside cover of the *cahier* is the list of works included in *O&P,* which was being prepared late that winter or spring for the Plain Edition.

discovery of the identifying evidence, and a happy ending. Stein follows a different scenario, recalling the *cahier* about "Myrtili" and the mysterious power of names of *A Play Without Roses*.

The immediate occasion for the novel is the Finnish servant girl, Margit Tulonen, who worked for the women for about a year, from late 1931 until January 1933.[6] I do not know whether she in fact was an orphan and adopted or whether Stein created these features for this text. She knew about orphans or adopted children already—Madame Récamier's niece, the cast-out child of Madame Déscôtes, and Madame de Monzie's adopted daughter; also, both Stein and Toklas were left motherless at a young age.

Orphaned, without family, though she knows her birthday (356) and has a first name, Marguerite is a waif, a lost soul with no history, no memory, no surname, who dares not ask the main question, who am I (354). She is born in Finland—at the end of the world—and adopted by an unidentified family. No linear narrative, history, or biography can be written about her, for she has no social identity, no sense of provenance, family, or country. She floats in the great, cold north full of ice, and leaves, a kind of wandering Jew, to go, like Stein, first to England, then to France.

In England, she meets no one, remains lonely, makes no friends. It is said that she had an adventure, meeting another Marguerite (349), another self, perhaps a lesbian lover.

> Now she went away. Older. After that please mind the cross. And be always with and might have missed her mother. Might not. She had no father. She had no mother.
>
> In England she did not like weddings either. She felt very well. (346)

Unless she is to remain a nobody, she must create herself, make a name for herself, as Stein has done as an artist. Marguerite has none of the adventures and none of the intense daily life we might expect in a novel; unlike Ida, who does something about her situation by creating a twin for herself, Marguerite does not ground herself in a daily life but lives an abstract, transparent existence. The simple novel about her raises questions of how hers can be created as a high life, how we can know her, how we can read her "life story."

> Many things that have happened in her life are these. She would not say. What is it when you ask. She was not born in vain in Finland nor did she in vain go to England nor in a way in vain did she come to France. All

6. When her work permit ran out, she had to return home. A few postcards from her are at Yale. In the *Cookbook* (193–94), Toklas calls her a competent cook, a somewhat depressed Hamlet figure, who avidly read Stein's books.

these succeeded one another. And oftentimes she would not be conscious that this was past. Because quite naturally these countries were there in a way to her they might since without calculation there is no prostration they might not only follow it alone. She who was not blind because she had that beauty thoughtfully could be not known. I have often said I will not mention her. (372)

Near the end of the novel,

> She was waiting for no dog. She had been left not by them but by leaving. She would be often found in tears not without reason. (372)

And Stein concludes,

> I can no longer remember how she says what she says. (373)

Narrative is always in Stein's mind as an unsolved problem. For example, the narrative of "Marguerite Or A Simple Novel Of High Life" is tied to questions of identity, which in turn connect with family, history, and time. Always Stein looks deeply into the landscape of utterances, facts, and events to reach beyond the moment; sometimes light lifts them in forms that reach for writing.

Margit, the adopted orphan, bears some resemblance to a dog; unlike a dog, however, she suffers from her situation, for her sense of who she is is tied to her frustrated sense of place, time, and history. Dogs, born of bitches, do not become members of dog families. As they grow, they are quickly freed of the physical need for family; psychologically they develop no sense of time, memory, or history. Once sold to or adopted by human families, they are given first names, to which they learn to respond, but no last names. Not driven by language, they have no need to ask, who am I.

"Undressed," emptied of reference, language makes *A Play Of Pounds* a text of pronouns and word forms of syntactical activity that do not send us into the world to look for what they point to. "Marguerite" portrays the movements through languages and space of the orphan from the north with no surname, no history, no country, and no social identity. Unlike other Stein novels, "Marguerite" has never received the attention it deserves.

"Bartholomew Arnold Or After The War Is Over" (*MR* 321–38)

It is not clear whether "Bartholomew Arnold" was written before or after "Marguerite." In the same *cahier* with this work are also "Waiting For What," the brief text about the young painter Sir Francis Rose,[7] and "Or A History Of The United States Of America,"[8] which date the *cahier* to late March or April 1932. The subtitle, "Or After The War Is Over," is revised from an earlier subtitle, "Which leads not singularly to ways of narration."

Stein opens with Basket as a personality, not Bartholomew.

> He was named Basket and he could have shaken hands and then what comes after that.

Is Basket Bartholomew? Is Bartholomew like Basket? Is this a portrait, a story, a history? And what comes after what?

> This is the life of Bartholomew who was born after.

He seems to be male, a kind of boy, though he is not a child with an identity; he already has a sister but does not know that and perhaps he "had not to be had by a mother" (326). With bits of disjunctive narrative and description, snippets from all sorts of corners of the language of children, pets, and families, she speaks of making "a very little one . . . tiny," "ruled by their rest" (323). She starts with linear writing but undercuts it, disrupting time sequences, mixing tenses from past to future, and slipping subject pronouns from "he" to "they" to "she" to "it." Bartholomew is and is not a "character." Perhaps he is an "it." Again and again Stein starts but then breaks off what seems to want to become a story of a life.

Twice on the second page appears a subhead, "The first meeting" (322). Is Bartholomew a new idea, a new expectation of words springing to life? Is he a new work about to be born, a new paper creature, an offspring similar to Virginia Woolf's Orlando? Is Bartholomew this new work, or is it a narrative about its birth and its becoming a life? How can such a narrative be written?

> Bartholomew comes to live half way through or just as they knew or they did not know.
>
> . . .
>
> It is often their intelligence which is at fault.
>
> Bartholomew can be called will he or may he they had called him in and it is not a change to sing signs it is by that that they afterward like it as new.

7. Used to introduce the Francis Rose exhibit at the Galerie Vignon, April 12–25, 1932, this text was later that spring incorporated in "Here. Actualities."
8. This text, with additions, was in the spring of 1934 incorporated in the George Washington section of *FIA*.

> Bartholomew can not complain. It is better than never.
> But it is always a nuisance.
> . . .
> . . .
> Bartholomew was easily not a name. (323–24)

Another intermediate subhead follows, "The birth of Bartholomew." It turns out that

> He is not born. A very pretty charming little girl came to be born in the place of which no one could fancy that it has come. Alright.
> Could all be here who heard that he was here and not here.
> And so Bartholomew cried. Not only. Within itself. Because alternately. He was not coming. Nor had he come. Nearly enough. (325)

And disruption continues,

> Bartholomew can be called one. And they will come tomorrow. Oh how horrid it is to be not allowed to have been both the younger and the elder. Which is it. Do you not like it. Will you not mind it. Will you not get it. Do you not have it. Bartholomew naturally could be in uniform. He was waiting. (325)

Stein knew no one named Bartholomew,[9] and he makes no sense as one of the twelve disciples, the sculptor Bartholomé, or one of the many French towns beginning with St. Barthélemy. What starts as his history, birth, youth, development, is ruptured as soon as it begins, his parents canceled out. He requires a different telling, partaking of but rejecting representation, a power of life that is never sure or predictable and that we cannot explain. Androgynous, anthropomorphic, with the thinnest ties to reality, he will be a work of words. His initials B A, with the *B* Stein so often uses and whose link to Basket, her pet and child, opens the text, are the first two letters of the alphabet reversed.

"Bartholomew" is full of concrete "story" details, representationally teasing but never completed. It sounds and reads like a history or story but keeps saying, "No, that's not what I am. I am an idea for which there is no model in the world. I am new, unlike my so-called siblings, and I mutate all the time." It is as if this work, like *A Play Of Pounds,* from which it yet radically differs, also moved in elemental features of composition, combining the utterly referential and the totally abstract.

9. Alone, the name Bartholomew occurs, not prominently, in a few texts written in Mallorca and after, where it may relate to a son; with different second names, it returns in 1932, in *A Manoir* (298) and *Short Sentences* (320, 326, 331).

> Bartholomew may marry a ball. (337)

He may toss a ball, play a game of catch of balls and words, and free new phrases, new sentences, new narratives. Is writing like dog catching or ball playing? For Stein the dog is baby and pet, but he also becomes a locus for meditating and writing. He requires attention but, unlike a child, does not talk back or make demands. He can become a pivot for her meditation that gathers everything into the present moment, as if the interaction with him allowed perceptions to lift off that returned to her in words.

For six pages out of the total sixteen (327–33), she abandons the name Bartholomew altogether; the name Arnold appears only in the title. Why? Has Bartholomew failed to become what he promised and become something else? Is he, as his name would almost inevitably suggest to an American, a traitor, a Benedict Arnold? Is Stein playing with that association here and in the George Washington section of *Four In America,* where she incorporates the "Bartholomew Arnold" passage into the Washington text but substitutes for his name almost consistently "George Washington" or "George"?[10]

Look at how Stein ends the narrative of Bartholomew:

> They stretch arrest arrests. No one need know Bartholomew.
> Why should Bartholomew be so persistent.
> Bartholomew this time did not know what it was like.
> Bartholomew to ask what news is there of you.
> Or not. Bartholomew.
> Kindred Kit to Bartholomew.
> It is of not any importance to arrange what they have Bartholomew or higher than if they did know that not only not but a valley could be more than if a wish it were below.
> Why did they guess that they would not have Bartholomew.
> It is true that Bartholomew never came through. (338)

10. "Bartholomew Arnold" will return in my discussion of *FIA*. Why Stein used him in the Washington section is open to speculation. Was she using the story of Benedict Arnold to create history for Washington as novelist? Was she, without giving it away, playing a game of associating Bartholomew with Benedict Arnold and in turn with Washington, all as the same character? Did she want to undercut our associations with Washington as father of the country by giving him narrative material as a novelist? After all, *FIA* works with but undercuts history, making the book's four heroes into something other than what they were historically.

    Did she need to complete Washington and *FIA* in the hope of a contract? She had already added "Scenery And George Washington" and "Or A History Of The United States Of America" to the Washington section.

Even with the last sentence visibly a later addition in the manuscript, it sounds as if Stein had produced in "Bartholomew Arnold" a piece about a writing project that failed to become a text—a dog. Many of my remarks take the form of questions, for I am not sure about this tantalizingly slippery work.

"Bartholomew Arnold" is even more problematic than *A Play Of Pounds*. It is an almost nonreferential text about a Bartholomew that turns more and more ambiguous and finally has no existence. His narrative is quite different from that of Marguerite, of Lucy Church, of the Georges and "Finally George."

George, including Washington, another George, is grounded in the many Georges and, in "Finally George," in the fullness of vocabulary and the dense paragraphs that rarely contribute to narrative progress.

> Some know how George is gentle and bewildering gentle and bewildering. His name is George. He is meant to be superfluous and he is very much more than in the meantime. And how often is it that they do not cry. In the place. Of many cases. Of what they might. Like just as well. (275)

Lucy Church, while also a church and a village, is a credible if mutating character lyrically embedded in real things, the place, the landscape, the water, the moving hills.

> Lucy Church additionally meant with it at all and having suddenly added number five to the number of those very well known here but not exactly.
>
> Trading very well known here but not exactly.
>
> Finally for them. Lucy Church and chickens she prefers fields to fields and she says so but necessity intervenes not necessity not obligation not assurance but the possibility of there being no neglect. Imagine she says. Imagine what I say. (49)

Marguerite is a person though, lacking an identity, she is only a first name. Stein traces her movements, but without the lively details of so many Stein figures. She makes her more real than Bartholomew, with a provenance we can follow in her attempt to build a history.

But Bartholomew, a product of her mind, has none of the reality of these figures and no referents. Only for a moment does Stein by analogy make him into a Basket who could have shaken hands—but he is not Basket. He remains only as an "it," dog or girl, existing by implication, without events, perhaps even without being born. As in "We Came. A History," the "readie" for Bob Brown, we read the fragmented sentences horizontally across the page in a kind of linear ticker tape form. As a result, the history disappears as soon as it is written, and the text keeps us perpetually in the present, although the fragmentation creates a syncopation that breaks up the linearity.

> Maybe she will. Be very well. If they like it. It is often as exhausted. (321)

Very soon Stein will write "Stanzas In Meditation," where her characters—nearly all pronouns like "they," "she," "it," except "I," which is always Stein—exist in a fluid space and time that undercuts all narrative. A year later, she will again labor to make a play, this time out of a real dog that failed to live.

A Play A Lion For Max Jacob (P&P 28–36)

Here is another portrait such as Stein, combining genres, writes at this time. "A Play To Believe A Poem," it opens with a play and ends with a portrait poem. The occasion for this airy filigree in tiny, simple words and lines is not clear, though suggestions of "wishes" and "winning" may connect with a birthday or an honor, we cannot be sure. Jacob's birthday was July 12, though, for astrological reasons, he tried to change it to July 11.

As far as I have been able to ascertain, he received the nomination as *chevalier* of the *Légion d'honneur* in 1933; however, perhaps preparatory to this event, important works honoring him were created in 1932: Darius Milhaud's opera, *Maximilian;* Virgil Thomson's *Stabat Mater* to Jacob's text; the Francis Poulenc secular cantata, *Le Bal Masqué,* on Jacob poems. I assume that Stein wrote her text in the early summer of 1932. Though its exact date and occasion are open to speculation, the text, charming and lyrical, is not difficult to follow. She plays lightly with rhyming repetitions of the lion's land as a space for the play and Jacob as a gentle lion with purring paws, winning and won. It is

> A play in which a great many actors say I mean. (30)

She juggles numbers, actors running with meaning and counting, in short lines, sometimes joined into fast extended series, sometimes slowed to one line per act, as in the "Scenes" of *A Play Of Pounds.*

Act II
Scene one
Max Jacob   Forty make three run
Forty make four among
Thirty make twenty-two and bring

Thirty make five of twenty-one
And six make twenty-six and sung. (30)

The final portrait, mostly in fast two-beat lines beginning with "Be," is a wonderfully skilled, tender, singing tribute to the poet.

Stein takes off from Jacob's devotion to Lafontaine by using a *cahier* about Lafontaine's "Le Lion et le Rat," with its moral, *Patience et longueur de temps / Font plus que force ni que rage.*[11] Is she lionizing Max Jacob? Her interest in names may have entered the text. Jacob's father changed his name from Alexandre to Jacob, his second first name becoming his last name. Also, Max Jacob wrote early art criticism under the pseudonym Léon David. The poem ends with a cryptic abbreviation,

One or two or not three
U. P.

"Stanzas In Meditation" (*SIM* 1–151)

Context

"Stanzas In Meditation," also called "Meditation In Stanzas," and once, rounding off the count, "200 Sonnets Of Meditation,"[12] is composed in six French notebooks, two thin *cahiers* for Part I, three identical larger *cahiers* for Parts II, III, IV, and a fat dummy notebook, more capacious than the preceding three, for Part V. The size of the *cahiers* determines the length of the five parts. Beginning in a small *cahier,* Stein may not at first have anticipated a large work, but she soon needed a second *cahier* to complete the first part; requiring still more scope, she switched to larger *cahiers* for the next four parts and one larger still for the last. She relied on the *cahiers* to organize her work.

These *cahiers* show no images or text such as often entered other works; it is as if the disembodied abstract language rose from internal energy with no external stimulus. Nor is there evidence that Stein took notes in *carnets;* not only are none preserved, but spacing and handwriting in the *cahiers* nowhere suggest copying.[13] In other words, the manuscript *cahiers* do explain the five-part design but do not answer questions about the nature of "Stanzas."

11. "The Lion and the Rat"
Hence, we see / that patience and the hour can be /
stronger than a brute ferocity.
trans. Christopher Wood

12. *LGS/CVV,* 18 March 1937, 537. "Sonnets" may recall her comments on Shakespeare's plays and sonnets in the Henry James section of *FIA.*

13. Errors in the numbering of the stanzas were transferred from the Toklas typescript to

On the inside cover of the fifth manuscript *cahier,* for Part IV, Stein entered, barely legibly, with revisions, a descriptive title,

of commonplace
Stanzas ~~of my ordinary~~ reflections.
Stanzas of Poetry[14]

The reflections do not let you go, lead to no conclusion with a name. Nothing tells you what is what and what it is. No sign or cornerstone to look up. Every word or group of words sends you back to the shifting architecture of the work, never to the world in which it is erected. The happening of "Stanzas" is in the evolving verbal landscape, which includes but does not represent the world.

I opened this chapter observing that by 1932, contexts almost vanish from Stein's work. In the stanzas, and even before, her language virtually empties out of references. How then do text and context now relate? What are these texts, which seem to culminate in the self-portrait of the abstract stanzas that create a voice composing words? And finally, what happens in the world of her words between "Stanzas" and *The Autobiography Of Alice B. Toklas,* where every word seems pinned to a fact, person, or circumstance as in a documentary movie, until you think you have the whole life and the whole person in your hands? The referential autobiography creates a magnificent, hollow personality, successful and famous, which explains nothing about the creative process. The stanzas, described by Sutherland as "articulate thoughts in meditation" (xvi), create a voice composing words.

Reading them in the 1956 posthumous Yale volume taught me to attend to verbal details in more concentrated form than ever. Many passages wrenched idiom and incipient sense, creating distortions so that time and again a door shut on reading. Only once I looked at the manuscripts and typescripts of "Stanzas" did I discover in Stein's handwritten revisions a context that took me aback. Some of the passages that had made reading so forbiddingly difficult and odd were those that Stein had revised.

---

print. Where such errors appear, I add "a" or "b" to the first or second of two stanzas that bear the same number, for example, in Part III, iia, iib, or xvia, xvib. Numbering in manuscript (which I call "ms") sometimes differs from the typescript. The editors' adjustment of numbering in the Library of America text of "Stanzas," based on the first typescript (which I call "ts 1"), without adjustment to the text in the 1956 posthumous volume, results in unfortunate changes in sequence. This text (which I call "ts 2") was also not proofread for errors against ms and ts 1. Where textual errors occur in print compared to ms, ts 1, or ts 2, I so indicate for passages I quote.

14. In *AABT,* Toklas calls "Stanzas" "her real achievement of the commonplace," adding that Stein hopes "it is not too commonplace" (276).

Throughout the stanzas, Stein, who was not in the habit of revising, had laboriously and consistently changed her original phrasing, replacing not only the *auxiliary verb* "may" with "can" but the *word* "may" or "May" in all its forms. For example, "this May in unison" is revised to "this day in unison" (I, vi), a comprehensible change. But what of "should they may be they might," recast as "should they can be they might" (I, xv), which sounds odd, particularly after one has seen the idiomatic original? Again, "or may be they shall be spared," revised to "can they shall be spared" (I, vii), sounds like a downright error. What of the rhyme "may / to-day" (I, vi), destroyed in revision to "can / to-day"?

Some of the revisions twist the language to incomprehensible, even un-English phrasing. When I first read some of these passages, before I saw the manuscript, I thought they were Stein language games. But once I saw how the revisions were done, many phrases with "may" in the original turned out to be fairly ordinary, idiomatic English, skewed by the changes in phrasing and meaning.

As I could find no discernible writing reasons for them, I asked on what authority this text was revised. Inked in by Stein sometimes over the original in the manuscript, the changes are also typed by Toklas or inked by Stein into the second typescript. As the most authoritative text of a work is usually thought to be the latest, most up-to-date revised version, the editors of the sixth posthumous Yale volume (published in 1956) understandably relied on this revised typescript of "Stanzas."[15] Yet there was also another typescript, presumably the first, which reproduced the stanzas in their original, handwritten form, before revisions.[16] Did a comparison of these two typescripts not suggest that there was something odd about the second? Was such a comparison undertaken? Or did readers at that time consider any Stein text brilliant but largely incomprehensible word play and did they from the start eliminate the first typescript from consideration as an alternative, with no sense that its language is plainer English and more accessible?

We know that Donald Sutherland, who wrote the preface for the posthumous volume and raised no questions about the language, did not see the manuscript and did not know that there were two typescripts. At that time, no one looked in detail at Stein's manuscripts and typescripts. "Stanzas" was

15. This is the typescript that Thornton Wilder in May 1939 received from Sir Robert Abdy, who tried but failed to publish the work in a fine edition; Wilder returned the typescript to Stein, who later, with his support, submitted a selection of stanzas, marked "Poetry" on the pages, for publication in *Poetry* (Chicago), February 1940. See *LGS/TW* 230–31 and n. 4.

16. This typescript was among the papers of Carl Van Vechten, who gave it to the Yale Collection in 1940 for the Stein exhibit; we do not know when Stein sent it to him.

produced and reviewed, and no questions were raised about the authority of the text. I myself came to consider the printed text adulterated only once I studied the revisions.

That is when I began to report my findings in a series of essays interpreting how this text came about. Stein always said her life was not important for her work. However, in 1932–33 for the first time, the life becomes a key element for following the texts. As Stein and Toklas left almost no clues to their life, I relied on other documents, manuscripts, typescripts, letters, argument, and late comments of Toklas. Here is a gradual biographical detective story of what offered itself as aids in reading. The scenario outlined in this chapter differs radically from and replaces the conclusions in my earlier essays,[17] whose errors in dating affected how I read and interpreted the events and texts of 1932.

To discover what actually happened with this text led to a strange way of following evidence. I knew already that in the spring of 1932, the manuscript of Stein's early novel, *Q. E. D.*, about her 1902 love affair with May Bookstaver and a triangle situation in which Stein was jilted, was discovered in Paris.[18] But it took me weeks of pondering the substitution of "can" for "may" and other changes until their meaning finally came to me in a dream that made the verb "may" and the name "May" one. It was more than recognition of a pun. With nothing spelled out by the words, I then groped for what happened by a kind of underground burrowing in texts until, after twists and turns that led me down blind alleys to dead ends and misinterpretations, I found passageways into the texts through contexts I had not known were there.

I undertook two tasks. The first was to to follow the biographical events for 1932 in the hope of discovering when the "Stanzas" were written, when

17. I list these essays to emphasize that the present chapter of my book, the result of more extensive research, corrects errors in them. "How to Read Gertrude Stein: The Manuscript of 'Stanzas In Meditation,'" *Text,* vol. 1 for 1981 (New York: AMS Press, 1984); "Stanzas In Meditation: The Other Autobiography," *Chicago Review* 35, no. 2 (winter 1985), reprinted in Richard Kostelanetz, ed., *Gertrude Stein Advanced: An Anthology of Criticism* (Jefferson, N.C.: McFarland, 1990). The headnote to the selection of "Stanzas" in *A Stein Reader,* 2d printing, summarizes the main facts but includes no details and is in error about the timing of events and texts discussed in this chapter.

18. The novel, not published until after Stein's death, first, with some textual changes, under the title *Things As They Are* (Pawlet, Vt.: Banyan Press, 1950). It was next printed under its original title, with the original text restored, in *Fernhurst, Q. E. D., and Other Early Writings* (New York: Liveright, 1971), with a note on the texts by Donald Gallup and an introduction by Leon Katz. Further details about the publication are in Donald Gallup, *Pigeons on the Granite: Memories of a Yale Librarian* (New Haven, Conn.: Beinecke Rare Book and Manuscript Library, 1988), 145–57.

completed, when typed, revised, and retyped, and why. I also followed in manuscript and typescript the other texts Stein wrote in 1932, especially the plays *A Manoir* and *Short Sentences,* where some changes of a different kind had also been made. The second task was to compare the manuscript and the two typescripts of "Stanzas" in order to find out how Stein and Toklas did the revisions.

The events in Paris of the spring of 1932 are described in the brief "Here. Actualities.," a title that translates French radio language introducing newscasts, "Ici les actualités." It announces four historic debuts: the first communion of Picasso's son Paulo in April, the first one-man show of Sir Francis Rose, April 12–25 at the Galerie Vignon, the inaugural lecture on April 11 at the Collège de France of Bernard Faÿ as Professor of American history, upon his appointment on February 29, and the discovery in Stein's studio, just before the April 30 birthday of Toklas and the women's departure for the country, of "the first thing that was written." Not identified by title in the newscast and not known to Toklas, it is the manuscript of *Q. E. D.*

About this first book the report asks, "was it hidden with intention," followed almost immediately by the cryptic, "There is no blindness in memory nor in happening." The mere question suggests that the answer is yes, but hidden from whom, why, when? Only from Toklas, at the hub of their joint daily life, could it have been intentionally hidden.[19] When I first followed and dated these details, I concluded that Toklas read the early novel as soon as it was found in Paris or upon arrival in Bilignin and that she flew into a jealous rage about the early love affair[20] of which she had not known and which she felt was absorbed in the many forms of "May," "may," and *M* words in the "Stanzas" that Stein began to write in the early summer. I was wrong. Even though Toklas later read the love affair into the poems, she knew nothing of it in the early summer, for she did not read *Q. E. D.* until much later in the year. How the affair returned to Stein's mind and

19. Before mid-July, Toklas had typed the little report. In a letter of July 17 to Henry McBride, Stein said she had written another piece of actualities, which she was "not giving away for nothing." The first such piece was "Left To Right," which was to be a definitive dismissal of the cooperative relationship with Hugnet. Not giving it away for nothing was a reminder to McBride that she had not yet been paid for "Genuine Creative Ability," which he had published in *Creative Art* for February 1930. Stein planned to submit the new text to *Harper's Bazaar,* London, which had in 1931 printed "Left To Right."
20. What apparently enraged Toklas was less the love affair itself than the fact that when in 1910 she and Stein, trying to obviate forever any need for jealousy, had sealed their love pact by exchanging confessions about all their earlier attachments, Stein had not told about this love affair whereas Toklas had supposedly told all. Toklas now accused Stein of breach of faith, going after her with paranoid recriminations.

whether it left traces in her writing is a separate matter of great but speculative interest.

With Stein and Toklas in the Paris studio the afternoon *Q. E. D.* was found were Bernard Faÿ[21] and Louis Bromfield, the novelist. Stein handed the manuscript to Bromfield, asking him to read it. She may have wished to remove it from Toklas or to enlist help from this best-selling novelist to get it published, for she made a publication project out of any opportunity that offered itself. When, then, did Toklas find out what *Q. E. D.* was about? The answer to this question is crucial, for it affects how we interpret the texts that follow.

The letters from Bromfield to Stein at the Yale Collection of American Literature and hers to him at the Ohio State University Library, nearly all from both undated, show that Bromfield in the summer of 1932 had the manuscript of *Q. E. D.* and praised it "for the presence in it of the ideas which later flowered in Lucy Church." He recognized its interest as well as the difficulties of publishing it.[22] Bromfield also placed *Lucy Church Amiably* on the summer list of recommended reading for the *New York Daily Tribune* and had written to Irita Van Doren about "her books," presumably the Plain Edition. Unsure about Stein's country address, he sent his letter to rue de Fleurus for forwarding. In her answer, perhaps late May or June, Stein carefully wrote out her address, thanking him for his efforts on her behalf, and continued,

> if the quod erat could be published to be sure I did not dare read it when I found it they won't lose it because it is the only copy that exists anywhere I am working a lot I am trying to write a long dull poem like the long ones of Wordsworth and it is very interesting to do.

Bromfield answered about July 17 or 18, after the Picasso *vernissage* of July 16,

> I still have the manuscript which I am guarding carefully hesitating to send it to the rue de Fleurus and fearful of sending it to your country address. . . . If this letter reaches you I'll send it along if you say so. However,

21. They may have been looking among Stein's early papers for material connected with *The Making Of Americans,* which Faÿ had contracted with Librairie Stock to issue in a translation by the Baroness Renée de Seillière and himself. It appeared in 1933 as *Américains d'Amérique.*

22. This letter, printed in *The Flowers of Friendship* (249), is misdated and excerpted with errors. The Bromfield novel referred to is *A Modern Hero* of 1932, not *Twenty-Four Hours* of 1930, as Stein's answers to Bromfield at Ohio State University Library make clear. That publication was problematic is hardly surprising if we remember that Radclyffe Hall's *The Well of Loneliness* (1928), in spite of favorable reviews, had been tried for obscenity.

> Cass Canfield of Harpers is coming out on Sunday [July 19 or 26] and I should like to talk to him about it . . . an extremely astute fellow. . . .

In her next letter, say late July, Stein again spoke of *Q. E. D.*,

> About the ms. do keep it I only meant if there was a question of somebody really taking it on we would have it type written but keep it until we get back and I have no prejudice against Harpers.

Though no letter announcing or acknowledging the shipment is preserved, I assumed that by August, when Bromfield was to go on vacation to Sweden or Salzburg, he must have returned the manuscript rather than leaving it in the empty *presbytère* at Senlis. As a result, I assumed that Toklas read *Q. E. D.* later that summer and difficulties began then. Only much later did I discover that I was wrong.

Among the papers of the W. A. Bradley Agency, now at the Humanities Research Center in Austin, is a one-page letter from Stein to Bradley, stamped "rcvd 16 December 1932." She was back in Paris after the summer, with the typescript of the *Autobiography* already delivered to Bradley, who had started to negotiate a contract for it with Harcourt Brace. In this very businesslike letter, she quotes to Bradley her endorsement of Charles Henri Ford's and Parker Tyler's gay novel, *The Young and Evil,* which Bradley, through Stein, had placed with Jack Kahane of Obelisk Press; a typed page with the endorsement is attached. As an afterthought, she adds,

> I have just received the ms of that early first book of mine and its title was Quod Erat Demonstrandum we were all young once. When you come the next time I will show it to you.[23]

Implied is that she has already told Bradley of the "early first book." Did she think that at a moment when Bradley was negotiating a lucrative contract with Harcourt Brace, he might even place *Q. E. D.* to ride in on what promised to become the success of the *Autobiography?* Was it from Bromfield that she had just received the novel and had he kept it until December rather than sending it to her? Now her late July answer to Bromfield, telling him he could hold on to the manuscript, returned to me, joining her note to Bradley. If this was correct, Toklas could indeed not have read *Q. E. D.* or known of the love affair in the summer unless Stein told her, a most unlikely possibility.

An interesting addition appears in the *Autobiography.* Without title,

23. How ironic that in a single letter Stein should write her endorsement for the young gay novel of Ford and Tyler and speak of her own young gay novel, written thirty years earlier, neither typed nor published.

Figure 10. Photograph by Charles Henri Ford, taken on 1 or 2 July 1933 upon his visit to Bilignin with Stein, Toklas, the "Widow Roux," their housekeeper, a local man, Bernard Fäy, and, in the foreground, Ford.

Q. E. D. is described three times in one paragraph on page 104[24] as "a completely forgotten first piece of writing." This idea, put by Stein in the mouth of her lover, who knew nothing of it, is to stop speculation, make the early book sound unimportant—or make Toklas sound naive. At the same time, in the comment of Toklas, *Q. E. D.,* not created through the power of her inspiration, is denied reality. A single sentence at the end of this paragraph in the manuscript of the *Autobiography* states,

> I I
>
> When ~~we~~ get home this autumn ~~we~~ will read it.

With "we" revised to "I," the sentence is then crossed out in red and not printed.[25] I now no longer read this canceled sentence as indicating that Toklas had read the novel before the *Autobiography* was finished and they returned to Paris but as an error in voice that Stein removed; the sentence

24. This is in the last section of the original Part III, "1907–1914," of the book, the end of what is now Chapter 4, "Gertrude Stein before she came to Paris."

25. I have not succeeded in finding the original typescript or the setting typescript of the *AABT.* They are not among the Stein papers. Harcourt Brace have assured me that setting typescripts are kept for no more than two years and normally returned to the author. Nor was the printer, Quinn and Boden Company, Inc., of Rahway, New Jersey, able to help; the original printer had died in 1978 and the firm has been disbanded.

Figure 11. Gertrude Stein, Bilignin, 4 July 1933, during Charles Henri Ford's visit. Photographer unknown.

appears to speak far more in Stein's voice than in that of both women (we) or Toklas (I), and Stein's voice is inappropriate for the *Autobiography.*

If the note to Bradley and the earlier statement to Bromfield imply that the novel was not returned and Toklas had not read it in the summer, how do we then look at the revisions of "Stanzas," when were they done, what do we make of the changes in the texts of *A Manoir* and *Short Sentences,* and does *Q. E. D.* enter the context of the *Autobiography?* If Toklas did not read the novel until after the *Autobiography* was written, typed, and delivered to Bradley, how do we read the texts, revisions, and events of that summer and fall?

There is no further reference to *Q. E. D.* in the Stein-Bromfield letters[26] and none, for that matter, in the Stein-Bradley letters. I considered whether

26. Only in his review of the *AABT,* "Gertrude Stein, Experimenter with Words," published upon the book's appearance in the *New York Herald Tribune,* Sunday, 3 September 1933, 1–2, does Bromfield briefly speak of the early novel, giving away nothing about its lesbian content.

> I had the interesting good fortune to read a novel, unpublished, and written in an old copy-book, set down when Gertrude Stein was in her early twenties. The struggle with these elements [i.e., to achieve a direct emotional contact with the reader and to create a sense of actuality] was already present. The faded writing had in it the same fierce intensity of purpose and evidence of the same battle with words and grammar and meanings which has occupied her steadily since then.

Bromfield might have given the manuscript to someone else, who could have returned it to her in December, but rejected the only possibility, Bernard Faÿ.[27]

The *Autobiography* may give us a clue to solving the mystery of a late statement, where she has spoken of landscapes and *Operas And Plays,* published in the Plain Edition, August 1932, and goes on,

> I am trying to be as commonplace as I can be, she used to say to me. And then sometimes a little worried, it is not too commonplace. The last thing that she has finished, Stanzas of Meditation, and which I am now typewriting, she considers her real achievement of the commonplace. (276)

If we take these words literally, they would mean that Toklas would have been typing the "Stanzas" at the end of October, shortly before submitting to Bradley the first and second part of the typescript of the *Autobiography,* on November 16 and 25. But if these words are put into the context of that summer and the writing of the "Stanzas," this is not at all what they mean.

If Stein began writing the "Stanzas" in May or June and finished them late July or mid-August, then, logically, given the women's usual working procedure, Toklas would have typed them when they were complete—say mid-August. But we know that the women had an August deadline to return the proofs for *Operas And Plays.* That deadline could have delayed the typing of "Stanzas."

The "Stanzas" were a major work, filling six *cahiers,* some very large. Therefore, considering that Stein, in the voice of Toklas, says that she is "now" typing the "Stanzas," it is clearly a physical impossibility. At that point in real time, Toklas must have been finishing the typescript of the *Autobiography.*

This could mean that she waited, given the constraints of proofreading

27. Bernard Faÿ had visited Stein in June and again from August 20 to 30, and had then from September 22 to December 10 been in America and returned in time for his first lecture at the Collège de France on December 12. The only likely confidant for the book or its matter, which she might have discussed with him, he never in his many letters mentions it, nor does Stein in hers to him; nor would he have taken it to America. Faÿ and Bromfield had planned but never produced a critical book about Stein; no letters from Faÿ to Bromfield are preserved among the Bromfield papers at Ohio State University. Nothing leads me to think that Bromfield, at her request, passed the novel to Faÿ.

Nor is it likely that she might have spoken of it or shown it to Charles Henri Ford, who visited her that summer; or to Paul Bowles, whom she saw only once, briefly. Both were young, preoccupied with their own work, and unaware of Stein's early work or life. Ford, in correspondence and interviews with me (May–June 1989; 5 February 1998), recalled no details about Stein, her work, or her moods; distrustful about his relationship to Tchelitchew, she would have been unlikely to reveal personal details.

Operas And Plays, to type the text of "Stanzas." Or was she typing them *as* Stein was writing them, or as Stein was writing the *Autobiography,* or did she in fact wait to begin typing until the *Autobiography* was finished?

Either way, it became clear that Toklas could not in this statement have been referring to typescript 2—the revised text—for she could not have read *Q. E. D.* until December. Therefore, the revisions had to be pushed forward. And not only the revisions of "Stanzas" but also the revisions in *A Manoir* and *Short Sentences.* Bromfield returned the manuscript in early December and, as the crossed-out sentence of the *Autobiography* said, "I will read it when I return."

When the stanzas were being purged, Stein had to review her text word for word as she may never have done before. In that process, she not only marked the "may/can" changes but also made other, literary revisions in certain stanzas that are distinct improvements.[28] The result is that typescript 2, the corrupt text, includes a number of true revisions. I add here only a few examples of these, in a footnote, to illustrate her care with the stanzas, even as she missed many of the "may's" that the eye, after all, barely notices in any text.[29]

Contrary to what I stated earlier in print, the writing of *The Autobiography Of Alice B. Toklas* does not appear to be related to the writing of "Stanzas" or *A Manoir* and *Short Sentences.* Toklas did not read *Q. E. D.* until after the *Autobiography* was written. Of course it is true that this book portrays and creates Toklas, joining her name forever to that of Stein and Stein's name to her voice, iconizing the two in the world. It becomes a marriage certificate more permanent than any legal marriage contract and made this marriage last as literature far beyond the life and death of the partners.

Typescript 1 of "Stanzas" was not destroyed but kept and in December

28. These can be followed by comparing ms, ts 1, and ts 2, a slow process, where one also discovers how Stein crossed out "may" and substituted "can" and how Toklas, apparently, sometimes got ahead of her in typing the revised or censored ts 2, which yielded the Yale text.

29. I show the replacements in these examples:

I, ii Often as evening is as light
As once for all
Think of how many ~~open~~ often
And they like it here.

I, iii He thought ~~that~~ they needed comfort
Which they did
And ~~they~~ he gave them ~~an~~ as assurance
That it would be all as well.

I, xii Could call meditation often in their willing
Just why they may can count how ~~may one~~ many are mistaken

1936 sent by Stein to Carl Van Vechten, who gave it to Yale and had no reason to check it against typescript 2.[30] We do not know for certain whether or when typescripts 1 of *A Manoir* and of *Short Sentences* were prepared or what happened to them. But it is striking that these three works have second typescripts, from which they were printed; we do not know how the first typescript of "Stanzas" came to be kept.

How are we to interpret the maddening evidence hidden in the documents about "Stanzas" and the following texts? The fact that Stein kept typescript 1 and gave it to Van Vechten, on whom she could rely to preserve it, suggests that she wanted to keep the evidence. Evidence of what? This remains the question behind this intricate biographical melodrama that leaves "blood on the dining room floor" at the end of 1932, long before Stein wrote her murder mystery the following summer.

The stanzas do echo tension between the women, but it is not about *Q. E. D.* Part of it is the frictions and swings of mood of daily life together. Much of it is the long years of unsuccessful efforts to make her work known, the inadequacy of the Plain Edition in compensating for the lack of readers. The tension entered the relationship with Toklas, whose great efforts for the Plain Edition could not satisfy Stein's enormous need for recognition. And yet in the stanzas, Stein appears to fly free of her obsessive needs into a land of language liberated from the world to rise, often beyond understanding, in a kind of song of singing. She was never again so free of audience. While she was in America, hostile distress sometimes shows up when Stein did not see her family or her old friends in New York, including Mary Knoblauch, just widowed, and Mabel Weeks. Monitoring Stein's engagements, Toklas kept her away from her past.

According to Leon Katz, who in 1953–54 discussed *Q. E. D.* with Toklas, the quarrel continued off and on until the second visit to Chicago, in March 1935, when Stein told Toklas she would leave her unless she stopped goading and bickering. Toklas told Katz she did stop. However, for years she entered small, sharp reminders in Stein's manuscripts. For example, in the typescript of *Byron A Play,* written soon after the troubles began, Toklas types "Byron. -ay we be left to any one" (377) and Stein, by hand, fills in the "M" that makes the word "May." In the same play, the section beginning "Let us think of a name" (364–65) is full of phrases that play with "May" and "may," suggesting that the goading may have been mutual. Again, in the manuscript of *Everybody's Autobiography,* Toklas many times in her red pencil circles "may" and, erasing or circling the "n," the word "many." In "An American And France" (1936), in the sentence "so many Spanish painters married Russians"

30. See *LGS/CVV* 528 and n.

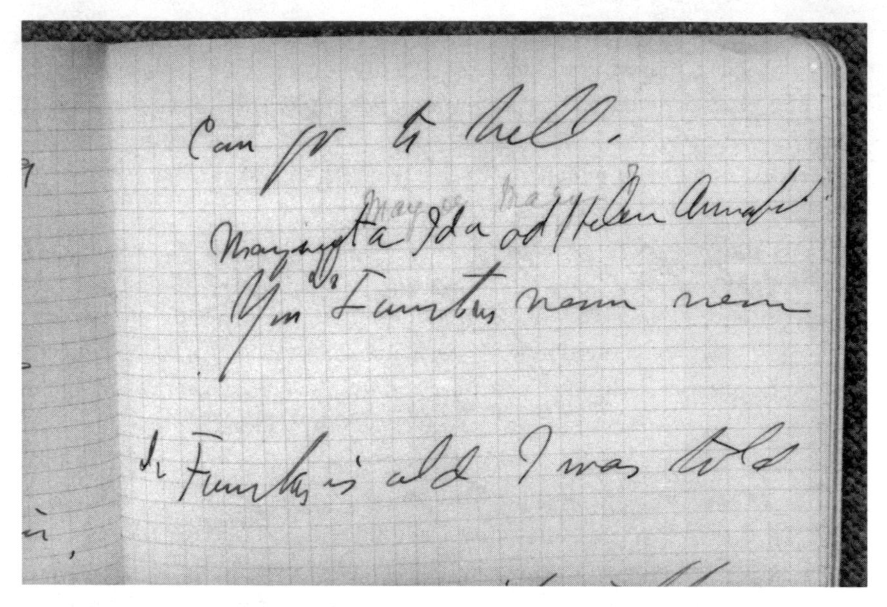

Figure 12. Alice Toklas sees hidden meanings in Stein's manuscript *cahier* of *Doctor Faustus Lights The Lights,* 1938. Courtesy YCAL.

(*WAM* 63), Stein wrote "may" instead of "many," whether by an oversight or to tease Toklas, who then with pointed pen added the missing "n." On the margin of *Doctor Faustus Lights The Lights* (1938), Toklas asks whether Marguerite Ida Helena Annabel is another *M* figure. Such exchanges appear for years as a red subtext in manuscripts.

Apparently after the discovery of the manuscript, Toklas destroyed the letters of May Bookstaver that Stein had kept and in part incorporated into the novel. Years later, upon an inquiry about the book by Donald Gallup, Toklas told him that Stein had given her the manuscript,[31] a sure way to see to its preservation.

Back in Paris, with the *Autobiography* about to become a sure success, Toklas would have read the novel. This would have been when Toklas was already, as she says in the *Autobiography,* typing the original, not the revised, text of "Stanzas." And it would have been then that she flew into a rage over her discovery, made Stein revise the text, and eventually retyped it, which gives us typescript 2. Also at this time, Toklas would have typed the delayed sum-

31. For further details about manuscript and publication of *Q. E. D.,* see Gallup, *Pigeons on the Granite,* 147–56.

mer texts of *A Manoir* and *Short Sentences* and would have made the small but dramatic changes in the typescripts that speak her mind.

My vast contextual excursion into the scenarios of 1932–33 identified the text of the first typescript as Stein's original "Stanzas In Meditation" but explained nothing about the nature of its poetry. The drama of who "may" and who "can" becomes the essence of the power play between the two women. With its astounding power to nail down misleading referential meanings, however, it was a biographical, not a literary, matter. Nor did the *Autobiography,* beyond naming and approximately dating it, tell us anything about the "last work that she has written."

The abstract, disembodied stanzas can be read in innumerable ways, especially as they also "bleed" one into the next, echoing across lines and works. That is why they are so seductive for those engaged in theory and decontextuated, authorless reading and so seductive as well for referential misreading.

A note is needed on the execution of the revisions of "Stanzas." Toklas must have demanded purgation from the start of the quarrel in December 1932 on. But how did that work? How did she go about enforcing her demands? The evidence of the changes from typescript 1 to typescript 2 and from manuscript presents an even more complicated scenario when looked at in detail. It was not so simple as changing every "may" to "can" in the "Stanzas."[32] How did the women manage the changes?

For the most part, the only revisions in typescript 1 are where Toklas missed a page in the manuscript and Stein wrote in the missing lines. So then typescript 2 must have been changed by going back to manuscript. But was it? It would seem that the quarrel erupted as Toklas was typing typescript 2 against manuscript and that she then demanded that Stein make the changes in the typescript. She then further demanded that Stein change the manuscript.

There is no consistent general procedure. Stein and Toklas seem to have tried to work things out as they went along but never quite managed to find a reasonable way. As a result, my comments vary from Part I to Part V. Also, the changes involve not only "may/can" but other textual, typographical errors, and misreadings.

32. The small but significant changes in *A Manoir* and *Short Sentences* were executed by Toklas alone; I assume that Stein, busy with readying the *AABT* for publication, did not participate in proofreading them.

Part I

In general, up to Stanza vi, Toklas typed "may" and Stein wrote in "can." In Stanza vi, in manuscript, Stein first changed "This May in unison" to "This day in unison." From then on, for the most part, every "may" is changed to "can" in manuscript. However, it appears that Stein may have entered that change in manuscript after she made it in typescript 2, for Toklas continued to type "may," which Stein amended to "can."

Also in Stanza vi, Toklas for the first time in typescript 2 left line spaces open, which Stein filled in. For example, she typed "All may be glory," leaving the rest of the line blank. Not changing the line in manuscript, Stein completed it in typescript 2 to read "All can be glory can be can be glory." This leaves open the possibility that all Stein's manuscript changes in Part I were made after she had amended typescript 2.

The revisions in Part I seem altogether mixed up—no method has been worked out.

Part II

Up to Stanza xi, Toklas types "may" and Stein changes it to "can." From Stanza xi on to the end of Part II, Toklas types "can."

Part III

Mostly Toklas typed "can" from the changed manuscript. In typescript 2, up to Stanza ix, there are no changes in Stein's hand. Then, in Stanzas ix, xi, xviii, and xix, Stein entered some changes that Toklas missed.

Part IV

Through Stanza x, the "may/can" changes are entered into manuscript and into typescript 2 by Stein. Beginning with the end of Stanza x, we rarely see Stein's hand in typescript 2 because nearly all the changes are typed in by Toklas.

"Can" in typescript 2, with few exceptions, reflects the changes entered in manuscript from Stanza x on.

Part V

We no longer see Stein's hand in manuscript at all. Toklas automatically, on her own, changes every "may" to "can."

Text

What allowed Stein to rise suddenly into writing at the edge of language the abstract, disembodied edifice of "Stanzas"? From the start, hers is the language of poetry—word play, homonyms, homophones, puns, double entendres, repetitions, variations, rhythms. She has written that language for years, though she has only recently, in part when working with the idea of the "Readies," started composing in lines, breaking up sentences, and using stops to monitor speed, movement, and rhythm in speech. Her unwavering interest in narrative never prevents her from relying on that language, whether in poetry, plays, portraits, or novels.

The narrative portraits of 1932 relate to the exploration of spaces, movement, and lines that we see in 1931. By the early summer of 1932, when she begins "Stanzas In Meditation," her ear is trained to work with line spaces, not the same as meter; she is free of the syncopating machinery of full stops and capitals, and her lines flow for whole stanzas in smooth continuity with virtually no punctuation at all. The discipline of 1931 has taught her new attention to words in movement. Her poetry now carries its grammar without punctuation, no longer an essential element. Periods can be used to stop writing arbitrarily, for they are no longer needed to support meaning in servile ways, as she said in "Poetry And Grammar" (*LIA* 218). Rarely, for emphasis in rhetorically prominent positions, do periods still turn up, as in the third and fourth lines here:

> Just why they joined for which they knelt
> They can call that they were fortunate.
> They may be after it is all given away.
> They may. Have it in mine. (I, vi)[33]

Each time I try to grasp a passage, phrase, or stanza, it changes shape, dissolving its boundaries and loosening the bounds of commentary. In this instability of shape, voice, and meaning lies the maddening magnificence of the stanzas. I want to read, not read into or pin down, the poems. I read aloud, listen to the changing permutations. The more the language empties out of references and antecedents, nouns to pronouns, the more new readings open.

As long as I look for consistency, each reading seems to cancel the last as a misreading. Yet each is a discovery, multiplying rather than striking out

33. Stein, in manuscript, made errors in numbering, which Toklas, not always correctly, adjusted. I quote text of "Stanzas" throughout from ts 1, indicating duplicate numbers with "a" or "b." The editors of the Library of America text regularized the numbering of the stanzas but did not take into account the numbering of the Yale text; where the Library of America numbering differs from that of ts 1 and the Yale text, I add "LA" followed by that stanza number. Where necessary, text is amended by checking against manuscript to correct errors.

possibilities. I read what I see and hear. How do I speak the second of these lines to discover what Stein was doing:

> See how one thing can mean another.
> Not another one no not any not another one. (IV, xi)

Passages enter eye and ear in different ways. Few make a continuous order the mind can grasp, be it in sentences, lines, images, or ideas.

A very few strike us with bright, sharp nouns, verbs naming concrete things, or perceptions in phrases that sing,

> All potatoes are even when they have flowers . . . (III, iib [LA iii])

> Let me see let me go let me be not only determined (II, xix)

Some verses laugh at familiar forms, like this one-stanza takeoff on nursery rhymes,

> Stanza ten make a hen
> Stanza third make a bird
> Stanza white make a dog
> Stanza first make it heard
> That I will not only go there
> But here (III, xii [LA xiii])

Or ask a little question, say about water, or is it about plurals and collectives; watch what she does with "kind" as adjective or noun:

> It comes to this I wish I knew
> Why water is not made of waters
> Which from which they well.
> Can they be kind if they are so inclined. (IV, xi)

Sometimes familiar asides appear, but whether such remarks come from the Stein-Toklas ménage or whether they are shrewd comments on how we mutter asides while writing is irrelevant.

> I have often thought that she meant what I said. (V, ii)

> Who is winning why the answer of course is she is. (IV, xxiv)

A little earlier in this stanza, at the point when five leaves remain before the end of the *cahier,* which will also be the end of Part IV and of this stanza, she looks ahead and says,

> It is very difficult to plan to write four pages.
> Four pages depend upon how many more you use.

You must be careful not to be wasteful.
That is one way of advancing being wasteful
It uses up the pages two at a time for four. . . . (IV, xxiv)

The four remaining pages will complete this section in the space left in the *cahier* that governs her format.

Such passages can be brilliant lyrics, observations, and epithets that show her working methods; they also provide relief from the almost uniform patterns of neutral, abstract language. But they do not open a total canvas for "Stanzas." It is almost impossible to quote complete sentences, full stop to full stop. To read a stanza, we must give up our reading habits, abandon expectations of language behavior, and read aloud word for word, literally, I am tempted to say naively, as if we did not know how to read. Such reading requires enormous effort against all our proud training as readers and writers. For the language in "Stanzas" is constantly in the process of mutation. The effort to follow it cleans out our minds and ears; sometimes it gives us access to the virgin territory of the making of poetry itself.

When speaking the stanzas aloud, we are beguiled by sound—that is why they are so hard to read. Stein relies on the "abstract," "disembodied" language to keep us from reading expressively, but we fall by habit into expressive reading and then end up lost in an expressiveness that does not work because her language prevents it. The only way in is by reading over and over, until the words begin to assemble themselves in patterns we can hear and see.

Sometimes details open the edifice of "Stanzas," an almost ghostly filigree transparency lifted from the everyday world, not visibly sustained by poles supporting its architecture. Shimmering screens of translucent words and reflecting, encircling figuration constantly change in meaning and function. The words echo and mirror. She called the poems "reflections," a term she had used for her translations of Hugnet's poems; anglicized French, it includes both *reflet,* from *refléter,* which is used for reflecting light, and the more abstract *réflexions,* from *réfléchir,* meaning to think or meditate.

Once again I think I am reflecting
And they may be patient in not why now
And more than if which they are reflecting
That if they with which they will be near now
Or not at all in the same better
Not for which they will be all called
By which they will may be as much as if wishing
But which each one has seen each one
Not at all now. . . . (I, xv)

How can we write about a large work whose importance we do not doubt even as it defies analysis, characterization, classification? How do we describe these "Stanzas," enter them, retrieve their intention, their sense, their grammar? Beyond useful comments on details, most attempts to speak about them have failed.

Stein rarely commented on her work; to her, a proper job of writing was self-explanatory and required no comment. Her most interesting comments on writing appear in letters to writers. In a letter to Lindley Hubbell that I date August 25, 1931, are two comments that may be related. Hubbell had sent her a book of his poems.[34] First, she insists, in commenting on Hubbell's poems ("they"), that sound and meaning in poetry must be deliberately divorced; but then she quickly shifts to the more general and personal writer's "you," "us," and "we," which includes herself and her own work. Next, she speaks about her new poem,

> Thanks for the book of poetry, I like it, it really is poetry . . . every now and then there is a perfect harmony of sound and sense, and they are simple and they bear rereading, just how meaning is related to sound and just how you must conceive meaning so that sound does not count, is the thing that endlessly holds us, because of course if the meaning has a certain emphasis, then the sound separates itself and it all goes to pot, and if the sound sounds then the meaning is annoyed, and after all the meaning is reliable only if it creates in and by itself the sound, and yet there should be no sound, well its all very difficult, but then it is what we do. I am at present trying a long narrative poem, I always had a passion in my youth for the long dull poems of Wordsworth and Crabbe and I want to do a long dull poem too and a bare one[35] and perhaps I am but anyway your sympathy and appreciation mean a lot to me and I know mine do to you.

34. At YCAL, his letter is dated May 1931. Hubbell's book, *The Tracing of a Portal* (New Haven, Conn.: Yale University Press, 1931), inscribed to Stein, who marked the poems she liked, is preserved at YCAL.

35. The long poem of which she speaks here, in 1931, seems to be "Winning His Way," her first trial effort on the way to "Stanzas." In his spirited defense of Stein, "The Plain Edition of Gertrude Stein," published in *Contempo* 3, no. 12 (25 October 1933), Hubbell compared the beginning of *Before The Flowers Of Friendship Faded Friendship Faded* to Wordsworth's "Ode: Intimations of Immortality."

The long dull poems of Crabbe must be his somber rural tales in verse, "Peter Grimes," "The Widow's Tale," "The Village." Wordsworth, with less somber realism, used similar themes, as in the dramatized sections of "The Excursion," "The Wanderer," "The Solitary," "The Pastor."

By early summer 1932, in the same phrase, she again likened her work to Wordsworth's, but this time it was "Stanzas In Meditation." To Louis Bromfield she commented,

> I am working a lot I am trying to write a long dull poem like the long ones of Wordsworth and it is very interesting to do I was always fond of these long dull poems well anyway make the weather better and come to see us. . . .

Stein may have felt that the voice of "Stanzas" was similar to that of "Winning His Way," and both to Wordsworth's.

These are Stein's only comments on the work in progress.

I try to describe Stein's language, her use of words and constructions, her changes in tone. She relies on a small vocabulary of mostly short, abstract, and "neutral" words, and she composes by repeating and varying them in form, as in music. This procedure moves her away from information to a free language of writing itself. Here is Stanza x of Part IV, where, starting from "think," she seizes word ideas to work with.

> This one which they think I think alone
> Two follow
> I think when they think
> Two think I think I think they will be too
> Two and one make two for you
> And so they need a share of happiness
> How are ours about to be one two or not three.
> This that I think is this.
> It is natural to think in numerals
> If you do not mean to think
> Or think or leave or bless or guess
> Not either so or yes once.

Always she starts with anything she can seize, often only for a moment. Stanza viii of Part II begins with *A* words but does not mechanically follow through the alphabet. She quickly moves on,

> She may be thought to be accurate with acacia
> Or by and by accustomed to be fairly. . . .

Or watch how she builds a mountain range in Stanza v of Part III,

> It is not a range of a mountain
> Of average of a range of a average mountain

Nor may they of which of which of arrange
To have been not which they which
May add a mountain to this.
Upper an add it then maintain
That if they were busy so to speak
Add it to end

The word "like" opens many games—liking it here, liking her, liking something, and "like" as preposition and conjunction. "Like it," richer in its playful permutations than we had known it could be, is central to "Stanzas," as statement, question, affirmation, doubt, and along with many other echoes of Shakespeare, *As You Like It* pervades the stanzas. "Like it" is always in the immediate present, but what is "it"? She opens "it," places "it" before us, studies it, never closes it by giving it another name.

What Stein does with pronouns goes far beyond replacing nouns. The "I" does not figure largely in these poems. In Part I, Stanza i, she reacts to the world, as does Wordsworth, in the poetic voice. Part I puts the personal "I" aside to focus on the here and now in meditation. Her meditative project, an "it" never defined, is to create meaning out of what is here. Perhaps for a moment or a stanza, we can say "it" is this or that, but "it" is not stable. Prose expresses that "it" in description and narrative, but poetry has no such mechanism—Stein is opening herself not to a subject but to whatever is here for her to receive. As she says to Hubbell, she tries to avoid being seduced by the sound of the words she might choose, for they might take over, removing her from the meditative stance and the experience she is trying to reach.

What "it" is, in these disembodied "Stanzas," depends on where we are, how we know what we think we know. It is totally different from what she does in "Winning His Way," where "it" is never indefinite and we always know what "it" is since it is variously referenced to fame, friendship, or poetry.

By itself, the "it" is indeed "disembodied." For Stein's work here this means that it is flexible, pliable, and open to receive what the mind perceives. Questions about "it" arise especially with the reality of landscape, hills, colors, light, always changing and never twice the same even as she remains in the same place.

When not referenced, "it," a neuter, is outside the dualistic categories that narrow perceptions of the world—up/down, in/out, for/against, good/evil, black/white, he/she. Perhaps Stein is especially receptive to "itnesses" as possibilities of a nonbinary world. Sexuality is one of its central aspects, but it also feeds into her constant questioning of hearing and seeing, writing and reading, sight and sense, sight and sound.

In the steady conversations about "Stanzas," I came at last to listen more and more for "it," the simplest, most common word that crops up not only in "Stanzas" but throughout Stein's texts. "It" has no reference, no meaning, rarely an antecedent, is never twice the same, keeps turning into something else: a pivot, a handle, an agent in the process of line and sentence making. Without color and almost without sound, "it" is absolutely necessary for turning phrases in writing: a motor to make the language move, opening and closing lines and stanzas though designating nothing. The job of "it" is not to mean but to keep meaning moving. Stein came to know that this openness was at the center of her work as an artist and at the center of what she would impart to us.[36]

Here is the whole of Stanza vii of Part III. The first six lines, and others later, end with "it," which also occurs in the lines, and once—not a printing error—"it" appears twice in succession. A stanza about "it"? What "it"? We recall the French grammar lesson about constructions with *il* and *le* that Stein had written into the 1929 portrait of the Dutch painter "Kristians Tonny," whose French was faulty (*P&P* 212). English "it" has no direct French equivalent, and there is no French neuter; so it follows rules for *il, le, ce, ceci, cela, ça,* and others.

But in this stanza she tries out lively uses of English "it," not by nailing down an antecedent or a grammar lesson but by adding prepositions, starting with "by it," asking "by which," confirming "by it," on to "for it," and "all call for in it." She follows "its" possibilities; knowing that "it" can be anything—what we hear, what we see, what we say when in anger we deny what is the matter and say "it" isn't anything: "Avoidance is a valley of pleasure." "It" is everything, "it" is something, "it" is here and now. Always changing, "it" is what she writes now, and in a moment it will be something else.

> By it by which by it
> As not which not which by it
> For it it is in an accessible with it
> But which will but which will not it

36. In "Poetry And Grammar" (1934), she returns to these ideas in the stanzas. "Pronouns are not as bad as nouns . . . they of course are not really the name of anything. They represent some one but they are not its or his name. In not being his or its or her name they already have a greater possibility of being something than if they were as a noun is the name of anything. . . ." (*LIA* 213–14).

Come to be not made not made one of it
By that all can tell all call for in it
That they can better call add
Can in add none add it.
It is not why she asked that anger
In an anger may they be frightened
Because for it they will be which in not
Not now.
Who only is not now.
I can look at a landscape without describing it. (III, vii)

Tiny details lead into a verbal maze. When the words compose no shapes we recognize, we face a heap of incomprehensible print that swims and shimmers or turns opaque as it rigidifies and freezes. We are so used to pursuing printed words as signs in mandated grammatical relations that we forget that they are our fragmentary talking and listening tools.

It is clear that the text of "Stanzas" in the posthumous Yale volume is corrupt. However, the story of the events in the earlier "Context" section of this chapter has also shown that the corruptions of "Stanzas" were not a part of the writing process but date to December 1932 or early 1933, when the poems were being retyped. Once I knew that, the corruptions gradually lost their power and ceased to enter my reading. "Stanzas" is not about "may/can" and not about the power of personality to corrupt. That power does not ruin what Stein was trying to do in this work. Nor are the stanzas about Stein and Toklas, who hover behind them but are not "they," "she," and "I." It is time to do some reading in the world of "it."

The opening stanza begins with fairly regular, unrhymed four-beat lines that soon turn into a loose five-beat, ten-syllable blank verse, the most common form in the poem, though she becomes increasingly free with lines as she goes on. In the early stanzas, grammatical breaks still coincide largely with line breaks, making for a regularity abandoned later, when lines and syntax take on separate lives of their own rather than supporting one another.

I caught a bird which made a ball
And they thought better of it.
But it is all of which they taught
That they were in a hurry yet
In a kind of a way they meant it best
That they should change in and on account
But they must not stare when they manage

Whatever they are occasionally liable to do
It is often easy to pursue them once in a while
And in a way there is no repose
They like it as well as they ever did
But it is very often just by the time
That they are able to separate
In which case in effect they could
Not only be very often present perfectly
In each way whichever they chose. (I, i)

Behind this beginning is an ordinary sentence, "I caught a ball"; in writing, she displaces the noun, "I caught a bird," and makes the bird a ball—no, "bird" is not a metaphor for "ball." The sentence is reversible, "I caught a ball which made a bird," with a different spin.[37] We are in the country, and Stein plays with dog and ball, two nouns of daily life, that become the stuff of a poem. Ball and bird fly through the air of the stanza without difficulty. Echoes come later,

To think how birds spell and do not spell well
And how could it do birds and words (IV, xxi)

Stein starts the new work restlessly, groping for its world and voice. Breathless opening lines, full of haste and hesitations, create a kind of in-between state, reaching for words that will fit, the wish to "kindly have it joined." "Hurry," "change," "often," "pursue," "once in a while," "no repose," "very often," "separate," "instigation" all push the lines ahead—to the sudden "present perfectly / In each way whichever they chose" and a first stop. She continues,

All of this never matters in authority
But this which they need if they are alike
Or in an especial case they will fulfill
Not only what they have at their instigation
Made for it as a decision in its entirety
Made that they minded as well as blinded
Lengthened for them welcome in repose
But which they open as a chance

37. While Marjorie Perloff was working on *Wittgenstein's Ladder* (Chicago: University of Chicago Press, 1996) and after, we considered this stanza in letters and discussions during summer and fall 1996, playing with how Wittgenstein's view of our assembling of sentences can open Stein texts and considering also what Neil Schmitz calls a "lyric complex" (*Of Huck and Alice: Humorous Writing in American Literature* [Minneapolis: University of Minnesota Press, 1983]).

But made it be perfectly their allowance
All which they antagonize as once for all
Kindly have it joined as they mind. (I, i)

Restlessness continues into the second stanza, which, like the end of the first, explores liking it now, liking it here, where writing proceeds. The question is not *where* they are or *what* they like, but what *liking it* is. Wealth and fame return:

They have not known that they will be in thought
Just as rich now or not known
Coming through with this as their plan
Always in arises.[38]
Liking it faintly[39] and fairly well
Which meant they do
Mine often comes amiss
Or liking strife awhile

Smoothly the sunset embraces this world to put the stanza to rest,

Often as evening is as light
As once for all
Think of how many often
And they like it here. (I, ii)

It is a shifting speaker's voice—I, we, they—choreographed often in countersteps to an opposite or partner, subject or object—you, he, me, us, which, who, them—but who these are we quickly cease to ask. Persons enter impersonally by pronouns, without antecedents. The words compose an internal monologue, imaginary dialogue, or conversation—or a kind of self-portraiture.

The many conjunctions, adverbs, prepositions, or adverbial and prepositional phrases start constructions that rarely complete themselves. Instead, by small permutations they flow steadily on in colorless horizontal lines, an austere visual monotony difficult to enter. Prepositions start to construct continuity, but pronominal prepositional phrases—"in which," "to which,"

38. Compare:

Coming through with this as their plan	*Hamlet,* act 3, scene 1, lines 88–89:
Always in arises.	Nymph, in thy orisons
	Be all my sins rememb'red.

The lines following also carry Shakespeare echoes.

39. Ms and ts 1 read "faintly," which I take to be Stein's intended word. Ts 2 reads "fairly," a typing error or misreading.

"from which"; coordinating and subordinating conjunctions—"but," "and," "not only," "where," "when"—break into it; neutral verbs—"change," "manage"—abound, and the few strong verbs—"stare," "pursue"—hitched to no objects, bring with them no sharp scenes or events.

Unfamiliar piled-up negatives, twisted, unfinished double negatives, and other incomplete double constructions—"not only" leads to "what else," not to "but also"—strike us as strange, incorrect, illogical. Yet they retain the Stein speaking power in their double and triple reflections by removing us from what we expect words to do, making us slow down, listen, hear and rehear, think and rethink.

Weak neutral words and a limited vocabulary can merge into a blur of almost inseparable syllables that the grammatical mind fails to take in. With minimal paraphrasable meaning, the words lose power as signs. Occasionally we are absorbed into fragments of landscape, weather, animals, tiny personal exchanges as parts of language and landscape. But mostly austere visual and auditory patterning prevails over meaning. With words weakened as signs and sentence parts, segments of words—sounds, letters, syllables, phonemes—gain freedom and power. Moving free of reference, they start to mean by punning—"auditory" to "ought" and "autocratic," "mead" to "meadow," "accurate" to "Acacia" to "anxiousness," "leaf" to "leave," "aisle" to "exile," "do" to "dew." Stein leads us into language by refusing its conventions.[40]

> I have thought that the bird makes the same noise
> differently
> Just as I said how will you do it if you like it
> And they will not stretch well from here to there
> If they know that in the full moon they should not plant
> it
> Just before.
> All might all mean that is the way to do
> Not better than they have lost
> But which they manage in their requital
> I have known that sound and this as known
> Which they will interlace with not only there

40. Norman Weinstein, in *Gertrude Stein and the Literature of Modern Consciousness* (New York: Frederick Ungar, 1970), starting from a different angle, describes the stanzas usefully, "the central device of the poem is the conscious maximization of semantic possibility. . . . Each line contains all the syntactical variants previously contained in separate poetic lines" (84, 85).

But the pale sky with the pale green leaves
Or which they will as they belong to trees
In this in their amount. (I, x)

"Interlacings" describes the activity of the mind or of a landscape in word weavings of sight and sound. "That" sound and "this," "here" and "there," "known" and "known," "pale sky" and "green leaves," with "pale" echoing the earlier "pail," "green" half-rhyming with "trees." A bird sings and she asks how it makes the landscape by filling sky and green leaves with sound. Farmer's wisdom appears, common in Stein, about when in the cycle of the moon to plant seedlings or how "not only red at night can deceive" (III, iib). Bits of nature interlace in a small landscape composition. Rarely do striking single lines like these stop us:

As they call a pail a pail and make a mountain cover
Not only their clouds but their own authority (I, x)

Further surprises follow: the adverb "closely," not "close," modifying "came"; the double negative, "no one was just yet not to be frightened"; the odd "neither . . . or better yet." Later still threads of verbal embroidery interlace love lines, flowers, petals, hand lines,

It came very closely but no one was just yet
Not to be frightened as they meant at all
I do not care that he should make threads so
Threads are tenderly heads as tenderly so and so
Very well merited
I should judge just inclined
Neither as disturbance or better yet
Might it be changed but once before
Left them to gather it wherever they can and will
Just the same. (I, x)

Interlace, interweave, boxes within boxes. Mountains, vegetation, pansies, meditative thought, enmeshed in a simultaneity of grammar that is a landscape, a flower-scape, a language-scape. Was she rehearing her own lines in her 1920 portrait "Next. Life And Letters Of Marcel Duchamp"?

To interlace a story with glass and with rope with color and roam. (*G&P* 405)

Or recalling the interlacings in Picasso's 1912 collage, "Still-Life with Chair-Caning"?

Throughout these poems, the countryside is a great presence, and a location for mood and voice. Yet what an abstract landscape this is. We do not collect daffodils here, though Stein slipped some four-leaf clovers into her *cahiers*. It is as if the landscape was a manuscript that Stein's stanzas were teaching us to read,

> A landscape is what when they that is I
> See and look. (V, xxxv)

Inside merges into outside, outdoors to indoors. Here are the views, the farmers, chickens, hay, talk on long walks, ducks, peas, beans, raspberries. Here she can "look at the landscape without describing it" (III, vii). And here is what makes landscape, mind and mood always new—the weather.

Take the opening of Part II, Stanza i, echoing Shakespeare again, and followed by deceptively simple monosyllables and "rain" the only concrete word. From what reading or remembering did that poetical opening, "full well," enter her lines?

> Full well I know that she is there
> Much as she will she can be there
> But which I know which I know when
> Which is my way to be there then
> Which she will know as I know here
> That it is now that it is there
> That rain is there and it is here
> That it is here that they are there
> They have been here to leave it now
> But how foolish to ask them if they like it
> Most certainly they like it because they like what they have
> But they might easily like something else
> And very probably just as well they will have it
> Which they like as they are very likely not to be
> Reminded that it is more than ever necessary
> That they should never be surprised at any one time
> At just what they have been given by taking what they have
> Which they are very careful not to add with
> As they may easily indulge in the fragrance
> Not only of which but by which they know
> That they tell them so.

With few and neutral words—"I," "she," "they"; "be there," "be here"; "know," "like"—she composes rain here, there, everywhere, place and time washed out. Do they hate the rain? How foolish—they like it here, even inundated in its pervasive fragrance. As long as we listen to the words, this narrow poem with its great economy of means is entirely accessible.

We know from a letter of Stein to Henry McBride of July 17 that the early summer was rainy and cold. Such tiny facts, of no interest in themselves or to a biographer, explain nothing of what she does with them in "Stanzas" but confirm how deeply the work is grounded in actuality. Landscape and weather set the life out of which she makes stanzas. She next moves from the rain to the domestic scene of a fire lit against the cold, smells in the house, and always "liking it here"—details of insignificant actuality of "it" made significant in words. Will they enjoy conviviality, share wine, be accepted by the neighbors? This theme recurs in many stanzas and other poems of this period.

> It is very often that they like to care
> That they have it there that the window is open
> If the fire which is lit and burning well
> Is not open to the air.
> Think well of that is open to the air
> Not only which but also nearly patiently there
> It is very often why they are nearly
> Not only with but also with the natural wine
> Of the country which does not impoverish
> Not only that but healthily with which they mean
> That they may be often with them long.
> Think of anything that is said
> How many times have they been in it
> How will they like what they have
> And will they invite you to partake of it
> And if they offer you something and you accept
> Will they give it to you and will it give you pleasure
> And if after a while they give you more
> Will you be pleased to have more
> Which in a way is not even a question
> Because after all they like it very much. (II, ii)

The authority of grammar, clauses, and phrases does not open this writing. Nor do lines or punctuation guide us. It is almost impossible to isolate or paraphrase passages. Over and over the stanzas demand speaking aloud, listening for words in relation and for lines that eye and mind, still bound by conventions Stein has abandoned, can enter. I slow down and down until, often in fragments, their voice can be heard.

Here is the opening section of the long, last poem of Part I, Stanza xv, filled with delight in what they see and doubts about its reality. What is direction in nature, in the landscape, the sky, north, south, east, west. Clouds moving arrest her eye and give her speech. The weather creates the unstable center of "it," here, now, how.

Should they may be they might if they delight
In which they must see it be there not only necessarily
But which they might in which they might
For which they might delight if they look there
And they see there that they look there
To see it be there which it is if it is
Which may be where where it is
If they do not occasion it to be different
From what it is.
In one direction there is the sun and the moon
In the other direction there are cumulous clouds and the sky
In the other direction there is why
They look at what they see
They look very long while they walk along
And they may be said to see that at which they look
Whenever there is no chance of its not being warmer
Than if they wish which they were. (I, xv)

Even if the following lines, midstanza, rise from weather, they hover among words we must hear and see moving, from "could" to "allowed" to "clouded," *in* the words, not in *what* the words *say,*

They could manage just what they did
But did they not feel that
They could be not only not allowed but not clouded
It was very different again
Just when they join that they look. (III, xvia [*LA* xvii])

The eye trained by paintings is always in the stanzas, as the next three sections show. The sense of space, distance, movement, and color carries her perceptions of landscape. This from the woman who knew that to compose she did not need to look at scenery and needed no model, the same who discovered as a part of a landscape painting the house she wanted, "which we never saw any nearer than across the valley" (*AABT* 282).

A change from rest or a change from the rest
Well and welcome as the day which when the sun shines
Makes water grow and covers others more

Than when they looked down there where they saw
All of which when they had not wondered
Would they like it there best
Might I ask were they disappointed. (II, v)

And it is well to state that the rain makes hills green
And the sky blue and the clouds dark
And the water water by them (II, iii)

It is often that they allow a cloud to be white
Or not only patently white but also just as green
Not only theirs in pleasure but theirs in case
Not only however but not only however
Or not at all in wishes that they had chickens
Which may be alternately well or ducks
Or will they spread for them alone
To be not only their care. (III, xix; xviii in ms, ts 1 [*LA* xx])

Strawberry plants are grown in a bed of straw to support and protect the delicate fruit. In the Rhône Valley, dried marsh grass, *blache,* is used for strawberry beds as well as litter for animals and bedding. This little pastoral song ends as an invitation to share a bed.

It will be often fortunately that strawberries need straw
Or may they yes indeed have marsh grass ready
It will support all who will have support
And she will kindly share hers with them
His with them (II, iv)

She abandons commas and uses very few periods. In the "readies" and "Winning His Way," she had slowed down the language and inserted stresses by adding periods, often in the middle of sentences. As she moves from Part I to Part V, she creates movement across lines, making them shorter, lighter, and faster, and abandoning the early largely iambic scheme. Internal and end rhymes create movement and lightness. With phrases like "Which I wish to say is this" (V, xxxviii), she seizes new topics right off, focusing on the immediate. Look at what she does here with "north" as an abstract idea, as direction relative to where I stand; north as north as against north in relation to south, east, west.

Which I wish to say is this
There is no beginning to an end
But there is a beginning and an end

To beginning.
Why yes of course.
Any one can learn north of course
Is not only north but north as north
Why were they worried.
What I wish to say is this.
Yes of course. (V, xxxviii)

This small, complete stanza perfectly shows her "occasional" procedure and her way of completing an idea.

Look what happens if we read by itself this astonishing one-line sentence that seems to lend itself to quoting:

They could recognize the sun if there was another one (IV, xviii [xxv in ms, ts1])

But see how it changes if you reach it from the preceding lines:

Could anyone influence anyone
One and one.
Or not.
If not why not.
Or if not would they not be more than
If they were changing which way any one
In which way any one would not need one
If not one and one.
Or not by them.
It is made why they do if they call them.
They could recognize the sun if there was another one

Now add the two lines that follow and listen to the whole passage:

Or not at all by me
When this you see.

Strange things happen to the sun of the initial line when it is reread in the sequence of the text.

Sunlight makes the colors in cloth fade, right? But here, someone, "she," seems to think no, the sun brings out the colors. Right, too. "Fade" appears as an intransitive and transitive verb, to fade or make something fade. The sun itself does not fade. At this moment, it brings out the colors of the cloth but over time makes them fade. Once again, a language problem becomes poetry.

She may be right to think that the sun
Not only does not fade but makes it less faded. (V, vii)

These two innocent lines are not merely about fading but are part of a long stanza between two, "she" and "I." They are no doubt abstracted from Toklas and Stein, but to reattach the words to the women and read them biographically narrows their range.

In her 1934 lecture, "Portraits And Repetition," Stein said that, in doing portraits, she had gradually moved toward a sense of "what poetry really is" (*LIA* 203). Her portraits—through all the years, for Stein as for Picasso, this is the word not only for pictures of people but for complex compositions completely realized—are self-contained, narrowly centered intensive word compositions, neither narrative nor descriptive, of people, objects, or spaces. Doing them moved her toward unemotional, nonreferential verbal realization.

Now she was writing in the wide, high landscape of the upper Rhône Valley that had first offered her the great view of plays as landscapes, always moving, always changing, and totally present. This world opened passageways into composition beyond its scenery, to the talking, listening, and looking of the mind and its own processes. "Stanzas" is composed through, not about, the weathered landscape in which she sits, looking in or out.

What she was writing here may also have returned her to the experience of St.-Rémy, in 1922–23, where she had also been immersed with devotion in a landscape, had written pastoral literature filled with singing, melody, opera, saints, angels, honey, birds, sheep, water, and colors of the bucolic scene.

> I created a melody of words that filled me with a melody that gradually made me do portraits easily by feeling the melody of anyone. And this then began to bother me because perhaps I was getting drunk with melody and I do not like to be drunk. . . . (*LIA* 199)

Looking back from 1934, she felt that in the work of what she called the early Spanish period, of "Mabel Dodge At The Villa Curonia," "Preciosilla," "Susie Asado," and in the writing of St.-Rémy, such as "Saints And Singing," she had created beauty through melody. This is the work with sound and sense of which she wrote to Hubbell in 1931. In the lecture she calls it drunk on honey and singing, self-indulgent, undisciplined.

> Melody should always be a by-product it should never be an end in itself it should not be a thing by which you live if you really and truly are

one who is to do anything and so as I say I very exactly began again. (*LIA* 201)

Now, ten years after the months at St.-Rémy, she had moved beyond immersion in the sight and melody of landscape. Soberly and dispassionately, she had studied language—vocabulary, grammar, sentences, paragraphs. She had reached a territory where she could touch the process of language itself as it makes poetry. Perhaps in the summer of 1932 she returned to St.-Rémy on one of the visits to the Riviera to see Picabia. Stanza Lxxi of Part V, the only one that names a person, includes "an introduction to Picabia."[41] A little beyond, Stanza Lxxvi, one of the very last, returns to St.-Rémy,

> I could not be in doubt
> About.
> The beauty of San Remy.
> That is to say
> The hills small hills
> Beside or really rather all behind.
> Where the Roman arches stay
> One of the Roman arches
> Is not an arch
> But a monument
> To which they mean
> Yes I mean I mean.
> Not only when but before.
> I can often remember to be surprised
> By what I see and saw.
> It is not only wonderfully
> But like before. (V, Lxxvi)

This exactingly sober view of scenery is far from her melodious St.-Rémy writing. The merging past and present times and tenses of the last five lines dramatize the difference between 1923 and 1932.

So far along in this large work, Stein apparently knew that she was finishing Part V and with it the whole of "Stanzas In Meditation." Three stanzas beyond the "Picabia" stanza, she already remarks, "Thank them for gathering all of it together."

By the end of the St.-Rémy stanza, with ten pages left in the *cahier,* she returns to accomplishment, identity, and love. The long Stanza Lxxviii of Part V speaks of cutting roses in the garden and concludes,

41. This is the stanza translated by Marcel Duchamp and printed in the catalog for the exhibition of Picabia drawings at Léonce Rosenberg's gallery, December 1–24, 1932.

> I can I wish I do love none but you.

The second and third stanzas thereafter end,

> I wish once more to say that I know the difference
> between two.
> The whole of this last end is to say which of two.

A one-liner laughs,

> Thank you for hurrying through.

The last stanza, Lxxxiii, tightly rhymed, returns to the door of private intimacy and, of course, writing. She ends with subtle play on the difference between "therefore," where it comes from, and "therefor," where it is going, looking backward and forward and doing away with the difference between inside and out,

> Why am I if I am uncertain reasons may inclose.
> Remain remain propose repose chose.
> I call carelessly that the door is open
> Which if they may refuse to open
> No one can rush to close.
> Let them be mine therefor.
> Everybody knows that I chose.
> Therefore if therefor before I close.
> I will therefor offer therefore I offer this.
> Which if I refuse to miss may be miss is mine.
> I will be well welcome when I come.
> Because I am coming.
> Certainly I come having come.

The final line is scribbled in as the very last in the *cahier,* ending Part V and "Stanzas,"

> These stanzas are done.

"Stanzas" is suffused with another landscape entirely. In the poetic, changeable Forest of Arden, where Jacques sings "stanzos," identities change, as do the names for things. In "Poetry And Grammar," Stein said that in Arden, Shakespeare "created a forest without mentioning the things that make a forest" (*LIA* 236). Here, in the land of comedy, subjects become objects, verbs nouns, and truth and convention, life and language are governed by the imagination. In 1903, *As You Like It* had yielded the epigraph for *Q. E. D.* with the pastoral scene of instruction in love between Phoebe,

Sylvius, Rosalind, and Orlando (act 5, scene 2, line 89), each of Sylvius' definitions followed by comments of Phoebe, Orlando, and Rosalind:

Phoebe: Good shepherd, tell this youth what 'tis to love.
Sylvius: It is to be all made of sighs and tears; . . .
It is to be all made of faith and service; . . .
It is to be all made of fantasy,
All made of passion, and all made of wishes;
All adoration, duty, and observance,
All humbleness, all patience, and impatience,
All purity, all trial, all obedience. . . .

As You Like It sings through Stanza vi of Part I, a striking example among the many that echo the poetry of Shakespeare's plays, of which Stein spoke in her lecture "Plays" (*LIA* 111, 114). Just as she values the liveliness created in his plays by poetry, she fills the stanzas with echoes of his spoken words. In addition, the play with "like" and "it," the center of it all, runs through all of "Stanzas."

To illustrate how Shakespeare is absorbed into "Stanzas," I quote the whole of Stanza vi,[42] which celebrates a wedding day,

I have not heard from him but they ask more
If with all which they merit with as well of
If it is not an ounce of which they measure
He has increased in weight by losing two
Namely they name as much.
Often they are obliged as it is by their way
Left more than they can add acknowledge
Come with the person that they do attack
They like neither best by them altogether
For which it is no virtue fortune all
Ours on account their with the best of all
Made it be in no sense other than exchange
By which they cause me to think the same
In finally alighting where they may have at one time
Made it best for themselves in their behalf.
Let me think well of a great many
But not express two so.
It is just neither why they like it

42. This is also the stanza where, in the process of revision, described at the end of the earlier "Context" section of this chapter, the first dramatic emendations were undertaken by the women.

Because it is by them in as they like
They do not see for which they refuse names
Articles which they like and once they hope
Hope and hop can be as neatly known
Theirs in delight or rather may they not
Cover it shone guessing in which they have
All may be glory may be may be glory
For not as ladling marguerites out.
It is best to know their share.
Just why they joined for which they knelt
They can call that they were fortunate.
They may be after it is all given away.
They may. Have it in mine.
And so it is a better chance to come
With which they know theirs to undo
Getting it better more than once alike
For which fortune favors me.
It is the day when we remember two.[43]
We two remember two two who are thin
Who are fat with glory too with two
With it with which I have thought twenty fair
If I name names if I name names with them,
I have not hesitated to ask a likely block
Of which they are attributed in all security
As not only why but also where they may
Not be unclouded just as yes to-day
They call peas beans and raspberries strawberries or two
They forget well and change it as a last
That they could like all that they ever get
As many fancies for which they have asked no one.
Might any one be what they liked before
Just may they come to be not only fastened
It should be should be just what they like
This May in unison

43. Stein revised this and the next line. I strike through words to show how they were changed in manuscript from the text originally typed in ts 1, to the text revised in manuscript and reproduced in ts 2:

It is the day when we remember ~~too~~ two
We two remember two two who are ~~theirs~~ thin
Who are fat with glory. . . .

All out of cloud. Come hither. Neither
Aimless and with a pointedly rested displeasure
She may be glad to be either in their resigning
That they have this plan I remember.
Well welcome in fancy
Or just need to better that they call
All have been known in name as call
They will call this day one for all
I know it may be shared by Tuesday
Gathered and gathered yes.
All who come will will come or come to be
Come to be coming that is in and see
See elegantly not without enjoin
See there there where is no share
Shall we be there I wonder now

Over and over, the language and the music of Shakespeare, not only *As You Like It,* can be heard in the stanzas. Stein did not copy, imitate, borrow, or allude. "Under the Greenwood Tree" sings here in permutations and echoes, not in allusion or quotation. Absorbed into the stanzas of 1932 is the language of Shakespeare and the world of this play with its capacity to mutate perceptions. And in the very last stanza, in

I will therefore offer therefore I offer this.
Which if I refuse to miss may be miss is mine.

we hear echoes of *Twelfth Night; Or, What You Will:*

O, mistress mine! where are you roaming
Oh! stay and hear; your true love's coming. (act 2, scene 3, line 42)

In 1932, in the Ain, she was in the upper reaches of the valley that had inspired and seduced her in 1922–23. The landscape of the Bugey was as captivating as the Rhône delta, but now, no longer the center of vision itself, it was a passageway grounding occasions for writing.

A Manoir (LO&P 277–316)

In the summer of 1932, perhaps late July, after finishing "Stanzas," Stein began a new play, *A Manoir.* Another play, *Short Sentences,* was written a little later, say August. The two share some textual features but differ radically in substance.

A Manoir is composed in a dummy book, filled to the end, similar to the one used for Part V of "Stanzas." It is subtitled "A historical play in which they are approached more often"; the designation "play," however, was revised in the manuscript from "novel," probably as soon as writing began since from the start words like "act" and "scene" appear. However, the play retains narrative and descriptive features, for example, in lines like these:

> Mary Cabell. She was soon to feel that they would
> account for which of them for which
> they were chosen. (300)

Are these Mary Cabell's own lines, someone else's about her, do they describe her, or are they stage directions, like the following?

> Scene one
>
> A house in which there is green paper put upon the kitchen shelves prettily which is for them not so many but a few and invention.
>
> The characters who come and go are all here. (278)

Stein plays with words that fall into joking lines and rhymes and finally lead to a description of a setting or "scene" that pokes fun at metaphorical language,

> Act II
>
> One one is a cloud
> One one one is out loud
> Three one one one is not tried
> But she is not why beside.
> It comes to this.
> At the foot of the hill not at the foot but very near the hill the beginning of the hill there is nothing to compare with this. (315)

The manoir starts from the Bilignin manor house, not named, with land in a walled garden, not a fortified castle with a dungeon (312). Etymologically related to manner, manners, the manoir is a substantial play space set in landscape and history. It is explored in descriptive and narrative detail and conversation. It is also a social space with innumerable names—characters, guests, acquaintances, local and beyond—many of which return in *Short Sentences.* We know Stein's preoccupation with names from other pieces; here are the new puppy, Byron, who must learn his name, Basket, who knows his, and the Finnish maid Marguerite, who does not know who she is,

Byron.	He called it his name
Basket.	He knew his name
Marguerite	She did not know the name (303)

Rather than at the manoir itself, the many names appear in the fields or on the road and paths near the manoir, which opens into the land and the historic social space. Names like Arthur Griffin Lands, Genevieve Land, and Mathilda Grant (287) even lead from the land and the manor to American land grants.

It is as if Stein was asking what the difference is between a landscape or view to look at and a scene or setting in a play, such as the house and the characters coming and going in the surrounding landscape. Is she working in new ways with the conventions of plays until characters and setting become one as do lines, stage directions, descriptive and narrative details?

We know that the lease to the Bilignin house was now at last securely in Stein's own name and Captain Bonhomme and his furnishings were removed (292). In the play, the manoir is a temporary habitation, not a year-round residence, just as it was for Stein and Toklas. As a summer house, it is like a theater, where visitors, spectators, neighbors temporarily assemble. Here is a concluding summation:

> Scene III
>
> In each country the guests as well as the owners are different. In their manners in their habits and in the change of address and also in their return to their place or wherever it is no effort either to go or not to go. And so as nothing changes why not come again. (316)

Discontinuity rules as sequence and permanence are refused; the many invented names that come and go display no known identities or histories, and the lines, if they are spoken, are not attached to personalities. As in *Short Sentences,* the next play, they often combine first and last names of different friends or local people, though there is here also a kind of family council, with nineteen different first names followed by the same last name, Julian, perhaps recalling her cousin, the banker Julian Stein (293). Local people include the farmer, M. Rosset, and M. St. Pierre, who had negotiated the lease.

Here is an example of the textual discontinuity in its indented setting with full stops, placed as Stein placed them. I am not sure of their function. The narrow width of the dummy *cahier* used for this text makes it difficult to distinguish the degrees of indentation for the play's elements on the smallish pages.

Scene IV

May Rhone. For which they could ask any across.
Will they
Anna Blaine. Of course not will they
Guy Foster. But which yes which will they like.
May Hilda. May Hilda like what they like.
A manoir is habitable.
I will never listen to one
Tell about a manoir being habitable
But this is the result
Of it all
That they will inevitably
Be not only softened but refused
To be admonished.
Why can no one not please bees
If you please
A scene in a manoir is often not a disturbance.

Scene I

I could just join with it. (308)

Perhaps Stein was particularly aware of how temporary her stay was, how tentative relationships, how unstable categories. Her stay becomes a play, temporary also. It is as if she was taking apart the idea of play, place, conversation, scenery, in narrative or descriptive lines like stage directions, rather than spoken lines. With the painter's or audience's eye, we see half the house on a hillside,

The upper land is below where they cut hay. (311)

And look at the looking at a view,

At the foot of the hill not at the foot but very near the hill the beginning of the hill there is nothing to compare with this. (315)

Sentences, word groups, lines, names, stage directions, sights are disassembled. The characters, guests, bystanders, so many that they become anonymous, contrast with the women's social life in the summer of 1932, when they were very busy with the Plain Edition and only one visitor, Bernard Faÿ, came twice for longer stays.

A Manoir is full of echoes of the spare language of "Stanzas"; it is also replete with puns, which remove context and fact and keep us from pinning down plot, events, and identities.

Now think plainly of a manoir.
She meant with or not without her consent.

Part one Act I

It could be sent that if they went they could not be sent without their consent one at a time. And how many cherries make a tree. Or if not how many pears have no consent.
And if not he was successful.
And if not will they grow.
And if not by that time not to have been mistaken
Nor if not will they not go. (310)

A Manoir

Once in the morning it was after
They looked after them.
A manoir is exceedingly rich.
And not fortified
And not a pleasure
And either or
Their own surprise
As they try
To believe why

Scene I

After one they came one
Just Henry Byron. Who had led him here
Ernest Fisher. But which they willed
Bertha Basket. But will they love William
Edith Arnold. She is my delight.
After any minute they went around.
Bertha Basket. It is very well to assume that a jacket
Edith Arnold. Is what they prefer to lose.
William Fisher. But which they please
Henry Byron. To lose
Oh why will they wail
Oh yes or why will they wail
She could not deny or destroy a veil
Or in plenty of time escape
Or end in an end
Or better not
Or for which they will reply

Scene I

> They feel that they will end one
> One and one.
> Henry Basket is all on edge (312–13)

The manuscript of *A Manoir* shows no revisions and no interference with the text, direct or indirect. The play is written in a dummy notebook, similar to the last of "Stanzas" though smaller in size.[44] There is no original typescript for it, though a later typescript, sent to Carl Van Vechten by Stein, was given by him to Yale in 1940; we do not know when he received it from Stein. The play was surely written before Toklas knew about *Q. E. D.* but typed after, as two details indicate. On page 284 of the text printed in *Last Operas And Plays* appears, as in the extant typescript, a sequence of double names such as Arthur Carler, Henrietta Adams, and one triple name, "May Maiden Hoar." The manuscript has only the double name "May Maiden." The extra word speaks volumes. Where is the original typescript, and who proofread this one?

The second interference is on page 300, where Mary Knight appears twice; in manuscript, the first *K* in her surname is underlined by Toklas in blue pencil, surely for Knoblauch, just as it is also in *Short Sentences.* The first name, "Mary" in typescript and print, is "May" in manuscript.

Short Sentences (LO&P 317–32)

Even visually, this is an organized piece, related to *A Manoir,* but starker and simpler. Recalling *A List,* another disciplined visual arrangement of names and "lines," it can be read in two columns down the page. In the left column are the many names, beginning with a mixture of first or first and last names, including a few with "Madame" and "Sir," but soon settling on first names of one and last names of another friend, such as Grace Church, Edith Acton. A good many carry echoes of Stein's early years: Arthur Grafton, Winifred Stanhope, Mabel Earle, Mildred Maine. A full stop follows each name. Down the right column run as many brief, one-

44. Perhaps the two dummies of bound blank pages, models for books to be published, were used for writing close together in time because both may have been samples for the next volume in the Plain Edition, *Matisse Picasso And Gertrude Stein With Two Shorter Stories,* issued in February 1933. Stein was frugal with paper and used what was at hand, often even reusing notebooks not completely filled. She relied in part on notebooks to suggest ways of handling her materials; an empty book without words or images on the cover, without lines or margins, seems particularly fitting for compositions as abstract and nonreferential as the long last part of "Stanzas" or *A Manoir.*

line phrases as there are names on the left—perhaps the short sentences of the title. The names suggest no cast of characters and no relationships; the phrases hardly sound like lines for speaking. Most of these are not end-stopped, though some make stopped sequences.

Both the names and the phrases of the play are replete with Mays, Marys, and may's—Ivan May, Mary Coburn, May Janes, May Welch. In the manuscript, every May or Mary and every auxiliary verb "may" is underlined in Toklas' indelible purple pencil. For Mary Knowlton, the initial *K* is also underlined, no doubt for Knoblauch. So is the very last complete name, May Helen; Helen Thomas is the pseudonym for May Bookstaver in *Q. E. D.* By the time Toklas underlined, she had read herself into a rage over *Q. E. D.*

Irregularly interrupting the columns and indented appears a "Chorus," aligned, like the names, with one of the chattering "short sentences," though whether these are spoken lines is unclear. The play opens like a lean, abstract dance or ballet, with the tripping, "The scene is one in which nicely they go."

Marie-Claire Pasquier speaks of this play in discussing the function of names for Stein.

> . . . one might say that for Stein the noun, especially the proper name, is the briefest form of portraiture, making her work music on the name of Stein. Thus under the title *Short Sentences* (1932) she wrote what Toklas came appropriately to call *A Play Of Nouns*. The list of proper names becomes the lay equivalent of the litany. Multiple associations which suggest a roll call. . . . Anyone who knows what it is to be held spellbound by reading a yearbook will know what it is to read a novel. As the saying goes, a writer's task is to rival the private citizen.[45]

Two names in *Short Sentences* differ in manuscript and in print, which means in the typescript from which the play was set: Henry Winthrop (322) and Anne Nicholson (325). In the manuscript, the first reads "Alice Winthrop," with "Alice" crossed out and "Henry" substituted in the hand of

45. . . . on pourrait dire que pour Stein le nom, et en particulier le nom propre, est la forme la plus brêve du portrait. Son oeuvre: la musique sur le nom de Stein. A titre d'expérience, Stein écrit sous le titre *Short Sentences* (1932) ce que Alice Toklas appellera justement *A Play of Nouns*. La liste des noms propres comme équivalent laïc de la litanie. Associations multiples qu'évoque l'expression "faire l'appel" . . . Qui n'a jamais été fasciné par la lecture d'un annuaire ne lira sans doute jamais un roman. L'écrivain, on l'a souvent dit, se donne pour tâche d'être l'émule de l'état-civil. (*Delta* 10 [May 1980]: 55–56)

I have found no documentation for the title, *A Play Of Nouns;* could it be the result of confusion, perhaps with *A Play Of Pounds?*

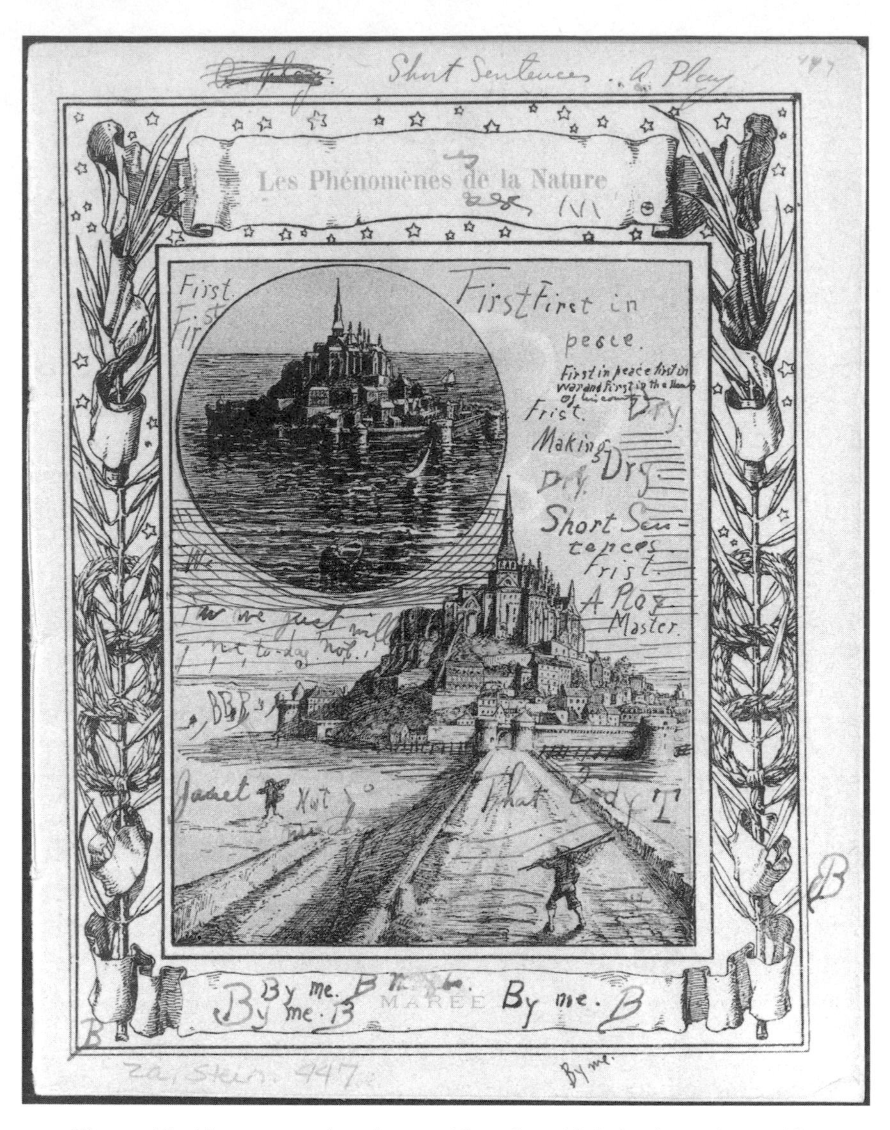

Figure 13. Manuscript *cahier* showing Mont-Saint-Michel at low tide, used for *Short Sentences. A Play,* with Stein doodles. Courtesy YCAL.

Toklas, not Stein; the second, "Babette Nicholson," with "Babette" crossed out and "Anne" written in by Toklas. In addition, on pages 327 and 331, a footnote by Van Vechten indicates that the first name to go with "May" is missing; in the manuscript, however, the name is "Alice," crossed out in the hand of Toklas; in the second case, a footnote says that the full name is missing in the third line of page 331; however, in the manuscript, crossed out, the name is "Alice Babette," leaving a double blank space in the extant typescript. As with *A Manoir,* where is the original typescript? The manuscript[46] defines some of our questions but does not yield full answers.

None of this was known to Carl Van Vechten, who edited *Last Operas And Plays* (1949) from the typescript. Plainly Toklas took herself out of this play of coupling couples. Are these changes related to the revisions of "Stanzas"? When were they made, and when was the play typed?

It is as if Stein was constructing a play made of names, people, words spoken or not spoken, thoughts completed or not, expressed or not, a jumble of materials that shake up the elements of a play. Is this procedure similar to that of *A Play Of Pounds?*

How to make sense of it all, and how to read the changes in the three works? Are the revisions related? The situation visible in the revisions of "Stanzas" seems at work in *A Manoir* and *Short Sentences* also. Did Toklas, back in Paris, read *Q. E. D.,* then begin typing the leftover manuscripts of the summer and, in doing so, act out her feelings and withdraw from the intimacy of living?

46. The play has never so far as I know been performed, but it offers a challenge to an enterprising director who might take its compounded names and lean phrases to build an exciting abstract production with no temptation to follow subject matter or references.

This is an autobiography of one of these. And only two.

—"Brim Beauvais" 288

Next to next to and does.
Does it join.
Does it mean does it join.
Does it mean does it mean does it join.
If after all they know
That I say so.

—"Stanzas In Meditation" V, Lx

10. 1932–34

The Autobiography Of Alice B. Toklas

"A Little Love Of Life" (*SIM* 277–82)

My main interest in this short, minor piece had never been in its play on writing with pen or pencil, its uneasy questioning of identity, or its work with pronouns, "I," "you," "she," "they," which sounds like "Stanzas," nor even in the love poem that ends the text and gives it its title. What had held my attention, after the first three lines, were two pages of penned notes in the manuscript, firmly crossed out and neither typed nor printed:

> Came to Paris after leaving the medical school without a degree and in between a winter in London in 1904 [*sic*].
> Began looking at everything and
> Was shown Cezanne in painting and began writing *Three Lives* under his direction. Then found Henri Matisse without their direction. Did nothing under
> Then [proposed / preferred] Picasso [early / only] [doing] which he [or] she [were / when]

I had assumed that these were notes for *The Autobiography Of Alice B. Toklas,* and that they dated the piece to early fall 1932. Then, however, I realized that they describe Stein herself, before she even met Toklas. Their voice is Stein's. There is nothing about Toklas. So I was forced to reconsider when "A Little Love" was written. Gradually these lines came to look like notes for Gertrude Stein's own autobiography. Yet those notes, the "Confessions" as she called them, were written as a follow-up on the success of *The Autobi-*

ography Of Alice B. Toklas in 1933, not 1932. They appear in the late 1933–34 piece entitled "And Now."

Finally, on reading "A Little Love" again and again, I gradually saw what appeared to be references to Byron, the dog Stein and Toklas received from Picabia in June 1932: "They went away to carry the dog to show him" (281); "sitting with a little dog upon her lap" (283); playing and baying and jealousy between the dogs. Is Picabia the "great painter" who is "not a genius" (282)?

We know of Stein's growing concerns with identity in "Marguerite Or A Simple Novel Of High Life," "Bartholomew Arnold," "Margit Marguerite Margherita," and in "Here. Actualities," which erupt in many forms in "Stanzas In Meditation." I began to wonder whether "A Little Love" might not emerge from Byron's entry into their household. His death in April 1933 became the occasion for Stein's last great work in her own voice—*Byron A Play.*

I place the piece here because I have no clear evidence that it was done before "Stanzas" or preparatory to the *Autobiography.* "A Little Love" raises more questions than I was able to answer. Slight as it is, I read it, including the crossed-out notes, as a warning—the problem of all Stein texts, about how we read what a work says and what questions its context raises.

The Autobiography Of Alice B. Toklas

From the text of "Stanzas In Meditation" I return, by way of the notes in "A Little Love Of Life," to the context for *The Autobiography Of Alice B. Toklas.* Nothing in the *Autobiography* itself answers the great question behind it, why the radical change in matter and manner, which makes Stein seem a different person from the earlier Stein. In "The Story Of A Book" (*HWW* 61) of April 1933 and in *Everybody's Autobiography* (9), when she was known to the world as its author, she forestalled questions with a light touch, suggesting that the book was going to be written sooner or later anyhow but was made possible in the fall of 1932 by exceptionally good weather.

Not very convincingly, this explains when it was written, but not why or how. She also said the idea of writing memoirs came from Sir Robert Abdy, a conventional, titled English friend associated with the Wildenstein Gallery in Paris. He may well have suggested it but was one of many who asked for such a book. Perhaps Stein singled him out as a member of a social world where she had friends to whom the autobiography might appeal.

I see the context of the making of the *Autobiography* in the growing need for success and fame, which the Plain Edition and the great labor of Toklas had not succeeded in satisfying. Only manuscripts, typescripts, and a few other papers open glimpses. In part the book is an offering to Toklas, written as an act of impersonation, with credit for its fame and success going to Toklas, not Stein. Stein is quoted suggesting that Toklas write her memoirs, and Toklas agrees "if during the summer [*she*] could find time" (309), as the reader immediately suspects she will not; a little later, when Toklas is not writing the book, Stein takes the initiative and offers to do it for her (309–10). This puts the best possible light on the affair and allows Stein, against all her earlier refusals, to get away with a book of memoirs, not her kind of writing, as a favor to Toklas.[1]

Text

No *carnets* for the *Autobiography* are preserved, but I doubt that there were any, for this book may have required lists of facts, dates, people in notes or outlines that we do find in the fifteen *cahiers* but not notations of actual composition such as Stein entered in *carnets*. Nor do there seem to have been other earlier drafts, subsequently revised. The manuscript *cahiers* at Yale show straightforward, steady writing, with few revisions. Some crossed-out sections are rewritten, but she neither edits nor polishes at length. Work flows well once she is in it.

The text in the fifteen fat *cahiers* at Yale is not exactly the same as the one printed. For example, the last sentence on page 34 reads,

> And now I will tell you how two americans happened to be in the heart of the art movement of which the outside world at that time knew nothing.

In manuscript, however, the sentence ends, "at that time had absolutely no conception." Such stylistic differences are slight, obviously the result of careful revisions. Where are the handwritten or typed revisions? There is no typescript at Yale, another oddity because Toklas usually made at least one carbon and often more. Once the book was published, of course, there was no need to retype, as she had so often done. But the absence of a typescript with author's corrections or revisions is odd.[2]

1. Impersonation in the name of an amateur returns in "And Now," where Stein tells of Janet Scudder submitting paintings under the name of Toklas to the spring salon. When they were accepted and Picasso saw the name Toklas in the catalog, he was distressed that a rank amateur should be accepted, for it upset his sense of standards (*HWW* 65–66; see also *Picasso* 4–5).
2. Trying to ascertain how changes were made and what the original setting typescript for the *Autobiography* was, I got in touch with Harcourt Brace and was assured that no setting typescripts were kept for more than two years, and nothing, to the firm's knowledge, was in their archive going back to the 1930s. I wanted to know how the careful revisions

Stein appears to have planned from the start to write the book "for" Toklas, perhaps thinking even then of the parallel to Defoe writing for Crusoe. Later, in her third *Narration* lecture, she recalls,

> Think of Defoe, he tried to write Robinson Crusoe as if it were exactly what did happen and yet after all he is Robinson Crusoe and Robinson Crusoe is Defoe and therefore after all it is not what is happening it is what is happening to him to Robinson Crusoe that makes what is exciting every one. (45)

Writing in early November 1932 to Bernard Faÿ, who was in America, she said, in exactly the words she had used in the text, she was doing the book for Toklas. On the last but one page of the book, she has Toklas say,

> For some time now, many people, and publishers, have been asking Gertrude Stein to write her autobiography and she had always replied, not possibly.
>
> She began to tease me and say that I should write my autobiography. . . . (309)

There follow sample titles from the ones jotted down on the inside covers of the *cahiers*. Then, in the last paragraph, comes the first reference to Defoe. I reproduce from manuscript, with strike-throughs for Stein's revisions, how she arrived at the conclusion:

> About ~~two months~~ six weeks ago Gertrude Stein said, it does not look to me as if you were ever going to write that autobiography. You know what I am going to do. I am going to write it for you. I am going to write it as simply as Defoe did the autobiography of Robinson Crusoe. And she ~~did~~ has and this is it.
>
> ~~Sincerely yours~~
> ~~Alice B. Toklas.~~

As Bridgman pointed out, she originally finished the book as Mark Twain finished *The Adventures of Huckleberry Finn.*[3] In the voice and name of Toklas, however, she ends with a weak close that does not fit the book. Catching the false close and crossing it out frees her to let the brilliant end-

---

of details visible in discrepancies between manuscript and print were made. So I tried to contact the printer, Quinn and Boden Company, Inc., of Rahway, New Jersey. The grandson of the original printer, Mr. Quinn, told me that his grandfather had died in 1978, after which the firm had been disbanded and all property liquidated.

3. Richard Bridgman, *Gertrude Stein in Pieces* (New York: Oxford University Press, 1970), 219n.

ing that precedes it stand. Far more than workmanlike draft and revision, the amended lines are a stunning, stage-worthy performance.

Picasso is central for the first decade, when painting and painters are more prominent for Stein than writing and writers, who become more important later. He is the firm, dominant spirit in the early years and beyond whereas Toklas is a neutral, intelligent observer and a voice that we take for granted. Picasso is dominant, Toklas transparent. The two are the most powerful figures in Stein's life, but with Picasso enter not only art and aesthetics but also male power.[4]

There is much in the book about Picasso and Fernande Olivier, his mistress in the first decade, whom Stein knew well. In the first *cahier* she included notes for Picasso's comment that money was needed to get rid of a woman (22–23), though Fernande may not have been in his mind when he made the statement. He was not the only one who got rid of a woman, for Derain, Pichot, and others also paid off their women or sent them away. By the fall of 1932, however, when Stein wrote the *Autobiography,* Fernande, destitute, was making efforts to publish her own autobiography, *Picasso et ses amis,* not of course mentioned by Stein. As a friend of Picasso, Stein had in the spring of 1931 declined to write a preface for the planned American edition of the book, which Fernande had shown her. That summer, however, Stein had put Fernande in touch with Bradley, who apparently made few efforts on her behalf.[5]

4. Beginning the last paragraph on page 64, there is in the manuscript, crossed out, one sentence,

   ~~It was this winter that Picasso made for Gertrude Stein a birthday surprize.~~

   We know nothing about this gift; if, as the context suggests, this is the winter of 1905–06, it cannot be the drawing of the swineherd with pigs, dated summer of 1906 in Gosol. One wonders why Stein decided to omit the reference.

5. Extracts of the memoir had appeared in five issues of *Le Soir,* up to 20 September 1930, when Picasso succeeded in stopping publication. After her appearance in *Le Soir,* Paul Léautaud of the *Mercure de France* contacted Fernande, developed a fascination with her, and, starting in June 1931, printed three installments in *Le Mercure de France.* Late in June he convinced Boutelleau of Librairie Stock to take the book on for publication, promising a preface. Endless revisions and delays postponed the publication repeatedly; according to a friend, Picasso paid off Stock.

   However, Stock at last, late in 1933, published the book. After the *Autobiography* was serialized in the *Atlantic Monthly,* Fernande accused Stein of plagiarism and threatened her with a lawsuit, which she never carried out. See Paul Léautaud, *Journal Littéraire,* vol. 1, *November 1893–June 1928* (Paris: Mercure de France, 1956; reprint, 1986), and vol. 2, *Correspondance générale* (Paris: Flammarion, 1972); Olivier to Stein, YCAL; Olivier to Bradley, Stein to Bradley, HRC; Fernande Olivier, *Souvenirs intimes: écrits pour Picasso* (Paris: Calman-Lévy, 1988); Fernande Olivier, *Picasso et ses amis* (Paris: Librairie

Certainly Stein knew that memoirs could be profitable. Near the end of the *Autobiography* (309), when she and Toklas talk of the book Toklas is to write, Stein quotes herself as saying,

> Just think, she would say, what a lot of money you would make.

On the margin, Toklas adds in heavy, red-penciled capitals, "NO." Stein kept the sentence. In manuscripts and typescripts appear Toklas' red page numbers, questions about facts, dates, etc., and marks for illegible or misspelled words, which Stein usually rewrites above the original. Sometimes Toklas adds sharp opinions, such as the "NO" about money; or about proofreading *The Making Of Americans,*

> Proof had to be corrected most of it four times and finally I broke my glasses, my eyes gave out, and Gertrude Stein finished it alone. (275)

"Never," Toklas adds in thick, large longhand. Stein retains the sentence unchanged.

But Toklas also effects changes, for example, about Hemingway. Originally this sentence was followed by another,

> I had been reading the Guide des Gourmets and I had found among other places where one ate well, Pernollet's Hotel in the town of Belley. (274)

Toklas crossed out the next sentence, and Stein left it out,

> I think it was Hemingway who first told me about these guide books.

Stein also includes comments of Toklas in the text, for example, the last sentence of a paragraph on Stein's driving,

> The only violent discussions we have had in connection with her driving a car have been on the subject of backing. (214)

Such details, on Toklas' margins and in Stein's text, become a subtext.

It is at the start of the book that Stein must find the voice she needs and settle into the new way of writing. She begins, as she often does, with no sure voice. She had always found her form and her voice by writing, not by predetermination. Her earlier work had not required thinking about voice, or about a narrator, apart from substance, but here voice is the key. The Toklas voice is familiar from details in many Stein pieces. Now, however, that voice must manage the substance throughout the book, an entirely new

---

Stock, 1933), published in English as *Picasso and His Friends,* trans. Jane Miller (New York: Appleton Century, 1965); John Richardson, *A Life of Picasso,* vol. 2, *1907–17* (New York: Random House, 1996).

affair. In joining the substance of Stein to the voice of Toklas, she is both distinguishing the two and making them one—one of two, two of two.

The fifteen fat, black oilcloth *cahiers* contain the full text of the *Autobiography.* But in addition, there is one preliminary *cahier,* with text and illustration on a rare American subject under the title *Châtiment Mérité* (*Deserved Punishment*): the story of a gold prospector during the gold rush, told as an example of the law of talion, the Mosaic law of an eye for an eye and a tooth for a tooth. A gold digger tries to rob and kill his companion but fails and flees. Two others join the victim in pursuit of the culprit, lassoing him. Vengeance is wrought when one of the captors—not the man he had tried to kill—puts a knife through him. The tale ends reassuring us: such customs no longer exist in America, where life is now more civilized.

When I first wrote about this *cahier,*[6] I said it could not have been chosen accidentally by the Californian Stein. I likened the violence of the gold diggers to the personal violence between the women in the summer of 1932, no matter how peaceful the words, the *Autobiography* emerging as a book of retaliation as well as a peace offering to Toklas. It all seemed to fit together perfectly. Though this is the only *cahier* on this subject that I have seen among the Stein papers, I no longer believe that the case is so simple and clear-cut, as the scenarios of the summer's events make clear.

Part I, paragraph 3, of the preliminary *cahier* includes three early, substantial deviations from the final text in print. The first two paragraphs tell, exactly as in the book, of the birth of Toklas in San Francisco, her mother's father, her father's father, who left his wife "just after their marriage to fight at the barricades in Paris, but . . . soon returned . . .". So far, except for minor differences in punctuation, the text is the same. But in paragraph 3, taking off from "violence," Stein loses control of voice and substance,

> I myself have had no liking for violence but in spite of that which is what I wish to say I have had some occasions to feel what violence is and when I do feel so I can and have thoroughly tempted there which is what there is to do. Moreover nobody can doubt if it is not to be considered [ ] to have which is the result I have had that I have what I have and I always have as I always will had to have that which I have. In this way there can be no doubt, no doubt, that in no way there is any doubt that having to have that which I have I have had and I have that which I have. . . .

The revised text keeps the first eight words, then continues with the charming description in the voice of Toklas,

6. Ulla Dydo, "*Stanzas In Meditation:* The Other *Autobiography,*" *Chicago Review* 35, no. 2 (winter 1985): 4–20.

> I myself have had no liking for violence and have always enjoyed the pleasures of needlework and gardening. I am fond of paintings, furniture, tapestry, houses and flowers even vegetables and fruit-trees. I like a view but I like to sit with my back turned to it. (3)

The second deviation, in paragraph four of the book, is the long, slow digression full of verbal interest about the fat aunt. The paragraph begins as in the final version, "I led in my childhood and youth the gently bred existence of my class and kind." The preliminary text continues,

> I had an aunt who was charming and she used to say Wido Bidot, and neither she nor I meant anything by that xcept drinking out of a saucer and any child does delight really does delight in drinking out of a saucer, and when my aunt, my charming aunt, she who afterwards was so large that she was unable to leave her [ ] without part of the door being removed, she and she was always charming, embroidered beautifully but never finished embroidering and sang so wonderfully and so slowly that she never sounded one note by another one but at any rate she did and about that there is no question she did say Widow Bidott and in saying Widow Bidotte she was charming.

Nothing is known of such an aunt in the Toklas or Stein family. The play with words about the widow who ends up too fat to move, with its nursery rhyme elements, is pure Stein—not Toklas.

The third deviation takes off from the very next sentence, just begun, "I had some intellectual adventures . . . ," and continues,

> . . . at this time, and these adventures as I [am] about to tell you were ones that were undoubtedly much as would [interest] any one. They consisted very largely in my having begun and I did begin preparing for anything. This was not an intellectual adventure it was an intellectual [escape] as any one knowing anything could and would know how to begin.
>
> How does one begin, one begins very well.
>
> At no time does one fail in beginning very well and having indeed having begun very well one can and one does [proceed] very well to have been begun. Then and thereafter I was charming I was delicate I was delicious I was attractive and it made of me what I was and need I say what that is and that was. I may say every one does and may know what there is what that was and what that will be and as such it is completely quite completely entirely completely [undoubtedly] entirely completely satisfying as completely charming. And so my life and so it goes on.

Rewritten, the text completes the initial sentence, and continues,

I had some intellectual adventures at this period but very quiet ones. When I was about nineteen years of age. . . . (3–4)

How powerfully Stein's manner demands its way, beginning again and again from the outset.

Even once she mastered the voice, she retained authorship. In the *cahiers* for the final text, after notebook number and title, "Autobiography of Alice B. Toklas" or "T F Y - W G S," for Twenty-Five Years With Gertrude Stein, she often adds, as elsewhere, "written by Gertrude Stein."

These three drastic but confined changes fill the preliminary *cahier.* They testify dramatically to Stein's difficulty in achieving a voice for this book. However, once these false starts are behind her, what is left becomes only the first page of the book. Now she begins again, in substantial new *cahiers,* and her flexible control of voice and substance hardly ever slips. She turns the private troubles of the summer into a brilliant writer's triumph, a winning book.

In the last week of November, after the election of Franklin Delano Roosevelt, Stein and Toklas returned to Paris for the opening of an exhibition of Picabia drawings from December 1 to 24, at Léonce Rosenberg's gallery. Stein's "Picabia Stanza," with Marcel Duchamp's translation, served as preface to the catalog. Stein had known Picabia since the early Saturday nights at rue de Fleurus, which he had attended with his first wife, Gabrielle Buffet-Picabia, but later, during his marriage to Germaine Everling, she had not maintained contact. By the spring of 1931, she was again friendly with him and Olga Mohler, his third wife, took to his painting, discussed ideas with him, and gave him support. She also shared his interest in cars and dogs.[7]

Back in Paris, Stein called Picasso to tell him about the *Autobiography,* which included so much about him. In "And Now," written between

7. The Picabias lived in Mougins, near mutual friends like the Guevaras and Francis Rose. Starting in 1931, on trips to Paris, they often stopped at Bilignin. In June 1932, Picabia gave them the chihuahua Byron that he had bred and, after Byron's death the following spring, his successor, Pépé ("And Now," *HWW* 65; *EA* 48–49, 56–59).

Through the efforts of Madame Marie Cuttoli, the wife of a senator from Philippeville, Algeria, and with support from Stein, Picabia was on July 14, 1933, elected chevalier of the *Légion d'honneur.* Madame Cuttoli, who owned the Galerie Vignon, had in 1930, upon Stein's recommendation, hired Georges Maratier to run her gallery. In the summer of 1933, Stein's renewed friendship with Picabia led to his portrait of her that is now at the Beinecke Library. See William Camfield, *Francis Picabia: His Art, Life and Times* (Princeton, N.J.: Princeton University Press, 1979), 245–46 & n. 3–10; Olga Mohler, *Francis Picabia* (Turin: Edizioni Notizie, 1975), 71; Picabia to Stein, YCAL; Stein to Picabia, Librairie Doucet, Paris.

November 1933 and March 1934, before the paragraph beginning, "I remember when there was the first big show," she added in manuscript a paragraph omitted upon publication:

> Picasso to whom I naturally translated it as soon as it was written was much excited, he began remembering all the things that were in the room that I had not mentioned, he said you forgot to mention the swords that were crossed at one end of the room between the two Italian angels, and he was very xcited and pleased, and then he went home and then he was furious and we have never seen each other again and now we never will. (*HWW* 64)

In *Everybody's Autobiography,* written in 1936, after Stein and Picasso had reconciled, Stein said that he came with his wife and Stein read to them in French. Picasso pointed out details omitted, but when Fernande Olivier appeared in the reading, his wife, in anger, rose to leave. Picasso wanted to stay but Stein insisted that he accompany his wife.

The Marketing of Gertrude Stein: Publication

Stein's agent, William Bradley, had been in contact about her with Harcourt, Brace and Company even before she wrote him, on November 13, that she had "a manuscript, Autobiography of Alice B. Toklas," and before she sent him the typescript, on November 16 and 24, 1932. Harcourt had on November 2 been assigned the leftover stock of Stein's *Useful Knowledge,* and on November 7, Bradley seized the opportunity of this assignment to propose to Harcourt that they publish *Three Lives* or *The Making Of Americans,* both out of print.[8]

On December 15, Harcourt rejected his proposal; Stein, they said, was established in America by "foreign editions" of her books whose importation had, "to a considerable extent, satisfied her following here." The foreign editions were the Contact Press edition of *The Making Of Americans* and the Plain Edition volumes. Bradley protested that readers could not be satisfied when Stein's two major works were out of print. By this time, however, he had informed Harcourt of the *Autobiography* and asked for a cabled response to his proposal that they consider the book. On December 22, Harcourt cabled, "OK send ms," and Bradley forwarded it on December 28; he wrote

8. *Useful Knowledge* was originally published in 1928 by Joseph Brewer under the imprint of Payson and Clarke. Later renamed Brewer and Warren, by late 1932 the firm went out of business. The practice then was to assign leftover stock for distribution to a major publisher.

that he counted on Alfred Harcourt to read the book right through to the very end, including the last page, "I do not think you will regret the time so spent." He added, "in my opinion with a little clever handling this book could be made into a best-seller."

Bradley knew how distressed Stein had been about publication. He also knew that she was ambitious and that she required good form and attention to her rights and royalties. She had reluctantly conceded that she needed his help in placing work. After Joseph Brewer rejected *Lucy Church Amiably,* writing in March 1929 that his firm could not risk another loss with a second book of hers, she wrote Bradley an unusually open letter,

> I have just had your letter and I am trying to tell you a little more which is rather difficult for a person of my nature to do. You see this publication business is not a thing I can so well dispense with, in the first place waiting and waiting to have the things you write printed and then they are not and hope deferred does make the heart sick, I cannot tell you the depth and bitterness of my disappointment when Brewer did not go on with Lucy Church I cannot yet think of it with any calm, and the other side, I did inherit a very small income on which I have lived with great care but one grows older and life is harder and it diminishes and the need of earning is definitely there, and so please don't take the attitude that I am aloof, I know you will understand the great difficulty I have in writing in this way but I do not mean anything xcept that I hope that you will sooner or later and I sometimes very much hope sooner do what I can not do for myself. . . .[9]

A little later, in June, she reassured him, "the successful publisher for me xists and you will find him, of that I am beginning to be sure." To Bradley she was a challenge, and he was eager to help her succeed. Once she hired him, with the charge that he was to make her rich and famous, he reviewed her contracts and royalty statements, even following up through Boston attorneys on royalties owed her by the Four Seas Company, which had gone out of business, for her 1922 collection, *Geography And Plays.*

For the Plain Edition, which Stein and Toklas managed on their own, he gave advice about promotion and bookstores in America. In letters, Stein was always positive and enthusiastic about her edition; new subscriptions were coming in daily, volumes were being shipped, and subscribers were impressed. In fact, of course, sales were limited, expenses were high, and efforts, especially on the part of Toklas, were enormous. Many copies were inscribed and given away. The project generated small profits for bookstores

9. N.d., probably May 1929, HRC.

and attracted no major reviews. As manager of the Plain Edition, Toklas tried to enlist readers for Stein's work, which submissions to publishers had not effectually done. Now, however, the *Autobiography,* joining as one the words of Stein and the voice of Toklas, created the key to publication, audience, fame, and money.

From 1929 on, Stein and Bradley negotiated with Lee Furman of the Macaulay Company in New York for a cut version, about one-third, of *The Making Of Americans,* which Stein thought of as a sampler, to be extended upon demand, eventually to its full length. Long negotiations led to a contract forwarded in June 1930 but canceled in August because the text submitted did not live up to Macaulay's conditions. Bradley was distressed, but Stein remained calm and positive: she was glad, she said, that Macaulay did not want the book, for they plainly did not understand it, which left Bradley and her free to go after more prestigious publishers.

Meanwhile, however, negotiations had also started through Bradley with Librairie Stock in Paris for a French translation of the short *The Making Of Americans.* By May 1, 1931, a contract was signed. From spring to summer, Stock's experienced translators, who had for years done books by major foreign authors, such as Joseph Conrad, discussed translation; they finally deemed Stein's work *irréalisable* in French. By August, therefore, Stock refused publication and returned the manuscript to Bradley.

Now Bernard Faÿ took the initiative and negotiated directly with Stock while also remaining in touch with Bradley. He proposed the Baroness Renée de Seillière as translator under his guidance. After repeated delays, he intimated that if the editors were unreasonable, he himself would translate the book. A respected historian, writer, and translator, Faÿ finally turned the Stock refusal into acceptance. Through the spring and summer of 1932, Renée de Seillière and Faÿ, with Stein reviewing, worked on the text. Completed by February 1, 1933, *Américains d'Amérique* was published on July 17.

Negotiations for French and American publications in Paris and New York went on side by side. Faÿ prepared the ground in France but also lectured on her at American colleges and universities and reviewed her work in France as well as America.[10] Close personal friends, Stein and Faÿ shared the triumph of publishing her as a French author and promoting her among the educated young, especially in America. On March 31, 1933, Faÿ wrote to

10. Three examples of his many essays on Stein, carefully timed to coincide advantageously with publications, are one about *Three Lives* in the *Chicago Tribune,* 19 August 1933, one about the *Autobiography* in the *Saturday Review of Literature,* 2 September 1933, and one in *Le Figaro,* 27 October 1934.

Stein from Evanston, Illinois, where he was teaching at Northwestern University, "I want to thank you, to tell you how much light, happiness and life you have put into my life this winter."

Meanwhile, Bradley skillfully negotiated on her behalf in New York. He kept in check her excessive demands and her aggressive need for recognition. At the same time, she herself perfectly understood business deals and often shrewdly calculated how and when work could be used to greatest advantage. Stein and Bradley shared in the success of her literary work and the publicity that testified to their triumph. On April 27, she wrote him,

> I do want to tell you how much I appreciate your kindness and patience and how comfortable I feel in my dependence on you. It has been a wonderful winter for me and it has given me something I never thought to have and I do want to thank you for it all. (HRC)

On May 4, Bradley responded,

> It has been a wonderful winter for me also, inasmuch as it has given me the most exciting episode in my life as an "author's representative." Everything else now seems a trifle tame by comparison, and probably will continue to do so until you entrust me with a second book to handle for you. . . . What will this summer bring forth? I shall live in expectations. . . . [Bradley's ellipses]

In 1933, the first great year of contracts and success, Bradley and Faÿ, who had regularly been in America and knew better than Stein what was happening there, supported and guided her, and she relied on them. Not until mid-1934 did Stein end up pitting Faÿ against Bradley, the intellectual against the commercial, in representing her interests.

With the delivery of the manuscript of the *Autobiography* to Harcourt Brace in December 1932 and its acceptance in January begins the next phase of Stein's life: the marketing of the *Autobiography,* indeed of Stein herself. This, and its effects on her next steps in writing, rather than the art of the *Autobiography,* which will continue to receive vast and valuable analysis, is the context I shall explore.

In January and February 1933, Bradley negotiated contracts for publication of the *Autobiography* by Harcourt in New York and, through Harcourt, by Allen Lane in London, where the plates were prepared at lower cost than in America; and for serialization in the *Atlantic Monthly.* In February, Bradley proposed to Harcourt that it reprint *Three Lives* and take on distribution of the Plain Edition; by June, Harcourt refused. From December until May, when the serialization of the *Autobiography* began, Stein was busy with illustrations and other decisions for the *Autobiography* and with projects started earlier—such as the Plain Edition *Matisse Picasso And Gertrude Stein With Two Shorter Stories,* published in February.[11] In April, the Literary Guild committed itself to the *Autobiography* for the fall.[12] The advances allowed Stein to buy a new Ford, a Hermés coat, studded dog collars, bathroom fixtures, a servant couple rather than the one maid of past years, and a telephone—Belley 168.

Upon the first installment in the *Atlantic Monthly* in May 1933, notes from friends and visitors to 27 rue de Fleurus, fan letters, and reviews started pouring in, continuing to the book's publication on September 1 and through the year into 1934. The Stein archive at Yale overflows with them, and Ray White's *Reference Guide,* after the small number of early reviews and none during World War I, lists pages and pages of commentary.[13] Orders for Plain Edition books increased. Calls came in for translations.

Stein had remained distant from Virgil Thomson since they quarreled three years earlier. However, Thomson had presented scenes from *Four Saints In Three Acts* at salons in New York and elsewhere, and the opera had become a matter of special interest.[14] In 1932, A. Everett Austin and the board of trustees of the Wadsworth Atheneum in Hartford decided to add to the existing museum a new wing for modern art, including a theater. The new

11. *Matisse Picasso And Gertrude Stein* is known as *GMP* and is so called in my list of abbreviations. The two shorter stories in this volume of early work are "A Long Gay Book" and "Many Many Women." A design for the title page of this volume, which the women were planning in the summer of 1932, appears in manuscript *cahier* 4 for Part III of "Stanzas In Meditation."

12. The following figures represent the documented plan for payment, though it may have been further adjusted in later, unrecorded negotiations, subject to conjecture. Bradley normally received a commission of 10 percent. According to the contract signed after January 18, 1933, Harcourt paid Stein an advance of $500 against royalties plus 10 percent for the first 5,000 copies, 15 percent thereafter; total Harcourt royalties were $4,495.31, probably by the end of 1933; *Atlantic Monthly* paid for serialization rights, for four installments and a maximum 60 percent of the text, $1,000. The Literary Guild paid a total of $6,000, to be divided half-and-half between Harcourt and Stein; with an August 20 cable from Harcourt, Stein received her $3,000 and a warning about the falling value of the dollar: "Buy francs Stein Guild payment" (William A. Bradley Collection, HRC).

13. Between 1909 and 1932, reviews averaged 1 to 20 annually, except in years when she published a book—38 in 1914 for *TB,* 34 in 1923 for *G&P,* 27 in 1928 for *UK;* in 1933 and 1934, they rose to 111 and 164, respectively.

14. I here give only the briefest account of negotiations for the production, because my focus is on Stein's movement into fame. For fuller accounts, see Virgil Thomson, *Virgil Thomson* (New York: Alfred A. Knopf, 1966), chaps. 18–20; Anthony Tommasini, *Virgil Thomson: Composer on the Aisle* (New York: W. W. Norton, 1997), chaps. 15–16; letters of Thomson, Stein, and Bradley, YCAL, HRC.

venture into modernism was to be launched with the Stein-Thomson opera and a Picasso exhibit. By the spring of 1933, funds had to be raised for a production of the opera, and both Stein and Bradley heard of the plan. Thomson returned to Paris from New York in April, hoping to secure her approval of the plans for the production.

Bradley now tried, as he said in his May 6 report to Stein, to act as "peacemaker" between her and Thomson. Although both she and Bradley distrusted Thomson, it was important to make a success of *Four Saints* and, in May and June, to negotiate with care for the production, for printing of the libretto, and for performances of other joint work. Negotiations were difficult, both about the plans for the production itself, including black actors, and about sharing profits 50–50, on which Stein insisted, even though it was not accepted practice between composer and librettist and it was Thomson who had promoted the opera. The appearance of the first serial printing of the *Autobiography* in May, in the middle of the negotiations, gave Stein's claim to the importance of her name for the production of the opera the extra backing that was needed. The contract was signed in the early autumn, and by October 31, Thomson was back in New York to attend to the production.

That spring, with prospects and honors accumulating even before the book was out, Stein again pressed for an American edition of the short *The Making Of Americans,* whether with Harcourt or another publisher. On May 6, Bradley wrote that he had proposed the matter to Harcourt, who had not so far responded. His long, formal answer barely conceals his frustration with his insistent client, "I do not think that you can possibly have any idea of what the state of affairs is over there in the US just now." With examples of bankruptcies, he spoke of the "prostration in publishing and bookselling" and warned,

> To hold the knife to anyone's throat at such a time as this, especially in dealing with one of the few completely solvent publishers, such as Harcourt, and attempt to force upon him a very expensive undertaking that might very well compromise the profits from a book like the AUTOBIOGRAPHY which must have seemed a veritable godsend to them, a well in the desert, would not only, to my mind, be almost a criminal act on our part but an act of folly as well. I do really pray you, very sincerely and seriously, to let me handle this whole matter as the circumstances seem to require. You know how eagerly interested I am to get the best results obtainable and to further your interests to the very farthest extent. But there are times when excessive zeal and eagerness defeat their own ends and bring about precisely the reverse of what we are aiming at.

> You say you think I should have forced Harcourt's hand at the moment of letting him have the AUTOBIOGRAPHY by putting THE MAKING OF AMERICANS into the contract. Personally, I am convinced that this would have been entirely impossible and that, even had I succeeded in doing so, it would have been a sterile victory, mitigating in every way against the AUTOBIOGRAPHY. For they would certainly have charged the whole cost of both books against that one book and thus reduced their budget in every way for the *lancement* of the AUTOBIOGRAPHY, as well as dampening their ardor and enthusiasm. No, the only reasonable thing to do at such a juncture is to wait till the latter is actually out, and on the way to a triumphant success.

What finally persuaded Harcourt to offer Stein a contract on October 23 was Faÿ's preface to *Américains d'Amérique.* Harcourt then asked him for a preface to the American edition, which he was happy to write. The book was published on February 8, 1934.[15]

Lindley Hubbell not only wrote a poem in praise of Stein but also gave her help with people he knew in the publishing world and with reviews.[16] To Bradley Stein forwarded a letter from Hubbell of May 11, identifying him as a librarian with the New York Public Library and, like Bradley himself, a New Englander. Hubbell wrote,

> Yesterday someone from the Modern Library called me up. A friend of mine, Ben Wasson [Hubbell's agent], had read my review of the Plain Edition, and remembering what I had said about the Modern Library he spoke to one of the editors. It didn't go over at the time but now that the Atlantic has capitulated, and the editors of the Modern Library decided that perhaps there was something to it after all. Anyway, he called me up yesterday & asked me for a copy of Three Lives. (HRC)

This is the beginning of Stein's association with Bennett Cerf of Random House, who on May 16 asked about the rights to *Three Lives,* first published

15. Harcourt had known Faÿ, long a popular expert on Franco-American relations, since 1929 when, through Bradley as agent, he and Avery Claflin published *The American Experiment.* Since 1923, before he became close to Stein, Faÿ had known Bradley, who had advised him as friend and steered him to American publishers.
16. Lindley Williams Hubbell, "A Letter to Gertrude Stein," *Pagany* 1, no. 2 (spring 1930): 37, reprinted in *A Gertrude Stein Companion: Content with the Example* (New York: Greenwood Press, 1988), 115; see also "The Plain Edition of Gertrude Stein," *Contempo* 3, no. 12 (25 October 1933): 1, 4–5, published alongside a review attacking Stein by Samuel D. Schmalhausen. See Stein to Hubbell, 6 August 1933, and Hubbell to Stein, 17 October 1933.

in 1909 by the Grafton Press and reprinted in 1927 by Albert and Charles Boni, who still had the plates. On May 29, Cerf offered to print the book in the Modern Library. A contract was signed by the last week of June. Carl Van Vechten provided an introduction, and the book was published in September.[17]

On October 23, the day Stein signed the contract with Harcourt for the short *The Making Of Americans,* Bennett Cerf inquired by letter about her plans for the long novel and offered to print it complete as a Modern Library Giant, exactly the kind of cheap, popular edition she had always hoped for. It was too late.

Always forward-looking, Stein immediately considered alternate options. She proposed to Cerf a collection of portraits spanning all the years of her writing; it was a book she had had in mind for years, and it allowed her to include important early work. Titled with her own phrase from "An Elucidation," *Portraits And Prayers* appeared on November 7, 1934, to celebrate the start of her American lecture tour.[18]

Stein wanted the same publisher to print both of what by the spring of 1934 she called her "open and public books," such as the *Autobiography,* and her "real kind of books." In addition, she wanted distribution of the Plain Edition. She had always been looking for a major trade publisher to take on all her work and become "her publisher," ready to print all her work. This wish sounds as if it came from an old patriarchal world, where she never ceased to look for a guiding mentor. How well Bennett Cerf played his part in that world when he asked to become her publisher by offering to print a book of hers every year—or everything.[19]

Byron A Play (LO&P 333–86)

Between November 1932 and summer 1933, Stein moved first to contracts and advances for the *Autobiography,* then to its reality with serialization, book publication, reviews. How ironic that after some thirty years of the world's refusal to listen to her she should have felt jolted into incapacity by the fame she had craved all those years. In the late autumn of 1933, she described her state of mind.

17. *LGS/CVV* 267–70; Columbia-Random House, YCAL. See also *EA* 99–100.
18. It was designed by Ernest Reichl, the distinguished German refugee artist who also designed Joyce's *Ulysses* and later Mann's *Doctor Faustus.* Published with Carl Van Vechten's photograph on the cover, it brilliantly displayed for readers who expected to see her a portrait of the author of portraits.
19. Gertrude Stein, *Everybody's Autobiography* (New York: Random House, 1937), 129.

What happened to me was this. When the success began and it was a success I got completely lost. You know the nursery rhyme, ~~when I am I I know~~[20] I am I because my little dog knows me. Well you see I did not know myself, I lost my personality. It has always been ~~so much~~ completely included in myself my personality as any personality naturally is, and here all of a sudden, I was not I just because so many people did know me. It was just the opposite of I am I because my little dog knows me. So many people knowing me I was I no longer and for the first time since I had begun to write I could not write and what was worse I could not worry about not writing and what was also worse I began to think about how my writing would sound to others, how could I make them understand, I who had always lived within myself and my writing.[21]

It sounds as if the success had poisoned her mind, cutting her off from herself and her work. It made her think of how to please her audience rather than how to write.

Later also, in *Everybody's Autobiography* (84), she said she was unable to write from November 1932 until *Blood On The Dining Room Floor,* late August 1933. Actually her silence was less long and not continuous. She wrote no new work from November 1932 until April 1933, though she was busy getting the *Autobiography* ready for publication. Also, with Toklas she ap-

20. Stein first wrote, "When I am I [my little dog knows me]," starting a form quite different from "I am I because my little dog knows me." The same form is used in "Saving The Sentence" (1929), "What is a sentence for if I am I then my little dog knows me" (*HTW* 19). Here the "I," not the dog, is the agent of recognition and identity. Stein relies on the nursery rhyme about the old woman who falls asleep on the king's highway, has her petticoat cut off by a peddler, and no longer knows who she is since her identity depends on her appearance. She therefore looks for confirmation of it from her little dog.

> "But if it be I, as I hope it be,
> I've a little dog at home, and he'll know me
> If I be I, he'll wag his little tail,
> And if it not be I, he'll loudly bark and wail."

The little dog does not recognize her and barks at her.

The song is printed as number 257 in William S. and Ceil Baring-Gould, comp., *The Annotated Mother Goose* (New York: Meridian Books, World Publishing Company, 1967), 159. This rhyme is also quoted by Josiah Royce in his discussion of Kant's "Transcendental Unity of Apperception" in *The Spirit of Modern Philosophy: An Essay in the Form of Lectures* (Boston: Houghton Mifflin and Company, 1892; reprint, New York: George Braziller, 1955), 128 (page citation is to the reprint edition). I assume that Stein, like Royce, relied on the folk rhyme, not that she got the line from Royce, as Richard Bridgman suggests (*Gertrude Stein in Pieces,* 242n). See also *EA* 297.

21. "And Now," *HWW* 63, quoted, with revisions marked, from manuscript.

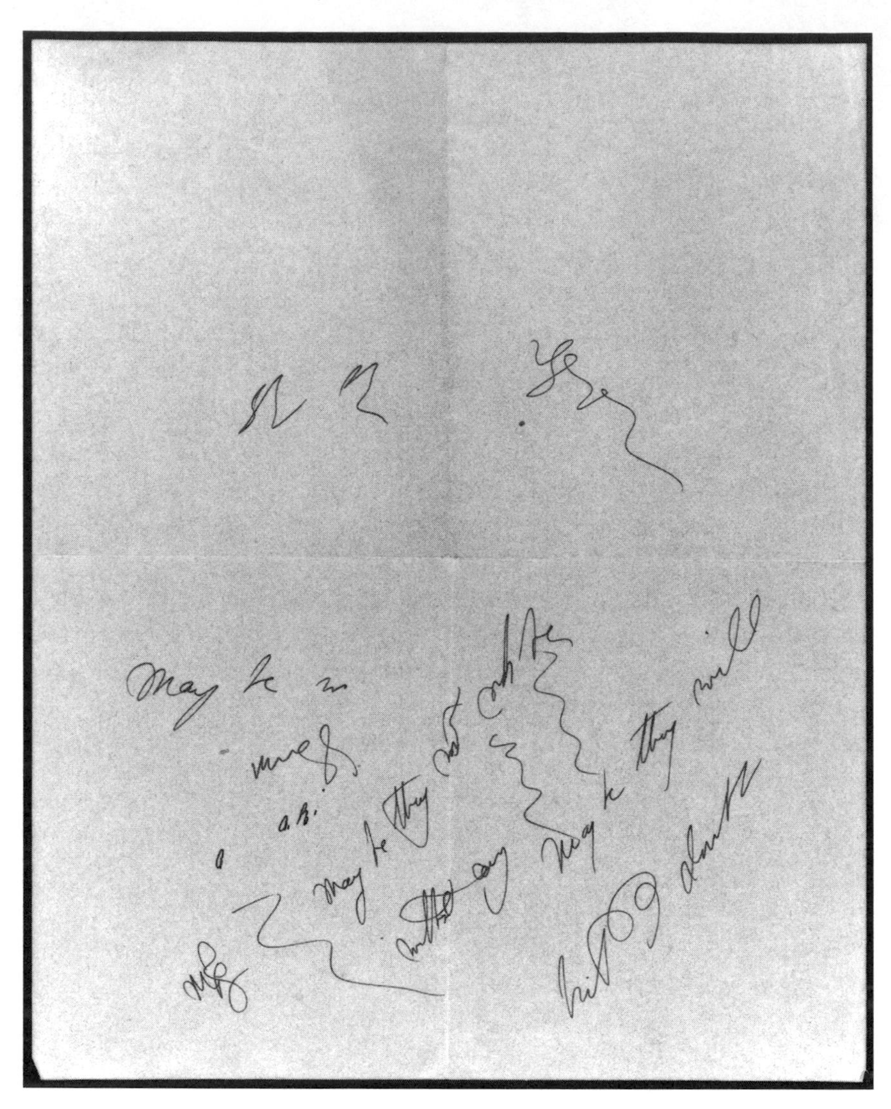

Figure 14. Alexander Calder to Gertrude Stein, 9 March 1932, with Stein doodles that become mobiles. YCAL Courtesy Estate of Alexander Calder / Artists Rights Society and Estate of Gertrude Stein.

parently entered the changes in the manuscript and the second typescript of "Stanzas In Meditation," and Toklas typed *Short Sentences* and perhaps other summer 1932 texts. Between May and late August 1933 she wrote some slight, short pieces, most about the *Autobiography.*

In mid-April, however, she wrote *Byron A Play,* perhaps the last work in the voice we know from "Stanzas In Meditation" as her very own. It was writ-

14 rue de la Colonie
Paris 13e
March 9/32

Dear Miss Stein

Would you and Miss Toklass care to come to tea next Monday (Mar. 14) We liked very much meeting you, and would like to do so again. I have arranged a few of the things from the show so that they work here.

Will you please drop us a card as to whether you will come or not

Very Cordially
Calder

ten before the effects of the *Autobiography* permanently affected her work. It was not that she lost her voice or, as Bridgman claims, experienced a writer's block. Incapacity now became the difficult matter of loss of *her own voice* and inability to recreate the *voice of the Autobiography* in a sequel to it that Bradley wanted.

Byron A Play was never mentioned in exchanges with Bradley or friends. It was not published until after Stein's death, when Van Vechten included it in *Last Operas And Plays* (1949). On December 22, 1935, she had written to him,

> Then there is this, in going over the ms. I found a play, about Byron, I think it is completely possible to do with Virgil [Thomson], who directly and indirectly wants it, it would take a lot of stage imagination to put it on, but it does move and it is a romantic tragedy, we will send it separate, I have not mentioned its xistence to anybody, I want to know what you say. . . . (*LGS/CVV* 467–68)

Van Vechten acknowledged it on January 9, 1936.[22]

Nothing about *Byron A Play* could be anticipated. It is not about the poet, though he is the stuff for drama and the name seems to put him in the play. But what led Stein to write it was the sudden death of the chihuahua puppy Byron.[23]

22. It is not clear whether Stein had shown it to Thomson or merely told him about it, although, ever since *Four Saints In Three Acts,* they had hoped to do another opera together. Van Vechten showed it to Thomson, who did not set it to music. His biographer, Anthony Tommasini, says Thomson told him he did not wish to do "another opera with a hermetic text" (*Virgil Thomson,* 480). But I wonder, was his choice of *Lord Byron* for his late opera the result of an unconscious memory, a transmuted regret about a work with Stein on which he missed out?
23. The dog, given to Stein by the Picabias at three months of age in June 1932, died in the early spring of 1933, probably April, in Paris. Madame Picabia says it was Stein who named him (William Camfield to author, 5 August 1986).

> They [i.e., the Picabias] called the two little Mexican dogs Monsieur and Madame and Byron was a son and a grandson. We called him Byron because he was to have as a wife his sister or his mother and so we called him Byron. Poor little Byron his name gave him a strange and feverish nature, he was very fierce and tender and he danced strange little war dances and frightened Basket. Basket was always frightened of Byron. And then Byron died suddenly one night of typhus. (*EA* 48–49)

Typhus is not a dog disease; perhaps it carried over from the typhus that sent Paul Bowles to the American Hospital in Paris that winter.

After Byron died, the Picabias on May 25 gave the women another chihuahua, Pépé, to replace the loss. Pépé lived with them for many years, into World War II; he seems to have died in 1943.

Byron appears in some works of 1932–33 and after: in "Stanzas In Meditation," two unnamed dogs (i.e., Basket and Byron), often with balls, are in Part II, Stanzas xvii, xviii, xix; Part IV, Stanza xi; Part V, Stanzas i, vi, Lxvii, Lxxii, Lxxviii, and elsewhere; Byron appears by name in Part II, Stanza xix. In *A Manoir* (*LO&P* 303, 358, 359, 364) and elsewhere, he appears numerous times as a "character," with a first name added; as someone spoken of; and even as "Byron a play" (*Blood On The Dining Room Floor,* 36); elements of Byron may enter the section on dogs in *Ida,* Vintage 97. Toklas speaks of him in the Ronald Duncan interview of November 1952. With a *B* name, like the many others she used, Byron was also a baby to rock (347) and nestle (339), and a Stein text. Because he was a gift from Picabia, two lines of the "Picabia" stanza (Part V, Stanza Lxxi) are in the play (357).

Read aloud and listen to this play, the longest Stein ever wrote, with its spare, narrowly centered vocabulary of short, neutral words and varied lines. Its language is mixed—light, short lines like jingles:

> I like Byron he likes me
> Byron will or will not be
> With me.
> Think of Byron. (368)

blocks of descriptive poetry resonating with his name:

> Byron. Because of Byron.
> Byron. By which Byron.
> Byron. May Byron.
> Byron Lay Byron down
> Byron Escaping Byron.
> Byron Byron makes no attempt to escape.
> Byron. If it may be Byron
> Then Byron Because Byron.
> Byron. By which Byron.
> Byron If Byron. (383)

questions about plays, often in prose:

> A play is a day or not to say so I wish to make a play not a day or even not what happened but only not what is seen.
> This is a play. (342)

> An hour in a play is not to-day.
> I have thought of a play.
> The difference between a play and not a play is this a play states that if they like they will come and leave a day. This which is a rejoinder. In a play there is no rejoinder because in a play they never tried. And so they may.
> What is a play to-day. (340)

passages that sound as if they came straight out of "Stanzas":

> I could be one with one of two
> But it may do to do what one can do
> For not for you to do but it is not gone where
> Make it be mine. (336)

The inventiveness of her lines is striking, their humor, their varied moods, the details about the little dog, and the thoughts about plays. But the design of *Byron A Play* for a long time eluded me. Why the many calls to Byron? Why all the talk about what a play is, why the assertions that she knows, never followed by what she knows?

> I can clearly understand now what a play is. (345)
>
> I feel I know now what a play is there are many kinds of them. (350)

And this from Stein, who was never one to theorize about genres, though she always raised questions about them.

What characters are in this play? There is Byron, of course, but he is dead and appears mostly as the subject of short descriptive and narrative sections or commentary. There are "I," "she," "they," some with echoes of Stein and Toklas. But what is she doing in this play that I hear moving in a Stein space with a Stein voice but cannot explain?

Gradually, reading aloud, I began to hear how she keeps the audience in the present. The designations Act I, Scene I—"Act" and "Scene" seem indistinguishable—repeated over and over, lead into very short sections of text, which never cumulatively build but remain in a single moment. Also, the title phrase, "Byron a play," appears over and over, in scene or act after scene or act, as a spoken line. But here and there it also moves into centered position offset as a title on the page. Finally I realized that the phrase is spoken by Stein and returns each time her effort to create *Byron A Play* fails and she begins again.

The name Byron is worked into line after line, a few times with new first names added—John, Henry, Irving, General, William (334–35), even George (362) and Lord (371)—but these are quickly discarded. Byron will not come if called by another name; only to the musical name "Byron," whose syllables rhythmically invoke him, will he respond. But when the name is twisted from "Byron" to "Bryon," we hear it broken in two separate syllables and losing the musical rhythm; will the dog respond to this name or not?

In the repeated phrases and names, Stein is doing what she has done from early years on: she is beginning again and again. But she is also developing in complex forms ideas of calling, calling up, calling by name, calling forth, and of identity in "I am I if my little dog knows me." When Byron was alive, she could call "Byron!" and he would come. He can no longer come when called. We can give dogs names and teach them to respond to a call. But they have no sense of identity, nor do they know our names. With this play, we have come a long way from the old woman and her little dog. Stein's preoccupation with names and identity will continue.

Slowly the repeated beginnings reach me and I hear what is happening. Stein is trying to write Byron into a work that she already knows will be *Byron A Play,* and she keeps failing, for the dog is dead and cannot come to her; only if she manages to invoke him successfully will she be able to create Byron and keep him in a text. For the first half of this play, she summons him, calling "Byron" and "Byron a play" without reaching him, only once or twice going beyond Act I, Scene I. She keeps talking to herself about how to put him into a play, how to write a play at all, even what a play is.

Why a play and not a novel, a poem? Because the essence of what dogs do is play, sit, run—all words that we also associate with the stage. So "Byron plays" or "Byron at play" becomes *Byron A Play,* the verb and the noun leading down a single path. His death is not mourned in an elegy but becomes the occasion for writing a play, an effort that leaves Stein frustrated.

> Byron a play.
> If in weakness can there be a play.
> It is doubtful if in weakness there can be a play.
> And so undoubtedly in weakness there is not a play.
> Byron a play.
> Not to-day
> Byron a play. (354)

Or,

> Act I
> Byron was brought when he came he drooped. (340)

The frustration leads her to look again and again, as she had done in *The Making Of Americans,* for a way to hold the present moment. She asks how she can write this play. The writing mirrors her hesitation and her questions about plays. In her statement of the problem is her gradual movement toward a solution.

> I wish now to say what the relation is of a play
> To words.
> Or not to words
> Does he understand words
> Or if he does not add to words
> Does he if he should win delight
> So that if all he might.
> . . .

A play then may be a day without words

Or indeed if they call at all they may call it a word with which they wish words were thirds. (348)

The fruitless efforts continue for thirty of the play's fifty-three pages. By the end of page 363, Stein says, presumably to Byron, "Read if you cannot run," an ironic revision of the biblical "Write the vision, and make it plain upon tables, that he may run that readeth it."[24] A few lines beyond,

Scene I

Byron I request you not to be fastidious in coming again fortunately.

It is very fortunate that you have found such a happy home.

Byron a play two months later

Act I

To Stein, a play cannot be made out of memory or the past; so she places it, after much manipulation of time, with a centered title, "two months later," in the future. With no further conjecture, halfway into the full text, the curtain goes up on *Byron A Play.*

And now, as it develops, the act and scene designations move from I to II, III, and beyond. With this new beginning ends Stein's dialogue with herself about how to make a play and her theorizing about plays, and we enter a domestic setting, where the dog is called by a pet name the women had actually used.

Byron May be called Byby.

May he not be angry. (364)

On the following page is a tableau,

In the room she is sitting by a new lamp reading a book and holding Byron.

He is not holding a basket he is sitting beside a table writing and if he sneezes he covers his shoulders with a shawl knitted for him as a new years present by a dear friend.

. . .

Byron cannot be punished for the sins of commission and omission because partly and happily he earns nothing for any one. (365)

Filled with pain upon the loss of her dog, a family baby, Stein had called

24. Hab. 2:2 AV. See also William Cowper, "Tirocinium," and Tennyson, "The Flower," Stanza 5. The phrase, which Stein knew from childhood, returns in the Henry James section of *Four In America,* 133.

him over and over by name. Her attempts to call him forth were unsuccessful and left her frustrated. Only once she seizes the voice she had lost is she able to write him into the text *Byron A Play,* one of her own babies. The search for Byron is over, he has entered the play, and she has overcome the loss (371).

> Byron who may mistake himself for himself all the time. (368)

> Scene III
> Richly believe that he is will he be.
> Renewed and put where he is or will he be.
> Byron. (369)

And she continues, in scenes and acts that move beyond I and II to III, IV, V, with more and more feeling,

> Scene VI
> In this long scene Byron soliloquizes.
> No one can say that a soliloquy is addressed to the world.
> And of course it is.
> Much less of course it is.
> Scene VI
> Byron could be careful to drink milk.
> Any Byron could be careful to drink milk without salt.
> Oh yes with tears or without tears any Byron could drink milk.
> Byron.
> Why do or does Byron drink milk without tears.
> Why does Byron drink milk without salt.
> Why does he turn angrily.
> Because he has been left with it.
> Scene VII
> Byron Byron Byron.
> Scene VIII
> I could if I felt like it stay here.
> Act III
> As much Byron as she liked.
> Byron was born Byron.
> He calls as if he came.
> And so without any doubt he may. (370)

She is at home, loving the dog who is here and hears her as she hears herself loving writing him on the moving paper.

Scene I

Byron, I love not cold nor freezing.
I love not following when a sound is coming
I do not love whether I love or whether paper is moving
I love and do not gather crumbs for birds which have been
Birds which have not been there
Once more I hear paper moving.
But whether which have more Byron.
Byron hears me hear Byron. (372)

Here, once again, is a piece of writing about writing the here and now. Unlike Bartholomew Arnold, who was never born, the little dog Byron was a real dog, and now, "dead is dead," he becomes a play. The women still have their big dog, Basket. But Stein has regained her voice in the struggle for *Byron A Play.*

She ends with a sequence of one-line scenes of Act IV:

Scene II
Byron. May be we are Byron.
Scene III
May be we have Byron
Scene IV
May be we do
Scene V
But may be you
Scene VI
Know Byron by Byron
Scene VII
Byron and clothing
Scene VIII
Byron and carrying.
Scene IX
Baby and Byron.

Short 1933 Texts

In the spring and summer of 1933, Stein also wrote a number of short pieces. The first, probably done in Paris, late April, was "The Story Of A Book," one of several about writing the *Autobiography.* A part of her contract with the Literary Guild, it was to introduce the Guild's edition of the *Autobiography* in its journal for members, *Wings.* Stein made the task easy for herself by writing a brief introduction and then quoting the enthusiastic letter about her book from Edward Aswell of the *Atlantic Monthly.* Bradley approved the sketch and forwarded it to *Wings.*[25]

The others are country work, slight occasional lyrics, observations, portraits. Some are fumbling attempts to resume the practice of daily writing, with titles for a new start, such as "Afterwards," "A Plan For Planting," and "First Page"; often she tries, in fidgety self-review, to return from the fame to herself, as in "First Page" or in "Afterwards,"

> I refer to what has happened. This is what has happened. Do not disguise what has happened. ("First Page," *SIM* 283)

> It is a strange thing one day you never heard of any one and the next day they live intimately in your house and everything. It's funny. ("Afterwards," *SIM* 290–91)

Comings and goings, being different and being the same carry through these pieces. In "Lucy La Fontaine,"

> So she came away to stay. . . . After a while she never went away but she did not stay. (*PL* 315)

People appear in incipient relationships that do not flourish, on the edge of marriages that will not succeed, in sentences that do not quite cohere. In "Or. And Then Silence,"

> Leontine married when she was a child. That is the reason she remained small. (*P&P* 242)

Some of these pieces anticipate the ominous uncertainties, dark moods, and broken grammar of *Blood On The Dining Room Floor.*

Not only a year of personal confusion over success, fame, money, and identity, 1933 was also the depth of the Great Depression. The banks had been closed in March, money was in short supply, further unemployment threatened, devaluation loomed. People were afraid of the future and looked for signs of improvement or calamity. From World War I, Stein knew predictions of hardship and signs of relief; she was to experience similar upheavals in World War II. Detective stories, thrillers, and mysteries offered distraction and became big sellers in the book trade. Stein and her friends had for years practiced fortune-telling, palmistry, and prediction, consulted

25. To correct errors in the Haas-Gallup listing, reprinted by Bridgman, *Gertrude Stein in Pieces,* I list the short texts here in the order in which they appear to have been written: "The Story Of A Book," "Afterwards," "A Poem," "First Page," which includes "Page IX," "A Plan For Planting," "Lucy La Fontaine," and "Or. And Then Silence A Portrait Of A Frenchman."

Ouija boards, and been interested in clairvoyance and occultism. She paid attention to eclipses of the sun and moon; she spotted four-leaf clovers and inserted some in her *cahiers.*

> Superstitions is believing that something means anything and that anything means something and that each thing means a particular thing and will mean a particular thing is coming.[26]

On August 22, the superstitious mood directly entered a letter to Lindley Hubbell,

> Did I ever tell you of a very curious thing that happened last summer or rather in the early spring of last year. We had just come down here and were sitting on the terrace, I happened to have in my pocket-book all the checks from money that I was to have for the summer and my voyage money beside. We were a little worried Alice and I because incomes were not what they were, and it was not a too bright prospect. All of a sudden down in the valley we heard a cuckoo call. I am very superstitious, naturally, anybody is, and I said to Alice, well anyway that means it is not going to be too awful, because the first cuckoo comes when I have money in my pocket, and then, and it is a thing I have never seen happen before, the cuckoo came flying up to the terrace sat upon the tree just at the corner and made one loud emphatic cuckoo right at me, and then left. I was quite overcome, I really was. And then late that fall I wrote the auto. I have just been putting this cuckoo into something I was writing, I thought you would like to know.

The cuckoo story also appears briefly in the Grant section of *Four In America,* just begun,

> He thanks and not only for a bird that is known to bring luck and money and came especially to say so, that is, I thank. He is not. (13)[27]

26. "The Superstitions Of Fred Anneday," *HWW* 28.
27. The story is also in Samuel Steward's *Dear Sammy: Letters from Gertrude Stein and Alice B. Toklas* (Boston: Houghton Mifflin, 1977), 20; the cuckoo singing in the cuckoo tree, a love song, on the other hand, is in *A Circular Play, LO&P* 147 and *Reader* 338; "A Sonatina Followed By Another," *BTV* 4; *A Lyrical Opera, O&P* 49 and "Arthur A Grammar," *HTW* 52, 56. In "The Superstitions Of Fred Anneday" (*HWW* 24), Stein works with the cuckoo story both as a love and a money story, and, because cuckoos take over other birds' nests, she also makes it a story of guilty displacement, perhaps the origin of money and success. In her 1940 wartime piece, "Les Superstitions," translated by Stein as "Superstitions" and incorporated into *Ida A Novel* (122–28), the cuckoo returns, along with a wealth of other superstitions. See *LGS/TW* 240n.

Then, in October, Stein was bitten by a snake. She told Bradley on October 24 and on November 4 wrote to Hubbell,

> I was bitten by a serpent, it was a very xciting experience, quite biblical, it made me want to reread Elsie Venner, it is a curious experience. . . .

No details are known about the snakebite, not an unexpected feature of daily life in the mountains and apparently not traumatic or dangerous. To Stein it seems to have fit the mood of 1933, the year of her great success and fame that return as a theme in *Doctor Faustus Lights The Lights* (1938). In the "wild world" (*R* 602) of that play Marguerite is "bitten by a viper" (*R* 604) though she does not die but seeks the help of Doctor Faustus. Later, she is approached by a man from over the seas, also referred to as Mr. Viper, who feels stung by Marguerite.

Blood On The Dining Room Floor

When Stein went to the country, about April 28, the summer may have promised new ease and new work. But it became an unnatural summer. A new work, *Blood On The Dining Room Floor,* arose, like *Byron A Play,* from an event that could not be foreseen, another death. But it also arose from her ambition—the wish to do another success book. She had for years been reading detective stories and had kept up with crime in the papers. A regular summer resident, she had come to know local families well; some of what she learned about them crops up, not as history but as verbal phantoms, in plays and other work of 1930–33 and later.

Notes and revisions in the manuscript of *Blood* show how many family stories seethe behind the details. With the mysterious death of Madame Pernollet of the hotel in Belley, Stein, a rank opportunist, saw her chance to use the death and her knowledge of the town and crime in a detective story of her own, perhaps another moneymaker.[28]

28. After completing *Blood,* she wrote to Louis Bromfield, "I was just reading Blood On The Common it reminded me of the American crimes you and I love, lets do one together, not the crime but about the crime, it would be fun." *Blood on the Common,* a mystery story by Anne Fuller and Marcus Allen, published by Dutton in May or June 1933, may have suggested the title *Blood On The Dining Room Floor.* Before Christmas 1933, having at Bromfield's suggestion followed the Wynekoop murder of November 22 in Chicago, she returned to the project, "We will do our detective story some day, . . . a dual one. . .". In December, she said they would "pull off our shilling shocker, I want . . . to get the essence of crime as America knows it." They never did collaborate, but the plan is another example of her interest in collaboration, for example, with Sherwood Anderson, Thornton Wilder, Lloyd Lewis (*EA* 270); see also *LGS/TW* 154, 158, 170, 175n, ff.

Unexpected writing at the edge of radical uncertainties, *Blood* has been seen as a psychological anomaly and has provoked exasperated controversy. Yet its shifting uncertainties are the very objects of her descriptive exploration; she refuses to put them to rest by naming a culprit, for they are the life of the story and the town. Not in subject matter or logic of events but in the twists of language is their explanation. For Stein, herself in a bewildered state of mind, the strange death, soon followed by another, meshed with the aftereffects of her success.[29]

Here are what "facts" are available about what happened. There are several separate clusters of events, linked by mysterious themes, hinted at but not made explicit; the crime, if crime it was, is not resolved.[30] One night in mid-August, Madame Pernollet, the wife of the hotelkeeper in Belley, fell from a window of the hotel onto the stone pavement below; five days later, she died of her injuries. Was the fall an accident from sleepwalking, a crime, suicide?[31]

At Stein's house in Bilignin, the day after the arrival of two guests, lady friends from Paris, there was odd trouble: the living room was in disarray, full of dust and dog hair, the cars would not start, and the telephone, new that summer, would not work (13; *EA* 60–62). One of a series of peculiar

29. Parts of *Blood* are summarized, with some variations, and lead to further meditations in *Everybody's Autobiography* (51–63, 65–70, 78–85). The short pieces "Is Dead" (*HWW* 33–36), "A Waterfall And A Piano" (*HWW* 31–33), and "The Horticulturists" are parts of the text of *Blood,* sometime later copied out by Stein onto loose sheets, with careful, small adjustments, to make separate "stories of the Ain." They were assigned 1936 dates in the HG listing because the first two were published in 1936 and 1937; the third, a family portrait that required extra adjustments to lift it from the story of Madame Pernollet's death, was not published; but all three are 1933 writing.

    "Why I Like Detective Stories" (*HWW* 146–50), on the other hand, was written after Stein's 1936 lecture trip to England, which led to thoughts about English detective stories; it was also prompted by a visit to the Abdys in Cornwall, where she saw the mysterious Druid stone monuments.
30. With the exception of the Pernollets, people in this story are not identified by last names; Stein used only a few ordinary first names but identified most by trade—"horticulturist," "hotelkeeper"—or by family relation—"brother," "sister," "mother"—which sets them at an eerie distance. Pseudonyms are used in the story of the Englishwoman, told briefly in one form in *Blood* (43ff.) and "A Waterfall And A Piano" and in another in *Everybody's Autobiography* (78–83).
31. Among the Stein papers is a black-edged note of 25 August 1933 from Monsieur Pernollet, with thanks for attendance at the funeral service (*Blood* 75; *EA* 54).

    I speculate whether the events of *Blood* could have returned Stein to the memory of Laura Riding's suicide attempt in London at the end of April 1929, when Stein had just seen her.

servant couples that Stein and Toklas employed that summer had wreaked the havoc, though it was not strictly a crime. The couple were dismissed, replaced by another, then another, all troubled, all troublemakers.

The death of Madame Pernollet starts gossip among the twenty-eight families of the town. Everyone has an opinion, not from observed and reasoned facts but from shady powers and interests that operate behind the closed doors of houses—family relations, property, class, and always, behind it all, war. The horticulturists, who run a nursery and flower business, are one of the prominent families. They live outside the town on their own property, which the four sons cultivate while the four daughters, who are employed nearby, come home in the evening. The father has been persuaded to leave the nursery to the sons and live elsewhere. The seven sons and daughters all resemble the eldest son, Alexander. Incest? The mother also has left the property that the sons cultivate, getting richer and richer; however, she remains a presence in the household. It was with one of the daughters, a maid at the Hotel Pernollet, that Monsieur Pernollet had a love affair. Does this fact have a bearing on the fall of Madame Pernollet? Not the maid but Alexander, her senior brother, says Madame Pernollet fell while walking in her sleep (21–28).

Other stories in *Blood* and "A Waterfall And A Piano" concern an orphan whose mother went crazy and was put away while her father, in despair over his wife, went to war to die. The orphan girl went to stay with a woman who bred dogs. To keep the many puppies alive, the woman bought a goat to supplement the milk the bitch produced. But Alexander, the senior horticulturist, refused to transport the goat to her in his car. So the puppies might not survive. The orphan will marry, as girls must, and will no doubt end up unhappy, whether as wife or servant. The ending of this story in "Waterfall" differs from that in *Blood,* but the themes of frustration and unpredictable behavior are constant.

A little later, beyond the time and scope of *Blood* but included in "A Waterfall And A Piano" and *Everybody's Autobiography* (78–83) comes the next death. A wealthy acquaintance of Stein, under the pseudonym Madame Caesar—the same woman who took in the orphan girl—lived with an "English-woman," Madame Steiner, also a pseudonym, in what sounds like a lesbian relationship. They went about in pants and caps, liked hunting, fishing, food, wine, and dogs, and cultivated first fish and then, in electric incubators, ducks and chickens. It is never entirely clear whether Madame Steiner is the Englishwoman, or whether she is an alternate lover or a kind of ghost. In the manuscript, erased above the name Madame Steiner, the actual name of the Englishwoman can still be read: Miss Milner. Also in the background is an odd man, a gardener and agent for everybody, a ghostly kind of liar about whom people talk. Women and men float about the property of Madame Caesar.

The Englishwoman went to England on a vacation, then returned. Soon after, on September 22, she was found in a ravine at nearby Améyzieu de Talissieu with two bullet holes in her head. Murder? Suicide? Accident? Stein was called and went to the scene with Bernard Faÿ, who was visiting. After this death, new relations developed among the people left behind. The gardener-agent and his wife ended up at Madame Caesar's place; inside her house, dressed in black, was the fat mother of the wife of an electrical engineer, not clearly identified, who perhaps tended the incubators. Eventually his wife went to stay with Madame Caesar. However, in a later letter, Stein tells Faÿ that his great admirer, the senior horticulturist, Fred Genevrey, named Alexander in *Blood,* is frequently at Madame Caesar's. All relations have changed. We are no longer sure who is whose lover, who lives with whom, even who is who.

The case of the Englishwoman's death is further complicated by the fact that she was foreign, Protestant, and perhaps illegitimate. Apparently Madame Caesar, a pseudonym for Madame Godet, saw to it that she was buried in the Catholic cemetery and paid for the grave.[32]

Throughout the story, living is about maintaining the façade of marriage and family, determined by money and class; individuals, especially women, live in frustration and suspicion.

> There was fear and indignation everywhere until there was nothing any longer to fear. There never had been. (12)

But fear and indignation are always here, whether or not there is anything to fear.

> The more you see the country the more you do not wonder why they shut the door. They never do in a way and yet if they did not it would be best. (46)

With no direct statements, everything, including the sentences, develops by indirection.

32. Bridgman, without documentation, says that the official verdict on both deaths was suicide (*Gertrude Stein in Pieces,* 278), an odd conclusion because suicide was a criminal offense and prevented burial in hallowed ground. I have not checked all the details or examined the local papers for this summer. A record of the Englishwoman's death is at the *mairie* in Talissieu, and a record of the death of Madame Pernollet is presumably in Belley. The Englishwoman was apparently born in 1886 in Southampton, the daughter of a woman named Champneys. In a letter to Bernard Faÿ of about November 17, Stein said that her case had been reopened by an English lawyer.

Not a part of the story of *Blood* but started though not completed in the manuscript of "And Now," the aborted "confession" of the writer of the *Autobiography* (*HWW* 63–66), begun that fall and described at length in *Everybody's Autobiography* (65–78), is a personal event, connected in theme: the sudden visit, the last week of August, of William Seabrook, a successful writer of popular anthropological books about primitive customs and magic rites. An alcoholic and a sadomasochist, Seabrook, unable to write, came from Toulon with his wife, Marjorie Worthington, to discover how Stein managed to keep writing when he could not; ironically, it was the moment when for the first time she herself had trouble writing. Stein told him he had been an expatriate too long and advised him to go home to America. After two or three days, the couple left.

Hearing from Seabrook of his closeness to his dead brother, Charlie, apparently led Stein to speak to him about her brother Leo. But even in "And Now" and in *Everybody's Autobiography,* she never reveals what passed between them, and we are left wondering.[33]

Also unexpected was a brief visit from Mougins of the painter Sir Francis Rose, a protégé whom Stein was not seeing that summer because he was a troublemaker. He presented Stein with a painting and left. Seabrook, a student of primitive societies, superstition, and magic, said the painting had qualities of black magic (*EA* 62, 66).

What Joan Retallack calls the "intricate incoherence" of *Blood*[34] takes us to a foreign country of the mind that is yet entirely familiar. From the start and the first pair of servants, there is something "queer" here. They behave peculiarly, these servants; they walk in an odd way and do not move right. In fact, everything is queer and nothing moves right.

Consistently parts or sequences of sentences do not hang together and do not progress logically or grammatically. Actions, phrases, clauses, details, comments seem bent to a queer way of moving in sentences. Perfectly good sentence bits, but is something missing? What happens to time here?

33. Seabrook's attempt to write about his brother eventually became his own autobiography, *No Hiding Place* (New York: J. B. Lippincott Company, 1942). It includes his account of meeting Stein (333–47). It also records that within the month, he sailed home and, with help from Alfred Harcourt, his publisher, signed himself into a hospital to dry out and take the cure. See also his *Witchcraft—Its Power in the World Today* (London: Harrap, 1940); Stella Bowen, *Drawn from Life: Reminiscences by Stella Bowen* (London: Collins Publishers, 1941); Marjorie Worthington, *The Strange World of Willie Seabrook* (New York: Harcourt, Brace, 1966).

34. Joan Retallack, "Accident . . . Aeroplane . . . Artichoke," *New American Writing* no. 10 (fall 1992): 120–35.

It is wonderful to be as strong when you are eighty as you will be when you are ninety, and as lively. (31)

What order does this follow?

And now when can I ask when I am answered. Which of course not. (71)

And where does Mabel come from, with her face against the pane, who often changed her name and whom we have met elsewhere in Stein, even recently in *Byron A Play* (380)?

You call the person you are kind to Mabel if her name is Mabel but the person who is kind is not called Mabel. Oh not at all. But to everybody's astonishment this time it was the other way around. (33)

The other way around what? For that matter, what of Lizzie, another name familiar to all that appears over and over, not only in *Blood,*

Lizzie do you understand.[35]

Or go back to the life story of one pair of those queer servants:

The next ones were found on the side of a mountain. She had a queer way of walking, he didn't. She had been married before but perhaps not only then, at any rate she was soon very sick and is still in a hospital lying on a chair and will not live long. He was like a sheep. He was not at all silly. He was like a sailor. He had been a waiter. He cried when he was disappointed and fell down when he was angry. (12)

The crisp logic of the traditional detective story—the engine of discovery—is bent out of its sharp shape. We have no culprit, no witnesses. We have only twisting whispers, changing scenarios, disconnected tenses, fragments dangling in a story and whispers of incessant, unspoken conversations behind half-open doors. Always we expect ratiocination, and always it gets cut off. Stein starts a topic but then turns a corner. She sets herself up as a detective to explain what happened, in the Stein way, not with step-by-step detection.

The deaths make language move in the town by gossip and suspicion, driven by family and money. Language is tampered with in the service of self-interest—preservation of family, power, wealth, reputation. Among

35. *Blood,* 14, 22, 51, 60, 79. John Herbert Gill, in the afterword to his edition of *Blood,* suggests that the 1892 murder of Lizzie Borden's parents returns in this phrase as an unsolved criminal mystery (88–90).

those who have the most money and power, *Blood*[36] works itself out in innuendoes inside, between, behind the houses.

> There is no further guess. Everybody knows, and they need not say. That is why everybody talks and nobody says, because everybody sees, and everybody says they do. Not by and by, there are no secrets about what everybody knows and still they do complain. Why if why not why do they not complain. Not here not in not choice not and not we. We like ate and late not we. (79)

Money makes the world go round in *Blood* far more than in any other Stein work. The one exception, sharp, clear, and, unlike *Blood,* not eerie, is "Business In Baltimore," a detached, ironic study of her family's city and society, where money, class, and business determine life. By 1933, money had become a strangely personal matter.

About August 24, Bradley came to the Bugey to enjoy a brief vacation and celebrate the publication of the *Autobiography* with Stein. He stayed nearby, at the *auberge* in Aiguebelette. There was a dinner with Bradley, Stein, Toklas, and the Seabrooks. On August 31 or September 1, Stein, Toklas, and Bradley celebrated the book with a bottle of an old Ain wine, a 1923 Arbin. During a boat ride that day or the next, Stein read him the beginning of the detective story, and he raised questions about transitions. They had a long personal talk. On September 2, she drove him to the train and the next day wrote,

> I immediately began to write some more, I fixed up the transitions, but anyway I don't seem to stop so that is something, if it does not make a book it will make short stories but perhaps it will make a book, anyway I am so full of writing these days I can't stop and I will write the three books just one after the other probably.

The three were *Blood On The Dining Room Floor* and two planned books, the confessions of the writer of the *Autobiography,* begun as "And Now," and what was to become *Four In America.*

On September 5, Bradley answered,

> I knew you would get your transitions fixed up easily and I believe you will eventually weld that rich and complicated matter into a perfect and

36. An opera based on *Blood* by Jonathan Sheffer of New York was presented as a work in process, October 11 and 12, 1999, at the Guggenheim Museum in New York City.

> balanced whole. I shall always be proud of having, as the French say, assisted at its *éclosion* and take a special interest in that particular book so closely allied with your life at Bilignin and the tragedy of the Pernollet family.

By October 11, again with reservations, he acknowledged *Blood:* "Personally, I feel it would do with a bit of cutting and condensing." He proposed to submit it to *Story* magazine, but on October 13, Stein refused, stating, "I sent it to you taking it for granted that you might have some ideas about placing it somewhere, more commercially." She inferred that he considered it not "worth money," not a best-seller; it left her worrying that she might have lost her genius (*EA* 84–85). Whether genius was unalterably given or could change came soon to preoccupy her in *Four In America.*

Three years later, in "Why I Like Detective Stories," she reviewed *Blood:*

> it was all very clear in my head but it did not get natural the trouble was that if it all had happened and it all had happened then you had to mix it up with other things that had happened. . . . A detective story has to have . . . an ending and my detective story did not have any. (*HWW* 148–49)

In *Everybody's Autobiography,* she said she was still caught up in success:

> I tried to write the story of Blood . . . and although I did it, I did not really do it and everyone was writing to me and I did not do any writing. (85)

"Qu'est-ce que je pense de la France" (*L'Intransigeant* 1–2)

Before Seabrook left, he made contact with Hector Ghilini, of the journal *L'Intransigeant,* who asked Stein for a short piece on what she thought of France. Her answer, written in French, appeared in the issue of January 6, 1934.[37] She sent the little article to Bradley, who on September 14 again responded as editor,

> As for your little article for l'Intran[sigeant], my wife feels that this would gain in effect if the French were touched up a bit. If you agree, she would be only too happy to do it for you, but perhaps, inasmuch as Bernard Faÿ is your "*traducteur attitré,*" you would prefer to have it left to him.

On September 16, Stein answered wryly that Madame Giraud and her daughter had already improved her French,

37. See also *EA* 102–3.

and it was such a slight thing I was afraid it might die of improvements so I did not let them go very far.

Unless Faÿ thought revision was needed, it should go "more or less like that." Bradley forwarded it unaltered.

By mid-September, the reviews had started to pour in at Bradley's office, and he was exuberant with delight. On September 24, he wrote,

> You have been elected by a landslide surpassing even that of our President, Mr. Roosevelt.

The Marketing of Gertrude Stein: Planning with Bradley

Bradley considered planning a part of his responsibility as authors' representative. He mapped out publication plans from the large stock of out-of-print and unpublished works not already included in projects for the Plain Edition. Most of the planning was done in talk in Paris, and only a few jottings survive. Inferences can be drawn from letters and from Stein's writing, however.

One short entry in a *carnet* of spring or early summer 1929 is discussed in connection with publication plans at the beginning of chapter 10. Apparently in the summer of 1929, she told Bradley in an undated letter that Elliot Paul was visiting and expecting for September to prepare a book about her work, "an amplification of the articles he did in the Chicago Tribune two years ago," presumably his 1927 column "From a Littérateur's Notebook." This project was never realized.

Attached to this letter is a publishing "Program" that "would certainly bring results with a little patience but it would have to be very well handled." This "Program" may date from a different time and may have been attached to Stein's letter by Bradley. It lists samples from *The Making Of Americans, Lucy Church Amiably, A Birthday Book, Portraits And Prayers,* and a reissue of *Three Lives,* followed by "going over and a real edition of *The Making Of Americans,* then How To Write, G. M. P., etc." Plans for trips to America were always tied to *The Making Of Americans.*

In the spring of 1933, with Stein, Bradley outlined a program to enhance her new reputation as the popular leader of modernism and produce continued financial rewards. It included *A Birthday Book,* written in 1924 for Paulo Picasso, Stein's godson, but not published because of Pablo Picasso's failure to do illustrations he had promised. It remained on her mind for years. Now she hoped to issue it as a small popular book, with images by the young artist Richard Jones, samples of whose work she sent to Bradley on June 2, saying,

> I think he has a rather unusual sense of balance, force of balance in his drawings to be more indeterminate as is the case in the one I have marked. I think this format is good but the thing to remember is that the effect is to be gay and not comic. The ~~illustrations~~ decorations should not be illustrations or tell a story the human figure and objects should not be any more definite than the drawing I have marked. The little page again should depend upon the lettering the decoration again should be made simply to balance the lettering and not illustrations. Of course once they are done I must see them before they are offered to the editor.

The book was not published, and the sketches are not among the Stein papers.

In 1933, however, Bradley entered discussions not only for printing completed work but also for new writing. Stein, always preoccupied with her art, had never written to plans or outlines. Blueprints, made in advance, were alien to her thinking. Bradley and Stein had made a bargain to create another commercial success, but both must have realized the extent of their gamble. At this time neither could have understood how completely impossible it would be for her, even with the incentive of the falling dollar, of which she speaks in "And Now" (64). A book became real for her only once it was being written from inside. During his visit they had talked about what she was doing; by September 5, from Paris, he reiterated his interest in her real work, not only in planning another success book,

> I had long wanted to talk with you more at length of your work on the literary side, with all its philosophical and psychological implications, and I shall look forward to resuming the conversation on your return to Paris.

The two new works she had written, *Blood On The Dining Room Floor* and *Byron A Play,* were not planned but arose from actual events. *Blood* starts from what happened that summer but self-consciously, in mixed voices, moves toward a model of detective writing and is affected by Stein's immersion in fame. *Byron A Play,* rising also from events, is almost certainly the last piece of great writing altogether in Stein's voice, and nowhere do we hear about it.

Two other works, quite different, were actually planned with Bradley and created difficulties apparent everywhere. They have a more theoretical ring, a review quality that often sounds labored. One, first identified by two names, "Grant" and "Shakespeare," eventually became *Four In America.* The other, spoken of as the "Confessions" or "Confessions of the writer of the Autobiography of Alice B. Toklas," was to be a second autobiographical volume in the voice of the *Autobiography.* An aborted affair, it became only a short piece published as "And Now." The two works involve different writing ideas but share important qualities.

"And Now" (*HWW* 63–66 and manuscript)

Written between late November 1933 and early spring of 1934, "And Now" is a strange, unfinished piece with a complicated history. About mid-November, Stein reported to Faÿ that William Heineman's representative, a Mr. Willert, on Faÿ's referral, had expressed an interest in printing *Three Lives* and *The Making Of Americans* in England; she told him that if he printed the two books, she would in return give him the "Confessions," if she ever wrote them. Of course, she could not make publishing commitments without Bradley. The reprints were not done, and "Confessions" was not completed.

What Bradley finally placed for publication, in *Vanity Fair* 43, no. 4, for September 1934, after *Harper's Bazaar* (New York) rejected it in mid-June, is a text cut from the heavily revised piece she had written. At the beginning of the manuscript she noted, "Vanity Fair used a part." Stein must have selected the part submitted, perhaps with Bradley, Toklas, or Faÿ. The word "confession" is appropriate for this troubled year; it appears also in *Blood,* where "The confessions of Mary M. in this case" (34) may trail elements of the drama between Stein and Toklas that give us pause.

In early December, Stein, who had been attending Faÿ's lectures at the Collège de France, wrote him after one of them,

My dear Bernard,

When I got home just a little tired I realized fully how moved and passionately interested I had been. It was an extraordinary experience. I was living in you and living in the thing and for once in my life almost not living in myself. A strange and very moving xperience and giving me quite a new point of view toward life. Thanks a thousand times for that and all. I am beginning to write the confessions of the writer of the autobiography of Alice B. Toklas and there will be much to confess but this is a new way to confess, listening to you to-day gave me distinctly a new way to confess, contact with your mind is comforting and stimulating, and nothing is more deeply satisfying to me than that. We do mean a great deal to each other.

Always,
Gtde.

I did like the way you told about my quarrels.

What she meant was that his lecture had lifted her out of her preoccupation with herself and, by placing her entirely within the substance he was discussing, offered her a new way of writing the confessions. The topic of his lecture is not known; however, Stein's postscript suggests that unless she was his subject, at the very least he must have referred to her as an example.

Bradley wanted another book like the *Autobiography,* in the brilliant voice Stein had amply proved she could invent and master. But she could not regain the Toklas voice. He did not understand that she was unable to repeat the successful impersonation and even tried to negotiate with Harcourt for the "Confessions" that he told them would be forthcoming. But the gay voice would not speak again. Not until three years later, after the triumph of the American lecture tour, did she get the impetus to write another autobiography. That was when she returned to the idea, not to expand the confessions of "And Now," or to produce a sequel to *Toklas,* but to write, in her own public voice, *Everybody's Autobiography.*[38]

An ironic mood makes an odd opening for a new work. She says the other book, the *Autobiography,* was gay but this one will not be so gay. The other one included war and peace but the new one has only peace. She sees the struggle for recognition recorded in the *Autobiography* as war and success as peace. Conflict was the stuff of life; she relished quarrels and battles. In the Grant section of *Four In America* (50ff.), on which she was working, she describes war as dance, always interesting because in motion, forward and back.

Success, on the other hand, she plays down as dull, passive peace that stands still. The gay war includes the quarrel with Toklas; it is underscored by the anecdote of Janet Scudder's submission of her paintings to the spring salon under the name of Alice Toklas and Picasso's shocked response to the admission of Toklas, an amateur, to a professional show.

Toklas always presented herself as amateur—secretary, typist, housekeeper—but never as writer, as if that was why Stein had to write her autobiography for her. As Carl Van Vechten put it,

> Gertrude invariably told Alice she could not write. Even a cookbook. When Alice suggested this she ridiculed and tortured her, to such an ex-

38. The many excisions and revisions in the manuscript of "And Now" suggest how much trouble the project gave her. On the cover of its *cahier* she wrote, and crossed out, "A Confession," then, "And Now," the title retained, and "Beginning of another biography." A fourth title, "A True Story," comes from an advertising flyer on which part of the text is written, for a contest for "True Stories," run by *Story* magazine, edited by Whit Burnett and Martha Foley; in the November 1933 issue they reprinted Stein's "Left To Right," which may explain why Stein had the contest materials.

tent that Alice never even wrote a long letter during Stein's lifetime. . . . On one occasion Alice was so upset and hurt that she did not speak to GS for a couple of days.[39]

This is the woman who after Stein's death wrote thousands of lively, memorable letters, an autobiography, and a cookbook, which ends,

> And now it amuses me to remember that the only confidence I ever gave was given twice, in the upper garden, to two friends. The first one gaily responded, How very amusing. The other asked, with no little alarm, But, Alice, have you ever tried to write. As if a cook-book had anything to do with writing.[40]

Now, Stein says, she will write "what happened from the day I wrote the autobiography to to-day. . ." (63). As if to push herself, she repeats this several times, down to the end of the piece, but tells only fragments of what happened. Her reaction to success and loss of identity sends her to Cézanne's late recognition and his wish to paint more carefully than ever, as he did in his late painterly canvases, "more than ever covered over painted and painted over" (64).

She speaks of Picabia's early relationship to Picasso and of what he learned from his photographer grandfather, evident in the transparencies he had started painting in 1927–28 and now in the superimpositions that followed in 1933.[41] Photography leads her to Stieglitz, Steichen, and, in manuscript but not retained in print, Man Ray. She observes that Steichen had always felt documentary photography could exactly reproduce traditional painting, which did not interest him. But he became fascinated with modern painting when he realized that photography could not compete with the accomplishments of the new painting, such as cubism. Photographs are in her mind;

39. Carl Van Vechten to Donald Gallup in Gallup, *Pigeons on the Granite: Memories of a Yale Librarian* (New Haven, Conn.: Beinecke Rare Book and Manuscript Library, 1988), 121.

40. Alice B. Toklas, *The Alice B. Toklas Cookbook* (London: Michael Joseph, 1954), 280. Edward Burns, who reminded me of this passage, says that Harold Knapik told him the first respondent was Picasso, the second Thornton Wilder.

41. The transparencies are collagelike layers, often multiplied, of outlined images that refer back to art of the past—Botticelli, Piero della Francesca. Picabia began to create transparencies after completing the film *Entr'acte* (1924), which also relied on shifting transparent imagery, for example, in the shots of Paris. He sometimes used cellophane in these paintings. By 1933, he began to do superimpositions, sometimes reworking his older paintings into new images that retained traces of what they had earlier held. Unlike the transparencies, they relied not only on outlines but on the solidity of painted surfaces. Picabia at this time went through doubt and turmoil about his painting, receiving support and interest from Stein. See Camfield, *Francis Picabia,* chaps. 16 and 17.

the Grant and Wright sections of *Four In America,* begun by now, recall memorable photographic portraits, and in Wright she looks at painting.[42]

The manuscript includes other brief anecdotes and comments not printed, and finally notes for further writing:

> Then the conversation with Picabia about the *paresse des peintres* [artists' indolence], and the picture held within the canvas they have to fall back on it, Cezanne and the early cubists left the canvas. I objected to Picabia because he was not [*paresseux*] [indolent] so Alice B. said.
>
> Conversation of Anatole and Pablo about his youthful pictures,—etc. they should have thrilled me then. And yet he does not want any one to know.
>
> In writing about Paris about the [Luxembourg] Gardens the queens and the wish to have a statue there because I like to look at them and so would they, each one is a pleasant surprise.
>
> Some time describe my New York experiences with May Mary [scratched across by Toklas] and with the political movement and Alfred Hodder and the Cleveland Roosevelt movement etc. etc.
>
> Also the early California and the street railroad and all the rest and the deaths and all the rest, tell everything and in a longish way simply.

These are tantalizing plans, barely spoken of in *Everybody's Autobiography,* which took up what was in her mind in 1936, especially the American tour. What her notes list was never written. Meanwhile, throughout what she does write in "And Now," Stein, without the voice to tell what happened and how, keeps changing course, starting over, and losing direction.

The printed piece ends affirming that she has returned to real writing, the way she used to write. Her words accurately render her method through the years. Yet they do not describe what she is doing here; rather, they sound like advice to herself about how she wants to write again. Here she also introduces the new work just begun,

> I write the way I used to write in Making of Americans, I wander around and I come home and I write, I write in one copy-book and I copy

42. Note also the many carryovers from "And Now" to the Henry James section. For example, "It was just the opposite of I am I because my little dog knows me. So many people knowing me I was I no longer. . . ." (*HWW* 63). "We had a motto. This is it. / I am I not any longer when I see" (*FIA* 125). Not only ideas but phrases echo through "And Now," *Four In America,* and the December letter to Faÿ. If "And Now" was begun in the fall of 1933, it may not have been completed, as far as it goes, until the spring, when Harcourt expressed a real interest in it.

> what I write in another copy-book and I write and I write. Just at present I write about American religion and Grant, Ulysses Simpson Grant, and I have come back to write the way I used to write and this is because now everything that is happening is once more happening inside, there is no use in the outside, if you see the outside you see just what you look at and that is no longer interesting. . . .[43]

Already in the spring of 1933, in a letter Bradley stamped as received on May 27, she had written,

> I am just beginning to work, I hope to do the Shakespeare thing we spoke of and the Grant, but as yet it has been so lovely that taking Basket and walking and digging in the garden makes me go to sleep.

She worried that after the preceding year's bounty of contracts, there might be no new ones. But on June 27, Bradley predicted that a new agreement might soon be signed for "Grant And Shakespeare." To Hubbell, in early July, she said,

> being so popular put me off for awhile but now I am started on Grant, U. S. Grant and it begins very well.

Planning for Grant was in her mind, and several times through the summer she mentioned the two projects, but only in late September did she in fact begin to write Grant.

Beginning *Four In America*

Exactly how she came to think about the new book and how far she planned it with Bradley are not clear. But as its substance did not arise spontaneously from the daily life, it could be conceived and outlined in advance. The title *Four In America* appeared only in the spring of 1934, but by October 1933 or earlier, she was planning a four-part study.

She saw herself as a representative American, aligned with major figures from history, especially with *The Making Of Americans* published in Paris and about to appear in New York. American leaders were also topics of conversation with Faÿ.[44] She wanted to consider her figures not historically, for

43. *HWW* 66; text quoted from manuscript.

44. His new books of 1933, *Roosevelt and His America* and *The Two Franklins: Fathers of American Democracy,* which Stein had read in manuscript, were both published in September 1933 by Little, Brown, and Company. The first, written mostly during the early months of Roosevelt's administration, while Faÿ was teaching at Northwestern Univer-

what they became, but speculatively, for what they might have become had they not become what they did. It was a new approach to portraiture and to the problem of identity and creativity. Always it included the duality of the historical person any reader would know and the one Stein imagined, a duality that also allowed her to think of herself as the writer she had always been and the one she had made of herself with the *Autobiography.*

Grant was to be examined as religious leader, Wright as painter, James as army general, Washington as novelist. In the preliminary *cahier,* of September 1933 or before, the name of Henry Ford also appears but is crossed out. It was a brilliant idea; as portrait narration, it also returned her to her abiding concern with narrative. "What They Thought And Bought," the book's supertitle, which is on all *cahiers,* may have been her original title.[45]

Given her deep American loyalty, *Four In America* was to define what was essentially American. Her love of France never implied expatriation from or

---

sity, rested on his conviction that America benefited from conflict. The second came out of his 1929 biography, *Franklin: The Apostle of Modern Times.*

When Faÿ was competing against André Siegfried for the chair at the Collège de France, he reported to Stein daily, discussing every political step with her. She interpreted and advised with relish, for her years of observing the workings of power in human beings had sharpened her judgment. His success in gaining the chair early in 1932 confirmed their friendship.

Faÿ, talented, learned, and ambitious, became a historian with a drive for work, reviewing, writing a novel and essays, and translating American writers (Sherwood Anderson, Glenway Wescott) into French. Paul Bowles, as a young writer and composer, had through Stein met Faÿ, who took him around Paris; he said, "He had the patience and charm that sometimes come as a result of prolonged physical suffering" (Paul Bowles, *Without Stopping: An Autobiography* [London: Peter Owen, 1972; New York: G. P. Putnam's Sons, 1972], 106).

Madeleine Boyd, the wife of the critic Ernest Boyd, who in part acted as agent, was less charitable, "Bernard Faÿ is pretty much disliked, as a snob, who has no rights to be, as he 'is only fils de notaire.' Of course it was a *comte* [count] who told me that, but then the French they are funny that way, they have more respect for a *maréchal ferrant* [farrier, blacksmith] than *un tabellion* [notary, scrivener]" (4 June 1938).

Stein's portrait picks up Faÿ's patience and charm,

> What is patience.
> Patience is amiable and amiably.
> What is amiable and amiably.
> What is impatience.
> Impatience is amiable and amiably. (*P&P* 42)

45. In the preliminary *cahier,* this title is followed by the fumbling "A historically [ ] adapted novel / or a history of these United States / which becomes afterwards a history of all the nations / that is a history of every nation of which I have known at least one. That is of its inhabitants." This tentative subtitle is not retained but echoes in "Or A History Of The United States Of America," incorporated in the Washington section.

rejection of America. Rather, she felt that by living abroad, she saw more clearly what it was to be American than she might have had she stayed at home. A book about great Americans might also help counteract the resentment many Americans at home felt about immigration, about Americans living abroad whom they considered unpatriotic, and about American men marrying foreign women, who then became American citizens.[46]

Four In America has been discussed mainly for its underlying idea. That idea unifies the book, but the parts differ in substance and style and require individual attention.[47] I follow the book here as one of the products of the fame that overwhelmed Stein in 1933–34. I make suggestions about readings but do not examine it in full detail.

She studied the four Americans first for their names and identities, then as geniuses. Grant changed his name from Hiram Ulysses Grant to U. S. Grant,[48] a change that must have resonated for the author of *The Autobiography Of Alice B. Toklas.* Wilbur Wright received a monument in the Sarthe for his flight in France.[49] The name of Henry James, aligned with that of his brother William and perhaps their father, Henry Sr., twice two first names, opens questions about names, identities, and relations.[50] Finally, there is

46. See Stein's "Thoughts On An American Contemporary Feeling," late 1931 or early 1932, in *Creative Art* 10, no. 2 (February 1932): 129; "Or A History Of The United States Of America," written in the notebook of "Bartholomew Arnold," 1932, and incorporated, with substantial additions, into the Washington section of *Four In America* (167–70). The latter title echoes in the subtitle she crossed out. Pieces like these addressed issues that preoccupied America.
47. Charles Caramello, in his study, *Henry James, Gertrude Stein, and the Biographical Act* (Chapel Hill, N.C.: University of North Carolina Press, 1996) goes to the other extreme, treating the Henry James section of *Four In America* virtually as a book in itself and focusing, with meticulous research, almost exclusively on James and Stein's relationship to him, largely to the exclusion of Stein's own broad purpose in *Four In America* and even of the problems of "Shakespeare" and "Flowers" that gave rise to the section.
48. Hiram Ulysses Grant—always called Ulysses—changed his name when he entered West Point at age seventeen. He planned to be Ulysses H[iram]. Grant. The congressman who made the appointment forgot his middle name and sent in the appointment under his mother's maiden name, for Ulysses S[impson]. Grant. The name was never corrected, and Grant signed himself "U. S. Grant," though he never used "Simpson." See William McFeely, *Grant: A Biography* (New York: W. W. Norton, 1981), 12–13 and n. 1, 2.
49. Orville (1871–1948) and Wilbur Wright (1867–1912), mechanics who operated a bicycle repair shop in Dayton, Ohio, used their skills and facilities to design airplanes. They first flew in 1903 and then refined their designs and achieved world renown in 1908, with flights by Orville in the United States and by Wilbur in France. The monument in Le Mans, Sarthe, was unveiled on July 17, 1920.
50. Names were not only in the mind of Stein but also in that of Henry James. Percy Lubbock's two-volume edition of *The Letters of Henry James* (New York: Charles Scribner's Sons, 1920), which Stein may have read, includes his letter of warning to his nephew,

Washington, a typical George, living on as the "father of his country" and in Robert E. Lee's phrase "first in war, first in peace, first in the hearts of his countrymen."[51] He becomes a novelist.

"Grant" (*FIA* 3–81)

She begins with Grant as a great name, a leader and genius, special to her since her youth, as the opening section makes clear.[52]

> I first became acquainted with U. S. Grant. After that for a long time I was acquainted with General U. S. Grant. How did I become acquainted with General U. S. Grant. By reading about him of course by seeing his photograph often of course, by feeling that he was a great man often of course, and not feeling that General Lee was a great man at all. And now I have not changed my mind. (49)

In her early notebooks, he is contrasted with Lee and later appears in texts, such as "A Diary" or "Regular Regularly In Narrative" (244), where she speaks of the name and her wish to collaborate on him with Sherwood Anderson; and "Grant Or Rutherford B. Hayes."

Then she looks at Grant[53] as leader and as the writer of his *Personal Memoirs,* the two-volume military history of 1885–86 in plain, colloquial speech filled with the flavor of religion and the bible that she recognized as a unique American style.[54] The basic idea of *Four In America*—that American genius is inevitably expressed and is not restricted to one calling—may have arisen from Stein's perception of the irony of Grant's many failures before his final success as a military leader. A reluctant soldier, albeit graduated from West

---

William James Junior, named after his father, about naming a child "Junior," a danger he wishes "to do *something* to conjure away." "Junior," of course, is only one invidiously social aspect of naming. James wrote the letter at a time of special awareness of identity, when Sargent was painting his portrait (18 June 1918, 2:214–17).

51. Caramello, *James, Stein,* 174–75 and n. 16.
52. A note among the Stein papers suggests that she and Leo may have contributed when funds were raised by ninety thousand subscribers to pay for Grant's Tomb, completed 1897. See *FIA* 74, 75, 76. The tomb is a national memorial dedicated not to President U. S. Grant but to General U. S. Grant.
53. On page 89 is a reference to a letter of 28 December 1933 from Ulysses Lee, a student at Howard University, Washington, D. C., who wrote to Stein on 28 December 1933 and 11 February 1934 about the opera and "Melanctha." The coincidence of names strikes her. If she here refers to his second letter, she would have started Wilbur Wright by February. See *LGS/CVV* 290n, 303n.
54. Cf. Edmund Wilson, *Patriotic Gore: Studies in the Literature of the American Civil War* (New York: Oxford University Press, 1962), 131–73, 648–51.

Point, Grant, the brilliant general, was a total failure as president—ruined by his success.

From his leadership in war she moves directly to camp meetings and religion.

> Hiram Ulysses Grant was a leader in religion. Remember that. A leader in American religion remember that. Not a leader in french religion. (35)

For Stein American religion is not authoritarian, not frightening, not filled with the fear of death.

> Do you see what American religion is and why there is no sky. Every where else there is a sky and why because there is no over all. But in American religion there is no sky because there is no over all. There is no all, there is no over all. (32)

> Religion is not vexing in a camp-meeting because whether seating, standing, walking, lying or moving or mourning everything, that is to say, anybody is something and is doing something. The woods have nothing to do with it. (14)

> Do you see how there is no kneeling in America, in American religion, not like that no waiting and no kneeling, no not like that. (58)

She considers him a genius and asks whether genius is an enduring feature of personality, regardless of change of name or occupation. Can one lose one's genius? Can it change? Such questions apply also to the author of *The Autobiography Of Alice B. Toklas,* who wonders whether she can still write, let alone write a masterpiece. The manuscript, filled with preliminary notes, scribbles, revisions, shows labored effort, especially at the beginning of the four sections, until she gradually finds a voice for each. There is stiffness in that voice, and she keeps reassuring herself against her own doubt that she is reaching her audience.

"Wilbur Wright" (*FIA* 83–117)

Wilbur Wright is already planned in "Grant,"

> Anybody can change their name and they do it too. But that is another question and can later express something as you will hear to see when I write about Wilbur Wright. Not that he did but someone else did, who was another Wilbur. But this is just to whet your appetite. (45)

Stein approaches his as the story not of one but two young Americans, unknown mechanics, who relied on their initiative and skill in bicycle repair to become inventors famous throughout the world. The brothers also share the same last name, and Wilbur has double initials, W. W. They are tied together.

In repeating, cogitating phrases, circling around questions of what would have happened if Wilbur Wright had become a painter rather than a flier, Stein explores ideas about personality and genius.[55] She faces difficulties because the Wright brothers did not attain to the same stature as the other three figures, but all the more questions of name, identity, and genius come up in new and perhaps freer forms. She takes off from the fact that Wright's monument and his photograph are what make him real in the mind.

As a flier and a bicycle repairman, he has seen movement, always of special interest to Stein as an American phenomenon.

> There is no need to see to move. But he did see not to move but what it is to move. Oh yes he saw.
> How many acts are there in moving. And this makes them feel better.
> He sees when he moves.
> He sees how he moves.
> He sees moving. (95)

She looks at him here not as the inventor he was but as a painter he might have been, though she takes into account his experience as inventor and the experience of the brothers as performers and actors at the great air show of 1912 at Brescia, where they appeared along with Curtiss and Blériot. In slow, musing steps she develops and characterizes personality types in a complex series of opposites: She begins with

> Painters and actors.
> American painters.
> American flyers. (88)

Into the triad of painters, actors, and fliers she also weaves the opposition of American and European characteristics. American actors typically are movie actors whereas European actors are play actors. In addition, she insists that actors, like painters, who see what they have painted, see themselves rather than hearing what they say (87). She supports the primacy of seeing with the acting technique of William Gillette, "silence, stillness and quick movement," which isolates single images on the stage, a matter she also discusses in her lecture "Plays" (*LIA* 116).

The difference between seeing and hearing is crucial, for it allows her to

55. That Stein should have considered Wilbur (1867–1912) rather than Orville (1871–1948) or both is because of Wilbur's flight in France on December 31, 1908, and, after his death, the monument at Le Mans planned but delayed by World War I, the cornerstone laid December 22, 1918, unveiled July 17, 1920.

posit that actors perceive themselves from outside, from the point of view of the audience, rather than by listening to their own voice and so identifying with themselves. Likewise, a painter will see his painting beside him, never extending himself personally into the picture. Preoccupations with identity do not interfere with the true artist's perception of a work.

> How do you do can be said regularly to a dog and he will always respond but not a painter not a painter of a picture. (112)

A dog, always in a personal relation, can be left alone and taught to wait for a master's return—not for nothing had she written a poem, "Left Alone. To Basket." But no painting is left alone and returned to:

> A painting is something seen after it has been done and in this way left alone nobody can say he or I left it alone. No painting is left alone. This is not possible. Insofar as it is a painting it is not left alone. (98)

The fact that the Wrights are brothers means, for Wilbur, that he may have been an inventor but could not have been an artist, who creates alone.

> He was never alone. This is what made him different from what he was and made it possible that as soon as he was dead they made a monument to him.
>
> I wish everybody could understand this. They would then see the importance as well as the unimportance of being alone. Alone I did it. This can never be said of Wilbur Wright but it might have been said of him if he had been different and what he had done had been differently done but it was not true of him there were always two of which he was one. (109)

This is a fascinating meditation about identity and the effect of sibling relations upon genius. Had she read studies of Wright that allowed her to speculate about his personality? Or is she thinking about how individuals free themselves—or are freed by their genius—to become themselves and follow their gift, as she implies in a single small sentence that she herself did? Wright, she insists, "did not paint pictures not as he might have done if he had only been one" (110). Seeing leads her to "looking," "looking at" and "looking like," and she muses how Wilbur Wright thought he was as old as he looked in his photograph and insists that he misperceived, looking at the picture with personal eyes,

> If he had been a painter he would not have had to die and so he would not have been dead and he would not have had a photograph of himself for all to see not he. (113)

This is a difficult study, in part because we, who know of the Wright brothers' fame, know little of their lives. Yet that is what allows Stein to pursue her "if-fiction" so lightly and personally, veering off again and again into new territory to make "Wilbur Wright" a series of tiny essays in perception.

Much of this section is instantly familiar to readers of her *Lectures In America.* Her interest in movement, in the "relation of what is painted and the painting of it" (*LIA* 79) takes us directly to "Pictures." Seeing and hearing and their mixture return in "Plays" as do movement, the cinema, and photography, of which she also speaks in "And Now." Reading *Four In America* becomes not only an exploration of the four figures and American genius but a voyage of discovery of germs of the lectures, already in her mind.

"Henry James": Shakespeare, Flowers (*FIA* 121–59)

The matter of Shakespeare comes up early, in a letter of September 22, 1933, to Hubbell about fame and success, long before she actually wrote the section on James:

> I am almost getting the better of these strange sensations and it is taking the form of meditations on Shakespeare's sonnets and Before the flowers which will be a treatise that I know will interest you. I have just begun it and it will be all about audiences, a very fearful subject and it is taking form.

Shakespeare's sonnets and *Before The Flowers,* then, are the beginning of what is here planned but only in the late winter or early spring of 1934 written as the Henry James section of *Four In America* (119). It includes a "motto" (125), which she has already written into "And Now," "I am I not any longer when I see." She opens a "Duet" (119) to follow further series of opposites, such as she had explored in the Wright section, now between Shakespeare's sonnets and plays, between accident and coincidence, between Hugnet's "Enfances" and her *Before The Flowers Of Friendship Faded Friendship Faded.* She differentiates between smooth-sounding writing, planned in advance, and "lively" writing, arising spontaneously.

The name of Henry James does not even appear until a reminder on the ninth page of this section, "Henry James nobody has forgotten Henry James even if I have but I have not" (128). Four pages later,

> You do understand that about hesitating, there is a waltz called Hesitation, but you do understand that sooner or later than this will then be then about Henry James and his having been a general. . . . (132)

Again,

> Remember I wish to say later what Henry James did but that has nothing to do with coincidences. . . . (133)

Only on page 136 does she begin to look at James. Exactly when he entered her thinking about "Shakespeare" and *Flowers* is not quite clear, though he is included in the preliminary *cahier* (number xiii); for a study of Americans, she needed an American as focus, even if the section included Shakespeare.

In a letter to Carl Van Vechten postmarked October 15, 1933, Stein says that she is "doing a long book all about four eminent Americans" (*LGS/CVV* 279–80). On October 7, from New York, Lincoln Kirstein asked her for a contribution to a special Henry James issue of *Hound and Horn;* he wanted her to expand her comment in the *Autobiography,* where she called James her forerunner and "the only nineteenth century writer who being an american felt the method of the twentieth century" (96).

On November 1, with enthusiasm, she agreed to write for the James number, and Kirstein sent her details. By January he set her a deadline of February 12, followed by two cables requesting the piece, but she did not produce it in time.[56] What she did write became the Henry James section of *Four In America.*

"Henry James" is the section most often anthologized, quoted, and discussed, for, unlike the others, it reviews Stein's own writing and includes a wealth of literary observations. Of the four figures, James, whom she called her precursor, is no doubt closest to her as a writer. Propelled by *Before The Flowers Of Friendship Faded Friendship Faded,* her version of Hugnet's "Enfances,"[57] this section raises questions of poetry and creativity and of "a poetic American thing" (147). At times, it is an exchange between James and Stein (and occasionally Toklas); at others it is ruminations, with rhetorical questions moving toward lectures to an imagined audience, "do you understand," "do you see what I mean," as she had already done in the Wright

56. No further letter from her is among the *Hound and Horn* or the Stein papers at YCAL. The editor's preface to the James number of *Hound and Horn* (April–May 1934) notes that "Miss Stein's study is not finished at this date." See also Lincoln Kirstein and Varian Fry, "The Hound and Horn 1927–1934," *Harvard Advocate* 121, no. 2 (Christmas 1934): 6–10, 92–94, "Gertrude Stein did not finish her piece in time for inclusion" (92).

57. After the falling-out in December 1930 of Hugnet and Stein, plans for a bilingual edition of their texts were canceled. In May 1931, Stein printed her text alone in the Plain Edition, as discussed earlier in chapter 8.

section. Central to this section is her discovery, through *Flowers,* of the difference between "Shakespeare's sonnets and Shakespeare's plays." They offer an analogy for her own experience.

She discovers in Shakespeare's work two radically different modes of writing: writing to order, bound by the conventions, as in the sonnets, and writing spontaneously, free of conventions, as in the plays. He chose both the strategic and the tactical route, as generals do. She says the differences in the emotion and tension of the two ways can be heard in the sound of writing (124).[58] She is not writing a study of Shakespeare but uses him to illustrate her own experience, which receives added grandeur from the illustration. She may have had the analogy in mind when discussing her plans with Bradley.[59] Some readers find her use of Shakespeare both inaccurate and arrogant, but he fits her topic of genius and allows her to explore her own case.

Playing with words as words and as names leads her to "Henry James," two first names, like those of his brother, and she wonders whether the brothers separated their identities.

> How could Henry James fancy that with his name it was not a similar name to that of his brother. Was his brother another.
>
> There now you see. It is not necessary never to mention never to have a brother.
>
> Fortunately many foil an instance of that.
>
> She bowed to her brother.
>
> That is coming in here. (153)

The last two lines, from her 1931 portrait of her brother, confirm her own separate sense of identity.

I briefly interrupt this comment on *Four In America* to take up a short novel, written late winter or early spring 1934, near the James section, many of whose preoccupations and devices it shares, before returning to the end of *Four In America* with Washington.

58. In *Narration,* Lecture IV, she describes the sonnets, unlike the plays, as words "with a smooth feeling with no vibration in them" (52).
59. Stein's friend W. G. Rogers, who escorted her on part of her tour through New England, refers to a statement remembered by another friend which she supposedly made in answer to a question at Wesleyan University: "I don't care to say whether I'm greater than Shakespeare, and he's dead and can't say whether he's greater than I am. Time will tell." William Garland Rogers, *When This You See Remember Me: Gertrude Stein in Person* (New York: Rinehart, 1948), 140–41. I have not found this comment in the reviews of her lecture at Wesleyan.

"The Superstitions Of Fred Anneday, Annday, Anday A Novel Of Real Life" (*HWW* 24–30)

"Fred Anneday" is a novel, Henry James was a novelist, and the George Washington section of *Four In America* is about novels. On the inside cover of the *cahier* for "Fred Anneday," Stein wrote, "What is poetry and if you know what poetry is what is prose," which becomes the opening of the lecture "Poetry And Grammar"; she is thinking about questions of poetry discussed in the Henry James section. She also relies on devices used in the James section.[60] "Fred Anneday" also returns to the superstitions of the summer of 1933, and even to the visit of the cuckoo of early summer 1932 and to material first used in the summer of 1933. Here she relates superstition and writing in new ways, investing Fred with her own experience of ambition and success.[61]

In exchanges with Bradley, plans for publications, and letters about her work, we do not hear about "Fred Anneday," just as we do not hear about "Brim Beauvais," "Bartholomew Arnold," or *Byron A Play.* This novel draws on the troubled summer of 1933; though its voice is mixed, it is not the public or audience voice but is real Stein writing. Like a fable, with a remote, legendary quality and moral overtones, it is self-critical and serious, as if she was reviewing personality in a distant territory of the mind.

The elements for the novel of Fred Anneday rise from but do not represent the village life of *Blood;* they center on Fred Genevrey, the eldest of the horticulturists, called Alexander in *Blood* and Fred or, since this is a novel, Fred Anneday here. Think of his name—Anneday, any day, a year and a day, Genevrey, aîné, anodyne, even everyman. The novel opens with three superstitions, tiny thematic vignettes about cuckoos, already spoken of in *Blood,* as guides to the novel.

> Superstition is believing that something means anything and that anything means something and that each thing means a particular thing and will mean a particular thing is coming. Oh yes it does. (28)

60. Like the James section, "Fred Anneday" uses the device of a motto, which is also in "Brim Beauvais," who returns here as a character. The first is the motto of "Brim Beauvais" (269), "How could it be a little whatever he liked" (27); the next, "Pens by hens" (29), also in "Brim Beauvais" (269), returns in "Les Superstitions" (1939–40). See *LGS/TW* 240 n. 4.

61. Stein considered the subject matter of "Fred Anneday" related to that of the series of stories of the Ain, which had started with *Blood* and included "A Waterfall And A Piano," "Is Dead," and "The Horticulturists." See Stein to James Laughlin, n.d., in response to his letter of 24 September 1936, Wake Forest University Library, Winston-Salem, N.C.

The first is the cuckoo bird singing a love song in the cuckoo tree, as in *A Lyrical Opera* and "A Sonatina. . .". At the beginning, the cuckoo song is beyond the experience of Fred Anneday-Gertrude Stein, an American who knows cuckoo clocks but not cuckoos. In Fiesole, with its gardens that fit the horticulturist, Anneday-Stein, in love, first hears the cuckoo as a love song.

The second, in France, happens when Fred hears the cuckoo while he has money in his pocket, the story Stein told Hubbell about the spring of 1932; now the cuckoo prompts superstitious hopes of riches and success, a miracle which promptly happens. We have already met these two versions.

In the third, the cuckoo occupies nests of other birds. Taking things from others, Stein says, may be how one becomes successful and rich, and she illustrates it with the displacement of monks from their monastery by outsiders. We will see Stein, in the Washington section, displacing sections of her own writing. Fred Anneday, a troubled man, sleepless, ambitious, nervous, controlling, has all his life pursued superstitions—ambitions, delusions, dreams—or been haunted by them. He wants everything, not only one woman, not only money, not only his mother, religion, power in all its forms.

He loved many women before he found the one woman he loved, who sounds like an image of his mother, though this is of course denied. Up to the one woman he loved, we know the outline of Fred's life from *Blood* and "The Horticulturists." Perhaps we have even met the one woman he loved as Madame Caesar. It does not matter, and we do not read this piece as local history. Perhaps she is a dream, a myth. Fred's story will exemplify the cuckoo legends.

Before it opens, Stein defines the novel in its relation to reality.

> A novel is what you dream in your night sleep. A novel is not waking thoughts although it is written and thought with waking thoughts. But really a novel goes as dreams go in sleeping at night and some dreams are like anything and some dreams are like something and some dreams change and some dreams are quiet and some dreams are not. And some dreams are just what any one would do only a little different always just a little different and that is what a novel is. (25)

Two friends of Fred appear. One is Brim Beauvais, not given to superstition, with a life less eventful than Fred's. Like Brim Beauvais, Fred also is a book creature.[62] The other is Enoch Mariner, a new name and a new person-

62. When Brim reappears, he carries elements of the earlier piece, but not all details are here. For example, his wife, Florence Anna, does not reappear. Stein fairly often brings back names—or partial names—used earlier. Such echoes must be heard, but it is an error to

age, who suggests to Fred's mother that at sixty, incidentally also Stein's age, she take a new lover; she does not. Dreams, ambitions, superstitions underlie love life and family life. Enoch and Brim are not characters interacting in events but figures with different personalities. Likewise, the novel Stein is writing here is not a story of village life.

> Fred Anday never said farewell to any one in a day no one ever does because every one sees every one every day which is a natural way for a day to be. Think of any village town or city or desert island or country house or anything. Of course no dream is like that because after all there has to be all day to be like that. And all day is like that. And there cannot be a novel like that because it is too confusing written down if it is like that so a novel is like a dream when it is not like that. (28–29)

This novel is a kind of legendary family history. Close to portrait narration, it has no plot, though it includes ideas about plot. It centers on Fred's personality. Family histories move by children—family—and by "love." Family spells frustration, which in Fred becomes excess ambition, hunger for power, sleeplessness; love frees him, eases frustration, releases the demon superstitions. Family history, love, and children also moved *The Making Of Americans,* in her mind as its short version appeared in February 1934 and she lectured about it in Paris on March 23.

Fred had no child; of the eight young Genevreys, only one had one child. Enoch and Brim had no children. Stein works with Fred, the eldest, in contrast to herself, the youngest. Childlessness leads to fear of death, equated with birth control. Once Fred-Stein finds the woman he loves, he ceases to be worried, nervous, sleepless, though in the background is his aging mother with her wig. The woman he loves is not like the mother, though it sounds as if any woman loved was like a mother, whether the lover knows it or not.

Fred's life gradually ceased to be exciting, but the way it ceased to be so was exciting—this is the material for a novel. Here Fred's life becomes the stuff for conversation and gossip; it lives on as the mystery of Fred Anday. Enoch Mariner proposes by letter to a girl he has met once and who rejects him. No one would know, but the girl shows the letter to friends and so he too becomes part of gossip.

> So many things happen that nobody knows that it is necessary to say that he was right to have his superstitions. Of course he is. What is the use of knowing what has happened if one is not to know what is to happen.

---

look for consistency in carryovers. The hotel and the Pernollet family also return in "Fred Anneday," with many features of *Blood,* but not as copies or to extend a plot.

But of course one is to know what is to happen because it does. Not like it might but might it not happen as it does of course it does. And Anday Fred Anday is never in tears. Not in consequence but never in tears. (30)

How love happens and how it changes Fred or anyone else we do not know, nor do first names or what we know of identities tell us. But first names are among the building blocks of 1934.

Do not bother. Do not bother about a story oh do not bother. Inevitably one has to know how a story ends even if it does not. Fred Anaday's story does not end but that is because there is no more interest in it. And in a way yes in a way that is yes that is always so. I can tell this story as I go. I like to tell a story so.

Anybody will have to learn that novels are like that. (30)

Returning to *Four In America*

"George Washington" (*FIA* 161–221)

In the July-September 1932 issue of *Hound and Horn* (vol. 5, no. 4) had appeared Stein's "Scenery And George Washington: A Novel Or A Play," a dream vision of Washington visiting Stein in the country, written in the fall of 1931.[63] This Washington piece did not include the change of calling that became the "if" feature of *Four In America,* but it may have been an impulse for that study. Stein used the whole piece, with title, to start the Washington section (161–66).

Next, she added into "Washington" (167–73) another earlier piece, "Or A History Of The United States Of America."[64] In *Four In America,* between quoted paragraphs of this text, she inserted substantial details about George Washington's name and his experience as a novelist. Only a few passages of "Or A History" are omitted; a few others are slightly altered in copying. Written in the same *cahier* as "Bartholomew Arnold," "Or A History" is in part about American men marrying foreign women who then become citizens, with narrative examples.[65] This transcription ends with the last sentence of this piece as the last of "Volume I" (173) of *Four In America.*

63. In the manuscript, the "or" of the title is revised to "and." The genre designation, novel and/or play, occurs also in *Byron A Play, A Manoir,* and other texts, perhaps to suggest that this material can become a novel or a play.
64. Of this text, unpublished at the time, there is also a typescript at YCAL. It includes a subtitle, absent from the manuscript but inked into the typescript by Stein, "Or An American Marrying." The subtitle is not transferred to *FIA,* which suggests that Stein copied from the manuscript.
65. See *EA* 127.

So far, so good. Stein seems to have relied on earlier texts to get off the ground and gain momentum for the final lap of the new big book. The inclusion of the first makes perfectly good sense. The second, entered in snippets and followed by sections composed for or by Washington, does not appear to fit well with Washington as novelist unless Stein thought that the many "pleasant scenes which are not scarce nowadays" (168), of which she speaks early in "Or A History," might make scenes for the novels.

I was startled to discover, however, that three pages beyond the end of "Or A History"—filled with her most direct comments on American politics and some on Washington as novelist—Stein began, on page 176, systematically but without identification, to copy into the Washington section from the very same *cahier* nearly the complete text of "Bartholomew Arnold."[66] She follows the order of "Bartholomew," inserting sentences and paragraphs, usually broken into indented sentences. Between the transcribed sentences, she again adds material on Washington the novelist, which also absorbs her own experience.

The early transcriptions are selective, with some changes, but the later ones become systematic and complete, even repeating the original subtitle from manuscript, "Which leads not singularly to ways of narrative" (187). The name "Bartholomew" of the original, however, in transfer becomes "George Washington"—except from the bottom of page 210 to midpage 212, where Bartholomew appears and she distinguishes him from Washington:

> Bartholomew has nothing to do with George Washington because Bartholomew did not know what a novel is and George Washington is he is to know what a novel is. (211)

Also, most pronouns are changed, from "she" to "he," "her" to "his," "he" to "they." "She," "girl," and "sister" are almost consistently cut. The few other changes in transcription do not look intentional; they may be errors—or play. Between the copied elements we return to Washington as novelist and person. Stein's method of transcription for "Or A History" and "Bartholomew Arnold" is almost the same, except that "Bartholomew" enters unannounced and unidentified. No reader would have made the connection

66. Also unpublished at the time, it was printed posthumously in *MR* 321–38. She starts copying with the second sentence because the first compares Bartholomew to Basket. In *EA* (85) she says that in the summer of 1933, she had done no writing except for a piece on war. I do not know which piece this is unless it is identified by the subtitle as "Bartholomew Arnold Or After The War Is Over."

The initials of Bartholomew Arnold strike me as significant play as do those of Brim Beauvais. In the background may hover the *ABC,* Alice B., and Stein's frequent play with *B* names.

between Bartholomew Arnold and George Washington. I myself discovered it only by hearing in this text phrases familiar from "Bartholomew."

She also adds fitting historical detail into the comments on Washington as novelist, such as his spy novel,

> This is exactly what he did. He had spies and they were faithful to him. He did write a novel about this.
>
> . . .
>
> George Washington in relation with a spy will not die. (181)

Later, we get to Fort Necessity, the entrenched camp Washington built at Great Meadows:

> Fort Necessity does not separate a novel from reality. (187)

In the last chapter I described "Bartholomew Arnold" as not a portrait of any person we know but the story of a creature of the *ABC*s, an "it," a work in gestation that attempts to join literary brothers and sisters but does not come off. It seems to be an abstract construction made out of a welter of concrete elements for which there is no model in the world. What is Stein doing? The last sentence of "Bartholomew," "It is true that Bartholomew never came through" (338) is in *Four In America* (221) as

> It is true that George Washington never came through.

It is followed by the last lines of the book,

> That is what a novel is.
> He knew.
> He knew what a novel is.
> It is true.
> How true.
> Through to you.

Here is a full example of her transfer of "Bartholomew Arnold," paginated to sources.

"Bartholomew Arnold"

> The simple story. Is. That a child who was born was which it came first. And neither how or. Perhaps more.
>
> I would like Bartholomew.
>
> The birth of Bartholomew
>
> He is not born. A very pretty charming little girl came to be born in the place of which no one could fancy that it had come. Alright.

Could all be here who heard that he was here not here.

And so Bartholomew cried. Not only. Within itself. Because alternately. He was not coming. Nor had he come. Nearly enough.

Has no one been to see Bartholomew. (*MR* 324–25)

Four In America

The simple story. Is. That as a child who was born, which, it, came first.

And neither how or. Perhaps never.

That makes it agreeable that, Good-bye George was not said to George Washington.

I would like George Washington.

The birth of George Washington.

He is not born.

A very pretty charming boy came to be born in the place of which no one could fancy that it had come.

Alright.

Could all be here who heard that he was here not here.

Volume XXI

Any evening that he went away some one could say good-bye George and could say Good-bye George was not what was said to George Washington.

And so George Washington cried.

Not only. Within itself. Because alternately. He was not coming. Nor had he come. Nearly enough.

Has no one been to see George Washington. (184–85)

This text changes in tone from the copied to the added material and makes odd reading. The amazing number of piecemeal inclusions from many sources, along with hesitations about uncertain progress, suggest how Stein cut and pasted the Washington section together. She may have been anxious to finish *Four In America* before going to the country, especially as she had already missed Lincoln Kirstein's deadline for the Henry James section for *Hound and Horn.*

The reason for the transfer into the Washington section must be more than cannibalizing. If "Bartholomew Arnold" is indeed about the gestation and naming of a new work, was she trying to give George Washington this work to make his own as a novel? I recall how deliberately she composes into "Fred Anneday" another abstract paper creature, Brim Beauvais, who, like Bartholomew Arnold (both have odd, untraceable names), is part of the family but not exactly as a child. Is playful, freewheeling Bartholomew meant to come to life here and make a name for himself—and for Washington?

If Stein was indeed writing into the Washington section the incarnation of Bartholomew, was she demonstrating what happens with names—Bartholomew becomes somebody by becoming George Washington? And what about the association of Washington with Benedict Arnold? The fact that the name "Arnold" appears only in the title of the "Bartholomew" piece would imply that she was undercutting the association with Benedict Arnold even in that piece. By the time she inserts it in the Washington section, there is no longer any trace of "Arnold." However, Benedict Arnold must have been in Stein's mind. Was she, by identifying Bartholomew Arnold with George Washington, creating a perverse link between "the father of our country" and America's arch-traitor, but giving nothing about it away?

Stein worked on Grant in the country in the fall of 1933 and continued after her return to Paris about November 19. By late October, Bradley, suffering from "the grippe" and overwork, was sent by his doctor to Locarno and did not return until early 1934. She finished Grant early in January, apparently gave it to Bradley, who read it, then reread it on the boat when sailing to America on March 20, to stay in New York until July 3. He told Stein that Grant gave him pleasure. In America that spring he was ill again, as was Alfred Harcourt, which slowed down negotiations.

On April 9, Bradley submitted the Grant section to Harcourt as a sample of the full study, in hopes of a contract and an advance for the whole. By April 14, Stein wrote to Bradley that Wright had been completed before he left, James was complete now, and she was working on Washington. She would send him the completed typescript before leaving for the country. What she wanted to publish now, she said, was *Four In America,* not the "Confessions."

On May 11, Harcourt rejected Grant as not in Stein's "open and public manner."

Writing may be made between the ear and the eye and the ear and the eye the eye will be well and the ear will be well.

—"Finally George" 277

I have just eaten one of the candies that [I] said I'll try I think perhaps it is a good thing to eat words.

—Stein to Bernard Faÿ (undated letter, 1934)

11. 1933–35

Lecturing

Everyone knows that it took the *Autobiography,* the potboiler written in the voice of Toklas, to give Stein popular fame. She became known for that book, and her audience, her agent, and her publishers wanted more work in that voice, which would sell. When the *Atlantic Monthly* agreed to print four installments of the *Autobiography,* the editor, Ellery Sedgwick, on February 11, 1933, said what many felt:

> During our long correspondence, I think you felt my constant hope that the time would come when the real Miss Stein would pierce the smokescreen with which she has always so mischievously surrounded herself. . . . Hail Gertrude Stein about to arrive!

But the voice of the *Autobiography* that publishers considered the real Stein voice was, in fact, a smoke screen for that voice, and the stark difference between the two would in the spring of 1934 split open Stein's own sense of who she was as a writer.

With its very personal illustrations, the *Autobiography* was read as a history of real people, real events, the art collection, the artists, the studio, the salon, and the writer. It failed to trail into publication the works she had spent a lifetime of total concentration writing. It displayed her and Toklas as personalities rather than making her work known and read, as she had hoped.

At the beginning of this book I spoke of Stein's two voices—the voice of words in meditation and the late, strident voice of personality that leads to audience writing, an aspect of personality display. Almost as soon as the

Autobiography appeared, the engine of personality began its job of publicity, and requests came in for Stein to appear personally in America. Her thirty-year absence from home made her more interesting and became a selling point. One might expect the book published on September 1, or even the four sections serialized from May to August, to lead to a claim for her personal appearance. Yet that is not how it began.

As soon as Bradley had negotiated the contract for the *Autobiography* with Harcourt, long before the book was published, he seems to have put out feelers for a lecture tour by Stein. In the early 1930s, he took an interest in American tours for speakers on a wide range of subjects, not only his clients; for example, as early as 1932, he suggested Hitler as a lecturer of interest. He also arranged engagements in America for numerous clients, including the journalist Sisley Huddleston, the princess Marthe Bibseco, and Stein's friend, the Duchesse de Clermont-Tonnerre, Elisabeth de Gramont; such tours could pay well for both speaker and agent.[1]

Among the Bradley papers is a cable dated February 1, 1933, from the Colston Leigh Bureau of Lectures and Entertainments in New York, apparently a response to an inquiry about a lecture tour for Stein from Bradley, who may have felt that a tour in the wake of what he knew would be a best-seller would add to her fame and her income. Leigh's response was negative; Stein was not "universally known" and so not a top-of-the-line speaker. No wonder — the *Autobiography* was not yet published or even heard of. On March 1, Bradley answered, announcing the *Autobiography* as a "first-class attraction." He added that Stein had decided not to tour but suggested that an "irresistible offer" might make her change her mind.

He must have discussed the matter with Stein, whose refusal is easy to understand even though years earlier she had planned, once successful, to return to America to speak and arrange for American publications, especially of *The Making Of Americans.* Now she thought of an American tour with

1. According to a 1931–32 Colston Leigh folder among the Bradley papers, it took about one year to prepare a tour, with photographs, catalog, synopses, publicity. Certain speakers of sure interest were guaranteed pay; others, whose success depended on the sociopolitical climate, received no guarantee. Among well-known American speakers were Michael Strange, Sherwood Anderson, Carl Van Doren, Mortimer Adler, Joseph Wood Krutch, and George Pierce Baker. Some desired speakers, such as Sigrid Undset and Georgette LeBlanc, refused.

   Foreign, but not American, speakers paid tax. The total spent by a lecture bureau on a speaker was calculated as 2*X*. Of this sum, the lecture bureau got 1*X* and the speaker 1*X* minus 10 percent of *X* for an agent (i.e., 5 percent of the total). Sisley Huddleston earned a high total of $2,887.50. Normally, rail travel, sleepers, and hotel accommodation were paid by the bureau but transatlantic crossing usually by the speaker.

the Plain Edition in mind, which she wanted to continue and distribute in America. Between March and early October 1933, there followed many exchanges between Leigh and Bradley, who shows up as a tough bargaining agent.[2]

On October 12, a month after the book had appeared, Leigh cabled a much better offer, for a January 1935 tour, ten weeks, five lectures weekly, at a minimum of 45 percent, with steamship and railroad paid. The next day, Stein wrote to Bradley,

> About the Colston Leigh offer you must just say no. I would never bind myself to do anything in the future, I never have and I never will. It is not unlikely that I will go to America one of these days but if I do I will decide then what I want to do and I am quite certain when that time comes I can make such detailed arrangements as will satisfy me. My dear Bradley after seeing so much of me in Bilignin and on the lake you must understand me well enough to know that putting myself in other people's hands is a thing that for me is quite and entirely impossible and that when I go over it will be largely in connection with the Plain Edition and its future, and all that needs much meditation and arrangement, you know that I have always made haste slowly and I will necessarily continue to do so.

By November 3, Leigh said he considered Stein worth more "now" than in a year. Her refusal notwithstanding, Bradley continued to negotiate for fewer than the usual five lectures weekly, mainly to college and university audiences, and not to women's clubs.

After the historic performance of *Four Saints In Three Acts* on February 8, with the libretto now in print[3] and the short *The Making Of Americans*

2. The problem of a Stein contract was the inclusion of Alice Toklas. In March 1933, Leigh refused a proposed 50-50 contract with ship passage and railroad travel paid for both women. By the end of March, Bradley inquired what view the bureau might take of a tour by Bernard Faÿ. It is not clear whether Bradley tried to arrange a tour for Faÿ, who had for some years been lecturing on the American college circuit and was to be in the United States to teach, speak, and do research from April 25 until September 5, or whether Bradley hoped to use an offer for Faÿ as a bargaining point for Stein.

    Faÿ, it turned out, had for years lectured in the United States under the auspices of the International Institute of Education and had made $8,000 by lecturing. Leigh could offer him at most $2,000 to $2,500. To this proposal Bradley responded sharply that Leigh did not understand the quality of Faÿ's work on Franklin or Washington: "I shall never attempt to force first rate men upon you when a second rate man will serve your purposes just as well" (9 April 1933). Leigh answered that Faÿ might be a brilliant scholar but was not a "drawing card." "I would rather have one Sisley Huddleston than three Bernard Faÿs . . ." (28 April 1933).

3. After Harcourt refused to print the libretto in time for the performance, saying it could

issued on that date and quickly reviewed, Stein's fame had spread beyond the *Autobiography.* Widespread reviews had generated growing interest in her. She had been invited to the premiere of the opera and the opening of the first American Picasso retrospective at the new Wadsworth Atheneum in Hartford but had refused; her absence no doubt added to the curiosity about who this woman was. By this time, she had not accommodated her fame and was trying, with difficulty, to work. When A. Everett Austin Jr., the director of the Wadsworth Atheneum, on November 16, 1933, asked if she would lend some of her Picassos, including her portrait, for an exhibit of the highest quality, she declined:

> About the Picasso show, I think your idea excellent but alas I cannot find it in my heart to part with all my pictures just as I have returned to them after a seven months absence, and in any case quite frankly I do not like to lend them and certainly not any of them so very far away. But you will understand.[4]

Also in February 1934 Bradley sounded Alfred Harcourt out about lecturing. In a first response of February 9, Harcourt said a "regular" tour sponsored by a lecture bureau might be an unpleasant surprise for Stein but asked whether she could afford not to do it. With strong ties to Columbia University, he promised to check on university lectureships. By March 7, he sent Bradley a "preliminary report": Columbia, Princeton, the New School for Social Research, and the Museum of Modern Art were all eager to have Stein, at a minimum of $100 per lecture, "which might be increased."

In addition, major New York clubs like the Colony and Cosmopolitan would want to have her, as would other colleges and universities, such as Vassar, Radcliffe, and Harvard; he was making inquiries at Johns Hopkins, Yale, Smith, the University of Chicago. He thought lecture bureaus charged too much for their services and might not be able to deal with "such a person as Miss Stein." He recommended a "competent lady agent" who might make suitable arrangements in New York.[5]

On March 20, 1934, Bradley sailed from Le Havre to New York on the SS *Champlain,* staying until July 3, when he was to return on the SS *Lafayette,* to be in Paris on July 10. His most important business was Stein, who had given

---

not be well done in the short time available, Bennett Cerf issued it on February 20; on April 28, Stein wrote to Bradley that Cerf, whom she had just seen in Paris, had already sold 2,500 copies.

4. Stein to A. Everett Austin Jr., n.d., Archive of the Wadsworth Atheneum, Hartford.
5. A Mrs. Mary Blankenhorn, on the staff of the *Nation,* of whom Bradley also approved when he met her.

him power of attorney to negotiate and make commitments in America. Agreements for further performances of the opera needed to be worked out with Virgil Thomson, Harry Moses, John Houseman, and Maurice Grosser,[6] as did publication of score and libretto with Thomson. New contracts for works Stein was readying for submission and texts she was writing required discussion with Harcourt, Brace or other publishers; illustrations needed attention; and the lecture tour was in question. Lengthy exchanges followed between Stein and Bradley in April and May, especially about further performances of collaborative work with Thomson, who both felt could not be trusted.

On Sunday, May 6, the *New York Times* published the subtle, humorous Lansing Warren interview with Stein, with details about the "sibylline" author's "cryptic" social and political views—prohibition, immigration—and her new book on four Americans:

> She promises that the new book will not be difficult to read, which seems to mean that the style she has chosen is less in the manner of "Capitols Capitols" [*sic*] and more on the order of the *Autobiography.* (23)[7]

6. From May 1933 on, Bradley negotiated a contract for the opera between Stein and Thomson; it was signed by the time Thomson returned to America in November. After the successful Hartford production on February 8, 1934, Harry Moses brought the show to New York for an unprecedented six-week Broadway run starting on February 20, at the Forty-fourth Street Theatre and the Empire Theatre. Moses wanted to take the production on the road for twenty-six weeks in the autumn.

   However, a demand was made that Grosser, who had not been paid for his scenario and his copying, be paid "one-half of 1% of royalties" for future productions or publications of the score, and it was suggested that this sum be deducted from Stein's share of royalties. A threat of injunction ensued, which Bradley and Stein considered Thomson's doing, not Grosser's. Stein, unwilling to give up her rights, fought vigorously, saying that Grosser had acted most intelligently as a friend but never as a coauthor entitled to royalties. In the end, the show did not go on the road, and the threat of injunction was not carried out. In November, four performances were given in Chicago. See Anthony Tommasini, *Virgil Thomson: Composer on the Aisle* (New York: W. W. Norton, 1997), chaps. 15, 16; Virgil Thomson, *Virgil Thomson* (New York: Alfred A. Knopf, 1966), chaps. 19, 20; Stein, Thomson, Bradley letters, YCAL; Stein-Bradley and Bradley-Thomson letters, HRC.

7. This is the interview that begins with provocative Stein statements such as, "Hitler should have received the Nobel Peace Prize." As a result, some who read her literally and partially have accused her of favoring National Socialism. See, for example, the report in the New York *Forward* of 2 February 1996, which relied on misinformation cited in the right-wing political journal *Nativ,* published in Israel.

   What Stein had said, later quoted in full by Warren, was clearly ironic:

   > "I say that Hitler ought to have the peace prize," she says, "because he is removing all elements of contest and struggle from Germany. By driving out the Jews and the

Bradley had taken with him the first section of *Four In America,* on Grant, for submission to Harcourt, in hopes of a contract for the complete work. Stein had in the meantime finished the Wright and James sections and by April the Washington; Bradley received the complete text on May 15. Her April letters are filled with impatient suggestions for further publications—not only *Four In America* but also *A Birthday Book* and a book of portraits—and productions, such as her film text "about Basket," "Deux Soeurs Qui Ne Sont Pas Soeurs." Bradley, however, wanted another autobiography, the "Confessions."

Throughout Bradley's absence, there were steady exchanges by letter and cable between him, his wife, Jenny, who managed the agency in Paris, and Stein, who conferred with Mrs. Bradley in Paris and, after May 5, from Bilignin but also wrote directly to Bradley.[8] In New York, Bradley negotiated with Harcourt, Leigh, and Cerf. He reported to Faÿ, who sent suggestions from Paris or America and was steadily in contact with Stein. Carl Van Vechten, in touch with publishers, was separately consulted about a lecture tour by Bradley and Faÿ, in New York and Paris; and of course he wrote to Stein. There were delays, misunderstandings, and growing uneasiness about what had or had not been agreed on, what might have been wiser, what advantages had been considered. It was a perfect scenario for trouble.

Neither the name nor the hand of Toklas appears in any correspondence until late July, although both Bradley and his wife always punctiliously sent greetings to both women. Not only in these letters but in virtually all of Stein's activities, including her writing, it is as if Toklas has vanished. In the wake of the book that had made the fame by making them one, they seemed to live in separate worlds. The cloud of the preceding winter had not lifted, but new writing, practical decisions, and varied activities kept them busy. In

---

democratic and left elements, he is driving out everything that conduces to activity. That means peace."

8. All Stein's letters were handwritten, and no copies were made, nor are notes preserved. Bradley's long letters from America were also handwritten. The fact that Stein did not date her letters added to the difficulties of exchange. Hers was not an idiosyncratic refusal of proper form but a deep disinclination to stop the steady flow of the daily life by pinning down a date; writing letters as she did positioned her absolutely in the here and now. A fair number of her letters to Bradley, in fact, are dated, no doubt because Bradley, with some success, insisted on dates for business and legal reasons. When she did not date, Bradley acknowledged *undated* letters, stamping them with date of receipt.

   Bradley's absence from Paris was not the only difficulty. After contracting the "grippe" in the fall of 1933 and a long rest in Locarno, he was again taken ill in America, suffered dental problems, and became homesick. Also that spring, Alfred Harcourt underwent surgery and was away from his office for some six weeks, although his partner, Donald Brace, attended to publications.

the events of the weeks that followed, however, Stein's anger rose, displacing itself from Toklas onto Bradley.

On May 11, Donald Brace wrote to Bradley for Alfred Harcourt:

> We have been a great deal puzzled by the new manuscript of Miss Stein's—the Grant section from a book to contain four similar pieces and to be called FOUR IN AMERICA. Of course, her enthusiasts will care for it, but I am afraid it is going to be hard reading for most of the readers of the AUTOBIOGRAPHY. I don't know whether you saw the article by Lansing Warren in last Sunday's New York Times Magazine. . . . [I]t is stated that Miss Stein is engaged in writing a book on four Americans. . . . It continues: "she promises that the new book will not be difficult to read . . . more on the order of the AUTOBIOGRAPHY." I wish this quotation were accurate, but from the manuscript of the Grant, it seems to us that this new work promises to be in Miss Stein's more involved manner rather than an open and public book.
>
> With the AUTOBIOGRAPHY, the American public had begun to realize what an extraordinary personality Miss Stein is and what a force she has been and is in modern art and literature. The title, the idea, and the subject matter of the new work promised something that would interest the same public and extend it. Actually, however, I can see only a small group of readers for it, and their comments and the comments of the press on it would, I fear, be likely to discourage readers and even interfere with future sales of the AUTOBIOGRAPHY and THE MAKING OF AMERICANS.
>
> . . . [W]e had hoped her next work would appeal to an even larger audience. As a matter of fact, the sale of THE MAKING OF AMERICANS has been roughly one-fourth of that of the AUTOBIOGRAPHY. The reason . . . must be that it is more difficult. . . . We want in general to confine ourselves to publishing what may be called Miss Stein's more open books. Certainly . . . the next book ought to be one of those. This, of course, is only a publishing viewpoint. . . .

He thought *Portraits And Prayers,* which Bradley had shown him, would have little chance for the same reasons. On May 13, Bradley warned Stein against flooding the market with excessive publications or in haste submitting *Four In America* to other publishers, who would realize that Harcourt had rejected it. Harcourt, he emphasized, was still interested in the "Confessions."

> That is why I am desperately sorry you could not have done the Grant along the lines first discussed by us. Not that I do not like it as it stands.

> . . . What good does it do you if we, personally, belong to the little body of the "elect," who like all manifestations of your open spirit if we are unable to translate that liking into results. . . .

Results, he added, were the real mandate he had received from her.

The terms "open and public books" and "real kind of books" stuck. Stein now insisted that the only publisher she would consider was one who printed all her books. Her "public" books were merely "illustrations" to accompany her "real" books.

> The body of my real work should be edited by the same man who does these other books.

On May 15, after discussions with Harcourt, Bradley cabled to Stein offers for lectures from Columbia University and the imminent likelihood of others. As the academic year was winding down, quick decisions were necessary. He also took up discussions with her friend William Rogers of Springfield, Massachusetts, for engagements in New England. By May 25, assuming that she was going to lecture in America, Stein submitted proposals to Bradley.

> 1. The gradual making of the Making of Americans and its gradual change into something else.
>
> The American W[omen's] Club lecture with the development into the Long Gay Book.
>
> 2. The conception of personality and its expression in portraits, poetry and Tender Buttons.
>
> 3. The question of tenses grammar, and its relation to telling a story. The later period.
>
> 4. Pictures that is paintings and what they mean to me.
>
> 5. The History of English literature as I understand it.
>
> 6. Plays and what they are.
>
> All to be illustrated by readings.

Soon she wanted the lectures to be printed when she was in America.

She discussed Bradley's plans and his and Harcourt's proposals for lectures with Faÿ, who was well liked at Columbia, where he had been a visiting lecturer. She respected the quality of his mind and his academic standing while also looking to students as her most promising audience; on the other hand, she came increasingly to see Bradley as a commercial agent interested in her work only for business and profit. Faÿ was committed to an American tour for Stein, but not under a lecture bureau. He agreed with Bradley that after thirty years abroad, Stein was out of touch with America. He wanted to

Figure 15. *Stein in the Garden at Bilignin with Pépé.*
Snapshot by unknown photographer, 1937. Courtesy YCAL.

protect her from commercialism, support her, and make sure that she earned the honors due her in her country; he would participate in her venture by speaking and writing about her work in French and English, in France and America. In the early summer of 1934 he was writing, lecturing in Paris and elsewhere, speaking about her, and reading proof for the French *Autobiography*. He planned visits with Stein in August and early September.

Stein was willing to leave after October 15, when Faÿ's French translation of the *Autobiography* was to be published.[9] Faÿ in the meantime had contacted a friend, Marvin Ross, a young art historian, about organizing Stein's lectures under his, not Bradley's, guidance; later Bradley attempted to dissuade Ross from taking on this assignment, a step that both Stein and Faÿ considered objectionable. Also in the wings as a possible helper for a tour was Walter H. Murphey, "Hub," the Northwestern University student Faÿ had hired as assistant and brought to Paris in the spring of 1932; he was to be back in America by June 20.

Finally, another friend of Faÿ, Rousseau Voorhies, a southerner who worked for the Chicago office of the Macmillan Company and whom Faÿ had introduced to Stein, was ready to act as advance man to do publicity

9. The original agreement for publication had been made with Librairie Stock, but, after repeated difficulties between Boutelleau and Faÿ, Mrs. Bradley arranged for publication by Gallimard in October, with a chapter to appear in September in *La Nouvelle Revue Française*.

work, broadcast, and lecture in Chicago about her and Faÿ. He tried to organize a Stein student club and a competition for writing "like Stein" at the University of Chicago. On March 14, without her permission, he printed in the *Chicago Daily News* a letter she had sent him in answer to his questions for a talk he planned to give about her work on March 23 at the Chicago College Club. This publication and his offensive attempts at publicity, including a lecture on May 13 about *Four Saints,* followed by a newspaper interview, created embarrassment for Stein that left her uncertain about lecturing in Chicago at all.[10]

Before the end of May, Faÿ wrote to Stein that Bradley was serving her poorly and behaving intolerably. Stein, while recognizing that his services were important, was reluctant to take the route of a commercial tour, and Faÿ warned her against becoming the star of a lecture bureau. She wanted *Four In America* published in time for her arrival and the lectures while she was there; in mid-May, she sent "And Now" to Bradley's office for submission to the New York and London *Harper's* provided they paid well.

On May 26, anticipating Bradley's return, Stein presented her objections to his wife. She accused him of having tried to find different publishers for her "real" and her "public" work—"a case of Hamlet with Hamlet left out." As a result, he was responsible for having "landed her in an impasse," especially now that he had failed to get Harcourt's commitment to *Four In America* and the lectures. "He has had the things I wanted accepted, refused." Later the same day, having received further letters from Bradley, she wrote again, emphasizing that everything had gone wrong—including the tour arranged by Bradley through Leigh for the Duchesse de Clermont-Tonnerre, who had just returned from her tour.[11]

Meanwhile, Faÿ wrote Stein on June 30 that he had made contact with "Mrs. Goodspeed, a good-looking, silly-clever Evanston lady, wife of the foremost trustee and lover of the wife of the president of the University of Chicago"; she visited Stein that summer, inviting her to Chicago for lectures and a planned production of *Four Saints.*[12] Faÿ was also in touch with Fanny

10. See also Fanny Butcher papers, Newberry Library, Chicago.
11. In June 1933, Leigh had been unable to arrange lectures for Paul Reynaud, appointed minister of finance by André Tardieu in 1930, because he had asked for repudiation of France's debt to the United States, which caused bitterness in America. Bradley, who was trying to arrange a tour for the Duchess for that October, felt that it would therefore be "practically a flat failure." By the time she did tour, in the spring of 1934, she spoke mainly on social and cultural topics and on the artistic role of women. She had hoped to speak about Stein but did not feel qualified.
12. "Bobsy" Goodspeed, wife of Charles Barney Goodspeed and president of the Arts Club of Chicago, was a powerful woman in the cultural affairs of Chicago.

Butcher, the literary editor of the *Chicago Tribune.* Both women wanted Stein in Chicago.

On May 31, Colston Leigh offered a Stein tour, exclusive of Columbia and the New School, already booked, but ready to pay 50–50 for train fare and accommodations for Stein and Toklas. Leigh in the meantime on his own approached Alfred Barr of the Museum of Modern Art, indicating that Stein would tour under his auspices, preempting Barr's already declared interest in a Stein lecture. The same happened with a late June offer of Stein's services to Mrs. Goodspeed, who had already contacted Stein and was on her way to see her. When Stein heard of Leigh's offers of her services, she was very angry and asked that he retract the offers, make clear that he had acted without authorization, and apologize.

On June 7 and 8, in "dismay," Bradley responded at length to Stein's accusations and defended his actions with publishers. He challenged her about continuing the publication plans he and she had worked out. He reminded her that she had hired him to make her "rich and famous," which he had done. To her claim that he had sold only her "public" books, he responded,

> You said in your letter that Harcourt should remember that your reputation was made by the *other* sort of books. But let me remind you that your *publishing* reputation was made by the *Autobiography.*

He was now submitting *Four In America* to other publishers.

> Please, now that I have erected a solid structure for you, don't try to tear it down as proof of your superior destination! It really isn't worthwhile.

He added that he had gone ahead on his own responsibility with Leigh and had now obtained most favorable terms from him.

On June 11, Faÿ advised Stein to go ahead with lectures, but not with a lecture bureau. He considered Marvin Ross "gentle, obedient and reliable" as agent and felt sure he would do the advance publicity responsibly. Regret-

---

Faÿ, with an honorary doctorate from Northwestern University (1932) and well connected in Chicago, had a plan, not known to Stein, for an honorary doctorate to be awarded her by the University of Chicago, just as Yale had given a doctorate to Edith Wharton. He knew that Stein would be asked to speak at the University of Chicago, as Harvard had asked T. S. Eliot. In June or July 1933, Bradley hoped that Stein might win a Pulitzer Prize. There was also talk about the Prix Femina. That summer, Stein also told Bradley, in confidence, that she was being considered for the *Légion d'honneur,* especially fitting with *Américains d'Amérique* about to appear. None of these honors came to her that year, although she finally made it into *Who's Who* for 1933 and onto the cover of *Time* for September 11, 1933.

tably, Stein might have to break with Harcourt.[13] At this time, Stein considered lecturing only from one or two centers in the East, such as New York, with trips to Springfield and Boston, Baltimore, and Chicago; these would not require extensive traveling. She felt there would be "plenty of publicity that comes naturally" through friends and acquaintances, saw no need for an agent, and for the first time in weeks spoke of Toklas,

> there is no reason why Miss Toklas should not make the traveling arrangements for us as she always has done.

On June 23, to Mrs. Bradley, Stein reviewed things as she saw them,

> Before Bradley left for New York I told him definitely that I was ready to go on with Harcourt if there was a decision on his part to print Four in America and other books of that character. If he were not willing to my great regret I must insist that Bradley find a new publisher that would. That I absolutely insisted that the lectures and the Confessions should go with the Four in America and a book of portraits should not be offered separately. Knowing that Bradley would be likely to be influenced by Harcourt once he was over there, I wrote him immediately after his departure repeating all this. I wrote him the same thing twice afterward, in all I wrote him this three times beside having told it to him and on top of this definite and repeated statement he after his stay in America sends me the contracts from Harcourt saying that Harcourt had definitely decided never to print any of my other type of books not even if they were moderately successful at the same time telling me that he was offering the Four in America alone and therefore meeting with the inevitable refusal of which I had warned him and him offering it alone which I had absolutely forbidden. The consequence of course of this is that in my opinion he has done my publishing programme incalculable harm. I do not wish to discuss the matter, there is nothing to discuss, my letters were clear and concise and he has acted in complete disregard of my repeated instructions. It is therefor that I have lost confidence in him.

No such letters from Stein are among the Bradley papers.

On June 24, she asked that Bradley not offer any more of her work in New York. Two days later, in a scathing letter, Mrs. Bradley rejected the abuse Stein was heaping on Bradley, who by now had ceased contact with Leigh. Faÿ already agreed with Stein, as a letter of June 28 makes clear,

13. On the back of this letter, Stein doodled, then played with names, including "H. P. Brace / H. G. Grace / May Grace / Henry Grace / Jenny Grace / Indy Grace / and Margaret Grace / This is all the Graces / there are."

> Bradley is getting impossible and you are wise in holding him in check. The Lee business was absurd and his tendency of selling books before they are written and before they are thought of is preposterous . . . for us authors there is practically nothing worse than this feeling that we have to follow a program and fulfill old promises.

Upset by Leigh's unauthorized selling and promotion of her, Stein on July 9 or 10 insisted to Mrs. Bradley,

> I am the only person authorized to act for myself.

On July 11, Faÿ agreed with Stein that she, and perhaps he also, would have to get rid of Bradley, with whom she was under contract, unlike Faÿ, who only occasionally consulted him. He answered her questions about her exact obligations to Bradley, who could be taken off unfulfilled contracts but not off commissions for fulfilled contracts. On July 13, in a typed letter, Stein asked that Bradley return the power of attorney she had given him on March 16.

> For the serious injury done to my affairs by this flagrant violation of my direct and positive cabled orders, I hold Mr. Bradley responsible.

On July 15 and 17, Faÿ reported to Stein on his meeting with Bradley, just back in Paris. "His voice was horrible," he looked "gaga and changed" but talked "a steady stream full of sweet feelings" about her, declaring himself proud of his handling of her affairs, heroic in choosing Leigh for thousands of dollars and facing people stirred up against Stein by Thomson. Meanwhile, Faÿ made plans with Ross, contacted Theodore Spencer at Harvard and Mrs. Goodspeed in Chicago for lectures, and looked forward to visiting Stein from August 1 or 2 to August 12 and the first week of September; that was when James Laughlin,[14] "a rather nice boy and very solemn," whom

14. James Laughlin IV (1914–97), later the founder of New Directions, had taken a leave from Harvard after his sophomore year to go to Europe and become a writer. Through Faÿ he was invited to Bilignin by Stein to help write abstracts of the lectures, a difficult task he later completed in Paris with Faÿ's help. A correspondence ensued that in 1936–37 led to publications of Stein's "A Waterfall And A Piano" and "Daniel Webster Eighteen in America: A Play" in *New Directions Prose and Poetry* for 1936 and 1937. It was also through Laughlin, a Choate School graduate, that Stein was invited by Dudley Fitts to speak at the Choate School on the American tour; and the (Princeton) *Nassau Lit.*, after exchanges with Laughlin, asked for a contribution and received "Fred Anneday."

    After meeting Stein, Laughlin planned a book about her, to be entitled *Understanding Gertrude Stein.* He took voluminous notes and prepared a working index but ended up feeling that it was not adequate. His notes are in his archive. See also "About Gertrude Stein," *Yale Review* 77, no. 4 (summer 1988) and an extended version of this essay in

he had met in Geneva or Lausanne and Salzburg, joined them to prepare summaries of the lectures and blurbs for publications.

By July 19, Bradley, back in Paris, examined all her letters, summarized what she had written, and defended himself vigorously against her accusations. Since she would have no copies of her letters, he sent her typed copies prepared by his office, now at Yale.

From that date on, all their letters observe perfect, polite form, with the appropriate thank-you's and acknowledgments: Bradley's letters were signed and sent by his secretary, and Stein's were typed and signed by her secretary—Alice Toklas.

On July 24, Bradley wrote to Harcourt that he was no longer Stein's agent and asked for separate, direct remission of her royalties and his 10 percent. In phrasing he was to use again, he concluded,

> Her success has turned her head completely and transformed her into the imperial despot she so strikingly resembles.

In a letter of July 26 from New York, Bennett Cerf of Random House, as Van Vechten knew, made the offer Stein had hoped for:

> It should hardly be necessary for me to tell you how happy we would be to become the American publisher of all your books.

Van Vechten on August 5 told Stein how happy he was with *Four In America;* she responded on August 16,

> I cannot tell you how happy you have made me by liking the Four in America. I do think it is one of my major works, and now I want to tell you all about it. . . . I refused [Harcourt's] contract, and split with Bradley about all that. You see I insist that I will not give my lectures to anybody who will not print the Four in America and then later a portrait book and I broke with Bradley and I refused Harcourt on that issue and I do think I am right. Now Cerf is trying it on but I think if I hold out and with your aid that I will find somebody who will be enthusiastic about doing all three . . .[15]

Scripsi 5, no. 3 (April 1989), Ormond College, University of Melbourne, Australia; "About Bilignin and Literature and the G B M," *Gotham Book Mart Catalogue # 36.* His first short story, "The River," was written while he was in Paris; his story "Partial Eclipse," *Story* 9, no. 51 (October 1936), is a satiric study of Bernard Faÿ and Brancusi. "New Words for Old: Notes on Experimental Writing," *Story* 9, no. 53 (December 1936) includes ideas he first met through Stein. Interview with author, Norfolk, Connecticut, 1 August 1983; Dydo-Laughlin letters, 5 February–28 August 1983; Stein-Laughlin letters, YCAL and New Directions Archive, now Houghton Library, Harvard University.

15. *LGS/CVV* 328, 329.

On July 27, upon a request from Toklas, Bradley forwarded all remaining papers and receipts and asked that any further questions be directed to his attorney.[16] Two days later, again at a request of Toklas, he sent dates, texts, and charges of all cables to and from America. He ended,

> In looking over these attentively, I note the use of a word, in two places, which it was not my intention to make you pay for. Therefore I send you stamps for frs. 4.65, in reembursement of same.
>
> Very truly yours,
> W. A. Bradley
>
> May 19 One word frs. 3.30
> May 14 One word $ 0.09 at 15.116 frs. 1.66
> frs. 4.66
>
> The "one word," ending both cables, was "LOVE."

16. On August 23, Bradley's office returned to Stein "nine short stories entrusted to Mr. A. Mervyn Davies" of New York for placing. In October 1933, Stein had asked Bradley urgently to place with magazines as many short things as he could. Bradley had earlier known Davies, who specialized in magazine work. On February 2, 1934, he asked him to handle Stein's "short things verse and prose . . . which she has been in the habit of giving away," of which he disapproved. Davies had tried, without success, to place them:

    "Gertrude Stein and Alice Toklas seen by a French friend," apparently an essay by Georges Maratier, not at YCAL
    "Lucy La Fontaine" (1933)
    "Harriet" (1910)
    "Procession" (1923)
    "A Man" (Edstrom, September 1911)
    "A Painter" (Manguin, October 1911)
    "Left Alone. To Basket" (1929)
    "Or. And Then Silence" (1933)
    "The Gradual Making Of The Making Of Americans" (1934)

    Leon Katz cites the dates of September 1911 for "A Man" and October 1911 for "A Painter," based on chronological alignment of details in Stein's early notebooks with her progress and stylistic changes in *The Making Of Americans* (telephone conversation with Leon Katz, New York City to Los Angeles, 20 August 1997).

    Also included in Bradley's original letter to Davies but not listed with the returned pieces were, "What Is This" (in "Selected Poems," 1918); "New" (1923); and three texts I have not been able to identify, "A Love Poem," "3 And 4," and "Gardner." The reason for the discrepancy between the two lists is not clear. See Bradley–A. Mervyn Davies letters, HRC.

Lectures for America

Context

After the *Autobiography* appeared in book form, Stein on September 22, 1933, described her sensations to Hubbell,

> as Henry James would say and what sensations. I am about getting the better of these strange sensations and it is taking the form of meditations on Shakespeare's sonnets and Before the flowers which will be a treatise that I know will interest you, I have just begun it, and it will be all about audiences a very fearful subject and it is taking form.[17]

She was already meditating about what some six months later she would write in the Henry James section of *Four In America* and carry over to the lectures for the American tour.

The lectures became the last of many steps that followed the strange new sensations of the success. Long known as an anomaly beyond comprehension, Stein had now suddenly written a popular book, and people wanted to hear what this woman had to say. For her, lecturing became not a chance to charm an audience but an opportunity to account for her work as a writer and to close the gap between the voice of Stein and that of Toklas.

She now had the money, success, and fame she had craved but not the understanding of the readers she needed. Henry McBride, who had long warned her that success would spoil her art, wrote with uneasy regret on October 27, 1933, "That book was doomed to be a bestseller. Doomed is my word, not yours. I don't like to give you up to the general public." The book and the reviews might give her up to the general public, but personal appearance might allow her to speak of her art and to correct the misleading impression left by the memoir. An American tour on her own terms might also sell more books, especially the Plain Edition.

She was uneasy about touring, but attending the lectures of Bernard Faÿ at the Collège de France had led her to think in new ways about lectures. Stein and Faÿ came from different generations and different worlds but shared a love of America. Their friendship had deepened, and they supported one another's efforts, each gaining from the other but never competing. On January 9, 1934, in phrasing obviously learned from her, he wrote,

> My lectures interest me because in a way they are a dialogue between your mind and my mind.

17. By summer 1933, Stein was planning the Grant and James sections and perhaps the others, but she did not begin writing until the winter.

Unlike Bradley, who had initiated the contact with the commercial lecture bureau, Faÿ understood what she wanted to achieve intellectually. He supported a tour on her own, avoiding the mercenary route of a lecture bureau. Experienced in speaking regularly at American colleges and universities, Faÿ made contacts for her and enlisted Marvin Chauncey Ross, a young friend, to act under his guidance as her agent and attend to bookings. Faÿ wanted her to reap the attention she deserved and to contribute to it.[18]

In the first months of 1934, Stein worked on new writing—*Four In America,* her study of issues larger than the daily life, including American genius, identity, poetry; "Fred Anneday," about storytelling, which arose from life in the country, with autobiographical overtones; and the aborted confessions of "And Now," never completed. On the inside cover of the *cahier* for "Fred Anneday," of about February, appears the opening question for the lecture "Poetry And Grammar," "What is poetry and if you know what poetry is what is prose." The lectures grow directly out of her writing of winter and spring 1934.

Stein always said she wrote the lectures in the summer, once the decision to undertake the tour was made, by mid-July. Various letters[19] speak of writing the three on general aesthetic topics—"Pictures," "Plays," "What Is English Literature"—by mid-July. But it is now clear that she was thinking about them earlier, especially while writing the Henry James section of *Four In America;* she may have taken notes even by the beginning of 1934.

By early March, on the back of a letter, she jotted down notes, including the title, for the first part of "The Gradual Making Of The Making Of Americans." The letter, from Pearl F. Clark, the chairwoman of the American Women's Club in Paris, invited her to speak to members of the club on March 23, 1934. The topic was the short *The Making Of Americans,* published in February, which the women were reading. This is how, long before the American tour, she wrote and delivered the first half of "The Gradual Making Of The Making Of Americans" in Paris. The invitation allowed her to formulate ideas and gave her practice in speaking.

18. Knowing what an honorary degree would mean to her, he made concerted efforts, not known to her, to have an honorary doctorate awarded to Stein, both at the University of Chicago and, according to Toklas, at Harvard. However, these efforts failed. Both in the United States and in France, Faÿ spoke and wrote about her, and he translated the short *The Making Of Americans* and the *Autobiography.* Stein also relied on support from friends in France and America. See, for example, her letter to Carl Van Vechten of 2 June 1934 (*LGS/CVV* 311).

19. See Stein to and from DuPoy, Faÿ, Hubbell, Scudder, Van Vechten, and quoted in W. G. Rogers, *When This You See Remember Me: Gertrude Stein in Person* (New York: Rinehart, 1948).

From a December 1933 lecture by Faÿ at the Collège de France, she had come away with a new sense of lecturing and audience. We do not know his topic, though it may have been Stein, or at least Stein was used as an example:

> I was living in you and living in the thing and for once in my life almost not living in myself. A strange and very moving xperience and giving me quite a new point of view toward life. Thanks a thousand times for that and all.

This idea returns in "Portraits And Repetition," after she speaks of writing *Flowers* and then the *Autobiography,*

> However the important thing was that for the first time in writing, I felt something outside me while I was writing, hitherto I had always had nothing but what was inside me while I was writing. Beside that I had been going for the first time since my college days to lectures. I had been going to hear Bernard Fay lecture about Franco-American things and I had become interested in the relation of a lecturer to his audience. I had never thought about an audience before not even when I wrote Composition As Explanation which was a lecture but now I suddenly began, to feel the outside inside and the inside outside[20] and it was perhaps not so exciting but it was very interesting. (*LIA* 205)

From Bilignin, on about September 12, Faÿ and Laughlin returned to Paris, where Laughlin, with Faÿ's help, completed the abstracts of the lectures. In its September 1 issue, *La Nouvelle Revue Française* printed a chapter of Faÿ's translation of the *Autobiography.* By October 5, the French Line

20. Echoes of the parodied Longfellow in

"The Modern Hiawatha"

When he killed the Mudjokivis,
Of the skin he made him mittens,
Made them with the fur side inside,
Made them with the skin side outside,
He, to get the warm side inside,
Put the inside skin side outside;
He, to get the cold side outside,
Put the warm side fur side inside.
That's why he put the fur side inside,
Why he put the skin side outside,
Why he turned them inside outside.

Anon., n.d., in Dwight McDonald, ed., *Parodies: An Anthology from Chaucer to Beerbohm—and After* (New York: Random House, 1960), 108.

confirmed the cabin on the SS *Champlain,* sailing on October 17, that Faÿ had selected for Stein and Toklas, and on October 15, there was a reception and book signing for the translation. When Faÿ sailed for New York on October 23, on the SS *Lafayette,* copies of *Autobiographie d'Alice Toklas* and *Américains d'Amérique,* which Faÿ was prepared to sign, were available on board.

In the September issue of *Vanity Fair* appeared "And Now," with a photograph of the studio. Editor Frank Crowninshield noted that Stein had not made up her mind about the tour but gave titles of some lectures, spoke of engagements at Columbia and the New School, and, if she came, of her wish to be back in Paris by Christmas.

> Certain it is that two ladies have not made such a sensation in the literary world since William Wordsworth and Sir Walter Scott paid pious visits to Lady Eleanor Butler and Miss Sarah Ponsonby, "the ladies of Llangollen." So please, Miss Stein and Miss Toklas, don't disappoint us: we do be expecting you.[21]

Sometime in September or early October, the lectures written and the women ready to leave for America, Stein wrote the short "Meditations On Being About To Visit My Native Land." It remained unpublished in her lifetime, an almost shy piece, quiet, half withdrawn, not great Stein writing.[22] Its two parts are not well fitted together, but it shows earnest if nervous effort, and some of her voice is here. It retains her sparse, narrow phrasing, as in the first sentence, made of four repeated, interwoven verbal elements: "busy," "visit native land," "meditating," "say to me say to them."

> I am being so very "busy" in being about to visit my native land that I have not been meditating not meditating very much but if I were not

21. The December issue of *Vanity Fair,* published when Stein was already in America, printed her letter of October 5,

> Dear *Vanity Fair,*
> It will be nice seeing you again because undoubtedly we will see you, if we come and we are coming, indeed we are coming on the Champlain sailing October 17th and it is getting near. I know I will like it but I am a little scared. And, more-over, you never sent me a copy of *Vanity Fair,* nor have any of my friends, assuming that you did. Please do, it is not yet too late, and I would like to see it. *Vanity Fair* was, after all, pretty well my first. Always, Gertrude Stein.

The editors added that they had indeed sent her a copy. Frank Crowninshield, the editor of *Vanity Fair,* published Stein as early as June 1917, June 1918, March 1919, and beyond. See Robert Wilson, comp., *Gertrude Stein: A Bibliography* (Rockville, Md.: Quill and Brush, 1994).

22. It is included in *PL* 254–56.

so busy and were to meditate I would meditate a great deal and I would and in a way do meditate upon what they are to say to me and what I am to say to them, those who make my native land my native land.

The public condition of being "busy" interferes with meditating and prevents real writing. She speaks of it as best she can, but not in her full and free voice. There is a "set" subject—the response she anticipates in America, what it will be like there, what they will say. The lectures, hovering between public discourse and private meditation, are written, virtually a new genre of Stein writing. Stein and Toklas arrived in New York on October 24.

Once in America, upon invitation, Stein wrote five further new lectures. The first was for the students at the Choate School in Wallingford, Connecticut. James Laughlin, an alumnus, had suggested it as a good venue but felt her lectures were too difficult for preparatory school students. Arrangements were made with Dudley Fitts, writer and teacher of classics at the school, and Stein on January 12 delivered a new lecture, "How Writing Is Written." No manuscript or typescript is preserved; the only text we have is a version typed and punctuated in standard form by Dudley Fitts from stenographic notes taken by a secretary during delivery at the school. As a result the text, which was not extemporized, looks quite unlike other Stein pieces while preserving the Stein voice.

With great simplicity and directness, she shapes anew for the boys ideas that are in her original lectures, such as the need to rely on direct observation, not memory or resemblance, discussed in "Portraits And Repetition." She stands before them as a senior writer but never talks down to them. Rather, she presents herself as one of their grandparents' generation, which allows them to feel less hostile than they might feel toward their parents and so to listen to her, and she acknowledges the difficulty of being young and wanting to speak of their own life and time.

None of this is new. Similar ideas are already in "Composition As Explanation" and in the present lectures. But from these Stein culls ideas cast into a language and tone so simple, fresh, and personal that they carry great power. What makes this talk so impressive is how she speaks.

The four *Narration* lectures, combined with assigned readings and student conferences, were written in Chicago between February 24 and March 13, 1935. They were designed for a course in narration for students at the University of Chicago, selected by her codirector, Thornton Wilder, from March 1 to 14, 1935.

The first lecture is recast from "What Is English Literature," distinguishes English from American narrative, and asks students to follow the project of an "American narrative." As examples, she adds details seen in America while touring. In America, words focus on moving; they

> began to have within themselves the consciousness of completely moving, they began to detach themselves from the solidity of anything, they began to excitedly feel themselves as if they were anywhere or anything. . . . (10)

She wants to make the students proud of being aspiring *American* writers who must find their own way without leaning on English models. Here also, nothing is new except the firm American emphasis.

The second lecture, based almost completely on "Poetry And Grammar," relies on a phrase read on a billboard in Georgia to open the question of narrative as it relates to poetry and prose:

> Let's make our flour meal and meat in Georgia. (16)

She concludes that traditional distinctions between prose and poetry in narrative no longer apply, for now writers and readers want to escape from succeeding and being tied to beginning, middle, and ending. As a result there is now, especially in America, "moving in every direction."

She offers a brilliant summary of her thinking about narrative, poetry, and prose, in a language charged with rhetoric, repetition, and variation that displays her capacity for pyrotechnics in writing and takes immense concentration to follow, even as it moves with great clarity of mind.

> [A] narrative is any kind of way of trying to tell anything any one has to tell about anything that is or was or will be happening, and any kind of telling is the telling of what is happening inside or outside but is the telling the natural the immediate the necessary telling of anything that is happening. (33)

> To know about this you have to look at country to see what it looks like, since land and water looks not like itself but is the whole of it, and therefore is there any beginning and ending to it. (32)

Only the third and fourth lectures add new material. In the third, given on March 8, 1935, she announces that she will discuss how we tell stories, newspaper and history writing, detective stories, biography, autobiography, and finally, audience. Instead she concentrates on newspaper writing, relying on what she had written in the first of her Herald Tribune Syndicate articles, published on March 3. Journalists, she says, write

> what happened the day before and so get the feeling that it has happened on the same day the newspaper appeared the day the news paper reader reads the newspaper and not the day before. (35–36)

The fourth lecture again opens with and later repeats American experience.

> After all anybody is as their land and air is. Anybody is as the sky is high or low, the air heavy or clear, anybody is as there is wind and no wind there. It is that which makes them and the arts they make and the work they do and the way they eat and the way they drink and the way they learn and everything. (46, 48)

In all the other lectures, she relied on ideas she had discussed before. However, they include some illustrations from her experience of being in America, which add a strong American emphasis and create a different tone.

As if she had come full circle, in this last new lecture she speaks very personally of audience, not only summarizing but virtually confessing what she had experienced and gradually developed in the Henry James section of *Four In America.*

> What makes writing writing is hearing what an audience is that is to say makes recognition while in the act of writing what he is writing. It is so easy to know no not so easy to know and it is so easy to say no so hard to say but hard or easy it is said and known this what I have to say and do so as I say that is as I write. (56)

The Lectures

Texts: *Lectures In America,* "How Writing Is Written," and *Narration*

For these many pages, I have followed Stein's work, tracing and elucidating her writing process. The *Lectures In America* that end this book take me back to its beginning. In them Stein returned to elucidating, not as in "An Elucidation," where she had spoken to an inside audience that was a part of her text, but as she could do it in addressing an actual audience outside. Here, in public, she lays out in new forms many of the core ideas this book has followed.

She composed them in the spring and summer of 1934. Only gradually, however, by a laborious process in the course of the winter, while working on *Four In America,* especially the Henry James section, had she clarified what she was about. Here, in the name of changing occupations and identities, she drags about a great welter of confusing ideas, including many about her own work, that she has trouble disentangling. Consider how many unwieldy pairs of opposites she assembles in this study: accident and coincidence, Shakespeare's plays and Shakespeare's sonnets, "I am I because my little dog knows me" and "I am I not any longer when I see," writing the way you are writing and writing the way you are going to be writing, Henry James as general and Henry James as novelist.

The James section is also dominated by a teaching voice. Often she seems to be making an effort to speak in a voice not or not yet her own. The ideas in the lectures are not the same as those she discusses in the James section, though they are related. With hindsight, however, I look at them as preparations for the clarity she reaches in the lectures. By the time she formulates them, she speaks about herself and her development in a new voice of her own, not that of an impersonated, changed other.

Rather than following her text by text, I here identify and comment on "bothers" that led her to core ideas that she discusses. Three cardinal concerns carry through all her work and, directly or indirectly, through all she said in America. The first two, not isolated for definition and discussion, she takes for granted, as do all who know her work. Behind everything she says is her commitment to the "present moment," the "here and now." It is in her advice to the boys at Choate, to rely on direct observation and not on memory or resemblance which, removed from experience, become inaccurate and dead. It is in her focus on words not only as signs but as things directly portraying concentrated apprehension, discussed along with representation in "Pictures,"

> how words which were the words that made whatever I looked at look like itself were not the words that had in them any quality of description . . . words that . . . as often as not had as I say nothing whatever to do with what any words would do that described that thing. (191–92)

And it is in the presentation of her discovery, in "The Gradual Making," that complete descriptions of people are developed gradually, over time, but the perceptions opening them are completely realized and present to the observer all at one time.

Related is the "beginning again and again" that we associate with all her efforts, as in "The Gradual Making," where it is the moving force behind the summary of her early development as, having stopped with the long novel, she began again with "A Long Gay Book," and then with *Tender Buttons*. Her concept of the "continuous present," not named but related, emerges from her struggle with methods of telling stories by experimenting with sentences stripped of dependent clauses and cast into a total present filled with "its own life" (61–62); this vitality reinforced a point she had made in *Four In America* when speaking of Owen Young's mistaken assumption about the need for clarity of expression rather than force (*FIA* 127).

The third core idea has to do with "movement," to Stein an essentially American and modernist quality. *The Making Of Americans,* she says in "The Gradual Making," is an essentially American book about

> a space that is filled with moving, a space of time that is filled always filled with moving and my first real effort to express this thing which is an American thing. (161)

This connects directly with her comments on movement at the end of "Pictures" and her study of movement in *Four In America.* Moving, she maintains, is existing (165).

> In short this generation has conceived an intensity of movement so great that it has not to be seen against something else to be known, and therefore, this generation does not connect itself with anything, . . . and that is why it is American. (166)

And in "Poetry And Grammar" she muses about the possibility of creating a new "American thing," "a new balance with movement of time in a given space" (224),

> the balance of a space completely not filled but created by something moving as moving is not as moving should be. (225)

And in the first *Narration* lecture she points out that in America, where she observed road signs, words focus on moving; they

> began to have within themselves the consciousness of completely moving, they began to detach themselves from the solidity of anything, they began to excitedly feel themselves as if they were anywhere or anything. . . . (10)

In *Everybody's Autobiography* she tells about seeing, on the highway near Olivet, Michigan,

> the shaving advertisements that delighted me one little piece on a board and then further on two more words and then further on two more words a whole lively poem. (225–26)

Among the Stein papers is a copy of Number Five of the *Burma Shave Jingle Book* with eighteen jingles that she may have picked up on the tour, a perfect emblem for movement:

> Holler
> Half a pound
> For half a dollar

Isn't that
A cheerful earful
Burma Shave

Stein's exploration, in "What Is English Literature" and at the beginning of the first *Narration* lecture, of the evolution of English literature and her description of the self-contained "English daily island life" in a circumscribed space contrasts with her emphasis on an independent "American literature" (50), in spite of its reliance on the same language—"discontinuous, fragmented, disembodied" in response to the geographical immensity of America. Her study of American leaders, language, and genius in *Four In America* helped prepare her for addressing Americans and aspiring writers as independent, creating not to English models but following James and herself on the new road to modernism.

In 1934, to present American writing as a separate literature in its own right had a force quite unlike today. She spoke to an audience not yet persuaded that there was an independent American literature, American language, American art. American literature was not taught or researched at colleges and universities until after World War II, when it became possible, at a small number of colleges and universities, to study and even major in American literature.[23] Returning home after thirty years, she presented herself not as an estranged expatriate but as a quintessentially American writer.

In "Plays," a lecture that underwent extensive revision and became the one least often delivered of the group, she explores two ideas central to her thinking. One is the bother of "syncopated time" in performances, which leaves us uneasy or "nervous" in relation to the excitement that is to be conveyed, when the action on stage does not go with the emotion of the audience. She looks at how we reach a high point of emotion in life, in books, and in plays. In life, as events move toward a climax, our excitement reaches completion and our reactions are at one with the events; in books, as we move toward climax, we experience the pleasure of relief, which we can repeat when we reread the book. But on stage, she says, we must meet the actors as characters and make sure we can identify them in the action; we

23. Vernon Parrington's *Main Currents of American Thought* had appeared in 1927, the journal *American Literature* was founded in 1929, Granville Hicks' *The Great Tradition* appeared in 1933, and the first volume of Perry Miller's *The New England Mind* was published in 1939. F. O. Matthiessen's *American Renaissance* came out in 1941 as did the first edition of *The Oxford Companion to American Literature* by James Hart, who had begun his research in 1936.

must also visually absorb scenery and costumes. As our eyes and ears are separately busy in the theater, that can present difficulties and inhibit our ability to experience relief.[24]

The other idea, which offers a partial solution to the problem of syncopated time, is the play as a "landscape," for

> if a play was exactly like a landscape then there would be no difficulty about the emotion of the person looking on at a play being behind or ahead of the play because the landscape does not have to make acquaintance. (122)

We can be in a play as we can be in a landscape, where everything is steadily "in relation."

> And of that relation I wanted to make a play and I did, a great number of plays. (125)

The landscape play has nothing to do with lovely valleys, sunsets over the mountains, and glittering streams; it is an essence, an abstract idea, connected with painting and including movement.

> Anyway the play as I see it is exciting and it moves but it also stays and that is as I said in the beginning might be what a play should do. (131)

Throughout the lectures Stein returned to her great discovery in "Sentences And Paragraphs" of 1929–30 of "non-emotional sentences" and "emotional paragraphs." Sentences are held together by the patternings of the parts of speech that compose them. Diagramming sentences reveals their shapes; we might say that diagrams make landscapes out of the linear sentences. In "Poetry And Grammar" she goes into detail about words and the parts of speech that make for "the inner life of sentences." As is well known, she objects to nouns and adjectives as stiff and dead; in sentences, she looks for words whose activity is not rigidly determined, from articles to verbs to pronouns, that always have "a great possibility of being something" but, unlike nouns, are not pinned down.

She carefully distinguishes emotional paragraphs and non-emotional sentences,

24. She speaks of how impressed she was by William Gillette's concept in his melodramas of the action being focused on "silence, stillness and quick movement," which did not impede the audience's sensation of relief.

Paragraphs are emotional not because they express an emotion but because they register or limit an emotion. (48)

English writers, in the eighteenth and nineteenth centuries, began to add more and more explanation and information, creating barriers to lively language. In terms close to the ones she uses in *Four In America,* she speaks in "What Is English Literature" of Henry James, and his work with the paragraph, building drama and suspense,

> He too needed the whole paragraph . . . but . . . his whole paragraph was detached from what it said from what it did, what it was from what it held, and over it all something floated not floated away but just floated, floated up there. (53)

About "repetition" and "insistence" Stein spoke at length in "Portraits And Repetition." Repetition, of course, is what she had been charged with over and over by resistant, uncomprehending readers. She says that human beings do not repeat themselves, for if they are alive, their emphasis is different with every statement, every movement. This is insistence. She made this discovery as a young girl, when moving from Oakland to Baltimore and meeting her eleven little aunts, who at first seemed to be copies of one another, repeating themselves, but it turned out that each had her own individual voice, gave her own kind of attention, even remained silent in her own way. Only in a state of fatigue did they repeat themselves; this observation carries over to Stein's experiments with fatigue among Harvard and Radcliffe students and her discovery that what was interesting about them as they talked was their individuality, not the repetitions that were conditioned by the nature of the laboratory experiment.

Her 1911–12 portrait "Orta," of the dancer Isadora Duncan reaching for self-definition as an integrated artist, shows Stein's rhythmic repetitions skillfully composing a dance of insistence,

> She was that one and being that one and being one feeling in believing completing being existing, and being one thinking in feeling in believing completing being existing, and being one thinking in feeling in meaning being existing and being one being of a kind of a one and being if that kind of them and they being of a kind of them and complete connection being existing in her being one dancing between dancing being existing and her being one not being one completing being one, she was one dancing and being that one she was that one and being that one she was that one the one dancing and being the one dancing being that one she was the one going on being that one the one dancing. (*R* 136)

Stein came to think of "talking and listening" as one—the great gift of the artist. She also called it the asset of "genius,"[25] in whose workings she felt simultaneous creative agilities rather than split and conflicting activities. Again and again the lectures return to this unity, which her language perfectly exemplifies.

These terms, which also mark Stein's progress over the years, are distributed and repeated throughout the lectures, for which Stein mined her own work. When she wrote the five new lectures in America, she added no new core terms.

For some years I thought of the lecture texts as audience writing—the last of the many steps she felt driven to take toward self-realization, publicity stunts to charm listeners. When she first thought about them, she was also uneasy and feared them as temptations to abandon god for mammon.

"Audience" is a central concern for her, not only for lecturing but in her own sense of herself as a writer. After all, here for the first time she was consciously speaking to listeners; she said that she had even written the 1926 lecture "Composition As Explanation" for herself, not for them.

In early September, after reading the lectures to Faÿ and the young Jay Laughlin, who was to prepare summaries for the press, she commented in a letter to W. G. Rogers,

> The lectures are good . . . but they are for a pretty intelligent audience and though they are very clear very clear they are not too easy.[26]

As a first step in making them accessible, she limited her audience to a maximum of five hundred, which allowed her to avoid shouting to an anonymous crowd.[27] To reach them, she had to maintain spontaneity. In the Henry James section of *Four In America,* when considering the difference between the smooth sound of planned writing and the forceful sound of spontaneous writing and speaking, she had already said,

> Mr. Owen Young made a mistake, he said the only thing he wished his son to have was the power of clearly expressing his ideas. Not at all. It is not clarity that is desirable but force.

25. The term "genius" has unfortunate connotations that may have worked against Stein, making her sound like a braggart. But it connects with her early search for a definition of the fully integrated personality, able both to create as artist and think as intellectual.
26. W. G. Rogers, *When This You See Remember Me: Gertrude Stein in Person* (New York: Rinehart, 1948), 118–19.
27. She also made sure that, before speaking, she would not be introduced with the usual encomiums for distinguished speakers that merely mixed voices and made listening difficult.

> Clarity is of no importance because nobody listens and nobody knows what you mean no matter what you mean, nor how clearly you mean what you mean. But if you have vitality enough of knowing enough of what you mean, somebody and sometime and sometimes a great many will have to realize that you know what you mean and so they will agree that you mean what you know, what you know you mean, which is as near as anybody can come to understanding any one. (*FIA* 127)[28]

If lecturing was to succeed, her words had to enter the minds of educated listeners with such immediacy of insight as would carry force and vitality. Stein wrote her talks with a double perspective, speaking both to herself as her inside audience and to the audience outside.

> Think of your ears as eyes. You can even think of your eyes as ears but not so readily perhaps. (*FIA* 129)

Two words spontaneously written next to each other have greater intensity of sound than two words smoothly and prettily joined.

What she says in "Portraits And Repetition" tells us a great deal about how she designed the lectures:

> No matter how complicated anything is, if it is not mixed up with remembering there is no confusion, but and that is the trouble with a great many so called intelligent people they mix up remembering with talking and listening, and as a result they have theories about anything but as remembering is repetition and confusion, and being existing that is listening and talking is action and not repetition intelligent people although they talk as if they knew something are really confusing, because they are so to speak keeping two times going at once, the repetition time of remembering and the actual time of talking but, and as they are rarely talking and listening, that is the talking being listening and the listening being talking, although they are clearly saying something they are not clearly creating something, because they are because they always are remembering, they are not at the same time talking and listening. Do you understand. Do you any or all of you understand. Anyway that is the way it is. And you hear it even if you do not say it in the way I say it as I hear it and say it. (*LIA* 179–80)

To her, remembering is the demon of the writing world, for it leads to dead repetition, which prevents the writer from perceiving and from reach-

28. See *FIA* 126–34. Owen Young (1874–1962), lawyer, counsel for General Electric, and lecturer at Boston University, created the Radio Corporation of America and was active at the 1924 reparations conference after World War I.

NARRATION (Miss Gertrude Stein)

Four Lectures and Classes

Lecture I

The relation of the literature that is narrative that is how is anything told
to the habit of doing anything and living which that country has.
The comparison between English literature and American literature, the comp
difference in their habits although they use the same language, and its connectio
with their narrative.

Lecture II

The difference between poetry and prose and the relation of that differe
the stating of events or what happens. Knowing thoroughly the difference betw
poetry and prose and its connection with vocabulary and grammar, what is the
ble effect of this upon narrative in prose and narrative in poetry and how ca
of them be done now.

Lecture III

History and is history narrative, and why does it generally speakin
method of literary expression. Is it due to its connection with past pre
future. The newspaper and its effort to create narrative and the connec
with the writing of history. What is the connection of all this with re
inevitable repetition which connects itself with daily life and with wa
because it is not sufficiently understood that war and catastrophe are
publicising of repetition of success and failure which as common knowl
already knows.

Lecture IV

Narrative and its relation to physical qualities of a country,
separating people from the country when the consciousness of the pe
made the two things one, its effect upon novels that is narrative,
tion to the time sense of the people in its relation to the countr
mystery stories what is the degree of consciousness of time sense
ing from being exciting to being soothing, has this not a great
present becoming past and the future becoming past although it i
present. Analysis of the difference of relating action to comp

Figure 16. Description of the Four *Narration* Lecture
Supplementary Reading List, Chicago, March
with Stein and Toklas revisions. Co

ing an audience; in the grip o
what they already know.

People who attended the lec
temporize. In fact, Carl Van Vec
and Mary she totally abandoned h
on February 25, 1935, that at Tulan
English Literature"; Donald Fessen
November 20, 1934, on her Radclif
quoted from the lecture her substitu
many so-called intelligent people . . .
listening," by "The essence of intellig
know it."[29]

One way Stein holds them is by a
which we react in conditioned ways, w
1935, almost one year after her lecture
Havre in time for sailing to America o
She was glad he liked her lectures,[30] she

> there is a thing that bothers me, in all
> happened, that you write with what y
> than what you say. We used to talk of
> and the minimum of form, and I do
> what bothers me is that you to me use y
> doing so, if you did it completely well alr
> serving god and mammon which canno
> me a lot.

She feared he was appealing to his audience
writing? As she had said at the end of "What

> The writer is to serve god or mammon b
> written or by writing the way it is being wr
> writing is writing. That is for writing the di
> and mammon. If you write the way it has a
> are serving mammon, because you are living
> already been earning or has earned. If you w
> then you are serving as a writer god because y
> (*LIA* 54–55)

29. See *LGS/TW*, Rice, Appendix I, "Gertrude Stein's Ame
30. This may refer to a typescript or advance copy of Stein's
the University of Chicago Press in December 1935.

She avoided dead familiar terms that relied on memory; to take examples from plays, she does not use such words as "plot," "action," "character," "setting," "climax." Instead, she relies on her own terms—few and simple ordinary words, many in opposing pairs, that require not a dictionary but careful listening as she repeats them in varying sentence patterns: "landscape," "repetition," "insistence," "inside and outside," "god and mammon," "remembering," "listening and talking."

Another way is by weaving extended yet simply constructed sentences with frequent repetitions and variations that rhythmically draw the listener in; she never works with the subordinations of complex-compound sentences. The long passage from "Portraits And Repetition," just cited, is an example of her skill in weaving "remembering," "talking," "listening" into rhythms that impress themselves on the mind receptive to sounded words or visual patterns on the page. Her long, evolving sentences and paragraphs balance and move rhythmically, never becoming humdrum, singsong, dead "repetition and confusion." The eye can sight-read repetitions rhythmically just as the ear receives the spoken words when we read Stein aloud. It takes more concentrated auditory attention than most of us are used to.

In most of her writing, her method is to proceed by meandering, seemingly disconnected observations, process talk in the present moment of the mind thinking, listening, hearing, speaking, weaving from inside to outside by tiny personal increments. In the lectures, however, she keeps apparent digressions narrowly within the bounds of her subject. This process creates a voice that requires concentration, intellectual by way of being playful, that is unfamiliar to most of us. It can be irritating—or exhilarating.

Yet the lectures are not audience writing. The experience of audience entered Stein's thought, extending her ideas about writing,[31] but in speaking, she concentrated on her work and her art. Self-portraits in a new voice, her talks were a new form of elucidation that grew out of her review of her own work.

When speaking, she both talked to herself as inside audience and addressed her outside audience. Listeners cannot concentrate only on *what* she has to say, for her ideas cannot be lifted from the words. They must listen to *how* she speaks of how she thinks as she elucidates. We are with her in the double process of her writing and our listening as her audience. She captivates this insight beautifully in the fourth *Narration* lecture:

31. For example, the concern with sounding out the outside self and the inside self, the relation of lecturer to audience, as in "Poetry And Grammar," *LIA* 205, and the long discussion of audience in Narration no. 4.

> . . . the writer writing knows what he is writing as he recognizes it as he is writing it and so he is actually having it happen that an audience is existing even if he as an audience is not an audience that is is one not having a feeling that he is an audience and yet that is just what a writer is. . . . What makes writing writing is hearing what an audience is that is to say makes recognition while in the act of writing what he is writing. . . .
> . . . Of course if you are reading what you are lecturing then you have a half in one of any two directions, you have been recognizing what you are writing when you were writing and now in reading you disassociate recognizing what you are reading from what you did recognize as being written while you were writing. In short you are leading a double life. (56–57)

She has incorporated the idea of audience not as a temptation to indulge in personality writing but as a part of a writer's serious business. She listens to herself speaking to us and recognizing, as we also do, what she is saying. This is a part of what she means by the phrase "listening and talking." As audience, we must abandon memory, abandon what we have learned, abandon as well our expectations of where a lecture will go next. In a sense, to listen to her, we must become illiterate, unknowing, expectationless.

Only in the lectures themselves and in part, indirectly, in the Henry James section, does she finally confront her work and her efforts as a modernist. Here, she faces the same writing problem that she faced throughout her life: how to write about what she was doing.

She does not abandon the ruminative stance but limits its scope, makes its movement more transparent and reduces digression since an audience cannot puzzle over a sentence or repeat a thought but must move on with her. She works with short, simple key words repeated and varied as building blocks for ideas, composing musically, by rhythm, as Marcel Brion had recognized when he likened her method to Bach's counterpoint. Because lecturing gives her set subjects—pictures, plays, portraiture—to follow toward a finish, she speaks with a narrower focus than in the wonderfully crooked paths of her meditations.

Even as the lectures compromise her usual ways by making her tighten and focus, they have a true Stein tone. She speaks to us—and herself—of what writing is, defining and explaining by repeating her terms in varying constructions, counterpointed for development. Her meaning is not only in the words chosen to argue her points but in her application, in forms she uses to display her intention—present participles, whose forms tell what they represent: we must listen to such active forms that themselves do some talking.

I have presented the core ideas as if they were a theoretical scaffold. Of course they were not. Indeed, Stein rarely stated them as ideas or theory but relied on them as working tools in writing. I close this book with her response to a writer about his craft—and hers.

On February 25, 1932, Lindley Hubbell sent Stein a copy of his story, "Homecoming,"[32] announcing also that he had started a novel. The story concerns the first return home from New York in some years of a young painter, a son of hardworking Czech farmers in the country. When he arrives, everyone is self-conscious and uncomfortable and he feels unwelcome. His mother berates him for not sending money and having gone to New York. The next morning, after church, everyone goes to Uncle Gus, where someone is already playing the accordion and Uncle Gus is singing and beginning to get drunk.

> After dinner we went back into the front room and sat around wherever we could find a place; on the bed, on chairs, on trunks, and some of the men leaned against the walls. They offered me a chair and I sat down. Then they brought in some more moonshine, with several bottles of beer and a big platter of dried cheese. The cheese tasted funny and crumbly in my mouth after not tasting it for so many years, but the beer was good. The moonshine was terrible, but they kept giving me glasses of it and looked hurt if I hesitated to take it, so I had to keep on drinking. I felt funny, but I was no longer ill at ease. I began to love everybody and to think that after all they were my own people. I had come back to them with love in my heart, but I had found a barrier of distrust and hostility between us, for I had gone away from them and had not shared their life as all the rest of us had done. But that didn't seem to matter any longer. (268)

He even ends up dancing with his mother while everyone sings. The next morning they all work in the fields and the narrator tells at length how very sick and hungover he feels. After another hostile encounter with his mother and further discomfort among the family, his brother Albert drives him back to the station.

On March 30, 1932, Stein responded,

> I like the idea of your writing a novel make it long enough and go very slow sometimes and go pretty fast sometimes but keep going and the thing you want to consider at all times and this a propos of your story is

32. Lindley Williams Hubbell, "Homecoming," *Hound & Horn* 5, no. 3 (April–June 1932): 265–71.

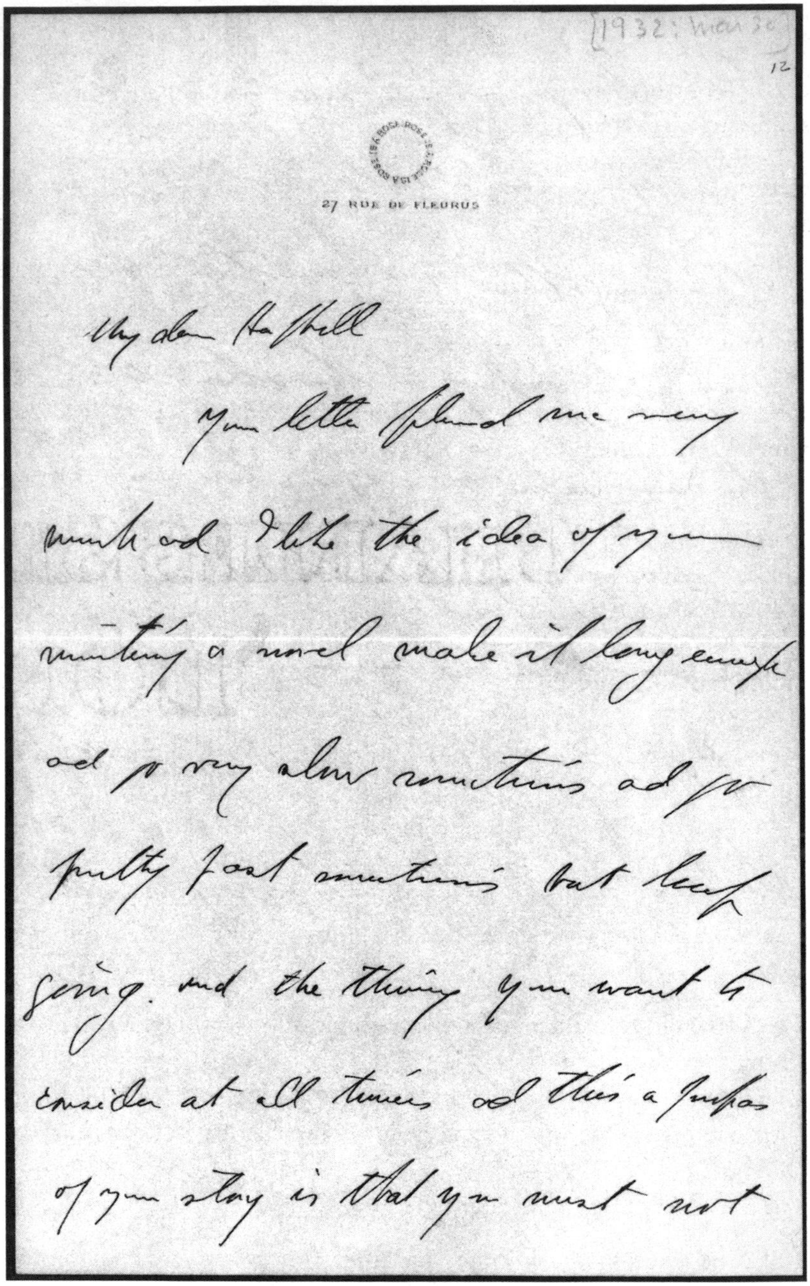

[1932: Mar 30]

12

ROSE IS A ROSE IS A ROSE IS A ROSE

27 RUE DE FLEURUS

My dear Hubbell

Your letter pleased me very much and I like the idea of your writing a novel make it long enough and go very slow sometimes and go pretty fast sometimes but keep going. and the thing you want to consider at all times and this a purpose of your story is that you must not

Figure 17. Stein, from Paris, to Lindley Hubbell, New York, postmarked 30 March 1932. Courtesy YCAL.

observe things and feel emotion, you can
write, your trouble will not be there,
it is in getting your emotion to have
imagination and your observation to have
the same value of imagination, now you
see when you say that the cheese tasted
creamy and crumbly in my mouth after
not tasting it for so many years but
the beer was good, that is imagination
but your long description of the next
morning is not imagination it is
a conceived observation and that fails.

that you must not observe things and feel emotion, you can write, your trouble will not be there, it is in getting your emotion to have imagination and your observation to have the same value of imagination, now you see when you say that the cheese tasted funny and crumbly in your mouth after not tasting it for so many years but the beer was good, that is imagination but your long description of the next morning is not imagination it is a conceived observation and that fails but after all all that there is to do is as the french say *continuez* and that you will do.

Chronological Listing 1923–34

This listing follows the writing, not the publication, of texts. Dates are given, when available, for beginning and end of composition, especially important for longer or several concurrently written pieces. For 1923 and 1924, only texts related to chapter 1 are listed; from chapter 2 on, all mid-1925 to 1935 texts are included and dated. Where indented titles follow titles printed to margin, as in "Virgil Thomson," "Bernard Fay," and others, these, with pages indicated, originate in the text listed to margin above, such as "Sentences." However, the indented titles are completed as self-contained texts in their own manuscript *cahiers.*

Included in the last column are the Haas-Gallup (HG) numbers, no longer used at YCAL but still one of the few important early resources; they are reprinted, with adjustments indicated, in Richard Bridgman's *Gertrude Stein in Pieces* (New York: Oxford University Press, 1970), 365–85.

Where Stein wrote, especially from 1925 on, followed her seasonal movement from Paris to Belley and, from 1929 on, Bilignin, making patterns that are also reflected in the texts. Locations are given after dates for texts.

Selected citations to printed texts are as follows: posthumous Yale edition volumes, out of print but available in libraries, are indicated, as are some other collections (e.g., *Portraits And Prayers*), especially for texts not otherwise available. Citations are given for texts reprinted in *Selected Writings, Library of America,* and in *A Stein Reader,* the only ones for whose textual correctness I can vouch. For all other printed versions, consult Robert Wilson's *Gertrude Stein: A Bibliography* (Rockville, Md.: Quill and Brush, 1994).

1923

Winter–Early Spring: St.-Rémy

March–April: St.-Rémy–Paris

Summer: Paris

July–August

September–November: Nice

December: Paris

1924

Early: Paris

Spring–Summer

Summer: Belley

Fall: Paris

1925–26

Spring 1925–Fall 1926: Paris–Belley–Paris

Spring 1925–Spring 1926: Paris–Belley–Paris

1925

Spring–Summer: Paris

Summer: Belley

“A Stitch In Time Saves Nine. Birds Of A Feather Flock Together. Chickens Come Home To Roost.” *RAB* 52 334a
“A Third.” *AFAM* 329 335
Review: *Troubadour* by Alfred Kreymborg. *RAB* 53 335a

November–December: Paris
“Lipchitz.” *P&P* 63, *R* 491 344

December–January
“Jean Cocteau.” *P&P* 80 338

1926

Late January–February: Paris
“An Address.” [= “Composition As Explanation.”] *R* 493, *SW* 511, *LA* 520 339

June–September: England–Belley
“Edith Sitwell And Her Brothers The Sitwells And Also To Osbert Sitwell And To S. Sitwell.” *PL* 293 340

August: Belley
“Allen Tanner.” *UK* 86 341

June–Late September: England–Belley–Paris
An Acquaintance With Description. R 504, *LA* 530 342

September–October: Paris
“Pavlik Tchelitchef or Adrian Arthur.” *Dix Portraits* 23, 59 343

Late 1926–Spring 1927: Paris
“Patriarchal Poetry.” *BTV* 251, *LA* 567 345

1927

Winter–May: Paris–Belley
“Regular Regularly In Narrative.” Plain Edition, Vol. 3, *HTW* 215–70 346

Spring: Paris
“Duchess de Rohan. A Writer.” *PL* 310 347
“A Diary.” *A&B* 199 348
“Three Sitting Here.” *P&P* 124 360

"The d'Aiguys." *P&P* 108 370
"George Hugnet." *R* 538 373

September–October: Belley–Paris

"Arthur A Grammar." *HTW* 37–101 368

November–December: Paris

"Christian Berard." *P&P* 73 374
"Why I Do Not Live In America." *HWW* 51 377

1928–29

December–January: Paris

"Bibliography." *transition* 15, 47–55 389

October–July

"Sentences." *HTW* 113–213 376

November–December

"Virgil Thomson." (116–17; 123) *Dix Portraits* 27, 63; *P&P* 198, *LA* 651 381

December–January

"Bernard Fay." (129–31) *Dix Portraits* 35–38; *P&P* 41 379

May–July: Bilignin

"Five Words In A Line." *RAB* 142 383
"Kristians Tonny." (132) *Dix Portraits* 38, 75; *P&P* 212 386
"Basket." (212) *P&P* 181 381

1929

Spring: Paris

"G. Maratier." *P&P* 183 387
Film. Deux Soeurs Qui Ne Sont Pas Soeurs. O&P 399 382

Spring–Summer: Bilignin

"For-Get-Me-Not." *SIM* 230 380

September–October

"More Grammar Genia Berman." *Dix Portraits* 43, 79; *P&P* 185 384
["G. Basketing."] = "Saving The Sentence." *HTW* 11–21 385

November–December: Paris

["Saving The Sentence Again."] = "Sentences And Paragraphs." *HTW* 23–35 390
"Genuine Creative Ability." (25; 34) *PGS* 104 424
"The Return." (26; 34) *PL* 66 391
"The Pilgrims. Thoughts About Master Pieces." (27) *PL* 145 404
"Pay Me." (28–29) *PL* 137 406
"Why Willows." (29) *RAB* 154 405
"Evidence." (30; 32) *R* 541, *RAB* 153 392
"Bravig Imbs." (30) (in "Evidence") *R* 544, *P&P* 210, *RAB* 153 396
"Madame Langlois." (in "Evidence") *R* 546 397
"Absolutely As Bob Brown Or Bobbed Brown." (30–32) *PL* 311 393

1930

January–February: Paris

"Sentences And Paragraphs."
"Eric de Hauleville." *P&P* 211 394
"How Are Fears." (34) *PL* 139 407
"Madame De Clermont-Tonnerre." (34–35) *P&P* 89 395
"Grace Or Yves de Longevialle." In Wendy Steiner, "The Steinian Portrait," *Yale University Library Gazette* 50, no. 1 (July 1975): 45 402

Spring

"To Kitty Or Kate Buss." *P&P* 103 408
"A Grammarian." *HTW* 103–11 400
Parlor. (107) *O&P* 325 398
At Present. A Play. Nothing But Contemporaries Allowed. (108–9) *O&P* 315 401
"Title Sub-Title." (111) *AFAM* 386 403

Spring–Early Summer: Bilignin

"More Grammar For A Sentence." *AFAM* 359, *R* 547 399
"Abel." *SIM* 222 415
"A French Rooster. A History." *SIM* 213 414
"To Pierre De Massot." *PL* 311 410

July–August

Before The Flowers Of Friendship Faded Friendship Faded. Plain Edition, Vol. 2; *Exact Change Yearbook # 1* (Boston, 1995), 41 409

Summer–Fall

"We Came. A History." *RAB* 148, *Readies For Bob Brown's Machine* 99 412
"History Or Messages From History." *A&B* 219 413

September

December: Paris

1930–31

December–January: Paris

1931

January: Paris

Winter–Spring

Summer: Bilignin

September
"A Ballad." *SIM* 256 439

October
"Scenery And George Washington. A Novel Or A Play." *FIA* 161–66 453

Early November
"Thoughts On An American Contemporary Feeling." *RAB* 159 440

1932

January–February: Paris
A Play Without Roses Portrait Of Eugene Jolas. P&P 200 441
A Play Of Pounds. LO&P 239 442
"Answer to Eugene Jolas' 'Metanthropological Crisis': A Manifesto." *transition* 21, 136. *HWW* 53 465

March–April
"Marguerite A Novel Of High Life." *MR* 339 443
"Bartholomew Arnold Or After The War Is Over." *MR* 321 444
A Play A Lion For Max Jacob. P&P 28 446
"Or A History Of The United States Of America." (printed with additions and revisions in *FIA* 166–73) 459

May: Bilignin
"Here. Actualities." [includes "Sir Francis Rose" *RAB* 56, HG 446a] *PL* 11 449
"Margite Marguerite Margherita." *SIM* 269 450

June–July
"Stanzas In Meditation." *SIM* 1–151 (corrupt text); *LA* 1–145 451

Late July
A Manoir. An Historic Play In Which They Are Approached More Often. LO&P 277 447

August–September
Short Sentences. LO&P 317 445

September?
"A Little Love Of Life." *SIM* 277 448

October–November
The Autobiography of Alice B. Toklas. SW 1, *LA* 653 452

December: Paris
"Letter to Bernard Faÿ on the Election of Franklin Roosevelt." 456

1933

April: Paris
Byron A Play But Which They Say Byron A Play. LO&P 333 455
"The Story Of A Book." *HWW* 61 457

Summer: Bilignin
"Afterwards." *SIM* 290 463
"A Poem." *SIM* 289 455a
"First Page." (includes "Page IX," HG 465a) *SIM* 282 460

Summer–Fall
"A Plan For Planting." *PL* 14 454
"Lucy La Fontaine." *PL* 315 462
"Or. And Then Silence. A Portrait Of A Frenchman." *P&P* 241 464a

Late August–September
Blood On The Dining Room Floor. 461

September
"Qu'est que je pense de la France." *L'Intransigeant,* 6 January 1934, 1 468

1933–34

November–Early Spring: Bilignin–Paris
"And Now." *HWW* 63 466

October–April
Four In America FIA 458

"Grant."	October–January
"Wilbur Wright."	January–February
"Henry James."	February–March
"George Washington."	March–April

1934

Late Winter: Paris

"The Superstitions Of Fred Anneday, Annday, Anday A Novel Of Real Life." *HWW* 24 — 467

March

"The Gradual Making Of The Making Of Americans." *LIA* 135, *SW* 239 — 469

June–August: Bilignin

Lectures In America. LIA 191–336 — 469

September–October

"Letter To *Vanity Fair.*" *Vanity Fair* 43 (December 1934): 13 — 471

"Meditations On Being About To Visit My Native Land." *PL* 254 — 472

1935

January: America

"How Writing Is Written." *HWW* 151 — 490

25 February–14 March: Chicago

Narration lectures. — 484

Selected Bibliography

Principal Works of Gertrude Stein

Included in this listing and in citations in notes are the first printed editions of Stein texts but reprints only for works difficult to find.

Alphabets And Birthdays. New Haven, Conn.: Yale University Press, 1957. Vol. 7 of Yale edition of the *Unpublished Writings of Gertrude Stein.*

An Acquaintance With Description. London: Seizin Press, 1929. In *A Stein Reader* and *Library of America Gertrude Stein.*

As Fine As Melancthu (1914–1939). New Haven, Conn.: Yale University Press, 1954. Vol. 4 of Yale edition of the *Unpublished Writings of Gertrude Stein.*

The Autobiography Of Alice B. Toklas. New York: Harcourt, Brace, 1933; London: John Lane, Bodley Head, 1933.

Bee Time Vine And Other Pieces (1913–1927). New Haven, Conn.: Yale University Press, 1953. Vol. 3 of Yale edition of the *Unpublished Writings of Gertrude Stein.*

Before The Flowers Of Friendship Faded Friendship Faded. Paris: Plain Edition, 1931. Reprint, with Georges Hugnet's poems "Enfances" on facing pages and with introduction by Juliana Spahr, *Exact Change Yearbook.* No. 1. Boston, 1995.

Blood On The Dining Room Floor. Pawlet, Vt.: Banyan Press, 1948. Reprint, Berkeley, Calif.: Creative Arts Book Co., 1982; London: Virago Press, 1985.

A Book Concluding With As A Wife Has A Cow A Love Story. Lithographs by Juan Gris. Paris: Galerie Simon, 1926. Reprint, West Glover, Vt.: Something Else Press, 1973. Text in *A Stein Reader.*

Brewsie And Willie. New York: Random House, 1946.

Composition As Explanation. London: Hogarth Press, 1926. The lecture, without

Stein's examples following, is in *Selected Writings, A Stein Reader,* and other collections.
Descriptions Of Literature. Cover drawing by Pavel Tchelitchew. Englewood, N.J.: As Stable Pamphlets, 1926. In *A Stein Reader.*
Dix Portraits. Paris: Editions de la Montagne, 1930. English texts with French translations.
"An Elucidation." *transition* no. 1 (April 1927): 64–78. In *A Stein Reader.*
Everybody's Autobiography. New York: Random House, 1937; London: Heineman, 1938. Reprint, New York: Vintage Books, 1973 (with index); London: Virago Press, 1985; Cambridge, Mass.: Exact Change, 1993.
Fernhurst, Q. E. D., and Other Early Writings. Introduction by Leon Katz and essays "A Note on the Texts" and "The Making of *The Making Of Americans*" by Donald Gallup. New York: Liveright, 1971. Reprint, London: Virago Press, 1995.
Four In America. Introduction by Thornton Wilder. New Haven, Conn.: Yale University Press, 1947.
Four Saints In Three Acts. Introduction by Carl Van Vechten. New York: Random House, 1934. Text also in *Selected Writings, Last Operas And Plays.*
———. Vocal score. Words by Gertrude Stein, music by Virgil Thomson, scenario by Maurice Grosser. New York: Music Press, 1948.
———. Complete recording. Elektra/Nonesuch Records, 1982. Joel Thome conducting Orchestra of Our Time.
The Geographical History Of America Or The Relation Of Human Nature To The Human Mind. New York: Random House, 1936.
Geography And Plays. Preface by Sherwood Anderson. Boston: Four Seas, 1922. Reprint, West Glover, Vt.: Something Else Press, 1968; Madison: University of Wisconsin Press, 1993. University of Wisconsin edition includes an introduction and notes by Cyrena N. Pondrom.
The Gertrude Stein First Reader & Three Plays. Dublin and London: Maurice Fridberg, 1946. Reprint, decorated by Sir Francis Rose, Boston: Houghton Mifflin, 1948.
Gertrude Stein on Picasso. Edited by Edward Burns and with an afterword by Leon Katz and Edward Burns. New York: Liveright, 1970. Reprint, with different illustrations, as *Picasso: The Complete Writings,* Boston: Beacon Press, 1985.
Have They Attacked Mary. He Giggled. New York: n.p. [privately printed by Henry McBride], 1917. In *Selected Writings.*
How To Write. Paris: Plain Edition, 1931. Reprint, West Glover, Vt.: Something Else Press, 1973; New York: Dover, 1975.
How Writing Is Written. Edited and with a preface by Robert Bartlett Haas. Los Angeles: Black Sparrow Press, 1974. Vol. 2 of the *Previously Uncollected Writings of Gertrude Stein.*

Ida A Novel. New York: Random House, 1941. Reprint, New York: Vintage Books, 1971.
In Savoy Or Yes Is For A Very Young Man. (Play Of the Resistance In France). London: Pushkin Press, 1946. In *Last Operas And Plays.*
Last Operas And Plays. Edited and with an introduction by Carl Van Vechten. New York and Toronto: Rinehart, 1949. Reprint, New York: Vintage Books, 1975. Reprint, with Stein's lecture "Plays" and a new introduction by Bonnie Marranca, but without the Van Vechten introduction, Baltimore: Johns Hopkins University Press, 1995.
Lectures In America. New York: Random House, 1935. Reprint, Boston: Beacon Press, 1957; New York: Vintage Books, 1975. Reprint, with an introduction by Wendy Steiner, Boston: Beacon Press, 1985; London: Virago Press, 1988.
Look At Me Now And Here I Am. Writings and Lectures 1909–45. Edited by Patricia Meyerowitz, with an introduction by Elizabeth Sprigge. New York and London: Penguin Books, 1971.
Lucy Church Amiably. Paris: Plain Edition, 1930. Reprint, New York: Something Else Press, 1969.
The Making Of Americans Being A History Of A Family's Progress. Paris: Contact Editions, 1925. Abridged edition, with a preface by Bernard Faÿ, New York: Harcourt, Brace, 1934. Reprint of 1925 edition, New York: Something Else Press, 1966. Reprint of 1925 edition, with a foreword by William Gass and an introduction by Steven Meyer, Normal, Ill.: Dalkey Archive Press, 1995. Selections with headnotes by Leon Katz in *A Stein Reader.*
Matisse Picasso And Gertrude Stein With Two Shorter Stories. Paris: Plain Edition, 1933. Abbreviated as *GMP,* this book also includes "A Long Gay Book" and "Many Many Women." Reprint, Millerton, N.Y.: Something Else Press, 1972. "A Long Gay Book" is in *A Stein Reader.*
The Mother Of Us All. Vocal score. Libretto by Gertrude Stein, music by Virgil Thomson, scenario by Maurice Grosser. New York: Music Press, 1947. Text in *Last Operas And Plays.*
———. Complete recording. New World Records, 1977. Raymond Leppard conducting Santa Fe Opera.
Motor Automatism. New York: Phoenix Book Shop, 1969. Includes "Normal Motor Automatism" by Leon Solomons and Gertrude Stein and "Cultivated Motor Automatism: A Study of Character in Its Relation to Attention" by Gertrude Stein. Originally published in *Psychological Review* 3, no. 5 (September 1896): 492–512; *Psychological Review* 5, no. 3 (May 1898): 295–306.
Mrs. Reynolds And Five Earlier Novelettes. New Haven, Conn.: Yale University Press, 1952. Vol. 2 of Yale edition of the *Unpublished Writings of Gertrude Stein.* Reprint of *Mrs. Reynolds* alone, Los Angeles: Sun and Moon Press, 1989.
Narration. Introduction by Thornton Wilder. Chicago: University of Chicago

Press, 1935. Reprint, Chicago: University of Chicago Press, 1969; New York: Greenwood Press, 1969; Folcroft, Penn.: Folcroft Library Editions, 1977.

A Novel Of Thank You. New Haven, Conn.: Yale University Press, 1958. Vol. 8 of Yale edition of the *Unpublished Writings of Gertrude Stein* (also includes 3 other short texts). Reprint of *A Novel Of Thank You* alone, with an introduction by Steven Meyer, Normal, Ill.: Dalkey Archive Press, 1994.

Operas And Plays. Paris: Plain Edition, 1932. Reprint, with a foreword by James Mellow, Barrytown, N.Y.: Station Hill Press, 1987.

Painted Lace and Other Pieces [1914–1937]. New Haven, Conn.: Yale University Press, 1955. Vol. 5 of Yale edition of the *Unpublished Writings of Gertrude Stein.*

Paris France. London: B. T. Batsford, 1938; New York: Charles Scribner's Sons, 1940. Reprint, New York: Liveright, 1970.

Picasso. Paris: Librairie Floury, 1938. In French.

———. London: B. T. Batsford, 1938; New York: Charles Scribner's Sons, 1939. Reprint, with different illustrations, Boston: Beacon Press, 1959. Reprint, with different illustrations, New York: Dover, 1984. In *Gertrude Stein On Picasso.*

Portrait Of Mabel Dodge At The Villa Curonia. Florence: n.p. [privately printed], 1912. In *Selected Writings.*

Portraits And Prayers. New York: Random House, 1934.

Previously Uncollected Writings of Gertrude Stein. 2 vols. Edited and with a preface by Robert Bartlett Haas. Los Angeles: Black Sparrow Press, 1973–74.

A Primer for the Gradual Understanding of Gertrude Stein. Edited and with a preface by Robert Bartlett Haas. Los Angeles: Black Sparrow Press, 1973.

Reflections On The Atomic Bomb. Edited and with a preface by Robert Bartlett Haas. Los Angeles: Black Sparrow Press, 1973. Vol. 1 of the *Previously Uncollected Writings of Gertrude Stein.*

Selected Writings of Gertrude Stein. Edited and with introduction and notes by Carl Van Vechten. New York: Random House, 1946. Reprint, with an introduction by F. W. Dupee, New York: Modern Library, 1962.

Stanzas In Meditation and Other Poems (1929–1933). Edited by Donald Sutherland. New Haven, Conn.: Yale University Press, 1956. Vol. 6 of Yale edition of the *Unpublished Writings of Gertrude Stein.* Selections, in unadulterated text, in *A Stein Reader* and in *LA.*

A Stein Reader. Edited and with an introduction by Ulla E. Dydo. Evanston, Ill.: Northwestern University Press, 1993. Texts checked against manuscript for accuracy.

Stein, Gertrude. *Writings.* 2 vols. New York: Library of America, 1998.

Tender Buttons. New York: Claire Marie, 1914. Reprint, Los Angeles: Sun and Moon Press, 1990. In *Selected Writings, Look At Me Now.*

Things As They Are. Pawlet, Vt.: Banyan Press, 1950. Corrected text, with the original title *Q. E. D.,* in *Fernhurst, Q. E. D., and Other Early Writings.*

Three Lives. New York: Grafton Press, 1909. Reprint, with an introduction by Carl

Van Vechten, New York: Modern Library, 1933. In *Selected Writings.* Several current reprints.
Two (Gertrude Stein And Her Brother) and Other Early Portraits (1908–1912). New Haven, Conn.: Yale University Press, 1951. Vol. 1 of Yale edition of the *Unpublished Writings of Gertrude Stein.*
The Unpublished Writings of Gertrude Stein. 8 vols. New Haven, Conn.: Yale University Press, 1951–58.
Useful Knowledge. New York: Payson and Clarke, 1928. Reprint, with a foreword by Edward Burns and an introduction by Keith Waldrop, Barrytown, N.Y.: Station Hill Press, 1988.
A Village Are You Ready Yet Not Yet A Play In Four Acts. Lithographs by Elie Lascaux. Paris: Galerie Simon, 1928.
Wars I Have Seen. New York: Random House, 1945.
A Wedding Bouquet. London: J. and W. Chester, 1938. Ballet with Chorus: music by Gerald Hugh Tyrwhitt-Wilson, Lord Berners, words by Gertrude Stein.
What Are Masterpieces. Foreword by Robert Bartlett Haas. Los Angeles: Conference Press, 1940. Reprint, with an afterword by Robert Bartlett Haas, New York: Pittman Publishing, 1970.
The World Is Round. Pictures by Clement Hurd. New York: William R. Scott, 1939. New edition, New York: Young Scott Books, 1967. Reprint of 1939 edition, with an afterword by Edith Thatcher Hurd, San Francisco: North Point Press, 1988.
———. Illustrations by Sir Francis Rose. London: B. T. Batsford, 1939. Reprint, New York: Haskell House, 1965.

Other Sources

My book is based on a close study of Stein's manuscripts and includes a selective bibliography of critical books, articles, and appreciations. My citations are no measure of the help I received from reading in the growing body of Stein criticism here and abroad over the years of working in the Stein backyard. I am indebted to all friends and colleagues who have read her, written about her, thought about her, talked about her, and wondered about her.

This bibliography could never possibly acknowledge my debt to contemporary poets. Reading them, listening to their readings, and talking with them has endlessly inspired me. Their work has helped keep Stein's work in focus and my study alive.

Andrews, Bruce, and Charles Bernstein, eds. *The L=A=N=G=U=A=G=E Book.* Carbondale: Southern Illinois University Press, 1984.
Antheil, George. *Bad Boy of Music.* Garden City, N.Y.: Doubleday Doran, 1945.

Antin, David. "Some Questions About Modernism." *Occident* 8 (spring 1974): 7–38.
Apollinaire, Guillaume. "Aesthetic Meditations on Painting: The Cubist Painters." Translated by Mrs. Charles Knoblauch. *Little Review* 8, no. 2 (spring 1922): 7–19; 9, no. 1 (autumn 1922): 41–59; and 9, no. 2 (winter 1922): 49–60.
Ashbery, John. "The Impossible." *Poetry* 90, no. 4 (July 1957): 250–54.
Baring-Gould, William, and Ceil Baring-Gould, comps. *The Annotated Mother Goose.* New York: Meridian Books, 1962.
Barney, Natalie. *Souvenirs Indiscrets: Aventures de l'Esprit.* Paris: Flammarion, 1960.
Beach, Sylvia. *Shakespeare and Company.* New York: Harcourt, Brace, 1956.
Beeson, Jack. "Virgil Thomson's *Aeneid.*" *Parnassus: Poetry in Review* 10, no. 2 (spring-summer 1977): 457–78.
Berger, John. *Ways of Seeing.* London: BBC and Penguin Books, 1972.
Bernstein, Charles. "Stein's Identity." In *My Way.* Chicago: University of Chicago Press, 1999.
Bowen, Stella. *Drawn from Life: Reminiscences of Stella Bowen.* London: Collins, 1941.
Bowers, Jane Palatini. *"They Watch Me As They Watch This": Gertrude Stein's Metadrama.* Philadelphia: University of Pennsylvania Press, 1991.
Brakhage, Stan. *Brakhage Scrapbook: Collected Writings 1964–80.* Edited by Robert Haller. New Paltz, N.Y.: Documentext, 1982.
———. *Metaphors on Vision.* New York: Film Culture, 1963.
Bridgman, Richard. *The Colloquial Style in America.* New York: Oxford University Press, 1966.
———. *Gertrude Stein in Pieces.* New York: Oxford University Press, 1970.
Brion, Marcel. *L'Art Abstrait.* Paris: Editions Albin Michel, 1956.
———. "Le Contrepoint Poétique de Gertrude Stein." *Échanges,* no. 3 (June 1930): 122–28.
Bromfield, Louis. *The Farm.* New York: Harper Brothers, 1933.
Brooks, Romaine. "No Pleasant Memories." *Life and Letters Today* 18, no. 12; and 19, no. 15.
Bryher, Winifred. *Heart of Artemis: A Writer's Memoirs.* New York: Harcourt, Brace, 1962.
Buss, Kate. *Jevons Block: A Book of Sex Enmity.* Boston: McGrath Sherrill Press, 1917.
Camfield, William. *Francis Picabia: His Art, Life, and Times.* Princeton, N.J.: Princeton University Press, 1979.
Cantacuzène, Princess, Countess Spéransky, née Grant. *Revolutionary Days: Recollections of Romanoffs and Bolsheviki 1914–1917.* Boston: Small Maynard, 1919.
Caramello, Charles. *Henry James, Gertrude Stein and the Biographical Act.* Chapel Hill: University of North Carolina Press, 1996.

Cather, Willa, and Georgine Milmine. *The Life of Mary Baker Eddy and the History of Christian Science.* Lincoln: University of Nebraska Press, 1993.

Chessman, Harriet Scott. *The Public Is Invited to Dance.* Stanford, Calif.: Stanford University Press, 1989.

Clermont-Tonnerre, the Ex-Duchesse de (Elisabeth de Gramont). *Memoires.* 4 vols. Paris: Editions de Grasset, 1928–37.

Coates, Robert. *The Eater of Darkness.* Paris: Contact Editions, 1926.

———. *Yesterday's Burdens.* New York: Macaulay, 1933.

Cocteau, Jean. *Le Potomak 1913–1914.* Paris: Librairie Stock, 1924.

Le Corbusier. *Towards a New Architecture.* New York: Dover, 1986.

Crane, Stephen. "Black Riders" [1895]. In *Prose and Poetry,* Library of America Series, no. 18. Edited by J. C. Levenson, 1299–1324. New York: Literary Classics of the United States, 1984.

Daix, Pierre, and Joan Rosselet. *Picasso: The Cubist Years 1907–16; Catalogue Raisonné of Paintings and Related Works.* London: Thames and Hudson, 1979.

Damon, Maria. *The Dark End of the Street.* Minneapolis: University of Minnesota Press, 1993.

Davenport, Guy. *The Geography of the Imagination.* San Francisco: North Point Press, 1981.

Davidson, Jo. *Between Sittings.* New York: Dial Press, 1951.

Davidson, Michael. *Ghostlier Demarcations: Modern Poetry and the Material World.* Berkeley: University of California Press, 1997.

DeKoven, Marianne. *A Different Language: Gertrude Stein's Experimental Writing.* Madison: University of Wisconsin Press, 1983.

Djikstra, Bram. *The Hieroglyphics of a New Speech: Cubism, Stieglitz, and the Early Poetry of William Carlos Williams.* Princeton, N.J.: Princeton University Press, 1969.

Dodge, Mabel [Mabel Dodge Luhan]. "Speculations, or Post-Impressionism in Prose." *Arts and Decoration* 3 (1913): 172–74.

Duncan, Isadora. *My Life.* New York: Liveright, 1927.

Elder, R. Bruce. *The Films of Stan Brakhage in the American Tradition of Ezra Pound, Gertrude Stein and Charles Olson.* Waterloo, Ont.: Wilfrid Laurier University Press, 1998.

Ewing, Max. *Going Somewhere.* London: Cassell, 1933.

Faÿ, Bernard. *Franklin: The Apostle of Modern Times.* Translated by Bravig Imbs. Boston: Little, Brown, 1929.

———. *George Washington, Gentilhomme.* Paris: Grasset, 1932.

———. *Les Précieux.* Paris: Librairie Académique Perrin, 1966.

———. *The Revolutionary Spirit in France and America.* New York: Harcourt, Brace, 1927.

———. *The Two Franklins: Fathers of American Democracy.* Boston: Little, Brown, 1933.

Fénéon, Felix. "Bulletin # 1, 29 janvier 1914," *Petits Bulletins.* In *Oeuvres plus que complètes,* Vol. 1, *Chronique d'art.* Edited by Joan Halperin. Geneva: Librairie Droz, 1970.
Fifer, Elizabeth. "Is Flesh Advisable? The Interior Theatre of Gertrude Stein." *Signs* 4 (spring 1979): 472–83.
Ford, Charles Henri, and Parker Tyler. *The Young and Evil.* Paris: Obelisk Press, 1933.
Ford, Ford Madox. *It Was the Nightingale.* Philadelphia: Lippincott, 1933.
Ford, Hugh. *Published in Paris.* New York: Macmillan, 1975.
Fry, Roger. *Cézanne: A Study of His Development.* New York: Noonday, 1968.
Gallup, Donald. "Always Gertrude Stein." *Southwest Review* 34, no. 4 (summer 1949): 254–58.
———. "A Book Is a Book." *New Colophon* 1, no. 1 (January 1948): 67–80.
———. "The Gertrude Stein Collection." *Yale University Library Gazette* 22, no. 2 (October 1947): 21–25.
———. *Pigeons on the Granite: Memoirs of a Yale Librarian.* New Haven, Conn.: Beinecke Rare Book and Manuscript Library, 1988.
———. "The Weaving of a Pattern: Marsden Hartley and Gertrude Stein." *Magazine of Art* 41, no. 7 (November 1948): 256–61.
———. *What Mad Pursuits! More Memoirs of a Yale Librarian.* New Haven, Conn.: Beinecke Rare Book and Manuscript Library, 1998.
———, ed. *The Flowers of Friendship: Letters Written to Gertrude Stein.* New York: Alfred A. Knopf, 1953.
Gallup, Donald, and Robert B. Haas. *Catalogue of the Published and Unpublished Writings of Gertrude Stein.* New Haven, Conn.: Yale University Library, 1941.
Gass, William H. "Gertrude Stein and the Geography of the Sentence." In *The World Within the Word: Essays by William Gass.* New York: Alfred A. Knopf, 1979.
———. "Gertrude Stein: Her Escape from Protective Language." *Accent* (autumn 1958): 233–44.
Gordon, Taylor. *Born to Be.* New York: Covici-Friede Publishers, 1929.
Grant, U. S. *Personal Memoirs.* New York: Charles L. Webster, 1885.
Graves, Robert. *Goodbye to All That.* London: Jonathan Cape, 1929.
Greenaway, Kate. *The Language of Flowers.* London: G. Routledge, 1886.
Griffiths, Paul. *On Being Mindless: Buddhist Meditation and the Mind-Body Problem.* New York: Open Court, 1986.
Gris, Juan. "On the Possibilities of Painting." *Transatlantic Review* 1, no. 6 (June 1924): 482–88; and 2, no. 1 (July 1924): 75–79.
Grosser, Maurice. *The Painter's Eye.* New York: Rinehart, 1951.
———. *Painting in Public.* New York: Alfred A. Knopf, 1948.
———. "Virgil Thomson Among the Painters." *Parnassus: Poetry in Review* 10, no. 2 (spring–summer 1977): 506–18.

Hall, Radclyffe. *The Well of Loneliness.* London: Jonathan Cape, 1928.
Hapgood, Hutchins. *A Victorian in the Modern World.* New York: Harcourt, Brace, 1939.
Harper, Allanah. *All Trivial Fond Records.* London: Grey Walls Press, 1950.
Hejinian, Lyn. "Two Stein Talks: Language and Realism, Grammar and Landscape." *Temblor* 3 (1986): 128–39.
———. *The Language of Inquiry.* Berkeley: University of California Press, 2000.
Herbert, Robert L., Eleanor S. Apter, and Elise K. Kenney, eds. *The Société Anonyme and the Dreier Bequest. A Catalogue Raisonné.* New Haven, Conn.: Yale University Press, 1984.
Hirsch, Nathaniel D. Mttron. *Genius and Creative Intelligence.* Cambridge, Mass.: Sci-Art Publishers, 1931.
Hoffman, Frederick J. *Gertrude Stein.* University of Minnesota Pamphlets on American Writers. Minneapolis: University of Minnesota Press, 1961.
Hoffman, Michael J. *Critical Essays on Gertrude Stein.* Boston: Hall, 1986.
———. *The Development of Abstractionism in the Work of Gertrude Stein.* Philadelphia: University of Pennsylvania Press, 1965.
Hoover, Kathleen, and John Cage. *Virgil Thomson: His Life and Music.* New York: Thomas Yoseloff, 1959.
Horowitz, Helen Lefkowitz. *The Power and Passion of M. Carey Thomas.* New York: Knopf, 1994.
Howe, Susan. *The Europe of Trusts.* Los Angeles: Sun and Moon Press, 1990.
Hubbell, Lindley Williams. *Autobiography.* Kobe, Japan: Ikuta Press, 1971.
———. "Homecoming." *Hound and Horn* 5, no. 3 (April–June 1932): 265–71.
———. "A Letter to Gertrude Stein." *Pagany* 1, no. 2 (spring 1930): 37.
———. "The Plain Edition of Gertrude Stein." *Contempo* 3, no. 12 (25 October 1933): 1, 4.
Hugnet, Georges. *Enfances.* Paris: Editions Cahiers d'Art, 1933.
———. *La Belle en dormant.* Paris: Editions des Cahiers Libres, 1933.
———. *La Perle.* Film directed by Henri d'Arche, starring Kissa Kouprine and Hugnet; scenario written 1928–29, opened June 1929.
———. *Le Droit de Varech.* Paris: Editions de la Montagne, 1930.
———. *Pleins et Déliés: Témoignages et Souvenirs.* La Chapelle-sur-Loîr: Guy Auteur, 1972.
———. "Portrait de Virgil Thomson." *Le Figaro littéraire* (21 August 1954): 9.
———. *Quarante Poésies de Stanislas Boutemer.* Paris: Théophile Briant Editeur, 1928.
———. "Virgil Thomson." *Pagany* 1, no. 1 (winter 1930): 37–38.
Imbs, Bravig. *Confessions of Another Young Man.* New York: Henkle-Yewdale House, 1936.
James, William. *The Principles of Psychology.* 2 vols. New York: Holt, 1890.
———. *Psychology: Briefer Course.* Cambridge: Harvard University Press, 1984.

———. *The Varieties of Religious Experience: A Study in Human Nature.* 1902. Reprint, New York: Modern Library, 1936.
———. *The Will to Believe and Other Essays in Popular Philosophy.* New York: Longmans, Green, 1927. Reprint, Cambridge: Harvard University Press, 1979.
———. *William James on Psychical Research.* Edited by Gardner Murphy and Robert Ballou. Clifton, N.J.: Augustus Kelley, 1973.
Jolas, Eugene. *Secession in Astropolis.* Paris: Black Sun Press, 1929.
———, ed. *Anthologie de la Nouvelle Poésie Américaine.* Paris: Kra, 1928.
Kahnweiler, Daniel-Henri. *Juan Gris: His Life and Work.* Translated by Douglas Cooper. New York: Harry N. Abrams, 1946.
———. *The Rise of Cubism.* New York: Wittenborn, 1949.
Katz, Leon. "The First Making of The Making of Americans: A Study Based on Gertrude Stein's Notebooks and Early Versions of Her Novel (1902–8)." Ph.D. diss., Columbia University, 1963.
Kawin, Bruce. *Telling It Again and Again: Repetition in Literature and Film.* Ithaca: Cornell University Press, 1972.
Kellner, Bruce. *Carl Van Vechten and the Irreverent Decades.* Norman: University of Oklahoma Press, 1968.
———. *A Gertrude Stein Companion: Content with the Example.* New York: Greenwood Press, 1988.
———, ed. *Letters of Carl Van Vechten.* New Haven, Conn.: Yale University Press, 1987.
King, Georgiana Goddard. "Free Among the Dead." In *The Book of Bryn Mawr Stories.* Philadelphia: George W. Jacobs and Company, 1901.
———. "Gertrude Stein." *International* 7, no. 6 (1913): 157.
———. *Heart of Spain.* Edited by Agnes Mongan. Cambridge: Harvard University Press, 1941.
Kirstein, Lincoln. *Tchelitchev.* Santa Fe, N.M.: Twelvetrees Press, 1994.
Kornfeld, Lawrence. "From a Director's Notebook." *Performing Arts Journal* 1, no. 1 (spring 1976): 33–39.
Kostelanetz, Richard, ed. *Gertrude Stein Advanced.* Jefferson, N.C.: McFarland, 1990.
Kramer, Andreas, and Rainer Rumold, eds. *Eugene Jolas: Man from Babel.* New Haven, Conn.: Yale University Press, 1998.
Kreymborg, Alfred. *Troubadour.* New York: Boni and Liveright, 1925.
Kreymborg, Alfred, Lewis Mumford, and Paul Rosenfeld. *The American Caravan.* New York: Macaulay, 1927.
Lake, Carlton, and Linda Ashton. *Henri-Pierre Roché: An Introduction.* Austin, Tex.: Harry Ransom Humanities Research Center, 1991.
Léautaud, Paul. *Correspondance générale.* Vol. 2. Paris: Flammarion, 1972.
———. *Journal littéraire.* Vol. 2. Paris: Mercure de France, 1936.
Le Rider, Jacques. *Der Fall Otto Weininger.* Vienna: Löcker Verlag, 1985.

Luhan, Mabel Dodge. *Intimate Memories.* 4 vols. New York: Harcourt, Brace, 1933–37.
Massot, Pierre de. *André Breton ou Le Septembriseur.* Paris: Eric Losfeld, 1967.
———. *Francis Picabia.* Paris: Seghers, 1966.
McCown, Eugene. *The Siege of Innocence.* New York: Doubleday, 1950.
McFeely, William S. *Grant: A Biography.* New York: W. W. Norton, 1981.
McGann, Jerome. *Black Riders: The Visible Language of Modernism.* Princeton, N.J.: Princeton University Press, 1993.
McGuffy, William Holmes. *Third Eclectic Reader.* New York: American Book Company, 1879.
———. *Fifth Eclectic Reader.* New York: American Book Company, 1879.
———. *Fourth Eclectic Reader.* Cincinnati, Ohio: Eclectic Press of Van Antwerp, Bragg, 1879.
Mellow, James. *Charmed Circle: Gertrude Stein and Company.* New York: Praeger, 1974.
Merleau-Ponty, Maurice. *The Phenomenology of Perception.* Translated by Colin Smith. London: Routledge and Kegan Paul, 1962.
Meyer, Stephen J. "Stein and Emerson." *Raritan* 10, no. 2 (fall 1990): 87–119.
Moad, Rosalind. "1914–1916: Years of Innovation in Gertrude Stein's Writing." Ph.D. diss., University of York, England, 1993.
Mohler, Olga. *Francis Picabia.* Turin: Edizioni Notizie, 1975.
Münsterberg, Hugo. *The Film: A Psychological Study; The Silent Photoplay in 1916.* 1916. Reprint, New York: Dover, 1970.
Neuman, Shirley. *Autobiography and the Problem of Narration.* English Literary Studies Monograph Series, no. 18. Victoria, B.C.: University of Victoria, 1979.
Neuman, Shirley, and Ira B. Nadel, eds. *Gertrude Stein and the Making of Literature.* London: Macmillan, 1988.
Nichol, B. P. *The Martyrology.* Vol. 1–2. Toronto: Coach House Press, 1977.
———. "When the Time Came." *Line* no. 1 (spring 1983): 46–61. Publication of Simon Fraser University Library, Burnaby, B.C.
Olivier, Fernande. *Picasso and His Friends.* Translated by Jane Miller. New York: Appleton-Century, 1965.
———. *Picasso et ses amis.* Paris: Librairie Stock, 1933.
———. *Souvenirs Intimes Ecrits pour Picasso.* Paris: Calman-Levy, 1988.
Paul, Elliot. "From a Litérateur's Notebook." *Chicago Tribune* (Paris), 15, 22, 29 May 1927.
Peers, E. Allison. *Behind That Wall: An Introduction to Some Classics of the Interior Life.* London: SCM Press, 1947.
Perelman, Bob. *The Trouble with Genius.* Berkeley: University of California Press, 1994.
Perera, Victor. *The Cross and the Pear Tree: A Sephardic Journey.* London: André Deutsch, 1996.

Teuber, Marianne L. "Helmholtzian Visual Science and the Dissolution of Perspective in Cubism." Paper presented at the 71st annual meeting of the College Art Association of America, Panel on Scientific Theory and Artistic Practice from Plato and Praxiteles to Einstein, Philadelphia, 17–19 February 1983.

———. "William James and Picasso's Cubism." Abstract of paper presented at Fourth European Conference on Visual Perception, Paris, September 1981.

Thomas, Martha Carey. *The Making of a Feminist: Early Journals and Letters.* Edited by Marjorie Housepian Dobkin. Kent, Ohio: Kent State University Press, 1979.

Toklas, Alice B. *The Alice B. Toklas Cookbook.* London: Michael Joseph, 1954; New York: Michael Joseph, 1954.

———. Interview by Ronald E. Duncan. Tape recording. Oral History, Bancroft Library, University of California at Berkeley, 28–29 November 1952.

———. *Staying On Alone: Letters of Alice B. Toklas.* Edited by Edward Burns, with an introduction by Gilbert Harrison. New York: Liveright, 1973.

———. *What Is Remembered.* New York: Holt, Rinehart and Winston, 1963.

Tufte, Virginia. "Gertrude Stein's Prothalamium: A Unique Poem in a Classical Mode." *Yale University Library Gazette* 42 (July 1968): 17–23.

Tyler, Parker. *The Divine Comedy of Pavel Tchelitchew.* New York: Fleet Publishing, 1967.

Ullman, Alice Woods. *The Thicket: A Novel.* New York: Mitchell Kennerly, 1913.

Vollard, Ambroise. *Souvenir d'un marchand de tableaux.* Paris: Albin Michel, 1937.

Walker, Jayne L. *Gertrude Stein: The Making of a Modernist.* Amherst: University of Massachusetts Press, 1984.

Watson, Steven. *Prepare for Saints.* New York: Random House, 1998.

Weininger, Otto. *Sex and Character.* 1903. Reprint, New York: AMS, 1975.

Weinstein, Norman. *Gertrude Stein and the Literature of Modern Consciousness.* New York: Frederick Ungar, 1970.

White, Ray Lewis, comp. *Gertrude Stein and Alice B. Toklas: A Reference Guide.* Boston: G. K. Hall, 1984.

———, ed. *Sherwood Anderson / Gertrude Stein: Conversations and Personal Essays.* Chapel Hill: University of North Carolina Press, 1972.

Whitehead, Alfred North. *Process and Reality: An Essay in Cosmology.* New York: Macmillan, 1929.

Wilcox, Wendell. "A Note on Gertrude Stein and Abstraction." *Poetry* 55, no. 5 (February 1940): 254–57. Reprinted in *Gertrude Stein Advanced: An Anthology of Criticism,* edited by Richard Kostelanetz, 190–203. Jefferson, N.C.: McFarland, 1990.

———. *Everything Is Quite All Right.* New York: Bernard Ackerman, 1945.

Williams, William Carlos. *Selected Essays of William Carlos Williams.* New York: Random House, 1954.

Wilson, Edmund. *Axel's Castle.* New York: Charles Scribner's Sons, 1931.
———. "A Guide to Gertrude Stein." *Vanity Fair* 21, no. 1 (September 1923): 60, 80.
Wilson, Robert A., comp. *Gertrude Stein: A Bibliography.* New York: Phoenix Bookshop, 1974.
———, comp., assisted by Arthur Uphill. *Gertrude Stein: A Bibliography.* Rockville, Md.: Quill and Brush, 1994.
Wineapple, Brenda. *Genêt: A Biography of Janet Flanner.* New York: Ticknor and Fields, 1989.
———. *Sister Brother: Gertrude Stein and Leo Stein.* New York: G. P. Putnam's Sons, 1996.
Worthington, Marjorie. *The Strange World of Willie Seabrook.* New York: Harcourt, Brace, 1966.

Index

Alice Toklas, whether identified or not, is a presence in Stein's life and work. As this book is not a biography, it would serve no purpose to cite every occurrence of the name Toklas with a page number.

ULLA E. DYDO is Professor Emerita at the City University of New York and is one of the world's foremost Gertrude Stein scholars. She is the editor of *A Stein Reader,* also published by Northwestern University Press, and the coeditor of *The Letters of Gertrude Stein and Thornton Wilder.*

WILLIAM RICE has worked with Edward Burns and Ulla Dydo on various editions of Stein's letters and on *A Stein Reader.* A painter, he is currently preparing a study of Picasso's notebooks for *Les Demoiselles d'Avignon.*